Francis Bacon

The physical and metaphysical works of Lord Bacon

Including the Advancement of learning and Novum organum

Francis Bacon

The physical and metaphysical works of Lord Bacon
Including the Advancement of learning and Novum organum

ISBN/EAN: 9783742806000

Manufactured in Europe, USA, Canada, Australia, Japa

Cover: Foto ©Andreas Hilbeck / pixelio.de

Manufactured and distributed by brebook publishing software (www.brebook.com)

Francis Bacon

The physical and metaphysical works of Lord Bacon

THE

PHYSICAL AND METAPHYSICAL

WORKS

OF

LORD BACON,

INCLUDING THE

ADVANCEMENT OF LEARNING AND NOVUM ORGANUM

EDITED BY

JOSEPH DEVEY, M.A.

LONDON: GEORGE BELL AND SONS, YORK STREET,
COVENT GARDEN.

1886.

PREFACE

Lord Bacon can only be said to have carried the three first parts of his *Instauratio Magna* to any degree of perfection. Of these the *Sylva Sylvarum* is but a dry catalogue of natural phenomena, the collection of which, however necessary it might be, Bacon viewed as a sort of mechanical labour, and would never have stooped to the task, had not the field been abandoned by the generality of philosophers, as unworthy of them. The two other portions of the *Instauratio Magna*, which this volume contains, unfold the design of his philosophy, and exhibit all the peculiarities of his extraordinary mind, enshrined in the finest passages of his writings.

Of the *De Augmentis*, though one of the greatest books of modern times, only three translations have appeared, and each of these strikingly imperfect. That of Wats, issued while Bacon was living, is singularly disfigured with solecisms, and called forth the just censures of Bacon and his friends. The version of Eustace Cary is no less unfortunate, owing to its poverty of diction, and antiquated phraseology. Under the public sense of these failures, another translation was produced about sixty years ago by Dr. Shaw, which might have merited approbation, had not the learned physician been impressed with the idea that he could improve Bacon by relieving his work of some of its choicest passages, and entirely altering the arrangement. In the present version, our task has been principally to rectify Shaw's mistakes, by restoring the author's own arrangement, and supplying the omitted portions. Such of Shaw's notes as were deemed of value have been retained, and others added where the text seemed to require illustration. Due care also has been taken to point out the sources whence Bacon drew his extraordinary stores of learning, by furnishing authorities for the quotations and allusions in the text, so that the reader may view at a glance the principal authors whom Bacon loved to consult, and whose agency contributed to the formation of his colossal powers.

The version of the *Novum Organum* contained in this volume is that by Wood, which is the best extant. The present edition of this immortal work has been enriched with an ample commentary, in which the remarks of the two Playfairs, Sir John Herschel, and the German and French editors, have been diligently consulted, that nothing may be wanting to render it as perfect as possible.

CONTENTS.

THE GREAT INSTAURATION

Author's Announcement, Preface, and Account of the Work .. .. *Pages* 1-20

I. THE DIGNITY AND ADVANCEMENT OF LEARNING, IN NINE BOOKS.

⁂ The Contents are given in full at pages 21-26.

II. NOVUM ORGANUM.

Preface 380
BOOK I.—ON THE INTERPRETATION OF NATURE AND THE EMPIRE OF MAN 383
BOOK II.—ON THE INTERPRETATION OF NATURE OR THE REIGN OF MAN 448

FRANCIS OF VERULAM'S

GREAT INSTAURATION.

Announcement of the Author.

FRANCIS OF VERULAM THOUGHT THUS, AND SUCH IS THE METHOD WHICH HE DETERMINED WITHIN HIMSELF, AND WHICH HE THOUGHT IT CONCERNED THE LIVING AND POSTERITY TO KNOW.

BEING convinced, by a careful observation, that the human understanding perplexes itself, or makes not a sober and advantageous use of the real helps within its reach, whence manifold ignorance and inconveniences arise, he was determined to employ his utmost endeavours towards restoring or cultivating a just and legitimate familiarity betwixt the mind and things.

But as the mind, hastily and without choice, imbibes and treasures up the first notices of things, from whence all the rest proceed, errors must for ever prevail, and remain uncorrected, either by the natural powers of the understanding or the assistance of logic; for the original notions being vitiated, confused, and inconsiderately taken from things, and the secondary ones formed no less rashly, human knowledge itself, the thing employed in all our researches, is not well put together nor justly formed, but resembles a magnificent structure that has no foundation.

And whilst men agree to admire and magnify the false powers of the mind, and neglect or destroy those that might be rendered true, there is no other course left but with better assistance to begin the work anew, and raise or rebuild the sciences, arts, and all human knowledge from a firm and solid basis.

This may at first seem an infinite scheme, unequal to human abilities, yet it will be found more sound and judicious than the course hitherto pursued, as tending to some issue; whereas all hitherto done with regard to the sciences is vertiginous, or in the way of perpetual rotation.

Nor is he ignorant that he stands alone in an experiment almost too bold and astonishing to obtain credit, yet he thought it not right to desert either the cause or himself, but to boldly enter on the way and explore the only path which is pervious to the human mind. For it is wiser to engage in an undertaking that admits of some termination, than to involve oneself in perpetual exertion and anxiety about what is interminable. The ways of contemplation, indeed, nearly correspond to two roads in nature, one of which, steep and rugged at the commencement, terminates in a plain; the other, at first view smooth and easy, leads only to huge rocks and precipices. Uncertain, however, whether these reflections would occur to another, and observing that he had never met any person disposed to apply his mind to similar thoughts, he determined to publish whatsoever he found time to perfect. Nor is this the haste of ambition, but anxiety, that if he should die there might remain behind him some outline and determination of the matter his mind had embraced, as well as some mark of his sincere and earnest affection to promote the happiness of mankind.

AUTHOR'S PREFACE.

Of the state of learning—That it is neither prosperous nor greatly advanced, and that a way must be opened to the human understanding entirely distinct from that known to our predecessors, and different aids procured, that the mind may exercise her power over the nature of things.

It appears to me that men know neither their acquirements nor their powers, but fancy their possessions greater and their faculties less than they are; whence, either valuing the received arts above measure, they look out no farther; or else despising themselves too much, they exercise their talents upon lighter matters, without attempting the capital things of all. And hence the sciences seem to have their Hercules' Pillars, which bound the desires and hopes of mankind.

But as a false imagination of plenty is among the principal causes of want, and as too great a confidence in things present leads to a neglect of the future, it is necessary we should here admonish mankind that they do not too highly value or extol either the number or usefulness of the things hitherto discovered; for, by closely inspecting the multiplicity of books upon arts and sciences, we find them to contain numberless repetitions of the same things in point of invention, but differing indeed as to the manner of treatment; so that the real discoveries, though at the first view they may appear numerous, prove upon examination but few. And as to the point of usefulness, the philosophy we principally received from the Greeks must be acknowledged puerile, or rather talkative than generative—as being fruitful in controversies, but barren of effects.

The fable of Scylla seems a civil representation of the present condition of knowledge; for she exhibited the countenance and expression of a virgin, whilst barking monsters encircled her womb. Even thus the sciences have their specious and plausible generalities; but when we descend to particulars, which, like the organs of generation, should produce fruits and effects, then spring up loud altercations and controversies, which terminate in barren sterility. And had this not been a lifeless kind of philosophy, it were scarce possible it should have made so little progress in so many ages, insomuch, that not only positions now frequently remain positions still, but questions remain questions, rather riveted and cherished than determined by disputes; philosophy thus coming down to us in the persons of master and scholar, instead of inventor and improver. In the mechanic arts the case is otherwise—these commonly advancing towards perfection in a course of daily improvement, from a rough unpolished state, sometimes prejudicial to the first inventors, whilst philosophy and the intellectual sciences are, like statues, celebrated and adored, but never advanced; nay, they sometimes appear most perfect in the original author, and afterwards degenerate. For since men have gone over in crowds to the opinion of their leader, like those silent senators of Rome,[a] they add nothing to the extent of learning themselves, but perform the servile duty of waiting upon particular authors, and repeating their doctrines.

It is a fatal mistake to suppose that the sciences have gradually arrived at a state of perfection, and then been recorded by some one writer or other; and that as nothing better can afterwards be invented, men need but cultivate and set off what is thus discovered and completed; whereas in reality, this registering of the sciences proceeds only from the assurance of a few and the sloth and ignorance of many. For after the sciences might thus perhaps in several parts be carefully cultivated; a man of an enterprising genius rising up, who, by the conciseness of his method, renders himself acceptable and famous, he in appearance erects an art, but in reality corrupts the labours of his predecessors. This, however, is usually well received by posterity, as readily gratifying their curiosity, and indulging their indolence. But he that rests upon established consent as the judgment approved by time, trusts to a very fallacious and weak foundation; for we have but an imperfect knowledge of the discoveries in arts and sciences, made public in different ages and countries, and still less of what has been done by particular persons, and transacted in private; so that neither the births nor miscarriages of time are to be found in our records.

Nor is consent, or the continuance thereof, a thing of any account; for however governments may vary, there is but one state of the sciences, and that will for ever be democratical or popular. But the doctrines in greatest vogue among the people, are either the contentious and quarrelsome, or the showy and empty; that is, such as may either entrap the assent, or lull the mind to rest: whence, of course, the greatest geniuses in all ages have suffered violence; whilst out of regard to their own character, they submitted to the judgment of the times, and the populace. And thus when any more sublime speculations happened to appear, they were commonly tossed and extinguished by the breath of popular opinion. Hence time, like a river, has brought down to us

---

[a] Pedarii senatores.

what is light and tumid, but sunk what was ponderous and solid. As to those who have set up for teachers of the sciences, when they drop their character, and at intervals speak their sentiments, they complain of the subtilty of nature, the concealment of truth, the obscurity of things, the entanglement of causes, and the imperfections of the human understanding; thus rather choosing to accuse the common state of men and things, than make confession of themselves. It is also frequent with them to adjudge that impossible in an art, which they find that art does not affect; by which means they screen indolence and ignorance from the reproach they merit. The knowledge delivered down to us is barren in effects, fruitful in questions, slow and languid in improvement, exhibiting in its generalities the counterfeits of perfection, but meagre in its details, popular in its aim, but suspected by its very promoters, and therefore defended and propagated by artifice and chicanery. And even those who by experience propose to enlarge the bounds of the sciences, scarce ever entirely quit the received opinions, and go to the fountainhead, but think it enough to add somewhat of their own; as prudentially considering, that at the time they show their modesty in assenting, they may have a liberty of adding. But whilst this regard is shown to opinions and moral considerations, the sciences are greatly hurt by such a languid procedure; for it is scarce possible at once to admire and excel an author: as water rises no higher than the reservoir it falls from. Such men, therefore, though they improve some things, yet advance the sciences but little, or rather amend than enlarge them.

There have been also bolder spirits, and greater geniuses, who thought themselves at liberty to overturn and destroy the ancient doctrine, and make way for themselves and their opinions; but without any great advantage from the disturbance; as they did not effectively enlarge philosophy and arts by practical works, but only endeavoured to substitute new dogmas, and to transfer the empire of opinion to themselves, with but small advantage; for opposite errors proceed mostly from common causes.

As for those who, neither wedded to their own nor others' opinions, but continuing friends to liberty, made use of assistance in their inquiries, the success they met with did not answer expectation, the attempt, though laudable, being but feeble; for pursuing only the probable reasons of things, they were carried about in a circle of arguments, and taking a promiscuous liberty, preserved not the rigour of true inquirers; whilst none of them duly conversed with experience and things themselves. Others again, who commit themselves to mechanical experience, yet make their experiments at random, without any method of inquiry. And the greatest part of these have no considerable views, but esteem it a great matter if they can make a single discovery; which is both a trifling and unskilful procedure, as no one can justly or successfully discover the nature of any one thing in that thing itself, or without numerous experiments which lead to farther inquiries. And we must not omit to observe, that all the industry displayed in experiment has been directed by too indiscreet a zeal at some prejudged effect, seeking those which produced fruit rather than knowledge, in opposition to the Divine method, which on the first day created time alone, delaying its material creations until the sun had illumined space.

Lastly, those who recommend logic as the best and surest instrument for improving the sciences, very justly observe, that the understanding, left to itself, ought always to be suspected. But here the remedy is neither equal to the disease, nor approved; for though the logic in use may be properly applied in civil affairs, and the arts that are founded in discourse and opinion, yet it by no means reaches the subtilty of nature; and by catching at what it cannot hold, rather serves to establish errors, and fix them deeper, than open the way of truth.[b]

Upon the whole, men do not hitherto appear to be happily inclined and fitted for the sciences, either by their own industry, or the authority of authors, especially as there is little dependence to be had upon the common demonstrations and experiments; whilst the structure of the universe renders it a labyrinth to the understanding; where the paths are not only everywhere doubtful, but the appearances of things and their signs deceitful; and the wreaths and knots of nature

[b] For exemplifications of these opinions, the reader may consult Morhof's "Polyhistor.," and the other writers upon polymathy and literary history. *Shaw.*

intricately turned and twisted :[c] through all which we are only to be conducted by the uncertain light of the senses, that sometimes shines, and sometimes hides its head ; and by collections of experiments and particular facts, in which no guides can be trusted, as wanting direction themselves, and adding to the errors of the rest. In this melancholy state of things, one might be apt to despair both of the understanding left to itself, and of all fortuitous helps ; as of a state irremediable by the utmost efforts of the human genius, or the often-repeated chance of trial. The only clue and method is to begin all anew, and direct our steps in a certain order, from the very first perceptions of the senses. Yet I must not be understood to say that nothing has been done in former ages, for the ancients have shown themselves worthy of admiration in everything which concerned either wit or abstract reflection ; but, as in former ages, when men at sea, directing their course solely by the observation of the stars, might coast along the shores of the continent, but could not trust themselves to the wide ocean, or discover new worlds, until the use of the compass was known: even so the present discoveries referring to matters immediately under the jurisdiction of the senses, are such as might easily result from experience and discussion ; but before we can enter the remote and hidden parts of nature, it is requisite that a better and more perfect application of the human mind should be introduced. This, however, is not to be understood as if nothing had been effected by the immense labours of so many past ages ; as the ancients have performed surprisingly in subjects that required abstract meditation, and force of genius. But as navigation was imperfect before the use of the compass, so will many secrets of nature and art remain undiscovered, without a more perfect knowledge of the understanding, its uses, and ways of working.

For our own part, from an earnest desire of truth, we have committed ourselves to doubtful, difficult, and solitary ways ; and relying on the Divine assistance, have supported our minds against the vehemence of opinions, our own internal doubts and scruples, and the darkness and fantastic

---

[c] By wreaths and knots, is understood the apparent complication of causes, and the superaddition of properties not essential to things ; as light to heat, yellowness to gold, pellucidity to glass, &c. *Shaw.*

images of the mind; that at length we might make more sure and certain discoveries for the benefit of posterity. And if we shall have effected anything to the purpose, what led us to it was a true and genuine humiliation of mind. Those who before us applied themselves to the discovery of arts, having just glanced upon things, examples, and experiments; immediately, as if invention was but a kind of contemplation, raised up their own spirits to deliver oracles: whereas our method is continually to dwell among things soberly, without abstracting or setting the understanding farther from them than makes their images meet; which leaves but little work for genius and mental abilities. And the same humility that we practise in learning, the same we also observe in teaching, without endeavouring to stamp a dignity on any of our inventions, by the triumphs of confutation, the citations of antiquity, the producing of authorities, or the mask of obscurity; as any one might do, who had rather give lustre to his own name, than light to the minds of others. We offer no violence, and spread no nets for the judgments of men, but lead them on to things themselves, and their relations; that they may view their own stores, what they have to reason about, and what they may add, or procure, for the common good. And if at any time ourselves have erred, mistook, or broke off too soon, yet as we only propose to exhibit things naked, and open, as they are, our errors may be the readier observed, and separated, before they considerably infect the mass of knowledge; and our labours be the more easily continued. And thus we hope to establish for ever a true and legitimate union between the experimental and rational faculty, whose fallen and inauspicious divorces and repudiations have disturbed everything in the family of mankind.

But as these great things are not at our disposal, we here, at the entrance of our work, with the utmost humility and fervency, put forth our prayers to God, that remembering the miseries of mankind, and the pilgrimage of this life, where we pass but few days and sorrowful, he would vouchsafe, through our hands, and the hands of others, to whom he has given the like mind, to relieve the human race by a new act of his bounty. We likewise humbly beseech him, that what is human may not clash with what is divine; and that when the ways of the senses are opened, and a greater natural light set up in the mind, nothing of incredulity and blindness towards divine mysteries may arise; but rather that the understanding, now cleared up, and purged of all vanity and superstition, may remain entirely subject to the divine oracles, and yield to faith, the things that are faith's: and lastly, that expelling the poisonous knowledge infused by the serpent, which puffs up and swells the human mind, we may neither be wise above measure, nor go beyond the bounds of sobriety, but pursue the truth in charity.

We now turn ourselves to men, with a few wholesome admonitions and just requests. And first, we admonish them to continue in a sense of their duty, as to divine matters; for the senses are like the sun, which displays the face of the earth, but shuts up that of the heavens: and again, that they run not into the contrary extreme, which they certainly will do, if they think an inquiry into nature any way forbid them by religion. It was not that pure and unspotted natural knowledge whereby Adam gave names to things, agreeable to their natures, which caused his fall; but an ambitious and authoritative desire of moral knowledge, to judge of good and evil, which makes men revolt from God, and obey no laws but those of their own will. But for the sciences, which contemplate nature, the sacred philosopher declares, "It is the glory of God to conceal a thing, but the glory of a king to find it out."[d] As if the Divine Being thus indulgently condescended to exercise the human mind by philosophical inquiries.

In the next place, we advise all mankind to think of the true ends of knowledge, and that they endeavour not after it for curiosity, contention, or the sake of despising others, nor yet for profit, reputation, power, or any such inferior consideration, but solely for the occasions and uses of life; all along conducting and perfecting it in the spirit of benevolence. Our requests are,—1. That men do not conceive we here deliver an opinion, but a work; and assure themselves we attempt not to found any sect or particular doctrine, but to fix an extensive basis for the service of human nature. 2. That, for their own sakes, they lay aside the zeal and

---

[d] Prov. xxv. 2.

prejudices of opinions, and endeavour the common good; and that being, by our assistance, freed and kept clear from the errors and hinderances of the way, they would themselves also take part of the task. 3. That they do not despair, as imagining our project for a grand restoration, or advancement of all kinds of knowledge, infinitely beyond the power of mortals to execute; whilst in reality, it is the genuine stop and prevention of infinite error. Indeed, as our state is mortal, and human, a full accomplishment cannot be expected in a single age, and must therefore be commended to posterity. Nor could we hope to succeed, if we arrogantly searched for the sciences in the narrow cells of the human understanding, and not submissively in the wider world. 4. In the last place, to prevent ill effects from contention, we desire mankind to consider how far they have a right to judge our performance, upon the foundations here laid down: for we reject all that knowledge which is too hastily abstracted from things, as vague, disorderly, and ill-formed; and we cannot be expected to abide by a judgment which is itself called in question.

DISTRIBUTION OF THE WORK.

IN SIX PARTS.

1. Survey and Extension of the Sciences; or, the Advancement of Learning.
2. Novum Organum; or, Precepts for the Interpretation of Nature.
3. Phenomena of the Universe; or, Natural and Experimental History, on which to found Philosophy.
4. Ladder of the Understanding.
5. Precursors, or Anticipators, of the Second Philosophy.
3. Second Philosophy; or, Active Science.

WE divide the whole of the work into six parts: the first whereof gives the substance, or general description of the knowledge which mankind at present possess; choosing to dwell a little upon things already received, that we may the easier perfect the old, and lead on to new; being equally inclined to cultivate the discoveries of antiquity, as to strike out fresh paths of science. In classing the sciences, we comprehend not only the things already invented and known, but also those omitted and wanted; for the intellectual globe, as well as the terrestrial, has both its frosts and deserts. It is therefore no wonder if we sometimes depart from the common divisions. For an addition, whilst it alters the whole, must necessarily alter the parts, and their sections; whereas the received divisions are only fitted to the received sum of the sciences, as it now stands. With regard to the things we shall note as defective; it will be our method to give more than the bare titles, or short heads of what we desire to have done; with particular care, where the dignity or difficulty of the subject requires it, either to lay down the rules for effecting the work, or make an attempt of our own, by way of example, or pattern, of the whole. For it concerns our own character, no less than the advantage of others, to know that a mere capricious idea has not presented the subject to our mind, and that all we desire and aim at is a wish. For our designs are within the power of all to compass, and we ourselves have certain and evident demonstrations of their utility. We come not hither, as augurs, to measure out regions in our mind by divination, but like generals, to invade them for conquest. And this is the first part of the work.

When we have gone through the ancient arts, we shall prepare the human understanding for pressing on beyond them. The second object of the work embraces the doctrine of a more perfect use of reason, and the true helps of the intellectual faculties, so as to raise and enlarge the powers of the mind; and, as far as the condition of humanity allows, to fit it to conquer the difficulties and obscurities of nature. The thing we mean, is a kind of logic, by us called The Art of interpreting Nature; as differing widely from the common logic, which, however, pretends to assist and direct the understanding, and in that they agree: but the difference betwixt them consists in three things, viz., the end, the order of demonstrating, and the grounds of inquiry.

The end of our new logic is to find, not arguments, but arts; not what agrees with principles, but principles themselves: not probable reasons, but plans and designs of works—a different intention producing a different effect. In one the adversary is conquered by dispute, and in the other nature by works. The nature and order of the demonstrations agree with this object. For in common logic, almost our whole labour is spent upon the syllogism. Logicians hitherto appear scarcely to have noticed induction, passing it over with some slight comment. But we reject the syllogistic method as being too confused, and allowing nature to escape out of our hands. For though nobody can doubt that those things which agree with the middle term agree with each other, nevertheless, there is this source of error, that a syllogism consists of propositions, propositions of words, and words are but the token and signs of things. Now, if the first notions, which are, as it were, the soul of words, and the basis of every philosophical fabric, are hastily abstracted from things, and vague and not clearly defined and limited, the whole structure falls to the ground. We therefore reject the syllogism, and that not only as regards first principles, to which logicians do not apply them, but also with respect to intermediate propositions, which the syllogism contrives to manage in such a way as to render barren in effect, unfit for practice, and clearly unsuited to the active branch of the sciences. Nevertheless, we would leave to the syllogism, and such celebrated and applauded demonstrations, their jurisdiction over popular and speculative acts; while, in everything relating to the nature of things, we make use of induction for both our major and minor propositions; for we consider induction as that form of demonstration which closes in upon nature and presses on, and, as it were, mixes itself with action. Whence the common order of demonstrating is absolutely inverted; for instead of flying immediately from the senses, and particulars, to generals, as to certain fixed poles, about which disputes always turn, and deriving others from these by intermediates, in a short, indeed, but precipitate manner, fit for controversy, but unfit to close with nature; we continually raise up propositions by degrees, and in the last place, come to the most general axioms, which are not notional, but well defined, and what nature allows of, as entering into the very essence of things.[a]

[a] This passage, though tersely and energetically expressed, is founded upon a misconception of deduction, or, as Bacon phrases it, syllogistic reasoning, and its relation to induction. The two processes are only reverse methods of inferences, the one concluding from a general to a particular, and the other from a particular to a general, and both

DISTRIBUTION OF THE WORK. 13

But the more difficult part of our task consists in the form of induction, and the judgment to be made by it ; for that form of the logicians which proceeds by simple enumeration, is a childish thing, concludes unsafely, lies open to contradictory instances, and regards only common matters, yet determines nothing : whilst the sciences require such a form of induction, as can separate, adjust, and verify experience, and come to a necessary determination by proper exclusions and rejections.

Nor is this all ; for we likewise lay the foundations of the sciences stronger and closer, and begin our inquiries deeper than men have hitherto done, bringing those things to the test which the common logic has taken upon trust. The logicians borrow the principles of the sciences from the sciences themselves, venerate the first notions of the mind, and acquiesce in the immediate informations of the senses, when rightly disposed; but we judge, that a real logic should enter every province of the sciences with a greater authority

schemata are resolvable into propositions, and propositions into words, which, as he says, are but the tokens and signs of things. Now if these first notions, which are as it were the soul of words and the basis of every philosophic fabric, be hastily abstracted from things, and vague and not clearly defined and limited, the whole structure, whether erected by induction or deduction, or both, as is most frequently the case, must fall to the ground. The error, therefore, does not lie in the deductive mode of proof, without which physical science could never advance beyond its empirical stage, but in clothing this method in the vulgar language of the day, and reasoning upon its terms as if they pointed at some fact or antithesis in nature, instead of previously testing the accuracy of such expressions by experiment and observation. As such notions are more general than the individual cases out of which they arise, it follows that this inquiry must be made through the medium of induction, and the essential merit of Bacon lies in framing a system of rules by which this ascending scale of inference may be secured from error. As the neglect of this important preliminary to scientific investigation vitiated all the Aristotelian physics, and kept the human mind stationary for two thousand years, hardly too much praise can be conferred upon the philosopher who not only pointed out the gap but supplied the materials for its obliteration. The ardency of his nature, however, urged him to extremes, and he confounded the accuracy of the deductive method with the straw and stubble on which it attempted to erect a system of physics. In censuring intermediate propositions, Bacon appears to have been unaware that he was condemning the only forms through which reason or inference can manifest itself, and lecturing mankind on the futility of an instrument which he was employing in every page of his book. *Ed.*

than their own principles can give; and that such supposed principles should be examined, till they become absolutely clear and certain. As for first notions of the mind, we suspect all those that the understanding, left to itself, procures; nor ever allow them till approved and authorized by a second judgment. And with respect to the informations of the senses, we have many ways of examining them; for the senses are fallacious, though they discover their own errors; but these lie near, whilst the means of discovery are remote.

The senses are faulty in two respects, as they either fail or deceive us. For there are many things that escape the senses, though ever so rightly disposed; as by the subtilty of the whole body, or the minuteness of its parts; the distance of place; the slowness or velocity of motion; the commonness of the object, &c. Neither do the senses, when they lay hold of a thing, retain it strongly; for evidence, and the informations of sense, are in proportion to a man, and not in proportion to the universe.[b] And it is a grand error to assert that sense is the measure of things.[c]

[b] Bacon held, that every perception is nothing more than the consciousness of some body acting either interiorly or from without upon that portion of the frame which is the point of contact. Hence all the knowledge we have of the material world arises from the movements which it generates in our senses. These sensations simply inform us that a wide class of objects exist independent of ourselves, which affect us in a certain manner, and do not convey into our minds the real properties of such objects so much as the effects of the relation in which they stand to our senses. Human knowledge thus becomes relative; and that which we call the relation of objects to one another, is nothing more than the relation which they have to our organization. Hence as these relations of objects, either internal or exterior to the mind vary, sensations must vary along with them, and produce, even in the same individual, a crowd of impressions either conflicting or in some measure opposed to each other. So far as these feelings concern morals, it is the business of ethics to bring them under the influence of reason, and, selecting out of them such as are calculated to dignify and elevate man's nature, to impart to them a trenchant and permanent character. As respects that portion which flow in upon the mind from the internal world, it is the peculiar province of induction as reformed by our author, to separate such as are illusory from the real, and to construct out of the latter a series of axioms, expressing in hierarchical gradation the general system of laws by which the universe is governed. *Ed.*

[c] The doctrine of the two last paragraphs may appear contradictory to the opinion of some philosophers, who maintain the infallibility of

To remedy this, we have from all quarters brought together, and fitted helps for the senses; and that rather by experiments than by instruments; apt experiments being much more subtile than the senses themselves, though assisted with the most finished instruments. We, therefore, lay no great stress upon the immediate and natural perceptions of the senses, but desire the senses to judge only of experiments, and experiments to judge of things: on which foundation, we hope to be patrons of the senses, and interpreters of their oracles. And thus we mean to procure the things relating to the light of nature, and the setting it up in the mind; which might well suffice, if the mind were as white paper. But since the minds of men are so strangely disposed, as not to receive the true images of things, it is necessary also that a remedy be found for this evil.

The idols, or false notions, which possess the mind, are either acquired or innate. The acquired arise either from the opinions or sects of philosophers, or from preposterous laws of demonstration; but the innate cleave to the nature of the understanding, which is found much more prone to error than the senses. For however men may amuse themselves, and admire, or almost adore the mind, it is certain, that like an irregular glass, it alters the rays of things, by its figure, and different intersections.

The two former kinds of idols may be extirpated, though with difficulty; but this third is insuperable. All that can be done, is to point them out, and mark, and convict that treacherous faculty of the mind; lest when the ancient errors are destroyed, new ones should sprout out from the rankness of the soil: and, on the other hand, to establish this for ever, that the understanding can make no judgment but by

the senses, as well as of reason; but the dispute perhaps turns rather upon words than things. Father Malbranche is express, that the senses never deceive us, yet as express that they should never be trusted, without being verified; charging the errors arising in this case upon human liberty, which makes a wrong choice. See "Recherches de la Vérité," liv. i. chaps. 5, 6, 7, 8. The difference may arise only from considering the senses in two different lights, viz. physically, or according to common use; and metaphysically, or abstractedly. The *Novum Organum* clears the whole. See also Marin Mersenus, "De la Vérité des Sciences." *Ed.*

induction, and the just form thereof. Whence the doctrine of purging the understanding requires three kinds of confutations, to fit it for the investigation of truth; viz., the confutation of philosophies, the confutation of demonstrations, and the confutation of the natural reason. But when these have been completed, and it has been clearly seen what results are to be expected from the nature of things, and the nature of the human mind, we shall have then furnished a nuptial couch for the mind and the universe, the divine goodness being our bridemaid. And let it be the prayer of our Epithalamium, that assistance to man may spring from this union, and a race of discoveries, which will contribute to his wants and vanquish his miseries. And this is the second part of the work.

But as we propose not only to pave and show the way, but also to tread in it ourselves, we shall next exhibit the phenomena of the universe; that is, such experience of all kinds, and such a natural history, as may afford a foundation to philosophy. For as no fine method of demonstration, or form of explaining nature, can preserve the mind from error, and support it from falling; so neither can it hence receive any matter of science. Those, therefore, who determine not to conjecture and guess, but to find out and know; not to invent fables and romances of worlds, but to look into, and dissect the nature of this real world, must consult only things themselves. Nor can any force of genius, thought, or argument, be substituted for this labour, search, and inspection; not even though all the wits of men were united: this, therefore, must either be had, or the business be deserted for ever.

But the conduct of mankind has hitherto been such, that it is no wonder nature has not opened herself to them. For the information of the senses is treacherous and deceitful; observation careless, irregular, and accidental; tradition idle, rumorous, and vain; practice narrow and servile; experience blind, stupid, vague, and broken; and natural history extremely light and empty: wretched materials for the understanding to fashion into philosophy and the sciences! Then comes in a preposterous subtilty of argumentation and sifting, as a last remedy, that mends not the matter one jot, nor separates the errors. Whence there are absolutely no hopes of enlarging and promoting the sciences, without rebuilding them.

The first materials for this purpose must be taken from a new kind of natural history. The understanding must also have fit subjects to work upon, as well as real helps to work with. But our history, no less than our logic, differs from the common in many respects; particularly, 1. In its end, or office; 2. Its collection; 3. Its subtilty; 4. Its choice; and 5. Its appointment for what is to follow.

Our natural history is not designed so much to please by its variety, or benefit by gainful experiments, as to afford light to the discovery of causes, and hold out the breasts to philosophy; for though we principally regard works, and the active parts of the sciences, yet we wait for the time of harvest, and would not reap the blade for the ear. We are well aware that axioms, rightly framed, will draw after them whole sheaves of works: but for that untimely and childish desire of seeing fruits of new works before the season, we absolutely condemn and reject it, as the golden apple that hinders the progress.

With regard to its collection; we propose to show nature not only in a free state, as in the history of meteors, minerals, plants, and animals; but more particularly as she is bound, and tortured, pressed, formed, and turned out of her course by art and human industry. Hence we would set down all opposite experiments of the mechanic and liberal arts, with many others not yet formed into arts; for the nature of things is better discovered by the torturings of art, than when they are left to themselves. Nor is it only a history of bodies that we would give; but also of their cardinal virtues, or fundamental qualities; as density, rarity, heat, cold, &c., which should be comprised in particular histories.

The kind of experiments to be procured for our history are much more subtile and simple than the common; abundance of them must be recovered from darkness, and are such as no one would have inquired after, that was not led by constant and certain tract to the discovery of causes; as being in themselves of no great use, and consequently not sought for their own sake, but with regard to works: like the letters of the alphabet with regard to discourse.

In the choice of our narratives and experiments we hope

to have shown more care than the other writers of natural history; as receiving nothing but upon ocular demonstration, or the strictest scrutiny of examination; and not heightening what is delivered to increase its miraculousness, but thoroughly purging it of superstition and fable. Besides this, we reject, with a particular mark, all those boasted and received falsehoods, which by a strange neglect have prevailed for so many ages, that they may no longer molest the sciences. For as the idle tales of nurses do really corrupt the minds of children, we cannot too carefully guard the infancy of philosophy from all vanity and superstition. And when any new or more curious experiment is offered, though it may seem to us certain and well founded; yet we expressly add the manner wherein it was made; that, after it shall be understood how things appear to us, men may beware of any error adhering to them, and search after more infallible proofs. We, likewise, all along interpose our directions, scruples, and cautions; and religiously guard against phantoms and illusions.

Lastly, having well observed how far experiments and history distract the mind; and how difficult it is, especially for tender or prejudiced persons, to converse with nature from the beginning, we shall continually subjoin our observations, as so many first glances of natural history at philosophy; and this to give mankind some earnest, that they shall not be kept perpetually floating upon the waves of history; and that when they come to the work of the understanding, and the explanation of nature, they may find all things in greater readiness. This will conclude the third part.

After the understanding has been thus aided and fortified, we shall be prepared to enter upon philosophy itself. But in so difficult a task, there are certain things to be observed, as well for instruction as for present use. The first is to propose examples of inquiry and investigation, according to our own method, in certain subjects of the noblest kind, but greatly differing from each other, that a specimen may be had of every sort. By these examples we mean not illustrations of rules and precepts, but perfect models, which will exemplify the second part of this work, and represent, as it were, to the eye, the whole progress of the mind, and the continued structure and order of invention, in the most chosen subjects, after the same manner as globes and machines facilitate the more abstruse and subtile demonstrations in mathematics. We assign the fourth part of our work to these examples, which are nothing else than a particular application of the second part of our undertaking.[d]

The fifth part is only temporary, or of use but till the rest are finished; whence we look upon it as interest till the principal be paid; for we do not propose to travel hoodwinked, so as to take no notice of what may occur of use in the way. This part, therefore, will consist of such things as we have invented, experienced, or added, by the same common use of the understanding that others employ. For as we have greater hopes from our constant conversation with nature, than from our force of genius, the discoveries we shall thus make may serve as inns on the road, for the mind to repose in, during its progress to greater certainties. But this, without being at all disposed to abide by anything that is not discovered, or proved, by the true form of induction. Nor need any one be shocked at this suspension of the judgment, in a doctrine which does not assert that nothing is knowable; but only that things cannot be known except in a certain order and method : whilst it allows particular degrees of certainty, for the sake of commodiousness and use, until the mind shall enter on the explanation of causes. Nor were those schools of philosophers,[e] who held positive truth to be unattainable, inferior to others who dogmatized at will. They did not, however, like us, prepare helps for the guidance of the senses and understanding, as we have done, but at once abolished all belief and authority, which is a totally different and almost opposite matter.

The sixth and last part of our work, to which all the rest are subservient, is to lay down that philosophy which shall flow from the just, pure, and strict inquiry hitherto proposed. But to perfect this, is beyond both our abilities and our hopes, yet we shall lay the foundations of it, and recommend

[d] This part is what the author elsewhere terms *scala intellectus*, or the progress of the understanding, and was intended to be supplied by him in the way of monthly productions. See his dedication of the "History of the Winds" to Prince Charles. *Shaw.*
[e] The later Academy, who held the ἀκαταληψία.

the superstructure to posterity. We design no contemptible beginning to the work; and anticipate that the fortune of mankind will lead it to such a termination as is not possible for the present race of men to conceive. The point in view is not only the contemplative happiness, but the whole fortunes, and affairs, and powers, and works of men. For man being the minister and interpreter of nature, acts and understands so far as he has observed of the order, the works and mind of nature, and can proceed no farther; for no power is able to loose or break the chain of causes, nor is nature to be conquered but by submission: whence those twin intentions, human knowledge and human power, are really coincident; and the greatest hinderance to works is the ignorance of causes.

The capital precept for the whole undertaking is this, that the eye of the mind be never taken off from things themselves, but receive their images truly as they are. And God forbid that ever we should offer the dreams of fancy for a model of the world; but rather in his kindness vouchsafe to us the means of writing a revelation and true vision of the traces and moulds of the Creator in his creatures.

May thou, therefore, O Father, who gavest the light of vision as the first fruit of creation, and who hast spread over the fall of man the light of thy understanding as the accomplishment of thy works, guard and direct this work, which, issuing from thy goodness, seeks in return thy glory! When thou hadst surveyed the works which thy hands had wrought, all seemed good in thy sight, and Thou restedst. But when man turned to the works of his hands, he found all vanity and vexation of spirit, and experienced no rest. If, however, we labour in thy works, Thou wilt make us to partake of thy vision and sabbath; we, therefore, humbly beseech Thee to strengthen our purpose, that Thou mayst be willing to endow thy family of mankind with new gifts, through our hands, and the hands of those in whom Thou shalt implant the same spirit.

FIRST PART

OF THE

GREAT INSTAURATION.

THE DIGNITY AND ADVANCEMENT OF LEARNING,

IN NINE BOOKS.

CONTENTS.

BOOK I.

The different Objections to Learning stated and confuted. Its Dignity and Merit maintained.

BOOK II.

CHAPTER I.

General Division of Learning into History, Poetry, and Philosophy, in relation to the Three Faculties of the Mind, Memory, Imagination, and Reason. The same Distribution applies to Theology.

CHAPTER II.

History divided into Natural and Civil;—Civil subdivided into Ecclesiastical and Literary. The Division of Natural History, according to the Subject-matter, into the History of Generations, Præter-generations, and the Arts.

CHAPTER III.

Second Division of Natural History, in relation to its Use and End, into Narrative and Inductive. The most important end of Natural History is to aid in erecting a Body of Philosophy which appertains to Induction. Division of the History of Generations into the History of the Heavens, the History of Meteors, the History of the Earth and Sea, the History of Massive or Collective Bodies, and the History of Species.

CHAPTER IV.

Civil History divided into Ecclesiastical and Literary. Deficiency of the latter. The absence of Precepts for its compilation.

CHAPTER V.
The Dignity of Civil History and the Obstacles it has to encounter.

CHAPTER VI.
Division of Civil History into Memoirs, Antiquities, and Perfect History.

CHAPTER VII.
Division of Perfect History into Chronicles, Biographies, and Relations. The Development of their parts.

CHAPTER VIII.
Division of the History of Times into Universal and Particular. The Advantages and Disadvantages of both.

CHAPTER IX.
Second Division of the History of Times, into Annals and Journals.

CHAPTER X.
Second Division of Special Civil History into Pure and Mixed.

CHAPTER XI.
Ecclesiastical History divided into the General History of the Church, History of Prophecy, and History of Providence.

CHAPTER XII.
The Appendix of History embraces the Words of Men, as the Body of History includes their Exploits. Its Division into Speeches, Letters, and Apophthegms.

CHAPTER XIII.
The Second leading Branch of Learning—Poetry. Its Division into Narrative, Dramatic, and Parabolic. Three Examples of the latter species detailed.

BOOK III.

CHAPTER I.
Division of Learning into Theology and Philosophy. The latter divided into the Knowledge of God, of Nature, and of Man. Construction of Philosophia Prima as the Mother of all the Sciences.

CHAPTER II.
Natural Theology with its Appendix, the Knowledge of Angels and Spirits.

CHAPTER III.
Natural Philosophy divided into Speculative and Practical. The Necessity of keeping these Two Branches distinct.

CHAPTER IV.

Division of the Speculative Branch of Natural Philosophy into Physics and Metaphysics. Physics relate to the Investigation of Efficient Causes and Matter; Metaphysics to that of Final Causes and the Form. Division of Physics into the Sciences of the Principles of Things, the Structure of Things, and the Variety of Things. Division of Physics in relation to the Variety of Things into Abstract and Concrete. Division of Concretes agrees with the Distribution of the Parts of Natural History. Division of Abstracts into the Doctrine of Material Forms and Motion. Appendix of Speculative Physics twofold: viz., Natural Problems and the Opinions of Ancient Philosophers. Metaphysics divided into the Knowledge of Forms and the Doctrine of Final Causes.

CHAPTER V.

Division of the Practical Branch of Natural Philosophy into Mechanics and Magic (Experimental Philosophy), which correspond to the Speculative Division—Mechanics to Physics, and Magic to Metaphysics. The word Magic cleared from False Interpretation. Appendix to Active Science twofold: viz., an Inventory of Human Helps and a Catalogue of Things of Multifarious Use.

CHAPTER VI.

The Great Appendix of Natural Philosophy both Speculative and Practical. Mathematics. Its Proper Position not among the Substantial Sciences, but in their Appendix. Mathematics divided into Pure and Mixed.

BOOK IV.

CHAPTER I.

Division of the Knowledge of Man into Human and Civil Philosophy. Human Philosophy divided into the Doctrine of the Body and Soul. The Construction of one General Science, including the Nature and State of Man. The latter divided into the Doctrine of the Human Person and the Connection of the Soul with the Body. Division of the Doctrine of the Person of Man into that of his Miseries and Prerogatives. Division of the Relations between the Soul and the Body into the Doctrines of Indications and Impressions. Physiognomy and the Interpretation of Dreams assigned to the Doctrine of Indications.

CHAPTER II.

Division of the Knowledge of the Human Body into the Medicinal, Cosmetic, Athletic and the Voluptuary Arts. Division of Medicine into Three Functions: viz., the Preservation of Health, the Cure of Diseases, and the Prolongation of Life. The last distinct from the two former.

CHAPTER III.

Division of the Doctrine of the Human Soul into that of the Inspired Essence and the Knowledge of the Sensible or Produced Soul. Second Division of the same philosophy into the Doctrine of the Substance and the Faculties of the Soul. The Use and Objects of the latter. Two Appendices to the Doctrine of the Faculties of the Soul: viz., Natural Divination and Fascination (Mesmerism). The Faculties of the Sensible Soul divided into those of Motion and Sense.

BOOK V.

CHAPTER I.

Division of the Use and Objects of the Faculties of the Soul into Logic and Ethics. Division of Logic into the Arts of Invention, Judgment, Memory, and Tradition.

CHAPTER II.

Division of Invention into the Invention of Arts and Arguments. The former, though the more important of them, is wanting. Division of the Invention of Arts into Literate (Instructed) Experience and a New Method (Novum Organum). An Illustration of Literate Experience.

CHAPTER III.

Division of the Invention of Arguments into Promptuary, or Places of Preparation, and Topical, or Places of Suggestion. The Division of Topics into General and Particular. An Example of Particular Topics afforded by an Inquiry into the Nature of the Qualities of Light and Heavy.

CHAPTER IV.

The Art of Judgment divided into Induction and the Syllogism. Induction developed in the Novum Organum. The Syllogism divided into Direct and Inverse Reduction. Inverse Reduction divided into the Doctrine of Analytics and Confutations. The Division of the latter into Confutations of Sophisms, the Unmasking of Vulgarisms (Equivocal Terms), and the Destruction of Delusive Images or Idols. Delusive Appearances divided into *Idola Tribûs, Idola Specûs,* and *Idola Fori.* Appendix to the Art of Judgment. The Adapting the Demonstration to the Nature of the Subject.

CHAPTER V.

Division of the Retentive Art into the Aids of the Memory and the Nature of the Memory itself. Division of the Doctrine of Memory into Prenotion and Emblem.

BOOK VI.

CHAPTER I.

Division of Tradition into the Doctrine of the Organ, the Method and the Illustration of Speech. The Organ of Speech divided into the Knowledge of the Marks of Things, of Speaking, and Writing. The two last comprise the two Branches of Grammar. The Marks of Things divided into Hieroglyphics and Real Characters. Grammar again divided into Literary and Philosophical. Prosody referred to the Doctrine of Speech and Ciphers to the Department of Writing.

CHAPTER II.

Method of Speech includes a Wide Part of Tradition. Styled the Wisdom of Delivery. Various kinds of Methods enumerated. Their respective Merits.

CHAPTER III.

The Grounds and Functions of Rhetoric. Three Appendices which belong only to the Preparatory Part, viz., the Colours of Good and Evil, both simple and composed; the Antithesis of Things (the *pro* and *con.* of General Questions); the Minor Forms of Speech (the Elaboration of Exordiums, Perorations, and Leading Arguments).

CHAPTER IV.

Two General Appendices to Tradition, viz., the Arts of Teaching and Criticism.

BOOK VII.

CHAPTER I.

Ethics divided into the Doctrine of Models and the Georgics (Culture) of the Mind. Division of Models into the Absolute and Comparative Good. Absolute Good divided into Personal and National.

CHAPTER II.

Division of Individual Good into Active and Passive. That of Passive Good into Conservative and Perfective. Good of the Commonwealth divided into General and Respective.

CHAPTER III.

The Culture of the Mind divided into the Knowledge of Characteristic Differences of Affections, of Remedies and Cures. Appendix relating to the Harmony between the Pleasures of the Mind and the Body.

BOOK VIII.

CHAPTER I.
Civil Knowledge divided into the Art of Conversation, the Art of Negotiation, and the Art of State Policy.

CHAPTER II.
The Art of Negotiation divided into the Knowledge of Dispersed Occasions (Conduct in Particular Emergencies), and into the Science of Rising in Life. Examples of the former drawn from Solomon. Precepts relating to Self-advancement.

CHAPTER III.
The Arts of Empire or State Policy omitted. Two Deficiencies alone noticed. The Art of Enlarging the Bounds of Empire, and the Knowledge of Universal Justice drawn from the Fountains of Law.

BOOK IX.

The Compartments of Theology omitted. Three Deficiencies pointed out. The Right Use of Reason in Matters of Faith. The Knowledge of the Degrees of Unity in the City of God. The Emanations of the Holy Scriptures.

ON THE DIGNITY AND
ADVANCEMENT OF LEARNING.

FIRST BOOK.

The Different Objections to Learning stated and confuted; its Dignity and Merit maintained.

TO THE KING.

As under the old law, most excellent king, there were daily sacrifices and free oblations[a]—the one arising out of ritual observance, and the other from a pious generosity, so I deem that all faithful subjects owe their kings a double tribute of affection and duty. In the first I hope I shall never be found deficient, but as regards the latter, though doubtful of the worthiness of my choice, I thought it more befitting to tender to your Majesty that service which rather refers to the excellence of your individual person than to the business of the state.

In bearing your Majesty in mind, as is frequently my custom and duty, I have been often struck with admiration, apart from your other gifts of virtue and fortune, at the surprising development of that part of your nature which philosophers call intellectual. The deep and broad capacity of your mind, the grasp of your memory, the quickness of your apprehension, the penetration of your judgment, your lucid method of arrangement, and easy facility of speech:— at such extraordinary endowments I am forcibly reminded of the saying of Plato, "that all science is but remembrance,"[b] and that the human mind is originally imbued with all knowledge; that which she seems adventitiously to acquire in life being nothing more than a return to her first conceptions, which had been overlaid by the grossness of the

---

[a] See Numb. xxviii. 23; Levit. xxii. 18.
[b] Plato's Phædo, i. 72 (Steph.); Theæt. i. 166, 191; Menon, ii. 81; and Aristot. de Memor. 2.

body. In no person so much as your Majesty does this opinion appear more fully confirmed, your soul being apt to kindle at the intrusion of the slightest object; and even at the spark of a thought foreign to the purpose to burst into flame. As the Scripture says of the wisest king, "That his heart was as the sands of the sea,"[c] which, though one of the largest bodies, contains the finest and smallest particles of matter. In like manner God has endowed your Majesty with a mind capable of grasping the largest subjects and comprehending the least, though such an instrument seems an impossibility in nature. As regards your readiness of speech, I am reminded of that saying of Tacitus concerning Augustus Cæsar, "Augusto profluens ut quæ principem virum deceret, eloquentia fuit."[d] For all eloquence which is affected or overlaboured, or merely imitative, though otherwise excellent, carries with it an air of servility, nor is it free to follow its own impulses. But your Majesty's eloquence is indeed royal, streaming and branching out in nature's fashion as from a fountain, copious and elegant, original and inimitable. And as in those things which concern your crown and family, virtue seems to contend with fortune—your Majesty being possessed of a virtuous disposition and a prosperous government, a virtuous observance of the duties of the conjugal state with most blessed and happy fruit of marriage, a virtuous and most Christian desire of peace at a time when contemporary princes seem no less inclined to harmony,—so likewise in intellectual gifts there appears as great a contention between your Majesty's natural talents and the universality and perfection of your learning. Nor indeed would it be easy to find any monarch since the Christian era who could bear any comparison with your Majesty in the variety and depth of your erudition. Let any one run over the whole line of kings, and he will agree with me. It indeed seems a great thing in a monarch, if he can find time to digest a compendium or imbibe the simple elements of science, or love and countenance learning; but that a king, and he a king born, should have drunk at the true fountain of knowledge, yea, rather, should have a fountain of

[c] 3 Kings iv. 29. We may observe that Bacon invariably quotes from the Vulgate, to which our references point.
[d] Tacitus, Annales, xiii. 3.

learning in himself, is indeed little short of a miracle. And the more since in your Majesty's heart are united all the treasures of sacred and profane knowledge, so that like Hermes your Majesty is invested with a triple glory, being distinguished no less by the power of a king than by the illumination of a priest and the learning of a philosopher.[e] Since, then, your Majesty surpasses other monarchs by this property, which is peculiarly your own, it is but just that this dignified pre-eminence should not only be celebrated in the mouths of the present age, and be transmitted to posterity, but also that it should be engraved in some solid work which might serve to denote the power of so great a king and the height of his learning.

Therefore, to return to our undertaking: no oblation seemed more suitable than some treatise relating to that purpose, the sum of which should consist of two parts,—the first of the excellence of learning, and the merit of those who labour judiciously and with energy for its propagation and development. The second, to point out what part of knowledge has been already laboured and perfected, and what portions left unfinished or entirely neglected; in order, since I dare not positively advise your Majesty to adopt any particular course, that by a detailed representation of our wants, I may excite your Majesty to examine the treasures of your royal heart, and thence to extract, whatever to your magnanimity and wisdom may seem best fitted to enlarge the boundaries of knowledge.

On the threshold of the first part it is advisable to sift the merits of knowledge, and clear it of the disgrace brought upon it by ignorance, whether disguised (1) in the zeal of divines, (2) the arrogance of politicians, or (3) the errors of men of letters.

Some divines pretend, 1. "That knowledge is to be received with great limitation, as the aspiring to it was the original sin, and the cause of the fall; 2. That it has somewhat of the serpent, and puffeth up;" 3. That Solomon says, "Of making books there is no end: much study is weariness of the flesh; for in much wisdom is much grief; and he that increaseth knowledge, increaseth sorrow:"[f] 4. "That

[e] Poemander of Hermes Trismegistus.
[f] Eccles. xii. 12, and i. 18

St. Paul cautions against being spoiled through vain philosophy:"[g] 5. "That experience shows learned men have been heretics; and learned times inclined to atheism; and that the contemplation of second causes takes from our dependence upon God, who is the first."

To this we answer, 1. It was not the pure knowledge of nature, by the light whereof man gave names to all the creatures in Paradise, agreeable to their natures, that occasioned the fall; but the proud knowledge of good and evil, with an intent in man to give law to himself, and depend no more upon God. 2. Nor can any quantity of natural knowledge puff up the mind; for nothing fills, much less distends the soul, but God. Whence as Solomon declares, "That the eye is not satisfied with seeing, nor the ear with hearing;"[h] so of knowledge itself he says, "God hath made all things beautiful in their seasons; also he hath placed the world in man's heart; yet cannot man find out the work which God worketh from the beginning to the end;"[i] hereby declaring plainly that God has framed the mind like a glass, capable of the image of the universe, and desirous to receive it as the eye to receive the light; and thus it is not only pleased with the variety and vicissitudes of things, but also endeavours to find out the laws they observe in their changes and alterations. And if such be the extent of the mind, there is no danger of filling it with any quantity of knowledge. But it is merely from its quality when taken without the true corrective, that knowledge has somewhat of venom or malignity. The corrective which renders it sovereign is charity, for according to St. Paul, "Knowledge puffeth up, but charity buildeth."[k] 3. For the excess of writing and reading books, the anxiety of spirit proceeding from knowledge, and the admonition, that we be not seduced by vain philosophy; when these passages are rightly understood, they mark out the boundaries of human knowledge, so as to comprehend the universal nature of things. These limitations are three: the first, that we should not place our felicity in knowledge, so as to forget mortality; the second, that we use knowledge so as to give ourselves ease and content, not distaste and repining; and the third, that we presume not by the con-

[g] 1 Cor. viii. 1.   [h] Eccles. i. 8.
[i] Eccles. iii. 11.   [k] 1 Cor. viii. 1.

templation of nature, to attain to the mysteries of God. As to the first, Solomon excellently says, "I saw that wisdom excelleth folly as far as light excelleth darkness. The wise man's eyes are in his head, but the fool walketh in darkness; and I myself perceived also that one event happeneth to them all."[1] And for the second, it is certain that no vexation or anxiety of mind results from knowledge, but merely by accident; all knowledge, and admiration, which is the seed of knowledge, being pleasant in itself; but when we frame conclusions from our knowledge, apply them to our own particular, and thence minister to ourselves weak fears or vast desires; then comes on that anxiety and trouble of mind which is here meant—when knowledge is no longer the dry light of Heraclitus, but the drenched one, steeped in the humours of the affections.[m] 4. The third point deserves to be more dwelt upon; for if any man shall think, by his inquiries after material things, to discover the nature or will of God, he is indeed spoiled by vain philosophy; for the contemplation of God's works produces knowledge, though, with regard to him, not perfect knowledge, but wonder, which is broken knowledge. It may, therefore, be properly said, "That the sense resembles the sun, which shows the terrestrial globe, but conceals the celestial;"[n] for thus the sense discovers natural things, whilst it shuts up divine. And hence some learned men have, indeed, been heretical, whilst they sought to seize the secrets of the Deity borne on the waxen wings of the senses. 5. As to the point that too much knowledge should incline to atheism, and the ignorance of second causes make us more dependent upon God, we ask Job's question, "Will ye lie for God, as one man will do for another, to gratify him?"[o] For certainly God works nothing in nature but by second causes;[p] and to assert the contrary is mere imposture, as it were, in favour of God, and offering up to the author of truth the unclean sacrifice of a lie. Undoubtedly a superficial tincture of philosophy may incline the mind to atheism, yet a farther knowledge brings

---

[1] Eccles. ii. 13, 14.
[m] Ap. Stob. Serm. v. 120, in Ritter's Hist. Phil. § 47.
[n] Phil. Jud. de Somnis, p. 41.
[o] Job xiii. 7.
[p] Hooker, Eccl. Pol. i. 2; Butler, Anal. part i c. 2.

it back to religion;[q] For on the threshold of philosophy, where second causes appear to absorb the attention, some oblivion of the highest cause may ensue; but when the mind goes deeper, and sees the dependence of causes and the works of Providence, it will easily perceive, according to the mythology of the poets, that the upper link of Nature's chain is fastened to Jupiter's throne.[r] To conclude, let no one weakly imagine that man can search too far, or be too well studied in the book of God's word, and works, divinity, and philosophy; but rather let them endeavour an endless progression in both, only applying all to charity, and not to pride—to use, not ostentation, without confounding the two different streams of philosophy and revelation together.[s]

The reflections cast upon learning by politicians, are these. 1. "That it enervates men's minds, and unfits them for arms; 2. That it perverts their dispositions for government and politics; 3. That it makes them too curious and irresolute, by variety of reading; too peremptory or positive by strictness of rules; too immoderate and conceited by the greatness of instances; too unsociable and incapacitated for the times, by the dissimilitude of examples; or at least, 4. That it diverts from action and business, and leads to a love of retirement; 5. That it introduces a relaxation in government, as every man is more ready to argue than obey; whence Cato the censor—when Carneades came ambassador to Rome, and the young Romans, allured with his eloquence, flocked about him,—gave counsel in open senate, to grant him his despatch immediately, lest he should infect the minds of the youth, and insensibly occasion an alteration in the state."[t]

The same conceit is manifest in Virgil, who, preferring the honour of his country to that of his profession, challenged the arts of policy in the Romans, as something superior to

---

[q] See the author's essay on Atheism, and Mr. Boyle's essays upon the Usefulness of Philosophy.
[r] Iliad, viii. 19; and conf. Plato, Theæt. i. 153.
[s] The dispute betwixt the rational and scriptural divines is still on foot: the former are for reconciling reason and philosophy with faith and religion; and the latter for keeping them distinct, as things incompatible, or making reason and knowledge subject to faith and religion. The author is clear, that they should be kept separate, as will more fully appear hereafter, when he comes to treat of theology. *Shaw.*
[t] Plutarch in M. Cato.

letters, the pre-eminence in which, he freely assigns to the Grecians.

> "Tu regere imperio populos, Romane memento:
> Hæ tibi erunt artes."—Æn. vi. 851.

And we also observe that Anytus, the accuser of Socrates, charged him in his impeachment with destroying, in the minds of young men, by his rhetorical arts, all authority and reverence for the laws of the country.[u]

1. But these and the like imputations have rather a show of gravity, than any just ground; for experience shows that learning and arms have flourished in the same persons and ages. As to persons, there are no better instances than Alexander and Cæsar, the one Aristotle's scholar in philosophy, and the other Cicero's rival in eloquence; and again, Epaminondas and Xenophon, the one whereof first abated the power of Sparta, and the other first paved the way for subverting the Persian monarchy. This concurrence of learning and arms, is yet more visible in times than in persons, as an age exceeds a man. For in Egypt, Assyria, Persia, Greece, and Rome, the times most famous for arms are likewise most admired for learning; so that the greatest authors and philosophers, the greatest leaders and governors, have lived in the same ages. Nor can it well be otherwise; for as the fulness of human strength, both in body and mind, comes nearly at an age; so arms and learning, one whereof corresponds to the body, the other to the soul, have a near concurrence in point of time.

2. And that learning should rather prove detrimental than serviceable in the art of government, seems very improbable. It is wrong to trust the natural body to empirics, who commonly have a few receipts whereon they rely, but who know neither the causes of diseases, nor the constitutions of patients, nor the danger of accidents, nor the true methods of cure. And so it must needs be dangerous to have the civil body of states managed by empirical statesmen, unless well mixed with others who are grounded in learning. On the contrary, it is almost without instance, that any government was unprosperous under learned governors

[u] Plato, Apol. Soc.

For however common it has been with politicians to discredit learned men, by the name of pedants, yet it appears from history, that the governments of princes in minority have excelled the governments of princes in maturity, merely because the management was in learned hands. The state of Rome for the first five years, so much magnified, during the minority of Nero, was in the hands of Seneca, a pedant: so it was for ten years, during the minority of Gordianus the younger, with great applause in the hands of Misitheus, a pedant; and it was as happy before that, in the minority of Alexander Severus, under the rule of women, assisted by preceptors. And to look into the government of the bishops of Rome, particularly that of Pius and Sextus Quintus, who were both at their entrance esteemed but pedantical friars, we shall find that such popes did greater things, and proceeded upon truer principles of state, than those who rose to the papacy from an education in civil affairs, and the courts of princes. For though men bred to learning are perhaps at a loss in points of convenience, and present accommodations, called[x] reasons of state, yet they are perfect in the plain grounds of religion, justice, honour, and moral virtue, which, if well pursued, there will be as little use of reasons of state, as of physic in a healthy constitution. Nor can the experience of one man's life furnish examples and precedents for another's: present occurrences frequently correspond to ancient examples, better than .to later. And lastly, the genius of any single man can no more equal learning, than a private purse hold way with the exchequer.

3. As to the particular indispositions of the mind for politics and government, laid to the charge of learning, if they are allowed of any force, it must be remembered, that learning affords more remedies than it breeds diseases; for if, by a secret operation, it renders men perplexed and irresolute, on the other hand, by plain precept, it teaches when, and upon what grounds, to resolve, and how to carry things in suspense, without prejudice: if it makes men positive and stiff, it shows what things are in their nature demonstrative, what conjectural; and teaches the use of distinctions and exceptions, as well as the rigidness of prin-

---

[x] By the Italians "Ragioni di stato."

ciples and rules. If it misleads, by the unsuitableness of examples, it shows the force of circumstances, the errors of comparisons, and the cautions of application; so that in all cases, it rectifies more effectually than it perverts: and these remedies it conveys into the mind much more effectually by the force and variety of examples. Let a man look into the errors of Clement the Seventh, so livelily described by Guicciardini; or into those of Cicero, described by himself in his epistles to Atticus, and he will fly from being irresolute: let him look into the errors of Phocion, and he will beware of obstinacy or inflexibility: let him read the fable of Ixion,[y] and it will keep him from conceitedness: let him look into the errors of the second Cato, and he will never tread opposite to the world.[z]

4. For the pretence that learning disposes to retirement, privacy, and sloth; it were strange if what accustoms the mind to perpetual motion and agitation should induce indolence; whereas no kind of men love business, for its own sake, but the learned; whilst others love it for profit, as hirelings for the wages; others for honour; others because it bears them up in the eyes of men, and refreshes their reputations, which would otherwise fade; or because it reminds them of their fortune, and gives them opportunities of revenging and obliging; or because it exercises some faculty, wherein they delight, and so keeps them in good humour with themselves. Whence, as false valour lies in the eyes of the beholders, such men's industry lies in the eyes of others, or is exercised with a view to their own designs; whilst the learned love business, as an action according to nature, and agreeable to the health of the mind, as exercise is to that of the body: so that, of all men, they are the most indefatigable in such business as may deservedly fill and employ the mind. And if there are any laborious in study, yet idle in business, this proceeds either from a weakness of body, or a softness of disposition, and not from learning itself, as Seneca remarks, "Quidam tam sunt umbratiles ut putent in turbido esse, quicquid in luce est."[a] The consciousness of such a disposition may indeed incline a man to learning, but learning does not breed any such temper in him.

[y] Pind. Pyth. ii. 21.   [z] Cic. ad Att l. 1.
[a] Seneca's Epistles, iii. near the end.

If it be objected, that learning takes up much time, which might be better employed, I answer that the most active or busy men have many vacant hours, while they expect the tides and returns of business; and then the question is, how those spaces of leisure shall be filled up, whether with pleasure or study? Demosthenes being taunted by Æschines, a man of pleasure, that his speeches smelt of the lamp, very pertly retorted, "There is great difference between the objects which you and I pursue by lamp-light."[b] No fear, therefore, that learning should displace business, for it rather keeps and defends the mind against idleness and pleasure, which might otherwise enter to the prejudice both of business and learning. 5. For the allegation that learning should undermine the reverence due to laws and government, it is a mere calumny, without shadow of truth; for to say that blind custom of obedience should be a safer obligation than duty, taught and understood, is to say that a blind man may tread surer by a guide than a man with his eyes open can by a light. And, doubtless, learning makes the mind gentle and pliable to government, whereas ignorance renders it churlish and mutinous; and it is always found that the most barbarous, rude, and ignorant times have been most tumultuous, changeable, and seditious.

6. As to the judgment of Cato the Censor, he was punished for his contempt of learning, in the kind wherein he offended, for when past threescore the humour took him to learn Greek, which shows that his former censure of the Grecian learning was rather an affected gravity than his inward sense.[c] And, indeed, the Romans never arrived at their height of empire till they had arrived at their height of arts; for in the time of the two first Cæsars, when their government was in its greatest perfection, there lived the best poet, Virgil; the best historiographer, Livy; the best antiquary, Varro; and the best, or second best orator, Cicero, that the world has known. And as to the persecution of Socrates, the time must be remembered in which it occurred, viz., under the reign of the Thirty Tyrants, of all mortals the bloodiest and basest that ever reigned, since the government

---

Plutarch's Life of Demosthenes, not said of Æschines, but Pytheas.
[c] Plutarch's M. Cato.

had no sooner returned to its senses than that judgment was reversed. Socrates, from being a criminal, started at once into a hero, his memory loaded with honours human and divine, and his discourses, which had been previously stigmatized as immoral and profane, were considered as the reformers of thought and manners.[d] And let this suffice as an answer to those politicians who have presumed, whether sportively or in earnest, to disparage learning.

We come now to that sort of discredit which is brought upon learning by learned men themselves; and this proceeds either (1) from their fortune, (2) their manners, or (3) the nature of their studies.

1. The disrepute of learning from the fortune or condition of the learned, regards either their indigence, retirement, or meanness of employ. As to the point, that learned men grow not so soon rich as others, because they convert not their labours to profit, we might turn it over to the friars, of whom Machiavel said, "That the kingdom of the clergy had been long since at an end, if the reputation and reverence towards the poverty of the monks and mendicants had not borne out the excesses of bishops and prelates."[e] For so the splendour and magnificence of the great had long since sunk into rudeness and barbarism, if the poverty of learned men had not kept up civility and reputation. But to drop such advantages, it is worth observing how reverend and sacred poverty was esteemed for some ages in the Roman state, since, as Livy says, " There never was a republic greater, more venerable, and more abounding in good examples than the Roman, nor one that so long withstood avarice and luxury, or so much honoured poverty and parsimony."[f] And we see, when Rome degenerated, how Julius Cæsar after his victory was counselled to begin the restoration of the state, by abolishing the reputation of wealth. And, indeed, as we truly say that blushing is the livery of virtue, though it may sometimes proceed from guilt,[g] so it holds true of poverty that it is the attendant of virtue, though sometimes it may proceed from mismanagement and accident.

[d] Plato, Apol. Socr. [e] Mach. Hist. de Firenza, b. 10.
[f] Livy's preface, towards the end.
[g] Diog. Cyn. ap. Laert. vi. 54 ; compare Tacitus, Agric. 45, of Domitian, "Sævus vultus et rubor, a quo se contra pudorem muniebat."

As for retirement, it is a theme so common to extol a private life, not taxed with sensuality and sloth, for the liberty, the pleasure, and the freedom from indignity it affords, that every one praises it well, such an agreement it has to the nature and apprehensions of mankind. This may be added, that learned men, forgotten in states and not living in the eyes of the world, are like the images of Cassius and Brutus at the funeral of Junia, which not being represented as many others were, Tacitus said of them that "they outshone the rest, because not seen."[h]

As for their meanness of employ, that most exposed to contempt is the education of youth, to which they are commonly allotted. But how unjust this reflection is to all who measure things, not by popular opinion, but by reason, will appear in the fact that men are more careful what they put into new vessels than into those already seasoned. It is manifest that things in their weakest state usually demand our best attention and assistance. Hearken to the Hebrew rabbins: "Your young men shall see visions, your old men shall dream dreams;"[i] upon which the commentators observe, that youth is the worthier age, inasmuch as revelation by vision is clearer than by dreams. And to say the truth, how much soever the lives of pedants have been ridiculed upon the stage, as the emblem of tyranny, because the modern looseness or negligence has not duly regarded the choice of proper schoolmasters and tutors; yet the wisdom of the ancientest and best times always complained that states were too busy with laws and too remiss in point of education. This excellent part of ancient discipline has in some measure been revived of late by the colleges of Jesuits abroad; in regard of whose diligence in fashioning the morals and cultivating the minds of youth, I may say, as Agesilaus said to his enemy Pharnabasus, "Talis quum sis, utinam noster esses."[k]

2. The manners of learned men belong rather to their individual persons than to their studies or pursuits. No doubt, as in all other professions and conditions of life, bad and good are to be found among them; yet it must be admitted that learning and studies, unless they fall in with

[h] Annals, iii. 76.   [i] Joel ii. 28.   [k] Plut. Life of Agesil.

very depraved dispositions, have, in conformity with the adage, "Abire studia in mores," a moral influence upon men's lives. For my part I cannot find that any disgrace to learning can proceed from the habits of learned men, inherent in them as learned, unless peradventure that may be a fault which was attributed to Demosthenes, Cicero, the second Cato, and many others, that seeing the times they read of more pure than their own, pushed their servility too far in the reformation of manners, and to seek to impose, by austere precepts, the laws of ancient asceticism upon dissolute times. Yet even antiquity should have forewarned them of this excess; for Solon, upon being asked if he had given his citizens the best laws, replied, "The best they were capable of receiving."[l] And Plato, finding that he had fallen upon corrupt times, refused to take part in the administration of the commonwealth, saying that a man should treat his country with the same forbearance as his parents, and recall her from a wrong course, not by violence or contest, but by entreaty and persuasion.[m] Cæsar's counsellor administers the same caveat in the words, "Non ad vetera instituta revocamus quæ jampridem corruptis moribus ludibrio sunt."[n] Cicero points out the same error in the second Cato, when writing to his friend Atticus:—" Cato optime sentit sed nocet interdum Reipublicæ ; loquitur enim tanquam in Republica Platonis, non tanquam in fæce Romuli."[o] The same orator likewise excuses and blames the philosophers for being too exact in their precepts. These preceptors, said he, have stretched the lines and limits of duties beyond their natural boundaries, thinking that we might safely reform when we had reached the highest point of perfection.[p] And yet himself stumbled over the same stone, so that he might have said, " Monitis sum minor ipse meis."[q]

3. Another fault laid to the charge of learned men, and arising from the nature of their studies, is, " That they esteem the preservation, good, and honour of their country before their own fortunes or safeties." Demosthenes said well to the Athenians, " My counsels are not such as tend to

[l] Plutarch, Solon.   [m] Epist. Z. iii. 331 ; and cf. Ep. Γ. iii. 316.
[n] Sallust, Cat. Conspiracy.   [o] Cicero to Atticus, epis. ii. 1.
[p] Oratio pro L. Muræna, xxxi. 65.
[q] "I am unequal to my teaching."—Ovid, Ars Amandi, ii. 549.

aggrandize myself and diminish you, but sometimes not expedient for me to give, though always expedient for you to follow."[r] So Seneca, after consecrating the five years of Nero's minority to the immortal glory of learned governors, held on his honest-course of good counsel after his master grew extremely corrupt. Nor can this be otherwise; for learning gives men a true sense of their frailty, the casualty of fortune, and the dignity of the soul and its office; whence they cannot think any greatness of fortune a worthy end of their living, and therefore live so as to give a clear and acceptable account to God and their superiors; whilst the corrupter sort of politicians, who are not by learning established in a love of duty, nor ever look abroad into universality, refer all things to themselves, and thrust their persons into the centre of the world, as if all lines should meet in them and their fortunes, without regarding in storms what becomes of the ship of the state, if they can save themselves in the cock-boat of their own fortune.

Another charge brought against learned men, which may rather be defended than denied, is, "That they sometimes fail in making court to particular persons." This want of application arises from two causes—the one the largeness of their mind, which can hardly submit to dwell in the examination and observance of any one person. It is the speech of a lover rather than of a wise man, "Satis magnum alter alteri theatrum sumus."[s] Nevertheless he who cannot contract the sight of his mind, as well as dilate it, wants a great talent in life. The second cause is, no inability, but a rejection upon choice and judgment; for the honest and just limits of observation in one person upon another extend no farther than to understand him sufficiently, so as to give him no offence, or be able to counsel him, or to stand upon reasonable guard and caution with respect to one's self; but to pry deep into another man, to learn to work, wind, or govern him, proceeds from a double heart, which in friendship is want of integrity, and towards princes or superiors want of duty. The eastern custom which forbids subjects to gaze upon princes, though in the outward ceremony bar-

---

[r] Oration on the Crown.   [s] Seneca, Ep. Mor. i. 7.

barous, has a good moral; for men ought not, by cunning and studied observations, to penetrate and search into the hearts of kings, which the Scripture declares inscrutable.[t]

Another fault noted in learned men is, "That they often fail in point of discretion and decency of behaviour, and commit errors in ordinary actions, whence vulgar capacities judge of them in greater matters by what they find them in small." But this consequence often deceives; for we may here justly apply the saying of Themistocles, who being asked to touch a lute, replied, "He could not fiddle, but he could make a little village a great city."[u] Accordingly many may be well skilled in government and policy, who are defective in little punctilios. So Plato compared his master Socrates to the shop-pots of apothecaries painted on the outside with apes and owls and antiques, but contained within sovereign and precious remedies.[x]

But we have nothing to offer in excuse of those unworthy practices, whereby some professors have debased both themselves and learning, as the trencher philosophers, who, in the decline of the Roman state, were but a kind of solemn parasites. Lucian makes merry with this kind of gentry, in the person of a philosopher riding in a coach with a great lady, who would needs have him carry her lapdog, which he doing with an awkward officiousness, the page said, "He feared the Stoic would turn Cynic."[y] But above all, the gross flattery wherein many abuse their wit, by turning Hecuba into Hellena, and Faustina into Lucretia, has most diminished the value and esteem of learning.[z] Neither is the modern practice of dedications commendable; for books should have no patrons but truth and reason. And the ancient custom was, to dedicate them only to private and equal friends, or if to kings and great persons, it was to such as the subject suited. These and the like measures, therefore, deserve

---

[t] Prov. xxv.   [u] Cicero, Tuscul. Quæst. i. 2; Plutarch, Themistocles.
[x] Conv. iii. 215; and cf. Xen. Symp. v. 7.
[y] Lucian de Merc. Cond. 33, 34. The raillery couched under the word cynic will become more evident if the reader will recollect the word is derived from κυνος, the Greek name for dog. Those philosophers were called Cynics who, like Diogenes, rather barked than declaimed against the vices and the manners of their age. *Ed.*
[z] Du Bartas Bethulian's Rescue, b. v. translated by Sylvester.

rather to be censured than defended. Yet the submission of learned men to those in power cannot be condemned. Diogenes, to one who asked him "How it happened that philosophers followed the rich, and not the rich the philosophers?" answered, "Because the philosophers know what they want, but the rich do not."[a] And of the like nature was the answer of Aristippus, who having a petition to Dionysius, and no ear being given him, fell down at his feet, whereupon Dionysius gave him the hearing, and granted the suit; but when afterwards Aristippus was reproved for offering such an indignity to philosophy as to fall at a tyrant's feet, he replied, "It was not his fault if Dionysius's ears were in his feet."[b] Nor was it accounted weakness, but discretion, in him[c] that would not dispute his best with the Emperor Adrian, excusing himself, "That it was reasonable to yield to one that commanded thirty legions."[d] These and the like condescensions to points of necessity and convenience, cannot be disallowed; for though they may have some show of external meanness, yet in a judgment truly made, they are submissions to the occasion, and not to the person.

We proceed to the errors and vanities intermixed with the studies of learned men, wherein the design is not to countenance such errors, but, by a censure and separation thereof to justify what is sound and good; for it is the manner of men, especially the evil-minded, to depreciate what is excellent and virtuous, by taking advantage over what is corrupt and degenerate. We reckon three principal vanities for which learning has been traduced. Those things are vain which are either false or frivolous, or deficient in truth or use; and those persons are vain who are either credulous of falsities or curious in things of little use. But curiosity consists either in matter or words, that is, either in taking pains about vain things, or too much labour about the delicacy of language. There are, therefore, in reason as well as experience, three distempers of learning; viz., vain affectations, vain disputes, and vain imaginations, or effeminate learning, contentious learning, and fantastical learning.

The first disease, which consists in a luxuriancy of style, has been anciently esteemed at different times, but strangely

[a] Laert. Life Diog.   [b] Laert. Life Arist.
[c] Demonax.   [d] Spartianus, Vit. Adriani, § 15.

prevailed about the time of Luther, who, finding how great a task he had undertaken against the degenerate traditions of the Church, and being unassisted by the opinions of his own age, was forced to awake antiquity to make a party for him; whence the ancient authors both in divinity and the humanities, that had long slept in libraries, began to be generally read. This brought on a necessity of greater application to the original languages wherein those authors wrote, for the better understanding and application of their works. Hence also proceeded a delight in their manner of style and phrase, and an admiration of this kind of writing, which was much increased by the enmity now grown up against the schoolmen, who were generally of the contrary party, and whose writings were in a very different style and form, as taking the liberty to coin new and strange words, to avoid circumlocution and express their sentiments acutely, without regard to purity of diction and justness of phrase. And again, because the great labour then was to win and persuade the people, eloquence and variety of discourse grew into request as most suitable for the pulpit, and best adapted to the capacity of the vulgar; so that these four causes concurring, viz., 1. admiration of the ancients; 2. enmity to the schoolmen; 3. an exact study of languages; and, 4. a desire of powerful preaching,—introduced an affected study of eloquence and copiousness of speech, which then began to flourish. This soon grew to excess, insomuch that men studied more after words than matter, more after the choiceness of phrase, and the round and neat composition, sweet cadence of periods, the use of tropes and figures, than after weight of matter, dignity of subject, soundness of argument, life of invention, or depth of judgment. Then grew into esteem the flowing and watery vein of Orosius,[e] the Portugal bishop; then did Sturmius bestow such infinite pains upon Cicero and Hermogenes; then did Car and Ascham, in their lectures and writings, almost deify Cicero and Demosthenes; then grew the learning of the schoolmen to be utterly despised as barbarous; and the whole bent of those times was rather upon fulness than weight.

[e] Neither a Portuguese or a bishop, but a Spanish monk born at Tarragona, and sent by St. Augustine on a mission to Jerusalem in the commencement of the fifth century.

Here, therefore, is the first distemper of learning, when men study words and not matter; and though we have given an example of it from later times, yet such levities have and will be found more or less in all ages. And this must needs discredit learning, even with vulgar capacities, when they see learned men's works appear like the first letter of a patent, which, though finely flourished, is still but a letter. Pygmalion's frenzy seems a good emblem of this vanity;[f] for words are but the images of matter, and unless they have life of reason and invention, to fall in love with them is to fall in love with a picture.

Yet the illustrating the obscurities of philosophy with sensible and plausible elocution is not hastily to be condemned; for hereof we have eminent examples in Xenophon, Cicero, Seneca, Plutarch, and Plato;[g] and the thing itself is of great use; for although it be some hinderance to the severe inquiry after truth, and the farther progress in philosophy, that it should too early prove satisfactory to the mind, and quench the desire of farther search, before a just period is made; yet when we have occasion for learning and knowledge in civil life, as for conference, counsel, persuasion, discourse, or the like, we find it ready prepared to our hands in the authors who have wrote in this way. But the excess herein is so justly contemptible, that as Hercules, when he saw the statue of Adonis, who was the delight of Venus, in the temple, said with indignation, "There is no divinity in thee;" so all the followers of Hercules in learning, that is, the more severe and laborious inquirers after truth, will despise these delicacies and affectations as trivial and effeminate.

The luxuriant style was succeeded by another, which, though more chaste, has still its vanity, as turning wholly upon pointed expressions and short periods, so as to appear concise and round rather than diffusive; by which contrivance the whole looks more ingenious than it is. Seneca

---

[f] Ovid, Metam. x. 243.

[g] M. Fontenelle is an eminent modern instance in the same way; who, particularly in his "Plurality of Worlds," renders the present system of astronomy agreeably familiar, as his "History of the Royal Academy" embellishes and explains the abstruse parts of mathematics and natural philosophy. *Shaw.*

used this kind of style profusely, but Tacitus and Pliny with greater moderation. It has also begun to render itself acceptable in our time. But to say the truth, its admirers are only the men of a middle genius, who think it adds a dignity to learning; whilst those of solid judgment justly reject it as a certain disease of learning, since it is no more than a jingle, or peculiar quaint affectation of words.[h] And so much for the first disease of learning.

The second disease is worse in its nature than the former; for as the dignity of matter exceeds the beauty of words, so vanity in matter is worse than vanity in words; whence the precept of St. Paul is at all times seasonable: "Avoid profane and vain babblings, and oppositions of science falsely so called."[i] He assigns two marks of suspected and falsified science: the one, novelty and strangeness of terms; the other, strictness of positions; which necessarily induces oppositions, and thence questions and altercations. And indeed, as many solid substances putrefy, and turn into worms, so does sound knowledge often putrefy into a number of subtle, idle, and vermicular questions, that have a certain quickness of life, and spirit, but no strength of matter, or excellence of quality. This kind of degenerate learning chiefly reigned among the schoolmen; who, having subtle and strong capacities, abundance of leisure, and but small variety of reading, their minds being shut up in a few authors, as their bodies were in the cells of their monasteries, and thus kept ignorant both of the history of nature and times; they, with infinite agitation of wit, spun out of a small quantity of matter, those laborious webs of learning which are extant in their books. For the human mind, if it acts upon matter, and contemplates the nature of things, and the works of God, operates according to the stuff, and is limited thereby; but if it works upon itself, as the spider does, then it has no end; but produces cobwebs of learning, admirable indeed for the fineness of the thread, but of no substance or profit.[k]

[h] Since the establishment of the French Academy, a studied plainness and simplicity of style begins to prevail in that nation.
[i] 1 Tim. vi. 20.
[k] For the literary history of the schoolmen, see Morhof's "Polyhist." tom. ii. lib. i. cap. 14; and Camden's "Remains."

This unprofitable subtilty is of two kinds, and appears either in the subject, when that is fruitless speculation or controversy, or in the manner of treating it, which amongst them was this: Upon every particular position they framed objections, and to those objections solutions; which solutions were generally not confutations, but distinctions; whereas the strength of all sciences is like the strength of a fagot bound. For the harmony of science, when each part supports the other, is the true and short confutation of all the smaller objections; on the contrary, to take out every axiom, as the sticks of the fagot, one by one, you may quarrel with them, and bend them, and break them at pleasure: whence, as it was said of Seneca, that he "weakened the weight of things by trivial expression,"[1] we may truly say of the schoolmen, "That they broke the solidity of the sciences by the minuteness of their questions." For, were it not better to set up one large light in a noble room, that to go about with a small one, to illuminate every corner thereof? Yet such is the method of schoolmen, that rests not so much upon the evidence of truth from arguments, authorities, and examples, as upon particular confutations and solutions of every scruple and objection; which breeds one question, as fast as it solves another; just as in the above example, when the light is carried into one corner, it darkens the rest. Whence the fable of Scylla seems a lively image of this kind of philosophy, who was transformed into a beautiful virgin upwards, whilst barking monsters surrounded her below,—

"Candida succinctam latrantibus inguina monstris."
Virg. Ecl. vi. 75.

So the generalities of the schoolmen are for a while fair and proportionable; but to descend into their distinctions and decisions, they end in monstrous altercations and barking questions. Whence this kind of knowledge must necessarily fall under popular contempt; for the people are ever apt to contemn truth, upon account of the controversies raised about it; and so think those all in the wrong way, who never meet. And when they see such quarrels about subtilties and matters of no use, they usually give into the

[1] Quinctilian, lib. x. cap. 1, § 130.

judgment of Dionysius, "That it is old men's idle talk."ᵐ But if those schoolmen, to their great thirst of truth, and unwearied exercise of wit, had joined variety of reading and contemplation, they would have proved excellent lights to the great advancement of all kinds of arts and sciences. And thus much for the second disease of learning.

The third disease, which regards deceit or falsehood, is the foulest; as destroying the essential form of knowledge, which is nothing but a representation of truth; for the truth of existence and the truth of knowledge are the same thing, or differ no more than the direct and reflected ray. This vice, therefore, branches into two; viz., delight in deceiving and aptness to be deceived; imposture and credulity, which, though apparently different, the one seeming to proceed from cunning, and the other from simplicity, yet they generally concur. For, as in the verse,

"Percontatorem fugito; nam garrulus idem est,"
Hor. lib. i. epis. xviii. v. 69.

an inquisitive man is a prattler; so a credulous man is a deceiver; for he who so easily believes rumours, will as easily increase them. Tacitus has wisely expressed this law of our nature in these words, "Fingunt simul creduntque."ⁿ

This easiness of belief, and admitting things upon weak authority, is of two kinds, according to the subject; being either a belief of history and matter of fact, or else matter of art and opinion. We see the inconvenience of the former in ecclesiastical history, which has too easily received and registered relations of miracles wrought by martyrs, hermits, monks, and their relics, shrines, chapels, and images. So in natural history, there has not been much judgment employed, as appears from the writings of Pliny, Carban, Albertus, and many of the Arabians; which are full of fabulous matters: many of them not only untried, but notoriously false, to the great discredit of natural philosophy with grave and sober minds. But the produce and integrity of Aristotle is here worthy our observation, who, having compiled an exact history of animals, dashed it very sparingly with fable or fiction, throwing all strange reports which he

---

ᵐ Diog. Laert. iii. 18, Life of Plato. ⁿ Tacit. Hist. b. i. 51

thought worth recording in a book by themselves,° thus wisely intimating, that matter of truth which is the basis of solid experience, philosophy, and the sciences, should not be mixed with matter of doubtful credit; and yet that curiosities or prodigies, though seemingly incredible, are not to be suppressed or denied the registering.

Credulity in arts and opinions, is likewise of two kinds; viz., when men give too much belief to arts themselves, or to certain authors in any art. The sciences that sway the imagination more than the reason, are principally three; viz., astrology, natural magic, and alchemy; the ends or pretensions whereof are however noble. For astrology pretends to discover the influence of the superior upon the inferior bodies; natural magic pretends to reduce natural philosophy from speculation to works; and chemistry pretends to separate the dissimilar parts, incorporated in natural mixtures, and to cleanse such bodies as are impure, throw out the heterogeneous parts, and perfect such as are immature. But the means supposed to produce these effects are, both in theory and practice, full of error and vanity, and besides, are seldom delivered with candour, but generally concealed by artifice and enigmatical expressions, referring to tradition, and using other devices to cloak imposture. Yet alchemy may be compared to the man who told his sons, he had left them gold buried somewhere in his vineyard; where they, by digging, found no gold, but by turning up the mould about the roots of the vines, procured a plentiful vintage. So the search and endeavours to make gold have brought many useful inventions and instructive experiments to light.ᵖ

Credulity in respect of certain authors, and making them

° Θαυμάσια Ἀκούσματα.

ᵖ As among the Egyptians, the Chinese, and the Arabians, if their histories are to be credited. In later times, they make copper out of iron, at Newsohl, in Germany. See Agricola "De Re Metallica," Morhof, Fr. Hoffman, &c. Whilst Brand of Hamburgh was working upon urine, in order to find the philosopher's stone, he stumbled upon that called Kunckel's burning phosphorus, in the year 1669. See Mém. de l'Acad. Royal. des Sciences, an 1692. And M. Homberg operating upon human excrement, for an oil to convert quicksilver into silver, accidentally produced what we now call the black phosphorus, a powder which readily takes fire and burns like a coal in the open air. See Mém. de l'Acad. an 1711. To give all the instances of this kind were almost endless. *Ed.*

dictators instead of consuls, is a principal cause that the sciences are no farther advanced. For hence, though in mechanical arts, the first inventor falls short, time adds perfection; whilst in the sciences, the first author goes farthest, and time only abates or corrupts. Thus artillery, sailing, and printing, were grossly managed at the first, but received improvement by time; whilst the philosophy and the sciences of Aristotle, Plato, Democritus, Hippocrates, Euclid, and Archimedes, flourished most in the original authors, and degenerated with time. The reason is, that in the mechanic arts, the capacities and industry of many are collected together; whereas in sciences, the capacities and industry of many have been spent upon the invention of some one man, who has commonly been thereby rather obscured than illustrated. For as water ascends no higher than the level of the first spring, so knowledge derived from Aristotle will at most rise no higher again than the knowledge of Aristotle. And therefore, though a scholar must have faith in his master, yet a man well instructed must judge for himself; for learners owe to their masters only a temporary belief, and a suspension of their own judgment till they are fully instructed, and not an absolute resignation or perpetual captivity. Let great authors, therefore, have their due, but so as not to defraud time, which is the author of authors, and the parent of truth.

Besides the three diseases of learning above treated, there are some other peccant humours, which, falling under popular observation and reprehension, require to be particularly mentioned. The first is the affecting of two extremes; antiquity and novelty: wherein the children of time seem to imitate their father; for as he devours his children, so they endeavour to devour each other; whilst antiquity envies new improvements, and novelty is not content to add without defacing. The advice of the prophet is just in this case: "Stand upon the old ways, and see which is the good way, and walk therein."q For antiquity deserves that men should stand awhile upon it, to view around which is the best way; but when the discovery is well made, they should stand no longer, but proceed with cheerfulness. And to speak the

---

q Jeremiah vi. 16.

truth antiquity, as we call it, is the young state of the world; for those times are ancient when the world is ancient; and not those we vulgarly account ancient by computing backwards; so that the present time is the real antiquity.

Another error, proceeding from the former, is, a distrust that anything should be discovered in later times that was not hit upon before; as if Lucian's objection against the gods lay also against time. He pleasantly asks why the gods begot so many children in the first ages, but none in his days; and whether they were grown too old for generation, or were restrained by the Papian law, which prohibited old men from marrying?[r] For thus we seem apprehensive that time is worn out, and become unfit for generation. And here we have a remarkable instance of the levity and inconstancy of man's humour; which, before a thing is effected, thinks it impossible, and as soon as it is done, wonders it was not done before. So the expedition of Alexander into Asia was at first imagined a vast and impracticable enterprise, yet Livy afterwards makes so light of it as to say, "It was but bravely venturing to despise vain opinions."[s] And the case was the same in Columbus's discovery of the West Indies. But this happens much more frequently in intellectual matters, as we see in most of the propositions of Euclid, which, till demonstrated, seem strange, but when demonstrated, the mind receives them by a kind of affinity, as if we had known them before.

Another error of the same nature is an imagination that of all ancient opinions or sects, the best has ever prevailed, and suppressed the rest; so that if a man begins a new search, he must happen upon somewhat formerly rejected; and by rejection, brought into oblivion; as if the multitude, or the wiser sort to please the multitude, would not often give way to what is light and popular, rather than maintain what is substantial and deep.

Another different error is, the over-early and peremptory reduction of knowledge into arts and methods, from which time the sciences are seldom improved; for as young men rarely grow in stature after their shape and limbs are fully

---

[r] Senec. imput. ap. Lact. Instit. 1. 26, 13.
[s] "Nihil aliud quam bene ausus est, vana contemnere."—Livy, b. 10, c. 17.

formed, so knowledge, whilst it lies in aphorisms and observations, remains in a growing state; but when once fashioned into methods, though it may be farther polished, illustrated, and fitted for use, it no longer increases in bulk and substance.

Another error is, that after the distribution of particular arts and sciences, men generally abandon the study of nature, or universal philosophy, which stops all farther progress. For as no perfect view of a country can be taken upon a flat, so it is impossible to discover the remote and deep parts of any science by standing upon the level of the same science, or without ascending to a higher.

Another error proceeds from too great a reverence, and a kind of adoration paid to the human understanding; whence men have withdrawn themselves from the contemplation of nature and experience, and sported with their own reason and the fictions of fancy. These intellectualists, though commonly taken for the most sublime and divine philosophers, are censured by Heraclitus, when he says, "Men seek for truth in their own little worlds, and not in the great world without them:"[t] and as they disdain to spell, they can never come to read in the volume of God's works; but on the contrary, by continual thought and agitation of wit, they compel their own genius to divine and deliver oracles, whereby they are deservedly deluded.

Another error is, that men often infect their speculations and doctrines with some particular opinions they happen to be fond of, or the particular sciences whereto they have most applied, and thence give all other things a tincture that is utterly foreign to them. Thus Plato mixed philosophy with theology;[u] Aristotle with logic; Proclus with mathematics;

---

[t] Text Empir. against St. Math. vii. 133.

[u] If it is true that God is the great spring of motion in the universe, as the theory of moving forces is a part of mechanics and mechanics a department of physics, we cannot see how theology can be entirely divorced from natural philosophy. Physicists are too apt to consider the universe as eternally existing, without contemplating it in its finite aspect as a series of existences to be produced, and controlled by the force of laws externally impressed upon them. Hence their theory of moving forces is incomplete, as they do not take the prime mover into account, or supply us, in case of denying him, with the equivalent of his action. *Ed.*

as these arts were a kind of elder and favourite children with them. So the alchemists have made a philosophy from a few experiments of the furnace, and Gilbert another out of the loadstone: in like manner, Cicero, when reviewing the opinions on the nature of the soul, coming to that of a musician, who held the soul was but an harmony, he pleasantly said, "This man has not gone out of his art."[x] But of such authors Aristotle says well: "Those who take in but a few considerations easily decide."[y]

Another error is, an impatience of doubting and a blind hurry of asserting without a mature suspension of judgment. For the two ways of contemplation are like the two ways of action so frequently mentioned by the ancients; the one plain and easy at first, but in the end impassable; the other rough and fatiguing in the entrance, but soon after fair and even: so in contemplation, if we begin with certainties, we shall end in doubts; but if we begin with doubts, and are patient in them, we shall end in certainties.

Another error lies in the manner of delivering knowledge, which is generally magisterial and peremptory, not ingenuous and open, but suited to gain belief without examination. And in compendious treatises for practice, this form should not be disallowed; but in the true delivering of knowledge, both extremes are to be avoided; viz., that of Velleius the Epicurean, who feared nothing so much as the non-appearance of doubting;"[z] and that of Socrates and the Academics, who ironically doubted of all things: but the true way is to propose things candidly, with more or less asseveration, as they stand in a man's own judgment.

There are other errors in the scope that men propose to themselves: for whereas the more diligent professors of any science ought chiefly to endeavour the making some additions or improvements therein, they aspire only to certain second prizes; as to be a profound commentator, a sharp disputant, a methodical compiler, or abridger, whence the returns or revenues of knowledge are sometimes increased, but not the inheritance and stock.

But the greatest error of all is, mistaking the ultimate end

[x] "Hic ab arte sua non recessit."—Tuscul. Quæst. i. c. 10.
[y] Arist. De Gener. et Corrup. lib. 1.
[z] Cicero, De Natura Deorum, i. c. 8.

BOOK I.]   THE TRUE END OF LEARNING MISTAKEN.   55

of knowledge; for some men covet knowledge out of a natural curiosity and inquisitive temper; some to entertain the mind with variety and delight; some for ornament and reputation; some for victory and contention; many for lucre and a livelihood; and but few for employing the Divine gift of reason to the use and benefit of mankind. Thus some appear to seek in knowledge a couch for a searching spirit; others, a walk for a wandering mind; others, a tower of state; others, a fort, or commanding ground; and others, a shop for profit or sale, instead of a storehouse for the glory of the Creator and the endowment of human life. But that which must dignify and exalt knowledge is the more intimate and strict conjunction of contemplation and action; a conjunction like that of Saturn, the planet of rest and contemplation; and Jupiter, the planet of civil society and action. But here, by use and action, we do not mean the applying of knowledge to lucre, for that diverts the advancement of knowledge, as the golden ball thrown before Atalanta, which, while she stoops to take up, the race is hindered.

"Declinat cursus, aurumque volubile tollit."—Ovid, Metam. x. 667.

Nor do we mean, as was said of Socrates, to call philosophy down from heaven to converse upon earth:[a] that is, to leave natural philosophy behind, and apply knowledge only to morality and policy: but as both heaven and earth contribute to the use and benefit of man, so the end ought to be, from both philosophies, to separate and reject vain and empty speculations, and preserve and increase all that is solid and fruitful.

We have now laid open by a kind of dissection the chief of those peccant humours which have not only retarded the advancement of learning, but tended to its traducement.[b] If we have cut too deeply, it must be remen-

[a] Cicero, Tuscul. Quæst. v. c. 4.
[b] To this catalogue of errors incident to learned men may be added, the frauds and impostures of which they are sometimes guilty, to the scandal of learning. Thus plagiarism, piracy, falsification, interpolation, castration, the publishing of spurious books, and the stealing of manuscripts out of libraries, have been frequent, especially among ecclesiastical writers, and the Fratres Falsarii. For instances of this kind, see Struvius "De Doctis Impostoribus," Morhof in "Polyhist. de Pseudonymis, Anonymis, &c.," Le Clerc's "Ars Critica," Cave's "His-

bered, "Fidelia vulnera amantis, dolosa oscula malignantis.[c] However, we will gain credit for our commendations, as we have been severe in our censures. It is, notwithstanding, far from our purpose to enter into fulsome laudations of learning, or to make a hymn to the muses, though we are of opinion that it is long since their rites were celebrated; but our intent is to balance the dignity of knowledge in the scale with other things, and to estimate their true values according to universal testimony.

Next, therefore, let us seek the dignity of knowledge in its original; that is, in the attributes and acts of God, so far as they are revealed to man, and may be observed with sobriety. But here we are not to seek it by the name of learning; for all learning is knowledge acquired, but all knowledge in God is original: we must, therefore, look for it under the name of wisdom or sapience, as the Scriptures call it.

In the work of creation we see a double emanation of virtue from God; the one relating more properly to power, the other to wisdom; the one expressed in making the matter, and the other in disposing the form. This being supposed, we may observe that, for anything mentioned in the history of the creation, the confused mass of the heavens and earth was made in a moment; whereas the order and disposition of it was the work of six days: such a mark of difference seems put betwixt the works of power and the works of wisdom; whence, it is not written that God said, "Let there be heaven and earth," as it is of the subsequent works; but actually, that "God made heaven and earth;" the one carrying the style of a manufacture, the other that of a law, decree, or counsel.

To proceed from God to spirits. We find, as far as credit may be given to the celestial hierarchy of the supposed Dionysius the Areopagite, the first place is given to the angels of love, termed Seraphim; the second, to the angels of light, called Cherubim; and the third and following places to thrones, principalities, and the rest, which are all angels of power and ministry; so that the angels of know-

toria Literaria Scriptorum Ecclesiasticorum," Father Simon, and Mabillon. *Ed.*

[c] Prov. xxvii. 6.

ledge and illumination are placed before the angels of office and domination.[d]

To descend from spiritual and intellectual, to sensible and material forms; we read the first created form was light,[e] which, in nature and corporeal things, hath a relation and correspondence to knowledge in spirits, and things incorporeal; so, in the distribution of days, we find the day wherein God rested and completed his works, was blessed above all the days wherein he wrought them.[f]

After the creation was finished, it is said that man was placed in the garden to work therein, which work could only be work of contemplation; that is, the end of his work was but for exercise and delight, and not for necessity: for there being then no reluctance of the creature, nor sweat of the brow, man's employment was consequently matter of pleasure, not labour. Again, the first acts which man performed in Paradise consisted of the two summary parts of knowledge, a view of the creature, and imposition of names.[g]

In the first event after the fall, we find an image of the two states, the contemplative and the active, figured out in the persons of Abel and Cain, by the two simplest and most primitive trades, that of the shepherd and that of the husbandman;[h] where again, the favour of God went to the shepherd, and not to the tiller of the ground.

So in the age before the flood, the sacred records mention the name of the inventors of music and workers in metal.[i] In the age after the flood, the first great judgment of God upon the ambition of man was the confusion of tongues,[k] whereby the open trade and intercourse of learning and knowledge was chiefly obstructed.

It is said of Moses, "That he was learned in all the wisdom of the Egyptians,"[l] which nation was one of the most ancient schools of the world; for Plato brings in the Egyptian priest saying to Solon, "You Grecians are ever children, having no knowledge of antiquity, nor antiquity of knowledge."[m] In the ceremonial laws of Moses we find, that

[d] See Dionys. Hierarch. 7, 8, 9.   [e] Gen. i. 3.
[f] Gen. ii. 3.   [g] Gen. ii. 19.   [h] Gen. iv. 2.   [i] Gen. iv. 21, 22.
[k] Gen. xi.   [l] Acts vii. 22.   [m] Plat. Tim. iii. 22.

besides the prefiguration of Christ, the mark of the people of
God to distinguish them from the Gentiles, the exercise of
obedience, and other divine institutions, the most learned of
the rabbis have observed a natural and some of them a
moral sense in many of the rites and ceremonies. Thus in
the law of the leprosy, where it is said, "If the whiteness
have overspread the flesh, the patient may pass abroad for
clean; but if there be any whole flesh remaining, he is to
be shut up for unclean,"[n]—one of them notes a principle of
nature, viz., that putrefaction is more contagious before
maturity than after. Another hereupon observes a position
of moral philosophy, that men abandoned to vice do not
corrupt the manners of others, so much as those who are but
half wicked. And in many other places of the Jewish law,
besides the theological sense, there are couched many philosophical matters. The book of Job[o] likewise will be found,
if examined with care, pregnant with the secrets of natural
philosophy. For example, when it says, "Qui extendit
Aquilonem super vacuum, et appendit terram super nihilum,"
the suspension of the earth and the convexity of the heavens
are manifestly alluded to. Again, "Spiritus ejus ornavit
cælos, et obstetricante manu ejus eductus est coluber tortu-
osus;"[p] and in another place, "Numquid conjungere valebis
micantes stellas Pleiadas, aut gyrum Arcturi poteris dis-
sipare?"[q] where the immutable[r] configuration of the fixed
stars, ever preserving the same position, is with elegance
described. So in another place: "Qui facit Arcturum, et
Oriona, et Hyadas,[s] et interiora Austri,"[t] where he again refers
to the depression of the south pole in the expression of "interiora Austri," because the southern stars are not seen in

[n] Leviticus xiii. 12.
[p] Job xxvi. 7, 13.
[o] See Job xxvi.—xxxviii.
[q] xxxviii. 31.
[r] That is, to Job, who cannot be supposed to know what telescopes
only have revealed, that stars change their declination with unequal
degrees of motion. It is clear, therefore, that their distances must be
variable, and that in the end the figures of the constellations will
undergo mutation; as this change, however, will not be perceptible for
thousands of years, it hardly comes within the limit of man's idea of
mutation, and therefore, with regard to him, may be said to have no
existence. *Ed.*

[s] The Hyades nearly approach the letter V in appearance.

[t] The crown of stars which forms a kind of imperfect circle near
Arcturus.

our hemisphere.[u] Again, what concerns the generation of living creatures, he says, "Annon sicut lac mulsisti me, et sicut caseum coagulasti me?"[x] and touching mineral subjects, "Habet argentum venarum suarum principia, et auro locus est, in quo conflatur; ferrum de terra tollitur, et lapis solutus calore in æs vertitur,"[y] and so forward in the same chapter.

Nor did the dispensation of God vary in the times after our Saviour, who himself first showed his power to subdue ignorance, by conferring with the priests and doctors of the law, before he showed his power to subdue nature by miracles. And the coming of the Holy Spirit was chiefly expressed in the gift of tongues, which are but the conveyance of knowledge.

So in the election of those instruments it pleased God to use for planting the faith, though at first he employed persons altogether unlearned, otherwise than by inspiration, the more evidently to declare his immediate working, and to humble all human wisdom or knowledge, yet in the next succession he sent out his divine truth into the world, attended with other parts of learning as with servants or handmaids; thus St. Paul, who was the only learned amongst the apostles, had his pen most employed in the writings of the New Testament.

Again, we find that many of the ancient bishops and fathers of the Church were well versed in all the learning of the heathens, insomuch that the edict of the Emperor Julian prohibiting Christians the schools and exercises, was accounted a more pernicious engine against the faith than all the sanguinary persecutions of his predecessors.[z] Neither could Gregory the First, bishop of Rome, ever obtain the opinion of devotion even among the pious, for designing, though otherwise an excellent person, to extinguish the memory of heathen antiquity.[a] But it was the Christian

---

[u] It is not true that all the southern stars are invisible in our hemisphere. The text applies only to those whose southern declination is greater than the elevation of the equator over their part of the horizon, or, which is the same thing, than the complement of the place's latitude. *Ed.*   [x] x. 10.   [y] xxviii. 1.
[z] Epist. ad Jamblic. Gibbon, vol. ii. c. 23.
[a] Gibbon, vol. iv. c. 45.

Church which, amidst the inundations of the Scythians from the north-west and the Saracens from the east, preserved in her bosom the relics even of heathen learning, which had otherwise been utterly extinguished. And of late years the Jesuits, partly of themselves and partly provoked by example, have greatly enlivened and strengthened the state of learning, and contributed to establish the Roman see.

There are, therefore, two principal services, besides ornament and illustration, which philosophy and human learning perform to faith and religion, the one effectually exciting to the exaltation of God's glory, and the other affording a singular preservative against unbelief and error. Our Saviour says, " Ye err, not knowing the Scriptures, nor the power of God;"[b] thus laying before us two books to study, if we will be secured from error; viz., the Scriptures, which reveal the will of God, and the creation, which expresses his power; the latter whereof is a key to the former, and not only opens our understanding to conceive the true sense of the Scripture by the general notions of reason and the rules of speech, but chiefly opens our faith in drawing us to a due consideration of the omnipotence of God, which is stamped upon his works. And thus much for Divine testimony concerning the dignity and merits of learning.

Next for human proofs. Deification was the highest honour among the heathens; that is, to obtain veneration as a god was the supreme respect which man could pay to man, especially when given, not by a formal act of state as it usually was to the Roman emperors, but from a voluntary, internal assent and acknowledgment. This honour being so high, there was also constituted a middle kind, for human honours were inferior to honours heroical and divine. Antiquity observed this difference in their distribution, that whereas founders of states, lawgivers, extirpers of tyrants, fathers of the people, and other eminent persons in civil merit, were honoured but with the titles of heroes, or demigods, such as Hercules, Theseus, Minos, Romulus, &c. Inventors, and authors of new arts or discoveries for the service of human life, were ever advanced amongst the gods, as in the case of Ceres, Bacchus, Mercury, Apollo, and others. And this

[b] Matt. xxii. 29.

appears to have been done with great justice and judgment, for the merits of the former being generally confined within the circle of one age or nation, are but like fruitful showers, which serve only for a season and a small extent, whilst the others are like the benefits of the sun, permanent and universal. Again, the former are mixed with strife and contention, whilst the latter have the true character of the Divine presence, as coming in a gentle gale without noise or tumult.

The merit of learning in remedying the inconveniences arising from man to man, is not much inferior to that of relieving human necessities. This merit was livelily described by the ancients in the fiction of Orpheus's theatre, where all the beasts and birds assembled, and forgetting their several appetites, stood sociably together listening to the harp, whose sound no sooner ceased, or was drowned by a louder, but they all returned to their respective natures; for thus men are full of savage and unreclaimed desires, which as long as we hearken to precepts, laws, and religion, sweetly touched with eloquence and persuasion, so long is society and peace maintained; but if these instruments become silent, or seditions and tumult drown their music, all things fall back to confusion and anarchy.

This appears more manifestly when princes or governors are learned; for though he might be thought partial to his profession who said, "States would then be happy, when either kings were philosophers, or philosophers kings;"[c] yet so much is verified by experience, that the best times have happened under wise and learned princes; for though kings may have their errors and vices, like other men, yet if they are illuminated by learning, they constantly retain such notions of religion, policy, and morality, as may preserve them from destructive and irremediable errors or excesses; for these notions will whisper to them, even whilst counsellors and servants stand mute. Such senators likewise as are learned proceed upon more safe and substantial principles than mere men of experience,—the former view dangers afar off, whilst the latter discover them not till they are at hand, and then trust to their wit to avoid them. This felicity of

---

[c] Plato (De Republica, b. 5) ii. 475.

times under learned princes appears eminent in the age between the death of Domitian and the reign of Commodus, comprehending a succession of six princes, all of them learned, or singular favourers and promoters of learning. And this age, for temporal respects, was the happiest and most flourishing that ever the Roman state enjoyed; as was revealed to Domitian in a dream the night before he was slain,[c] when he beheld a neck and head of gold growing upon his shoulders; a vision which was, in the golden times succeeding this divination, fully accomplished. For his successor Nerva was a learned prince, a familiar friend and acquaintance of Apollonius, who expired reciting that line of Homer,—" Phœbus, with thy darts revenge our tears."[d] Trajan, though not learned himself, was an admirer of learning, a munificent patron of letters, and a founder of libraries. Though the taste of his court was warlike, professors and preceptors were found there in great credit and admiration. Adrian was the greatest inquirer that ever lived, and an insatiable explorer into everything curious and profound. Antoninus, possessing the patient and subtile mind of a scholastic, obtained the *soubriquet* of Cymini Sector, or splitter of cumin-seed.[e] Of the two brothers who were raised to the rank of gods, Lucius Commodus was versed in a more elegant kind of learning, and Marcus was surnamed the philosopher. These princes excelled the rest in virtue and goodness as much as they surpassed them in learning. Nerva was a mild philosopher, and who, if he had done nothing else than give Trajan to the world, would have sufficiently distinguished himself. Trajan was most famous and renowned above all the emperors for the arts both of peace and war. He enlarged the bounds of empire, marked out its limits and its power. He was, in addition, so great a builder, that Constantine used to call him Parietaria, or Wallflower,[f] his name being carved upon so many walls. Adrian strove with time for the palm of duration, and repaired its decays and ruins wherever the touch of its scythe had appeared. Antoninus was pious in name and nature. His nature and innate goodness gained him the reverence and affection of all classes,

---

[c] Suetonius, Life of Domitian, c. 23. [d] Iliad, i. 42.
[e] "Unum de istis puto qui cuminum secant."—Julian. Cæs.
[f] βοτάνη τοίχου. He called Adrian ἐργαλεῖον ζωγραφικόν.

ages, and conditions; and his reign, like his life, was long and unruffled by storms. Lucius Commodus, though not so perfect as his brother, succeeded many of the emperors in virtue. Marcus, formed by nature to be the model of every excellence, was so faultless, that Silenus, when he took his seat at the banquet of the gods, found nothing to carp at in him but his patience in humouring his wife.g Thus, in the succession of these six princes, we may witness the happy fruits of learning in sovereignty painted in the great table of the world.

Nor has learning a less influence on military genius than on merit employed in the state, as may be observed in the lives of Alexander the Great and Julius Cæsar, a few examples of which it will not be impertinent here to notice.

Alexander was bred under Aristotle,h certainly a great philosopher, who dedicated several of his treatises to him. He was accompanied by Calisthenes and several other learned persons both in his travels and conquests. The value this great monarch set upon learning appears in the envy he expressed of Achilles's great fortune in having so good a trumpet of his actions and prowess as Homer's verses; in the judgment he gave concerning what object was most worthy to be inclosed in the cabinet of Darius found among his spoils, which decided the question in favour of Homer's works; in his reprehensory letter to Aristotle, when chiding his master for laying bare the mysteries of philosophy, he gave him to understand that himself esteemed it more glorious to excel others in learning and knowledge than in power and empire. As to his own erudition, evidences of its perfection shine forth in all his speeches and writing, of which, though only small fragments have come down to us, yet even these are richly impressed with the footsteps of the moral sciences. For example, take his words to Diogenes, and judge if they do not inclose the very kernel of one of the greatest questions in moral philosophy, viz., whether the enjoyment or the contempt of earthly things leads to the greatest happiness; for upon seeing Diogenes contented with so little, he turned round to his courtiers, who were deriding the cynic's condition, and said, "If I were not Alexander, I

g Julian. *Cæsares.*
h For these anecdotes see Plutarch's life of Alex.

would be Diogenes." (But Seneca, in his comparison, gives the preference to Diogenes, saying that Diogenes had more things to refuse than it was in the disposition of Alexander to confer.)[i] For his skill in natural science, observe his customary saying, that he felt his mortality chiefly in two things—sleep and lust.[k] This expression, pointing as it does to the indigence and redundance of nature manifested by these two harbingers of death, savours more of an Aristotle and a Democritus than of an Alexander. In poesy, regard him rallying in his wounds one of his flatterers, who was wont to ascribe unto him Divine honour. "Look," said he, "this is the blood of a man—not such liquor as Homer speaks of, which ran from Venus's hand when it was pierced by Diomedes."[l] In logic, observe, in addition to his power of detecting fallacies and confuting or retorting arguments, his rebuke to Cassander, who ventured to confute the arraigners of Antipater, his father, Alexander having incidentally asked, "Do you think these men would come so far to complain, except they had just cause?" Cassander replied, "That was the very thing which had given them courage, since they hoped that the length of the journey would entirely clear them of calumnious motives." "See," said Alexander, "the subtilty of Aristotle, taking the matter *pro* and *con*." Nevertheless he did not shrink to turn the same art to his own advantage which he reprehended in others; for, bearing a secret grudge to Calisthenes, upon that rhetorician having drawn down great applause by delivering, as was usual at banquets, a spontaneous discourse in praise of the Macedonian nation, Alexander remarked, that it was easy to be eloquent upon a good topic, and requested him to change his note, and let the company hear what he could say against them. Calisthenes obeyed the request with such sharpness and vivacity, that Alexander interrupted him, saying, "That a perverted mind, as well as a choice topic, would breed eloquence." As regards rhetoric, consider his rebuke of Antipater, an imperious and tyrannous governor, when one of Antipater's friends ventured to extol his moderation to Alexander, saying that he had not fallen into the Persian pride of wearing the purple, but still retained the Macedonian habit. "But

---

[i] Seneca de Benef. v. 5.   [k] Vid. Seneca, Ep. Mor. vi. 7.
[l] Iliad, iv. 340.

Antipater," replied Alexander, "is all purple within."[m] Consider also that other excellent metaphor which he used to Parmenio, when that general showed him, from the plains of Arbella, the innumerable multitude of his enemies, which, viewed as they lay encamped in the night, represented a host of stars; and thereupon advised Alexander to assail them at once. The hero rejected the proposition, saying, " I will not steal a victory." As concerns policy, weigh that grave and wise distinction, which all ages have accepted, which he made between his two chief friends, Hephæstion and Craterus, saying, " That the one loved Alexander, and the other the king." Also observe how he rebuked the error ordinary with counsellors of princes, which leads them to give advice according to the necessity of their own interest and fortune, and not of their master's. When Darius had made certain proposals to Alexander, Parmenio said, "I would accept these conditions if I were Alexander." Alexander replied, " So surely would I were I Parmenio." Lastly, consider his reply to his friends, who asked him what he would reserve for himself, since he lavished so many valuable gifts upon others. " Hope," said Alexander, who well knew that, all accounts being cleared—"hope is the true inheritance of all that resolve upon great enterprises." This was Julius Cæsar's portion when he went into Gaul, all his estate being exhausted by profuse largess. And it was also the portion of that noble prince, howsoever transported with ambition, Henry, duke of Guise; for he was pronounced the greatest usurer in all France, because all his wealth was in names, and he had turned his whole estate into obligations. But perhaps the admiration of this prince in the light, not of a great king, but as Aristotle's scholar, has carried me too far.

As regards Julius Cæsar, his learning is not only evinced in his education, company, and speeches, but in a greater degree shines forth in such of his works as have descended to us. In the Commentary, that excellent history which he has left us, of his own wars, succeeding ages have admired the solidity of the matter, the vivid passages and the lively images of actions and persons, expressed in the greatest propriety of diction and perspicuity of narration. That this

---

[m] ὁλοπόρφυρος. Apop Reg. et Imp.

excellence of style was not the effect of undisciplined talent, but also of learning and precept, is evident from that work of his, entitled De Analogia,[n] in which he propounds the principles of grammatical philosophy, and endeavours to fashion mere conventional forms to congruity of expression, taking, as it were, the picture of words from the life of reason. We also perceive another monument of his genius and learning in the reformation of the Calendar, in accomplishing which he is reported to have said that he esteemed it as great a glory to himself to observe and know the law of the heavens, as to give laws to men upon earth. In his Anti-Cato,[o] he contended as much for the palm of wit as he strove in his battles for victory, and did not shrink from confronting the greatest champion of the pen in those times, Cicero the orator. Again, in his book of apophthegms, he deemed it more honourable to note the wise sayings of others, than to record every word of his own as an oracle or apophthegm, as many vain princes are by flattery urged to do.[p] And yet, should I enumerate any of them, as I did before those of Alexander, we should find them to be such as Solomon points to in the saying, "Verba sapientum tanquam aculei, et tanquam clavi in altum defixi."[q] Of these, however, I shall only relate three, not so remarkable for elegance as for vigour and efficacy. He who could appease a mutiny in his army by a word, must certainly be regarded as a master of language. This Cæsar performed under the following circumstances. The generals always addressed the army as milites; the magistrates, on the other hand, in their charges to the people used the word Quirites. Now the soldiers being in tumult, and feignedly praying to be disbanded, with a view to draw Cæsar to other conditions, the latter resolved not to succumb, and after a short pause, began his speech with "Ego, Quirites,"[r] which implied they were at once cashiered: upon which, the soldiers were so astonished and confused that they relinquished their demands, and begged to be addressed by the old appellation of milites. The second saying thus transpired. Cæsar extremely affected the name

[n] Vid. Cic. *Brutus*, 72.
[o] Vid. Cic. ad Att. xii. 40, 41 ; xiii. 50 ; and Top. xxv.
[p] Cic. ad Fam. ix. 16. [q] Eccl. xii. 11.
[r] Suet. Life Jul. Cæs. c. 70.

of king, and some were set on to salute him with that title as he passed by. Cæsar, however, finding the cry weak and poor, put it off thus in a kind of jest, as if they had mistaken his surname : "Non rex sum, sed Cæsar," [s] I am not king, but Cæsar,[t] an expression, the pregnancy of which it is difficult to exhaust ; for first, it was a refusal of the name, though not serious ; again, it displayed infinite confidence and magnanimity in presuming Cæsar to be the greater title, a presumption which posterity has fully confirmed. But chiefly the expression is to be admired as betraying a great incentive to his designs, as if the state strove with him for a mere name, with which even mean families were invested. For Rex was a surname with the Romans, as well as King is with us. The last saying I shall mention, refers to Metellus : as soon as Cæsar had seized Rome, he made straightway to the ærarium to seize the money of the state ; but Metellus being tribune, forestalled his purpose, and denied him entrance : whereupon Cæsar threatened, if he did not desist, to lay him dead on the spot. But presently checking himself, added, "Adolescens, durius est mihi hoc dicere quam facere ;" Young man, it is harder for me to say this than to do it.[u] A sentence compounded of the greatest terror and clemency that could proceed out of the mouth of man. But to conclude with Cæsar. It is evident he was quite aware of his proficiency in this respect, from his scoffing at the idea of the strange resolution of Sylla, which some one expressed about his resignation of the dictatorship ; "Sylla," said Cæsar, "was unlettered, and therefore knew not how to dictate." [x]

And here we should cease descanting on the concurrence of military virtue with learning, as no example could come with any grace after Alexander and Cæsar, were it not for an extraordinary case touching Xenophon, which raised that philosopher from the depths of scorn to the highest pinnacle of admiration. In his youth, without either command or experience, that philosopher followed the expedition of

[s] Suet. Life Jul. Cæs. 79.
[t] The point of this expression arises from the absence of the article in the Latin tongue, which made rex, a king, exactly convertible with the title of those families who bore Rex for their surname. With us, also, there are many individuals who bear the name of King, and among the French the name Roi is not uncommon. *Ed.*
[u] Plutarch ; cf. Cic. ad Att. x. 8. [x] Suet. Life, lxxvii.

Cyrus the younger against Artaxerxes, as a volunteer, to enjoy the love and conversation of his friend Proxenus.[y] Cyrus being slain on the field, Falinus came to the remnant of his army with a message from the king, who, presuming on the fewness of their number, and the perilous nature of their position in the midst of foreign enemies, cut off from their country by many navigable rivers, and many hundred miles, had dared to command them to surrender their army, and submit entirely to his mercy. Before an answer was returned, the heads of the army conferred familiarly with Falinus, and among the rest Xenophon happened to say, "Why, Falinus, we have only these two things left, our arms and our virtue, and if we yield up our arms, how can we make use of our virtue?" Falinus, with an ironical smile, replied, "If I be not deceived, young man, you are an Athenian; and I believe you study philosophy, as you talk admirably well. But you grossly deceive yourself if you think your courage can withstand the king's power."[z] Here was the scorn, but the wonder followed. This young philosopher, just emerged from the school of Socrates, after all the chieftains of the army had been murdered by treason, conducted those ten thousand foot through the heart of the king's territories, from Babylon to Græcia, untouched by any of the king's forces. The world, at this act of the young scholar, was stricken with astonishment, and the Greeks encouraged in succeeding ages to invade the kings of Persia. Jason the Thessalian proposed the plan, Agesilaus the Spartan attempted its execution, and Alexander the Macedonian finally achieved the conquest.

To proceed from imperial and military, to moral and private virtue; it is certain that learning softens the barbarity and fierceness of men's minds, according to the poet,

"Scilicet ingenuas didicisse fideliter artes
Emollit mores, nec sinit esse feros."[a]

But then it must not be superficial, for this rather works a contrary effect. Solid learning prevents all levity, temerity, and insolence, by suggesting doubts and difficulties, and

[y] Xen. Anab. ii. towards the end.   [z] Xen. Anab. ii. 1—12.
[a] Ovid. Ep. Pont. ii. ix. 47.

inuring the mind to balance the reasons on both sides, and reject the first offers of things, or to accept of nothing but what is first examined and tried. It prevents vain admiration, which is the root of all weakness : things being admired either because they are new, or because they are great. As for novelty, no man can wade deep in learning, without discovering that he knows nothing thoroughly; nor can we wonder at a puppet-show, if we look behind the curtain. With regard to greatness; as Alexander, after having been used to great armies, and the conquests of large provinces in Asia, when he received accounts of battles from Greece, which were commonly for a pass, a fort, or some walled town, imagined he was but reading Homer's battle of the frogs and the mice; so if a man considers the universal frame, the earth and its inhabitants will seem to him but as an ant-hill, where some carry grain, some their young, some go empty, and all march but upon a little heap of dust.

Learning also conquers or mitigates the fear of death and adverse fortune, which is one of the greatest impediments to virtue and morality; for if a man's mind be deeply seasoned with the consideration of the mortality and corruptibility of things, he will be as little affected as Epictetus, who one day seeing a woman weeping for her pitcher that was broken, and the next day a woman weeping for her son that was dead, said calmly, "Yesterday I saw a brittle thing broken, and to-day a mortal die."[b] And hence Virgil excellently joined the knowledge of causes and the conquering of fears together as concomitants:—

> "Felix qui potuit rerum cognoscere causas,
> Quique metus omnes, et inexorabile fatum,
> Subjecit pedibus; strepitumque Acherontis avari."[c]

It were tedious to enumerate the particular remedies which learning affords for all the diseases of the mind, sometimes by purging the morbific humours, sometimes by opening obstructions, helping digestion, increasing the appetite, and sometimes healing exulcerations, &c. But to sum up all, it disposes the mind not to fix or settle in defects, but to remain ever susceptible of improvement and reformation;

[b] See Epictetus, Enchir. c. 33, with the comment of Simplicius.
[c] Georg. ii. 490.

for the illiterate person knows not what it is to descend into himself, or call himself to an account, nor the agreeableness of that life which is daily sensible of its own improvement; he may perhaps learn to show and employ his natural talents, but not increase them; he will learn to hide and colour his faults, but not to amend them, like an unskilful mower, who continues to mow on without whetting his scythe. The man of learning, on the contrary, always joins the correction and improvement of his mind with the use and employment thereof. To conclude, truth and goodness differ but as the seal and the impression; for truth imprints goodness, whilst the storms of vice and perturbation break from the clouds of error and falsehood.

From moral virtue we proceed to examine whether any power be equal to that afforded by knowledge. Dignity of command is always proportionable to the dignity of the commanded. To have command over brutes as a herdsman is a mean thing; to have command over children as a schoolmaster is a matter of small honour; and to have command over slaves is rather a disgrace than an honour. Nor is the command of a tyrant much better over a servile and degenerate people; whence honours in free monarchies and republics have ever been more esteemed than in tyrannical governments, because to rule a willing people is more honourable than to compel. But the command of knowledge is higher than the command over a free people, as being a command over the reason, opinion, and understanding of men, which are the noblest faculties of the mind that govern the will itself; for there is no power on earth that can set up a throne in the spirits of men but knowledge and learning; whence the detestable and extreme pleasure wherewith arch-heretics, false prophets, and impostors are transported upon finding they have a dominion over the faith and consciences of men, a pleasure so great, that if once tasted scarce any torture or persecution can make them forego it. But as this is what the Apocalypse calls the depths of Satan,[d] so the just and lawful rule over men's understanding by the evidence of truth and gentle persuasion, is what approaches nearest to the Divine sovereignty.

With regard to honours and private fortune, the benefit

[d] Rev. ii. 24.

of learning is not so confined to states as not likewise to reach particular persons; for it is an old observation, that Homer has given more men their livings than Sylla, Cæsar, or Augustus, notwithstanding their great largesses. And it is hard to say whether arms or learning have advanced the greater numbers. In point of sovereignty, if arms or descent have obtained the kingdom, yet learning has obtained the priesthood, which was ever in competition with empire.

Again, the pleasure and delight of knowledge and learning surpass all others; for if the pleasures of the affections exceed the pleasures of the senses as much as the obtaining a desire or a victory exceeds a song or a treat, shall not the pleasures of the understanding exceed the pleasures of the affections? In all other pleasures there is a satiety, and after use their verdure fades; which shows they are but deceits and fallacies, and that it was the novelty which pleased, not the quality; whence voluptuous men frequently turn friars, and ambitious princes melancholy. But of knowledge there is no satiety, for here gratification and appetite are perpetually interchanging, and consequently this is good in itself, simply, without fallacy or accident. Nor is that a small pleasure and satisfaction to the mind, which Lucretius describes to this effect:[e]—" It is a scene of delight to be safe on shore and see a ship tossed at sea, or to be in a fortification and see two armies join battle upon a plain. But it is a pleasure incomparable for the mind to be seated by learning in the fortress of truth, and from thence to view the errors and labours of others."

To conclude. The dignity and excellence of knowledge and learning is what human nature most aspires to for the securing of immortality, which is also endeavoured after by raising and ennobling families, by buildings, foundations, and monuments of fame, and is in effect the bent of all other human desires. But we see how much more durable the monuments of genius and learning are than those of the hand. The verses of Homer have continued above five and twenty hundred years without loss, in which time numberless palaces, temples, castles, and cities have been demolished and are fallen to ruin. It is impossible to have the true pic-

[e] " Suave mari magno turbantibus æquora ventis," &c. De Rerum Natura, ii. 1.—13.

tures or statues of Cyrus, Alexander, Cæsar, or the great personages of much later date, for the originals cannot last, and the copies must lose life and truth; but the images of men's knowledge remain in books, exempt from the injuries of time, and capable of perpetual renovation. Nor are these properly called images; because they generate still, and sow their seed in the minds of others, so as to cause infinite actions and opinions in succeeding ages. If, therefore, the invention of a ship was thought so noble, which carries commodities from place to place and consociateth the remotest regions in participation of their fruits, how much more are letters to be valued, which, like ships, pass through the vast ocean of time, and convey knowledge and inventions to the remotest ages? Nay, some of the philosophers who were most immersed in the senses, and denied the immortality of the soul, yet allowed that whatever motions the spirit of man could perform without the organs of the body might remain after death, which are only those of the understanding, and not of the affections, so immortal and incorruptible a thing did knowledge appear to them.[f] And thus having endeavoured to do justice to the cause of knowledge, divine and human, we shall leave Wisdom to be justified of her children.[g]

[f] The merits of learning have been incidentally shown by many, but expressly by few. Among the latter may be included Johannes Wouwerius de Polymathia, Gulielmus Budæus de Philologia, Morhof in "Hist. Polyhister," and Stollius in "Introduct. in Historiam Literariam." To these may be added, Baron Spanheim, M. Perault, Sir William Temple, Gibbon, and Milton. *Ed.*

[g] Matt. xi. 19.

SECOND BOOK.

CHAPTER I.

General Divisions of Learning into History, Poetry, and Philosophy, in relation to the Three Faculties of the Mind—Memory, Imagination, and Reason. The same Distribution applies to Theology.

TO THE KING.

It is befitting, excellent King, that those who are blessed with a numerous offspring, and who have a pledge in their descendants that their name will be carried down to posterity, should be keenly alive to the welfare of future times, in which their children are to perpetuate their power and empire. Queen Elizabeth, with respect to her celibacy, was rather a sojourner than an inhabitant of the present world, yet she was an ornament to her age and prosperous in many of her undertakings. But to your Majesty, whom God has blessed with so much royal issue, worthy to immortalize your name, it particularly appertains to extend your cares beyond the present age, which is already illuminated with your wisdom, and extend your thoughts to those works which will interest remotest posterity. Of such designs, if affection do not deceive me, there is none more worthy and noble than the endowment of the world with sound and fruitful knowledge. For why should a few favourite authors stand up like Hercules' Columns, to bar further sailing and discovery, especially since we have so bright and benign a star in your Majesty to guide and conduct us?

It remains, therefore, that we consider the labours which princes and others have undertaken for the advancement of learning, and this markedly and pointedly, without digression or amplification. Let it then be granted, that to the completion of any work munificent patronage is as essential as soundness of direction and conjunction of labours. The first multiplies energy, the second prevents error, and the third compensates for human weakness. But the principal of these is direction, or the pointing out and the delineation of the direct way to the completion of the object in view. For " claudus in via antevertit cursorem extra viam ;" and Solomon appositely says, "If the iron is not pointed, greater strength is to be used ;"[a]—so what really prevaileth over everything is wisdom, by which he insinuates that a wise selection of means leads us more directly to our object than a straining or accumulation of strength. Without wishing to derogate from the merit of those who in any way have advanced learning, this much I have been led to say, from perceiving that their works and acts have tended rather to the glory of their name than the progression or proficiency of the sciences,—to augment the man of learning in the minds of philosophers, rather than reform or elevate the sciences themselves.

The institutions which relate to the extension of letters are threefold, viz., schools and universities, books, and professors. For as water, whether of the dew of heaven or spring of the earth, would speedily lose itself in the ground unless collected into conduits and cisterns, so it seemeth this excellent liquor of knowledge, whether it descend from Divine inspiration or spring from human sense, would soon hide itself in oblivion, unless collected in books, traditions, academies, and schools, it might find a permanent seat, and a fructifying union of strength.

The works which concern the seats of learning are four,—buildings, endowments, privileges, and charters, which all promote quietness and seclusion, freedom from cares and anxieties. Such stations resemble those which Virgil prescribes for beehiving :—

> " Principio sedes apibus, statioque petenda
> Quo neque sit ventis aditus."[b]

The works which relate to books are two,—first, libraries, which are as the shrines where the bones of old saints full of virtue lie buried ; secondly, new editions of writers, with correcter impressions, more faultless versions, more useful commentaries, and more learned annotations.

Finally, the works which pertain to the persons of the learned are, besides the general patronage which ought to be extended to them, twofold. The foundation of professor-

[a] Ecc. x. 10. [b] Georg. iv. 8.

ships in sciences already extant, and in those not yet begun or imperfectly elaborated.

These are, in short, the institutions on which princes and other illustrious men have displayed their zeal for letters. To me, dwelling upon each patron of letters, that notion of Cicero occurs, which urged him upon his return not to particularize, but to give general thanks,—" Difficile non aliquem, in gratum quenquam, præterire."[c] Rather should we, conformably to Scripture, look forward to the course we have yet to run, than regard the ground already behind us.

First, therefore, I express my surprise, that among so many illustrious colleges in Europe, all the foundations are engrossed by the professions, none being left for the free cultivation of the arts and sciences. Though men judge well who assert that learning should be referred to action, yet by reposing too confidently in this opinion, they are apt to fall into the error of the ancient fable,[d] which represented the members of the body at war with the stomach, because it alone, of all the parts of the frame, seemed to rest, and absorb all the nourishment. For if any man esteem philosophy and every study of a general character to be idle, he plainly forgets that on their proficiency the state of every other learning depends, and that they supply strength and force to its various branches. I mainly attribute the lame progress of knowledge hitherto to the neglect or the incidental study of the general sciences. For if you want a tree to produce more than its usual burden of fruit, it is not anything you can do to the branches that will effect this object, but the excitation of the earth about its roots and increasing the fertility of the soil; nor must it be overlooked that this restriction of foundations and endowments to professional learning has not only dwarfed the growth of the sciences, but been prejudicial to states and governments themselves. For since there is no collegiate course so free as to allow those who are inclined to devote themselves to history, modern languages, civil policy, and general literature; princes find a dearth of able men to manage their affairs and efficiently conduct the business of the commonwealth.

Since the founders of colleges plant, and those who endow

[c] Apocryphal Orat. post Redit. in Sen. xii. 30 ; cf. pro Pl. xxx. 74.
[d] Speech of Menenius Agrippa, Livy, ii. 32.

them water, we are naturally led to speak in this place of the mean salaries apportioned to public lectureships, whether in the sciences or the arts. For such offices being instituted not for an ephemeral purpose, but for the constant transmission and extension of learning, it is of the utmost importance that the men selected to fill them be learned and gifted. But it is idle to expect that the ablest scholars will employ their whole energy and time in such functions unless the reward be answerable to that competency which may be expected from the practice of a profession. The sciences will only flourish on the condition of David's military law,—that those who remain with the baggage shall have equal part with those who descend to the fight, otherwise the baggage will be neglected. Lecturers being in like manner guardians of the literary stores whence those who are engaged in active service draw, it is but just that their labours should be equally recompensed, otherwise the reward of the fathers of the sciences not being sufficiently ample, the verse will be realized,—

"Et patrum invalidi referent jejunia nati."*

The next deficiency we shall notice is, the want of philosophical instruments, in crying up which we are aided by the alchemists, who call upon men to sell their books, and to build furnaces, rejecting Minerva and the Muses as barren virgins, and relying upon Vulcan. To study natural philosophy, physic, and many other sciences to advantage, books are not the only essentials,—other instruments are required; nor has the munificence of men been altogether wanting in their provisions. For spheres, globes, astrolabes, maps, and the like, have been provided for the elucidation of astronomy and cosmography; and many schools of medicine are provided with gardens for the growth of simples, and supplied with dead bodies for dissection. But these concern only a few things. In general, however, there will be no inroad made into the secrets of nature unless experiments, be they of Vulcan or Dædalus, furnace, engine, or any other kind, are allowed for; and therefore as the secretaries and spies of princes and states bring in bills for intelligence, so you must allow the spies and intelligences of nature to bring in their bills, or else you will be ignorant of

* Virg. Georg. iii. 128.

many things worthy to be known. And if Alexander placed so large a treasure at Aristotle's command, for the support of hunters, fowlers, fishers, and the like, in much more need do they stand of this beneficence who unfold the labyrinths of nature.

Another defect I discover is the neglect in vice-chancellors, heads of houses, princes, inspectors, and others, of proper supervision or diligent inquiry into the course of studies, with a view to a thorough reformation of such parts as are ill suited to the age, or of unwise institution. For it is one of your Majesty's sage maxims, that as respects customs and precedents, we must consider the times in which they took their rise, since much is detracted from their authority, if such are found feeble and ignorant. It is, therefore, all the more requisite, since the university statues were framed in very obscure times, to institute an inquiry into their origin. Of errors of this nature I will give an example or two from such objects as are most obvious and familiar. The one is, that scholars are inducted too early into logic and rhetoric,—arts which, being the cream of all others, are fitter for graduates than children and novices. Now, being the gravest of the sciences, these arts are composed of rules and directions, for setting forth and methodizing the matter of the rest, and, therefore, for rude and blank minds, who have not yet gathered that which Cicero styles *sylva* and *supellex*[f] matter, and fecundity, to begin with those arts is as if one were to paint or measure the wind, and has no other effect than to degrade the universal wisdom of these arts into childish sophistry and contemptible affectation. This error has had the inevitable result of rendering the treatises on those sciences superficial, and dwarfing them to the capacities of children. Another error to be noticed in the present academical system is the separation between invention and memory, their exercises either being nothing but a set form of words, where no play is given to the understanding, or extemporaneous, in the delivery of which no room is left to the memory. In practical life, however, a blending of the powers of judgment and memory is alone put into requisition, so that these practices, not being adapted to the life of action, rather pervert than

[f] Sylva de Orat. iii. 26; Supellex Orat. xxiv.

discipline the mind. This defect is sooner discovered by scholars than by others, when they come to the practice of the civil professions. We may conclude our observations on university reform, with the expression of Cæsar in his letter to Oppius and Balbus: " Hoc quemadmodum fieri possit, nonnulla mihi in mentem veniunt, et multa reperiri possunt: de iis rebus rogo vos, ut cogitationem suscipiatis."[g]

The next want I discover is the little sympathy and correspondence which exists between colleges and universities, as well throughout Europe as in the same state and kingdom. In this we have an example in many orders and sodalities, which, though scattered over several sovereignties and territories, yet enter into a kind of contract, fraternity, and correspondence with one another, and are associated under common provincials and generals. And, surely, as nature creates brotherhood in families, and trades contract brotherhood in communities,[h] and the anointment of God establishes a brotherhood in kings and bishops, in like manner there should spring up a fraternity in learning and illumination, relating to that paternity which is attributed to God, who is called the Father of lights.

Lastly, I may lament that no fit men have been engaged to forward those sciences which yet remain in an unfinished state. To supply this want it may be of service to perform, as it were, a lustrum of the sciences, and take account of what have been prosecuted and what omitted. For the idea of abundance is one of the causes of dearth; and the multitude of books produces a deceitful impression of superfluity. This, however, is not to be remedied by destroying the books already written, but by making more good ones, which, like the serpent of Moses, may devour the serpents of the enchanters.[i] The removal of the defects I have enumerated, except the last, are indeed opera basilica, towards which the endeavours of one man can be but as an image on a cross road, which points out the way, but cannot tread it. But as the survey of the sciences which we have proposed lies within the power of a

[g] Cic. ad Att. ix. 7.

[h] The original is sodality, or guild societies, which had their origin in the middle ages, when members of the same calling formed a common fund and joined in certain spiritual exercises, taking a saint for their patron out of the Roman calendar. These institutions have since become commercial. *Ed.*   [i] Exod. vii. 10.

CHAP. I.]   IN WHAT RESPECTS WORKS ARE POSSIBLE.   77

private individual, it is my intention to make the circuit of knowledge, noticing what parts lie waste and uncultivated, and abandoned by the industry of man, with a view to engage, by a faithful mapping out of the deserted tracks, the energies of public and private persons in their improvement. My attention, however, is alone confined to the discovery, not to the correction of errors. For it is one thing to point out what land lies uncultivated, and another thing to improve imperfect husbandry.

In completing this design, I am ignorant neither of the greatness of the work nor my own incapacity. My hope, however, is, that, if the extreme love of my subject carry me too far, I may at least obtain the excuse of affection. It is not granted to man to love and be wise : " amare et sapere." On such topics opinion is free, and that liberty of judgment which I exercise myself lies equally at the disposition of all. And I for my part shall be as glad to receive correction from others as I am ready to point out defects myself. It is the common duty of humanity : " nam qui erranti comiter monstrat viam."[k] I, indeed, foresee that many of the defects and omissions I shall point out will be much censured, some as being already completed, and others as too difficult to be effected. For the first objection I must refer to the details of my subject ; with regard to the last, I take it for granted that those works are possible which may be accomplished by some person, though not by every one ; which may be done by many, though not by one ; which may be completed in the succession of ages, though not within the hour-glass of one man's life ; and which may reached by public effort, though not by private endeavour. Nevertheless, if any man prefer the sentence of Solomon—" Dicit piger, Leo est in via ;"[l] to that of Virgil, " possunt, quia posse videntur"[m]—I shall be content to have my labours received but as the better kind of wishes. For as it requires some knowledge to ask an apposite question, he also cannot be deemed foolish who entertains sensible desires.

The justest division of human learning is that derived from the three different faculties of the soul, the seat of learning : history being relative to the memory, poetry to the

[k] Cic. de Off. i. 16.   [l] Prov. xxii. 13.   [m] Virg. Æn. v. 231.

imagination, and philosophy to the reason. By poetry we understand no more than feigned history or fable, without regard at present to the poetical style. History is properly concerned about individuals, circumscribed by time and place; so likewise is poetry, with this difference, that its individuals are feigned, with a resemblance to true history, yet like painting, so as frequently to exceed it. But philosophy, forsaking individuals, fixes upon notions abstracted from them, and is employed in compounding and separating these notions according to the laws of nature and the evidence of things themselves.

Any one will easily perceive the justness of this division that recurs to the origin of our ideas. Individuals first strike the sense, which is as it were the port or entrance of the understanding. Then the understanding ruminates upon these images or impressions received from the sense, either simply reviewing them, or wantonly counterfeiting and imitating them, or forming them into certain classes by composition or separation. Thus it is clearly manifest that history, poetry, and philosophy flow from the three distinct fountains of the mind, viz., the memory, the imagination, and the reason; without any possibility of increasing their number. For history and experience are one and the same thing; so are philosophy and the sciences.

Nor does divine learning require any other division; for though revelation and sense may differ both in matter and manner, yet the spirit of man and its cells are the same; and in this case receive, as it were, different liquors through different conduits. Theology, therefore, consists—1. of sacred history; 2. parable, or divine poesy; and 3. of holy doctrine or precept, as its fixed philosophy. As for prophecy, which seems a part redundant, it is no more than a species of history; divine history having this prerogative over human, that the narration may precede, as well as succeed the fact.

CHAPTER II.

History divided into Natural and Civil ;—Civil subdivided into Ecclesiastical and Literary. The Division of Natural History according to the subject matter, into the History of Generations, of Præter-Generations, and the Arts.

History is either natural or civil: the natural records the works and acts of nature; the civil, the works and acts of men. Divine interposition is unquestionably seen in both, particularly in the affairs of men, so far as to constitute a different species of history, which we call sacred or ecclesiastical. But such is the dignity of letters and arts, that they deserve a separate history, which, as well as the ecclesiastical, we comprehend under civil history.

We form our division of natural history upon the threefold state and condition of nature; which is, 1. either free, proceeding in her ordinary course, without molestation; or 2. obstructed by some stubborn and less common matters, and thence put out of her course, as in the production of monsters; or 3. bound and wrought upon by human means, for the production of things artificial. Let all natural history, therefore, be divided into the history of generations, prætergenerations, and arts; the first to consider nature at liberty; the second, nature in her errors; and the third, nature in constraint.

The history of arts should the rather make a species of natural history, because of the prevalent opinion, as if art were a different thing from nature, and things natural different from things artificial: whence many writers of natural history think they perform notably, if they give us the history of animals, plants, or minerals, without a word of the mechanic arts. A farther mischief is to have art esteemed no more than an assistant to nature, so as to help her forwards, correct or set her free, and not to bend, change, and radically affect her; whence an untimely despair has crept upon mankind; who should rather be assured that artificial things differ not from natural in form or essence, but only in the efficient: for man has no power over nature in anything but motion, whereby he either puts bodies together, or separates them. And therefore, so far as natural bodies may be separated or conjoined, man may do anything.

Nor matters it, if things are put in order for producing effects, whether it be done by human means or otherwise. Gold is sometimes purged by the fire, and sometimes found naturally pure: the rainbow is produced after a natural way, in a cloud above; or made artificially, by the sprinkling of water below. As nature, therefore, governs all things by means,—1. of her general course; 2. her excursion; and 3. by means of human assistance; these three parts must be received into natural history, as in some measure they are by Pliny.

The first of these parts, the history of creatures, is extant in tolerable perfection; but the two others, the history of monsters and the history of arts, may be noted as deficient. For I find no competent collection of the works of nature digressing from the ordinary course of generations, productions, and motions; whether they be singularities of place and region, or strange events of time and chance; effects of unknown properties, or instances of exceptions to general rules. We have indeed many books of fabulous experiments, secrets, and frivolous impostures, for pleasure and strangeness; but a substantial and well-purged collection of heteroclites, or irregularities of nature, carefully examined and described, especially with a due rejection of fable and popular error, is wanting: for as things now stand, if false facts in nature be once on foot, through the neglect of examination, the countenance of antiquity, and the use made of them in discourse, they are scarce ever retracted.

The design of such a work, of which we have a precedent in Aristotle, is not to content curious and vain minds, but— 1. to correct the depravity of axioms and opinions, founded upon common and familiar examples; and 2. to show the wonders of nature, which give the shortest passage to the wonders of art: for by carefully tracing nature in her wanderings, we may be enabled to lead or compel her to the same again. Nor would we in this history of wonders have superstitious narrations of sorceries, witchcrafts, dreams, divinations, &c. totally excluded, where there is full evidence of the fact; because it is not yet known in what cases, and how far effects attributed to superstition, depend upon natural causes. And, therefore, though the practice of such things is to be condemned; yet the consideration of them may afford light, not only in judging criminals, but in a deeper disclosure of nature. Nor should men scruple examining into these things, in order to discover truth : the sun, though it passes through dirty places, yet remains as pure as before. Those narrations, however, which have a tincture of superstition, should be kept separate, and unmixed with others, that are merely natural. But the relations of religious prodigies and miracles, as being either false or supernatural, are unfit to enter into a history of nature.

As for the history of nature wrought or formed, we have some collections of agriculture and manual arts, but commonly with a rejection of familiar and vulgar experiments, which yet are of more service in the interpretation of nature than the uncommon ones: an inquiry into mechanical matters being reputed a dishonour to learning; unless such as appear secrets, rarities, and subtilties. This supercilious arrogance, Plato justly derides in his representation of the dispute between Hippias and Socrates touching beauty. Socrates is represented, in his careless manner, citing first an example of a fair virgin, then a fine horse, then a smooth pot curiously glazed. This last instance moved Hippias's choler, who said, "Were it not for politeness' sake, I would disdain to dispute with any that alleged such low and sordid examples." Whereupon Socrates replied, "You have reason, and it becomes you well, being a man so sprucely attired, and so trim in your shoes."[a] And certainly the truth is, that they are not the highest instances that always afford the securest information; as is not unaptly expressed in the tale so common of the philosopher,[b] who, while he gazed upwards to the stars, fell into the water.[c] For had he looked down, he might have discovered the stars in the water; but looking up to heaven, he could not see the water in the stars; for mean and small things often discover great ones, better than great can discover the small; and therefore Aristotle observes, "That the nature of everything is best seen in its smallest portions."[d] Whence he seeks the nature of a commonwealth, first in a family; and so the nature of the world, and the policy thereof must be sought in mean relations and small portions.

---

[a] Plato, Hipp. Maj. iii. 291.
[b] Laertius, "Life of Thales."
[c] Thales; see Plato, Theæt. i. 174.
[d] Arist. Polit. i. and Phys. i

The magnetic virtue of iron was not first discovered in bars, but in needles.

But in my judgment the use of mechanical history is, of all others, the most fundamental towards such a natural philosophy as shall not vanish in the fume of subtile, sublime, or pleasing speculations; but be operative to the endowment and benefit of human life; as not only suggesting, for the present, many ingenious practices in all trades, by connecting and transferring the observations of one art to the uses of another, when the experience of several arts shall fall under the consideration of one man; but as giving a more true and real illumination with regard to causes and axioms, than has hitherto appeared. For as a man's temper is never well known until he is crossed; in like manner the turns and changes of nature cannot appear so fully, when she is left at her liberty, as in the trials and tortures of art.

We add, that the body of this experimental history should not only be formed from the mechanic arts, but also from the operative and effective part of the liberal sciences, together with numerous practices, not hitherto brought into arts; so that nothing may be omitted which has a tendency to inform the understanding.[e]

[e] And therefore the history of sophistications, or adulterations and frauds practised in arts and trades, ought to be inserted, which the learned Morhof adds as a fourth part of this experimental history, though it may seem sufficiently included under the history of arts, as being the secret part essential to every art, and properly called the mystery or craft thereof. Of these impositions, a large number may be readily collected, and serve not only to quicken the understanding and enrich experimental history, but also to contribute to perfect the science of economical prudence. For contraries illustrate each other, and to know the sinister practices of an art gives light to the art itself, as well as puts men upon their guard against being deceived. See Morhof's "Polybist." tom. ii. p. 128. *Shaw.*

CHAPTER III.

Second Division of Natural History, in relation to its Use and End, into Narrative and Inductive. The most important end of Natural History is to aid in erecting a Body of Philosophy which appertains to Induction. Division of the History of Generations into the History of the Heavens, the History of Meteors, the History of the Earth and Sea, the History of Massive or Collective Bodies, and the History of Species.

As natural history has three parts, so it has two principal uses, and affords,—1. a knowledge of the things themselves that are committed to history; and 2. the first matter of philosophy. But the former, though it has its advantages, is of much more inferior consideration than the other, which is a collection of materials for a just and solid induction, whereon philosophy is to be grounded. And in this view, we again divide natural history into narrative and inductive; the latter whereof is wanting. If the natural history extant, though apparently of great bulk and variety, were to be carefully weeded of its fables, antiquities, quotations, frivolous disputes, philology, ornaments, and table-talk, it would shrink to a slender bulk. But besides, a history of this kind is far from what we require, as wanting the two above-mentioned parts of a natural history, viz. prætergenerations and arts, on which we lay great stress; and only answers one part in five of the third, viz. that of generations. For the history of generations has five subordinate parts; viz. 1. The celestial bodies, considered in their naked phenomena, stripped of opinions; 2. Meteors, comets,[a] and the regions of the air; 3. The earth and sea, as integral parts of the universe, including mountains, rivers, tides, sands, woods, and islands, with a view to natural inquiries rather than cosmography; 4. The elements, or greater assemblages of matter, as I call them,—viz. fire, air, water, and earth; and 5. The species of bodies, or more exquisite collections of matter, by us called the smaller assemblages, in which alone the industry of

Bacon, in the original, classes comets among meteors, yet fifteen hundred years before, Seneca had placed them among planets, predicting that the time would arrive when their seemingly erratic motions would be found to be the result of the same laws. We need hardly remind the reader of the realization of this sage conjecture in the magnificent discoveries of Sir Isaac Newton. *Ed.*

writers has appeared, and that too rather in a luxurious than solid manner; as rather abounding in things superfluous, viz. the representation of plants and animals, &c., than careful observations, which should ever be subjoined to natural history. In fine, all the natural history we have is absolutely unfit for the end we propose, viz. to build philosophy upon; and this both in the manner and matter thereof; hence we set down inductive history as deficient.

CHAPTER IV.

Civil History divided into Ecclesiastical and Literary. Deficiency of the latter. The Absence of Precepts for its Compilation.

CIVIL history, in general, may be divided into three particular kinds, viz. sacred, civil, and literary; the latter whereof being wanting, the history of the world appears like the statue of Polyphemus, without its eye; the part that best shows the life and spirit of the person. In many particular sciences indeed, as the law, mathematics, and rhetoric, there are extant some short memoirs, and jejune relations of sects, schools, books, authors, and the successions of this kind of sciences, as well as some trivial accounts of the inventors of things and arts; but we say, that a just and universal literary history has not hitherto been published.

The design of this work should be, to relate from the earliest accounts of time,—1. what particular kinds of learning and arts flourished, in what ages, and what parts of the world; 2. their antiquities, progress, and travels on the globe; 3. their decline, disappearance, and restoration. In each art should be observed, 4. its origin and occasion of invention; 5. the manner and form of its delivery; and 6. the means of its introduction, exercise, and establishment. Add to these, 7. the most famous sects and controversies of learned men; 8. the calumnies they suffered, and the praises and honours they received; 9. all along let the best authors and books be noted; with 10. the schools, successions, academies, societies, colleges, orders, and whatever regards the state of learning: but 11. principally let events be throughout coupled with their causes (which is the soul, as it were, of civil history), in relating the nature of countries and people, and 12. their disposition and indisposition to different kinds of learning; 13. the accidents of time, whether favourable or destructive to the sciences ; 14. the zeal and mixture of religion ; 15. the severity and lenity of laws ; 16. the remarkable patronage, efforts, and endowments of illustrious men, for the promotion of learning and the like. All which we would have handled, not in the manner of critics, who barely praise and censure ; but historically, or in the way of a naked delivery of facts, with but a sparing use of private judgment.

For the manner of writing this history, we particularly advise the materials of it to be drawn, not only from histories and critical works, but also that the principal books of every century be regularly consulted downwards ; so far we mean, as that a taste may be had, or a judgment formed, of the subject, style, and method thereof ; whence the literary genius of every age may at pleasure be raised, as it were, from the dead.

The use and end of this work is not to derive honour and pomp to learning, nor to gratify an eager curiosity and fondness of knowing and preserving whatever may relate thereto ; but chiefly to make learned men wise, in the prudent and sober exercise and administration of learning, and by marking out the virtues and vices of intellectual things, as well as the motions and perturbations of states, to show how the best regulation and government may be thence derived ; for as the works of St. Austin or St. Ambrose will not make so wise a divine as a thorough reading of Ecclesiastical History, the same will hold true of learned men with regard to particular books and literary history : for whoever is not supported by examples and the remembrance of things, must always be exposed to contingencies and precipitancy.

CHAPTER V.

The Dignity of Civil History and the Obstacles it has to encounter.

CIVIL history, particularly so called, is of prime dignity and authority among human writings ; as the examples of antiquity, the revolutions of things, the foundations of civil prudence, with the names and reputations of men, are committed to its trust. But it is attended with no less difficulty than dignity; for it is a work of great labour and judgment, to throw the mind back upon things past, and store it with antiquity; diligently to search into, and with fidelity and freedom relate, 1. the commotions of times; 2. the characters of persons; 3. the instability of counsels; 4. the courses of actions; 5. the bottoms of pretences; 6. the secrets of state; and 7. to set all this to view in proper and suitable language: especially as ancient transactions are uncertain, and late ones exposed to danger. Whence such a civil history is attended with numerous defects; the greater part of historians writing little more than empty and vulgar narrations, and such as are really a disgrace to history; while some hastily draw up particular relations and trivial memoirs, some only run over the general heads of actions; and others descend to the minutest particular, which have no relation to the principal action. These, in compliance with their genius, boldly invent many of the things they write; whilst those stamp the image of their own affections upon what they deliver; thus preserving fidelity to their party, but not to things themselves. Some are constantly inculcating politics, in which they take most pleasure, and seek all occasions of exhibiting themselves, thus childishly interrupting the thread of their history; whilst others are too tedious, and show but little judgment in the prolixity of their speeches, harangues, and accounts of actions; so that in short, nothing is so seldom found among the writings of men as true and perfect civil history.

CHAPTER VI.

Division of Civil History into Memoirs, Antiquities, and Perfect History.

THIS civil history is of three kinds, and bears resemblance to three kinds of pictures; viz., the unfinished, the finished, and the defaced: thus civil history, which is the picture of times and things, appears in memoirs, just history, and antiquities; but memoirs are history begun, or the first strokes and materials of it; and antiquities are history defaced, or remnants that have escaped the shipwreck of time.

Memoirs, or memorials, are of two kinds; whereof the one may be termed commentaries, the other registers. In commentaries are set down naked events and actions in sequence, without the motives, designs, counsels, speeches, pretexts, occasions, &c.; for such is the true nature of a commentary, though Cæsar, in modesty mixed with greatness, called the best history in the world a commentary.

Registers are of two kinds; as either containing the titles of things and persons in order of time, by way of calendars and chronicles, or else after the manner of journals, preserving the edicts of princes, decrees of council, judicial proceedings, declarations, letters of state, and public orations, without continuing the thread of the narration.

Antiquities are the wrecks of history, wherein the memory of things is almost lost; or such particulars as industrious persons, with exact and scrupulous diligence, can any way collect from genealogies, calendars, titles, inscriptions, monuments, coins, names, etymologies, proverbs, traditions, archives, instruments, fragments of public and private history, scattered passages of books no way historical, &c.; by which means something is recovered from the deluge of time. This is a laborious work; yet acceptable to mankind, as carrying with it a kind of reverential awe, and deserves to come in the place of those fabulous and fictitious origins of nations we abound with; though it has the less authority, as but few have examined and exercised a liberty of thought about it.

In these kinds of imperfect history, no deficiency need be noted, they being of their own nature imperfect: but epitomes of history are the corruption and moths that have fretted and corroded many sound and excellent bodies of history, and reduced them to base and unprofitable dregs; whence all men of sound judgment declare the use of them ought to be banished.

CHAPTER VII.
Division of History into Chronicles, Biographies, and Perfect Relations.
The Development of their parts.

JUST history is of three kinds, with regard to the three objects it designs to represent; which are either a portion

of time, a memorable person, or an illustrious action. The
first kind we call writing annals or chronicles; the second,
lives; and the third, narratives or relations. Chronicles
share the greatest esteem and reputation, but lives excel in
advantage and use, as relations do in truth and sincerity.
For chronicles represent only grand public actions, and external shows and appearances to the people, and drop the
smaller passages and motions of men and things. But as the
divine artificer hangs the greatest weight upon the smallest
strings, so such histories rather show the pomp of affairs,
than their true and inward springs. And though it in-
tersperses counsel, yet delighting in grandeur, it attributes
more gravity and prudence to human actions, than really
appears in them; so that satire might be a truer picture of
human life, than certain histories of this kind: whereas
lives, if wrote with care and judgment, proposing to represent a person, in whom actions, both great and small, public
and private, are blended together, must of necessity give a
more genuine, native, and lively representation, and such as
is fitter for imitation.

Particular relations of actions, as of the Peloponnesian
war, and the expedition of Cyrus, may likewise be made with
greater truth and exactness than histories of times; as
their subject is more level to the inquiry and capacity of the
writer, whilst they who undertake the history of any large
portion of time must need meet with blanks and empty
spaces, which they generally fill up out of their own invention.
This exception, however, must be made to the sincerity of
relations, that, if they be wrote near the times of the actions
themselves, they are, in that case, to be greatly suspected of
partiality or prejudice. But as it is usual for opposite parties
to publish relations of the same transactions, they, by this
means, open the way to truth, which lies betwixt the two
extremes: so that, after the heat of contention is allayed, a
good and wise historian may hence be furnished with matter
for a more perfect history.

As to the deficiencies in these three kinds of history,
doubtless many particular transactions have been left unre-
corded, to the great prejudice, in point of honour and glory,
of those kingdoms and states wherein they passed. But to
omit other nations, we have particular reason to complain to

your Majesty of the imperfection of the present history of England, in the main continuance of it, and the partiality and obliquity of that of Scotland, in the most copious and recent account that has been left us. As this island of Great Britain will now, as one united monarchy, descend to future ages, we cannot but deem it a work alike honourable to your Majesty, and grateful to posterity, that exploits were collected in one history, in the style of the ancient Testament, which hands down the story of the ten tribes and the two tribes as twins together. If the greatness of the undertaking, however, should prove any obstacle to its perfect execution, a shorter period of time, fraught with the greatest interest, occurs from the junction of the roses to the union of the two kingdoms—a space of time which to me appears to contain a crowd of more memorable events than ever occurred in any hereditary monarchy of similar duration. For it commences with the conjoint adoption of a crown by arms, and title, an entry by battle, and a marriage settlement. The times which follow, partaking of the nature of such beginnings, like waters after a tempest, full of workings and swellings, though without boisterous storms, being well navigated by the wisdom of the pilot,[a] one of the most able of his predecessors. Then succeeded the reign of a king, whose policy, though rather actuated by passion than counsel, exercised great influence upon the courts of Europe, balancing and variably inclining their various interests; in whose time, also, began that great change of religion, an action seldom brought on the stage. Then the reign of a minor. Then an attempt at usurpation, though it was but as a " febris ephemera :" then the reign of a queen, matched with a foreigner : then the reign of a queen, solitary and unmarried. And now, as a close, the glorious and auspicious event of the union of an island, divided from the rest of the world : so that we may say the old oracle which gave rest to Æneas, " antiquam exquirite matrem,"[b] is fulfilled in the union of England and Scotland under one sceptre. Thus as massive bodies, drawn aside from their course, experience certain waverings and trepidations before they fix and settle, so this monarchy, before it was to settle in your Majesty and your

[a] Henry VII. [b] Æn. iii. 96.

heirs, in whom I hope it is established for ever, seems by the providence of God to have undergone these mutations and deflections as a prelude to stability.

With regard to lives, we cannot but wonder that our own times have so little value for what they enjoy, as not more frequently to write the lives of eminent men. For though kings, princes, and great personages are few, yet there are many other excellent men who deserve better than vague reports and barren elogies. Here the fancy of a late poet, who has improved an ancient fiction, is not inapplicable. He feigns that at the end of the thread of every man's life, there hung a medal, on which the name of the deceased is stamped; and that Time, waiting upon the shears of the fatal sister, as soon as the thread was cut, caught the medals, and threw them out of his bosom into the river Lethe. He also represented many birds flying over its banks, who caught the medals in their beaks, and after carrying them about for a certain time, allowed them to fall in the river. Among these birds were a few swans, who used, if they caught a medal, to carry it to a certain temple consecrated to immortality. Such swans, however, are rare in our age. And although many, more mortal in their affections than their bodies, esteem the desire of fame and memory but a vanity, and despise praise, whilst they do nothing that is praiseworthy,—" animos nil magnæ laudis egentes;"[c] yet their philosophy springs from the root, " non prius laudes contempsimus quam laudanda facere desivimus;" and does not alter Solomon's judgment,—" the memory of the just shall be with praises; but the name of the wicked shall rot;"[d] the one flourishing, whilst the other consumes or turns to corruption. So in that laudable way of speaking of the dead, " of happy memory! of pious memory!" &c., we seem to acknowledge, with Cicero and Demosthenes, " that a good name is the proper inheritance of the deceased;"[e] which inheritance is lying waste in our time, and deserves to be noticed as a deficiency.

In the business of relations it is, also, to be wished that greater diligence were employed; for there is no signal action, but has some good pen to describe it. But very few

[c] Æn. v. 751.   [d] Prov. x. 7.   [e] Demosth. adv. Lept. 488.

being qualified to write a complete history, suitable to its dignity (a thing wherein so many have failed), if memorable acts were but tolerably related as they pass, this might lay the foundations, and afford materials for a complete history of times, when a writer should arise equal to the work.

CHAPTER VIII.

Division of the History of Times into Universal and Particular. The Advantages and Disadvantages of both.

History of times is either general or particular, as it relates the transactions of the whole world, or of a certain kingdom or nation. And there have been those who would seem to give us the history of the world from its origin; but, in reality, offer only a rude collection of things, and certain short narratives instead of a history; whilst others have nobly, and to good advantage, endeavoured to describe, as in a just history, the memorable things, which in their time happened over all the globe. For human affairs are not so far divided by empires and countries, but that in many cases they still preserve a connection: whence it is proper enough to view, as in one picture, the fates of an age. And such a general history as this may frequently contain particular relations, which, though of value, might otherwise either be lost, or never again reprinted: at least, the heads of such accounts may be thus preserved. But upon mature consideration, the laws of just history appear so severe as scarcely to be observed in so large a field of matter, whence the bulkiness of history should rather be retrenched than enlarged; otherwise, he who has such variety of matter everywhere to collect, if he preserve not constantly the strictest watch upon his informations, will be apt to take up with rumours and popular reports, and work such kind of superficial matter into his history. And, then, to retrench the whole, he will be obliged to pass over many things otherwise worthy of relation, and often to contract and shorten his style; wherein there lies no small danger of frequently cutting off useful narrations, in order to oblige mankind in their favourite way of compendium; whence such accounts, which might otherwise live of themselves, may come to be utterly lost.

CHAPTER IX.

Second Division of the History of Times into Annals and Journals.

HISTORY of times is likewise divisible into annals and journals, according to the observation of Tacitus, where, mentioning the magnificence of certain structures, he adds, "It was found suitable to the Roman dignity that illustrious things should be committed to annals, but such as these to the public journals of the city;"[a] thus referring what related to the state of the commonwealth to annals, and smaller matters to journals. And so there should be a kind of heraldry in regulating the dignities of books as well as persons: for as nothing takes more from the dignity of a state than confusion of orders and degrees, so it greatly takes from the authority of history to intermix matters of triumph, ceremony, and novelty, with matters of state. And it were to be wished that this distinction prevailed; but in our times journals are only used at sea and in military expeditions, whereas among the ancients it was a regal honour to have the daily acts of the palace recorded, as we see in the case of Ahasuerus, king of Persia.[b] And the journals of Alexander the Great contained even trivial matters;[c] yet journals are not destined for trivial things alone, as annals are for serious ones, but contain all things promiscuously, whether of greater or of less concern.

CHAPTER X.

Second Division of Special Civil History into Pure and Mixed.

THE last division of civil history is into pure and mixed. Of the mixed there are two eminent kinds,—the one principally civil, and the other principally natural: for a kind of writing has been introduced that does not give particular narrations in the continued thread of a history, but where the writer collects and culls them, with choice, out of an author, then reviewing and as it were ruminating upon them, takes occasion to treat of political subjects; and this

[a] Annals, xiii. 31.   [b] Esther vi. 1.
[c] Plutarch's Symposium, i. qu. 6; and Alex. Life, xxiii. 76.

kind of ruminated history we highly esteem, provided the writers keep close to it professedly, for it is both unseasonable and irksome to have an author profess he will write a proper history, yet at every turn introduce politics, and thereby break the thread of his narration. All wise history is indeed pregnant with political rules and precepts, but the writer is not to take all opportunities of delivering himself of them.

Cosmographical history is also mixed many ways,—as taking the descriptions of countries, their situations and fruits, from natural history; the accounts of cities, governments, and manners, from civil history; the climates and astronomical phenomena, from mathematics: in which kind of history the present age seems to excel, as having a full view of the world in this light. The ancients had some knowledge of the zones and antipodes,—

"Nosque ubi primus equis oriens afflavit anhelis,
Illic sera rubens accendit lumina vesper,"[a]—

though rather by abstract demonstration than fact. But that little vessels, like the celestial bodies, should sail round the whole globe, is the happiness of our age. These times, moreover, may justly use not only plus ultra, where the ancients used non plus ultra, but also imitabile fulmen where the ancients said non imitabile fulmen,—

"Demens qui nimbos et non imitabile fulmen."[b]

This improvement of navigation may give us great hopes of extending and improving the sciences, especially as it seems agreeable to the Divine will that they should be coeval. Thus the prophet Daniel foretells, that "Many shall go to and fro on the earth, and knowledge shall be increased,"[c] as if the openness and thorough passage of the world and the increase of knowledge were allotted to the same age, which indeed we find already true in part: for the learning of these times scarce yields to the former periods or returns of learning,—the one among the Greeks and the other among the Romans, and in many particulars far exceeds them.

[a] Virgil, Georgics, i. 251. [b] Virgil, Æneid, vi. 590.
[c] Dan. xii. 4.

CHAPTER XI.

Ecclesiastical History divided into the General History of the Church, History of Prophecy, and History of Providence.

ECCLESIASTICAL history in general has nearly the same divisions with civil history: thus there are ecclesiastical chronicles, lives of the fathers, accounts of synods, and other ecclesiastical matters; but in propriety it may be farther divided,—1. Into the general history of the Church; 2. The history of prophecy; and, 3. The history of providence. The first describes the times of the Church militant, whether fluctuating, as the ark of Noah; moveable, as the ark in the wilderness; or at rest, as the ark in the temple; that is, in the states of persecution, migration, and peace. And in this part there is a redundancy rather than a deficiency, but it were to be wished the goodness and sincerity of it were equal to the bulk.

The second part, viz. the history of prophecy, consists of two relatives,—the prophecy and the accomplishment; whence the nature of it requires, that every Scripture prophecy be compared with the event, through all the ages of the world, for the better confirmation of the faith and the better information of the Church with regard to the interpretation of prophecies not yet fulfilled. But here we must allow that latitude which is peculiar and familiar to divine prophecies, which have their completion not only at stated times, but in succession, as participating of the nature of their author, "with whom a thousand years are but as one day,"[a] and therefore are not fulfilled punctually at once, but have a growing accomplishment through many ages, though the height or fulness of them may refer to a single age or moment. And this is a work which I find deficient; but it should either be undertaken with wisdom, sobriety, and reverence, or not at all.

The third part,—the history of providence, has been touched by some pious pens, but not without a mixture of party. This history is employed in observing that Divine agreement which there sometimes is betwixt the revealed and secret will of God. For although the counsels and judgments of

[a] Psalm lxxxix. 4.

God are so secret as to be absolutely unsearchable to man,[b] yet the Divine goodness has sometimes thought fit, for the confirmation of his own people, and the confutation of those who are as without God in the world, to write them in such capital letters, as they who run may read them.[c] Such are the remarkable events and examples of God's judgments, though late and unexpected, sudden and unhoped for deliverances and blessings, Divine counsels dark and doubtful at length opening and explaining themselves, &c. All which have not only a power to confirm the minds of the faithful, but to awaken and convince the consciences of the wicked.

CHAPTER XII.

The Appendix of History embraces the Words of Men, as the Body of History includes their Exploits. Its Division into Speeches, Letters, and Apophthegms.

AND not only the actions of mankind, but also their sayings, ought to be preserved, and may doubtless be sometimes inserted in history, so far as they decently serve to illustrate the narration of facts; but books of orations, epistles, and apophthegms, are the proper repositories of human discourse. The speeches of wise men upon matter of business, weighty causes, or difficult points, are of great use, not only for eloquence, but for the knowledge of things themselves. But the letters of wise men upon serious affairs are yet more serviceable in points of civil prudence, as of all human speech nothing is more solid or excellent than such epistles, for they contain more of natural sense than orations, and more ripeness than occasional discourses: so letters of state affairs, written in the order of time by those that manage them, with their answers, afford the best materials for civil history.

Nor do apophthegms only serve for ornament and delight, but also for action and civil use, as being the edge-tools of speech,—

"Secures aut mucrones verborum,"[a]

which cut and penetrate the knots of business and affairs:

---

[b] 1 Cor. ii.   [c] Epis. to the Ephesians ii. and Habak. ii.
[a] Cicero's Epis. Fam. ix.

for occasions have their revolutions, and what has once been advantageously used may be so again, either as an old thing or a new one. Nor can the usefulness of these sayings in civil affairs be questioned, when Cæsar himself wrote a book upon the subject, which we wish were extant; for all those we have yet seen of the kind appear to be collected with little choice and judgment.

CHAPTER XIII.

The Second leading Branch of Learning—Poetry. Its Division into Narrative, Dramatic, and Parabolic. Three Examples of the latter species detailed.

POETRY is a kind of learning generally confined to the measure of words, but otherwise extremely licentious, and truly belonging to the imagination, which, being unrestrained by laws, may make what unnatural mixtures and separations it pleases. It is taken in two senses, or with respect to words and matter. The first is but a character of style and a certain form of speech not relating to the subject, for a true narration may be delivered in verse and a feigned one in prose; but the second is a capital part of learning, and no other than feigned history. And here, as in our divisions, we endeavour to find and trace the true sources of learning, and this frequently without giving way to custom or the established order,—we shall take no particular notice of satire, elegy, epigram, ode, &c., but turn them over to philosophy and the arts of speech, and under the name of poetry treat nothing more than imaginary history.

The justest division of poetry, except what it shares in common with history (which has its feigned chronicles, feigned lives, and feigned relations), is,—1. Into narrative; 2. Dramatic; and, 3. Allegorical. Narrative poetry is such an exact imitation of history as to deceive, did it not often carry things beyond probability. Dramatic poetry is a kind of visible history, giving the images of things as if they were present, whilst history represents them as past. But allegorical poetry is history with its type, which represents intellectual things to the senses.

Narrative poetry, otherwise called heroic poetry, seems,

with regard to its matter, not the versification, raised upon a noble foundation, as having a principal regard to the dignity of human nature. For as the active world is inferior to the rational soul, so poetry gives that to mankind which history denies, and in some measure satisfies the mind with shadows when it cannot enjoy the substance. For, upon a narrow inspection, poetry strongly shows that a greater grandeur of things, a more perfect order, and a more beautiful variety is pleasing to the mind than can anywhere be found in nature after the fall. So that, as the actions and events, which are the subjects of true history, have not that grandeur which satisfies the mind, poetry steps in and feigns more heroical actions. And as real history gives us not the success of things according to the deserts of virtue and vice, poetry corrects it, and presents us with the fates and fortunes of persons rewarded or punished according to merit. And as real history disgusts us with a familiar and constant similitude of things, poetry relieves us by unexpected turns and changes, and thus not only delights, but inculcates morality and nobleness of soul. Whence it may be justly esteemed of a Divine nature, as it raises the mind, by accommodating the images of things to our desires, and not, like history and reason, subjecting the mind to things. And by these its charms, and congruity to the mind, with the assistance also of music, which conveys it the sweeter, it makes its own way, so as to have been in high esteem in the most ignorant ages, and among the most barbarous people, whilst other kinds of learning were utterly excluded.

Dramatic poetry, which has the theatre for its world, would be of excellent use if it were sound; for the discipline and corruption of the theatre is of very great consequence. And the corruptions of this kind are numerous in our times, but the regulation quite neglected. The action of the theatre, though modern states esteem it but ludicrous, unless it be satirical and biting, was carefully watched by the ancients, that it might improve mankind in virtue : and indeed many wise men and great philosophers have thought it to the mind as the bow to the fiddle; and certain it is, though a great secret in nature, that the minds of men in company are more open to affections and impressions than when alone.

But allegorical poetry excels the others, and appears a

solemn sacred thing, which religion itself generally makes use of, to preserve an intercourse between divine and human things; yet this, also, is corrupted by a levity and indulgence of genius towards allegory. Its use is ambiguous, and made to serve contrary purposes; for it envelops as well as illustrates,—the first seeming to endeavour at an art of concealment, and the other at a method of instructing, much used by the ancients. For when the discoveries and conclusions of reason, though now common, were new, and first known, the human capacity could scarce admit them in their subtile state, or till they were brought nearer to sense, by such kind of imagery and examples; whence ancient times are full of their fables, their allegories, and their similes. From this source arise the symbol of Pythagoras, the enigmas of Sphinx, and the fables of Æsop. Nay, the apophthegms of the ancient sages were usually demonstrated by similitudes. And as hieroglyphics preceded letters, so parables preceded arguments; and the force of parables ever was and will be great, as being clearer than arguments, and more apposite than real examples.

The other use of allegorical poetry is to envelop things whose dignity deserves a veil; as when the secrets and mysteries of religion, policy, and philosophy, are wrapped up in fables and parables. But though some may doubt whether there be any mystical sense concealed in the ancient fable of the poets, we cannot but think there is a latent mystery intended in some of them: for we do not, therefore, judge contemptibly of them, because they are commonly left to children and grammarians; but as the writings that relate these fables are, next to the sacred ones, the most ancient and the fables themselves much older still, being not delivered as the inventions of the writers, but as things before believed and received, they appear like a soft whisper from the traditions of more ancient nations, conveyed through the flutes of the Grecians. But all hitherto attempted toward the interpretation of these parables proving unsatisfactory to us, as having proceeded from men of but common-place learning, we set down the philosophy of ancient fables as the only deficiency in poetry. But lest any person should imagine that any of these deficiencies are rather notional than real, and that we, like augurs, only measure countries i our mind, and know not how to invade them, we will proceed to subjoin examples of the work we recommend. These shall be three in number,—one taken from natural philosophy, one from politics, and another from morals.

PAN, OR NATURE.
Explained of Natural Philosophy.

"THE ancients have, with great exactness, delineated universal nature under the person of Pan. They leave his origin doubtful: some asserting him the son of Mercury, and others the common offspring of all Penelope's suitors. The latter supposition doubtless occasioned some later writers to entitle this ancient fable, Penelope—a thing frequently practised when the early relations are applied to more modern characters and persons, though sometimes with great absurdity and ignorance, as in the present case: for Pan was one of the ancientest gods, and long before the time of Ulysses: besides, Penelope was venerated by antiquity for her matronal chastity. A third sort will have him the issue of Jupiter and Hybris, that is, Reproach. But whatever his origin was, the Destinies are allowed his sisters.

"He is described by antiquity with pyramidal horns reaching up to heaven, a rough and shaggy body, a very long beard, of a biform figure, human above, half-brute below, ending in goat's feet. His arms, or ensigns of power, are a pipe in his left hand, composed of seven reeds; in his right a crook; and he wore for his mantle a leopard's skin.

"His attributes and titles were, the god of hunters, shepherds, and all the rural inhabitants; president of the mountains, and after Mercury the next messenger of the gods. He was also held the leader and ruler of the Nymphs, who continually danced and frisked about him, attended with the Satyrs, and their elders the Sileni. He had also the power of striking terrors, especially such as were vain and superstitious; whence they came to be called panic terrors.[b]

"Few actions are recorded of him; only a principal one is, that he challenged Cupid at wrestling, and was worsted. He also catched the giant Typhon in a net, and held him fast. They relate farther of him, that when Ceres growing

[a] Hymn to Pan, Hom. Odyss. *ver. fin.* [b] Cicero, Epis. to Atticus, 5.

disconsolate for the rape of Proserpine, hid herself, and all the gods took the utmost pains to find her, by going out different ways for that purpose, Pan only had the good fortune to meet her as he was hunting, and discovered her to the rest. He likewise had the assurance to rival Apollo in music; and in the judgment of Midas was preferred: but the judge had, though with great privacy and secrecy, a pair of ass's ears fastened on him for his sentence.[c]

"There is very little said of his amours, which may seem strange among such a multitude of gods, so profusely amorous. He is only reported to have been very fond of Echo, who was also esteemed his wife; and one nymph more called Syrinx, with the love of whom Cupid inflamed him for his insolent challenge; so he is reported, once, to have solicited the moon to accompany him apart into the deep woods.

"Lastly, Pan had no descendant, which also is a wonder, when the male gods were so extremely prolific; only he was the reputed father of a servant girl, called Iambe, who used to divert strangers with her ridiculous and prattling stories."

This fable is, perhaps, the noblest of all antiquity, and pregnant with the mysteries and secrets of nature. Pan, as the name imports, represents the universe, about whose origin there are two opinions; viz., that it either sprung from Mercury, that is, the Divine Word, according to the Scriptures and philosophical divines; or from the confused seeds of things. For some of the philosophers[d] held that the seeds and elements of nature were infinite in their substance; whence arose the opinion of homogeneous primary parts, which Anaxagoras either invented or propagated. Others more accurately maintain that the variety of nature can equally spring from seeds, certain and definite in substance, but only diversified in form and figure, and attribute the remaining varieties to the interior organization of the seeds themselves. From this source the doctrine of atoms is derived, which Democritus maintained, and Leucippus found out. But others teach only one principle of nature—Thales, water; Anaximenes, air; Heraclitus, fire[e]—and defined this

[c] Ovid, Metamorphoses, ii.   [d] Anaxagoras, in Diog. Laert.
[e] This difference between the three philosophies is nothing else, as Hippocrates has observed (De Dicta, lib. i.), than a mere dispute about

CHAP. XIII.] THE FABLE OF PAN INTERPRETED. 101

principle, which is one in act, to be various and dispensable in powers, and involving the seeds of all natural essences. They who introduced,—as Aristotle and Plato,[f]—primordial matter, every way disarranged, shapeless, and indifferent to any form, approached nearer to a resemblance of the figure of the parable. For they conceived matter as a courtezan, and the forms as suitors; so that the whole dispute comes to these two points: viz., either that nature proceeds from Mercury, or from Penelope and all her suitors.[g]

The third origin of Pan seems borrowed by the Greeks from the Hebrew mysteries, either by means of the Egyptians, or otherwise; for it relates to the state of the world, not in its first creation, but as made subject to death and corruption after the fall: and in this state it was and remains the offspring of God and Sin, or Jupiter and Reproach. And, therefore, these three several accounts of Pan's birth may seem true, if duly distinguished in respect of things and times. For this Pan, or the universal nature of things, which we view and contemplate, had its origin from the divine word, and confused matter, first created by God himself, with the subsequent introduction of sin, and consequently corruption.

The Destinies are justly made Pan's sisters; for the rise, preservation, and dissolution of things; their depressions, exaltations, processes, triumphs, and whatever else can be ascribed to individual natures, are called fates and destinies, but generally pass unnoticed, except indeed in striking examples, as in men, cities, and nations. Pan, or the nature of things, is the cause of these several changes and effects, and in regard to individuals as the chain of natural causes, and the thread of the Destinies, links them together. The ancients likewise feigned that Pan ever lived in the

---

words. For if there be but one single element or substance identical in all its parts, as the primary mover of things, it follows, as this substance is equally indifferent to the forms of each of the three elements, that one name may attach to it quite as philosophically as the other. In strict language, such a substance could not be defined by any of these terms; as fire, air, or water, appear only as its accidental qualities, and it is not allowable to define anything whose essential properties remain undiscovered. *Ed.*   [f] Plato's Timæus.

[g] Bacon directs his interpretation here to the confused mixture of things, as sung by Virgil, Ecl. vi. 31.

open air; but the Parcæ or the Destinies in a large subterraneous cave, from which they emerged with inconceivable swiftness, to operate on mankind, because the common face of the universe is open; but the individual fates, dark, swift, and sudden. The analogy will also correspond if fate be enlarged above its ordinary acceptation as applicable to inanimate nature. Since, also, in that order nothing passes without a cause, and nothing is so absolutely great as to be independent, nature holding in her lap and bosom every event either small or great, and disclosing them in due season, it is, therefore, no marvel that the Parcæ are introduced as the sisters of Pan: for Fortune is the daughter of the foolish vulgar, and finds favour only with the more unsound philosophers. And the words of Epicurus savour less of dotage than profanity—" Præstare credere fabulam Deorum quam fatum asserere [h]—as if anything in the frame of nature could, like an island, stand apart from the rest. But Epicurus framed his natural philosophy on his moral, and would hear of no opinion which might press or sting his conscience, or in any way trouble that euthymia or tranquillity of mind which he had received from Democritus. Hence, being more indulgent to his own fancies than patient of truth, he fairly cast off the yoke, and abandoned as well the necessity of fate as the fear of the gods.

Horns are given him broad at the roots, but narrow and sharp a-top, because the nature of all things seems pyramidal: for individuals are infinite; but being collected into a variety of species, they rise up into kinds; and these again ascend, and are contracted into generals, till at length nature may seem collected to a point, which is signified by the pyramidal figure of Pan's horns. And no wonder if Pan's horns reach to the heavens, since the sublimities of nature, or abstract ideas, reach in a manner to things divine. Thus Homer's famous chain of natural causes is tied to the foot of Jupiter's chain;[i] and indeed no one can treat of metaphysics, or of the internal and immutable in nature, without rushing at once into natural theology.

Pan's body, or the body of nature, is, with great propriety and elegance, painted shaggy and hairy, as representing the

[a] Seneca's Epistles. [i] Iliad, ix.

rays of things: for rays are as the hair or fleece of nature, and more or less worn by all bodies. This evidently appears in vision, and in all effects or operations at a distance: for whatever operates thus may be properly said to emit rays.[k] But particularly the beard of Pan is exceeding long, because the rays of the celestial bodies penetrate, and act to a prodigious distance, and have descended into the interior of the earth so far as to change its surface;[l] and the sun himself, when clouded on its upper part, appears to the eye bearded.

Again, the body of nature is justly described biform, because of the difference between its superior and inferior parts; as the former, for their beauty, regularity of motion, and influence over the earth, may be properly represented by the human figure, and the latter, because of their disorder, irregularity, and subjection to the celestial bodies, are by the brutal. This biform figure also represents the participation of one species with another, for there appear to be no simple natures, but all participate or consist of two: thus man has somewhat of the brute, the brute somewhat of the plant, the plant somewhat of the mineral; so that all natural bodies have really two faces, or consist of a superior and an inferior species.

There lies a curious allegory in the making of Pan goat-footed, on account of the motion of ascent, which the terrestrial bodies have towards the air and heavens: for the goat is a clambering creature, that delights in climbing up rocks and precipices; and in the same manner the matters destined to this lower globe strongly affect to rise upwards, as appears from the clouds and meteors. And it was not without reason that Gilbert, who has written a painful and elaborate work upon the magnet, doubted whether ponderous bodies, after being separated a long distance from the earth, do not lose their gravitating tendency towards it.

---

[k] This is always supposed to be the case in vision, the mathematical demonstrations in optics proceeding invariably upon the assumption of this phenomenon. *Ed.*

[l] Bacon had no idea of a central fire, and how much it has contributed to work these interior revolutions. The thermometer of Drebbel, which he describes in the second part of the Novum Organum, has shown that down to a certain depth beneath the earth's surface the temperature (in all climates) undergoes no change, and beyond that limit, that the heat augments in proportion to the descent. *Ed.*

Pan's arms, or the ensigns he bears in his hands, are of two kinds; the one an emblem of harmony, the other of empire. His pipe, composed of seven reeds, plainly denotes the consent and harmony, or the concords and discords of things, produced by the motion of the seven planets. If there be other planets yet concealed, or any greater mutations in the heavens, as in superlunary comets, they seem like pipes either altogether united or silent for a time, because their influence either does not reach so low as us, or leaves uninterrupted the harmony of the seven pipes of Pan. His crook also contains a fine representation of the ways of nature, which are partly straight and partly crooked: thus the staff, having an extraordinary bend towards the top, denotes that the works of Divine Providence are generally brought about by remote means, or in a circuit, as if somewhat else were intended, rather than the effect produced; as in the sending of Joseph into Egypt. So, likewise, in human government, they who sit at the helm manage and wind the people more successfully by pretext and oblique courses than they could by such as are direct and straight; so that in effect all sceptres are crooked on the top. Nay, in things strictly natural you may sooner deceive nature than force her, so improper and self-convicting are open direct endeavours, whereas an oblique and insinuating way gently glides along, and secretly accomplishes the purpose.

Pan's mantle, or clothing, is with great ingenuity made of a leopard's skin, because of the spots it has: for, in like manner, the heavens are sprinkled with stars, the sea with islands, the earth with flowers, and almost each particular thing is variegated, or wears a mottled coat.

The office of Pan could not be more livelily expressed than by making him the god of hunters: for every natural action, every motion and process, is no other than a chase; thus arts and sciences hunt out their works, and human schemes and counsels their several ends, and all living creatures either hunt out their aliment, pursue their prey, or seek their pleasures, and this in a skilful and sagacious manner.[m] He is also styled the god of the rural inhabitants,

---

[m] "Torva leæna lupum sequitur, lupus ipse capellam:
Florentem cytisum sequitur lasciva capella."
Virgil, Ecl. ii. 63.

because men in this situation live more according to nature than they do in cities and courts, where nature is so corrupted with effeminate arts, that the saying of the poet may be verified:—

" —— pars minima est ipsa puella sui."[a]

He is likewise particularly styled president of the mountains, because in mountains and lofty places the nature of things lies more open and exposed to the eye and the understanding.

In his being called the messenger of the gods, next after Mercury, lies a divine allegory; as, next after the word of God, the image of the world is the herald of the divine power and wisdom, according to the expression of the Psalmist: "The heavens declare the glory of God, and the firmament showeth his handy-work."[b]

Pan is delighted with the company of the Nymphs: that is, the souls of all living creatures are the delight of the world, and he is properly called their governor, because each of them follows its own nature as a leader, and all dance about their own respective rings with infinite variety and never-ceasing motion. Hence one of the moderns has ingeniously reduced all the power of the soul to motion, noting the precipitancy of some of the ancients, who, fixing their thoughts prematurely on memory, imagination, and reason, have neglected the cogitative faculty, which, however, plays the chief rôle in the work of conception. For he that remembers, cogitates, as likewise he who fancies or reasons; so that the soul of man in all her moods dances to the musical airs of the cogitations, which is that rebounding of the Nymphs. And with these continually join the Satyrs and Sileni, that is, youth and age; for all things have a kind of young, cheerful, and dancing time; and again their time of slowness, tottering, and creeping. And whoever, in a true light, considers the motions and endeavours of both these ages, like another Democritus, will perhaps find them as odd and strange as the gesticulations and antic motions of the Satyrs and Sileni.

The power he had of striking terrors contains a very sensible doctrine, for nature has implanted fear in all living

[a] Ovid, Rem. Amoris, v. 343. Mart. Epist. [b] Psalm xix. 1.

creatures, as well to keep them from risking their lives as to guard against injuries and violence; and yet this nature or passion keeps not its bounds, but with just and profitable fears always mixes such as are vain and senseless; so that all things, if we could see their insides, would appear full of panic terrors. Nor is this superstition confined to the vulgar, but sometimes breaks out in wise men. As Epicurus, "Non Deos vulgi negare profanum; sed vulgi opiniones Diis applicare profanum."[p]

The presumption of Pan in challenging Cupid to the conflict, denotes that matter has an appetite and tendency to a dissolution of the world, and falling back to its first chaos again, unless this depravity and inclination were restrained and subdued by a more powerful concord and agreement of things, properly expressed by love or Cupid; it is therefore well for mankind, and the state of all things, that Pan was thrown and conquered in the struggle.

His catching and detaining Typhon in the net receives a similar explanation; for whatever vast and unusual swells, which the word Typhon signifies, may sometimes be raised in nature, as in the sea, the clouds, the earth, or the like; yet nature catches, entangles, and holds all such outrages and insurrections in her inextricable net, wove as it were of adamant.

That part of the fable which attributes the discovery of lost Ceres to Pan, whilst he was hunting, a happiness denied the other gods, though they diligently and expressly sought her, contains an exceeding just and prudent admonition; viz. that we are not to expect the discovery of things useful in common life, as that of corn, denoted by Ceres, from abstract philosophies, as if these were the gods of the first order,—no, not though we used our utmost endeavours this way,—but only from Pan, that is, a sagacious experience and general knowledge of nature, which is often found, even by accident, to stumble upon such discoveries, whilst the pursuit was directed another way.

The event of his contending with Apollo in music, affords us an useful instruction, that may help to humble the human reason and judgment, which is too apt to boast and glory in itself. There seem to be two kinds of harmony; the one of Divine Providence, the other of human reason: but the

[p] Laertius's Life of Epicurus.

government of the world, the administration of its affairs, and the more secret divine judgments, sound harsh and dissonant to human ears or human judgment; and though this ignorance be justly rewarded with ass's ears, yet they are put on and worn, not openly, but with great secrecy; nor is the deformity of the thing seen or observed by the vulgar.

We must not find it strange if no amours are related of Pan, besides his marriage with Echo; for nature enjoys itself, and in itself all other things: he that loves, desires enjoyment; but in profusion there is no room for desire; and therefore Pan, remaining content with himself, had no passion, unless it be for discourse, which is well shadowed out by Echo, or talk; or when it is more accurate, by Syrinx, or writing.[q] But Echo makes a most excellent wife for Pan, as being no other than genuine philosophy, which faithfully repeats his words, or only transcribes exactly as nature dictates; thus representing the true image and reflection of the world, without adding a tittle. The calling the moon aside into a deeply embrowned wood, seems to refer to the convention between the sense and spiritual things. For the ear of Endymion and Pan are different, the moon of her own accord in the latter case stooping down from her sphere as Endymion lay asleep, intimating that divine illuminations oft glide gently into the understanding, cast asleep and withdrawn from the senses. But if they be called by sense, representing Pan, they afford no other light than that

"Quale, per incertam lunam, sub luce malignâ,
Est iter in sylvis."[r]

It tends also to the support and perfection of Pan or nature, to be without offspring; for the world generates in its parts, and not in the way of a whole, as wanting a body external to itself wherewith to generate.

Lastly, for the supposed or spurious prattling daughter of Pan, it is an excellent addition to the fable, and aptly represents the talkative philosophies that have at all times been stirring, and filled the world with idle tales; being ever barren, empty, and servile, though sometimes indeed diverting and entertaining, and sometimes again troublesome and importunate.

[q] Syrinx signifying a reed, or the ancient pen.   [r] Æneid, vi. 270.

PERSEUS,[*] OR WAR.

Explained of the Preparation and Conduct necessary to War.

"THE fable relates, that Perseus was despatched from the east by Pallas, to cut off Medusa's head, who had committed great ravage upon the people of the west; for this Medusa was so dire a monster, as to turn into stone all those who but looked upon her. She was a Gorgon, and the only mortal one ot the three; the other two being invulnerable. Perseus, therefore, preparing himself for this grand enterprise, had presents made him from three of the gods: Mercury gave him wings for his heels; Pluto, a helmet; and Pallas, a shield and a mirror. But though he was now so well equipped, he posted not directly to Medusa, but first turned aside to the Greæ, who were half-sisters to the Gorgons. These Greæ were gray-headed, and like old women from their birth, having among them all three but one eye, and one tooth, which, as they had occasion to go out, they each wore by turns, and laid them down again upon coming back. This eye and this tooth they lent to Perseus, who, now judging himself sufficiently furnished, he, without farther stop, flies swiftly away to Medusa, and finds her asleep. But not venturing his eyes, for fear she should wake, he turned his head aside, and viewed her in Pallas's mirror, and thus directing his stroke, cut off her head; when immediately, from the gushing blood, there darted Pegasus winged. Perseus now inserted Medusa's head into Pallas's shield, which thence retained the faculty of astonishing and benumbing all who looked on it."

This fable seems invented to show the prudent method ot choosing, undertaking, and conducting a war. The chief thing to consider in undertaking war is a commission from Pallas, certainly not from Venus, as the Trojan war was, or other slight motive. Because the designs of war ought to be justified by wise counsels. As to the choice of war, the fable propounds three grave and useful precepts.

The first is, that no prince should be over-solicitous to subdue a neighbouring nation: for the method of enlarging an empire is very different from that of increasing an estate. Regard is justly had to contiguity or adjacency in private lands and possessions; but in the extending of empire, the

---

[*] Ovid, Metam. iv.

occasion, the facility, and advantage of a war, are to be regarded instead of vicinity. Thus Perseus, though an eastern prince, readily undertook an expedition into the remotest parts of the western world. An opposite instance of the wisdom of this precept occurs in the different strategy of war practised by Philip and Alexander. For Philip urged war only on the frontiers of his empire, and with great strife and peril barely succeeded in bringing a few cities under his rule, but Alexander carried his invading arms into distant countries; and with a felicitous boldness undertook an expedition against Persia, and subduing multitudinous nations on his journey, rested at last rather fatigued with conquest than with arms. This policy is further borne out by the propagation of the Roman power; for at the time that the arms of this martial people on the side of the west stretched no further than Liguria, they had brought under their dominion all the provinces of the East as far as Mount Taurus. In like manner, Charles the Eighth, finding a war with Great Britain attended with some dangers, directed his enterprise against Naples, which he subdued with wonderful rapidity and ease. One of the causes of these wonderful successes in distant wars, is the low state of discipline and equipment, which invites the attack of the invading power, and the terror which is generally struck into the enemy from the bold audacity of the enterprise. Nor can the enemy retaliate or effect any reciprocal invasion, which always results from a war waged with the frontier nations. But the chief point is, that in subduing a neighbouring state the choice of stratagems is narrowed by circumstances; but in a distant expedition, a man may roll the tide of war where the military discipline is most relaxed, or where the strength of the nation is most torn and wasted by civil discord, or in whatever part the enemy can be the most easily subjugated.

The second precept is, that the cause of the war be just and honourable; for this adds alacrity both to the soldiers and the people who find the supplies, procures aids, alliances, and numerous other conveniences. Now, there is no cause of war more just and laudable than the suppressing of tyranny, by which a people are dispirited, benumbed, or left without life and vigour, as at the sight of Medusa. Such heroic acts transformed Hercules into a divinity. It was undoubtedly a point of religion with the Romans to aid with valour and speed such of their allies and confederates as were in any way distressed. So just and vindictive wars have generally met with success; as the war of the triumvirate in revenge for the death of Cæsar, the war of Severus for the death of Pertinax, and of Junius Brutus for the death of Lucretia; for they who take up arms to relieve and revenge the calamities of men fight under the standard of Perseus.

Lastly, it is prudently added, that as there were three of the Gorgons who represent war, Perseus singled her out for his expedition that was mortal; which affords this precept, that such kind of wars should be chosen as may be brought to a conclusion without pursuing vast and infinite hopes.

Again, Perseus's setting out is extremely well adapted to his undertaking, and in a manner commands success,—he received despatch from Mercury, secrecy from Pluto, and foresight from Pallas. It also contains an excellent allegory, that the wings given him by Mercury were for his heels, not for his shoulders, because expedition is not so much required in the first preparations for war as in the subsequent matters that administer to the first; for there is no error more frequent in war than, after brisk preparations, to halt for subsidiary forces and effective supplies.

The allegory of Pluto's helmet rendering men invisible and secret, is sufficiently evident of itself; for secretness appertains to celerity, inasmuch as speed prevents the disclosure of counsels: it therefore succeeds in importance. Pluto's helmet also seems to imply, that authority over the army is to be lodged in one chief; as directing committees in such cases are too apt to scatter dissensions among the troops, and to be swayed by paltry freaks and jealousies rather than by patriotism. It is not of less importance to discover the designs of the enemy, for which purpose the mirror of Pallas must be joined to the helmet of Pluto to disclose the weakness, the divisions, counsels, spies, and factions of the enemy. But as these arms are not sufficient to cope with all the casualties of war, we must grasp the shield of Pallas, *i.e.* of Providence, as a defence from the caprices of fortune. To this belong the despatch of spies, the fortification of camps, the equipment and position of the army, and whatever tends to promote the success of a just defensive war. For in the issue of contests the shield of Pallas is of greater consequence than the sword of Mars.

But though Perseus may now seem extremely well prepared, there still remains the most important thing of all,—before he enters upon the war he must of necessity consult the Greæ. These Greæ are treasons, half but degenerate sisters of the Gorgons, who are representatives of wars; for wars are generous and noble, but treasons base and vile. The Greæ are elegantly described as hoary-headed, and like old women from their birth, on account of the perpetual cares, fears, and trepidations attending traitors. Their force also, before it breaks out into open revolt, consists either in an eye or a tooth; for all faction alienated from a state is both watchful and biting, and this eye and tooth is as it were common to all the disaffected, because whatever they learn and know is transmitted from one to another, as by the hands of faction. And for the tooth they all bite with the same, and clamour with one throat, so that each of them singly expresses the multitude.

These Greæ, therefore, must be prevailed upon by Perseus to lend him their eye and their tooth,—the eye to give him indications and make discoveries, the tooth for sowing rumours, raising envy, and stirring up the minds of the people. And when all these things are thus disposed and prepared, then follows the action of the war.

He finds Medusa asleep; for whoever undertakes a war with prudence generally falls upon the enemy unprepared, and nearly in a state of security; and here is the occasion for Pallas's mirror, for it is common enough, before the danger presents, to see exactly into the state and posture of the enemy; but the principal use of the glass is in the very instant of danger, to discover the manner thereof and prevent consternation, which is the thing intended by Perseus's turning his head aside and viewing the enemy in the glass.[b]

Two effects here follow the conquest,—1. The darting forth of Pegasus, which evidently denotes fame, that flies abroad, proclaiming the victory far and near. 2. The bear-

[b] Thus it is the excellence of a general early to discover what turn the battle is likely to take, and looking prudently behind, as well as before, to pursue a victory so as not to be unprovided for a retreat.

ing of Medusa's head in the shield, which is the greatest possible defence and safeguard; for one grand and memorable enterprise, happily accomplished, bridles all the motions and attempts of the enemy, stupifies disaffection, and quells commotions.

DIONYSUS, OR BACCHUS.*
Explained of the Passions.

"THE fable runs, that Semele, Jupiter's mistress, having bound him by an inviolable oath to grant her an unknown request, desired he would embrace her in the same form and manner he used to embrace Juno; and the promise being irrevocable, she was burnt to death with lightning in the performance. The embryo, however, was sewed up, and carried in Jupiter's thigh, till the complete time of its birth; but the burden thus rendering the father lame, and giving him pain, the child was thence called Dionysus. When born, he was committed for some years to be nursed by Proserpina; and when grown up, appeared with such an effeminate face, that his sex seemed somewhat doubtful. He also died and was buried for a time, but afterwards revived. When a youth, he first introduced the cultivation and dressing of vines, the method of preparing wine, and taught the use thereof; whence becoming famous, he subdued the world, even to the utmost bounds of the Indies. He rode in a chariot drawn by tigers: there danced about him certain deformed demons called Cobali, &c.; the Muses also joined in his train. He married Ariadne, who was deserted by Theseus. The ivy was sacred to him. He was also held the inventor and institutor of religious rites and ceremonies, but such as were wild, frantic, and full of corruption and cruelty. He had also the power of striking men with frenzies. Pentheus and Orpheus were torn to pieces by the frantic women at his orgies, the first for climbing a tree to behold their outrageous ceremonies, and the other for the music of his harp. But the acts of this god are much entangled and confounded with those of Jupiter."

This fable seems to contain a little system of morality, so that there is scarce any better invention in all ethics. Un-

---

* Ovid's Metamorphoses, iii. iv. and vi.; and Fasti, iii. 767.

ler the history of Bacchus is drawn the nature of unlawful desire, or affection and disorder; for the appetite and thirst of apparent good is the mother of all unlawful desire, though ever so destructive; and all unlawful desires are conceived in unlawful wishes or requests, rashly indulged or granted before they are well understood or considered; and when the affection begins to grow warm, the mother of it (the nature of good) is destroyed and burnt up by the heat. And whilst an unlawful desire lies in the embryo, or unripened in the mind, which is its father, and here represented by Jupiter, it is cherished and concealed, especially in the inferior part of the mind, corresponding to the thigh of the body, where pain twitches and depresses the mind so far as to render its resolutions and actions imperfect and lame. And even after this child of the mind is confirmed, and gains strength by consent and habit, and comes forth into action, it must still be nursed by Proserpina for a time; that is, it skulks and hides its head in a clandestine manner, as it were underground, till at length, when the checks of shame and fear are removed, and the requisite boldness acquired, it either assumes the pretext of some virtue, or openly despises infamy. And it is justly observed, that every vehement passion appears of a doubtful sex, as having the strength of a man at first, but at last the impotence of a woman. It is also excellently added, that Bacchus died and rose again; for the affections sometimes seem to die and be no more; but there is no trusting them, even though they were buried, being always apt and ready to rise again whenever the occasion or object offers.

That Bacchus should be the inventor of wine carries a fine allegory with it; for every affection is cunning and subtile in discovering a proper matter to nourish and feed it; and of all things known to mortals, wine is the most powerful and effectual for exciting and inflaming passions of all kinds, being indeed like a common fuel to them all.

It is again with great elegance observed of Bacchus, that he subdued provinces and undertook endless expeditions; for the affections never rest satisfied with what they enjoy, but with an endless and insatiable appetite thirst after somewhat further. And tigers are prettily feigned to draw the chariot; for as soon as any affection shall, from going on foot, be ad vanced to ride, it triumphs over reason, and exerts its cruelty, fierceness, and strength against all that oppose it.

It is also humorously imagined, that ridiculous demons should dance and frisk about this chariot; for every passion produces indecent, disorderly, interchangeable, and deformed motions in the eyes, countenance, and gesture,—so that the person under the impulse whether of anger, insult, love, &c., though to himself he may seem grand, lofty, or obliging, yet in the eyes of others appears mean, contemptible, or ridiculous.

The Muses also are found in the train of Bacchus; for there is scarce any passion without its art, science, or doctrine to court and flatter it; but in this respect the indulgence of men of genius has greatly detracted from the majesty of the Muses, who ought to be the leaders and conductors of human life, and not the handmaids of the passions.

The allegory of Bacchus falling in love with a cast mistress is extremely noble; for it is certain that the affections always court and covet what has been rejected upon experience. And all those who, by serving and indulging their passions immensely raise the value of enjoyment, should know, that whatever they covet and pursue, whether riches, pleasure, glory, learning, or anything else, they only pursue those things that have been forsaken, and cast off with contempt by great numbers in all ages, after possession and experience.

Nor is it without a mystery that the ivy was sacred to Bacchus; and this for two reasons,—First, because ivy is an evergreen, or flourishes in the winter; and, secondly, because it winds and creeps about so many things, as trees, walls, and buildings, and raises itself above them. As to the first, every passion grows fresh, strong, and vigorous by opposition and prohibition, as it were by a kind of contrast or antiperistasis,[b] like the ivy in the winter. And for the

[b] The word ἀντιπερίστασις, used by the Greeks to express the forces of activity and resistance, which are continually producing all the variegated tissue of phenomena which mark the history of the moral and physical world, and are necessary to their preservation. Without reaction, action could not take place, as force can be only displayed in overcoming resistance, and we can have no idea of its existence except from its effect upon the antagonistic force it attempts to subdue. In

second, the predominant passion of the mind throws itself, like the ivy, round all human actions, entwines all our resolutions, and perpetually adheres to and mixes itself in, among, or even overtops them.

And no wonder that superstitious rites and ceremonies are attributed to Bacchus, when almost every ungovernable passion grows wanton and luxuriant in corrupt religions; nor again, that fury and frenzy should be sent and dealt out by him, because every passion is a short frenzy, and if it be vehement, lasting, and take deep root, it terminates in madness. And hence the allegory of Pentheus and Orpheus being torn to pieces is evident; for every headstrong passion is extremely bitter, severe, inveterate, and revengeful upon all curious inquiry, wholesome admonition, free counsel and persuasion.

Lastly, the confusion between the persons of Jupiter and Bacchus will justly admit of an allegory, because noble and meritorious actions may sometimes proceed from virtue, sound reason, and magnanimity, and sometimes again from a concealed passion and secret desire of ill, however they may be extolled and praised; insomuch that it is not easy to distinguish betwixt the acts of Bacchus and the acts of Jupiter.

But perhaps we remain too long in the theatre,—it is time we should advance to the palace of the mind.

mechanics, Newton has observed that reaction is always equal to action, and we may observe a similar principle in the antiperistasis of the moral world. The reactions in communities and individuals against any dominant principle are generally marked with excesses proportionally antagonistic to the fashions over which they prevail; and though no precise certainty can be acquired in the interpretation of phenomena connected with the human will, yet we think a vast amount of proximate truth might be elicited, and a flood of light thrown upon the springs of our spiritual nature by a philosophic attempt to generalize such movements and connect them with the higher laws of our mental constitution. Physically speaking, the force of the body resisting only augments the effect of the force which endeavours to conquer it; while in the moral world it increases both the effect and the power, as resistance irritates the assailing force and consequently excites it to redouble its efforts: hence may be seen the wisdom of that Providence who has hidden the springs of the universe from ocular vision to sharpen man's faculties in their discovery, and who ordinarily surrounds the course of genius with difficulties, in order that it may burst through them with purer flame. *Ed.*

THIRD BOOK.

CHAPTER I.

Division of Learning into Theology and Philosophy. The latter divided into the Knowledge of God, of Nature, and of Man. Construction of Philosophia Prima as the Mother of all the Sciences.

TO THE KING.

ALL history, excellent king, treads the earth, performing the office of a guide rather than of a light: and poetry is, as it were, the stream of knowledge,—a pleasing thing full of variations, and affects to be inspired with divine rapture, to which treasures also pretend. But now it is time I should awake and raise myself from the earth, and explore the liquid regions of philosophy and the sciences. Knowledge is like waters; some descend from the heavens, some spring from the earth. For all knowledge proceeds from a twofold source,—either from divine inspiration or external sense. As for that knowledge which is infused by instruction, that is cumulative, not original, as it is in waters, which, besides the head-springs, are increased by the reception of other rivers which fall into them. We shall, therefore, divide sciences into theology and philosophy. In the former we do not include natural theology, of which we are to speak anon, but restrict ourselves to inspired divinity, the treatment of which we reserve for the close of the work, as the fruit and sabbath of all human contemplations. Philosophy has three objects; viz., God, nature, and man; as also three kinds of rays—for nature strikes the human intellect with a direct ray, God with a refracted ray, from the inequality of the medium betwixt the Creator and the creatures, and man, as exhibited to himself, with a reflected ray: whence it is proper to divide philosophy into the doctrine of the deity, the doctrine of nature, and the doctrine of man.

But as the divisions of the sciences are not like different lines that meet in one angle, but rather like the branches of trees that join in one trunk,[a] it is first necessary that we con-

This observation is the foundation of Father Castel's late piece De Mathématique Universelle, wherein, by the help of sensible representa-

stitute an universal science as a parent to the rest, and as making a part of the common road to the sciences before the ways separate. And this knowledge we call "philosophia prima," primitive or primative or summary philosophy; it has no other for its opposite, and differs from other sciences rather in the limits whereby it is confined than in the subject as treating only the summits of things. And whether this should be noted as wanting may seem doubtful, though I rather incline to note it; for I find a certain rhapsody of natural theology, logics, and physics, delivered in a certain sublimity of discourse, by such as aim at being admired for standing on the pinnacles of the sciences; but what we mean is, without ambition, to design some general science, for the reception of axioms, not peculiar to any one science, but common to a number of them.

Axioms of this kind are numerous; for example, if equals be added to unequals, the wholes will be unequal. This is a rule in mathematics, which holds also in ethics, with regard to distributive justice. For in commutative justice, equity requires, that equal portions be given to unequal persons; but in distributive justice, that unequal portions should be distributed to unequals. Things agreeing to the same third, agree also with one another: this, likewise, is an axiom in mathematics, and, at the same time, so serviceable in logic as to be the foundation of syllogism.[b] Nature shows herself best in her smallest works. This is a rule in philosophy, that produced the atoms of Democritus, and was justly employed by Aristotle in politics, when he begins the consideration of a commonwealth in a family. All things change, but nothing is lost.[c] This is an axiom in physics, and holds in natural theology; for as the sum of matter neither diminishes nor increases, so it is equally the work of omnipotence to create or to annihilate it, which even the Scripture testifies: "Didici quod omnia opera, quæ fecit Deus, perseverent in perpetuum : non possumus eis quicquam addere, nec auferre."[d] Things are preserved from destruction, by bringing them back to their principles. This is an axiom in physics, but holds

tions and divisions, he proposes to teach the sciences readily, and even abstract mathematics, to common capacities. *Shaw.*
[b] Whately's Logic, ii. 3, § 1. [c] Cf. Plat. Theæt. i. 152.
[d] Eccl. iii. 14, and xlii. 21.

equally in politics; for the preservation of states, as is well observed by Machiavel,[e] depends upon little more than reforming and bringing them back to their ancient customs. A putrid malady is more contagious in its early than in its more matured stages, holds in natural as in moral philosophy; for wicked and desperately impious persons do not corrupt society so much as they who blend with their vices a mixture of virtue. What tends to preserve the effects of the greatest laws of nature, displays the strongest action, is a rule in natural philosophy. For the first and universal motion, that preserves the chain and contexture of nature unbroken, and prevents a vacuum, as they call it, or empty discontinuity in the world, controls the more particular law which draws heavy bodies to the earth, and preserves the region of gross and compacted natures. The same rule is good in politics; for those things which conduce to the conservation of the entire commonwealth, control and modify those made for the welfare of particular members of a government. The same principle may be observed in theology; for, among the virtues of this class, charity is the most communicative, and excels all the rest. The force of an agent is augmented by the antiperistatis of the counteracting body,[f] is a rule in civil states as in nature, for all faction is vehemently moved and incensed at the rising of a contrary faction.

A discord ending immediately in a concord sets off the harmony. This is a rule in music that holds also true in morals. A trembling sound in music gives the same pleasure to the ear, as the coruscation of water or the sparkling of a diamond to the eye,—

"—— splendet tremulo sub lumine pontus."[g]

The organs of the senses resemble the organs of reflection, as we see in optics and acoustics, where a concave glass resembles the eye, and a sounding cavity the ear. And of these axioms an infinite number might be collected; and thus the celebrated Persian magic was, in effect, no more than a notation of the correspondence in the structure and fabric of things natural and civil. Nor let any one under-

[e] Discorso sopra la Prima Deca di Tito Livio, libro 3.
[f] Aristotle, Meteors, Problem 1, § 11.   [g] Æneid, vii. 9.

stand all this of mere similitudes, as they might at first appear, for they really are one and the same footsteps, and impressions of nature, made upon different matters and subjects. And in this light the thing has not hitherto been carefully treated. A few of these axioms may indeed be found in the writings of eminent men, here and there interspersed occasionally; but a collected body of them, which should have a primitive and summary tendency to the sciences, is not hitherto extant, though a thing of so great moment as remarkable to show nature to be one and the same, which is supposed the office of a primary philosophy.

There is another part of this primary philosophy regarding the adventitious or transcendental condition of things; as little, much, like, different, possible, impossible, entity, nonentity, &c. For as these things do not properly come under physics, and as their logical consideration rather accommodates them to argumentation than existence, it is proper that this point be not quite deserted, as being of considerable dignity and use, so as to have some place in the arrangement of the sciences. But this should be done in a manner very different from the common: for example, no writer who has treated of much and little, endeavours to assign the cause why some things in nature are so numerous and large, and others so rare and small; for, doubtless, it is impossible in the nature of things, that there should be as great a quantity of gold as of iron, or roses as plenty as grass, and as great a variety of specific as of imperfect or non-specific nature.[h] So, likewise, nobody that treats of like and different has sufficiently explained, why betwixt particular species there are almost constantly interposed some things that partake of both; as moss[i] betwixt corruption and a plant; motionless fish betwixt a plant and an animal; bats betwixt birds and quadrupeds, &c. Nor has any one hitherto discovered why iron does not attract iron, as the loadstone does; and why gold does not attract gold, as quicksilver does, &c. But of these

[h] Specific bodies; that is, those which have a certain homogeneous form and regularity in their organization, and which exist in such variety as to urge the mind to form them into species. *Ed.*

[i] By the aid of the microscope, moss has been discovered to be only a collection of small plants, with parts as distinct and regular in their conformation as the larger plants. The vervain which generally covers the surface of moist bodies long exposed to the air presents similar appearances. **Ed.**

particulars we find no mention in the discourses of transcendentals; for men have rather pursued the quirks of words than the subtilities of things. And, therefore, we would introduce into primary philosophy a real and solid inquiry into these transcendentals, or adventitious conditions of beings, according to the laws of nature, not of speech.

CHAPTER II.
Natural Theology with its Appendix, the Knowledge of Angels and Spirits.

THUS having first seated the common parent of the sciences, as Berecynthia rejoicing over her celestial offspring,—

"Omnes cœlicolas, omnes supera alta tenentes,"[a]—

we return to our division of philosophy into divine, natural, and human; for natural theology may be justly called divine philosophy. Divine philosophy is a science, or rather the rudiments of a science, derivable from God by the light of nature, and the contemplation of his creatures; so that with regard to its object, it is truly divine; but with regard to its acquirement, natural. The bounds of this knowledge extend to the confutation of atheism, and the ascertaining the laws of nature, but not to the establishing of religion. And, therefore, God never wrought a miracle to convert an atheist, because the light of nature is sufficient to demonstrate a deity; but miracles were designed for the conversion of the idolatrous and superstitious, who acknowledged a God, but erred in their worship of him—the light of nature being unable to declare the will of God, or assign the just form of worshipping him. For as the power and skill of a workman are seen in his works, but not his person, so the works of God express the wisdom and omnipotence of the Creator, without the least representation of his image. And in this particular, the opinion of the heathens differed from the sacred verity, as supposing the world to be the image of God, and man a little image of the world. The Scripture never gives the world that honour, but calls it the work of his hands; making only man the image of God.[b] And, therefore, the being of a God, that he governs the world, that he

[a] Æneid, vi. 787.   [b] Ps. viii. 3, cii. 25, et al.

is all-powerful, wise, prescient, good, a just rewarder and punisher, and to be adored, may be shown and enforced from his works; and many other wonderful secrets, with regard to his attributes, and much more as to his dispensation and government over the universe, may also be solidly deduced, and made appear from the same. And this subject has been usefully treated by several.[c]

But from the contemplation of nature, and the principles of human reason, to dispute or urge anything with vehemence, as to the mysteries of faith, or over-curiously to examine and sift them, by prying into the manner of the mystery, is no safe thing: "Give unto faith the things that are faith's." And the heathens grant as much in that excellent and divine fable of the golden chain, where "men and gods are represented as unable to draw Jupiter to earth, but Jupiter able to draw them up to heaven."[d] So that it is a vain attempt to draw down the sublime mysteries of religion to our reason, but we should rather raise our minds to the adorable throne of heavenly truth. And in this part of natural theology, we find rather an excess than any defect; which we have however turned a little aside to note, on account of the extreme prejudice and danger which both religion and philosophy hence incur, because a mixture of these makes both an heretical religion and a fantastic and superstitious philosophy.[e]

It is otherwise, as to the nature of spirits and angels; this being neither unsearchable nor forbid, but in a great part level to the human mind, on account of their affinity. We are, indeed, forbid in Scripture to worship angels, or to entertain fantastical opinions of them,[f] so as to exalt them

[c] And more particularly since, by Cudworth, in his "Intellectual System of the Universe;" Mr. Boyle, in his "Christian Virtuoso;" Mr. Ray, in his "Wisdom of the Creation;" Dr. Bentley, in his "Discourse of the Folly and Unreasonableness of Atheism;" Dr. Clarke, in his "Demonstration of the Being and Attributes of God;" and by Derham, in his "Physico-Theology." See also Raphson's "De Deo;" Dr. Nieuwentyt's "Religious Philosopher;" Mr. Whiston's "Astronomical Principles of Religion;" Commenius's "Physicæ ad lumen divinum reformatæ Synopsis;" Paley's "Natural Religion;" the Bridgewater Treatises, and Cardinal Wiseman's "Connection of Science with Revealed Religion." *Ed.* [d] Iliad, ix.
[e] See above, Prelim. sec. iii. 8, and hereafter of Theology, sec. ult.
[f] St. Paul, Coloss. ii. 5, 18.

above the degree of creatures, or to think of them higher than we have reason; but the sober inquiry about them, which either ascends to a knowledge of their nature by the scale of corporeal beings, or views them in the mind, as in a glass, is by no means forbid. The same is to be understood of revolted or unclean spirits: conversation with them, or using their assistance, is unlawful; and much more in any manner to worship or adore them: but the contemplation and knowledge of their nature, power, and illusions, appears from Scripture, reason, and experience, to be no small part of spiritual wisdom. Thus says the apostle, "Strategematum ejus non ignari sumus."[g] And thus it is as lawful in natural theology to investigate the nature of evil spirits, as the nature of poisons in physics, or the nature of vice in morality. But this part of knowledge relating to angels and spirits, which we call the appendage to natural theology, cannot be noted for deficient, as having been handled by many; but we may justly tax no small part of the writers in this way, either with levity, superstition, or fruitless speculation.

CHAPTER III.

Natural Philosophy divided into Speculative and Practical. The Necessity of keeping these Two Branches distinct.

BUT to leave natural theology, and proceed to natural philosophy; as it was well said by Democritus, that "the knowledge of nature lies concealed in deep mines and caves;"[a] and by the alchemists, that "Vulcan is a second nature, imitating concisely what the first takes time and circuit to effect;"[b] suppose natural philosophy were divided, as it regards the mine and the furnace, and two offices of philosophers, miners and smelters introduced? This, indeed, may appear jocular, yet such a kind of division we judge extremely useful, when proposed in just and familiar terms; so that the doctrine of nature be divided into speculative and practical, or the search after causes, and the production of effects: the one entering into the bowels of nature, and the other forming her upon the anvil. Nor are we insensible of

[g] 2 Cor. ii. 11.   [a] Laertius, Life of Seneca.
[b] Paracelsus de Philos. Sagac.

the strict union betwixt causes and effects ; so that the explanation of them must, in some measure, be coupled together : but as all solid and fruitful natural philosophy hath both an ascending and a descending scale of parts, leading from experience to axioms, and from axioms to new discoveries, it seems most advisable here, in the division of sciences, to separate speculation from operation, and treat them distinct.

CHAPTER IV.

Division of the Speculative Branch of Natural Philosophy into Physics and Metaphysics. Physics relate to the Investigation of Efficient Causes and Matter ; Metaphysics to that of Final Causes and the Form. Division of Physics into the Sciences of the Principles of Things, the Structure of Things, and the Variety of Things. Division of Physics in relation to the Variety of Things into Abstract and Concrete. Division of Concretes agrees with the Distribution of the Parts of Natural History. Division of Abstracts into the Doctrine of Material Forms and Motion. Appendix of Speculative Physics twofold : viz., Natural Problems and the Opinions of Ancient Philosophers. Metaphysics divided into the Knowledge of Forms and the Doctrine of Final Causes.

THE speculative or theoretical part of natural philosophy we divide into physics and metaphysics ; taking the word metaphysics in a sense different from that received. And here we must, once for all, declare, as to our use of words, that though our conceptions and notions are new, and different from the common, yet we religiously retain the ancient forms of speech ; for as we hope that the method, and clear explanation, we endeavour at, will free us from any misconstruction that might arise from an ill choice of words ; so in everything else, it is our desire, as much as possible, without prejudice to truth and the sciences, not to deviate from ancient opinions and forms of speech. And here I cannot but wonder that Aristotle should proceed in such a spirit of contradiction, as he did to all antiquity ; not only coining new terms of science at pleasure, but endeavouring to abolish all the knowledge of the ancients ; so that he never mentions any ancient author but to reprove him, nor opinion but to confute it ; which is the ready way to procure fame and followers. For certainly it happens in philosophical, as it does in divine truth : "I came in the name of my Father, and ye received me not; but if one came in his own name, ye would receive him."[a] Which divine aphorism, as applied to Antichrist, the great deceiver, plainly shows us that a man's coming in his own name, without regard to antiquity or paternity, is no good sign of truth, though joined with the fortune and success of being received. But for so excellent and sublime a genius as Aristotle, one would think he caught this ambition from his scholar, and affected to subdue all opinions, as Alexander did all nations; and thus erect himself a monarchy in his own contemplation. Though for this, perhaps, he may not escape the lash of some severe pen, no more than his pupil; and be called a successful ravager of learning, as the other was of countries.[b] Some are doubtless disposed to treat him with the same courtesy as his scholar, in saying,

> "Fœlix doctrinæ prædo, non utile mundo
> Editus exemplum."[c]

But on the other hand, desiring, by all possible means, to cultivate and establish a free commerce betwixt ancient and modern learning, we judge it best religiously to side with antiquity, and therefore to retain ancient terms, though we frequently alter their sense, according to that moderate and laudable usage in politics, of introducing a new state of things, without changing the styles and titles of government.[d]

Thus then we distinguish metaphysics, as may appear by what was above delivered, from primary philosophy,[e] which has hitherto been taken from it, making this the common parent of the sciences, and that a part of natural philosophy

[a] St. John v. 43.
[b] We should rather say that Alexander caught the fire of ambition from his master, as Aristotle put forth his pretensions to mental empire long before his pupil overran Egypt. In addition, it may be observed that Aristotle was an Athenian, and that the strong antipathies which his countrymen bore to the king of Persia were increased by the ties of blood and friendship which bound him to Hermius, king of Atarné, whom the eastern despot had abused. It is most likely, therefore, that Aristotle never missed an opportunity of exciting his royal pupil to that conquest, which the Athenians had previously attempted to execute; as affording him the satisfaction of retaliating the injuries of a departed friend, as well as an opportunity of collecting a store of natural facts on which he might erect the superstructure of the physical sciences. *Ed.*
[c] Lucan, x. 21.   [d] Tacitus, Annals, i.
[e] Concerning primary philosophy, see above.

We have assigned the common and promiscuous axioms of the sciences to primitive philosophy; and all relative and accidental conditions of essences, which we call transcendant, as multitude, paucity, identity, diversity, possible, impossible, and the like, we have included in the same province, with this understanding, that they be handled according to their effects in nature, and not logically. We have referred the inquiry concerning God, unity, goodness, angels, and spirits, to natural philosophy. But to assign the proper office of metaphysics, as contradistinguished from primary philosophy, and natural theology, we must note, that as physics regards the things which are wholly immersed in matter and moveable, so metaphysics regards what is more abstracted and fixed; that physics supposes only existence, motion, and natural necessity, whilst metaphysics supposes also mind and idea. But to be more express: as we have divided natural philosophy into the investigation of causes, and the production of effects, and referred the investigation of causes to theory, which we again divide into physical and metaphysical; it is necessary that the real difference of these two be drawn from the nature of the causes they inquire into, and therefore, plainly, physics inquires into the efficient and the matter, and metaphysics into the form and the end. Physics, therefore, is vague and unstable as to causes, and treats moveable bodies as its subjects, without discovering a constancy of causes in different subjects. Thus the same fire gives hardness to clay and softness to wax, though it be no constant cause either of hardness or softness.[f]

"Limus ut hic durescit, et hæc ut cera liquescit
Uno eodemque igni."[g]

We divide physics into three parts; for nature is either collected into one total, or diffused and distributed. Nature is directed in its collocations either by the common elements in the diversity of things, or by the unity which prevails in the one integral fabric of the universe. Whence this union

[f] Physics, therefore, may be defined that part of universal philosophy which observes and considers the procedure of nature in bodies, so as to discover her laws, powers, and effects; and the material origins, and causes thereof, in different subjects; and thence form rules for imitating, controlling, or even excelling her works, in the instances it considers. *Shaw.*   [g] Virgil's Eclogues, viii. 80.

of nature produces two parts of physics; the one relating to the principles of things, and the other to the structure of the universe; whilst the third exhibits all the possible varieties and lesser collections of things. And this latter is like a first gloss, or paraphrase in the interpretation of nature. None of the three are deficient entirely, but how justly and solidly they have been treated is another question.

The third part we again divide into two others, with regard to concretes and abstracts, or into physics of creatures and physics of natures: the one inquiring into substances, and all the variety of their accidents; the other into accidents through all the variety of substances. Thus if inquiry be made about a lion or an oak; these support many different accidents: so if the inquiry were about heat or gravity; these are found in many different substances. But as all physics lies in the middle, betwixt natural history and metaphysics; so the former part approaches nearer to natural history, and the latter to metaphysics.

Concrete physics has the same division with natural history; being conversant either about celestial appearances, meteors, and the terrestrial globe; or about the larger assemblages of matter, called the elements; and the lesser or particular bodies: as also about prætergenerations and mechanics. For in all these, natural history examines and relates the matters of fact; and physics their instable, or material and efficient causes. And among these parts of physics, that is absolutely lame and incomplete, which regards the celestial bodies, though for the dignity of the subject it claims the highest regard. Astronomy, indeed, is well founded in phenomena; yet it is low and far from solid. But astrology is in many things destitute of all foundation. And to say the truth, astronomy itself seems to offer Prometheus's sacrifice to the understanding; for as he would have imposed upon Jupiter a fair large hide, stuffed with straw, and leaves, and twigs, instead of the ox itself, so astronomy gives us the number, situation, motion, and periods of the stars, as a beautiful outside of the heavens, whilst the flesh and the entrails are wanting; that is, a well-fabricated system, or the physical reasons and foundations for a just theory, that should not only solve phenomena, as almost any ingenious theory may do, but show the substance, motions, and influences of the heavenly bodies, as they really are. For

CHAP. IV.] PHYSICAL ASTRONOMY DEFICIENT. 127

those dogmas are long since exploded, which asserted the rapture of the first morn and the solidity of the heavens, in which the stars were supposed fastened like nails in the vaulted roof of a hall, and other opinions almost as silly; viz., that the zodiac has several poles; that there exists a movement of resilience against the rapture of the first motion; that all parts of the firmament are wheeled round in perfect circles, with eccentric and epicycles to preserve their circular rotation; that the moon has no influence over bodies higher in the heavens; the absurdity of which notions have thrown men upon the extravagant idea of the diurnal motion of the earth, an opinion which we can demonstrate to be most false.[h] But scarce any one has inquired into the physical causes of the substance of the heavens, stellar and interstellar; the different velocities of the celestial bodies with regard to one another; the different accelerations of motion in the same planet; the sequences of their motion from east to west;[i] the progressions, stations, and retrogradations of the planets, the stoppage and accidents of their motion in perigee and apogee, the obliquity of their motions; why the poles of rotation are principally in one quarter of the heavens; why certain planets keep a fixed distance from the sun, &c. Inquiries of this kind have hitherto been hardly touched upon, but the pains have been chiefly bestowed in mathematical observations and demonstrations; which indeed may show how to account for all these things ingeniously, but not how they actually are in nature: how to represent the apparent motions of the heavenly bodies, and machines of them, made according to particular fancies; but not the real causes and truth of things. And therefore astronomy, as it now stands, loses its dignity by being reckoned among the mathematical arts, for it ought in justice to make the most noble part of physics.[k]

[h] That doctrine had been recently demonstrated by Galileo, and defended by Gilbert.

[i] That is, from west to east, according to the Copernican system. *Ed.*

[k] Bacon maps out the entire region of human knowledge, breaking up the old sections, and assigning to each science new boundaries more conformable in his view to strict philosophical notions than the old; yet he capriciously enough makes mathematics an essential part of metaphysics, or inquiry into forms, and astronomy a compartment of mathematics, and then decries this absurd arrangement as the notion of the age. It is evident, however, that the age was innocent of the charge, and that Bacon snatched up the idea from the demonstrations which Copernicus,

And whoever despises the imaginary separation between terrestrial and celestial things, and well understands the more general appetites and passions of matter,[1] which are powerful in both, may receive a clear information of what happens above from that which happens below; and from what passes in the heavens, he may become acquainted with some inferior motions hitherto undiscovered, not as these are governed by those, but as they both have the same common passions. We, therefore, report this physical part of astronomy as wanting, in comparison of which the present animated astronomy is but as the stuffed ox of Prometheus —aping the form but wanting the substance.

But for astrology, it is so full of superstition, that scarce anything sound can be discovered in it; though we judge it should rather be purged than absolutely rejected. But if any one shall pretend that this science is founded, not in reason

---

Kepler, and Gilbert employed to dethrone the Ptolemaic theory of the heavens. Bacon was too jealous of Gilbert to entertain one moment any doctrine that he advanced; and a little further on he alludes to his mathematical thesis in favour of the earth's diurnal motion as proofs contradicted by natural philosophy, though incapable of being confuted by observation. From such demonstrations, however, astronomy could no more be regarded as a branch of mathematics than commerce or politics, because they sometimes call in the aid of arithmetic; and if Bacon had followed out this strange notion, he must have made, with Iamblicus, numbers the parent of all knowledge, as there is no department of science advanced beyond mere empiricism which does not rest upon the basis of figures. The degradation which Bacon imputes to astronomy from its association with mathematics shows that the most acute minds are no more privileged than the weakest to decide questions in relation to things of which they are perfectly ignorant. It is needless to say that a science only advances beyond empiricism to those intermediate or general axioms which Bacon so ardently desired to reach, so far as its phenomena admit of being extended and corrected by mathematical forms, and that it was only through such agencies that astronomy, almost in the space of a single age, was transformed from a mere empiric colligation of facts into the highest of the deductive sciences. The confusion arose from the consequences of Bacon's fundamental division of the sciences, which confounded those which are purely formal with the substantive sciences of which they are in some measure a universal condition, and hindered Bacon from seizing with precision upon the functions and limits of these sciences, and comprehending the important part the mathematical portion of them perform, in extending and corroborating physical discovery. *Ed.*

[1] Tendencies, forces, efforts, and effects. *Ed.*

and physical contemplations, but in the direct experience and observation of past ages, and therefore not to be examined by physical reasons, as the Chaldeans boasted, he may at the same time bring back divination, auguries, soothsaying, and give in to all kinds of fables; for these also were said to descend from long experience. But we receive astrology as a part of physics, without attributing more to it than reason and the evidence of things allow, and strip it of its superstition and conceits. Thus we banish that empty notion about the horary reign of the planets, as if each resumed the throne thrice in twenty-four hours, so as to leave three hours supernumerary: and yet this fiction produced the division of the week, a thing so ancient and so universally received. Thus likewise we reject, as an idle figment, the doctrine of horoscopes, and the distribution of the houses, though these are the darling inventions of astrology, which have kept revel, as it were, in the heavens. And we are surprised that some eminent authors in astrology should rest upon so slender an argument for erecting them, as because it appears by experience that the solstices, the equinoxes, the new and full moon, &c. have a manifest operation upon natural bodies, therefore the more curious and subtile positions of the stars must produce more exquisite and secret effects: whereas, laying aside those operations of the sun, which are owing to manifest heat, and a certain attractive virtue of the moon, which causes the spring tide; the other effects of the planets upon natural bodies are, so far as experience reaches, exceeding small, weak, and latent. Therefore the argument should run thus: since these greater revolutions are able to effect so little, those more nice and trifling differences of positions will have no force at all. And lastly, for the calculation of nativities, fortunes, good or bad hours of business, and the like fatalities, they are mere levities that have little in them of certainty and solidity, and may be plainly confuted by physical reasons.

And here we judge it proper to lay down some rules for the examination of astrological matters, in order to retain what is useful therein, and reject what is insignificant. Thus, 1. Let the greater revolutions be retained, but the lesser of horoscopes and houses be rejected,—the former being like ordnance, which shoot to a great distance, whilst the other are but like small bows, that do no execution. 2. The celestial operations affect not all kinds of bodies, but only the more sensible, as humours, air, and spirits.[m] Here we except the operations of the sun's heat, which may doubtless penetrate metals and other subterraneous bodies, and confine the other operations chiefly to the air, the humours, and the spirits of things. 3. All the celestial operations rather extend to masses of things than to individuals. Though they may obliquely reach some individuals also, which are more sensible than the rest, as a pestilent constitution of the air affects those bodies which are least able to resist it. 4. All the celestial operations produce not their effects instantaneously and in a narrow compass, but exert them in large portions of time and space. Thus predictions as to the temperature of a year may hold good, but not with regard to single days. 5. There is no fatal necessity in the stars; and this the more prudent astrologers have constantly allowed. 6. We will add one thing more, which, if amended and improved, might make for astrology, viz., that we are certain the celestial bodies have other influences besides heat and light, but these influences act not otherwise than by the foregoing rules, though they lie so deep in physics as to require a fuller explanation. So that, upon the whole, we must register as defective an astrology wrote in conformity to these principles, under the name of Astrologia Sana.

This just astrology should contain,—1. The doctrine of the commixture of rays, viz., the conjunctions, oppositions, and other situations, or aspect of the planets with regard to one another, their transits through the signs of the zodiac, and their situation in the same signs, as the situation of planets in a sign is a certain conjunction thereof with the stars of that sign; and as the conjunctions, so likewise should the oppositions and other aspects of the planets, with regard to the celestial signs, be remarked, which has not hitherto been fully done. The commixtures of the rays of the fixed stars with one another are of use in contemplating the fabric of the world, and the nature of the subjacent regions, but in

---

[m] But if celestial bodies act upon humours, air, and spirits, and these in turn affect solid bodies, it follows that they also act on solid bodies. *Ed.*

no respect for predictions, because at all times alike. 2. This astrology should take in the nearest approaches and the farthest removes of each planet to and from the zenith, according to the climate; for all the planets have their summer and winter, wherein they dart their rays stronger or weaker, according to their perpendicular or oblique direction. So we question not but the moon in Leo has, in the same manner as the sun, a greater effect upon natural bodies with us than when in Pisces, not because the moon in Leo moves the head, and under Pisces affects the feet, but by reason of her greater perpendicular elevation and nearer approach to the larger stars. 3. It should receive the apogees and perigees of the planets, with a proper inquiry into what the vigour of the planets may perform of itself, and what through their nearness to us; for a planet is more brisk in its apogee, but more communicative in its perigee. 4. It should include all the other accidents of the planets' motions, their accelerations, retardations, courses, stations, retrogradations, distances from the sun, increase and diminutions of light, eclipses, &c. For all these things affect the rays of the planets, and cause them to act either weaker, stronger, or in a different manner. 5. This astrology should contain all that can by any means be known or discovered of the nature of the stars, both erratic and fixed, considered in their own essence and activity, viz., their magnitude, colour, aspect, sparkling and vibrating of light; their situation with regard to the poles or equinoctial; the constellations, which thicker set and which thinner, which higher, which lower; what fixed stars are in the zodiac, and what out of it; the different velocities of the planets, their different latitudes, which of them are retrograde, and which not; their different distances from the sun; which move swiftest in their apogee, and which in their perigee; the irregularities of Mars, the excursions of Venus, and the extraordinary phases, accidents, and appearances observable in Venus and the sun; with other things of this kind. 6. Lastly, let it contain, from tradition, the particular natures and alterations of the planets and fixed stars; for as these are delivered with general consent, they are not lightly to be rejected, unless they directly contradict physical reasons.. And of such observations let a just astrology be formed: and according to these alone should schemes of the heavens be made and interpreted.

Such an astrology should be used with greater confidence in prediction, but more cautiously in election, and in both cases with due moderation. Thus predictions may be made of comets, and all kinds of meteors, inundations, droughts, heats, frosts, earthquakes, fiery eruptions, winds, great rains, the seasons of the year, plagues, epidemic diseases, plenty, famine, wars, seditions, sects, transmigrations of people, and all commotions or great innovations of things natural and civil. Predictions may possibly be made more particular, though with less certainty, if when the general tendencies of the times are found, a good philosophical or political judgment applies them to such things as are most liable to this kind of accidents. For example, from a foreknowledge of the seasons of any year they might be apprehended more destructive to olives than grapes, more hurtful in distempers of the lungs than the liver, more pernicious to the inhabitants of hills than valleys, and, for want of provisions, to monks than courtiers, &c. Or if any one, from a knowledge of the influence which the celestial bodies have upon the spirits of mankind, should find it would affect the people more than their rulers, learned and inquisitive men more than the military, &c. For there are innumerable things of this kind that require not only a general knowledge, gained from the stars, which are the agents, but also a particular one of the passive subjects.

Nor are elections to be wholly rejected, though not so much to be trusted as predictions; for we find in planting, sowing, and grafting, observations of the moon are not absolutely trifling, and there are many particulars of this kind. But elections are more to be curbed by our rules than predictions; and this must always be remembered, that election only holds in such cases where the virtue of the heavenly bodies, and the action of the inferior bodies also, is not transient, as in the examples just mentioned; for the increase of the moon and planets are not sudden things. But punctuality of time should here be absolutely rejected. And perhaps there are more of these instances to be found in civil matters than some would imagine.

There are but four ways of arriving at this science, viz., 1. By future experiments; 2. Past experiments; 3. Traditions; and, 4. Physical reasons. But, 1. It is in vain at present to think of future experiments, because many ages are required to procure a competent stock of them. And, 2. As for the past, it is true they are within our reach, but it is a work of labour and much time to procure them. Thus astrologers may, if they please, draw from real history all greater accidents, as inundations, plagues, wars, seditions, deaths of kings, &c., as also the positions of the celestial bodies, not according to fictitious horoscopes, but the abovementioned rules of their revolutions, or such as they really were at the time, and where the event conspires, erect a probable rule of prediction. 3. All traditions should be well sifted, and those thrown out that manifestly clash with physical reasons, leaving such in their full force as comport well therewith. And, 4. Those physical reasons are best suited to this inquiry which search into the universal appetites and passions of matter, and the simple genuine motions of the heavenly bodies. And this we take for the surest guide to astrology.

There remains another piece of wild astrology, though usually separated from it, and transferred to celestial magic as they call it. It is a strange fiction of the human brain, the receiving the benign action of the stars upon seals and signets of gems or metal suited to the purpose, so as to detain and fix, as it were, the felicity of that hour which would otherwise be volatile and fugitive. The poet passionately complains of a similar art among the ancients long since buried in oblivion,—

> "Annulus infuso non vivit mirus Olympo,
> Non magis ingentes humili sub lumine Phœbos,
> Fert gemma, aut celso divulsas cardine lunas."

Indeed the Roman Church has upheld the venerableness of saints' relics and their virtues, since the flux of time has no power to abate the force and efficacy of spiritual things; but to assert that the relics of persons might be so determined as to continue and perpetuate the virtue of an hour which

[a] Agrippa, Mystical Philosophy.

is past, and as it were dead, is mere superstition and imposture.

Abstract physics may be justly divided into two parts,—the doctrine of the schemes of matter, and the doctrine of appetites and motions. The schemes of matter are density, rarity, gravity, levity, heat, cold, tangibility, intangibility, volatile, fixed, determinate, fluid, humid, dry, unctuous, crude, hard, soft, fragile, tensile, porous, united, spirituous, jejune, simple, compound, absolute, imperfectly mixed, fibrous and veiny, simple position, or equable, similar, dissimilar, specificate, unspecificate, organical, inorganical, animate and inanimate; and farther than this we proceed not. For sensible and insensible, rational and irrational, we refer to the doctrine of man.

Appetites and motions are of two kinds,—as being either simple motions, wherein the spring of all natural actions is contained, that is, in respect of their schemes of matter; or motions compounded or produced, and with these the common philosophy, which enters but little into the body of nature, begins. But these compound motions, such as generation, corruption, &c., should be esteemed certain results or effects of simple motions, rather than primitive motions themselves. The simple motions are,—1. Motion of resistance, or preventive of penetration of dimensions; 2. Motion of connection, preventive of a vacuum, as it is called; 3. Motion of liberty, preventive of preternatural compression, or extension; 4. Motion in a new orb, with regard to rarefaction and condensation; 5. Motion of the second connection, or preventive of solution of continuity; 6. Motion of the greater congregation, or with regard to masses of connatural bodies, commonly called natural motion; 7. Motion of the lesser congregation, vulgarly termed motion of sympathy and antipathy; 8. Disponent motion, with regard to the just placing of parts in the whole; 9. Motion of assimilation, or multiplicative of its own nature upon another body; 10. Motion of excitation, where the noble agent excites the latent and benumbed motion in another thing; 11. Motion of the seal, or impression, by an operation without communication of substance; 12. Regal motion, or the restraint of other motions by a predominant one; 13. Endless motion, or spontaneous rotation; 14. Motion of trepidation, or the motion of systole and diastole, with regard to bodies placed betwixt things advantageous and hurtful; 15. And lastly, Motion couchant, or a dread of motion, which is the cause of many effects. And such are the simple motions that really proceed out of the inward recesses of nature; and which being complicated, continued, used alternately, moderated, repeated, and variously combined, produce those compound motions or results of motion we call generation, corruption, increase, diminution, alteration, translation, mixtion, separation, and conversion.

The measures of motions are an attendant on physics, as showing the effects of quantity, distance, or the sphere of activity, intension and remission, short and long continuance, activity, dulness, and incitation. And these are the genuine parts of abstract physics, which wholly consists,—1. In the schemes of matter; 2. Simple motions; 3. The results or sums of motions; and, 4. The measures of motions. As for voluntary motion in animals,—the motion in the action of the senses, the motions of the imagination, appetite, and will, the motion of mind, the determination, and other intellectual faculties,—they have their own proper doctrines under which we range them, confining the whole of physics to matter and efficient, and assigning over forms and ends to metaphysics.

We must annex two remarkable appendages to physics, with regard rather to the manner, than the matter of inquiry; viz., natural problems, and the opinions of the ancient philosophers. The first is an appendage of nature at large, and the other of nature united or summed up; both relating to a diligent kind of doubting, which is no contemptible part of knowledge. Now, problems contain particular doubts and opinions, general ones, as to principles and structure. In the books of Aristotle we have a noble example of problems, deserving not only the praises but the imitation of posterity, since new doubts are daily arising. But the utmost caution is to be used in such an undertaking. The recording and proposing of doubts has two advantages; the one, as it defends philosophy against errors, when that which is not clear is neither judged nor asserted, lest error thus should multiply error, but judgment is suspended upon it, and not made positive; the other is, that doubts once registered are like so many sponges, which perpetually suck and draw to themselves the increases of knowledge; whence those things which would have been slightly passed over, unless they had been doubted of before, come now from this very doubting to be more attentively considered. But these two advantages will scarce balance this single inconvenience, unless well provided against; viz., that when a doubt is once admitted for just, and becomes, as it were, authentic, it presently raises up disputants on both sides, who transmit to posterity the same liberty of doubting still; so that men seem to apply their wits rather to nourish the doubt than solve it. And of this we everywhere meet with examples in lawyers and scholars; who, when a doubt once gains admittance, would have it remain a doubt for ever, and engage themselves in doubting as well as asserting; whereas the true use of wit is to render doubtful things certain, and not certain ones doubtful. And therefore I set down as wanting a calendar of doubts or problems in nature, and recommend it to be undertaken, with care to blot out daily, as knowledge increases, those that are clearly discussed and settled. And this calendar we would have attended with another of no less utility; for as in every inquiry there are things plainly true, things doubtful, and things plainly false, it were exceeding proper that along with a calendar of doubts should go a calendar of falsehoods and vulgar errors, both in natural history and opinions, that they may no longer disturb the sciences.

As to the opinions of the ancient philosophers, for example those of Pythagoras, Philolaus, Xenophanes, Anaxagoras, Parmenides, Leucippus, Democritus, and others, which men usually pass slightly over, it is proper to cast a modest eye upon them. For though Aristotle, after the Ottoman manner, thought he could not reign secure without putting all his brethren to death, yet those who do not affect dominion and rule, but the inquiry and illustration of truth, will find their account in beholding, at one view, the different opinions of different philosophers, as to the nature of things. But there is no room to expect any pure truth from these or the like theories: for as the celestial appearances are solved both upon the suppositions of Ptolemy and Copernicus; so common experience, and the obvious face of things, may be applied to many different theories: whilst a much stricter procedure is required in the right discovery of truth. For as Aristotle accurately remarks, that children, when they first begin to speak, call every woman mother; but afterwards learn to distinguish their own:[o] so a childish experience calls every philosophy its mother, but when grown up, will easily distinguish its true one. In the mean time, it is proper to read the disagreeing philosophies, as so many different glosses of nature. We could therefore wish there were, with care and judgment, drawn up a work of the ancient philosophies,[p] from the lives of old philosophers, Plutarch's collection of their opinions, the citations of Plato, the confutations of Aristotle, and the scattered relations of other books, whether ecclesiastical or heathen; as Lactantius, Philo, Philostratus, &c. For such a work is not yet extant; and we would advise it to be done distinctly; so that each philosophy be drawn out and continued separate, and not ranged under titles and collections, as Plutarch has done. For every philosophy, when entire, supports itself, and its doctrines thus add light and strength to each other; which, if separated, sound strange and harsh. Thus, when we read in Tacitus the acts of Nero or Claudius, clothed with the circumstances of times, persons, and occasions, everything seems plausible; but when the same are read in Suetonius, distributed under chapters and common-places, and not described in the order of time, they look monstrous, and absolutely incredible. And the case is the same with philosophy proposed entire, and dismembered, or cut into articles. Nor do we exclude from this calendar the modern theories and opinions, as those of Paracelsus, elegantly reduced by

[o] Aristotle's Physics.
[p] The work here proposed is of vast extent, and a fit undertaking for a society, as intended to include all the ancient and modern systems of philosophy, or the history of knowledge through all ages and countries. Considerable progress has, however, been made in it, particularly by Vossius "De Philosophia, et Philosophorum Sectis," continued with a supplement by Russel, printed at Jena, in the year 1705; by Pancirollus, "De Rebus inventis et perditis;" by Paschius, "De Novis Inventis, quibus facem prætulit antiquitas;" by Stanley in his "Lives of the Philosophers;" by Herbelot in his "Bibliothèque Universelle;" by M. Bayle in his "Dictionary," &c. For more collections, histories, and writings to this purpose, see "Struvii Bibliotheca Philosophica," Morhof's "Polyhistor," and "Stolli Introductio in Historiam Litorariam." *Shaw.*

Severinus into a body and harmony of philosophy; or of Telesius, who, in restoring the philosophy of Parmenides, has turned their own weapons against the Peripatetics; or of Gilbert, who revived the doctrines of Philolaus; or of any other, provided he be worthy. But as there are whole volumes of these authors extant, we would only have the result drawn out and joined to the rest. And so much for physics and its appendages.

To metaphysics we assign the inquiry of formal and final causes. But an opinion has prevailed, as if the essential forms, or real differences of things, were absolutely undiscoverable by human means; granting, at the same time, that if they could be discovered, this, of all the parts of knowledge, would be the most worthy of inquiry. As to the possibility of the thing, there are indolent discoverers, who see nothing but sea and sky, absolutely deny there can be any land beyond them. But it is manifest that Plato, a man of a sublime genius, who took a view of everything as from a high rock, saw in his doctrine of ideas, that "forms were the true object of knowledge;"[q] though he lost the advantage of this just opinion by contemplating and grasping at forms totally abstracted from matter, and not as determined in it;[r] whence he turned aside to theological speculations, and therewith infected all his natural philosophy. But if with diligence, seriousness, and sincerity, we turn our eyes to action and use, we may find, and become acquainted with those forms, the knowledge whereof will wonderfully enrich and prosper human affairs.

The forms of substances, indeed, viz. the species of creatures,[s] are so complicated and interwoven, that the inquiry into them is either vain, or should be laid aside for a time, and resumed after the forms of a more simple nature have been duly sifted and discovered. For as it were neither easy nor useful to discover the form of a sound that shall make a word, since words, by the composition and transpositions

---

[q] In the Timæus, *passim*, et Rep. x. *init.* Cf. Hooker, i. 3, 4; compare also Hallam's Literature of Europe, part iii. c. 3, p. 402.

[r] As Mr. Boyle has excellently shown, by a large induction of experiments and crucial instances, wherewith most of his physical inquiries are enriched.

[s] As plants, animals, minerals; the elements fire, air, water, earth, &c.

of letters are infinite; but practicable, easy, and useful to discover the form of a sound expressing a single letter, or by what collision or application of the organs of the voice, it was made; and as these forms of letters being known, we are thence directly led to inquire the forms of words: so, to inquire the form of an oak, a lion, gold, water, or air, were at present vain; but to inquire the form of density, rarity, heat, cold, gravity, levity, and other schemes of matter and motions, which, like the letters of the alphabet, are few in number, yet make and support the essences and forms of all substances, is what we would endeavour after, as constituting and determining that part of metaphysics we are now upon.

Nor does this hinder physics from considering the same natures in their fluxile causes only; thus, if the cause of whiteness in snow, or froth, were inquired into, it is judged to be a subtile intermixture of air with water; but this is far from being the form of whiteness, since air intermixed with powdered glass or crystal is also judged to produce whiteness no less than when mixed with water: this, therefore, is only the efficient cause, and no other than the vehicle of the form. But if the inquiry be made in metaphysics, it will be found that two transparent bodies, intermixed in their optical portions, and in a simple order, make whiteness. This part of metaphysics I find defective; and no wonder; because in the method of inquiry hitherto used, the forms of things can never appear. The misfortune lies here, that men have accustomed themselves to hurry away, and abstract their thoughts too hastily, and carry them too remote from experience and particulars, and have given themselves wholly up to their own meditations and arguments.

The use of this part of metaphysics is recommended by two principal things: first, as it is the office and excellence of all sciences to shorten the long turnings and windings of experience, so as to remove the ancient complaint of the scantiness of life, and the tediousness of art;[t] this is best performed by collecting and uniting the axioms of the sciences into more general ones, that shall suit the matter of all individuals. For the sciences are like pyramids, erected upon the single basis of history and experience, and therefore

---

[t] Compare Plat. Thæet. i. 155, 156.

a history of nature is, 1. the basis of natural philosophy; and 2. the first stage from the basis is physics; and 3. that nearest the vertex metaphysics; but 4. for the vertex itself, "the work which God worketh from the beginning to the end,"[u] or the summary law of nature, we doubt whether human inquiry can reach it. But for the other three, they are the true stages of the sciences, and are used by those men who are inflated by their own knowledge, and a daring insolence, as the three hills of the giants to invade heaven.

"Ter sunt conati imponere Pelio Ossam
 Scilicet, atque Ossæ frondosum involvere Olympum."[x]

But to the humble and the meek they are the three acclamations, Sanctus, sanctus, sanctus; for God is holy in the multitude of his works, as well as in their order and union,[y] and therefore the speculation was excellent in Parmenides and Plato, that all things by defined gradations ascend to unity.[z] And as that science is the most excellent, which least burthens the understanding by its multiplicity; this property is found in metaphysics, as it contemplates those simple forms of things, density, rarity, &c., which we call forms of the first class; for though these are few, yet, by their commensurations and co-ordinations, they constitute all truth.

The second thing that ennobles this part of metaphysics, relating to forms, is, that it releases the human power, and leads it into an immense and open field of work; for physics direct us through narrow rugged paths, in imitation of the crooked ways of ordinary nature; but the ways of wisdom, which were anciently defined as "rerum divinarum et humanarum scientia,"[a] are everywhere wide, and abounding in plenty, and variety of means. Physical causes, indeed, by means of new inventions, afford light and direction in a like case again; but he that understands a form knows the ultimate possibility of superinducing that nature upon all kinds of matter, and is therefore the less restrained or tied down in his working, either as to the basis of the matter or the condition of the efficient. Solomon also describes this

[u] Eccles. iii. 1.   [x] Virgil, Georgics, i. 281.   [y] Apocalypse iv.
[z] See conclusion of the Dialogue entitled Parmenides.
[a] Plato's Phædo; Cicero, Tuscul. Quæst. 4. Defin. 2.

kind of knowledge, though in a more divine manner: "Non arctabuntur gressus tui, et currens non habebis offendiculum."[b] Thus denoting that the paths of wisdom are not liable to straits and perplexities.

The second part of metaphysics, is the inquiry of final causes, which we note not as wanting, but as ill-placed; these causes being usually sought in physics, not in metaphysics, to the great prejudice of philosophy; for the treating of final causes in physics has driven out the inquiry of physical ones, and made men rest in specious and shadowy causes, without ever searching in earnest after such as are real and truly physical. And this was not only done by Plato, who constantly anchors upon this shore; but by Aristotle, Galen, and others, who frequently introduce such causes as these: "The hairs of the eyelids are for a fence to the sight.[c] The bones for pillars whereon to build the bodies of animals. The leaves of trees are to defend the fruit from the sun and wind. The clouds are designed for watering the earth," &c. All which are properly alleged in metaphysics; but in physics are impertinent, and as remoras to the ship, that hinder the sciences from holding on their course of improvement, and introducing a neglect of searching after physical causes. And therefore the natural philosophies of Democritus and others, who allow no God or mind in the frame of things, but attribute the structure of the universe to infinite essays and trials of nature, or what they call fate or fortune, and assigned the causes of particular things to the necessity of matter without any intermixture of final causes, seem, so far as we can judge from the remains of their philosophy, much more solid, and to have gone deeper into nature, with regard to physical causes, than the philosophy of Aristotle or Plato; and this only because they never meddled with final causes, which the others were perpetually inculcating. Though in this respect Aristotle is more culpable than Plato, as banishing God,[d] the fountain of final causes, and substituting nature

---

[b] Prov. iv. 12. [c] Cf. *e. g.* Arist. Phys. ii. 8.

[d] From the text it must not be judged that Aristotle invested nature with the general powers usually attributed to a divine intelligence, in designing and executing her various ends with wisdom and precision, but only that he regarded nature as an active and intelligent principle performing her agencies by means palpable to herself, yet according to the laws and faculties conferred upon her by the prime mover of things. The

in his stead; and, at the same time, receiving final causes through his affection to logic, not theology.

These final causes, however, are not false, or unworthy of inquiry in metaphysics, but their excursion into the limits of physical causes hath made a great devastation in that province; otherwise, when contained within their own bounds,

Spinozist principle which the text attributes to the Stagyrite has been understood by many critics or the sensational school to intimate that Aristotle was of their way of thinking, though the idea of an independent material intelligence is expressly contradicted by numerous passages in his Metaphysics. In book xii. chap. 5, of the works which go under this name, the principal being is held to exclude the idea of matter from his nature: ἔτι τοίνυν ταύτας δεῖ οὐσίας εἶναι ἄνευ ὕλης· ἀϊδίους γὰρ δεῖ· κ.τ.λ.; and (ibid. 8) τὸ δέ τι ἦν εἶναι οὐκ ἔχει ὕλην τὸ πρῶτον· ἐντελέχεια γάρ. In chap. 7 he affirms this principle to be spirit,—ἀρχὴ ἡ νόησις; that matter cannot move of itself, but needs the action of an exterior agent,—οὐ γὰρ ἡ γε ὕλη κινήσει αὐτὴ ἑαυτήν, ἀλλὰ τεκτονική· and that this principle must be eternal and active,—Ἀΐδιον καὶ οὐσία καὶ ἐνέργεια οὖσα. Aristotle further proceeds to show that all other beings are only a species of means transmitting the motion to others which have been communicated to them, but that this primary being, possessing the spring of motion in itself, moves without being moved; illustrating this kind of action by the emotions and deeds that spring from the love, pity, or hatred that agents at rest excite in others. In another place he affirms that this being is not only eternal in duration but immutable in essence, and quite distinct from sensible things: ὅτι γὰρ ἔστιν οὐσία τις ἀΐδιος καὶ ἀκίνητος καὶ κεχωρισμένη τῶν αἰσθητῶν, φανερὸν ἐκ τῶν εἰρημένων· and that heaven and nature hang upon its behests,—ἐκ τοιαύτης ἄρα ἀρχῆς ἤρτηται ὁ οὐρανὸς καὶ ἡ φύσις. He further shows that life belongs to it by essence, and as the action of intelligence is life, and *vice versâ*, essential action constitutes the eternal life of this being. Aristotle then calls this independent principle God, and assigns to it endless duration: φαμὲν δὲ τὸν ΘΕΟ'Ν εἶναι ζῶον ἀΐδιον ἄριστον. "It remains," says the Stagyrite, "to determine whether this principle be one or several; but upon this point we need only remember that those who have decided for a plurality have advanced nothing worthy of consideration in support of their belief."—Ἀλλὰ μεμνῆσθαι καὶ τὰς τῶν ἄλλων ἀποφάσεις ὅτι περὶ πλήθους οὐδὲ εἰρήκασιν ὅ τι καὶ σαφὲς εἰπεῖν. (Ibid. chap. 8.) "For the principle of existence, or the immovable being which is the source of all movement, being pure action, and consequently foreign to matter, is one in reason and number . . . . all the rest is the creation of a mythology invented by politicians to advance the public interest and occupy the attention of mankind." Τὸ δέ τι ἦν εἶναι οὐκ ἔχει ὕλην τὸ πρῶτον· ἐντελέχεια γάρ. (Supp. note 1.) Ἐν μὲν ἄρα καὶ λόγῳ καὶ ἀριθμῷ τὸ πρῶτον κινοῦν ἀκίνητον. (Ibid. chap. 8.) Τὰ δὲ λοιπὰ μυθικῶς ἤδη προσήχθη πρὸς τὴν πειθὼ τῶν πολλῶν καὶ πρὸς τὴν εἰς τοὺς νόμους καὶ τὸ σύμφερον χρῆσιν. (Ibid.) *Ed.*

they are not repugnant to physical causes; for the cause, that "the hairs of the eyelids are to preserve the sight," is no way contradictory to this, that "pilosity is incident to the orifices of moisture,"—"Muscosi fontes," &c.;[e] nor does the cause which assigns the firmness of hides in beasts to a protection against the injuries of extreme weather, militate against the other cause, which attributes the firmness to the contraction of the pores on the exterior of the skin, through cold and deprivation of air; and so of the rest: these two kinds of causes agreeing excellently together; the one expressing the intention, and the other the consequence only.

Nor does this call Divine Providence in question, but rather highly confirms and exalts it; for as he is a greater politician, who can make others the instruments of his will, without acquainting them with his designs, than he who discloses himself to those he employs; so the wisdom of God appears more wondrous, when nature intends one thing, and Providence draws out another, than if the characters of Providence were stamped upon all the schemes of matter and natural motions. So Aristotle had no need of a God, after having once impregnated nature with final causes, and laid it down that "nature does nothing in vain; always obtains her ends when obstacles are removed,"[f] &c. But Democritus and Epicurus, when they advanced their atoms, were thus far tolerated by some, but when they asserted the fabric of all things to be raised by a fortuitous concourse of these atoms, without the help of mind, they became universally ridiculous. So far are physical causes from drawing men off from God and Providence, that, on the contrary, the philosophers employed in discovering them can find no rest, but by flying to God or Providence at last.

[e] Virg. Eclogues, vii. 45.   [f] Aristotle on the Heavens, 1.

CHAPTER V.

Division of the Practical Branch of Natural Philosophy into Mechanics and Magic (Experimental Philosophy), which correspond to the Speculative Division—Mechanics to Physics, and Magic to Metaphysics. The word Magic cleared from False Interpretation. Appendix to Active Science twofold; viz., an Inventory of Human Helps and a Catalogue of Things of Multifarious Use.

THE practical doctrine of nature we likewise necessarily divide into two parts, corresponding to those of speculative; for physics, or the inquiry of efficient and material causes, produces mechanics; and metaphysics, the inquiry of forms, produces magic; whilst the inquiry of final causes is a barren thing, or as a virgin consecrated to God. We here understand that mechanics which is coupled with physical causes; for besides the bare effective or empirical mechanics, which has no dependence on physics, and belongs to natural history, there is another not absolutely operative, and yet not strictly philosophical. For all discoveries of works either had their rise from accident, and so were handed down from age to age, or else were sought by design; and the latter were either discovered by the light of causes and axioms, or acquired by extending, transferring, or compounding some former inventions, which is a thing more ingenious and sagacious than philosophical. But the mechanics here understood is that treated by Aristotle promiscuously, by Hero in his Pneumatics, by that very diligent writer in metallics, George Agricola, and by numerous others in particular subjects; so that we have no omission to note in this point, only that the miscellaneous mechanics, after the example of Aristotle, should have been more carefully continued by the moderns, especially with regard to such contrivances whose causes are more obscure, or their effects more noble; whereas the writers upon these subjects hitherto have only coasted along the shore,—"premendo littus iniquum."[a] And it appears to us that scarce anything in nature can be fundamentally discovered, either by accident, experimental attempts, or the light of physical causes, but only by the discovery of forms.[b] Since, therefore, we have set down as wanting that part of

[a] Hor. Odes, b. ii. ode x. 3.
[b] Bacon means by forms general laws which co-operate with certain agents in producing the qualities of bodies. *Shaw.*

metaphysics which treats of forms, it follows that natural magic, which is relative to it, must also be wanting.

We here understand magic in its ancient and honourable sense,—among the Persians it stood for a sublimer wisdom, or a knowledge of the relations of universal nature, as may be observed in the title of those kings who came from the East to adore Christ. And in the same sense we would have it signify that science, which leads to the knowledge of hidden forms, for producing great effects, and by joining agents to patients setting the capital works of nature to view. The common natural magic found in books gives us only some childish and superstitious traditions and observations of the sympathies and antipathies of things, or occult and specific properties, which are usually intermixed with many trifling experiments, admired rather for their disguise than for themselves; but as to the truth of nature, this differs from the science we propose as much as the romances of Arthur of Britain, Hugh of Bordeaux, or other imaginary heroes, do from the Commentaries of Cæsar in truth of narration. Cæsar in reality performed greater things, though not by romantic means, than such fabulous heroes are feigned to do. This kind of learning is well represented by the fable of Ixion,[c] who, thinking to enjoy Juno, the goddess of power, embraced a cloud, and thence produced centaurs and chimæras; for so those who, with a hot and impotent desire, are carried to such things as they see only through the fumes and clouds of imagination, instead of producing works, beget nothing but vain hopes and monstrous opinions. This degenerate natural magic has also an effect like certain sleepy medicines which procure pleasing dreams; for so it first lays the understanding asleep, by introducing specific properties and occult virtues,—whence men are no longer attentive to the discovery of real causes, but rest satisfied in such indolent and weak opinions; and thus it insinuates numberless pleasing fictions, like so many dreams.

And here we may properly observe, that those sciences which depend too much upon fancy and faith, as this degenerate magic, alchymy, and astrology, have their means and their theory more monstrous than their end and action. The conversion of quicksilver into gold is hard to conceive,

[c] Pind. Pyth. ii. 21.

though it may much more probably be effected by a man acquainted with the nature of gravity, colour, malleability, fixedness, volatility, the principles of metals and menstruums, than by one who is ignorant of these natures, by the bare projection of a few grains of the elixir. The same may be understood of the prolongation of youth or retarding of old age, which may more rationally be expected by dietary, regimen, bathings, anointing, and proper medicines, directed by an accurate knowledge of the human frame, the nature of rarefaction, sustention, assimilation, and the reciprocal action of the mind upon the body, than by a few drops or scruples of some precious liquor or quintessence. But men are so headstrong and notional, as not only to promise themselves things impossible, but also hope to obtain the most difficult ends without labour or exertion.

This practical doctrine of nature requires two appendages of very great consequence. The first is, that an inventory be made of the stock of mankind, containing their whole possessions and fortunes, whether proceeding from nature or art, with the addition also of things formerly known, but now lost; so that he who goes upon new discoveries may have a knowledge of what has already been done. This inventory will be the more artificial and useful, if it also contain things of every kind, which, according to common opinion, are impossible; as likewise such as seemed next to impossible, yet have been effected, the one to whet the human invention, and the other to direct it, so that from these optatives and potentials actives may the more readily be deduced.

The second thing is, that a calendar be made of such experiments as are most extensively useful, and that lead to the discovery of others. For example, the experiment of artificial freezing, by means of ice and bay salt, is of infinite extent, and discovers a secret method of condensation of great service to mankind; fire is ready at hand for rarefaction, but the means of condensation are wanted. And it would greatly shorten the way to discoveries, to have a particular catalogue of these leading experiments.

CHAPTER VI.

The Great Appendix of Natural Philosophy both Speculative and Practical. Mathematics. Its Proper Position not among the Substantial Sciences, but in their Appendix. Mathematics divided into Pure and Mixed.

It was well observed by Aristotle, that physics and mathematics produce practice, or mechanics;[a] therefore, as we have treated both the speculative and practical part of the doctrine of nature, we should also consider mathematics as an auxiliary science to both, which being revived into philosophy, comes in as a third part after physics and metaphysics. But upon due recollection, if we designed it as a substantial and principal science, it were more agreeable to method and the nature of the thing to make it a part of metaphysics. For quantity, the subject of mathematics applied to matter, is as the dose of nature, and productive of numerous effects in natural things, and therefore ought to be reckoned among essential forms. And so much did the power of figures and numbers prevail with the ancients, that Democritus chiefly placed the principles of the variety of things in the figures of their atoms;[b] and Pythagoras asserted that the nature of things consisted of numbers.[c] Thus much is true, that of natural forms, such as we understand them, quantity is the most abstracted and separable from matter; and for this reason it has been more carefully cultivated and examined into by mankind than any other forms, which are all of them more immersed in matter. For, as to the great disadvantage of the sciences, it is natural for men's minds to delight more in the open fields of generals, than in the inclosures of particulars, nothing is found more agreeable than mathematics, which fully gratifies this appetite of expatiating and ranging at large. But as we regard not only truth and order, but also the benefits and advantages of mankind, it seems best, since mathematics is of great use in physics, metaphysics, mechanics, and magics, to make it an appendage or auxiliary to them all. And this we are in some measure obliged to do, from the fondness and towering notions of mathematicians, who would have their science preside over

---

[a] Metaphysics, i. and xi.   [b] Laertius, Life of Democritus.
[c] Iamblicus, Life of Pythagoras.

physics. It is a strange fatality, that mathematics and logic, which ought to be but handmaids to physics, should boast their certainty before it, and even exercise dominion against it. But the place and dignity of this science is a secondary consideration with regard to the thing itself.

Mathematics is either pure or mixed. To the pure belong the sciences employed about quantity, wholly abstracted from matter and physical axioms. This has two parts,—geometry and arithmetic; the one regarding continued, and the other discrete quantity. These two sciences have been cultivated with very great subtilty and application; but in plain geometry there has nothing considerable been added to the labours of Euclid, though he lived many ages since. The doctrine of solids has not been prosecuted and extended equal to its use and excellency, neither by the ancients nor the moderns; and in arithmetic there is still wanting a sufficient variety of short and commodious methods of calculation, especially with regard to progressions, whose use in physics is very considerable.[d] Neither is algebra brought to

[d] In nature no two beings exist perfectly equal, and the same being cannot retain its qualities unchanged for an instant of time together. In the universe everything moves in a constant progression and series, and it probably was the presentiment of this truth that led the greatest mathematicians after Bacon's time to turn nearly all their attention to this department of mathematics. Beyond the analogy, however, there is nothing in these phenomena which has any relation with the reality of things; nor have any philosophers since Flud's day ever dealt with them except as pure conditional verities. With data sufficiently determinate, we may approach the solution of any question to which they refer; but if these facts are not given, the problem must remain unresolved. The mathematician may draw consequences; but it is not allowed him to form principles, and if he attempt to apply figures to any hypothesis not warranted by facts, he must be content with the fate of the Samian who constructed the world out of arithmetic, and has been rewarded by the derision of ages for his pains.

No part of learning has perhaps been more cultivated since this author wrote than mathematics, as every other science, or the body of philosophy itself, seems rendered mathematical. The doctrine of solids has been improved by several; the shorter ways of calculation here noted as deficient are in a great measure supplied by the invention of logarithms. Algebra has been so far improved and applied as to rival, or almost prejudice, the ancient geometry; add to this the new discoveries of the Method of Fluxions, the Method of Tangents, the Doctrine of Infinites, the Squaring of Curves, &c. For the general system of mathematical learning, see " Wolfii Elementa Matheseos Uni-

perfection. As for the Pythagorical and mystical arithmetic, which began to be recovered from Proclus,[e] and certain remains of Euclid, it is a speculative excursion, the mind having this misfortune, that when it proves unequal to solid and useful things, it spends itself upon such as are unprofitable.

Mixed mathematics has for its subject axioms and the parts of physics, and considers quantity so far as may be assisting to illustrate, demonstrate, and actuate those; for without the help of mathematics many parts of nature could neither be sufficiently comprehended, clearly demonstrated, nor dexterously fitted for use. And of this kind are perspective, music, astronomy, cosmography, architecture, and mechanics. In mixed mathematics we at present find no entire parts deficient, but foretell there will be many found hereafter, if men are not wanting to themselves; for if physics be daily improving, and drawing out new axioms, it will continually be wanting fresh assistances from mathematics; so that the parts of mixed mathematics must gradually grow more numerous.

We have now gone through the physical sciences, and marked out the waste ground in them. If, however, we have departed from the ancient and received opinions, and arrayed opponents against us, we have not affected contradiction, and therefore will not enter into the lists of contention. If we have spoken the truth,

"Non canimus surdis; respondent omnia sylvæ,"[f]—

the voice of nature will cry it up, though the voice of man should cry it down; and as Alexander Borgia was wont to say of the expedition of the French against Naples, that they came with chalk in their hands to mark up their lodg-

versæ," in two volumes 4to., printed at Halle in the year 1715; or for a more cursory view, Father Castel's "Mathématique Universelle," published in the year 1731; but for the history of mathematics, see Vossius "De Universæ Matheseos Natura et Constitutione;" the "Almagest" of Ricciolus; Morhof's "Polyhist. Mathemat.;" and Wolfius's "Commentatio de Scriptis Mathematicis," at the end of the second volume of his "Elementa Matheseos Universæ;" Montucla's "Hist. Math.;" and De la Croix's "Analysis of Infinites." *Ed.*

[e] He ought to have said from Iamblicus. Proclus was, like himself, totally ignorant even of the little mathematical learning extant in his day. *Ed.*   [f] Virg. Eclogues, x. 8.

ings, and not with weapons to fight, so we prefer that entry of truth which comes peaceably, when the minds of men capable of lodging so great a guest are signed as it were with chalk, than that which comes with pugnacity, and forces its way by contentions and controversies. Wherefore, having gone through the two parts of philosophy that relate to God and to Nature, we come to the third, which is man himself.

FOURTH BOOK.

CHAPTER I.

Division of the Knowledge of Man into Human and Civil Philosophy. Human Philosophy divided into the Doctrine of the Body and Soul. The Construction of one General Science, including the Nature and State of Man. The latter divided into the Doctrine of the Human Person and the Connection of the Soul with the Body. Division of the Doctrine of the Person of Man into that of his Miseries and Prerogatives. Division of the Relations between the Soul and the Body into the Doctrines of Indications and Impressions. Physiognomy and the Interpretation of Dreams assigned to the Doctrine of Indications.

IF any man, excellent king, shall assault or wound me for any of these precepts, let him know that he infringes the code of military honour; for in addition to being under the gracious protection of your Majesty, I do not begin the fight, but am only one of those trumpeters of whom Homer speaks,—

Χαίρετε κήρυκες Διὸς ἄγγελοι, ἠδὲ καὶ ἀνδρῶν,[a]—

who pass inviolate even between enraged armies. Nor does our trumpet summon men to tear one another in frenzied combat, but rather to conclude a peace, that they who are now divided may direct their united forces against nature herself; and by taking her high towers and dismantling her fortified holds, enlarge as far as God will permit the borders of man's dominion. We now come to the knowledge of ourselves, whither we are directed by the ancients,[b] which

---

[a] Iliad, i. 334.   [b] Plato's Alcibiades.

merits a closer examination, since the knowledge of himself is to man the end and time of the sciences, of which nature only forms a portion. And here we must admonish mankind, that all divisions of the sciences are to be understood and employed, so as only to mark out and distinguish, not tear, separate, or make any solution of continuity in their body;[c] the contrary practice having rendered particular sciences barren, empty, and erroneous, whilst they are not fed, supported, and kept right by their common parent. Thus we find Cicero complaining of Socrates, that he first disjoined philosophy from rhetoric, which is thence become a frothy, talkative art.[d] And it is likewise evident, that although the opinion of Copernicus about the earth's rotation cannot be confuted by astronomical principles, because it agrees with phenomena, yet it may easily be exploded by natural philosophy. In like manner the art of medicine, without the assistance of natural philosophy, differs but little from empiricism.

The doctrine of man divides itself into two parts, or into human and civil philosophy, as it considers man separate, or joined in society. Human philosophy consists in the sciences that regard the body, and those that regard the soul of man. But before we descend to a more particular distribution, it is proper to make one general science of the nature and state of man, which certainly deserves to be freed from the rest, and reduced to a science by itself. And this will consist of such things as are common both to the body and the soul. It may, likewise, be divided into two parts; viz., according to the individual nature of man, and the connection of the soul and body. The former we call the doctrine of the person of man, and the other the doctrine of union. All which, being common and mixed matters, cannot be separately referred to the sciences that regard the body, nor to those that regard the soul.

The doctrine of the human person principally consists in two things: the consideration of the miseries of mankind, and its prerogatives or excellencies. There are many writings, both philosophical and theological, that elegantly and copiously bewail the human miseries, and it is an agree-

---

[c] Seneca's Epistles, § 89.   [d] De Oratore.

able and wholesome topic; but the prerogatives of mankind are not hitherto described. Pindar, in his praise of Hiero, says, with his usual elegance, that he cropped the tops of every virtue;[e] and methinks it would greatly contribute to the encouragement and honour of mankind, to have these tops, or utmost extents of human nature, collected from faithful history: I mean the greatest length whereto human nature of itself has ever gone, in the several endowments of body and mind. Thus it is said of Cæsar,[f] that he could dictate to five amanuenses at once. We read, also, of the ancient rhetoricians, as Protagoras and Gorgias; and of the ancient philosophers, as Callisthenes, Possidonius, and Carneades, who could with eloquence and copiousness dispute off hand, on either side of an argument,[g] which shows the power of the mind to advantage. So does, also, what Cicero relates of his master Archias, viz., that he could make extempore a large number of excellent verses upon the common transactions of life. It is a great honour to the memory, that Cyrus or Scipio could call so many thousands of men by their names.[h] Nor are the victories gained in the moral virtues less signal than those of the intellectual faculties. What an example of patience is that of Anaxarchus, who, when put to the torture, bit off his own tongue, and spit it in the tyrant's face! Nor, to come to our own times, is that a less example of scorn of suffering, which the murderer of the prince of Orange displayed in the midst of his tortures. This Burgundian, though scourged with iron thongs and torn with red-hot pincers, did not heave a sigh; and when a broken fragment of the scaffold fell on the heads of one of the bystanders, he, even girt around with flames, could not repress his laughter. We have many instances of great serenity and composure of mind at the time of death, as particularly in the centurion mentioned by Tacitus, who being bid by his executioner to stretch out his neck, valiantly replied, "I would thou wouldst strike as strongly."[i] John, duke of Saxony,[k] whilst playing at chess, received the order for his

[e] Pindar, Olymp. i. The triumphs of men, and the summits of human nature. [f] Suetonius's Life.
[g] Quintilian's Institutes, iii., and Laertius's Lives.
[h] Xenophon's Cyropædia, v.; and Quintilian's Institutes, xi.
[i] Annals, xv. 67.
[k] Meteren, History of the Civil Wars in the Netherlands.

execution the following day; whereupon, turning round to one that stood by him, he said, with a smile, "Judge, whether so far I am not the winner of the game. For as soon as I am dead, he," pointing to his antagonist, "will say that the game was his own." Sir Thomas More, the day before his execution, being waited upon by his barber, to know if he would have his hair off, refused it; with this answer, that "the king and he had a dispute about his head, and till that were ended he would bestow no cost upon it." And even when he had laid his head upon the block, he raised himself again a little, and gently putting his long beard aside, said, "This surely has not offended the king." By these examples it will appear that the miracles of human nature, and the utmost powers and faculties, both of mind and body, are what we would have collected into a volume, that should be a kind of register of human triumphs. And with regard to such a work, we commend the design of Valerius Maximus and Pliny, but not their care and choice.

The doctrine of union, or of the common tie of soul and body, has two parts: for as, in all alliances, there is mutual intelligence and mutual offices, so the union of the mind and body requires a description of the manner wherein they discover, and act upon each other by notices, or indication and impression. The description by indication has produced two arts of prediction: the one honoured with the inquiry of Aristotle, and the other with that of Hippocrates. And though later ages have debased these arts with superstitious and fantastical mixtures, yet, when purged and truly restored, they have a solid foundation in nature, and use in life. The first of these is physiognomy, which, by the lineaments of the body, discovers the dispositions of the mind; the second is the interpretation of natural dreams, which, from the agitations of the mind, discovers the state and dispositions of the body. I find the former deficient in one part; for though Aristotle has, with great ingenuity and diligence, treated the structure of the body at rest, he dropped the consideration of it in motion or gesture,[1] which is no less subject to the observations of art, and more useful

---

[1] Bacon's memory here fails him; for Aristotle in his Physiognomia Corporis in Motu, has treated the matter elaborately, though without going much into detail. *Ed.*

than the other. For the lineaments of the body show the general inclinations and dispositions of the mind, whilst the motions of the face, and the gestures of the other parts, not only do the same, but also express the present disposition and inclination: for, if I may use one of your Majesty's most forcible and elegant expressions, "as the tongue applies to the ear, so does gesture to the eye." And this is well known to many subtile and designing persons, who watchfully observe the countenance and gestures of others, and value themselves for their talent of turning such discoveries to their own advantage; and it must be acknowledged an excellent way of discovering dissimulation in others, and of admonishing men to choose proper times and opportunities for their addresses, which is no small part of civil prudence. A work upon this doctrine of gesture would not only prove useful in particular cases, but serve as a general rule; for all men laugh, weep, blush, frown, &c., alike: and this holds of nearly all the more subtile motions. But for chiromancy, it is absolutely a vain thing, and unworthy to be mentioned among those we are now treating.

The interpretation of natural dreams has been much laboured; but mixed with numerous extravagancies. We shall here only observe of it, that at present it stands not upon its best foundation; which is, that where the same thing happens from an internal cause, as also usually happens from an external one, there the external action passes into a dream. Thus the stomach may be oppressed by a gross internal vapour, as well as by an external weight; whence those who have the night-mare dream that a weight is laid upon them, with a great concurrence of circumstances. So, again, the viscera being equally tossed by the agitation of the waves at sea, as by a collection of wind in the hypochondria, hence melancholy persons frequently dream of sailing and tossing upon the waters; and instances of this kind are numerous.

The second part of the doctrine of union, which we call impression, is not yet reduced to an art; and but occasionally mentioned by writers. This also has two parts: as considering, 1st, how, and to what degree, the humours and constitution of the body may affect the soul, or act upon it; and 2nd, how, and to what degree, the passions and apprehensions of the soul may affect and work upon the body.

The first of these we sometimes find touched in medicine; but it has strangely insinuated itself into religion. Physicians prescribe remedies for the diseases of the mind, viz., madness, melancholy, &c., as also to cheer the spirits, strengthen the memory, &c.; but for diet, choice of meats and drinks, washings, and other observances relating to the body, they are found immoderately in the sect of the Pythagoreans, the Manichean heresy, and the law of Mahomet There are, also, numerous and strict ordinances in the ceremonial law, prohibiting the eating of blood and fat, and distinguishing the unclean animals from the clean for food.[m] Even the Christian religion, though it has thrown off the veil of ceremonies, still retains the use of fasting, abstinence, and other things that regard the subjection and humiliation of the body; as things not merely ritual, but advantageous. The root of all these ordinances, besides the ceremony and exercise of obedience, is, that the soul should sympathize and suffer with the body. And if any man of weaker judgment thinks that such macerations question the immortality, or derogate from the sovereignty of the soul, let him find an answer in the instances, either of an infant in its mother's womb, which shares in the vicissitudes, and yet is distinct from its mother's body, or of monarchs, who, though in possession of absolute power, are frequently influenced and swayed by their servants.

The other part, which considers the operations of the soul upon the body, has likewise been received into medicine; for every prudent physician regards the accidents of the mind as a principal thing in his cures, that greatly promote or hinder the effects of all other remedies. But one particular has been hitherto slightly touched, or not well examined, as its usefulness and abstruse nature require; viz., how far a fixed and riveted imagination may alter the body of the imaginant; for though this has a manifest power to hurt, it does not follow, it has the same to relieve: no more than because an air may be so pestilent as suddenly to destroy, another air should be so wholesome as suddenly to recover. This would be an inquiry of noble use; but, as Socrates would say, it requires a Delian diver, for it is deep plunged.[n]

[m] Deut. xii.   [n] Laertius's Life.

But among these doctrines of union, or consent of soul and body, there is none more necessary than an inquiry into the proper seat and habitation of each faculty of the soul in the body and its organs. Some, indeed, have prosecuted this subject; but all usually delivered upon it is either controverted or slightly examined, so as to require more pains and accuracy. The opinion of Plato, which seats the understanding in the brain, courage in the heart, and sensuality in the liver, should neither be totally rejected nor fondly received.[o]

CHAPTER II.

Division of the Knowledge of the Human Body into the Medicinal, Cosmetic, Athletic, and the Voluptuary Arts. Division of Medicine into Three Functions: viz., the Preservation of Health, the Cure of Diseases, and the Prolongation of Life. The last distinct from the two former.

THE doctrine of the human body divides itself according to the perfections of the body, whereto it is subservient. These perfections are four: viz., 1st, health; 2nd, comeliness; 3rd, strength; and 4th, pleasure: to which correspond as relatives: 1st, the arts of medicine; 2nd, beautifying; 3rd, gymnastics; and 4th, the art of elegance, which Tacitus calls eruditum luxum.[a] Medicine is a noble art, and honourably descended, according to the poets, who make Apollo the primary god, and his son Æsculapius, whom they also deify, the first professor thereof: for as, in natural things, the sun is the author and fountain of life, so the physician, who preserves life, seems a second origin thereof. But medicine receives far greater honour from the works of our Saviour, who was physician both to soul and body, and made the latter the standing subject of his miracles, as the soul was the constant subject of his doctrine.

Of all the things that nature has created, the human body is most capable of relief, though this relief be the most liable to error. For as the subtilty and variety of the subject affords many opportunities of cure, so likewise a great facility of mistake. And, therefore, as this art, especially at present,

[o] Plato's Timæus, and Aristotle on the Generation of Animals.
[a] Annals, xvi. 18.

stands among the most conjectural ones, so the inquiry into it is to be placed among the most subtile and difficult. Neither are we so senseless as to imagine, with Paracelsus and the alchymists, that there are to be found in man's body definite analogies to all the variety of specific natures in the world, perverting very impertinently that emblem of the ancients, that man was a microcosm or model of the whole world, to countenance their idle fancies. Of all natural bodies, we find none so variously compounded as the human: vegetables are nourished by earth and water; brutes by herbs and fruits; but man feeds upon the flesh of living creatures, herbs, grain, fruits, different juices and liquors; and these all prepared, preserved, dressed, and mixed in endless variety. Besides, the way of living among other creatures is more simple, and the affections that act upon the body fewer and more uniform; but man in his habitation, his exercises, passions, &c., undergoes numberless changes. So that it is evident that the body of man is more fermented, compounded, and organized, than any other natural substance; the soul, on the other side, is the simplest, as is well expressed :—

"—— purumque reliquit
Æthereum sensum, atque auraï simplicis ignem;"[b]—

so that we need not marvel that the soul so placed enjoys no rest, since it is out of its place: " Motus rerum extra locum est rapidus, placidus in loco."[c] This variable and subtile composition, and fabric of the human body, makes it like a kind of curious musical instrument, easily disordered; and therefore, the poets justly joined music and medicine in Apollo; because the office of medicine is to tune the curious organ of the human body, and reduce it to harmony.

The subject being so variable has rendered the art more conjectural, and left the more room for imposture. Other arts and sciences are judged of by their power and ability, and not by success or events. The lawyer is judged by the ability of his pleading, not the issue of the cause; the pilot, by directing his course, and not by the fortune of the voyage; whilst the physician and statesman have no particular act that clearly demonstrates their ability, but are

[b] Virg. Æneid, vi. 746.   [c] Arist. on the Heavens.

principally censured by the event, which is very unjust: for who can tell, if a patient die or recover, or a state fall into decay, whether the evil is brought about by art or by accident? Whence imposture is frequently extolled, and virtue decried. Nay, the weakness and credulity of men is such, that they often prefer a mountebank, or a cunning woman, to a learned physician. The poets were clear-sighted in discerning this folly, when they made Æsculapius and Circe brother and sister, and both children of Apollo, as in the verses:—

> " Ille repertorem medicinæ talis et artis,
> Fulmine Phœbigenam Stygias detrusit ad undas:"

and similarly of Circe, daughter of the sun:—

> " Dives inaccessis ubi Solis filia lucis
> Urit odoratam nocturna in lumina cedrum."[d]

For in all times, witches, old women, and impostors, have, in the vulgar opinion, stood competitors with physicians. And hence physicians say to themselves, in the words of Solomon, " If it befall to me, as befalleth to the fools, why should I labour to be more wise?"[e] And, therefore, one cannot greatly blame them, that they commonly study some other art, or science, more than their profession. Hence, we find among them poets, antiquaries, critics, politicians, divines, and in each more knowing than in medicine. Nor does this fall out, because as a certain declamour against physicians suggests,[f] being so often in contact with loathsome spectacles, that they seize the first hour of leisure to draw their minds from such contemplations. For as they are men—" Nihil humani à se alienum putent"—no doubt, because they find that mediocrity and excellency in their own art makes no difference in profit or reputation: for men's impatience of diseases, the solicitations of friends, the sweetness of life, and the inducement of hope, make them depend upon physicians with all their defects. But when this is seriously considered, it turns rather to the reproach than the excuse of physicians, who ought not hence to despair, but to use greater diligence. For we see what a power the subtilty of the understanding has over the variety both of the matter and form of things.

[d] Æneid, vii. 772, 11.   [e] Eccles. ii. 15.
[f] Agrippa, Scientia Vana.

There is nothing more variable than men's faces, yet we can remember infinite distinctions of them; and a painter with a few colours, the practice of the hand and eye, and help of the imagination, could imitate thousands if brought before him. As variable as voices are, yet we can easily distinguish them in different persons, and a mimic will express them to the life. Though the sounds of words differ so greatly, yet men can reduce them to a few simple letters. And certainly it is not the insufficiency or incapacity of the mind, but the remoteness of the object that causes these perplexities and distrusts in the sciences: for as the sense is apt to mistake at great distances, but not near at hand, so is the understanding. Men commonly take a view of nature as from a remote eminence, and are too much amused with generalities: whereas, if they would descend, and approach nearer to particulars, and more exactly and considerately examine into things themselves, they might make more solid and useful discoveries. The remedy of this error, therefore, is to quicken or strengthen the organ, and thus to approach the object. No doubt, therefore, if physicians, leaving generalities for a while, and suspending their assent, would advance towards nature, they might become masters of that art of which the poet speaks:—

"Et quoniam variant morbi, variabimus artes
Mille mali species mille salutis erunt."[g]

They should the rather endeavour this, because the philosophies whereon physicians, whether methodists or chemists, depend, are trifling, and because medicine, not founded on philosophy, is a weak thing. Therefore, as too extensive generals, though true, do not bring men home to action, there is more danger in such generals as are false in themselves, and seduce instead of directing the mind. Medicine, therefore, has been rather professed than laboured, and yet more laboured than advanced, as the pains bestowed thereon were rather circular than progressive; for I find great repetition, and but little new matter, in the writers of physic.

We divide medicine into three parts, or offices: viz., 1st, the preservation of health; 2nd, the cure of diseases; and 3rd, the prolongation of life. For this last part, physicians seem

[g] Ovid, Remedia Amoris, 525.

to think it no capital part of medicine, but confound it with the other two; as supposing, that if diseases be prevented, or cured after invasion, long life must follow of course. But, then, they do not consider that both preservation and cure regard only diseases, and such prolongation of life as is intercepted by them: whence the means of spinning out the full thread of life, or preventing, for a season, that kind of death which gradually steals upon the body by simple resolution, and the wasting of age, is a subject that no physician has treated suitably to its merit. Let none imagine we are here repealing the decrees of fate and Providence, by establishing a new office of medicine; for, doubtless, Providence alike dispenses all kinds of deaths, whether they proceed from violence, diseases, or the course and period of age; yet without excluding the use of remedies and preventions, for art and industry do not here overrule, but administer to nature and fate.

Many have unskilfully written upon the preservation of health, particularly by attributing too much to the choice, and too little to the quantity of meats. As to quantity, they, like the moral philosophers, highly commend moderation; whereas, both fasting changed to custom, and full feeding, where a man is used to it, are better preservatives of health than those mediocrities they recommend, which commonly dispirit nature, and unfit her to bear excess, or want, upon occasion. And for the several exercises, which greatly conduce to the preservation of health, no physician has well distinguished or observed them, though there be scarce any tendency to a disease, that may not be corrected by some appropriate exercise. Thus bowling is suited to the diseases of the kidneys, shooting with the long bow to those of the lungs, walking and riding to those of the stomach, &c.

Great pains have been bestowed upon the cure of diseases, but to small purpose. This part comprehends the knowledge of the diseases incident to the human body, together with their causes, symptoms, and cures. In this second office of medicine there are many deficiencies. And first, we may note the discontinuance of that useful method of Hippocrates,[b] in writing narratives of particular cures with

[b] Narrationes Medicales.

CHAP. II.] PHYSICIANS' NEGLECT OF ANATOMY. 161

diligence and exactness, containing the nature, the cure, and event of the distemper. And this remarkable precedent of one accounted the father of his art, need not to be backed with examples derived from other arts, as from the prudent practice of the lawyers, who religiously enter down the more eminent cases and new decisions, the better to prepare and direct themselves in future. This continuation, therefore, of medicinal reports we find deficient, especially in form of an entire body, digested with proper care and judgment. But we do not mean, that this work should extend to every common case that happens every day, which were an infinite labour, and to little purpose; nor yet to exclude all but prodigies and wonders, as several have done: for many things are new in their manner and circumstances, which are not new in their kind; and he who looks attentively will find many particulars worthy of observation, in what seems vulgar.

So in anatomy, the general parts of the human body are diligently observed, and even to niceness: but as to the variety found in different bodies, here the diligence of physicians fails. And, therefore, though simple anatomy has been fully and clearly handled, yet comparative anatomy is deficient. For anatomists have carefully examined into all the parts, their consistencies, figures, and situations; but pass over the different figure and state of those parts in different persons. The reason of this defect I take to be, that the former inquiry may terminate upon seeing two or three bodies dissected; but the other being comparative, and casual, requires attentive and strict application to many different dissections: besides, the first is a subject wherein learned anatomists may show themselves to their audience; but the other a rigorous knowledge, to be acquired only by silent and long experience. And no doubt but the internal parts, for variety and proportions, are little inferior to the external; and that hearts, livers, and stomachs, are as different in men, as foreheads, noses, and ears. And in these differences of the internal parts are often found the immediate causes of many diseases, which physicians not observing, sometimes unjustly accuse the humours, when the fault lies only in the mechanic structure of a part. And in such diseases it is in vain to use alteratives, as the case admits not of being altered by them, but must be affected, accommodated, or palliated by a regimen, and familiar medicines.

Again, comparative anatomy requires accurate observations upon all the humours, and the marks and impressions of diseases in different bodies upon dissection; for the humours are commonly passed over in anatomy, as loathsome and excrementitious things; whereas it is highly useful and necessary to note their nature and the various kinds that may sometimes be found in the human body, in what cavities they principally lodge, and with what advantage, disadvantage, and the like. So the marks and impressions of diseases, and the changes and devastations they bring upon the internal parts, are to be diligently observed in different dissections; viz. imposthumes, ulcerations, solutions of continuity, putrefactions, corrosions, consumptions, contractions, extensions, convulsions, luxations, dislocations, obstructions, repletions, tumours; and preternatural excrescences, as stones, carnosities, wens, worms, &c., all which should be very carefully examined, and orderly digested in the comparative anatomy we speak of; and the experiments of several physicians be here collected and compared together. But this variety of accidents, is by anatomists either slightly touched or else passed over in silence.

That defect in anatomy, owing to its not having been practised upon live bodies, needs not be spoken to, the thing itself being odious, cruel, and justly condemned by Celsus;[1] yet the observation of the ancients is true, that many subtile pores, passages, and perforations appear not upon dissection, because they are closed and concealed in dead bodies, that might be open and manifest in live ones. Wherefore, if we would consult the good of mankind, without being guilty of cruelty, this anatomy of live creatures should be entirely deserted or left to the casual inspection of chirurgeons, or may be sufficiently performed upon living brutes, notwithstanding the dissimilitude between their parts and those of men, so as to answer the design, provided it be done with judgment.

Physicians, likewise, when they inquire into diseases, find so many which they judge incurable, either from their first

---

[1] De Re Medica, i. 5.

appearance, or after a certain period, that the proscriptions of Sylla and the Triumvirate were trifling to the proscriptions of the physicians, by which, with an unjust sentence, they deliver men over to death; numbers whereof, however, escape with less difficulty than under the Roman proscriptions. A work, therefore, is wanting upon the cures of reputed incurable diseases, that physicians of eminence and resolution may be encouraged and excited to pursue this matter as far as the nature of things will permit; since to pronounce diseases incurable, is to establish negligence and carelessness, as it were by a law, and screen ignorance from reproach.

And farther, we esteem it the office of a physician to mitigate the pains and tortures of diseases, as well as to restore health; and this not only when such a mitigation, as of a dangerous symptom, may conduce to recovery; but also, when there being no farther hopes of recovery, it can only serve to make the passage out of life more calm and easy. For that complacency in death, which Augustus Cæsar so much desired, is no small felicity.[k] This was also observed in the death of Antoninus Pius, who seemed not so much to die as to fall into a deep and pleasing sleep. And it is delivered of Epicurus, that he procured himself this easy departure; for after his disease was judged desperate, he intoxicated himself with wine, and died in that condition, which gave rise to the epigram :—

"Hinc Stygias ebrius transit aquas."[l]

But the physicians of our times make a scruple of attending the patient after the disease is thought past cure, though, in my judgment, if they were not wanting to their own profession and to humanity itself, they should here give their attendance to improve their skill, and make the dying person depart with greater ease and tranquillity. We therefore set down as deficient an inquiry after a method of relieving the agonies of the dying, calling it by the name of euthanasia exteriori, to distinguish it from the internal composure, procured to the soul in death.

Again, we generally find this deficiency in the cures of diseases, that though the present physicians tolerably pursue

[k] Suetonius's Life Aug. Cæs. 100.   [l] Laertius's Life Epic. x. § 16.

the general intentions of cures, yet they have no particular medicines, which, by a specific property regard particular diseases; for they lose the benefit of traditions and approved experience by their authoritative procedure in adding, taking away, and changing the ingredients of their receipts at pleasure, after the manner of apothecaries substituting one thing for another, and thus haughtily commanding medicine, so that medicine can no longer command the disease. For except Venice treacle, mithridate, diascordium, the confection of alkermes, and a few more, they commonly tie themselves strictly to no certain receipts: the other saleable preparations of the shops being in readiness, rather for general purposes, than accommodated to any particular cures; for they do not principally regard some one disease, but have a general virtue of opening obstructions, promoting concoction, &c. And hence it chiefly proceeds, that empirics and women are often more successful in their cures than learned physicians, because the former keep strictly and invariably to the use of experienced medicines, without altering their compositions. I remember a famous Jew physician in England would say, "Your European physicians are indeed men of learning, but they know nothing of particular cures for diseases." And he would sometimes jest a little irreverently, and say, "Our physicians were like bishops, that had the keys of binding and loosing, but no more." To be serious; it might be of great consequence if some physicians, eminent for learning and practice, would compile a work of approved and experienced medicines in particular diseases. For though one might speciously pretend, that a learned physician should rather suit his medicines occasionally, as the constitution of the patient, his age, customs, the seasons, &c. require, than rest upon any certain prescriptions; yet this is a fallacious opinion that underrates experience and overrates human judgment. And as those persons in the Roman state were the most serviceable, who being either consuls, favoured the people, or tribunes, and inclined to the senate; so are those the best physicians, who being either learned, duly value the traditions of experience; or men of eminent practice, that do not despise methods and the general principles of the art. But if medicines require, at any time, to be qualified, this may rather be done in the vehicles than in the body of the medicine, where nothing should be altered without apparent necessity. Therefore, this part of physic which treats of authentic and positive remedies, we note as deficient; but the business of supplying it is to be undertaken with great judgment, and as by a committee of physicians, chosen for that purpose.

And for the preparation of medicines; it seems strange, especially as mineral ones have been so celebrated by chemists, though safer for external than internal use, that nobody hath hitherto attempted any artificial imitations of natural baths and medicinal springs, whilst it is acknowledged that these receive their virtues from the mineral veins through which they pass; and especially since human industry can, by certain separations, discover with what kind of minerals such waters are impregnated, as whether by sulphur, vitrol, iron, &c. And if these natural impregnations of waters are reducible to artificial compositions, it would then be in the power of art to make more kinds of them occasionally, and at the same time to regulate their temperature at pleasure. This part, therefore, of medicine, concerning the artificial imitation of natural baths and springs, we set down as deficient, and recommend as an easy as well as useful undertaking.

The last deficiency we shall mention seems to us of great importance; viz., that the methods of cure in use are too short to effect anything that is difficult or very considerable. For it is rather vain and flattering, than just and rational, to expect that any medicine should be so effectual, or so successful, as by the sole use thereof to work any great cure. It must be a powerful discourse, which though often repeated, should correct any deep-rooted and inveterate vice of the mind. Such miracles are not to be expected; but the things of greatest efficacy in nature, are order, perseverance, and an artificial change of applications, which, though they require exact judgment to prescribe, and precise observance to follow, yet this is amply recompensed by the great effects they produce. To see the daily labours of physicians in their visits, consultations, and prescriptions, one would think that they diligently pursued the cure, and went directly in a certain beaten track about it; but whoever looks attentively into their prescriptions and directions, will find, that the most of what they do is full of uncertainty, wavering, and irresolution, without any certain view or fore-knowledge or the course of the cure. Whereas they should from the first, after having fully and perfectly discovered the disease, choose and resolve upon some regular process or series of cure, and not depart from it without sufficient reason. Thus physicians should know, for example, that perhaps three or four remedies rightly prescribed in an inveterate disease, and taken in due order, and at due distances of time, may perform a cure; and yet the same remedies taken independently of each other, in an inverted order, or not at stated periods, might prove absolutely prejudicial. Though we mean not, that every scrupulous and superstitious method of cure should be esteemed the best, but that the way should be as exact as it is confined and difficult. And this part of medicine we note as deficient, under the name of the physicians' clue or directory. And these are the things wanting in the doctrine of medicine, for the cure of diseases; but there still remains one thing more, and of greater use than all the rest; viz., a genuine and active natural philosophy, whereon to build the science of physic.

We make the third part of medicine regard the prolongation of life: this is a new part, and deficient, though the most noble of all; for if it may be supplied, medicine will not then be wholly versed in sordid cures, nor physicians be honoured only for necessity, but as dispensers of the greatest earthly happiness that could well be conferred on mortals; for though the world be but as a wilderness to a Christian travelling through it to the promised land, yet it would be an instance of the divine favour, that our clothing, that is, our bodies, should be little worn while we sojourn here. And as this is a capital part of physic, and as we note it for deficient, we shall lay down some directions about it.

And first, no writer extant upon this subject has made any great or useful discovery therein. Aristotle,[m] indeed, has left us a short memoir, wherein there are some admonitions after his manner, which he supposes to be all that can be said of the matter; but the moderns have here written so weakly and

---

[m] De Longitudine et Novitate Vitæ.

superstitiously, that the subject itself, through their vanity, is reputed vain and senseless. 2. The very intentions of physicians upon this head are of no validity, but rather lead from the point than direct to it. For they talk as if death consisted in a destitution of heat and moisture, and therefore that natural heat should be comforted, and radical moisture cherished; as if the work were to be effected by broths, lettuce, and mallows; or again, by spices, generous wines, spirits, or chemical oils; all which rather do hurt than good. 3. We admonish mankind to cease their trifling, and not weakly imagine that such a great work as retarding the course of nature can be effected by a morning's draught, the use of any costly medicines, pearls, or aurum potabile itself; but be assured, that the prolongation of life is a laborious work, that requires many kinds of remedies, and a proper continuation and intermixture thereof; for it were stupidity to expect, that what was never yet done, should be effected, otherwise than by means hitherto unattempted. 4. Lastly, we admonish them rightly to observe and distinguish betwixt what conduces to health, and what to a long life; for some things, though they exhilarate the spirits, strengthen the faculties, and prevent diseases, are yet destructive to life, and, without sickness, bring on a wasting old age; whilst there are others which prolong life and prevent decay, though not to be used without danger to health; so that when employed for the prolongation of life, such inconveniences must be guarded against, as might otherwise happen upon using them.

Things seem to us preservable either in their own substance or by repair; in their own substance, as a fly, or an ant, in amber; a flower, an apple, &c. in conservatories of snow; or a corps of balsam; by repair, as in flame and mechanic engines. He who attempts to prolong life, must practise both these methods together; for separate, their force is less. The human body must be preserved as bodies inanimate are; again, as flame; and lastly, in some measure as machines are preserved. There are, therefore, three intentions for the prolongation of life; viz., 1. to hinder waste; 2. secure a good repair; and 3. to renew what begins to decay. I. Waste is caused by two depredations; viz., that of the internal spirit, and that of the external air; and both are prevented two ways; viz., by making these agents less predatory, or the patients, that is the juices of the body, less apt to be preyed on. The spirit is rendered less predatory, if either its substance be condensed; as, 1. by the use of opiates, preparations of nitre, and in contristation; or, 2. if it be lessened in quantity, as by fasting and diet; and 3. if it be moderated in its motion, as by rest and quiet. The ambient air becomes less predatory, either when it is less heated by the sun, as in the cold countries, caves, hills; or kept from the body, as by close skins, the plumage of birds, and the use of oil and unguents, without spices. The juices of the body are rendered less subject to be preyed on, if made more hardy, or more oleaginous, as by a rough astringent diet, living in the cold, robust exercises, the use of certain mineral baths, sweet things, and abstaining from such as are salt or acid; but especially by means of such drinks as consist of subtile parts, yet without acrimony or tartness. II. Repair is procured by nourishment, and nourishment is promoted four ways: 1. by forwarding internal concoction, which drives forth the nourishment, as by medicines that invigorate the principal viscera; 2. by exciting the external parts to attract the nourishment, as by exercise, proper frictions, unctions, and baths; 3. by preparing the aliment itself, that it may more easily insinuate, and require less digestion; as in many artificial ways of preparing meats, drinks, bread, and reducing the effects of these three to one: again, 4. by the last act of assimilation, as in seasonable sleep and external applications. III. The renovation of parts worn out is performed two ways; either by softening the habit of the body, as with suppling applications, in the way of bath, plaster, or unction, of such qualities as to insinuate into the parts, but extract nothing from them; or by discharging the old, and substituting new moisture, as in seasonable and repeated purging, bleeding, and attenuating diets, which restore the bloom of the body.

Several rules for the conduct of the work are derivable from these indications; but three of the more principal are the following. And first, prolongation of life is rather to be expected from stated diets, than from any common regimen of food, or the virtues of particular medicines; for those things that have force enough to turn back the course of nature, are commonly too violent to be compounded into a medicine, much more to be mixed with the ordinary food, and must therefore be administered orderly, regularly, and at set periods. 2. We next lay it down as a rule, that the prolongation of life be expected, rather from working upon the spirits, and mollifying the parts, than from the manner of alimentation. For as the human body, and the internal structure thereof, may suffer from three things, viz. the spirits, the parts, and aliments; the way of prolonging life by means of alimentation is tedious, indirect, and winding; but the ways of working upon the spirits and the parts, much shorter; for the spirits are suddenly affected, both by effluvia and the passions, which may work strangely upon them; and the parts also by baths, unguents, or plasters, which will likewise have sudden impressions. 3. Our last precept is, that the softening of the external parts be attempted by such things as are penetrating, astringent, and of the same nature with the body; the latter are readily received and entertained, and properly soften; and penetrating things are as vehicles to those that mollify, and more easily convey, and deeply impress the virtue thereof; whilst themselves also, in some measure, operate upon the parts: but astringents keep in the virtue of them both, and somewhat fix it, and also stop perspiration, which would otherwise be contrary to mollifying, as sending out the moisture; therefore the whole affair is to be effected by these three means used in order and succession, rather than together. Observe only, that it is not the intention of mollifying to nourish the parts externally, but only to render them more capable of nourishment; for dry things are less disposed to assimilate. And so much for the prolongation of life, which we make the third, or a new part of medicine.

The art of decoration, or beautifying, has two parts, civil and effeminate. For cleanliness and decency of the body were always allowed to proceed from moral modesty and reverence; first, towards God, whose creatures we are; next, towards society, wherein we live; and lastly, towards ourselves, whom we ought to reverence still more than others. But false decorations, fucuses, and pigments, deserve the imperfections that constantly attend them; being neither exquisite enough to deceive, nor commodious in application, nor wholesome in their use. And it is much that this depraved custom of painting the face should so long escape the penal laws both of the church and state, which have been very severe against luxury in apparel and effeminate trimming of the hair. We read of Jezebel, that she painted her face; but not so of Esther and Judith.

We take gymnastics, in a large sense, to signify whatever relates to the hability whereto the human body may be brought, whether of activity or suffering. Activity has two parts, strength and swiftness; so has endurance or suffering, viz., with regard to natural wants, and fortitude under torture. Of all these, we have many remarkable instances in the practices of rope-dancers, the hardy lives of savages, surprising strength of lunatics, and the constancy and resolution of many under exquisite torments. Any other faculties that fall not within the former division, as diving, or the power of continuing long under water without respiration, and the like, we refer them also to gymnastics. And here, though the things themselves are common, yet the philosophy and causes thereof are usually neglected, perhaps because men are persuaded that such masteries over nature are only obtainable either from a peculiar and natural disposition in some men, which comes not under rules, or by a constant custom from childhood, which is rather imposed than taught. And though this be not altogether true, yet it is here of small consequence to note any deficiency, for the Olympic games are long since ceased, and a mediocrity in these things is sufficient for use, whilst excellency in them serves commonly but for mercenary show.

The arts of elegance are divided with respect to the two senses of sight and hearing. Painting particularly delights the eye; so do numerous other magnificent arts, relating to buildings, gardens, apparel, vessels, gems, &c. Music pleases the ear with great variety and apparatus of sounds, voices, strings, and instruments; and anciently water-organs were esteemed as great master-pieces in this art, though now grown into disuse. The arts which relate to the eye and ear, are, above the rest, accounted liberal; these two senses being the more pure, and the sciences thereof more learned, as having mathematics to attend them. The one also has some relation to the memory and demonstrations; the other, to manners and the passions of the mind. The pleasures of the other senses, and the arts employed about them, are in less repute, as approaching nearer to sensuality than magnificence. Unguents, perfumes, the furniture of the table, but principally incitements to lust, should rather be censured than taught. And it has been well observed, that while states were in their increase, military arts flourished; when at their heights, the liberal arts; but when upon their decline, the arts of luxury. With the arts of pleasure, we join also the jocular arts: for the deception of the senses may be reckoned one of their delights.

And now, as so many things require to be considered with relation to the human body, viz. the parts, humours, functions, faculties, accidents, &c., since we ought to have an entire doctrine of the body of man, which should comprehend them all; yet lest arts should be thus too much multiplied, or their ancient limits too much disordered, we receive into the system of medicine, the doctrines of the parts, functions, and humours of the body; respiration, sleep, generation; the fœtus, gestation in the womb; growth, puberty, baldness, fatness, and the like; though these do not properly belong either to the preservation of health, the cure of diseases, or the prolongation of life, but because the human body is, in every respect, the subject of medicine. But for voluntary motion and sense, we refer them to the doctrine of the soul as two principal parts thereof. And thus we conclude the doctrine of the body, which is but as a tabernacle to the soul.

CHAPTER III.

Division of the Doctrine of the Human Soul into that of the Inspired Essence and the Knowledge of the Sensible or Produced Soul. Second Division of the same philosophy into the Doctrine of the Substance and the Faculties of the Soul. The Use and Objects of the latter. Two Appendices to the Doctrine of the Faculties of the Soul: viz. Natural Divination and Fascination (Mesmerism). The Faculties of the Sensible Soul divided into those of Motion and Sense.

WE now come to the doctrine of the human soul, from whose treasures all other doctrines are derived. It has two parts,—the one treating of the rational soul, which is divine, the other of the irrational soul, which we have in common with brutes. Two different emanations of souls are manifest in the first creation, the one proceeding from the breath of God, the other from the elements. As to the primitive emanation of the rational soul, the Scripture says, God formed man of the dust of the earth, and breathed into his nostrils the breath of life; but the generation of the irrational and brutal soul was in these words,—Let the water bring forth; let the earth bring forth. And this irrational soul in man is only an instrument to the rational one, and has the same origin in us as in brutes, viz. the dust of the earth; for it is not said, God formed the body of man, of the dust of the earth, but God formed man, that is, the whole man, the breath of life excepted, of the dust of the earth. We will, therefore, style the first part of the general doctrine of the human soul the doctrine of the inspired substance, and the other part the doctrine of the sensitive or produced soul. But as we are here treating wholly of philosophy, we would not have borrowed this division from divinity, had it not also agreed with the principles of philosophy. For there are many excellencies of the human soul above the souls of brutes, manifest even to those who philosophize only according to sense. And wherever so many and such great excellencies are found, a specific difference should always be made. We do not, therefore, approve that confused and promiscuous manner of the philosophers in treating the functions of the soul, as if the soul of man differed in degree rather than species from the soul of brutes, as the sun differs from the stars, or gold from other metals.

There may also be another division of the general doctrine of the human soul into the doctrine of the substance and faculties of the soul, and that of the use and objects of the faculties. And these two divisions being premised, we come to particulars.

The doctrine of the inspired substance, as also of the substance of the rational soul, comprehends several inquiries with relation to its nature, as whether the soul be native or adventitious, separable or inseparable, mortal or immortal; how far it is subject to the laws of matter, how far not, and the like. But the points of this kind, though they might be more thoroughly sifted in philosophy than hitherto they have been, yet in the end they must be turned over to religion, for determination and decision; otherwise they will lie exposed to various errors and illusions of sense. For as the substance of the soul was not, in its creation, extracted or deduced from the mass of heaven and earth, but immediately inspired by God; and as the laws of heaven and earth are the proper subjects of philosophy, no knowledge of the substance of the rational soul can be had from philosophy, but must be derived from the same Divine inspiration, whence the substance thereof originally proceeded.[a]

But in the doctrine of the sensitive or produced soul, even its substance may be justly inquired into, though this inquiry seems hitherto wanting. For of what significancy are the terms of actus ultimus and forma corporis, and such logical trifles, to the knowledge of the soul's substance? The sensitive soul must be allowed a corporeal substance, attenuated by heat and rendered invisible, as a subtile breath or aura, of a flamy and airy nature, having the softness of air in receiving impressions, and the activity of fire in exerting its action, nourished partly by an oily and partly by a watery substance, and diffused through the whole body; but in perfect creatures, residing chiefly in the head, and thence running through the nerves, being fed and recruited by the spirituous blood of the arteries, as Telesius[b] and his follower Donius in some measure have usefully shown. Therefore let this doctrine be more diligently inquired into,[c] because the

[a] To separate God from human reason, appears to be one of the great aims of one of the modern schools of philosophy, and sometimes the theory has received indirect confirmations from quarters by no means favourable to its advocates. Pascal wrote, "Selon les lumières naturelles, nous sommes incapable de connaître ce que Dieu est." In the edition of this philosopher's works, by Voltaire and Condorcet, the text was enriched with the addition of the phrase, "Ni s'il est;" and the following note appended to the passage, by Voltaire:— "Il est étrange que Pascal ait cru qu'on pouvait deviner le péché originel par la raison, et qu'il dise qu'on ne peut connaître par la raison si Dieu est." At this specimen of deistic candour, Condorcet exclaims, in a subsequent note, "How marvellous to behold Voltaire contending with Pascal for the existence of God!" *Ed.*

[b] Rerum Natura, book 5.

[c] This inquiry is greatly embroiled by the moderns; some seeking the soul all over the body, some in the blood, some in the animal spirits; some in the heart, some in the ventricles of the brain, and some, with Des Cartes, in the Glandula Pinealis. M. Petit wrote a curious piece

ignorance of it has produced superstitious and very corrupt opinions, that greatly lessen the dignity of the human soul, —such as the transmigration and lustration of souls through certain periods of years, and the too near relation in all respects of the human soul to the soul of brutes. For this soul in brutes is a principal soul, whereof their body is the organ; but in man it is itself an organ of the rational soul, and may rather be called by the name spirit than soul.

The faculties of the soul are well known;[d] viz., the understanding, reason, imagination, memory, appetite, will, and all those wherewith logic and ethics are concerned. In the doctrine of the soul the origin of these faculties must be physically treated, as they may be innate and adhering to the soul, but their uses and objects are referred to other arts; and in this part nothing extraordinary has hitherto appeared, though we do not indeed report it as wanting. This part of the faculties of the soul has also two appendages, which as they have yet been handled, rather present us with smoke than any clear flame of truth,—one being the doctrine of natural divination, the other of fascination.

Divination has been anciently and properly divided into artificial and natural. The artificial draws its predictions by reasoning from the indication of signs; but the natural predicts from the internal foresight of the mind, without the

relating to this subject, entitled, "De Animâ Corpori coextensâ;" printed at Paris, 1665. See also "Hobokenius de Sede Animæ in Corpore Humano." *Ed.*

[d] The text is indistinct. We are not told whether the faculties here enumerated belong to the produced or to the rational soul. Though from the language of the text, and the order of inquiry, the former appears to be the most probable opinion: yet we do not see how the origin of conscience to which they refer can be physically treated, or how the same substance can unite appetite, and the principle to which it is almost invariably opposed. To obviate such difficulties, Aristotle and Plato made a similar distinction between the rational and the sensitive principle in man, and assigned reason, imagination, and memory to the one, while they restricted appetite and sensational feeling to the other. Bacon, however, seems to place all these faculties in the sensitive soul, and leaves the inspired substance a mere breath or aura, without either faculties or functions. By thus implying the cogitative power of matter, he has in some measure countenanced the dangerous belief of the corruptibility of the human soul and its expiration with the body; at least, sceptics have not been slow in putting this interpretation upon his doctrine. *Ed.*

assistance of signs. Artificial divination is of two kinds,—
one arguing from causes, the other only from experiments
conducted by blind authority. The latter is generally superstitious. Such were the heathen doctrines about the inspection of entrails, the flight of birds, &c.; and the formal astrology of the Chaldeans was little better. Both kinds of
artificial divination spread themselves into various sciences.
The astrologer has his predictions from the aspects of the
stars; the physician, too, has his, as to death, recovery, and
the subsequent symptoms of diseases, from the urine, pulse,
aspect of the patient, &c.; the politician also is not without
his predictions,—" O urbem venalem, et cito perituram si
emptorem invenerit!"[e]—the event of which prophecy happened soon after, and was first accomplished in Sylla and
again in Cæsar. But the predictions of this kind being not
to our present purpose, we refer them to their proper arts,
and shall here only treat of natural divination, proceeding
from the internal power of the soul.

This also is of two kinds,—the one native, the other by
influx. The native rests upon this supposition, that the
mind abstracted or collected in itself, and not diffused in the
organs of the body, has from the natural power of its own
essence some foreknowledge of future things; and this appears chiefly in sleep, ecstasies, and the near approach of
death; but more rarely in waking, or when the body is in
health and strength. And this state of the mind is commonly procured or promoted by abstinence, and principally
such things as withdraw the mind from exercising the functions of the body, that it may thus enjoy its own nature
without any external interruption. But divination by influx
is grounded upon another supposition, viz., that the mind,
as a mirror, may receive a secondary illumination from the
foreknowledge of God and spirits, whereto likewise the above-
mentioned state and regimen of the body are conducive.
For the same abstraction of the mind causes it more powerfully to use its own nature, and renders it more susceptive
of divine influxes, only in divinations by influx the soul is
seized with a kind of rapture, and as it were impatience of

---

[e] "O city set to sale, whose destruction is at hand, if it find
a purchaser!" uttered by Jugurtha, on leaving Rome. Sallust's
Jugurtha, 35.

the Deity's presence, which the ancients called by the name of sacred fury, whereas in native divination the soul is rather at its ease and free.

Fascination is the power and intense act of the imagination upon the body of another. And here the school of Paracelsus, and the pretenders to natural magic, abusively so called, have almost made the force and apprehension of the imagination equal to the power of faith, and capable of working miracles; others keeping nearer to truth, and attentively considering the secret energies and impressions of things, the irradiations of the senses, the transmissions of thought from one to another, and the conveyances of magnetic virtues, are of opinion that impressions, conveyances, and communications, might be made from spirit to spirit, because spirit is of all things the most powerful in operation and easiest to work on; whence many opinions have spread abroad of master spirits, of men ominous and unlucky, of the strokes of love, envy, and the like. And this is attended with the inquiry, how the imagination may be heightened and fortified; for if a strong imagination has such power, it is worth knowing by what means to exalt and raise it.[f]

But here a palliative or defence of a great part of ceremonial magic would slily and indirectly insinuate itself, under a specious pretence that ceremonies, characters, charms, gesticulations, amulets, and the like, have not their power from any tacit or binding contract with evil spirits, but that these serve only to strengthen and raise the imagination of such as use them, in the same manner as images have prevailed in religion for fixing men's minds in the contemplation of things and raising the devotion in prayer. But allowing the force of imagination to be great, and that ceremonies do raise and strengthen it; allowing also, that ceremonies may be sincerely used to that end, as a physical remedy, without the least design of thereby procuring the assistance of spirits; yet ought they still to be held unlawful,

---

[f] The ways of working upon or with the imagination, are touched by the author, in his "Sylva Sylvarum," under the article Imagination. See more to this purpose in "Des Cartes upon the Passions," "Casaubon upon Enthusiasm," Father Malbranche's "Recherche de la Vérité," and Lord Shaftesbury's "Letter upon Enthusiasm." *Shaw.*

because they oppose and contradict that Divine sentence passed upon man for sin: "In the sweat of thy brow thou shalt eat thy bread." For this kind of magic offers those excellent fruits which God had ordained should be procured by labour at the price of a few easy and slight observances.

There are two other doctrines which principally regard the faculties of the inferior or sensitive soul, as chiefly communicating with the organs of the body,—the one is of voluntary motion, the other of sense and sensibility. The former has been but superficially inquired into, and one entire part of it is almost wholly neglected. The office and proper structure of the nerves, muscles, &c., requisite to muscular motion, what parts of the body rest while others move, and how the imagination acts as director of this motion, so far that when it drops the image whereto the motion tended, the motion itself presently ceases,—as in walking, if another serious thought come across our mind, we presently stand still; with many other such subtilties, have long ago been observed and scrutinized. But how the compressions, dilatations, and agitations of the spirit, which, doubtless, is the spring of motion, should guide and rule the corporeal and gross mass of the parts, has not yet been diligently searched into and treated. And no wonder, since the sensitive soul itself has been hitherto taken for a principle of motion and a function, rather than a substance.[g] But as

[g] The original is, *pro entelechia et functione quadam*, alluding to the technical term entelechy, which Aristotle introduced into his Physics (iii. 1) to denote the act through which any substance exercises its power. The rational soul was never taken in the sense of a simple act, or entelechy, as Bacon would insinuate, but was affirmed even by Aristotle, who introduced the phrase, to be a certain power apart and distinguished from the rest of the human system, as the eternal is distinguishable from the incorruptible. His words are: περὶ δὲ τοῦ νοῦ καὶ τῆς θεωρητικῆς δυνάμεως οὐδέπω φανερόν. Ἀλλ' ἔοικε ψυχῆς γένος ἕτερον εἶναι, καὶ τοῦτο μόνον ἐνδέχεται χωρίζεσθαι καθάπερ ἀΐδιον τοῦ φθαρτοῦ (Arist. De An. ii. 2); and as this power is not a simple act, but the effect of a vital substance, possessing the principle of activity virtually in itself, he implies its capability to communicate motion to surrounding bodies even in a state of immobility; ἴσως γὰρ οὐ μόνον ψεῦδός ἐστι τὸ τὴν οὐσίαν αὐτῆς τοι αὐτὴν εἶναι οἷαν φασίν οἱ λέγοντες εἶναι τὴν ψυχὴν τὸ κινοῦν αὐτὸ ἢ δυνάμενον κινεῖν· ἀλλ' ἔν τι τῶν ἀδυνάτων τὸ ὑπάρχειν αὐτῇ κίνησιν. (Arist. ibid. iii. 1.) With regard to the precise meaning of the word entelechy there have been many disputes among the learned. The origin of the term ought to be allowed

it is now known to be material, it becomes necessary to inquire by what efforts so subtile and minute a breath can put such gross and solid bodies in motion. Therefore, as this part is deficient, let due inquiry be made concerning it.

Sense and sensibility have been much more fully and diligently inquired into, as well in general treatises upon the subject as in particular arts; viz., perspective, music, &c.; but how justly, is not to the present intention. And, therefore, we cannot note them as deficient; yet there are two excellent parts wanting in this doctrine: one upon the difference of perception and sense, and the other upon the form of light. In treating of sense and sensibility, philosophers should have premised the difference between perception and sense, as the foundation of the whole: for we find there is a manifest power of perception in most natural bodies, and a kind of appetite to choose what is agreeable, and to avoid what is disagreeable to them. Nor is this meant of the more subtile perceptions only; as when the loadstone attracts iron, or flame flies to petreol, or one drop of water runs into another; or when the rays of light are reflected from a white object, or when animal bodies assimilate what is proper for them, and reject what is hurtful; or when a sponge attracts water, and expels air, &c.; for in all cases, no one body placed near to another can change that other, or be changed by it, unless a reciprocal perception precede the operation. A body always perceives the passages by which it insinuates; feels the impulse of another body, where it yields thereto; perceives the removal of any body that with-

---

to indicate its signification; but Aristotle used it in distinct senses, as signifying not only a simple act or function of an unsubstantial quality, but also as the act of a substantial power; and his followers have never hit upon a generic term capable of uniting the two notions. Many have abandoned it as untranslatable. Budæus uses the word efficacia; Cicero paraphrases it as a certain continuous and eternal motion (Tusc. i. 10), which only implies the motion of unsubstantial qualities, to which Bacon confined it. This signification, however, was but the exceptional use of the term, and does not coincide with the general applications of it in the Greek schools. Hermonlaus Barbarus is said to have been so much oppressed with this difficulty of translation, that he consulted the evil spirit by night, entreating to be supplied with a more common and familiar substitute for this word; the mocking fiend, however, suggested only a word equally obscure, and the translator discontented with this, invented for himself the word perfectibilia. *Ed.*

held it, and thereupon recovers itself; perceives the separation of its continuity, and for a time resists it; in fine, perception is diffused through all nature. But air has such an acute perception of heat and cold, as far exceeds the human touch, which yet passes for the measure of heat and cold. This doctrine, therefore, has two defects: one, in that men have generally passed it over untouched, though a noble subject; the other, that they who did attend to it have gone too far, attributed sense to all bodies, and made it almost a sin to pluck a twig from a tree, lest the tree should groan, like Polydorus in Virgil.[h] But they ought carefully to have searched after the difference betwixt perception and sense; not only in comparing sensible with insensible things, in the entire bodies thereof, as those of plants and animals, but also to have observed in the sensible body itself, what should be the cause that so many actions are performed without any sense at all. Why the aliments are digested and discharged, the humours and juices carried up and down in the body; why the heart and pulse beat; why the viscera act as so many workshops, and each performs its respective office; yet all this, and much more, be done without sense. But men have not yet sufficiently found of what nature the action of sense is, and what kind of body, what continuance, what repetitions of the impression are required to cause pain or pleasure. Lastly, they seem totally ignorant of the difference between simple perception and sense, and how far perception may be caused without sense. Nor is this a controversy about words, but a matter of great importance. Wherefore let this doctrine be better examined, as a thing of capital, and very extensive use: for the ignorance of some ancient philosophers in this point, so far obscured the light of reason, that they thought there was a soul indifferently infused into all bodies; nor did they conceive how motion of election could be caused without sense, or sense exist without a soul.

That the form of light should not have been duly inquired into, appears a strange oversight, especially as men have bestowed so much pains upon perspective: for neither has this art, nor others, afforded any valuable discovery in the subject

---

- Virg. Æneid, iii.

of light. Its radiations, indeed, are treated, but not its origin; and the ranking of perspective with mathematics has produced this defect, with others of the like nature, because philosophy is thus deserted too soon. Again, the doctrine of light, and the causes thereof, have been almost superstitiously treated in physics, as a subject of a middle nature, betwixt natural and divine; whence certain Platonists would have light prior to matter itself: for they vainly imagined, that space was first filled with light, and afterwards with body; but the Scriptures plainly say, that the mass of heaven and earth was dark before the creation of light. And as for what is physically delivered upon this subject, and according to sense, it presently descends to radiations, so that very little philosophical inquiry is extant about it. And men ought here to lower their contemplations a little, and inquire into the properties common to all lucid bodies, as this relates to the form of light; how immensely soever the bodies concerned may differ in dignity, as the sun does from rotten wood, or putrefied fish. We should likewise inquire the cause why some things take fire, and when heated throw out light; and others not. Iron, metal, stones, glass, wood, oil, tallow, by fire yield either a flame, or grow red-hot. But water and air, exposed to the most intense heat they are capable of, afford no light, nor so much as shine. That it is not the property of fire alone to give light; and that water and air are not utter enemies thereto, appears from the dashing of salt-water in a dark night, and a hot season, when the small drops of the water, struck off by the motion of the oars in rowing, seem sparkling and luminous. We have the same appearance in the agitated froth of the sea, called sea-lungs. And, indeed, it should be inquired what affinity flame and ignited bodies have with glow-worms, the Luciola, the Indian fly, which casts a light over a whole room; the eyes of certain creatures in the dark; loaf-sugar in scraping or breaking; the sweat of a horse hard ridden, &c. Men have understood so little of this matter, that most imagine the sparks, struck betwixt a flint and steel, to be air in attrition. But since the air ignites not with heat, yet apparently conceives light, whence owls, cats, and many other creatures see in the night (for there is no vision without light), there must be a native light in air; which, though weak and feeble, is proportioned to the visual organs of such creatures, so as to suffice them for sight. The error, as in most other cases, lies here, that men have not deduced the common forms of things from particular instances, which is what we make the proper business of metaphysics. Therefore let inquiry be made into the form and origins of light; and, in the mean time, we set it down as deficient. And so much for the doctrine of the substance of the soul, both rational and sensitive, with its faculties, and the appendages of this doctrine.

FIFTH BOOK.

CHAPTER I.

Division of the Use and Objects of the Faculties of the Soul into Logic and Ethics. Division of Logic into the Arts of Invention, Judgment, Memory, and Tradition.

THE doctrine of the human understanding, and of the human will, excellent king, are like twins; for the purity of illumination, and the freedom of will, began and fell together: nor is there in the universe so intimate a sympathy, as that betwixt truth and goodness. The more shame for men of learning, if in knowledge they are like the winged angels, but in affections like the crawling serpents, having their minds indeed like a mirror; but a mirror foully spotted.

The doctrine of the use and objects of the mental faculties has two parts, well known and generally received; viz., logic and ethics. Logic treats of the understanding and reason, and ethics of the will, appetite, and affections; the one producing resolutions, the other actions. The imagination, indeed, on both sides, performs the office of agent, or ambassador, and assists alike in the judicial and ministerial capacity. Sense commits all sorts of notions to the imagination, and the reason afterwards judges of them. In like manner reason transmits select and approved notions to the imagination before the decree is executed: for imagination always precedes and excites voluntary motion, and is therefore a common instrument both to the reason and the will, only it has two faces: that turned towards reason bearing the effigy of truth; but that towards action the effigy of goodness: yet they are faces:—

—— " quales decet esse sororum."[a]

But the imagination is more than a mere messenger; as being invested with, or, at least, usurping no small authority, besides delivering the message. Thus, Aristotle well observes, that the mind has the same command over the body, as the master over the slave; but reason over the imagination, the same that a magistrate has over a free citizen, who may come to rule in his turn.[b] For in matters of faith and religion, the imagination mounts above reason. Not that divine illumination is seated in the imagination, but, as in divine virtues, grace makes use of the motions of the will; so in illumination it makes use of the motions of the imagination; whence religion solicits access to the mind, by similitudes, types, parables, dreams, and visions. Again, the imagination has a considerable sway in persuasion, insinuated by the power of eloquence: for when the mind is soothed, enraged, or any way drawn aside by the artifice of speech, all this is done by raising the imagination; which, now growing unruly, not only insults over, but, in a manner, offers violence to reason, partly by blinding, partly by incensing it. Yet there appears no cause why we should quit our former division: for in general, the imagination does not make the sciences; since even poetry, which has been always attributed to the imagination, should be esteemed rather a play of wit than a science. As for the power of the imagination in natural things, we have already ranged it under the doctrine of the soul; and for its affinity with rhetoric, we refer it to the art of rhetoric.

This part of human philosophy which regards logic, is disagreeable to the taste of many, as appearing to them no other than a net, and a snare of thorny subtilty. For as knowledge is justly called the food of the mind, so in the desire and choice of this food, most men have the appetite

---

[a] Ovid, Metam. ii. 14.   [b] Aristotle's Politics, i. 5, 6.

of the Israelites in the wilderness, who, weary of manna, as a thin though celestial diet, would have gladly returned to the fleshpots: thus generally those sciences relish best that are subjective, and nearer related to flesh and blood; as civil history, morality, politics, whereon men's affections, praises, and fortunes turn, and are employed, whilst the other dry light offends, and dries up the soft and humid capacities of most men. But if we would rate things according to their real worth, the rational sciences are the keys to all the rest; for as the hand is the instrument of instruments, and the mind the form of forms, so the rational sciences are to be esteemed the art of arts. Nor do they direct only, but also strengthen and confirm; as the use and habit of shooting not only enables one to shoot nearer the mark, but likewise to draw a stronger bow.

The logical arts are four, being divided according to the ends they lead to: for in rational knowledge man endeavours, 1. either to find what he seeks; 2. to judge of what he finds; 3. to retain what he has approved; or 4. to deliver what he has retained: whence there are as many rational arts; viz., 1. the art of inquiry or invention; 2. the art of examination or judging; 3. the art of custody or memory; and 4. the art of elocution or delivery.

CHAPTER II.

Division of Invention into the Invention of Arts and Arguments. The former, though the more important of them, is wanting. Division of the Invention of Arts into Literate (Instructed) Experience and a New Method (Novum Organum). An Illustration of Literate Experience.

INVENTION is of two very different kinds: the one of arts and sciences, the other of arguments and discourse. The former I set down as absolutely deficient. And this deficiency appears like that, when, in taking the inventory of an estate, there is set down, in cash, nothing: for as ready money will purchase all other commodities, so this art, if extant, would procure all other arts. And as the immense regions of the West Indies had never been discovered, if the use of the compass had not first been known, it is no wonder that the discovery and advancement of arts hath made no greater progress, when the art of inventing and discovering the sciences remains hitherto unknown. That this part of knowledge is wanting, seems clear: for logic professes not, nor pretends to invent, either mechanical or liberal arts, nor to deduce the operations of the one, or the axioms of the other; but only leaves us this instruction in passage, to believe every artist in his own art.[a] Celsus, a wise man, as well as a physician, speaking of the empirical and dogmatical sects of physicians, gravely and ingenuously acknowledges, that medicines and cures were first discovered, and the reasons and causes of them discoursed afterwards,[b] not that causes, first derived from the nature of things, gave light to the invention of cures and remedies. And Plato, more than once, observes, that particulars are infinite, that the highest generalities give no certain directions; and, therefore, that the marrow of all sciences, whereby the artist is distinguished from the unskilful workman, consists in middle propositions, which experience has delivered and taught in each particular science.[c] Hence those who write upon the first inventors of things, and the origin of the sciences, rather celebrate chance than art, and bring in beasts, birds, fishes, and serpents, rather than men, as the first teachers of arts.

> "Dictamnum genitrix Cretæa carpit ab Ida,
> Puberibus caulem foliis, et flore comantem
> Purpureo: non illa feris incognita capris
> Gramina, cum tergo volucres hæsere sagittæ."[d]

No wonder, therefore, as the manner of antiquity was to consecrate the inventors of useful things, that the Egyptians, an ancient nation, to which many arts owe their rise, had their temples filled with the images of brutes, and but a few human idols amongst them.

> "Omnigenûmque Deûm monstra et lator Anubis
> Contra Neptunum et Venerem, contraque Minervam."[e]

And if we should, according to the traditions of the Greeks, ascribe the first invention of arts to men, yet we cannot say that Prometheus studied the invention of fire; or that when

---

[a] See Whately's Intro. § 5, b. iii. (on Fallacies) § 2, and b. iv.; also Arist. Eth. Mag. i. 1-17.   [b] Re Medica, i. 3.
[c] The Timæus.   [d] Æneid. xii. 412.   [e] Æneid. viii. 698.

he first struck the flint he expected sparks, but that he fell upon it by accident, and, as the poets say, stole it from Jupiter. So that as to the invention of arts, we are rather beholden to the wild goat for chirurgery, to the nightingale for music, to the stork for glysters, to the accidental flying off of a pot's cover for artillery, and, in a word, to chance, or anything else, rather than to logic. Nor does the manner of invention, described by Virgil, differ much from the former; viz., that practice and intent thought by degrees struck out various arts.

> " Ut varias usus meditando extunderet artes
> Paulatim."[f]

For this is no other than what brutes are capable of, and frequently practise; viz., an intent solicitude about some one thing, and a perpetual exercise thereof, which the necessity of their preservation imposes upon them; for Cicero truly observed, that practice applied wholly to one thing, often conquers both nature and art:—" Usus uni rei deditus, et naturam et artem sæpe vincit."[g] And therefore, if it may be said with regard to men, that continued labour and cogent necessity master everything,

> —— " Labor omnia vincit
> Improbus, et duris urgens in rebus egestas;"[h]—

so it may be asked with regard to brutes, who taught them instinct,

> " Quis expedivit Psittaco suum Χαῖρε?"[i]

Who taught the raven, in a drought, to drop pebbles into a hollow tree, where she chanced to spy water, that the water might rise for her to drink? Who taught the bee to sail through the vast ocean of air, to distant fields, and find the way back to her hive?[k] Who taught the ant to gnaw every grain of corn that she hoards, to prevent its sprouting? And if we observe in Virgil the word extundere, which implies difficulty, and the word paulatim, which imports slowness, this brings us back to the case of the Egyptian gods; since men have hitherto made little use of their rational faculties, and none at all of art, in the investigation of things.

[f] Georg. i. 133. [g] Oratio pro L. Cor. Balbo, xx.
[h] Virg. Georg. i. 145. [i] Perseus, Prol. 8.
[k] Pliny's Natural History.

And this assertion, if carefully attended to, is proved from the form of logical induction, for finding and examining the principles of the sciences; which form being absolutely defective and insufficient, is so far from perfecting nature, that it perverts and distorts her. For whoever attentively observes how the ethereal dew of the sciences, like that of which the poet speaks,

"Aërii mellis cœlestia dona,"[1]

is gathered (the sciences being extracted from particular examples, whether natural or artificial, as from so many flowers), will find that the mind of its own natural motion makes a better induction than that described by logicians. From a bare enumeration of particulars in the logical manner, where there is no contradictory instance, follows a false conclusion; nor does such an induction infer anything more than probable conjecture. For who will undertake, when the particulars of a man's own knowledge or memory appear only on one side, that something directly opposite shall not lie concealed on the other? as if Samuel should have taken up with the sons of Jesse brought before him, and not have sought David, who was in the field. And to say the truth, as this form of induction is so gross and stupid, it might seem incredible that such acute and subtile geniuses as have been exercised this way, could ever have obtruded it upon the world, but that they hasted to theories and opinions, and, as it were, disdained to dwell upon particulars; for they have used examples and particular instances but as whifflers to keep the crowd off and make room for their own opinions, without consulting them from the beginning, so as to make a just and mature judgment of the truth of things. And this procedure has, indeed, struck me with an awful and religious wonder, to see men tread the same paths of error, both in divine and human inquiries. For as in receiving divine truths men are averse to become as little children, so in the apprehending of human truths, for men to begin to read, and, like children, come back again to the first elements of induction, is reputed a low and contemptible thing.

But, allowing the principles of the sciences might be justly

[1] Virgil, Georg. iv. 1.

formed by the common induction, or by sense and experience, yet it is certain that the lower axioms cannot, in natural things, be with certainty deduced by syllogism from them. For syllogism reduces propositions to principles by intermediate propositions. And this form, whether of invention or proof, has place in the popular sciences, as ethics, politics, law, &c., and even in divinity, since God has been pleased to accommodate himself to the human capacity; but in physics, where nature is to be caught by works, and not the adversary by argument, truth in this way slips through our fingers, because the subtilty of the operations of nature far exceeds the subtilty of words. So that syllogism thus failing, there is everywhere a necessity for employing a genuine and correct induction, as well in the more general principles, as the inferior propositions. For syllogisms consist of propositions, propositions of words, but words are the signs of notions; wherefore if these notions, which are the souls of words, be unjustly and unsteadily abstracted from things, the whole structure must fall. Nor can any laborious subsequent examination of the consequences of arguments, or the truth of propositions, ever repair the ruin; for the error lies in the first digestion, which cannot be rectified by the secondary functions of nature.

It was not, therefore, without cause, that many of the ancient philosophers, and some of them eminent in their way, became academics and sceptics, who denied all certainty of human knowledge, and held that the understanding went no further than appearance and probability. It is true, some are of opinion that Socrates, when he declared himself certain of nothing, did it only in the way of irony, and put on the dissimulation of knowledge, that by renouncing what he certainly knew, he might be thought to know what he was ignorant of. Nor in the latter academy, which Cicero followed, was this opinion held with much reality; but those who excelled in eloquence, commonly chose this sect as the fittest for their purpose, viz., acquiring the reputation of disputing copiously on both sides of the question, thus leaving the high road of truth for private walks of pleasure. Yet it is certain there were some few, both in the old and new academies, but more among the Sceptics, who held this principle of doubting in simplicity and sincerity of heart.

But their chief error lay in accusing the perceptions of the senses, and thus plucked up the sciences by their roots. For though the senses often deceive or fail us, yet, when industriously assisted, they may suffice for the sciences, and this not so much by the help of instruments, which also have their use, as of such experiments, as may furnish more subtile objects than are perceivable by sense. But they should rather have charged the defects of this kind upon the errors and obstinacy of the mind, which refuses to obey the nature of things; and again, upon corrupt demonstrations, and wrong ways of arguing and concluding, erroneously inferred from the perceptions of sense. And this we say, not to detract from the human mind, or as if the work were to be deserted, but that proper assistances may be procured and administered to the understanding, whereby to conquer the difficulties of things and the obscurities of nature. What we endeavour is, that the mind, by the help of art, may become equal to things, and to find a certain art of indication or direction, to disclose and bring other arts to light, together with their axioms and effects. And this art we, upon just ground, report as deficient.

This art of indication has two parts; for indication proceeds, 1. from experiment to experiment; or 2. from experiments to axioms, which may again point out new experiments. The former we call learned experience, and the latter the interpretation of nature, Novum Organum, or new machine for the mind. The first, indeed, as was formerly intimated, is not properly an art, or any part of philosophy, but a kind of sagacity; whence we sometimes call it the chase of Pan, borrowing the name from the fable of that god. And as there are three ways of walking, viz., either by feeling out one's way in the dark; or 2. when being dimsighted, another leads one by the hand; and 3. by directing one's steps by a light: so when a man tries all kinds of experiments without method or order, this is mere groping in the dark; but when he proceeds with some direction and order in his experiments, it is as if he were led by the hand; and this we understand by learned experience: but for the light itself, which is the third way, it must be derived from the Novum Organum.

The design of learned experience, or the chase of Pan, is

to show the various ways of making experiments; and as we note it for deficient, and the thing itself is none of the clearest, we will here give some short sketch of the work. The manner of experimenting chiefly consists in the variation, production, translation, inversion, compulsion, application, conjunction, or any other manner of diversifying, or making chance experiments. And all this lies without the limits of any axiom of invention; but the interpretation of nature takes in all the transitions of experiments into axioms, and of axioms into experiments.

Experiments are varied first in the subject, as when a known experiment, having rested in one certain substance, is tried in another of the like kind; thus the making of paper is hitherto confined to linen, and not applied to silk, unless among the Chinese,[d] nor to hair-stuffs and camblets, nor to cotton and skins; though these three seem to be more unfit for the purpose, and so should be tried in mixture rather than separate. Again, engrafting is practised in fruit-trees, but rarely in wild ones; yet an elm grafted upon an elm is said to produce great foliage for shade. Incision likewise in flowers is very rare, though now the experiment begins to be made upon musk-roses, which are successfully inoculated upon common ones. We also place the variations on the side of the thing among the variations in the matter. Thus we see a scion grafted upon the trunk of a tree thrives better than if set in earth; and why should not onion-seed set in a green onion grow better than when sown in the ground by itself, a root being here substituted for the trunk, so as to make a kind of incision in the root?

An experiment may be varied in the efficient. Thus, as the sun's rays are so contracted by a burning-glass, and heightened to such a degree as to fire any combustible matter, may not the rays of the moon, by the same means, be actuated to some small degree of warmth, so as to show whether all the heavenly bodies are potentially hot? and as luminous heats are thus increased by glasses, may not opaque heats, as of stones and metals, before ignition, be increased likewise, or is there not some proportion of light here also?

---

[m] The Chinese also manufacture their paper out of the interior bark of cane. *Ed.*

Amber and jet, chafed, attract straws, whence query, if they will not do the same when warmed at the fire?

An experiment may be varied in quantity, wherein very great care is required, as being subject to various errors. For men imagine, that upon increasing the quantity the virtue should increase proportionably; and this they commonly postulate as a mathematical certainty, and yet it is utterly false. Suppose a leaden ball of a pound weight, let fall from a steeple, reaches the earth in ten seconds, will a ball of two pounds, where the power of natural motion, as they call it, should be double, reach it in five? No, they will fall almost in equal times, and not be accelerated according to quantity.[n] Suppose a drachm of sulphur would liquefy half a pound of steel, will, therefore, an ounce of sulphur liquefy four pounds of steel? It does not follow; for the stubbornness of the matter in the patient is more increased by quantity than the activity of the agent.[o] Besides, too much as well as too little may frustrate the effect,—thus, in smelting and refining of metals it is a common error to increase the heat of the furnace or the quantity of the flux; but if these exceed a due proportion, they prejudice the operation, because by their force and corrosiveness they turn much of the pure metal into fumes, and carry it off, whence there ensues not only a loss in the metal, but the remaining mass becomes more sluggish and intractable. Men should therefore remember how Æsop's housewife was deceived, who expected that by doubling her feed her hen should lay two eggs a day; but the hen grew fat, and laid none. It is absolutely unsafe to rely upon any natural experiment before proof be made of it, both in a less and a larger quantity.

[n] Because its surface in relation to its solidity is less than the first fall, and consequently encounters less resistance from the air, with respect to the entire quantity of its motion. *Ed.*

[o] This only happens when the increased content is attended with augmentation of surface. It may be accepted as a principle, that bodies are exposed to the action of external agents in proportion as their surface is extended, an increased size presenting a greater quantity of pores, through which the agent may insinuate itself. As surfaces are only as the squares of their diameters, and the contents increase in the ratio of the cubes of their diameters, it follows that, in the same subject matter, those bodies are more extended in relation to their solidity, which have less bulk, and consequently more liable to the action of external bodies, as Bacon remarks. *Ed.*

An experiment is produced two ways; viz., by repetition and extension, the experiment being either repeated or urged to a more subtile thing. It may serve for an example of repetition, that spirit of wine is made of wine by one distillation, and thus becomes much stronger and more acrid than the wine itself,—will likewise spirit of wine proportionally exceed itself in strength by another distillation? But the repetition also of experiments may deceive; thus here the second exaltation does not equal the excess of the first; and frequently, by repeating an experiment after a certain pitch is obtained, nature is so far from going farther, that she rather falls back. Judgment, therefore, must be used in this affair. So quicksilver put into melted lead, when it begins to grow cold, will be arrested, and remain no longer fluid; but will the same quicksilver, often served so, become fixed and malleable?

For an example of extension, water made pendulous above, by means of a long glass stem, and dipped into a mixture of wine and water, will separate the water from the wine, the wine gently rising to the top, and the water descending and settling at the bottom. Now, as wine and water, being two different bodies, are separable by this contrivance, may likewise the more subtile parts of wine, which is an entire body, be separated from the more gross by this kind of distillation, performed as it were by gravity, so as to have floating a-top a liquor like spirit of wine, or perhaps more subtile? Again, the loadstone draws iron in substance, but will loadstone plunged into a solution of iron attract the iron and cover itself with it? So the magnetic needle applies to the poles of the world; but does it do this after the same course and order that the celestial bodies move? Suppose the needle held at the south point, and then let go, would it now turn to the north by the west or east?[p] Thus gold imbibes quicksilver contiguous to it; but does the gold do this without increasing its own bulk, so as to become a mass specifically heavier than gold? Thus men help their memories by setting up pictures of persons in certain places; but would

---

[p] This question is impossible to decide, as we are never certain at the moment of the experiment that the needle has not been deflected from the south point, and the slightest imperceptible degree, too fine for human instrument to discover, would render the trial nugatory. *Ed.*

they obtain the same end if, neglecting their faces, they only imagined the actions or habits of the persons?

An experiment may be transferred three ways; viz., By nature or chance into an art; 2. from one art or practice to another; and, 3. from one part of an art to another. There are innumerable examples of the transferring of experiments from nature or chance to arts, as nearly all the mechanical arts owe their origins to slender beginnings afforded by nature or accident. It is authorized by a proverb, that grapes among grapes ripen sooner. And our cyder-makers observe the rule; for they do not stamp and press their apples without laying them on heaps for a time, to ripen by mutual contact, whereby the liquor is prevented from being too tart. So the making of artificial rainbows by the thick sprinkling of little drops of water, is an easy translation from natural rainbows made in a rainy cloud. So the art of distillation might be taken either from the falling of rain and dew, or that homely experiment of boiling water, where drops adhere to the cover of the vessel. Mankind might have been afraid to imitate thunder and lightning by the invention of great guns, had not the chemical monk received the first hint of it by the impetuous discharge and loud report of the cover of his vessel. But if mankind were desirous to search after useful things, they ought attentively, minutely, and on set purpose, to view the workmanship and particular operations of nature, and be continually examining and casting about which of them may be transferred to arts; for nature is the mirror of art.

Nor are there fewer experiments transferable from one art or practice to another, though this be rarely used. For nature lies everywhere obvious to us all, though particular arts are only known to particular artists. Spectacles were invented for weak sights,—might not, therefore, an instrument be discovered that applied to the ears should help the hearing? Embalming preserves dead bodies,—could not, therefore, something or like kind be transferred to medicine, for the preservation of live ones? So the practice of sealing in wax, cements, and lead, is ancient, and paved the way to the printing on paper, or the art of the press. So in cookery, salt preserves meats better in winter than in summer,— might not this be usefully transferred to baths, and the occasional regulation of their temperature? So by late experience salt is found of great efficacy in condensing, by the way of artificial freezing,—might not this be transferred to the condensing of metals, since it is found that the aquæ-fortes, composed of salts, dissolve particles of gold out of some lighter metals? So painting refreshes the memory by the image of a thing; and is not this transferred in what they call the art of memory? And let it be observed, in general, that nothing is of greater efficacy in procuring a stock of new and useful inventions, than to have the experiments of numerous mechanic arts known to a single person, or to a few, who might mutually improve each other by conversation; so that by this translation of experiments arts might mutually warm and light up each other, as it were, by an intermixture of rays. For although the rational way, by means of a new machine for the mind, promises much greater things; yet this sagacity, or learned experience, will in the mean time scatter among mankind many matters, which, as so many missive donatives among the ancients, are near at hand.

The transferring of experiments from one part of an art to another differs little from the transferring one art to another. But because some arts are so extensive as to allow of the translation of experiments within themselves, it is proper to mention this kind also, especially as it is of very great moment in some particular arts. Thus it greatly contributes to enlarge the art of medicine to have the experiments of that part which treats of the cures of diseases, transferred to those parts which relate to the preservation of health and the prolongation of life. For if any famous opiate should, in a pestilential distemper, suppress the violent inflammation of the spirits, it might thence seem probable that something of the same kind, rendered familiar by a due dose, might in good measure check that wasting inflammation which steals on with age.

An experiment is inverted when the contrary of what the experiment shows is proved; for example, heat is increased by burning-glasses; but may cold be so too? So heat in diffusing itself rather mounts upwards, but cold in diffusing itself rather moves downwards. Thus, if an iron rod be heated at one end, then erected upon its heated end, and the hand be applied to the upper part of the rod, the hand will presently be burnt; but if the heated end be placed upward and the hand applied below, it will be burnt much slower. But if the whole rod were heated, and one end of it wet with snow or a sponge dipped in cold water, would the cold be sooner propagated downwards than upwards if the sponge were applied below? Again, the rays of the sun are reflected from a white body, but absorbed by a black one. Are shadows also scattered by black and collected by white bodies? We see in a dark place, where light comes in only at a small hole, the images of external objects are received upon white paper, but not upon black.

An experiment is compelled where it is urged or produced to the annihilation or destruction of the power, the prey being only caught in the other chases, but killed in this. Thus the loadstone attracts iron,—urge, therefore, the iron, or urge the loadstone, till they attract no longer; for example, if the loadstone were burnt, or steeped in aquafortis, would it entirely, or only in part, lose its virtue? So if iron were reduced to a crocus, or made into prepared steel, as they call it, or dissolved in aquafortis, would the loadstone still attract it? The magnet draws iron through all known mediums,—gold, silver, glass, &c. Urge the medium, therefore, and, if possible, find out one that intercepts the virtue. Thus make trial of quicksilver, oil, gums, ignited gold, and such things as have not yet been tried. Again, microscopes have been lately introduced which strangely magnify minute objects; urge the use of them, either by applying them to objects so small that their power is lost, or so large till it is confounded. Thus, for example, can microscopes clearly discover those things in urine which are not otherwise perceptible? Can they discover any specks or clouds in gems that are perfectly clear and bright to appearance? Can they magnify the motes of the sun, which Democritus mistook for atoms and the principles of things?[a] Will they show a mixed powder of vermilion and ceruse in distinct grains of red and white? Will they magnify larger objects,—as the face, the eye, &c.,—as much as they do a gnat or a mite, or represent a piece of fine linen open as a net? But we need

---

[a] Epistles of Hippocrates, or Pliny's Nat. History.

not insist longer on compulsory experiments, as they do not justly come within the limits of literate experience, but are rather referred to axioms, causes, and the New Organum.

The application of an experiment is no more than an ingenious translation of it to some other experiment of use; for example, all bodies have their own dimensions and gravities. Gold has more gravity and less bulk than silver, and water than wine,—hence an useful experiment is derived for discovering what proportion of silver is mixed with gold, or of water with wine, from a knowledge of their measure and weight, which was the grand discovery of Archimedes.[1] Again, as flesh putrefies sooner in some cellars than in others, it were useful to transfer this experiment to the examination of airs, as to their being more or less wholesome to live in, by finding those wherein flesh remains longest unputrefied; and the same experiment is applicable to discover the more wholesome or pestilential seasons of the year. But examples of this kind are endless, and require that men should have their eyes continually turned one while to the nature of things and another while to human uses.

The conjunction of an experiment is a connection and chain of applications, when those things which were not useful single, are made useful by connection; for example, to have roses or fruits come late, the way is to pluck off the early buds, or to lay bare the roots and expose them to the open air, towards the middle of spring; but it is much better to do both together. So ice and nitre separate have a great power of cooling, but a much greater when mixed together. But there may be a fallacy in this obvious affair, as in all cases where axioms are wanting, if the conjunction be made in things that operate by different and, as it were, contrary ways.[2]

---

[1] The means that Bacon proposes, and to which the chemists still adhere, is the reverse of that of Archimedes. The ancient compared, in his experiment, three bodies of the same weight, but of different volume, while the text advises three bodies of the same volume, but of different weight. This reversion, however, does not affect the result. *Ed.*

[2] Such are the compounds of very active substances, which chemists designate neuter: for example, the greater part of salts, as nitre, sea-salt, the salt of Glauber, and generally all those substances composed of an acid united to an alkaline or earthy base. *Ed.*

As for chance experiments, these are plainly an irrational and wild procedure, when the mind suggests the trial of a thing, not because any reason or experiment persuades it, but only because nothing of the kind has been tried before; yet even here, perhaps, some considerable mystery lies concealed, provided no stone in nature were left unturned; for the capital things of nature generally lie out of the beaten paths, so that even the absurdness of a thing sometimes proves useful. But if reason also be here joined, so as to show that the like experiment never was attempted, and yet that there is great cause why it should be; then this becomes an excellent instrument, and really enters the bosom of nature. For example, in the operation of fire upon natural bodies it hath hitherto always happened that either something flies off, as flame and smoke in our common fires, or at least that the parts are locally separated to some distance, as in distillation, where the vapour rises and the fæces are left behind; but no man hath hitherto tried close distillation. Yet it seems probable, that if the force of heat may have its action confined in the cavities of a body, without any possibility of loss or escape, this Proteus of matter will be manacled, as it were, and forced to undergo numerous transformations, provided only the heat be so moderated and changed as not to break the containing vessel. For this is a kind of natural matrix, where heat has its effect without separating or throwing off the parts of a body. In a true matrix, indeed, there is nourishment supplied; but in point of transmutation the case is the same. And here let none despair or be confounded, if the experiments they attempt should not answer their expectation; for though success be indeed more pleasing, yet failure, frequently, is no less informing; and it must ever be remembered, that experiments of light are more to be desired than experiments of profit. And so much for learned experience, as we call it, which thus appears to be rather a sagacity, or a scenting of nature, as in hunting, than a direct science.[t]

[t] This section appears to have been little understood even by some eminent men, who censure the scheme of the author, and think that experiments must need be casual, and the human understanding unable to direct and conduct them to useful purposes unless by accident. The misfortune seems to lie here, that few converse so familiarly with nature,

As regards the Novum Organum, we shall state here nothing either summarily or in detail, it being our intention, with the Divine assistance, to devote an entire treatise to that subject, which is more important than all the rest.

CHAPTER III.

Division of the Invention of Arguments into Promptuary, or Places of Preparation, and Topical, or Places of Suggestion. The Division of Topics into General and Particular. An Example of Particular Topics afforded by an Inquiry into the Nature of the Qualities of Light and Heavy.

The invention of arguments is not properly an invention; for to invent, is to discover things unknown before, and not to recollect or admit such as are known already. The office and use of this kind of invention seems to be no more than dexterously to draw out from the stock of knowledge laid up in the mind such things as make to the present purpose; for one who knows little or nothing of a subject proposed, has no use of topics or places of invention, whilst he who is provided of suitable matter, will find and produce arguments, without the help of art and such places of invention, though not so readily and commodiously; whence this kind of invention is rather a bare calling to memory, or a suggestion with application, than a real invention. But since the term is already received, it may still be called invention, as the hunting in a park may be called hunting no less than that in the open field. But not to insist upon the word, the scope and the end of the thing itself, is a quick and ready use of our thoughts, rather than any enlargement or increase of them.

There are two methods of procuring a stock of matter for discourse; viz., 1. either by marking out, and indicating the parts wherein a thing is to be searched after, which is what we call the topical way; or 2. by laying up arguments for use, that were composed beforehand, relating to such things

as to judge what may be done in this way; or how the numerous discoveries of Lord Bacon, Mr. Boyle, Dr. Hook, Sir Isaac Newton, &c., were made. An attentive perusal of the Novum Organum, where this subject is largely prosecuted, will unravel the mystery. *Shaw.*

as frequently happen and come in dispute; and this we call the promptuary way: but the latter can scarce be called a part of science, as consisting rather in diligence than any artificial learning. Aristotle on this head ingeniously derides the sophists of his time, saying, they acted like a professed shoemaker, who did not teach the art of shoemaking, but set out a large stock of shoes, of different shapes and sizes.[a] But it might be replied, that the shoemaker who should have no shoes in his shop, and only make them as they were bespoke, would find few customers. Our Saviour speaks far otherwise of divine knowledge, saying, "Therefore every scribe which is instructed into the kingdom of heaven, is like unto a man that is an householder, which brings forth out of his treasure things new and old."[b]

We find also that the ancient rhetoricians gave it in precept to the orators to be always provided of various commonplaces, ready furnished and illustrated with arguments on both sides; as for the intention of the law against the words of the law; for the truth of arguments against testimonies, and vice versa.[c] And Cicero himself, being taught by long experience, roundly asserts, that a diligent and experienced orator should have such things as come into dispute, ready laboured and prepared, so as that in pleading there should be no necessity of introducing anything new or occasional, except new names, and some particular circumstances.[d] But as the first opening of the cause has a great effect in preparing the minds of the audience, the exactness of Demosthenes judged it proper to compose beforehand, and have in readiness, several introductions to harangues and speeches;[e] and these examples and authorities may justly overrule the opinion of Aristotle, who would have us change a whole wardrobe for a pair of shears. This promptuary method, therefore, should not be omitted; but as it relates as well to rhetoric as to logic, we shall here touch it but slightly; designing to consider it more fully under rhetoric.[f]

We divide topical inventions into general and particular. The general is so copiously and diligently treated in the

[a] De Reprehen. Soph. ii. 9. [b] St. Matt. xiii. 52.
[c] De Oratore. [d] Epistles to Atticus, vi. 16.
[e] The prefaces alluded to are of doubtful authority.
[f] See hereafter, sect. 18.

common logics, tnat we need not dwell upon its explanation: we only observe by the way, that this topical method is not only used in argumentation and close conference, but also in contemplation, when we meditate or revolve anything alone. Nor is its office only confined to the suggesting or admonishing us of what should be affirmed or asserted, but also what we should examine or question; a prudent questioning being a kind of half-knowledge; for, as Plato justly observes, a searcher must have some general notion of the thing he searches after, otherwise he could never know it when he had found it;[g] and therefore, the more comprehensive and sure our anticipation is, the more direct and short will be the investigation. And hence the same topics which conduce to the close examining into our own understandings, and collecting the notices there treasured up, are likewise assistant in drawing forth our knowledge. Thus, if a person, skilful in the point under question, were at hand, as we might prudently and advantageously consult him upon it; in like manner, we may usefully select and turn over authors and books, to instruct and inform ourselves about those things we are in quest of.

But the particular topical invention is much more conducive to the same purposes, and to be esteemed a highly fertile thing. Some writers have lately mentioned it, but it is by no means treated according to its extent and merit. Not to mention the error and haughtiness which have too long reigned in the schools, and their pursuing with infinite subtilty such things as are obvious, without once touching upon those that lie remote, we receive this topical invention as an extremely useful thing, that affords certain heads of inquiry and investigation appropriated to particular subjects and sciences. These places are certain mixtures of logic and the peculiar matter of each science. It is an idle thing, and shows a narrow mind, to think that the art of discovering the sciences may be invented and proposed in perfection from the beginning, so as to be afterwards only exercised and brought into use; for men should be made sensible that the solid and real arts of invention grow up and increase along with inventions themselves; so that when any one first comes to

[g] In Menone, ii. 80.

the thorough examination of a science, he should have some useful rules of discovery; but after he hath made a considerable progress in the science itself, he may, and ought, to find out new rules of invention, the better to lead him still further. The way here is like walking on a flat, where, after we have gone some length, we not only approach nearer the end of our journey, but also have a clearer view of what remains to be gone of it; so in the sciences, every step of the way, as it leaves some things behind, also gives us a nearer prospect of those that remain: and as we report this particular topical invention deficient, we think proper to give an example of it in the subject of gravity and levity.

1. Let inquiries be made what kind of bodies are susceptible of the motion of gravity; what of levity; and if there be any of a middle or neutral nature.

2. After the simple inquiry of gravity and levity, proceed to a comparative inquiry; viz., which heavy bodies weigh more, and which less, in the same dimensions; and of like ones, which mount upwards the swifter, and which the slower.

3. Inquire what effect the quantity of the body has in the motion of gravity. This at first sight may appear a needless inquiry, because motion may seem proportionable to quantity; but the case is otherwise. For although in scales quantity is equal to the gravity, yet where there is a small resistance, as in the falling of bodies through the air, quantity has but little force to quicken the descent; but twenty pounds of lead, and a single pound, fall nearly in the same time.

4. Inquire whether the quantity of a body may be so increased as that the motion of gravity shall be entirely lost, as in the globe of the earth, which hangs pendulous without falling. Quære, therefore, whether other masses may be so large as to sustain themselves? For that bodies should move to the centre of the earth is a fiction; and every mass of matter has an aversion to local motion, till this be overcome by some stronger impulse.

5. Inquire into the effects and nature of resisting mediums, as to their influencing the motion of gravity; for a falling body either penetrates and cuts through the body it meets in its way, or else is stopped by it. If it pass through, there is a penetration, either with a small resistance, as in air, or

with a greater, as in water. If it be stopped, it is stopped by an unequal resistance, where there is a preponderancy, as when wood is laid upon wax; or by an equal resistance, as when water is laid upon water, or wood upon wood of the same kind; which is what the schools pretend, when they idly imagine that bodies do not gravitate in their own places. And all these circumstances alter the motion of gravity; for heavy bodies move after one way in the balance, and after another in falling: and, which may seem strange, after one way in a balance suspended in the air, and after another in a balance plunged in water; after one way in falling through water, and after another when floating upon it.

6. Inquire into the effects of the figure of the descending body, in directing the motion of gravity: suppose of a figure broad and thin, cubical, oblong, round, pyramidal, &c.; and how bodies turn themselves whilst they remain in the same position as when first let go.

7. Inquire into the effects of the continuation and progression of the fall or descent itself, as to the acquiring a greater impulse or velocity, and in what proportion and to what length this velocity is increased; for the ancients, upon slender consideration, imagined that this motion, being natural, was always upon the increase.

8. Inquire into the effects of distance, or the near approach of a body descending to the earth, so as to fall swifter, slower, or not at all, supposing it were to be out of the earth's sphere of activity, according to Gilbert's opinion; as also the effects of plunging the falling body deeper into the earth, or placing it nearer the surface; for this also varies the motion, as is manifest to those who work in mines.

9. Inquire into the effects of the difference of bodies, through which the motion of gravity is diffused and communicated; and whether it is equally communicated through soft and porous bodies, as through hard and solid ones. Thus if the beam of a scale were one half of wood, and the other half of silver, yet of the same weight; inquire whether this would not make an alteration in the scales: and again, whether metal laid upon wool, or a blown bladder, would weigh the same as in the naked scale

10. Inquire into the effects of the distance of **a body from**

the point of suspension in the communication of the motion of gravity; that is, into the earlier or later perception of its inclination or depression : as in scales, where one side of the beam is longer, though of the same weight with the other, whether this inclines the beam; or in siphons, where the longer leg will draw the water, though the shorter, being made wider, contains a greater weight of water.

11. Inquire into the effects of intermixing or coupling a light body and a heavy one, for lessening the gravity of bodies; as in the weight of creatures alive and dead.

12. Inquire into the ascents and descents of the lighter and heavier parts of one entire body : whence curious separations are often made, as in the separation of wine and water, the rising of cream from milk, &c.

13. Inquire what is the line and direction of the motion of gravity, and how far it respects the earth's centre, that is, the mass of the earth; or the centre of its own body, that is, the appetite of its parts. For these centres are properly supposed in demonstrations, but are otherwise unserviceable in nature.

14. Inquire into the comparative motion of gravity, with other motions, or to what motions it yields, and what it exceeds. Thus in the motion they call violent, the motion of gravity is withheld for a time; and so when a large weight of iron is raised by a little loadstone, the motion of gravity gives way to the motion of sympathy.

15. Inquire concerning the motion of the air, whether it rises upwards, or be as it were neutral, which is not easy to be discovered without some accurate experiments; for the rising up of air at the bottom of water, rather proceeds from a resistance of the water, than the motion of the air, since the same also happens in wood. But air mixed with air makes no discovery; for air in air may seem as light, as water in water seems heavy : but in bubbles, which are air surrounded with a thin pellicle of water, it stands still for a time.

16. Let the bounds of levity be inquired after; for though men make the centre of the earth the centre of gravity, they will perhaps hardly make the ultimate convexity of the heavens the boundary of levity; but rather, perhaps, as heavy bodies seem to be carried so far, that they rest, and

grow as it were immovable; light bodies are carried so far, that they begin a rotation or circular motion.

17. Inquire the cause why vapours and effluvia are carried so high as that called the middle region of the air, since the matter of them is somewhat gross, and the rays of the sun cease alternately by night.

18. Inquire into the tendency of flame upwards, which is the more abstruse, because flame perishes every moment, unless perhaps in the midst of larger flames; for flames broken from their continuity are of small duration.

19. Inquire into the motion and activity of heat upwards; as when heat in ignited iron sooner creeps upwards than downwards. And thus much by way of example of our particular topical inquiry. We must, for a conclusion, admonish mankind to alter their particular topics in such manner, as after some considerable progress made in the inquiry, to raise topic after topic, if they desire to ascend to the pinnacle of the sciences. For my own part, I attribute so much to these particular topics, that I design a particular work upon their use, in the more eminent and obscure subjects of nature; for we are masters of questions, though not of things. And here we close the subject of invention.

CHAPTER IV.

The Art of Judgment divided into Induction and the Syllogism. Induction developed in the Novum Organum. The Syllogism divided into Direct and Inverse Reduction. Inverse Reduction divided into the Doctrine of Analytics and Confutations. The Division of the latter into Confutations of Sophisms, the Unmasking of Vulgarisms (Equivocal Terms), and the Destruction of Delusive Images or Idols. Delusive Appearances divided into *Idola Tribûs, Idola Specûs*, and *Idola Fori*. Appendix to the Art of Judgment. The Adapting the Demonstration to the Nature of the Subject.

WE come now to the art of judgment, which treats of the nature of proof or demonstration. This art, as it is commonly received, concludes either by induction or syllogism: for enthymemes and examples are only abridgments of these two.[a] As to judgment by induction, we need not be large

---

[a] An enthymeme is no other than a syllogism of two propositions, the third being supplied by the mind, as the word itself imports. *Ed.*

upon it, because what is sought we both find and judge of, by the same operation of the mind. Nor is the matter here transacted by a medium, but directly almost in the same manner as by the sense; for sense, in its primary objects, at once seizes the image of the object, and assents to the truth of it. It is otherwise in syllogism, whose proof is not direct, but mediate; and, therefore, the invention of the medium is one thing, and judgment, as to the consequence of an argument, another: for the mind first casts about, and afterwards acquiesces. But for the corrupt form of induction, we entirely ignore it, and refer the genuine one to our method of interpreting nature. And thus much of judgment by induction.

The other by syllogism is worn by the file of many a subtile genius, and reduced to numerous fragments, as having a great sympathy with the human understanding; for the mind is wonderfully bent against fluctuating, and endeavours to find something fixed and unmovable, upon which, as a firm basis, to rest in its inquiries. And as Aristotle endeavours to prove that, in all motion of bodies, there is something still at rest, and elegantly explains the ancient fable of Atlas, sustaining the heavens on his shoulders, of the poles of the world, about which the revolutions are performed:[b] so men have a strong desire to retain within themselves an atlas, or pole for their thoughts, in some measure to govern the fluctuations and revolutions of the understanding, as otherwise fearing their heaven should tumble. And hence it is, that they have been ever hasty in laying the principles of the sciences, about which all the variety of disputes might turn without danger of falling; not at all regarding, that whoever too hastily catches at certainties shall end in doubts, as he who seasonably withholds his judgment shall arrive at certainties.

It is therefore manifest that this art of judging by syllogism is nothing more than a reduction of propositions to their principles by middle terms.[c] But principles are

[b] Animal. Mot. 3.

[c] Bacon here only gives us a loose translation of the *Dictum de omne et nullo*, as inclosing the essentiality of the syllogism. Thus, to develop his thought, when a certain attribute does not appear to belong to a proposed subject, the logician presents another subject, in which the contested quality is admitted by his hearers to enter, and having shown that

supposed to be received by consent, and exempt from question, whilst the invention of middle terms is freely permitted to the subtilty and investigation of the wit. This reduction is of two kinds, direct and inverse. It is direct when the proposition itself is reduced to the principle, and this is called ostensive proof: it is inverse when the contradictory of the proposition is reduced to the contradictory of the principle, which they call proof by absurdity: but the number or scale of the middle term is diminished, or increased, according to the remoteness of the proposition from the principle.[d]

Upon this foundation we divide the art of judgment nearly, as usual, into analytics, and the doctrine of elenches, or confutations; the first whereof supplies direction, and the other caution: for analytics directs the true forms of the consequences of arguments, from which, if we vary, we make a wrong conclusion. And this itself contains a kind of elench, or confutation; for what is right shows not only itself, but also what is wrong. Yet it is safest to employ elenches as monitors, the easier to discover fallacies, which would otherwise ensnare the judgment. We find no deficiency in

this new subject—the middle term—may be affirmed of the original subject with which he set out, he concludes that its inseparable attribute must also belong to it. If these two primary propositions, viz. those which affirm the attribute of the middle term, and connect this term with the original subject, need proof, he is obliged to seek other middle terms, and employ them in the same manner, until he establish his disputed premises on the basis of experience or consentaneous principles. If such fundaments, common to the minds of the disputants, do not exist, the argument is nugatory, and rational conviction impossible. *Ed.*

[d] For no proof can be considered conclusive, unless the conclusion be an immediate consequence from the propositions which involve the last middle term. Now, if the proposition we seek to establish be particular (singular), and the principle from which we set out general (universal), it is clear that, to connect principle and consequent, we must either climb gradually from principles less general to ones more enlarged, until we reach a proposition which connects the last consequent with the general principle in question; or we must descend by a similar gradation from principles less general to others more particular, until we reach the proposition which affirms the last consequence of the particular conclusion. The number, therefore, of these intermediate links, must augment or diminish in proportion to the interval which separates the principle and consequent. *Ed.*

analytics; for it is rather loaded with superfluities than deficient.[e]

We divide the doctrine of confutations into three parts; viz., 1. The confutation of sophisms; 2. The confutation of interpretation; and 3. The confutation of images or idols. The doctrine of the confutation of sophisms is extremely useful: for although a gross kind of fallacy is not improperly compared, by Seneca, to the tricks of jugglers,[f] where we know not by what means the things are performed, but are well assured they are not as they appear to be, yet the more subtile sophisms not only supply occasions of answer, but also in reality confound the judgment. This part concerning the confutation of sophisms is, in precept, excellently treated by Aristotle, but still better by Plato, in example; not only in the persons of the ancient sophists, Gorgias, Hippias, Protagoras, Euthydemus, &c., but even in the person of Socrates himself,[g] who, always professing to affirm nothing, but to confute what was produced by others, has ingeniously expressed the several forms of objections, fallacies, and confutations. Therefore in this part we find no deficiency, but only observe by the way, that though we place the true and principal use of this doctrine in the confutation of sophisms, yet it is plain that its degenerate and corrupt use tends to the raising of cavils and contradictions, by means of those sophisms themselves; which kind of faculty is highly esteemed, and has no small uses, though it is a good distinction made between the orator and the sophist, that the former excels in swiftness, as the greyhound, the other in the turn, as the hare.

With regard to the confutations of interpretation, we must here repeat what was formerly said of the transcendental and adventitious conditions of beings, such as greater, less, whole, parts, motion, rest, &c. For the different way of considering these things, which is either physically or logically, must be remembered.[h] The physical treatment of

---

[e] Upon the subject of analytics, see Weigelius in his "Analysis Aristotelica, ex Euclide restituta;" and Morhof in his "Polyhistor," tom. i. lib. ii. c. 7, de Methodis variis.

[f] Epist. 45, c. 7.   [g] See the opening of the Theætetus.

[h] He might have added, mathematically, as greater and less have different significations in arithmetic and algebra. *Ed.*

them we have allotted to primary philosophy, but their logical treatment is what we here call the confutation of interpretation. And this we take for a sound and excellent part of learning, as general and common notions, unless accurately and judiciously distinguished from their origin, are apt to mix themselves in all disputes, so as strangely to cloud and darken the light of the question, and frequently occasion the controversy to end in a quarrel about words: for equivocations and wrong acceptations of words, especially of this kind, are the sophisms of sophisms;[1] wherefore it is better to treat of them separate than either to receive them into primary philosophy or metaphysics, or again, to make them a part of analytics, as Aristotle has confusedly done. We give this doctrine a name from its use, because its true use is indeed redargution and caution about the employing of words. So, likewise, that part concerning predicaments, if rightly treated, as to the cautions against confounding or transposing the terms of definitions and divisions, is of principal use, and belongs to the present article. And thus much for the confutation of interpretation.

As to the confutations of images, or idols, we observe that idols are the deepest fallacies of the human mind; for they do not deceive in particulars, as the rest, by clouding and ensnaring the judgment; but from a corrupt predisposition, or bad complexion of the mind, which distorts and infects all the anticipations of the understanding. For the mind, darkened by its covering the body, is far from being a flat, equal, and clear mirror that receives and reflects the rays without mixture, but rather a magical glass, full of superstitions and apparitions. Idols are imposed upon the understanding, either, 1. by the general nature of mankind; 2. the nature of each particular man; or 3. by words, or commucative nature. The first kind we call idols of the tribe; the second kind, idols of the den; and the third kind, idols of the market. There is also a fourth kind, which we call idols of the theatre, being superinduced by false theories, or philosophies, and the perverted laws of demonstration. This last kind we are not at present concerned with, as it may be

[1] Rather, vulgarisms; since sophisms imply a use of the intellect, though a perverted use; but the wrong acceptations of words imply no use at all. *Ed.*

rejected and laid aside; but the other's seize the mind strongly, and cannot be totally eradicated. Therefore no art of analytics can be expected here, but the doctrine of the confutation of idols is the primary doctrine of idols. Nor indeed can the doctrine of idols be reduced to an art, but can only be employed by means of a certain contemplative prudence to prevent them.

For the idols of the tribe,[k] it is observable, that the nature of the understanding is more affected with affirmatives and actives than with negatives and privatives, though in justness it should be equally affected with them both; but if things fall out right, or keep their course, the mind receives a stronger impression of this than of a much greater number of failures, or contrary events, which is the root of all superstition and credulity. Hence Diagoras, being shown in Neptune's temple many votive pictures of such as had escaped shipwreck, and thereupon asked by his guide, if he did not now acknowledge the divine power? answered wisely, "But first show me where those are painted that were shipwrecked, after having thus paid their vows."[l] And the case is the same, in the similar superstitions of astrological predictions, dreams, omens, &c. Again, the mind, being of itself an equal and uniform substance, presupposes a greater unanimity and uniformity in the nature of things than there really is, as may be observed in astronomical mathematicians, who, rejecting spiral lines, assert that the heavenly bodies move in perfect circles;[m] whence our thoughts are continually drawing parallels, and supposing relations in many things that are truly different and singular. Hence the chemists have fantastically imagined their four principles correspond-

---

[k] These might otherwise be called partial idols, as owing to the partiality or obliquity of the mind, which has its particular bent, and admits of some things more readily than others, without a manifest reason assigned for it to the understanding. However this be, they manifestly belong to the tribe of mankind. *Shaw.*

[l] Cicero, Natur. Deor. v. 9.

[m] The observations of Bradley and Molyneux directly establish the elliptical orbit, in which the earth performs its yearly revolution. The spiral lines, which Bacon suggests in place of the concentric and elliptical theory, are only the apparent paths which the planets seem to follow when viewed by the naked eye, and have long since, with the cumbersome machinery of Ptolemy, been swept from the heavens. *Ed.*

ing to the heavens, air, earth, and water; dreaming that the series of existences formed a kind of square battalion, and that each element contained species of beings corresponding to each other, and possessing, as it were, parallel properties.[n] And again, men make themselves, as it were, the mirror and rule of nature. It is incredible what a number of idols have been introduced into philosophy by the reduction of natural operations to a correspondence with human actions; that is, by imagining nature acts as man does, which is not much better than the heresy of the anthropomorphites, that sprung up in the cells and solitude of ignorant monks;[o] or the opinion of Epicurus, who attributed a human figure to the gods. Velleius the Epicurean need not, therefore, have asked why God should have adorned the heavens with stars and lights, as master of the works? For if the grand architect had acted a human part, he would have ranged the stars into some beautiful and elegant order, as we see in the vaulted roofs of palaces; whereas we scarce find among such an infinite multitude of stars any figure either square, triangular, or rectilinear; so great a difference is there betwixt the spirit of man, and the spirit of the universe.

The idols of the den have their origin from the peculiar nature, both of mind and body, in each person; as also from education, custom, and the accidents of particular persons. It is a beautiful emblem, that of Plato's den;[p] for, to drop the exquisite subtilty of the parable, if any one should be educated from his infancy in a dark cave till he were of full age, and should then of a sudden be brought into broad daylight, and behold this apparatus of the heavens and of things, no doubt but many strange and absurd fancies would arise in his mind; and though men live indeed in the view of the heavens, yet our minds are confined in the caverns of our bodies; whence of necessity we receive infinite images of errors and falsehoods, if the mind does but seldom, and only for a short continuance, leave its den, and not constantly dwell in the contemplation of nature, as it were, in the open daylight. And with this emblem of Plato's den agrees the

---

[n] This hypothesis gave rise to the romance of Lamekis.
[o] Epiphanius, adv. Hær. p. 811, in which the heresy of Audius is explained.   [p] Repub. vii.

saying of Heraclitus; viz., that men seek the sciences in their own narrow worlds, and not in the wide one.

But the idols of the market give the greatest disturbance, and from a tacit agreement among mankind, with regard to the imposition of words and names, insinuate themselves into the understanding: for words are generally given according to vulgar conception, and divide things by such differences as the common people are capable of: but when a more acute understanding, or a more careful observation, would distinguish things better, words murmur against it. The remedy of this lies in definitions; but these themselves are in many respects irremediable, as consisting of words: for words generate words, however men may imagine they have a command over words, and can easily say they will speak with the vulgar, and think with the wise. Terms of art also, which prevail only among the skilful, may seem to remedy the mischief, and definitions premised to arts in the prudent mathematical manner, to correct the wrong acceptation of words; yet all this is insufficient to prevent the seducing incantation of names in numerous respects, their doing violence to the understanding, and recoiling upon it, from whence they proceeded. This evil, therefore, requires a new and a deeper remedy; but these things we touch lightly at present, in the mean time noting this doctrine of grand confutations, or the doctrine of the native and adventitious idols of the mind, for deficient.

There is also wanting a considerable appendix to the art of judgment. Aristotle indeed marks out the thing, but has nowhere delivered the manner of effecting it. The design is to show what demonstrations should be applied to what subjects, so that this doctrine should contain the judging of judgments. For Aristotle well observes, that we should not require demonstrations from orators, nor persuasion from mathematicians;[q] so that if we err in the kind of proof, judgment itself cannot be perfect. And as there are four kinds of demonstration, viz., 1. by immediate consent and common notions; 2. by induction; 3. by syllogism; and 4. by congruity,[r] which Aristotle justly calls demonstration in

[q] Ethics, xiii. 1.

[r] Analogical demonstration, or proof *à latere*, to which Bacon seems to refer, consists in showing that the disputed attribute may be affirmed

circle,[a] each of these demonstrations has its peculiar subjects, and parts of the sciences, wherein they are of force, and others again from which they are excluded; for insisting upon too strict proofs in some cases, and still more the facility and remissness in resting upon slight proofs in others, is what has greatly prejudiced and obstructed the sciences. And so much for the art of judgment.

CHAPTER V.

Division of the Retentive Art into the Aids of the Memory and the Nature of the Memory itself. Division of the Doctrine of Memory into Prenotion and Emblem.

WE divide the art of memory, or the keeping and retaining of knowledge, into two parts; viz., the doctrine of helps

of several subjects analogical to the one proposed, and thence proceeds to draw the inference that such attribute enters also into the subject in question. In addition to these three last kinds of mediate positive proof, there are three others, which may be called mediate negative; viz., 1. *à posteriori*, which in inferring conclusions erroneous from the contradictory of that which is sought to be maintained, shows that the opposition is formed on false principles, and establishes the truth of their contradictories. 2. *à priori*, which in showing that the contradictory of the original proposition is a necessary consequence of some exploded principle, and also contradictory to the principle of which the contested proposition is also a consequence, infers the truth of such proposition with the principle of which it is a corollary. 3. *à latere*, whose object is to show that the attribute diametrically opposite to the one in question, agrees with a subject also diametrically opposite to the one proposed, that the last attribute may be inferred to agree with the last subject. *Ed.*

[a] Bacon seems to imply that Aristotle not only admitted demonstration in a circle, but even understood it in the sense of analogical proof or demonstration *à latere;* whereas the Stagyrite only introduced the term for the purpose of controverting it. Some of the ancient materialists, in order to rid themselves of the illogical consequences of a series of proofs ad infinitum, in which the denial of first principles involved them, asserted the possibility of demonstrating all things from each other, a line of argument in which the chain of proof would run into itself: ἀλλὰ πάντων εἶναι, ἀπόδειξιν οὐδὲν κωλύει· ἐνδέχεται γὰρ κύκλῳ γενέσθαι τὴν ἀπόδειξιν καὶ ἐξ ἀλλήλων. (Arist. Anal. Post. i. 3.) The Stagyrite, however, confronted this assertion with the reason, that demonstration could only be effected by evolving new truths out of things prior and more known, and pronounced the formation of a body of scientific truths without admitting first principles more palpable to the mind than any proof could make them, impossible. See, also, Arist. Analyt. Pri. ii. 5, 1. *Ed.*

for the memory, and the doctrine of the memory itself. The help for the memory is writing; and we must observe, that the memory, without this assistance, is unequal to things of length and accuracy, and ought not otherwise to be trusted. And this holds particularly in inductive philosophy, and in the interpretation of nature; for one might as well undertake to make an almanack by the memory, without writing, as to interpret nature by bare contemplation. Scarce anything can be more useful in the ancient and popular sciences than a true and solid help for the memory, that is, a just and learned digest of common-places. Some, indeed, condemn this method as prejudicial to erudition, hindering the course of reading, and rendering the memory indolent; but as it is a wrong procedure in the sciences to be over-hasty and quick, we judge it is of great service in studies, unless a man be solid, and completely instructed, to bestow diligence and labour in setting down common-places; as it affords matter to invention, and collects and strengthens the judgment. But among all the methods and common-place books we have hitherto seen, there is not one of value;[a] as savouring of the school rather than the world, and using rather vulgar and pedantical divisions than such as any way penetrate things.

And for the memory itself, it seems hitherto to have been negligently and superficially inquired into. There is, indeed, some art of memory extant; but I know that much better precepts for confirming and enlarging the memory may be had than this art contains, and that a better practice of the art itself may be formed than what is at present received. And I doubt not, if any one were disposed to make an ostentatious show of this art, that many surprising things might be performed by it; and yet, as now managed, it is but barren and useless. We do not, however, pretend that it spoils or surcharges the natural memory, which is the common objection, but that it is not dexterously applied for assisting the memory in real business, and serious affairs. But this turn,

[a] Upon the subject of common-place, consult Morhof's "Polyhistor," tom. i. lib. i. cap. 21, de Locorum Communium Scriptoribus; Mr. Locke's common-place, in his "Discourse of the Conduct of the Understanding;" and Julian's "Emploi du Temps." *Shaw.*

perhaps, I may receive from the political course of life I have led, never to value what has the appearance of art without any use. For immediately to repeat a multitude of names, or words, once repeated before, or off-hand to compose a great number of verses upon a subject, or to touch any matter that occasionally turns up with a satirical comparison, or to turn serious things into jest, or to elude anything by contradiction, or cavil, &c., of all which faculties there is a great fund in the mind, and which may, by a proper capacity and exercise, be carried to almost a miraculous height; yet I esteem all the things of this kind no more than rope-dancing, antic postures, and feats of activity. And indeed they are nearly the same things, the one being an abuse of the bodily, as the other is of the mental powers; and though they may cause admiration, they cannot be highly esteemed.

This art of memory has two intentions; viz., prenotion and emblem. By prenotion we understand the breaking off of an endless search; for when one endeavours to call anything to mind without some previous notion, or perception of what is sought for, the mind strives and exerts itself, endeavours and casts about in an endless manner; but if it hath any certain notion beforehand, the infinity of the search is presently cut short, and the mind hunts nearer home as in an inclosure. Order, therefore, is a manifest help to memory; for here there is a previous notion, that the things sought for must be agreeable to order. And thus verse is easier remembered than prose; because if we stick at any word in verse, we have a previous notion that it is such a word as must stand in the verse, and this prenotion is the first part of artificial memory. For in artificial memory we have certain places digested, and proposed beforehand; but we make images extemporary as they are required, wherein we have a previous notion that the image must be such as may, in some measure, correspond to its place; while this stimulates the memory, and, as it were, strengthens it to find out the thing sought for.

But emblems bring down intellectual to sensible things; for what is sensible always strikes the memory stronger, and sooner impresses itself than what is intellectual. Thus the memory of brutes is excited by sensible, but not by intellectual things. And, therefore, it is easier to retain the image of a sportsman hunting the hare, of an apothecary ranging his boxes, an orator making a speech, a boy repeating verses, or a player acting his part, than the corresponding notions of invention, disposition, elocution, memory, and action. There are also other things that contribute to assist the memory, but the art at present in use consists of the two above mentioned;[b] and to treat of the particular defects of the arts is foreign to our present purpose.

SIXTH BOOK.

CHAPTER I.

Division of Tradition into the Doctrine of the Organ, the Method and the Illustration of Speech. The Organ of Speech divided into the Knowledge of the Marks of Things, of Speaking, and Writing. The two last comprise the two Branches of Grammar. The Marks of Things divided into Hieroglyphics and Real Characters. Grammar again divided into Literary and Philosophical. Prosody referred to the Doctrine of Speech, and Ciphers to the Department of Writing.

ANY man may, excellent King, when he pleases, take the liberty to jest and laugh at himself or his own projects. Who, then, knows,—as there is a book in the famous library of St. Victor, entitled "Formicarum Artium,"[a] whether our book may not be an accidental transcript of its contents. We have indeed only accumulated a little heap of dust, and deposited therein many grains of the arts and sciences whereto ants may creep to repose awhile, and then betake themselves to their labours: nay, the wisest of kings points out the ant as an example to those whose only care is to

---

[b] I suppose that the art of memory, now commonly taught by memory-masters, is little more than a lecture upon the foundations here laid down; and perhaps their secrets are disclosed in Sir Hugh Plat's "Jewel House of Art and Nature," printed in London in the year 1653. See page 77—80 of that edition. Consult also upon the means of improving the memory, Morhof's "Polyhistor," tom. i. lib. ii. cap. 4, de Subsidiis dirigendi Judicii. *Shaw.* [Grey's "Memoria Technica" and Feinagle's "Art of Memory" are the modern works on the same subject. *Ed.*]   [a] Pantagruel, ii. 7, p. 76.

live upon the main stock, neglecting to cultivate the fields of science, and reap a new harvest of discoveries.[b]

We next proceed to the art of delivering, uttering, and communicating such things as are discovered, judged of, and treasured up in the memory; and this we call by the general name of traditive doctrine, which takes in all the arts relating to words and discourse. For although reason be as the soul of discourse, yet they ought both to be treated separate, no less than the soul and body. We divide this traditive doctrine into three parts; viz., with regard, 1. to the organ; 2. the method; and 3. the illustration or ornament of speech and discourse.

The vulgar doctrine of the organ of speech called grammar is of two kinds, the one having relation to speaking, the other to writing. For, as Aristotle well observed, words are the marks of thoughts, and letters of words; and we refer both of these to grammar.[c] But before we proceed to its several parts, it is necessary to say something in general of the organ of this traditive doctrine, because it seems to have more descendants besides words and letters. And here we observe, that whatever may be split into differences, sufficiently numerous for explaining the variety of notions, provided these differences are sensible, may be a means of conveying the thoughts from man to man; for we find that nations of different languages hold a commerce, in some tolerable degree, by gestures. And from the practice of some persons born deaf and dumb, but otherwise ingenious, we see conversation may be held betwixt them and such of their friends as have learned their gestures. And it is now well known, that in China and the more eastern provinces, they use at this day certain real, not nominal characters,[d] to

---

[b] Pantagruel, ii. 6, 6.   [c] Interpret. i. 2.
[d] The original is, "nec literas nec verba," which in Latin signify oral as well as written language; so that, to avoid equivocation, we should annex the two adjectives, sonorous and written, to fix their signification. With regard to the relation which exists between the oral and written speech of the Chinese, it is, as the text would imply, not different from that which prevails among us. In articulating, we pronounce as the Chinese the sonorous signs which correspond to the written words, and their art of reading, no less than ours, consists in the struggle to transplant this correspondence in our minds, and learn its reciprocal relations. Even allowing that the Chinese, in addition to their vulgar tongue, had

express, not their letters or words, but things and notions; insomuch, that numerous nations, though of quite different languages, yet, agreeing in the use of these characters, hold correspondence by writing.[e] And thus a book written in such characters, may be read and interpreted by each nation in its own respective language.

The signs of things significative without the help or interposition of words are therefore of two kinds, the one congruous, the one arbitrary. Of the first kind, are hieroglyphics and gestures; of the second, real characters. The use of hieroglyphics is of great antiquity, being held in veneration, especially among that most ancient nation, the Egyptians, insomuch that this seems to have been an early kind of writing, prior to the invention of letters, unless, perhaps, among the Jews.[f] And gestures are a kind of transitory hieroglyphics; for as words are fleeting in the pronunciation, but permanent when written down, so hieroglyphics, expressed by gesture, are momentary; but when

adopted hieroglyphical writing, so designed as to convey, without the interposition of oral signs, the exact ideas which they represent, yet each of these signs would invariably awaken the idea which represented it in the oral language, as well as the vocal word refer to the idea indicated by the written hieroglyphic. The only persons who appear not to intrude intermediate signs between the hieroglyphic and the idea which it conveys to the mind, are those who are incapacitated by nature. But in this respect there is no resemblance between the deaf and dumb and our Asiatic contemporaries.

Bacon therefore has not seized the exact distinction between the Chinese writing and our own, which consists not in dispensing with vocal signs, but in the diversified elements of which it is composed. Our language contains only twenty-five letters, while the Chinese letters are as innumerable as our words; and what makes the distinction perhaps more startling, there never has been an attempt on the part of that nation to analyze this infinite series of words, or to reduce them to the common elements of vocal sounds. Through this want of philosophic analysis, which characterizes nearly all the Asiatic tribes, the Chinese may be said never perfectly to understand their own language. *Ed.*

[e] See Spizelius "De Re Literaria Chinensium," ed. Lugd. Bat. 1660; Webb's "Historical Essay upon the Chinese Language," printed at London, 1669; Father Besnier's "Réunion des Langues;" Father le Compe, and other of the Missionaries' Letters. *Ed.*

[f] See Causinus's "Polyhistor Symbolicus," and "Symbolica Ægyptiorum Sapientia," ed. Par. 1618. And for other writers upon this subject, see Morhof's "Polyhistor," tom. i. lib. iv. cap. 2, de Variis Scripturæ Modis. *Ed.*

painted, durable. When Periander, being consulted how to preserve a tyranny newly usurped, bid the messenger report what he saw; and going into the garden, cropped all the tallest flowers;[g] he thus used as strong an hieroglyphic as if he had drawn it upon paper.

Again, it is plain that hieroglyphics and gestures have always some similitude with the things signified, and are in reality emblems; whence we call them congruous marks of things: but real characters have nothing of emblem, as being no less mute than the elementary letters themselves, and invented altogether at discretion, though received by custom as by a tacit agreement. Yet it is manifest that a great number of them is required in writing; for they must be as numerous as the radical words. This doctrine, therefore, concerning the organ of speech, that is, the marks of things, we set down as wanting; for although it may seem a matter of little use, whilst words and writing with letters are much more commodious organs of delivery; yet we think proper here to mention it as no inconsiderable thing. For whilst we are treating, as it were, of the coin of intellectual matters, it is not improper to observe that as money may be made of other materials besides gold and silver, so other marks of things may be invented besides words and letters.[h]

Grammar holds the place of a conductor in respect of the other sciences; and though the office be not noble, it is extremely necessary, especially as the sciences in our times are chiefly derived from the learned languages. Nor should this art be thought of small dignity, since it acts as an antidote against the curse of Babel, the confusion of tongues. Indeed, human industry strongly endeavours to recover those

---

[g] Arist. Polit. iii. 13. The person who sent to consult Periander was Thrasybulus of Miletus. Herodotus (v. 92) gives the opposite version of the story, making Periander consult Thrasybulus. Compare the story of Tarquin, told by Ovid, Fast. ii. 701.

[h] On this foundation, Bishop Wilkins undertook his laborious treatise of a real character, or philosophical language; though Dalgarn published a treatise on the same subject before him; viz. at London, in the year 1661 In the same year, Becher also published another to the same purpose at Frankfort, entitled "Character pro Notitia Linguarum Universali." See more upon this subject in Joachim Fritschii "Lingua Ludovicea," Kircher's "Polygraphia," Paschius's "Inventa Nova·Antiqua," and Morhof's "Polyhistor." *Shaw.*

enjoyments it lost through its own default. Thus it guards against the first general curse, the sterility of the earth, and the eating our bread in the sweat of the brow, by all the other arts ; as against the second, the confusion of languages, it calls in the assistance of grammar. Though this art is of little use in any maternal language, but more serviceable in learning the foreign ones, and most of all in the dead ones, which now cease to be popular, and are only preserved in books.

We divide grammar also into two parts,—literary and philosophical; the one employed simply about tongues themselves, in order to their being more expeditiously learned or more correctly spoken, but the other is in some sort subservient to philosophy; in which view Cæsar wrote his books of Analogy,[i] though we have some doubt whether they treated of the philosophical grammar now under consideration. We suspect, however, that they contained nothing very subtile or sublime, but only delivered precepts of pure and correct discourse, neither corrupted by any vulgar, depraved phrases, and customs of speech, nor vitiated by affectation ; in which particular the author himself excelled. Admonished by this procedure, I have formed in my thoughts a certain grammar, not upon any analogy which words bear to each other, but such as should diligently examine the analogy or relation betwixt words and things, yet without any of that hermeneutical doctrine, or doctrine of interpretation, which is subservient to logic. It is certain that words are the traces or impressions of reason ; and impressions afford some indication of the body that made them. I will, therefore, here give a small sketch of the thing.

And first, we cannot approve that curious inquiry, which Plato however did not contemn, about the imposition and original etymology of names,[k] as supposing them not given arbitrarily at first, but rationally and scientifically derived and deduced. This indeed is an elegant, and, as it were, a waxen subject, which may handsomely be wrought and twisted ; but because it seems to search the very bowels of antiquity, it has an awful appearance, though attended with but little truth and advantage. But it would be a noble

---

[i] Suetonius's Life.   [k] Cratyl.

kind of a grammar, if any one, well versed in numerous languages, both the learned and vulgar, should treat of their various properties, and show wherein each of them excelled and fell short; for thus languages might be enriched by mutual commerce, and one beautiful image of speech, or one grand model of language for justly expressing the sense of the mind, formed, like the Venus of Apelles, from the excellencies of several. And thus we should, at the same time, have some considerable marks of the genius and manners of people and nations from their respective languages. Cicero agreeably remarks, that the Greeks had no word to express the Latin ineptum;[1] "Because," says he, "the fault it denotes was so familiar among them, that they could not see it in themselves;" a censure not unbecoming the Roman gravity. And as the Greeks used so great a licentiousness in compounding words, which the Romans so religiously abstained from, it may hence be collected that the Greeks were better fitted for arts, and the Romans for exploits; as variety of arts makes compound words in a manner necessary, whilst civil business, and the affairs of nations, require a greater simplicity of expression. The Jews were so averse to these compositions, that they would rather strain a metaphor than introduce them. Nay, they used so few words and so unmixed, that we may plainly perceive from their language they were a Nazarite people, and separate from other nations. It is also worth observing, though it may seem a little ungrateful to modern ears, that the ancient languages are full of declensions, cases, conjugations, tenses, and the like; but the later languages, being almost destitute of them, slothfully express many things by prepositions and auxiliary verbs. For from hence it may easily be conjectured, that the genius of former ages, however we may flatter ourselves, was much more acute than our own. And there are things enough of this kind to make a volume. It seems reasonable, therefore, to distinguish a philosophical grammar from a simple literary one, and to set it down as deficient.[m]

---

[1] Orator. ii. 4.
[m] Considerable pains have been bestowed upon this subject by various authors; an account whereof is given by Morhof in his "Polyhistor." See tom. i. lib. iv. cap. 3, 4, 5; or more particularly, Abraham Mylii "De Linguæ Belgicæ cum aliis Linguis Communitate;" Henrici Schævii

All the accidence of words,—as sound, measure, accent,—likewise belong to grammar; but the primary elements of simple letters, or the inquiry with what percussion of the tongue, opening of the mouth, motion of the lips, and use of the throat, the sound of each letter is produced, has no relation to grammar, but is a part of the doctrine of sounds, to be treated under sense and sensible objects.[n] The grammatical sound we speak of regards only sweetness and harshness. Some harsh and sweet sounds are general; for there is no language but in some degree avoids the chasms of concurring vowels or the roughness of concurring consonants. There are others particular or respective, and pleasing or displeasing to the ears of different nations. The Greek language abounds in diphthongs, which the Roman uses much more sparingly, and so of the rest. The Spanish tongue avoids letters of a shrill sound, and changes them into letters of a middle tone. The languages of the Teutonic stock delight in aspirates, and numerous others which we have not space to cite.

But the measure of words has produced a large body of art; viz., poetry, considered not with regard to its matter, which was considered above, but its style and the structure of words; that is, versification; which, though held as trivial, is honoured with great and numerous examples. Nor should this art, which the grammarians call prosodia, be confined only to teaching the kinds of verse and measure; but precepts also should be added, as to what kind of verse is agreeable to every subject. The ancients applied heroic verse to encomium, elegy to complaint, iambic to invective, and lyric to ode and hymn; and the same has been prudently observed by the modern poets, each in his own language: only they deserve censure in this, that some of them, through affectation of antiquity, have endeavoured to set the modern languages to ancient measure; as sapphic, elegiac, &c., which is both disagreeable to the ear, and con-

---

"Dissertationes Philologicæ de Origine Linguarum et quibusdam earum attributis;" Thom. Hayne "De Linguis in genere, et de variarum Linguarum Harmonia," in the appendix to his "Grammaticæ Latinæ Compendium," and Dr. Wallis's "Grammatica Linguæ Anglicanæ." *Ed.*

[n] This is the subject which J. Conrad. Amman has prosecuted with great diligence, in his "Surdus loquens," and "Dissertatio de Loquela;" first printed at Amsterdam in 1692, and the last in 1700. *Shaw.*

trary to the structure of such languages.º And in these cases, the judgment of the sense is to be preferred to the precepts of art. As the poet says,

—— " Cœnæ Ferculæ nostræ
Mallem convivis quam placuisse cocis."ᵖ

Nor is this an art, but the abuse of art, as it does not perfect nature, but corrupt her. As to poetry, both with regard to its fable and its verse, it is like a luxuriant plant, sprouting not from seed, but by the mere vigour of the soil; whence it everywhere creeps up, and spreads itself so wide, that it were endless to be solicitous about its defects. And as to the accents of words, there is no necessity for taking notice of so trivial a thing; only it may be proper to intimate, that these are observed with great exactness, whilst the accents of sentences are neglected; though it is nearly common to all mankind to sink the voice at the end of a period, to raise it in interrogation, and the like.ᑫ And so much for that part of grammar which regards speaking.

Writing is practised either by means of the common alphabet, now vulgarly received, or of a secret and private one, agreed upon betwixt particular persons, and called by the name of cipher. But here a question arises about the common orthography; viz., whether words should be wrote as they are pronounced, or after the common manner? Certainly that reformed kind of writing, according to the pronunciation, is but an useless speculation, because pronunciation itself is continually changing, and the derivations of words, especially from the foreign languages, are very obscure; and lastly, as writing in the received manner no way obstructs the manner of pronunciation, but leaves it free, an innovation in it is to no purpose.

There are several kinds of ciphers, as the simple,ʳ those mixed with non-significants,ˢ those consisting of two kinds

º For some examples of this kind, see Southey's Epics.
ᵖ Martial, Epig. ix. 82.
ᑫ The stage having cultivated the accentuation of sentences more than the school, the rules of the art might, perhaps, to advantage, be borrowed from thence, in order to form an early habit of graceful speaking. *Shaw.*
ʳ In which each letter corresponds to a different letter of the alphabet. *Ed.*
ˢ That is, joined to other letters and words, the juncture of which

of characters,[t] wheel-ciphers,[u] key-ciphers,[x] word-ciphers,[y] &c. There are three properties required in ciphers; viz., 1. that they be easy to write and read; 2. that they be trusty and undecipherable; and 3. if possible, clear of suspicion. For if a letter should come into the hands of such as have a power over the writer or receiver, though the cipher itself be trusty and impossible to decipher, it is still subject to examination and question, unless there be no room to suspect or examine it.

There is a new and useful invention to elude the examination of a cipher; viz., to have two alphabets, the one of significant, and the other of non-significant letters; and folding up two writings together, the one conveying the secret, whilst the other is such as the writer might probably send without danger. In case of a strict examination about the cipher, the bearer is to produce the non-significant alphabet for the true, and the true for the non-significant; by which means the examiner would fall upon the outward writing, and finding it probable, suspect nothing of the inner.[z]

But to prevent all suspicion, we shall here annex a cipher of our own, that we devised at Paris in our youth, and which has the highest perfection of a cipher—that of signifying

---

destroys the sense to an ordinary observer, which the first letters and words are intended to convey. *Ed.*

[t] Abbreviated writing, or short-hand. *Ed.*

[u] This is a kind of dial, on which are drawn the circumferences of two concentric circles, bordered by the letters of the alphabet. Each letter being marked with a sign, we know to what letter of the exterior circle, each of the interior corresponds in relation to its rank in the alphabet. For example, suppose that it had been previously determined that the letter f should represent *a*, g *b*, and h *c*, the receiver of the missive should turn the interior circle of the dial round until the *a* in this circle pointed to *f* in the exterior, and then in the place of the letters in the note he had received, he would read those which corresponded to them in the interior circle. *Ed.*

[x] The key-ciphers are those figures which explain the latent sense of the letter, and are either conveyed with it, or previously concerted by those who are parties to the communication. *Ed.*

[y] Verbal ciphers are those which represent entire words. *Ed.*

[z] The publishing of this secret frustrates its intention; for the examiner, though he should find the outward letter probable, would doubtless, when thus advertised, examine the inner, notwithstanding its alphabet were delivered to him for non-significants. *Shaw.*

WRITING BY CIPHER EXPLAINED.

omnia per omnia (anything by everything),[a] provided only the matter included be five times less than that which includes it, without any other condition or limitation. The invention is this: first let all the letters of the alphabet be resolved into two only, by repetition and transposition; for a transposition of two letters through five places, or different arrangements, will denote two and thirty differences, and consequently fewer, or four and twenty, the number of letters in our alphabet, as in the following example.

A BILITERAL ALPHABET,

Consisting only of a and b changed through five places, so as to represent all the letters of the common alphabet.

A	=	aaaaa	I	=	abaaa	R	=	baaaa
B	=	aaaab	K	=	abaab	S	=	baaab
C	=	aaaba	L	=	ababa	T	=	baaba
D	=	aaabb	M	=	ababb	V	=	baabb
E	=	aabaa	N	=	abbaa	W	=	babaa
F	=	aabab	O	=	abbab	X	=	babab
G	=	aabba	P	=	abbba	Y	=	babba
H	=	aabbb	Q	=	abbbb	Z	=	babbb

Thus, in order to write an A, you write five *a*'s, or aaaaa; and to write a B, you write four *a*'s and one *b*, or aaaab; and so of the rest.

And here, by the way, we gain no small advantage, as this contrivance shows a method of expressing and signifying one's mind to any distance, by objects that are either visible or audible—provided only the objects are but capable of two differences, as bells, speaking-trumpets, fireworks, cannon, &c. But for writing, let the included letter be resolved into this biliteral alphabet; suppose that letter were the word FLY, it is thus resolved:

F   L   Y
aabab ababa babba.

Let there be also at hand two other common alphabets, differing only from each other in the make of their letters; so that, as well the capital as the small be differently shaped or cut at every one's discretion: as thus, for example, in Roman and Italic; each Roman letter constantly representing A, and each Italic letter B.

---

[a] For this cipher is practicable in all things that are capable of two differences.

THE FIRST, OR ROMAN ALPHABET.

A, a	H, h	O, o	V, v
B, b	I, i	P, p	U, u
C, c	K, k	Q, q	W, w
D, d	L, l	R, r	X, x
E, e	M, m	S, s	Y, y
F, f	N, n	T, t	Z, z
G, g			

All the letters of this Roman alphabet are read or deciphered, by translating them into the letter A only.

THE SECOND, OR ITALIC ALPHABET.

A, a	*H, h*	*O, o*	*V, v*
B, b	*I, i*	*P, p*	*U, u*
C, c	*K, k*	*Q, q*	*W, w*
D, d	*L, l*	*R, r*	*X, x*
E, e	*M, m*	*S, s*	*Y, y*
F, f	*N, n*	*T, t*	*Z, z*
G, g			

All the letters of this Italic alphabet are read by translating them into the letter B only.

Now adjust or fit any external double-faced writing, letter by letter, to the internal writing, first made biliterate; and afterwards write it down for the letter or epistle to be sent. Suppose the external writing were, "Stay till I come to you," and the internal one were, "Fly;" then, as we saw above, the word "Fly," resolved by means of the biliteral alphabet, is

<pre>
    F   L   Y
  aabab   ababa   babba
</pre>

whereof I fit, letter by letter, the words "Stay till I come to you," observing the use of my two alphabets of differently shaped letters, thus:

<pre>
  aabab   ababa   babba
  Stay t   il i co   me to you.
</pre>

Having now adjusted my writing according to all my alphabets, I send it to my correspondent, who reads the secret meaning by translating the Roman letters into *a*'s, and the Italic ones into *b*'s, according to the Roman and Italic alphabets, and comparing each combination of five of them with the biliteral alphabet.[b]

---

[b] Those who desire a fuller explanation may consult Bishop Wilkins's "Secret and Swift Messenger," or rather Mr. Falconer's "Cryptomenysis Patefacta, or Art of Secret Information disclosed without a

We herewith annex a fuller example of the cipher of writing "omnia per omnia," viz., an interior letter once sent by the Ephores of Sparta in a scytale or round ciphered staff:—

"Perditæ res. Minidarus cecidit. Milites esuriunt, neque hinc nos extricare, neque hic diutius manere possumus."

The exterior letter in which the above is involved is taken from the first epistle of Cicero. We adjoin it:—

"Ego omni officio ac potius pietate erga te, cæteris satisfacio omnibus; mihi ipse numquam satisfacio. Tanta est enim magnitudo tuorum erga me meritorum, ut quoniam tu nisi perfecta re, de me non conquiesti. Ego quia non idem tu tua causa efficio, vitam mihi esse acerbam putem. In causa hæc sunt; Ammonius regis legatus aperte pecunia non oppugnat. Res agitur per eosdem creditores per quos, cum tu aderas, agebatur regis causa, si qui sunt, qui velint qui pauci sunt, omnes ad Pompeium rem deferri volunt. Senatus religionis calumniam, non religione, sed malevolentia, et illius regiæ largitionis invidia, comprobat, &c."

The doctrine of ciphers has introduced another, relative to it, viz., the art of deciphering without the alphabet of the cipher, or knowing the rules whereby it was formed. This indeed is a work of labour and ingenuity, devoted, as well as the former, to the secret service of princes. Yet by a diligent precaution it may be rendered useless, though, as matters now stand, it is highly serviceable: for if the ciphers in use were good and trusty, several of them would absolutely elude the labour of the decipherer, and yet remain commodious enough, so as to be readily written and read. But through the ignorance and unskilfulness of secretaries and clerks in the courts of princes, the most important affairs are generally committed to weak and treacherous ciphers.[c]—And thus much for the organ of speech.

Key." The trustiness of this cipher depends upon a dexterous use of two hands, or two different kinds of letters, in the same writing, which the skilful decipherer, being thus advertised of, will be quicksighted enough to discern, and consequently be able to decipher, though a foundation seems here laid for several other ciphers, that perhaps could neither be suspected nor deciphered. *Shaw.*

[c] The art of ciphering is doubtless capable of great improvement. It is said that King Charles I. had a cipher consisting only of a straight line differently inclined; and there are ways of ciphering by the mere

CHAPTER II.

Method of Speech includes a wide Part of Tradition. Styled the Wisdom of Delivery. Various kinds of Methods enumerated. Their respective Merits.

THE doctrine concerning the method of speech has been usually treated as a part of logic; it has also found a place in rhetoric, under the name of disposition; but the placing of it in the train of other arts has introduced a neglect of many useful things relating to it. We, therefore, think proper to advance a substantial and capital doctrine of method, under the general name of traditive prudence. But as the kinds of method are various, we shall rather enumerate than divide them; but for one only method, and perpetually splitting and subdividing, it scarce need be mentioned, as being no more than a light cloud of doctrine that soon blows over, though it also proves destructive to the sciences, because the observers thereof, when they wrest things by the laws of their method, and either omit all that do not justly fall under their divisions, or bend them contrary to their own nature, squeeze, as it were, the grain out of the sciences, and grasp nothing but the chaff,—whence this kind of method produces empty compendiums, and loses the solid substance of the sciences.[a]

punctuation of a letter, whilst the words of the letter shall be non-significants, or sense, that leave no room for suspicion. It may also be worth considering, whether the art of deciphering could not be applied to languages, so as to translate, for instance, a Hebrew book without understanding Hebrew. See Morhof, De variis Scripturæ Modis, "Polyhist." tom. i. lib. iv. cap. 2. and Mr. Falconer's "Cryptomenysis Patefacta." *Shaw.*

[a] The design of Ramus, whose method of Dichotomies is here censured, was to reduce all divisions and subdivisions to two members, with a view to obtain a basis for the construction of dilemmas and disjunctive syllogisms. We are never certain that these species of reasoning are legitimate, except when the divisions out of which they rise are exact; and the only test of this accuracy is to be sought in a dichotomous contradictory division, where the supposition of one member necessarily leads to the exclusion of the other. This method of exhausting a subject by an analytic exhaustion of its parts, which he mainly derived from Plato, has its proper sphere in logic; and though condemned in the text, was employed by Bacon in many of his prerogative instances. The error of Ramus consisted in taking only a part for the whole of logic, and applying what is strictly applicable to subjects of a peculiar nature, to the whole range of inference.

CHAP. II.] METHOD DOCTRINAL AND INITIATIVE.

Let the first difference of method be, therefore, betwixt the doctrinal and initiative. By this we do not mean that the initiative method should treat only of the entrance into the sciences, and the other their entire doctrine; but borrowing the word from religion, we call that method initiative which opens and reveals the mysteries of the sciences; so that as the doctrinal method teaches, the initiative method should intimate, the doctrinal method requiring a belief of what is delivered, but the initiative rather that it should be examined. The one deals out the sciences to vulgar learners, the other as to the children of wisdom,—the one having for its end the use of the sciences as they now stand, and the other their progress and further advancement. But this latter method seems deserted; for the sciences have hitherto been delivered as if both the teacher and the learner desired to receive errors by consent,—the teacher pursuing that method which procures the greatest belief to his doctrine, not that which most commodiously submits it to examination, whilst the learner desires present satisfaction without waiting for a just inquiry, as if more concerned not to doubt than not to mistake. Hence the master, through desire of glory, never exposes the weakness of his own science, and the scholar, through his aversion to labour, tries not his own strength; whereas knowledge, which is delivered to others as a web to be further wove, should if possible be introduced into the mind of another in the manner it was first procured; and this may be done in knowledge acquired by

It is evident, however, that the dichotomous process can only be employed in the investigation of subjects which admit of a twofold contradictory division, and that where the primitive elements are composed of four or five distinct members, the method is totally inapplicable. Its use, therefore, ought to be attended with the greatest caution, as the Ramist can hardly be certain that the twofold division, in many cases, is not more apparent than real, and that a further analysis would not necessitate a multiform classification. For want of this foresight, Ramus, with all his subtilty, falls into inconceivable errors, and a great many of Bacon's exemplifications of his method in the crucial instance are direct paralogisms. Milton framed a logic on the model of Ramus's method, seduced rather by the bold antagonism of the latter against Aristotle, than by its philosophic justness. Both the original and the copy are now forgotten, and Ramus is committed to the judgment of posterity rather on his absurdities than his merits. See Hooker, i. 6, with Keble's note. *Ed.*

induction; but for that anticipated and hasty knowledge we have at present it is not easy for the possessor to say by what road he came at it. Yet in a greater or less degree any one might review his knowledge, trace back the steps of his own thoughts, consent afresh, and thus transplant his knowledge into the mind of another as it grew up in his own. For it is in arts as in trees,—if a tree were to be used, no matter for the root, but if it were to be transplanted, it is a surer way to take the root than the slips. So the transplantation now practised of the sciences makes a great show, as it were, of branches, that without the roots may be fit indeed for the builder, but not for the planter. He who would promote the growth of the sciences should be less solicitous about the trunk or body of them, and bend his care to preserve the roots, and draw them out with some little earth about them. Of this kind of transplantation there is some resemblance in the method of mathematicians;[b] but in general we do not see that it is either used or inquired after; we therefore place it among the deficiencies, under the name of the traditive lamp, or a method for posterity.[c]

There is another difference of method, bearing some relation to the former intention, though in reality almost opposite to it; both of them have this in common, that they separate the vulgar audience from the select; but herein they are opposite, that the former introduces a more open and the other a more secret way of instruction than the common; hence let them be distinguished, by terming the former plain or open, and the latter the learned or concealed method, thus transferring to the manner of delivery the difference made use of by the ancients, especially in publishing their books. This concealed or enigmatical method was itself also employed by the ancients with prudence and judgment, but is of late dishonoured by many, who use it as a false light to set off their counterfeit wares. The design of it seems to

[b] To this purpose see Wolfius's "Brevis Commentatio de Methodo Mathematica," prefixed to his "Elementa Matheseos Universæ;" as also his "Logics and Metaphysics." *Shaw.*

[c] Perhaps M. Tschirnhaus's "Medicina Mentis, sive Tentamen genuinæ Logicæ, in qua disseritur de Methodo detegendi incognitas Veritates," may pave the way for supplying this desideratum; proceeding as it does upon a mathematical and algebraical foundation, to raise a method of discovering unknown truths. *Shaw.*

have been, by the veil of tradition to keep the vulgar from the secrets of sciences, and to admit only such as had, by the help of a master, attained to the interpretation of dark sayings, or were able, by the strength of their own genius, to enter within the veil.

The next difference of method is of great moment with regard to the sciences, as these are delivered either in the way of aphorism or methodically. It highly deserves to be noted, that the general custom is, for men to raise as it were a formal and solemn art from a few axioms and observations upon any subject, swelling it out with their own witty inventions, illustrating it by examples, and binding the whole up into method. But that other way of delivery by aphorisms has numerous advantages over the methodical. And first, it gives us a proof of the author's abilities, and shows whether he hath entered deep into his subject or not. Aphorisms are ridiculous things, unless wrought from the central parts of the sciences; and here all illustration, excursion, variety of examples, deduction, connection, and particular description, is cut off, so that nothing besides an ample stock of observations is left for the matter of aphorisms. And, therefore, no person is equal to the forming of aphorisms, nor would ever think of them, if he did not find himself copiously and solidly instructed for writing upon a subject. But in methods so great a power have order, connection, and choice,—

"Tantum series juncturaque pollet ;
Tantum de medio sumptis accedit honoris,"[d]—

that methodical productions sometimes make a show of I know not what specious art, which, if they were taken to pieces, separated, and undressed, would fall back again almost to nothing. Secondly, a methodical delivery has the power of enforcing belief and consent, but directs not much to practical indications, as carrying with it a kind of demonstration in circle, where the parts mutually enlighten each other, and so gratifies the imagination the more; but as actions lie scattered in common life, scattered instructions suit them the best. Lastly, as aphorisms exhibit only certain scraps and fragments of the sciences, they carry with them an invitation

[d] Hor. Art. Poet. 242.

to others for adding and lending their assistance, whereas methods dress up the sciences into bodies, and make men imagine they have them complete.

There is a farther difference of method, and that too very considerable; for as the sciences are delivered either by assertions with their proofs, or by questions with their answers, if the latter method be pursued too far, it retards the advancement of the sciences no less than it would the march of an army, to be sitting down against every little fort in the way; whereas, if the better of the battle be gained, and the fortune of the war steadily pursued, such lesser places will surrender of themselves, though it must be allowed unsafe to leave any large and fortified place at the back of the army. In the same manner confutations are to be avoided or sparingly used in delivering the sciences, so as only to conquer the greater prejudices and prepossessions of the mind, without provoking and engaging the lesser doubts and scruples.

Another difference of method lies in suiting it to the subject; for mathematics, the most abstract and simple of the sciences, is delivered one way, and politics, the more compound and perplexed, another. For an uniform method cannot be commodiously observed in a variety of matter. And as we approve of particular topics for invention, so we must in some measure allow of particular methods of delivery.

There is another difference of method to be used with judgment in delivering the sciences, and this is governed by the informations and anticipations of the science to be delivered that are before infused and impressed upon the mind of the learner. For that science which comes as an entire stranger to the mind is to be delivered one way, and that which is familiarized by opinions already imbibed and received another. And therefore, Aristotle, when he thought to chastise, really commended Democritus, in saying, "If we would dispute in earnest, and not hunt after comparisons," &c.; as if he would tax Democritus with being too full of comparisons; whereas they whose instructions are already grounded in popular opinion have nothing left them but to dispute and prove, whilst others have a double task whose doctrines transcend the vulgar opinions; viz., first to render what they deliver intelligible, and then to prove it; whence they must of necessity have recourse to simile and metaphor, the better to enter the human capacity.[c] Hence we find in the more ignorant ages, when learning was in its infancy, and those conceptions which are now trite and vulgar were new and unheard of, everything was full of parables and similitudes, otherwise the things then proposed would either have been passed over without due notice and attention, or else have been rejected as paradoxes. For it is a rule in the doctrine of delivery, that every science which comports not with anticipations and prejudices must seek the assistance of similes and allusions. And thus much for the different kinds of methods, which have not hitherto been observed; but for the others, as the analytic, systatic, diæretic, cryptic, homeric, &c., they are already justly discovered and ranged.

Method has two parts, one regarding the disposition of a whole work or the subject of a book, and the other the limitation of propositions. For architecture not only regards the fabric of the whole building, but also the figure of the columns, arches, &c.; for method is as it were the architecture of the sciences. And herein Ramus has deserved better, by reviving the ancient rules of method,[f] than by obtruding his own dichotomies. But I know not by what fatality it happens that, as the poets often feign, the most precious things have the most pernicious keepers. Doubtless the endeavours of Ramus about the reduction of propositions threw him upon his epitomes, and the flats and shallows of the sciences: for it must be a fortunate and well-directed genius that shall attempt to make the axioms of the sciences convertible, and not at the same time render them circular, that is, keep them from returning into themselves.[g] And yet the attempt of Ramus in this way has not been useless.

[e] The reader will bear in mind that this was the situation of the author in his time, and on that account dispense with his figurative style, though it may not be altogether so necessary at present, when we are accustomed to the freest range of philosophical inquiry. *Ed.*

[f] Κάθολον πρῶτον, κατὰ παντὸς, καθ' αὐτὸ, κ.τ.λ.; relation to the first principle, relation to all, and relation to one's self.

[g] The axioms in the text must not be understood as applying to the mathematical sciences, which being, as Condillac observes, purely ideal, exact in their conversion nothing more than a detailed exposition of the properties we have already included in their definition; but of the

There are still two other limitations of propositions, besides that for making them convertible,—the one for extending and the other for producing them. For if it be just that the sciences have two other dimensions, besides depth, viz. length and breadth, their depth bearing relation to their truth and reality, as these are what constitute their solidity; their breadth may be computed from one science to another, and their length from the highest degree to the lowest in the same science,—the one comprehends the ends and true boundaries of the sciences, whence propositions may be treated distinctly, and not promiscuously, and all repetition, excursion, and confusion avoided; the other prescribes a rule how far and to what particular degree the propositions of the sciences are to be reduced. But no doubt something must here be left to practice and experience; for men ought ot avoid the extreme of Antoninus Pius, and not mince cumin-seed in the sciences, nor multiply divisions to the utmost. And it is here well worth the inquiry, how far we should check ourselves in this respect; for we see that too extensive generals, unless they be reduced, afford little information, but rather expose the sciences to the ridicule of practical men, as being no more fitted for practice than a general map of the world to show the road from London to York. The best rules may well be compared to a metalline speculum, which represents the images of things, but not before it is polished; for so rules and precepts are useful after having undergone the file of experience. But if these rules could be made exact and clear from the first, it were

objective sciences, where, since our knowledge of the subject is generally so imperfect as to render any direct definition uncertain, we are obliged to involve ourselves in a chain of reasoning to prove that the interchangeable attribute can be affirmed of the subject in its whole extent, and that both possess no qualities which are not convertible with each other. In establishing this reciprocal accordance of parts, it frequently happens that, having to connect a series of propositions in a chain of mutual dependence on each other, the first being proved by the second and the second by the third, &c., we arrive at and rest the whole proof upon a conclusion which is nothing else than the enunciation of the very proposition which we are labouring to establish, instead of grounding the argument upon some universally admitted principle or well-ascertained fact. This fallacy logicians term a vicious circle, and is the error to which Bacon alludes in the text. *Ed.*

better, because they would then stand in less need of experience.

We must not omit that some men, rather ostentatious than learned, have laboured about a certain method not deserving the name of a true method, as being rather a kind of imposture, which may nevertheless be acceptable to some busy minds. This art so scatters the drops of the sciences, that any pretender may misapply it for ostentation, with some appearance of learning. Such was the art of Lully, and such the typocosmia cultivated by some; for these are only a collection of terms of art heaped together, to the end that those who have them in readiness may seem to understand the arts whereto the terms belong. Collections of this kind are like a piece-broker's shop, where there are many slips, but nothing of great value. And thus much for the science which we call traditive prudence.[h]

CHAPTER III.

The Grounds and Functions of Rhetoric. Three Appendices which belong only to the Preparatory Part, viz., the Colours of Good and Evil, both simple and composed; the Antithesis of Things (the pro and con. of General Questions); the Minor Forms of Speech (the Elaboration of Exordiums, Perorations, and Leading Arguments).

WE next proceed to the doctrine of ornament in speech, called by the name of rhetoric or oratory. This in itself is certainly an excellent science, and has been laudably culti-

---

[h] Concio, who preceded Bacon, anticipates, in his treatise "De Methodo," many of the fundamental principles of the inductive logicians, and discriminates many branches of analysis, which they confound. Descartes, in his book on the same subject, has endeavoured to reduce the whole business of method to four rules, which, however, are found in the precepts of Aristotle. Johan. Beyer undertook to write upon this subject, in his "Filum Labyrinthi," according to the design of Bacon, but appears not to have understood the author, and has rather obscured his doctrine than improved it. M. Tschirnhaus, however, has treated the subject more suitably to its merit, in his "Medicina Mentis," mentioned above, in the note to § 2. A great variety of methods have been advanced by different authors, an ample catalogue of whom may be found in Morhof's "Polyhist." tom. i. lib. ii. cap. 7, "De Methodis Variis." *Ed.*

vated by writers. But to form a just estimate, eloquence is certainly inferior to wisdom. The great difference between them appears in the words of God to Moses upon his refusing, for want of elocution, the charge assigned him: "Aaron shall be thy speaker, and thou shalt be to him as God."[a] But for advantage and popular esteem, wisdom gives place to eloquence. "The wise in heart shall be called prudent, but the sweet of tongue shall find greater things," says Solomon:[b] clearly intimating that wisdom procures a name and admiration, but that eloquence is of greater efficacy in business and civil life. And for the cultivation of this art, the emulation betwixt Aristotle and the rhetoricians of his time, the earnest study of Cicero, his long practice and utmost endeavour every way to dignify oratory, hath made these authors even exceed themselves in their books upon the subject. Again, the great examples of eloquence found in the orations of Demosthenes and Cicero, added to the perfection and exactness of their precepts, have doubled its advancement. And therefore the deficiencies we find in it rather turn upon certain collections belonging to its train, than upon the doctrine and use of the art itself.

But in our manner to open and stir the earth a little about the roots of this science, certainly rhetoric is subservient to the imagination, as logic is to the understanding. And if the thing be well considered, the office and use of this art is but to apply and recommend the dictates of reason to the imagination, in order to excite the affections and will. For the administration of reason is disturbed three ways; viz., 1. either by the ensnaring of sophistry, which belongs to logic; 2. the delusion of words, which belongs to rhetoric; or 3. by the violence of the affections, which belongs to ethics. For as in transacting business with others, men are commonly over-reached, or drawn from their own purposes either by cunning, importunity, or vehemence; so in the inward business we transact with ourselves, we are either, 1. undermined by the fallacy of arguments; 2. disquieted and solicited by the assiduity of impressions and observations; or 3. shaken and carried away by the violence of the passions. Nor is the state of human nature so unequal, that these arts

---

[a] Exodus iv. 14, 15, 16.   [b] Prov. i. 21.

and faculties should have power to disturb the reason, and none to confirm and strengthen it; for they do this in a much greater degree. The end of logic is to teach the form of arguments for defending, and not for ensnaring, the understanding. The end of ethics is so to compose the affections, that they may co-operate with reason, and not insult it. And lastly, the end of rhetoric is to fill the imagination with such observations and images as may assist reason, and not overthrow it. For the abuses of an art come in obliquely only, and not for practice, but caution. It was therefore great injustice in Plato, though it proceeded from a just contempt of the rhetoricians of his time, to place rhetoric among the voluptuary arts,[c] and resemble it to cookery, which corrupted wholesome meats, and, by variety of sauces, made unwholesome ones more palatable. For speech is, doubtless, more employed to adorn virtue than to colour vice. This faculty is always ready, for every man speaks more virtuously than he either thinks or acts. And it is excellently observed by Thucydides, that something of this kind was usually objected to Cleon;[d] who, as he always defended the worst side of a cause, was ever inveighing against eloquence and the grace of speech, well knowing that no man could speak gracefully upon a base subject, though every man easily might upon an honourable one : for Plato elegantly observed, though the expression is now grown trite, that if virtue could be beheld, she would have great admirers.[e] But rhetoric, by plainly painting virtue and goodness, renders them, as it were, conspicuous ; for as they cannot be seen by the corporeal eye, the next degree is to have them set before us as lively as possible by the ornament of words and the strength of imagination. The Stoics, therefore, were deservedly ridiculed by Cicero for endeavouring to inculcate virtue upon the mind by short and subtile sentences and conclusions,[f] which have little or no relation to the imagination and the will.

Again, if the affections were orderly and obedient to reason, there would be no great use of persuasion and insinuation to gain access to the mind ; it would then be

[c] As it was in Bacon to place painting and music in the same category.
[d] B. iii. 42.   [e] Phedias.
[f] Orator. ii. 38 ; Tusc. Disp. ii. 18. 42.

sufficient that things themselves were nakedly and simply proposed and proved ; but, on the contrary, the affections revolt so often, and raise such disturbances and seditions—

―― " Video meliora, proboque ;
Deteriora sequor,"ᵍ—

that reason would perfectly be led captive, did not the persuasion of eloquence win over the imagination from the side of the passions, and promote an alliance betwixt it and reason against the affections. For we must observe that the affections themselves always aim at an apparent good, and in this respect have something common with reason. But here lies the difference, that the affections principally regard a present good, whilst reason, seeing far before it, chooses also the future and capital good. And therefore, as present things strike the imagination strongest, reason is generally subdued; but when eloquence and the power of persuasion raise up remote and future objects, and set them to view as if they were present ; then imagination goes over to the side of reason, and renders it victorious.

Hence we conclude, that rhetoric can no more be accused of colouring the worst part, than logic of teaching sophistry. For we know that the doctrines of contraries are the same, though their use be opposite ; and logic does not only differ from rhetoric, according to the vulgar notion, as the first is like the hand clenched, and the other like the hand open ; but much more in this, that logic considers reason in its natural state, and rhetoric as it stands in vulgar opinion ; whence Aristotle prudently places rhetoric between logic and ethics, along with politics, as partaking of them both. For the proofs and demonstrations of logic are common to all mankind, but the proof and persuasion of rhetoric must be varied according to the audience, like a musician suiting himself to different ears.

" Orpheus in sylvis, inter Delphinas Arion."ʰ

And this application and variation of speech should, if we desire its perfection, extend so far, that if the same things were to be delivered to different persons, yet a different set of words should be used to each.ⁱ Though it is certain that

ᵍ Ovid, Metam. vii. 20.   ʰ Virg. Ecl. viii. 56.
ⁱ For one of the most perfect exemplifications of this rule, see Lord

the greatest orators, generally, have not this political and sociable eloquence in private discourse; for whilst they endeavour at ornament and elegant forms of speech, they fall not upon that ready application and familiar style of discourse which they might with more advantage use to particulars. And it were certainly proper to begin a new inquiry into this subject; we therefore place it among the deficiencies under the title of prudential conversation,[k] which the more attentively a man considers, the higher value he will set upon it; but whether this be placed under rhetoric or politics is of no great significance.

We have already observed that the desiderata in this art are rather appendages than parts of the art itself; and all of them belong to the repository thereof, for the furnishing of speech and invention. To proceed in this view; first, we find no writer that hath carefully followed the prudent example of Aristotle, who began to collect popular marks or colours of apparent good and evil, as well simple as comparative.[l] These, in reality, are but rhetorical sophisms, though of excellent use, especially in business and private discourse. But the labour of Aristotle about these colours has three defects; for 1. though they are numerous, he recites but few; 2. he has not annexed their redargutions; and 3. he seems not to have understood their full use: for they serve as well to affect and move as to demonstrate. There are many forms of speech which, though significative of the same things, yet affect men differently; as a sharp instrument penetrates more than a blunt one, supposing both of them urged with equal force. There is nobody but would be more affected by hearing this expression, How your enemies will triumph upon this:

"Hoc Ithacus velit, et magno mercentur Atridæ,"[m]

than if it were simply said, This will injure your affairs: therefore these stings and goads of speech are not to be

Brougham's discourse to the Glasgow University and to the Manchester Mechanics' Institution. *Ed.*
[k] The foundations for this are, in some measure, laid by the learned Morhof in the sketch of his "Homiletice Erudita." See "Polyhistor," tom. i. lib. i. cap. 25. See also Jo. Andr. Bosii "De Prudentia et Eloquentia Civili comparanda," ed. Jenæ, 1698; and "Prudentia Consultatoria in Usum Auditorii Thomasiani," ed. Halæ Magdeburg, 1721. *Ed.* [l] Rhetor. ii. 3–8. [m] Æneid, ii. 104.

neglected. And since we propose this as a desideratum, we will, after our manner, give a sketch of it, in the way of examples; for precepts will not so well illustrate the thing. In deliberatives, we inquire what is good, what evil; and of good, which is the greater, and of evil, which the less. Whence the persuader's task is to make things appear good or evil, and that in a higher or lower degree; which may be performed by true and solid reasons, or represented by colours, popular glosses, and circumstances of such force as to sway an ordinary judgment; or even a wise man that does not fully and considerately attend to the subject. But besides this power to alter the nature of the subject in appearance, and so lead to error, they are of use to quicken and strengthen such opinions and persuasions as are true; for reasons nakedly delivered, and always after one manner, enter but heavily, especially with delicate minds; whereas, when varied and enlivened by proper forms and insinuations, they cause a stronger apprehension, and often suddenly win the mind to a resolution. Lastly, to make a true and safe judgment, nothing can be of greater use and preservation to the mind than the discovery and reprehension of these colours, showing in what cases they hold and in what not; which cannot be done without a comprehensive knowledge of things; but when performed, it clears the judgment, and makes it less apt to slip into error.[n]

SOPHISM I.—*What men praise and celebrate, is good; what they dispraise and censure, evil.*

This sophism deceives four ways; viz., either through ignorance, deceit, party, or the natural disposition of the praiser or dispraiser. 1. Through ignorance; for what signifies the judgment of the rabble in distinguishing good and evil? Phocion took it right, who, being applauded by the multitude, asked, What he had done amiss?[o] 2. Through

[n] This paragraph is taken from the fragment of the Colours of Good and Evil, usually printed as an appendix to the author's essays. That fragment was reconsidered, better digested, and finished by the author, in order to fit it for this place, in the De Augmentis Scientiarum; to which himself assigned it in the Latin edition. The reason of its being called a fragment was, that the author had made a large collection of such kind of sophisms in his youth; but could only find time in his riper years, to add the fallacies and confutations of the following twelve. *Shaw*   [o] Plutarch.

deceit; for those who praise or dispraise commonly have their own views in it, and speak not their real sentiments.

"*Laudat venales, qui vult extrudere, merces.*"[p]

"It is faulty, it is faulty, says the buyer; but when he is gone, he congratulates himself upon the bargain."[q] 3. Through party; for men immoderately extol those of their own and depress those of the opposite party. 4. Through disposition or temper; for some men are naturally formed servile and fawning, and others captious and morose; so that when such persons praise or dispraise, they do but gratify their humour, without much regard to truth.

II.—*What is commended, even by an enemy, is a great good; but what is censured, even by a friend, a great evil.*

The fallacy seems to lie here, that it is easily believed the force of truth extorts from us what we speak against our inclination.

This colour deceives through the subtilty both of friends and enemies. For praises of enemies are not always against their will, nor forced from them by truth; but they choose to bestow them where they may create envy or danger to their adversary. Hence the foolish conceit was current among the Greeks, that he who was praised by another with malicious intent, never failed to have his nose disfigured with a pustule. Again this colour deceives, because enemies sometimes use praises like prefaces, that they may the more freely calumniate afterwards. On the other side, it deceives by the craft of friends, who also sometimes acknowledge our faults, and speak of them not as compelled thereto by any force of truth, but touch only such as may do little hurt, and make us, in everything else, the best men in the world. And lastly, it deceives, because friends also use their reproofs, as enemies do their commendations, by way of preface, that they may afterwards launch out more fully in our praises.

III.—*To be deprived of a good, is an evil; and to be deprived of an evil, a good.*

This colour deceives two ways; viz., either by the comparison of good and evil, or by the succession of good to good, or evil to evil. 1. By comparison: thus if it were good for mankind to be deprived of acorns, it follows not

[p] Hor. Epist. ii. 11. [q] Prov. xx.

that such food was bad, but that acorns were good, though bread be better. Nor, if it were an evil for the people of Sicily to be deprived of Dionysius the Elder, does it follow that the same Dionysius was a good prince, but that he was less evil than Dionysius the Younger. 2. By succession: for the privation of a good does not always give place to an evil, but sometimes to a greater good,—as when the blossom falls, the fruit succeeds. Nor does the privation of an evil always give place to a good, but sometimes to a greater evil; for Milo, by the death of his enemy Clodius, lost a fair harvest of glory.

IV.—*What approaches to good, is good; and what recedes from good, is evil.*

It is almost universal, that things agreeing in nature agree also in place, and that things disagreeing in nature differ as widely in situation; for all things have an appetite of associating with what is agreeable, and of repelling what is disagreeable to them.

This colour deceives three ways; viz., by depriving, obscuring, and protecting. 1. By depriving; for the largest things, and most excellent in their kind, attract all they can to themselves, and leave what is next them destitute; thus the underwood growing near a large tree is the poorest wood of the field, because the tree deprives it of sap and nourishment,—whence it was well said, that the servants of the rich are the greatest slaves;[r] and it was witty of him who compared the inferior attendants in the courts of princes to the vigils of feast-days, which, though nearest to feast-days, are themselves but meagre. 2. By obscuring: for it is also the nature of excellent things in their kind, though they do not impoverish the substance of what lies near them, yet to overshadow and obscure it; whence the astrologers say, that though in all the planets conjunction is the most perfect amity, yet the sun, though good in aspect, is evil in conjunction. 3. By protecting: for things come together, not only from a similitude of nature, but even what is evil flies to that which is good (especially in civil society) for concealment and protection. Thus hypocrisy draws near to religion for shelter:

"Sæpe latet vitium proximitate boni."[s]

Divitis servi maxime servi.   [s] Ovid, Ars Amandi, ii. 662.

So sanctuary-men, who were commonly malefactors, used to be nearest the priests and prelates; for the majesty of good things is such, that the confines of them are reverend. On the other side, good draws near to evil, not for society, but for conversation and reformation; and hence physicians visit the sick more than the sound, and hence it was objected to our Saviour, that he conversed with publicans and sinners.[t]

V.—*As all parties challenge the first place, that to which the rest unanimously give the second seems the best; each taking the first place out of affection to itself, but giving the second where it is really due.*

Thus Cicero attempted to prove the Academics to be the best sect; for, saith he, "Ask a Stoic which philosophy is best, and he will prefer his own; then ask him which is the next best, and he will confess, the Academics. Ask an Epicurean the same question, who can scarce endure the Stoic, and as soon as he hath placed his own sect, he places the Academics next him."[u] So if a prince separately examined several competitors for a place, perhaps the ablest and most deserving man would have most second voices.

This colour deceives in respect of envy; for men are accustomed, next after themselves and their own faction, to prefer those that are softest and most pliable, with intent to exclude such as would obstruct their measures; whence this colour of meliority and pre-eminence becomes a sign of enervation and weakness.

VI.—*That is absolutely best the excellence whereof is greatest.*

This colour has these forms,—let us not wander in generals, let us compare particular with particular, &c., and though it seem strong, and rather logical than rhetorical, yet it is sometimes a fallacy:—1. Because many things are exposed to great danger, but if they escape, prove more excellent than others; whence their kind is inferior, as being subject to accident and miscarriage, though more noble in the individual. Thus, to instance, in the blossoms of March, one whereof, according to the French proverb, is, if it escape accidents, worth ten blossoms of May; so that though in general the blossoms of May excel the blossoms of March, yet in individuals the best blossoms of March may be preferred to the best of May. 2. Because the nature of things

---

[t] Matt. ix.   [u] Academ. Frag. By Varro.

in some kinds or species is more equal, and in others more unequal. Thus warm climates generally produce people of a sharper genius than cold ones; yet the extraordinary geniuses of cold countries usually excel the extraordinary geniuses of the warmer. So in the case of armies, if the cause were tried by single combat, the victory might often go on the one side, but if by a pitched battle, on the other; for excellencies and superiorities are rather accidental things, whilst kinds are governed by nature or discipline. 3. Lastly, many kinds have much refuse, which countervails what they have of excellent; and, therefore, though metal be generally more precious than stone, yet a diamond is more precious than gold.

VII.—*What keeps a matter safe and entire, is good; but what leaves no retreat, is bad: for inability to retire is a kind of impotency, but power is a good.*

Thus Æsop feigned that two frogs consulting together in a time of drought what was to be done, the one proposed going down into a deep well, because probably the water would not fail there, but the other answered, "If it should fail there too, how shall we get up again?" And the foundation of the colour lies here, that human actions are so uncertain and exposed to danger, that the best condition seems to be that which has most outlets. And this persuasion turns upon such forms as these,—You shall engage yourself; You shall not be your own carver; You shall keep the matter in your hands, &c.[x]

The fallacy of the sophism lies here:—1. Because fortune presses so close upon human affairs, that some resolution is necessary; for not to resolve is to resolve, so that irresolution frequently entangles us in necessities more than resolving. And this seems to be a disease of the mind, like to that of covetousness, only transferred from the desire of possessing riches to the desire of free will and power; for as the covetous man enjoys no part of his possessions, for fear of lessening them, so the unresolved man executes no-

---

[x] Sertorius having so far obstructed Pompey as to burn one of the towns of his allies in his sight, without experiencing from him the slightest opposition, added, with scorn, "I will teach this young scholar of Sylla, that it is more necessary for a general to look behind than before him;"—a piece of advice, we need hardly say, since the whole of life is a combat, as applicable to civil as to military warfare. *Ed.*

thing, that he may not abridge his freedom and power of acting. 2. Because necessity and the fortune of the throw adds a spur to the mind; whence that saying, "In other respects equal, but in necessity superior."y

VIII.—*That evil we bring upon ourselves, is greater; and that proceeding from without us, less.*

Because remorse of conscience doubles adversity, as a consciousness of one's own innocence is a great support in affliction,—whence the poets exaggerate those sufferings most, and paint them leading to despair, wherein the person accuses and tortures himself.

"Seque unam clamat causamque, caputque malorum."z

On the other side, persons lessen and almost annihilate their misfortunes, by reflecting upon their own innocence and merit. Besides, when the evil comes from without, it leaves a man to the full liberty of complaint, whereby he spends his grief and eases his heart; for we conceive indignation at human injuries, and either meditate revenge ourselves, or implore and expect it from the Divine vengeance. Or if the injury came from fortune itself, yet this leaves us to an expostulation with the Divine Powers,—

"Atque Deos, atque astra, vocat crudelia mater."a

But if the evil be derived from ourselves, the stings of grief strike inwards, and stab and wound the mind the deeper.

This colour deceives,—1. By hope, which is the greatest antidote to evils; for it is commonly in our power to amend our faults, but not our fortunes; whence Demosthenes said frequently to the Athenians, "What is worst for the past is best for the future, since it happens by neglect and misconduct that your affairs are come to this low ebb. Had you, indeed, acted your parts to the best, and yet matters should thus have gone backward, there would be no hopes of amendment; but as it has happened principally through your own errors, if these are corrected, all may be recovered."b So Epictetus, speaking of the degrees of the mind's tranquillity, assigns the lowest place to such as accuse others, a higher to those who accuse themselves, but the highest to those who neither accuse themselves nor others. 2. By pride, which so cleaves to the mind that it will scarce suffer men to acknow-

y Livy, iv. 28. z Æneid, xii. 600. a Virg. Ecl. v. 23. b Philip. i.

ledge their errors; and to avoid any such acknowledgment they are extremely patient under those misfortunes which they bring upon themselves; for as, when a fault is committed, and before it be known who did it, a great stir and commotion is made; but if at length it appears to be done by a son or a wife, the bustle is at an end. And thus it happens when one must take a fault to one's self. And hence we frequently see that women, when they do anything against their friends' consent, whatever misfortune follows, they seldom complain, but set a good face on it.

IX.—*The degree of privation seems greater than that of diminution, and the degree of inception greater than that of increase.*

It is a position in mathematics, that there is no proportion between something and nothing, and therefore the degrees of nullity and quiddity seem larger than the degrees of increase and decrease, as it is for a monoculus to lose an eye than for a man who has two. So if a man has lost several children, it gives him more grief to lose the last than all the rest, because this was the hope of his family. Therefore, the Sibyl, when she had burned two of her three books, doubled her price upon the third, because the loss of this would only have been a degree of privation, and not of diminution.

This colour deceives,—1. in things whose use and service lie in a sufficiency, competency, or determinate quantity: thus if a man were to pay a large sum upon a penalty, it might be harder upon him to want twenty shillings for this than ten pounds for another occasion. So in running through an estate, the first step towards it—viz., breaking in upon the stock—is a higher degree of mischief than the last, viz., spending the last penny. And to this colour belong those common forms—It is too late to pinch at the bottom of the purse; As good never a whit as never the better, &c. 2. It deceives from this principle in nature, that the corruption of one thing is the generation of another; whence the ultimate degree of privation itself is often less felt, as it gives occasion and a spur to some new course. So when Demosthenes rebuked the people for hearkening to the dishonourable and unequal conditions of King Philip, he called those conditions the food of their sloth and indolence, which they had better be without, because then their industry would be excited to procure other remedies. So a blunt physician whom I knew, when the delicate ladies complained to him, they were they could not tell how, yet could not endure to take physic, he would tell them their way was to be sick, for then they would be glad to take anything. 3. Nay, the degree of privation itself, or the extremest indigence, may be serviceable, not only to excite our industry, but to command our patience.

The second part of this sophism stands upon the same foundation, or the degrees betwixt something and nothing; whence the common-place of extolling the beginnings of everything, Well-begun is half-done, &c.

"Dimidium facti, qui cœpit, habet."[c]

And hence the superstition of the astrologers, who judge the disposition and fortune of a man from the instant of his nativity or conception.

This colour deceives,—1. because many beginnings are but imperfect offers and essays, which vanish and come to nothing without repetition and farther advancement; so that here the second degree seems more worthy and powerful than the first, as a body-horse in a team draws more than the fore-horse: whence it is not ill said, The second word makes the quarrel; for the first might perhaps have proved harmless if it had not been retorted; therefore the first gives the occasion indeed, but the second makes reconciliation more difficult. 2. This sophism deceives by weariness, which makes perseverance of greater dignity than inception; for chance or nature may give a beginning, but only settled affection and judgment can give continuance. 3. It deceives in things whose nature and common course carries them contrary to the first attempt, which is therefore continually frustrated, and gets no ground unless the force be redoubled: hence the common forms—Not to go forwards is to go backwards—running up hill—rowing against the stream, &c. But if it be with the stream, or with the hill, then the degree of inception has by much the advantage. 4. This colour not only reaches to the degree of inception from power to action, compared with the degree from action to increase, but also to the degree from want of power to power, com-

[c] Hor. Epist. 1, ii. 40.

pared with the degree from power to action; for the degree from want of power to power seems greater than that from power to action.

X.—*What relates to truth is greater than what relates to opinion; but the measure and trial of what relates to opinion is what a man would not do if he thought he were secret.*

So the Epicureans pronounce of the stoical felicity placed in virtue, that it is the felicity of a player, who, left by his audience, would soon sink in his spirit; whence they in ridicule call virtue a theatrical good; but it is otherwise in riches—

"Populus me sibilat; at mihi plaudo,"[d]

and pleasure,

—— "Grata sub imo
Gaudia corde premens, vultu simulante pudorem,"[e]

which are felt more inwardly.

The fallacy of this colour is somewhat subtile, though the answer to the example be easy, as virtue is not chosen for the sake of popular fame, and as every one ought principally to reverence himself; so that a virtuous man will be virtuous in a desert as well as a theatre, though perhaps virtue is made somewhat more vigorous by praise, as heat by reflection. But this only denies the supposition, and does not expose the fallacy. Allowing, then, that virtue, joined with labour, would not be chosen but for the praise and fame which usually attend it, yet it is no consequence that virtue should not be desired principally for its own sake, since fame may be only an impellent, and not a constituent or efficient cause. Thus, if when two horses are rode without the spur, one of them performs better than the other, but with the spur the other far exceeds, this will be judged the better horse: and to say that his mettle lies in the spur, is not making a true judgment; for since the spur is a common instrument in horsemanship, and no impediment or burthen to the horse, he will not be esteemed the worse horse that wants it, but the going well without it is rather a point of delicacy than perfection. So glory and honour are the spurs to virtue, which, though it might languish without them, yet since they are always at hand unsought, virtue is

[d] Hor. i. Sat. i. 66. [e] Ibid.

not less to be chosen for itself, because it needs the spur of fame and reputation, which clearly confutes the sophism.

XI.—*What is procured by our own virtue and industry is a greater good; and what by another's, or by the gift of fortune, a less.*

The reasons are,—1. Future hope, because in the favours of others, or the gifts of fortune, there is no great certainty; but our own virtue and abilities are always with us: so that when they have purchased us one good, we have them as ready, and by use better edged to procure us another. 2. Because what we enjoy by the benefit of others carries with it an obligation to them for it, whereas what is derived from ourselves comes without clog or incumbrance. Nay, when the Divine Providence bestows favours upon us, they require acknowledgments and a kind of retribution to the Supreme Being; but in the other kind, men rejoice (as the prophet speaks), and are glad; they offer to their toils, and sacrifice to their nets.[f] 3. Because what comes to us unprocured by our own virtue, yields not that praise and reputation we affect; for actions of great felicity may produce much wonder, but no praise: so Cicero said to Cæsar, "We have enough to admire, but want somewhat to praise."[g] 4. Because the purchases of our own industry are commonly joined with labour and struggle, which have not only some sweetness themselves, but give an edge and relish to enjoyment. Venison is sweet to him that kills it.[h]

There are four opposites or counter-colours to this sophism, and may serve as confutations to the four preceding colours respectively. 1. Because felicity seems to be a work of the Divine favour, and accordingly begets confidence and alacrity in ourselves, as well as respect and reverence from others. And this felicity extends to casual things, which human virtue can hardly reach. So when Cæsar said to the master of the ship in a storm, "Thou carriest Cæsar and his fortune;" if he should have said, "Thou carriest Cæsar and his virtue," it had been but a small support against the danger. 2. Because those things which proceed from virtue and industry are imitable, and lie open to others; whereas felicity is inimitable, and the prerogative of a singular person:

[f] Habac. i. 15, 16.
[g] "Quæ miremur habemus, quæ laudemus expectamus."—Orat. pro Marcellus.   [h] Suavis cibus à venatu.

whence, in general, natural things are preferred to artificial, because incapable of imitation; for whatever is imitable seems common, and in every one's power. 3. The things that proceed from felicity seem free gifts unpurchased by industry, but those acquired by virtue seem bought: whence Plutarch said elegantly of the successes of Timoleon (an extremely fortunate man), compared with those of his contemporaries Agesilaus and Epaminondas, "that they were like Homer's verses, and besides their other excellencies, ran peculiarly smooth and natural." 4. Because what happens unexpectedly is more acceptable, and enters the mind with greater pleasure; but this effect cannot be had in things procured by our own industry.

XII.—*What consists of many divisible parts is greater, and more one than what consists of fewer; for all things when viewed in their parts seem greater, whence also a plurality of parts shows bulky; but a plurality of parts has the stronger effect, if they lie in no certain order, for thus they resemble infinity and prevent comprehension.*

This sophism appears gross at first sight; for it is not plurality of parts alone, without majority, that makes the total greater; yet the imagination is often carried away, and the sense deceived with this colour. Thus to the eye the road upon a naked plain may seem shorter, than where there are trees, buildings, or other marks, by which to distinguish and divide the distance. So when a monied man divides his chests and bags, he seems to himself richer than he was; and therefore a way to amplify anything is to break it into several parts, and examine them separately. And this makes the greater show, if done without order; for confusion shows things more numerous than they are. But matters ranged and set in order appear more confined, and prove that nothing is omitted; whilst such as are represented in confusion not only appear more in number, but leave a suspicion of many more behind.

This colour deceives,—1. if the mind entertain too great an opinion of anything; for then the breaking of it will destroy that false notion, and show the thing really as it is, without amplification. Thus if a man be sick or in pain, the time seems longer without a clock than with one; for though the irksomeness of pain makes the time seem longer than it is, yet the measuring it corrects the error, and shows it shorter than that false opinion had conceived it. And so in a naked plain, contrary to what was just before observed, though the way to the eye may seem shorter when undivided, yet the frustration of that false expectation will afterwards cause it to appear longer than the truth. Therefore, if a man design to encourage the false opinion of another as to the greatness of a thing, let him not divide and split it, but extol it in the general. This colour deceives,—2. if the matter be so far divided and dispersed as not all to appear at one view. So flowers growing in separate beds show more than if they grow in one bed, provided all the beds are in the same plot, so as to be viewed at once; otherwise they appear more numerous when brought nearer than when scattered wider; and hence landed estates that lie contiguous are usually accounted greater than they are; for if they lie in different counties, they could not so well fall within notice. 3. This sophism deceives through the excellence of unity above multitude; for all composition is an infallible sign of deficiency in particulars,—

"Et quæ non prosunt singula, multa juvant."[i]

For if one would serve the turn, it were best; but defects and imperfections require to be pieced and helped out. So Martha, employed about many things, was told that one was sufficient.[k] And upon this foundation Æsop invented the fable how the fox bragged to the cat what a number of devices and stratagems he had to get from the hounds, when the cat said she had one, and that was to climb a tree, which in fact was better than all the shifts of reynard; whence the proverb, "Multa novit vulpes, sed felis unum magnum."[l] And the moral of the fable is this, that it is better to rely upon an able and trusty friend in difficulty than upon all the fetches and contrivances of one's own wit.

It were easy to collect a large number of this kind of sophisms,—which we collected in our youth, but without their illustrations and solutions. These at last we have found time to digest, and think the performance of considerable service,—whereto if their fallacies and detections were annexed, it might be a work of considerable service, as launching into primary philosophy and politics as well as

[i] Ovid, Remedia Amoris, 429. [k] Luke x. 41.
[l] The fox had many shifts, but the cat a capital one.

rhetoric. And so much for the popular marks or colours of apparent good and evil, both simple and comparative.

A second collection wanting to the apparatus of rhetoric is that intimated by Cicero, when he directs a set of common-places, suited to both sides of the question, to be had in readiness: such are, "pro verbis legis," et "pro sententia legis." But we extend this precept farther, so as to include not only judicial, but also deliberate and demonstrative forms. Our meaning is, that all the places of common use, whether for proof, confutation, persuasion, dissuasion, praise, or dispraise, should be ready studied, and either exaggerated or degraded with the utmost effort of genius, or, as it were, perverse resolution beyond all measure of truth. And the best way of forming this collection, both for conciseness and use, we judge to be that of contracting and winding up these places into certain acute and short sentences; as into so many clues, which may occasionally be wound off into larger discourses. And something of this kind we find done by Seneca;[m] but only in the way of suppositions or cases. The following examples will more fully illustrate our intention:—

For.   BEAUTY.[n]   *Against.*

For.	Against.
The deformed endeavour, by malice, to keep themselves from contempt.	Virtue, like a diamond, is best plain set.
Deformed persons are commonly revenged of nature.	As a good dress to a deformed person, so is beauty to a vicious man.
Virtue is internal beauty, and beauty external virtue.	Those adorned with beauty, and those affected by it, are generally shallow alike.
Beauty makes virtue shine, and vice blush.	

For.   BOLDNESS.   *Against.*

For.	Against.
A bashful suitor shows the way to deny him.	Boldness is the verger to folly.
Boldness in a politician is like action in an orator—the first, second, and third qualification.	Impudence is fit for nothing but imposture.
	Confidence is the fool's empress and the wise man's buffoon.
Love the man who confesses his modesty; but hate him who accuses it.	Boldness is a kind of dulness, joined with a perverseness.
A confidence in carriage soonest unites affections.	
Give me a reserved countenance and open conversation.	

---

[m] Controversia.

[n] In the original there is a different arrangement. We have followed the alphabetical order.

| *For.* | CEREMONIES. | *Against.* |

For. CEREMONIES. *Against.*

A graceful deportment is the true ornament of virtue.

If we follow the vulgar in the use of words, why not in habit and gesture?

He who observes not decorum in smaller matters may be a great man, but is unwise at times.

Virtue and wisdom, without all respect and ceremony, are, like foreign languages, unintelligible to the vulgar.

He who knows not the sense of the people, neither by congruity nor observation, is senseless.

Ceremonies are the translation of virtue into our own language.

What can be more disagreeable than in common life to copy the stage?

Ingenuous behaviour procures esteem, but affectation and cunning, hatred.

Better a painted face and curled hair, than a painted and curled behaviour.

He is incapable of great matters who breaks his mind with trifling observations.

Affectation is the glossy corruption of ingenuity.

For. CONSTANCY. *Against.*

Constancy is the foundation of virtue.

He is miserable who has no notion of what he shall be.

If human judgment cannot be constant to things, let it at least be true to itself.

Even vice is set off by constancy.

Inconstancy of fortune with inconstancy of mind makes a dark scene.

Fortune, like Proteus, is brought to herself by persisting.

Constancy, like a churlish porteress, turns away many useful informations.

It is just that constancy should endure crosses, for it commonly brings them.

The shortest folly is the best.

For. CRUELTY. *Against.*

No virtue is so often delinquent as clemency.

Cruelty proceeding from revenge is justice; if from danger, prudence.

He who shows mercy to his enemy denies it to himself.

Phlebotomy is as necessary in the body politic as in the body natural.

He who delights in blood is either a wild beast or a fury.

To a good man, cruelty seems a mere tragical fiction.

For. DELAY. *Against.*

Fortune sells many things to the hasty which she gives to the slow.

Hurrying to catch the beginnings of things is grasping at shadows.

Opportunity offers the handle of the bottle first, then the belly.

Opportunity, like the Sibyl, diminishes the commodity but enhances the price.

When things hang wavering, mark them, and work when they incline.

Commit the beginning of actions to Argus, with his hundred eyes, the end to Briareus, with his hundred hands.

DISSIMULATION.

For.

Dissimulation is a short wisdom.

We are not all to say, though we all intend, the same thing.

Nakedness, even in the mind, is uncomely.

Dissimulation is both a grace and a guard.

Dissimulation is the bulwark of counsels.

Some fall a prey to fair dealing.

The open dealer deceives as well as the dissembler; for many either do not understand him or not believe him.

Open dealing is a weakness of mind.

Against.

Dispatch is Pluto's helmet.

Things undertaken speedily are easily performed.

If we cannot think justly, at least let us speak as we think.

In shallow politicians, dissimulation goes for wisdom.

The dissembler loses a principal instrument of action, belief.

Dissimulation invites dissimulation.

The dissembler is a slave.

EMPIRE.

For.

To enjoy happiness is a great blessing, but to confer it a greater.

Kings are more like stars than men, for they have a powerful influence.

To resist God's vicegerents is to war against heaven.

Against.

It is a miserable state to have few things to desire and many to fear.

Princes, like the celestial bodies, have much veneration but no rest.

Mortals are admitted to Jupiter's table only for sport.

ENVY.

For.

It is natural to hate those who reproach us.

Envy in a state is like a wholesome severity.

Against.

Envy has no holidays.

Death alone reconciles envy to virtue.

Envy puts virtue to the trial, as Juno did Hercules.

EVIDENCE AGAINST ARGUMENTS.

For.

To rely upon arguments is the part of a pleader, not a judge.

He who is swayed more by arguments than testimony, trusts more to wit than sense.

Arguments might be trusted, if men committed no absurdities

Against.

If evidence were to prevail against arguments, a judge would need no sense but his hearing.

Arguments are an antidote against the poison of testimonies.

Those proofs are safest believed which seldomest deceive.

Arguments against testimonies make the case appear strange, but not true.

FACILITY.

For.

Give me the man who complies to another's humour without flattery.

The flexible man comes nearest to the nature of gold.

Against.

Facility is want of judgment.

The good offices of easy natures seem debts, and their denials, injuries.

He thanks only himself who prevails upon an easy man.

All difficulties oppress a yielding nature, for he is engaged in all.

Easy natures seldom come off with credit.

FLATTERY.

For.

Flattery proceeds from custom rather than ill design.

To convey instruction with praise is a form due to the great.

Against.

Flattery is the style of a slave.

Flattery is the varnish of vice.

Flattery is fowling with a bird-call.

The deformity of flattery is comedy; but the injury, tragedy.

To convey good counsel is a hard task.

FORTITUDE.

For.

Nothing is terrible but fear itself.

Pleasure and virtue lose their nature where fear disquiets.

To view danger is looking out to avoid it.

Other virtues subdue vice, but fortitude even conquers fortune.

Against.

A strange virtue that, to desire to destroy, to secure destruction.

A goodly virtue truly, which even drunkenness can cause.

A prodigal of his own life threatens the lives of others.

Fortitude is a virtue of the iron age.

FORTUNE.

For.

Public virtues procure praise; but private ones, fortune.

Fortune, like the milky way, is a cluster of small, twinkling, nameless virtues.

Fortune is to be honoured and respected, though it were but for her daughters, Confidence and Authority.

Against.

The folly of one man is the fortune of another.

This may be commended in fortune, that if she makes no election, she gives no protection.

The great, to decline envy, worship fortune.

FRIENDSHIP.

For.

Friendship does the same as fortitude, but more agreeably.

Against.

To contract friendship is to procure incumbrance.

Friendship gives the relish to happiness.

The worst solitude is to want friendship.

It is just that the hollow-hearted should not find friendship.

It is a weak spirit that divides fortune with another.

For.   **HEALTH.**   *Against.*

The care of health subjects the mind to the body.

A healthy body is the tabernacle, but a sickly one the prison of the soul.

A sound constitution forwards business, but a sickly one makes many holidays.

Recovery from sickness is rejuvenescency.

Pretence of sickness is a good excuse for the healthy.

Health too strongly cements the soul and body.

The couch has governed empires, and the litter, armies.°

For.   **HONOURS.**   *Against.*

Honours are the suffrages, not of tyrants, but Divine Providence.

Honours make both virtue and vice conspicuous.

Honour is the touchstone of virtue.

The motion of virtue is rapid to its place, but calm in it; but the place of virtue is honour.

To seek honour is to lose liberty.

Honours give command where it is best not to will; and next, not to be able.

The steps of honour are hard to climb, slippery a-top, and dangerous to go down.

Men in great place borrow others' opinions, to think themselves happy.

For.   **JESTS.**   *Against.*

A jest is the orator's altar.

Humour in conversation preserves freedom.

It is highly politic to pass smoothly from jest to earnest, and *vice versâ.*

Witty conceits are vehicles to truths that could not be otherwise agreeably conveyed.

Hunters after deformities and comparisons are despicable creatures.

To divert important business with a jest is a base trick.

Judge of a jest when the laugh is over.

Wit commonly plays on the surface of things, for surface is the seat of a jest.

For.   **INGRATITUDE.**   *Against.*

Ingratitude is but perceiving the cause of a benefit.

The desire of being grateful neither does justice to others nor leaves one's self at liberty.

A benefit of an uncertain value merits the less thanks.

The sin of ingratitude is not made penal here, but left to the furies.

The obligations for benefits exceed the obligation of duties; whence ingratitude is also unjust.

No public fortune can exclude private favour.

° As happened in the persons of Charles V. and the Maréchal De Saxe.

INNOVATION.

For.

Every remedy is an innovation.

He who will not apply new remedies must expect new diseases.

Time is the greatest innovator: and why may we not imitate time?

Ancient precedents are unsuitable, and late ones corrupt and degenerate.

Let the ignorant square their actions by example.

As they who first derive honour to their family are commonly more worthy than those who succeed them, so innovations generally excel imitations.

An obstinate adherence to customs is as turbulent a thing as innovation.

Since things of their own course change for the worse, if they are not by prudence altered for the better, what end can there be of the ill?

The slaves of custom are the sport of time.

Against.

New births are deformed things.

No author is accepted till time has authorized him.

All novelty is injury, for it defaces the present state of things.

Things authorized by custom, if not excellent, are yet comfortable and sort well together.

What innovator follows the example of time, which brings about new things so quietly as to be almost imperceptible?

Things that happen unexpected are less agreeable to those they benefit and more afflicting to those they injure.

JUSTICE.

For.

Power and policy are but the appendages of justice; for if justice could be otherwise executed, there were no need of them.

It is owing to justice that man to man is a god, not a wolf.

Though justice cannot extirpate vice, it keeps it under.

Against.

If justice consist in doing to another what we would have done to ourselves, then mercy is justice.

If every one must receive his due, then surely mortals must receive pardon.

The common justice of a nation, like a philosopher at court, renders rulers awful.

KNOWLEDGE AND CONTEMPLATION.

For.

That pleasure only is according to nature, which never cloys.

The sweetest prospect is that below, into the errors of others.

It is best to have the orbits of the mind concentric with those of the universe.

All depraved affections are false valuations, but goodness and truth are ever the same.

Against.

A contemplative life is but a specious laziness.

To think well is little better than to dream well.

Divine Providence regards the world, but man regards only his country.

A political man sows even his thoughts.

For.	LAW.	Against.

For. — It is not expounding, but divining, to recede from the letter of the law.

To leave the letter of the law makes the judge a legislator.

Against. — Generals are to be construed so as to explain particulars.

The worst tyranny is law upon the rack.

For.	LEARNING.	Against.

For. — To write books upon minute particulars were to render experience almost useless.

Reading is conversing with the wise, but acting is generally conversing with fools.

Sciences of little significance in themselves may sharpen the wit and marshal the thoughts.

Against. — Men in universities are taught to believe.

What art ever taught the seasonable use of art?

To be wise by precept and wise by experience are contrary habits, the one sorts not with the other.

A vain use is made of art, lest it should otherwise be unemployed.

It is the way of scholars to show all they know and oppose farther information.

For.	LIFE.	Against.

For. — It is absurd to love the accidents of life above life itself.

A long course is better than a short one, even for virtue.

Without a compass of life, we can neither learn, nor repent, nor perfect.

Against. — The philosophers, by their great preparation for death, have only rendered death more terrible.

Men fear death through ignorance, as children fear the dark.

There is no passion so weak but, if a little urged, will conquer the fear of death.

A man would wish to die, even through weariness of doing the same things over and over again.

For.	LOQUACITY.	Against.

For. — Silence argues a man to suspect either himself or others.

All restraints are irksome, but especially that of the tongue.

Silence is the virtue of fools.

Silence, like the night, is fit for treacheries.

Thoughts, like waters, are best in a running stream.

Silence is a kind of solitude.

He who is silent exposes himself to censure.

Against. — To speak little gives grace and authority to what is delivered.

Silence is like sleep, it refreshes wisdom.

Silence is the fermentation of the thoughts.

Silence is the style of wisdom and the candidate for truth.

For.	LOVE.	Against.

For. — Every man seeks, but the lover only finds, himself.

Against. — The stage is more beholden to love than civil life.

The mind is best regulated by the predominancy of some powerful affection.

He who is wise will pursue some one desire; for he that affects not one thing above another, finds all flat and distasteful.

Why should not one man rest in one individual?

I like not such men as are wholly taken up with one thing.

Love is but a narrow contemplation.

For. MAGNANIMITY. *Against.*

When the mind proposes honourable ends, not only the virtues but the deities are ready to assist.

Virtues proceeding from habit or precept are vulgar, but those that proceed from the end, heroical.

Magnanimity is a poetical virtue.

For. NATURE. *Against.*

Custom goes in arithmetical, but nature in geometrical progression.

As laws are to custom in states, so is nature to custom in particular persons.

Custom against nature is a kind of tyranny, but easily suppressed.

Men think according to nature, speak according to precept, but act according to custom.

Nature is a kind of schoolmaster; custom, a magistrate.

For. NOBILITY. *Against.*

Where virtue is deeply implanted from the stock, there can be no vice.

Nobility is a laurel conferred by time.

If we reverence antiquity in dead monuments, we should do it much more in living ones.

If we despise nobility in families, what difference is there betwixt men and brutes?

Nobility shelters virtue from envy and recommends it to favour.

Nobility seldom springs from virtue, and virtue seldomer from nobility.

Nobles oftener plead their ancestors for pardon than promotion.

New rising men are so industrious as to make nobles seem like statues.

Nobles, like bad racers, look back too often in the course.

For. POPULARITY. *Against.*

Uniformity commonly pleases wise men, yet it is a point of wisdom to humour the changeable nature of fools.

To honour the people is the way to be honoured.

Men in place are usually awed not by one man but the multitude.

He who suits with fools may himself be suspected.

He who pleases the rabble is commonly turbulent.

No moderate counsels take with the vulgar.

To fawn on the people is the basest flattery.

PRAISE.

For.

Praise is the reflected ray of virtue.

Praise is honour obtained by free voices.

Many states confer honours, but praise always proceeds from liberty.

The voice of the people hath something of divine, else how should so many become of one mind?

No wonder if the commonalty speak truer than the nobility, because they speak with less danger.

Against.

Fame makes a quick messenger but a rash judge.

What has a good man to do with the breath of the vulgar?

Fame, like a river, buoys up things light and swollen, but drowns those that are weighty.

Low virtues gain the praise of the vulgar, ordinary ones astonish them, but of the highest they have no feeling.

Praise is got by bravery more than merit, and given rather to the vain and empty than to the worthy and substantial.

PREPARATION.

For.

He who attempts great matters with small means hopes for opportunity to keep him in heart.

Slender provision buys wit, but not fortune.

Against.

The first occasion is the best preparation.

Fortune is not to be fettered in the chains of preparation.

The interchange of preparation and action are politic, but the separation of them ostentatious and unsuccessful.

Great preparation is a prodigal both of time and business.

PRIDE.

For.

Pride is inconsistent even with vice; and as poison expels poison, so are many vices expelled by pride.

An easy nature is subject to other men's vices, but a proud one only to its own.

Pride, if it rise from a contempt of others to a contempt of itself, at length becomes philosophy.

Against.

Pride is the ivy of virtue.

Other vices are only opposites to virtues, but pride is even contagious.

Pride wants the best condition of vice, concealment.

A proud man, while he despises others, neglects himself.

READINESS.

For.

That is unseasonable wisdom which is not ready.

He who errs suddenly, suddenly reforms his error.

To be wise upon deliberation, and not upon present occasion, is no great matter.

Against.

That knowledge is not deep fetched which lies ready at hand.

Wisdom is like a garment, lightest when readiest.

They whose counsels are not ripened by deliberation have not their prudence ripened by age.

What is suddenly invented suddenly vanishes.

EXAMPLES OF ANTITHETA.

For. REVENGE. *Against.*

Private revenge is a kind of wild justice.

He who returns injury for injury violates the law, not the person.

The fear of private revenge is useful, for laws are often asleep.

He who does the wrong is the aggressor, but he who returns it the protractor.

The more prone men are to revenge, the more it should be weeded out.

A revengeful man may be slow in time, though not in will.

For. RICHES. *Against.*

They despise riches who despair of them.

Envy at riches has made virtue a goddess.

Whilst philosophers dispute whether all things should be referred to virtue or pleasure, let us be collecting the instruments of both.

Riches turn virtue into a common good.

The command of other advantages are particular, but that of riches universal.

Great riches are attended either with care, trouble, or fame, but no use.

What an imaginary value is set upon stones and other curiosities, that riches may seem to be of some service.

Many who imagine all things may be bought by their riches, forget they have sold themselves.

Riches are the baggage of virtue, necessary though cumbersome.

Riches are a good servant but a bad master.

For. SUPERSTITION. *Against.*

They who err out of zeal, though they are not to be approved, should yet be pitied.

Mediocrity belongs to morality, extremes to divinity.

A superstitious man is a religious formalist.

I should sooner believe all the fables and absurdities of any religion than that the universal frame is without a deity.

As an ape appears the more deformed for his resemblance to man, so the similitude of superstition to religion makes it the more odious.

What affectation is in civil matters such is superstition in divine.[p]

It were better to have no belief of a God than such an one as dishonours him.

It was not the school of Epicurus, but the Stoics, that disturbed the states of old.

The real atheists are hypocrites, who deal continually in holy things without feeling.

---

[p] Superstition is anything but affectation. They are hypocrites who dissemble: those who believe too much are generally over earnest. *Ed.*

For.   SUSPICION.   *Against.*

Distrust is the sinew of prudence, and suspicion a strengthener of the understanding.

That sincerity is justly suspected which suspicion weakens.

Suspicion breaks a frail integrity, but confirms a strong one.

Suspicion breaks the bonds of trust.

To be overrun with suspicion is a kind of political madness.

For.   TACITURNITY.   *Against.*

Nothing is concealed from a silent man, for all is safely deposited with him.

He who easily talks what he knows, will also talk what he knows not.

Mysteries are due to secrets.

From a silent man all things are concealed, because he returns nothing but silence.

Change of customs keeps men secret.

Secrecy is the virtue of a confessor.

A close man is like a man unknown.

For.   TEMPERANCE.   *Against.*

To abstain and sustain are nearly the same virtue.

Uniformity, concords, and the measure of motions, are things celestial and the characters of eternity.

Temperance, like wholesome cold, collects and strengthens the force of the mind.

When the senses are too exquisite and wandering, they want narcotics, so likewise do wandering affections.

I like not bare negative virtues; they argue innocence, not merit.

The mind languishes that is not sometimes spirited up by excess.

I like the virtues which produce the vivacity of action, not the dulness of passion.

The sayings, "Not to use, that you may not desire;" "Not to desire, that you may not fear," &c., proceed from pusillanimous and distrustful natures.

For.   VAIN-GLORY.   *Against.*

He who seeks his own praise at the same time seeks the advantage of others.

He who is so strait-laced as to regard nothing that belongs to others, will perhaps account public affairs impertinent.

Such dispositions as have a mixture of levity, more easily undertake a public charge.

The vain-glorious are always factious, false, fickle, and upon the extreme.

Thraso is Gnatho's prey.

It is shameful in a lover to court the maid instead of the mistress, but praise is only virtue's handmaid.

For.   UNCHASTITY.   *Against.*

It is jealousy that makes chastity a virtue.

He must be a melancholy mortal who thinks Venus a grave lady.

Why is a part of regimen, pre-

Incontinence is one of Circe's worst transformations.

The unchaste liver has no reverence for himself, which is slackening the bridle of vice.

tended cleanness, and the daughter of pride, placed among the virtues?

In amours, as in wild fowl, there is property; but the right is transferred with possession.

They who, with Paris, make beauty their wish, lose, as he did, wisdom and power.

Alexander fell upon no popular truth when he said that sleep and lust were the earnest of death.

For. WATCHFULNESS. Against.

More dangers deceive by fraud than force.

It is easier to prevent a danger than to watch its approach.

Danger is no longer light if it once seem light.

He bids danger advance, who buckles against it.

Even the remedies of dangers are dangerous.

It is better to use a few approved remedies than to venture upon many unexperienced particulars.

For. WIFE AND CHILDREN. Against.

Charity to the commonwealth begins with private families.

Wife and children are a kind of discipline, but unmarried men are morose and cruel.

A single life and a childless state fit men for nothing but flight.

He sacrifices to death who begets no children.

The happy in other respects are commonly unfortunate in their children, lest the human state should too nearly approach the divine.

He who hath wife and children hath given hostages to fortune.

Generation and issue are human acts, but creation and its works are divine.

Issue is the eternity of brutes; but fame, merit, and institutions the eternity of men.

Private regards generally prevail over public.

Some affect the fortune of Priam, in surviving his family.

For. YOUTH. Against.

The first thoughts and counsels of youth have somewhat divine.

Old men are wise for themselves, but less for others and the public good.

If it were visible, old age deforms the mind more than the body.

Old men fear all things but the gods.

Youth is the field of repentance.

Youth naturally despises the authority of age, that every one may grow wise at his peril.

The counsels whereat time did not assist are not ratified by him.

Old men commute Venus for the graces.[q]

The examples of antithets here laid down may not, perhaps, deserve the place assigned them; but as they were collected in my youth, and are really seeds, not flowers, I was unwilling they should be lost. In this they plainly show a

---

[q] Understand propriety and decorum.

juvenile warmth, that they abound in the moral and demonstrative kind, but touch sparingly upon the deliberative and judicial.

A third collection wanting to the apparatus of rhetoric, is what we call lesser forms. And these are a kind of portals, postern-doors, outer rooms, back-rooms, and passages of speech, which may serve indifferently for all subjects; such as prefaces, conclusions, digressions, transitions, &c. For as in building, a good distribution of the frontispiece, staircases, doors, windows, entries, passages, and the like, is not only agreeable but useful; so in speeches, if the accessories or under-parts be decently and skilfully contrived and placed, they are of great ornament and service to the whole structure of the discourse. Of these forms, we will just propose one example or two; for though they are matters of no small use, yet because here we add nothing of our own, and only take naked forms from Demosthenes, Cicero, or other select authors, they may seem of too trivial a nature to spend time therein.

EXAMPLES OF LESSER FORMS.

A CONCLUSION IN THE DELIBERATIVE.

So the past fault may be at once amended, and future inconvenience prevented.

COROLLARY OF AN EXACT DIVISION.

That all may see I would conceal nothing by silence, nor cloud anything by words.

A TRANSITION, WITH A CAVEAT.

But let us leave the subject for the present, still reserving to ourselves the liberty of a retrospection.

A PREPOSSESSION AGAINST AN INVETERATE OPINION.

I will let you understand to the full what sprung from the thing itself, what error has tacked to it, and what envy has raised upon it.

And these few examples may serve to show our meaning as to the lesser forms of speech.[r]

---

[r] Though the ancients may seem to have perfected rhetoric, yet the moderns have given it new light. Gerhord Vossius bestowed incredible pains upon this art, as appears by his book "De Natura et Constitu-

CHAPTER IV.

Two General Appendices to Tradition, viz., the Arts of Teaching and Criticism.

THERE remain two general appendages to the doctrine of delivery; the one relating to criticism, the other to school-learning. For as the principal part of traditive prudence turns upon the writing; so its relative turns upon the reading of books. Now reading is either regulated by the assistance of a master, or left to every one's private industry; but both depend upon criticism and school-learning.

Criticism regards, first, the exact correcting and publishing of approved authors; whereby the honour of such authors is preserved, and the necessary assistance afforded to the reader. Yet the misapplied labours and industry of some have in this respect proved highly prejudicial to learning; for many critics have a way, when they fall upon anything they do not understand, of immediately supposing a fault in the copy. Thus, in that passage of Tacitus, where a certain colony pleads a right of protection in the senate, Tacitus tells us they were not favourably heard; so that the ambassadors distrusting their cause, endeavoured to procure the favour of Titus Vinius by a present, and succeeded; upon which Tacitus has these words: "Tum dignitas et antiquitas coloniæ valuit:" "Then the honour and antiquity of the colony had weight," in allusion to the sum received.[a] But a considerable critic here expunges "tum," and substitutes "tantùm," which quite corrupts the sense. And from this ill practice of the critics, it happens that the most corrected copies are often the least correct. And to say the truth, unless a critic

---

tione Rhetoricæ;" and still more by his "Institutiones Oratoriæ." See also Wolfgang; Schoensleder's "Apparatus Eloquentiæ;" "Tesmari Exercitationes Rhetoricæ," &c. Several French authors have likewise cultivated this subject; particularly Rapin, in his "Réflexions sur l'Eloquence;" Bohour, in his "Manière de bien Penser dans les Ouvrages de l'Esprit;" and his "Pensées Ingénieuses;" Father Lamy, in his "Art de Parler." See also M. Cassander's French translation of Aristotle's Rhetorics; the anonymous pieces, entitled, "L'Art de Penser," and "L'Art de Persuader;" Le Clerc's "Historia Rhetoricæ," in his "Ars Critica;" and "Stollius de Arte Rhetoricæ," in his "Introductio in Historiam Literariam." *Shaw.*

[a] Hist. b. i. c. 66.

is well acquainted with the sciences treated in the books he publishes, his diligence will be attended with danger.

A second thing belonging to criticism is the explanation and illustration of authors, comments, notes, collections, &c. But here an ill custom has prevailed among the critics of skipping over the obscure passages, and expatiating upon such as are sufficiently clear, as if their design were not so much to illustrate their author, as to take all occasions of showing their own learning and reading. It were therefore to be wished, that every original writer who treats an obscure or noble subject, would add his own explanations to his own work, so as to keep the text continued and unbroken by digressions or illustrations, and thus prevent any wrong interpretation by the notes of others.

Thirdly, there belongs to criticism the thing from whence its name is derived; viz., a certain concise judgment or censure of the authors published, and a comparison of them with other writers who have treated the same subject. Whence the student may be directed in the choice of his books, and come the better prepared to their perusal; and this seems to be the ultimate office of the critic, and has indeed been honoured by some greater men in our age than critics are usually thought.

For the doctrine of school-learning, it were the shortest way to refer it to the Jesuits, who, in point of usefulness, have herein excelled; yet we will lay down a few admonitions about it. We highly approve the education of youth in colleges, and not wholly in private houses or schools.[b] For in colleges, there is not only a greater emulation of the youth among their equals, but the teachers have a venerable aspect and gravity, which greatly conduces towards insinuating a modest behaviour, and the forming of tender minds from the first, according to such examples; and besides these, there are many other advantages of a collegiate education. But for the order and manner of discipline, it is of capital use to avoid too concise methods and too hasty an opinion of learning, which give a pertness to the mind, and rather make a show of improvement than procure it. But excursions of genius are to be somewhat favoured; so that if a scholar perform his usual exercises, he may be suffered

[b] See Osborn's Advice to a Son.

to steal time for other things whereto he is more inclined. It must also be carefully noted, though it has, perhaps, hitherto escaped observation, that there are two correspondent ways of enuring, exercising, and preparing the genius; the one beginning with the easier, leads gradually on to more difficult things; and the other, commanding and imposing such as are the harder at first; so that when these are obtained, the easier may be more agreeably despatched. For it is one method to begin swimming with bladders, and another to begin dancing with loaded shoes. Nor is it easy to see how much a prudent intermixture of these two ways contributes to improve the faculties both of body and mind. Again, the suiting of studies to the genius is of singular use; which masters should duly attend to, that the parent may thence consider what kind of life the child is fittest for. And further, it must be carefully observed, not only that every one makes much greater progress in those things whereto he is naturally inclined, but also, that there are certain remedies in a proper choice of studies for particular indispositions of mind. For example, inattention and a volatility of genius may be remedied by mathematics, wherein, if the mind wander ever so little, the whole demonstration must be begun anew. Exercises, also, are of great efficacy in teaching, but few have observed that these should not only be prudently appointed, but prudently changed. For, as Cicero well remarks, "faults as well as faculties are generally exercised in exercises;" whence a bad habit is sometimes acquired and insinuated together with a good one. It is therefore safer that exercises should be intermitted, and now and then repeated, than always continued and followed. These things, indeed, may at first sight appear light and trivial, yet they are highly effectual and advantageous. For as the great increase of the Roman empire has been justly attributed to the virtue and prudence of those six rulers, who had, as it were, the tuition of it in its youth, so proper discipline, in tender years, has such a power, though latent and unobserved, as neither time nor future labour can any way subdue in our riper age. It also deserves to be remarked, that even ordinary talents in great men, used on great occasions, may sometimes produce remarkable effects. And of this we will give an eminent instance, the rather because the

Jesuits judiciously retain the discipline among them. And though the thing itself be disreputable in the profession of it, yet it is excellent as a discipline; we mean the action of the theatre, which strengthens the memory, regulates the tone of the voice and the efficacy of pronunciation; gracefully composes the countenance and the gesture; procures a becoming degree of assurance; and lastly, accustoms youth to the eye of men. The example we borrow from Tacitus, of one Vibulenus, once a player, but afterwards a soldier in the Pannonian army. This fellow, upon the death of Augustus, raised a mutiny; so that Blesus, the lieutenant, committed some of the mutineers; but the soldiers broke open the prison and released them. Upon which, Vibulenus thus harangued the army: "You," says he, "have restored light and life to these poor innocents; but who gives back life to my brother, or my brother to me? He was sent to you from the German army for a common good, and that man murdered him last night, by the hands of his gladiators, whom he keeps about him to murder the soldiers. Answer, Blesus, where hast thou thrown his corpse? Even enemies refuse not the right of burial. When I shall, with tears and embraces, have performed my duty to him, command me also to death; but let our fellow-soldiers bury us, who are murdered only for our love to the legions."[c] With which words, he raised such a storm of consternation and revenge in the army, that unless the thing had presently appeared to be all a fiction, and that the fellow never had a brother, the soldiers might have murdered their leader; but he acted the whole as a part upon the stage. And thus much for the logical sciences.

We now come to that portion of our treatise which we have allotted to rational knowledge. Let no one, however, think that we hold the received division of the sciences of small account, because we have wandered out of the beaten paths. In so digressing we have been influenced by a twofold necessity, — First, to unite two methods, which both in their end and nature are altogether different, viz., the ranging in the same class those things which are naturally related to each other, and to throw into one heap all those things which are likely to be called immediately

[c] Annal. i. 22.

into use. Thus, as a secretary of a prince or of some civil department ranges his papers according to their distinct heads,—treaties, instructions, foreign and domestic letters,—each occupying a separate corner of his study, and yet does not fail to collect in some particular cabinet those papers he is likely to use together, so in this general cabinet of knowledge we have selected our divisions according to the nature of things themselves; but if any particular science required to be treated at length, we have followed those divisions which are most conformable to use and practice. The second necessity arose from supplying the addenda to the sciences, and reducing them to an entire body, which completely changed the old boundaries. For, say that the existing arts are fifteen in number, and that the deficiencies increase the number to twenty, as the parts of fifteen are not the parts of twenty, two, four, and three being prime numbers in each, it is plain that a new division was forced upon us.

SEVENTH BOOK.

CHAPTER I.

Ethics divided into the Doctrine of Models and the Georgics (Culture) of the Mind. Division of Models into the Absolute and Comparative Good. Absolute Good divided into Personal and National.

WE next, excellent King, proceed to ethics, which has the human will for its subject. Reason governs the will, but apparent good seduces it: its motives are the affections, and its ministers the organs and voluntary motions. It is of this doctrine that Solomon says, "Keep thy heart with all diligence,[a] for out of it are the actions of life." The writers upon this science appear like writing-masters, who lay before their scholars a number of beautiful copies, but give them no directions how to guide their pen or shape their letters; for so the writers upon ethics have given us shining draughts, descriptions, and exact images of goodness, virtue, duties, happiness, &c., as the true objects and scope of the human

[a] Prov. iv. 23.

will and desire; but for obtaining these excellent and well-described ends, or by what means the mind may be broke and fashioned for obtaining them, they either touch this subject not at all or slightly.[b] We may dispute as much as we please, that moral virtues are in the human mind by habit, not by nature; that generous spirits are led by reason, but the herd by reward and punishment; that the mind must be set straight, like a crooked stick, by bending it the contrary way, &c.[c] But nothing of this kind of glance-and-touch can in any way supply the want of the thing we are now in quest of.

The cause of this neglect I take to be that latent rock whereon so many of the sciences have split, viz., the aversion that writers have to treat of trite and vulgar matters, which are neither subtle enough for dispute nor eminent enough for ornament. It is not easy to see how great a misfortune hath proceeded hence,—that men, through natural pride and vain-glory, should choose such subjects and methods of treating them, as may rather show their own capacities, than be of use to the reader. Seneca says excellently, "Eloquence is hurtful to those it inspires with a desire of itself, and not of things;"[d] for writings should make men in love with the subject, and not with the writer. They, therefore, take the just course who can say of their counsels as Demosthenes did,—"If you put these things in execution, you shall not only praise the orator for the present, but yourselves also soon after, when your affairs are in a better posture."[e] As for myself, excellent King, to speak the truth, I have frequently neglected the glory of my order, name, and learning, both in the works I now publish and those which I have already designed to execute, in following out my direct purpose of advancing the happiness of mankind; so that I may fairly say, though marked out by nature to be the architect of philosophy and the sciences, I have submitted to become a common workman and labourer, there being many mean

---

[b] For the History of Morality, consult Scheurlius's "Bibliographia Moralis," ed. 1686; Placcius's "Epitome Bibliothecæ Moralis;" "Paschius de variis Moralia tradendi Modis Formisque," 1707; Barbeyrac's Preface to his French translation of Puffendorf "De Jure Naturæ et Gentium;" and "Stollii Introductio in Historiam Literariam," pp. 692—752. *Ed.*

[c] Arist. Ethics, ii.   [d] Epist. 100, towards the end.

[e] Olynthias 25, towards the end.

things necessary to the erection of the structure, which others, out of a natural disdain, refused to attend to. But in ethics the philosophers have culled out a certain splendid mass of matter, wherein they might principally show their force of genius or power of eloquence; but for other things that chiefly conduce to practice, as they could not be so gracefully set off, they have entirely neglected them. Yet so many eminent men, surely, ought not to have despaired of a like success with Virgil, who procured as much glory for eloquence, ingenuity, and learning, by explaining the homely observations of agriculture as in relating the heroic acts of Æneas,—

> "Nec sum animi dubius, verbis ea vincere magnum
> Quam sit, et angustis hunc addere rebus honorem."[f]

And certainly, if men were bent, not upon writing at leisure what may be read at leisure, but really to cultivate and improve active life, the georgics of the mind ought to be as highly valued as those heroical portraits of virtue, goodness, and happiness wherein so much pains have been taken.

We divide ethics into two principal doctrines,—the one of the model or image of good, the other of the regulation and culture of the mind, which I commonly express by the word georgics. The first describes the nature of good, and the other prescribes rules for conforming the mind to it. The doctrine of the image of good, in describing the nature of good, considers it either as simple or compounded, and either as to the kinds or degrees thereof. In the latter of these the Christian faith has at length abolished those infinite disputes and speculations as to the supreme degree of good, called happiness, blessedness, or the "summum bonum," which was a kind of heathen theology. For, as Aristotle said, "Youth might be happy, though only in hope;"[g] so, according to the direction of faith, we must put ourselves in the state of minors, and think of no other felicity, but that founded in hope. Being, therefore, thus delivered from this ostentatious heaven of the heathens, who, following Seneca, "Vere magnum habere fragilitatem hominis, securitatem Dei,"[h] exaggerated the perfectibility of man's nature,—we

---

[f] Georg. iii. 289.   [g] Nic. Ethics, i. 10; Rhet. ii. 12, 8.
[h] Epist. 53, § 12.

may, with less offence to truth and sobriety, receive much of what they deliver about the image of good. As for the nature of positive and simple good, they have certainly drawn it beautifully and according to the life, in several pieces exactly representing the form of virtue and duty,—their order, kinds, relations, parts, subjects, provinces, actions, and dispensations. And all this they have recommended and insinuated to the mind with great vivacity and subtilty of argument, as well as sweetness of persuasion, at the same time faithfully guarding, as much as was possible by words, against depraved and popular errors and insults. And in deducing the nature of comparative good they have not been wanting, but appointed three orders thereof,—they have compared contemplative and active life together;[1] distinguished between virtue with reluctance, and virtue secured and confirmed; represented the conflict betwixt honour and advantage; balanced the virtues, to show which overweighed, and the like,—so that this part of the image of good is already nobly executed; and herein the ancients have shown wonderful abilities. Yet the pious and strenuous diligence of the divines, exercised in weighing and determining studies, moral virtues, cases of conscience, and fixing the bounds of sin, have greatly exceeded them. But if the philosophers, before they descended to the popular and received notions of virtue and vice, pain and pleasure, &c., had dwelt longer upon discovering the roots and fibres of good and evil, they would, doubtless, have thus gained great light to their subsequent inquiries, especially if they had consulted the nature of things, as well as moral axioms, they would have shortened their doctrines and laid them deeper. But as they have entirely omitted this or confusedly touched it, we will here briefly touch it over again, and endeavour to open and cleanse the springs of morality, before we come to the georgics of the mind, which we set down as deficient.

All things are endued with an appetite to two kinds of good,—the one as the thing is a whole in itself, the other as it is a part of some greater whole; and this latter is more worthy and more powerful than the other, as it tends to the conservation of a more ample form. The first may be called

---

[1] See Arist. Eth. Nic. i. 3, sq.

individual or self-good, and the latter, good of communion. Iron by a particular property moves to the loadstone, but if the iron be heavy, it drops its affection to the loadstone and tends to the earth, which is the proper region of such ponderous bodies. Again, though dense and heavy bodies tend to the earth, yet rather than nature will suffer a separation in the continuity of things, and leave a vacuum, as they speak, these heavy bodies will be carried upwards, and forego their affection to the earth, to perform their office to the world. And thus it generally happens, that the conservation of the more general form regulates the lesser appetites. But this prerogative of the good of communion is more particularly impressed upon man, if he be not degenerate, according to that remarkable saying of Pompey, who, being governor of the city purveyance at a time of famine in Rome, and entreated by his friends not to venture to sea whilst a violent storm was impending, answered, "My going is necessary, but not my life;"[k] so that the desire of life, which is greatest in the individual, did not with him outweigh his affection and fidelity to the state. But no philosophy, sect, religion, law, or discipline, in any age, has so highly exalted the good of communion, and so far depressed the good of individuals, as the Christian faith; whence it may clearly appear that one and the same God gave those laws of nature to the creatures and the Christian law to men. And hence we read that some of the elect and holy men, in an ecstasy of charity and impatient desire of the good of communion, rather wished their names blotted out of the book of life than that their brethren should miss of salvation.[l]

This being once laid down and firmly established, will put an end to some of the soberest controversies in moral philosophy. And first, it determines that question about the preference of a contemplative to an active life, against the opinion of Aristotle; as all the reasons he produces for a contemplative life regard only private good, and the pleasure or dignity of an individual person, in which respects the contemplative life is doubtless best, and like the comparison made by Pythagoras,[m] to assert the honour and reputation

[k] Plut. Life Pomp.   [l] St. Paul, Rom. ix.
[m] Jamblycus's life, in the Tus. Quæst. v 3. Cicero substitutes Leontius, prince of the Phœnicians, for Hieron.

of philosophy, when being asked by Hiero who he was, he answered, "I am a looker-on; for as at the Olympic games some come to try for the prize, others to sell, others to meet their friends and be merry, but others again come merely as spectators, I am one of the latter." But men ought to know that in the theatre of human life it is only for God and angels to be spectators. Nor could any doubt about this matter have arisen in the Church, if a monastic life had been merely contemplative and unexercised in ecclesiastical duties, —as continual prayer, the sacrifice of vows, oblations to God, and the writing of theological books, for propagating the Divine law—as Moses retired in the solitude of the mount, and Enoch, the seventh from Adam, who, though the Scripture says he walked with God, intimating he was the first founder of the spiritual life, yet enriched the Church with a book of prophecies cited by St. Jude. But for a mere contemplative life, which terminates in itself, and sends out no rays either of heat or light into human society, theology knows it not.

It also determines the question that has been so vehemently controverted between the schools of Zeno and Socrates on the one side, who placed felicity in virtue, simple or adorned, and many other sects and schools on the other, —as particularly the schools of the Cyrenaics and Epicureans, who placed felicity in pleasure;[n] thus making virtue a mere handmaid, without which pleasure could not be well served. Of the same side is also that other school of Epicurus, as on the reformed establishment, which declared felicity to be nothing but tranquillity and serenity of mind. With these also joined the exploded school of Pyrrho and Herillus, who placed felicity in an absolute exemption from scruples, and the allowing no fixed and constant nature of good and evil, but accounting all actions virtuous or vicious, as they proceed from the mind by a pure and undisturbed motion, or with aversion and reluctance.[o] But it is plain that all things of this kind relate to private tranquillity and complacency of mind, and by no means to the good of communion.

[n] For an account of these sects, consult Ritter's "Geschichte der Philosophie alter Zeit."
[o] This opinion has been revived in the Anabaptist heresy, who measure everything by the humours and instincts of the spirit and constancy or vacillation of faith. *Ed.*

Again, upon the foundation above laid we may confute the philosophy of Epictetus, which rests upon supposing felicity placed in things within our power, lest we should otherwise be exposed to fortune and contingence,[p] as if it were not much happier to fail of success in just and honourable designs, when that failure makes for the public good, than to secure an uninterrupted enjoyment of those things which make only for our private fortune. Thus Gonsalvo at the head of his army, pointing to Naples, nobly protested he had much rather, by advancing a step, meet certain death, than by retiring a step prolong his life. And to this agrees the wise king, who pronounces " a good conscience to be a continual feast;"[q] thereby signifying that the consciousness of good intentions, however unsuccessful, affords a joy more real, pure, and agreeable to nature, than all the other means that can be furnished, either for obtaining one's desires or quieting the mind.

It likewise censures that abuse which prevailed about the time of Epictetus, when philosophy was turned into a certain art or profession of life, as if its design were not to compose and quiet troubles, but to avoid and remove the causes and occasions thereof, whence a particular regimen was to be entered into for obtaining this end, by introducing such a kind of health into the mind as was that of Herodicus in the body, mentioned by Aristotle,[r] whilst he did nothing all his life long but take care of his health, and therefore abstained from numberless things, which almost deprived him of the use of his body; whereas, if men were determined to perform the duties of society, that kind of bodily health is most desirable which is able to suffer and support all sorts of attacks and alterations. In the same manner, that mind is truly sound and strong which is able to break through numerous and great temptations and disorders; whence Diogenes seems to have justly commended the habit which did not warily abstain, but courageously sustain,[s]—which could check the sallies of the soul on the steepest precipice, and make it, like a well-broken horse, stop and turn at the shortest warning.

Lastly, it reproves that delicacy and unsociable temper

[p] Enchir. Arrian. i.   [q] Prov. xv. 15.   [r] Rhet. i. 5, 10.
[s] ἀνέχου ἀπέχου. Summa Stoic. Philos.

observed in some of the most ancient philosophers of great repute, who too effeminately withdrew from civil affairs, in order to prevent indignities and trouble to themselves, and live the more free and unspotted in their own opinions; as to which point the resolution of a true moralist should be such as Gonsalvo required of a soldier,—viz., "Not to weave his honour so fine, as for everything to catch and rend it."

CHAPTER II.

Division of Individual Good into Active and Passive. That of Passive Good into Conservative and Perfective. Good of the Commonwealth divided into General and Respective.

WE divide individual or self-good into active and passive. This difference of good is also found impressed upon the nature of all things, but principally shows itself in two appetites of the creatures; viz.,—1. That of self-preservation and defence; and, 2. That of multiplying and propagating. The latter, which is active, seems stronger and more worthy than the former, which is passive; for throughout the universe the celestial nature is the principal agent, and the terrestrial the patient; and in the pleasures of animals that of generation is greater than that of feeding; and the Scripture says, "It is more blessed to give than to receive."[a] And even in common life, no man is so soft and effeminate, as not to prefer the performing and perfecting of anything he had set his mind upon before sensual pleasures. The pre-eminence of active good is also highly exalted from the consideration of the state of mankind, which is mortal and subject to fortune; for if perpetuity and certainty could be had in human pleasures, this would greatly enhance them; but as the case now stands, when we count it a happiness to die late, when we cannot boast of to-morrow, when we know not what a day may bring forth, no wonder if we earnestly endeavour after such things as elude the injuries of time: and these can be no other than our works. Accordingly it is said, "Their works follow them."[b]

Another considerable pre-eminence of active good is given

[a] Acts Ap. xx. 35,   [b] Apoc. xiv. 13.

it, and supported by that inseparable affection of human nature—the love of novelty or variety. But this affection is greatly limited in the pleasures of the senses, which make the greatest part of passive good. To consider how often the same things come over in life,—as meals, sleep, and diversion,—it might make not only a resolute, a wretched, or a wise, but even a delicate person wish to die.[c] But in actions, enterprises, and desires, there is a remarkable variety, which we perceive with great pleasure, whilst we begin, advance, rest, go back to recruit, approach, obtain, &c.: whence it is truly said, "That life without pursuit is a vague and languid thing;"[d] and this holds true both of the wise and unwise indifferently. So Solomon says, "Even a brain-sick man seeks to satisfy his desire, and meddles in everything."[e] And thus the most potent princes, who have all things at command, yet sometimes choose to pursue low and empty desires, which they prefer to the greatest affluence of sensual pleasures: thus Nero delighted in the harp, Commodus in fencing, Antonius in racing, &c. So much more pleasing is it to be active than in possession!

It must, however, be well observed, that active, individual good differs entirely from the good of communion, notwithstanding they may sometimes coincide; for although this individual active good often produces works of beneficence, which is a virtue of communion, yet herein they differ, that these works are performed by most men, not with a design to assist or benefit others, but wholly for their own gratification or honour, as plainly appears when active good falls upon anything contrary to the good of communion; for that gigantic passion wherewith the great disturbers[f] of the world are carried away, as in the case of Sylla and others, who would render all their friends happy and all their enemies miserable, and endeavour to make the world carry their image, which is really warring against heaven,—this passion, I say, aspires to an active individual good, at least in appear-

[c] Seneca. [d] Seneca, Epist. xxiv. § 23—25. [e] Prov. xxi. 25.
[f] So Barrow, "Sermon iii. on Redemption." There are some persons of that wicked and gigantic disposition, contracted by evil practice, that should one offer to instruct them in truth or move them to piety, would exclaim with Polyphemus—
Νήπιός εἰς, ὦ ξεῖν', ἢ τηλόθεν εἰλήλουθας,
Ὅς με θεοὺς κέλεαι ἢ δειδίμεν, ἢ ἀλέασθαι.—Odyss. ix. 273.

ance, though it be infinitely different from the good of communion.

We divide passive good into conservative and perfective; for everything has three kinds of appetite with regard to its own individual good,—the first to preserve itself, the second to perfect itself, and the third to multiply and diffuse itself. The last relates to active good, of which we have spoken already; and of the other two the perfective is the most excellent; for it is a less matter to preserve a thing in its state, and a greater to exalt its nature. But throughout the universe are found some nobler natures, to the dignity and excellence whereof inferior ones aspire, as to their origins;—whence the poet said well of mankind, that "they have an ethereal vigour and a celestial origin:"

"Igneus est ollis vigor et cœlestis origo;" [g]

for the perfection of the human form consists in approaching the Divine or angelic nature. The corrupt and preposterous imitation of this perfective good is the pest of human life, and the storm that overturns and sweeps away all things, whilst men, instead of a true and essential exaltation, fly with blind ambition only to a local one; for as men in sickness toss and roll from place to place, as if by change of situation they could get away from themselves, or fly from the disease, so in ambition, men hurried away with a false imagination of exalting their own nature, obtain no more than change of place or eminence of post.

Conservative good is the receiving and enjoying things agreeable to our nature; and this good, though it be the most simple and natural, yet of all others it seems the lowest and most effeminate. It is also attended with a difference, about which the judgment of mankind has been partly unsettled and the inquiry partly neglected; for the dignity and recommendation of the good of fruition or pleasure, as it is commonly called, consists either in the reality or strength thereof,—the one being procured by uniformity, and the other by variety. The one has a less mixture of evil, the other a stronger and more lively impression of good: which of these is the best, is the question; but whether human nature be not capable of both at once, has not been examined.

[g] See Virgil, Æneid, vi. 730.

FELICITY—IN WHAT PLACED.

As for the question, it began to be debated between Socrates and a Sophist. Socrates asserted that felicity lay in a constant peace and tranquillity of mind, but the Sophist placed it in great appetite and great fruition. From reasoning they fell to railing, when the Sophist said, the felicity of Socrates was the felicity of a stock or a stone; Socrates, on the other hand, said, the felicity of the Sophist was the felicity of one who is always itching and always scratching. And both opinions have their supporters;[h] for the school even of Epicurus, which allowed that virtue greatly conduced to felicity, is on the side of Socrates; and if this be the case, certainly virtue is more useful in appeasing disorders than in obtaining desires. The Sophist's opinion is somewhat favoured by the assertion above mentioned, viz., that perfective good is superior to conservative good, because every obtaining of a desire seems gradually to perfect nature, which though not strictly true, yet a circular motion has some appearance of a progressive one.

As for the other point, whether human nature is not at the same time capable both of tranquillity and fruition, a just determination of it will render the former question unnecessary. And do we not often see the minds of men so framed and disposed, as to be greatly affected with present pleasures, and yet quietly suffer the loss of them?—Whence that philosophical progression, "Use not, that you may not wish; wish not, that you may not fear," seems an indication of a weak, diffident, and timorous mind. And, indeed, most doctrines of the philosophers appear to be too distrustful, and to take more care of mankind than the nature of the thing requires. Thus they increase the fears of death by the remedies they bring against it; for whilst they make the life of man little more than a preparation and discipline for death, it is impossible but the enemy must appear terrible, when there is no end of the defence to be made against him. The poet did better for a heathen, who placed the end of life among the privileges of nature,—

"Qui spatium vitæ extremum inter munera ponat
Naturæ."[i]

Thus the philosophers, in all cases, endeavour to render the mind too uniform and harmonical, without enuring it to

[h] Plato, Gorgias, i. 492.   [i] Juvenal, Sat. x. 360.

extreme and contrary motions; and the reason seems to be, that they give themselves up to a private life, free from disquiet and subjection to others; whereas men should rather imitate the prudence of a lapidary, who, finding a speck or a cloud in a diamond, that may be ground out without too much waste, takes it away, or otherwise leaves it untouched; and so the serenity of the mind is to be consulted without impairing its greatness. And thus much for the doctrine of self-good.

The good of communion, which regards society, usually goes by the name of duty, a word that seems more properly used of a mind well disposed towards others; whilst the term virtue is used of a mind well formed and composed within itself. Duty, indeed, seems at first to be of political consideration; but if thoroughly weighed, it truly relates to the rule and government of one's self, not others. And as in architecture it is one thing to fashion the pillars, rafters, and other parts of the building, and prepare them for the work, and another to fit and join them together, so the doctrine of uniting mankind in society differs from that which renders them conformable and well affected to the benefits of society.

This part concerning duties is likewise divided into two, —the one treating of the duties of man in common, and the other of respective duties, according to the profession, vocation, state, person, and degree of particulars.[k] The first of these, we before observed, has been sufficiently cultivated and explained by the ancient and later writers. The other also has been touched here and there, though not digested and reduced into any body of science.[l] We do not, however, except to its being treated piecemeal, as judging it the best way to write upon this subject in separate parts; for who will pretend he can justly discourse and define upon the peculiar and relative duties of all orders and conditions of

---

[k] For the modern writers in this way, see Morhof's "Polyhistor," tom. iii. lib. i. "De Philosophiæ moralis Scriptoribus;" and "Stollii Introductio in Historiam Literariam, de Philosophia generatim morali;" in particular, consult Puffendorf, "De Officio Hominis and Civis." *Shaw.*

[l] This appears to be attempted by Grotius, in his book "De Jure Belli ac Pacis;" and by Puffendorf, in his "De Jure Naturæ et Gentium." See M. Barbeyrac's translation of the latter into French, with annotations. *Shaw.*

men? But for treatises upon this subject, which have no tincture of experience, and are only drawn from general and scholastic knowledge, they commonly prove empty and useless performances; for though a bystander may sometimes see what escaped the player, and although it be a kind of proverb, more bold and true with regard to prince and people, "that a spectator in the valley takes the best view of a mountain," yet it were greatly to be wished that none but the most experienced men would write upon subjects of this kind; for the contemplations of speculative men in active matters appear no better to those who have been conversant in business than the dissertations of Phormio upon war appeared to Hannibal, who esteemed them but as dreams and dotage. One fault, however, dwells with such as write upon things belonging to their own office or art, viz., that they hold no mean in recommending and extolling them.

In speaking of books of this kind, it would indeed be sacrilege in me to omit mention of your Majesty's excellent work on the duty of a king. This work incloses the leading treasures of divinity, politics, and ethics, besides a sprinkling of all other arts; and I am not afraid to pronounce it one of the soundest and most profitable works I have ever read. It does not swell with the heat of invention, or flag with the coldness of negligence. The author is nowhere seized with that dizziness which confuses his sight of the main subject, and consequently avoids those digressions which, by a sort of circuitous method, descants on matter foreign to the purpose. Neither are its pages disfigured with the arts of rhetorical perfumes and paintings, designed rather to please the reader than to corroborate the argument. But they contain life and spirit, as well as solidity and bulk, containing excellent precepts, adapted as well to theoretical truth as to the expediency of use and action. The work is also entirely exempt from that vice even more censured, and which, if it were tolerable, it were so in kings, and in works on regal majesty, viz., that it does not exaggerate the privileges of the crown or invidiously exalt their power. For your Majesty has not described a king of Persia or Assyria, shining forth in all their pomp and glory, but a Moses and a David, pastors as well as rulers of their people. Nor can I forget that memorable saying which your Majesty delivered on an important point of judicature,—That kings rule by the laws of their kingdoms, as God by the laws of nature, and ought as rarely to exercise their prerogative, which transcends law, as God exercises his power of working miracles. And in your Majesty's other book on a free monarchy, you give all men to understand that your Majesty knows and comprehends the plenitude of the regal power, as well as its limits; I, therefore, have not shrunk from citing this book as one of the best treatises ever published upon particular and respective duties. I can also assure your Majesty, that had the book been a thousand years in existence it would not have lost any of the praises I have bestowed upon it; nor am I prescribed by the adage which forbids praise in presence; since this rule of decorum applies only to unseasonable and excessive eulogy. Surely Cicero, in his excellent oration in defence of Marcellus, is only bent upon drawing a picture with singular art, of Cæsar's virtues, though in his presence, as the second Pliny did for Trajan. But let us proceed with our subject.

To this part of the respective duties of vocations and particular professions belongs another, as a doctrine relative or opposite to it, viz., the doctrine of cautions, frauds, impostures, and their vices; for corruptions and vices are opposite to duties and virtues; not but some mention is already made of them in writings, though commonly but cursorily and satirically, rather than seriously and gravely; for more labour is bestowed in invidiously reprehending many good and useful things in arts and exposing them to ridicule, than in separating what is corrupt and vicious therein from what is sound and serviceable. Solomon says excellently, "A scorner seeks wisdom, and finds it not; but knowledge is easy to him that understands;"[m] for whoever comes to a science with an intent to deride and despise, will doubtless find things enough to cavil at, and few to improve by. But the serious and prudent treatment of the subject we speak of may be reckoned among the strongest bulwarks of virtue and probity; for as it is fabulously related of the basilisk, that if he sees a man first, the man presently dies; but if the man has the first glance, he kills the basilisk: so frauds, impostures, and tricks do not hurt, if first discovered; but if they strike

[m] Prov. xiv. 6.

first, it is then they become dangerous, and not otherwise: hence we are beholden to Machiavel, and writers of that kind, who openly and unmasked declare what men do in fact, and not what they ought to do;[n] for it is impossible to join the wisdom of the serpent and the innocence of the dove, without a previous knowledge of the nature of evil; as without this, virtue lies exposed and unguarded. And farther, a good and just man cannot correct and amend the vicious and the wicked, unless he has first searched into all the depths and dungeons of wickedness; for men of a corrupt and depraved judgment ever suppose that honesty proceeds from ignorance, or a certain simplicity of manners, and is rooted only in a belief of our tutors, instructors, books, moral precepts, and vulgar discourse, whence,—unless they plainly perceive that their perverse opinions, their corrupt and distorted principles, are thoroughly known to those who exhort and admonish them as well as to themselves,—they despise all wholesome advice; according to that admirable saying of Solomon, "A fool receives not the words of the wise, unless thou speakest the very things that are in his heart."[o] And this part of morality, concerning cautions and respective vice, we set down as wanting, under the name of sober satire, or the insides of things.

To the doctrine of respective duties belong also the mutual duties between husband and wife, parent and child, master and servant, as also the laws of friendship, gratitude, and the civil obligations of fraternities, colleges, neighbourhoods, and the like, always understanding that these things are to be treated, not as parts of civil society, in which view they belong to politics, but so far as the minds of particulars ought to be instructed and disposed to preserve these bonds of society.

The doctrine of the good of communion, as well as of self-good, treats good not only simply, but comparatively, and thus regards the balancing of duty betwixt man and man, case and case, private and public, present and future, &c.,—

---

[n] Perhaps the treatise of Hieron. Cardan "De Arcanis Prudentiæ Civilis," is a capital performance in this way; as exposing numerous tricks, frauds, and stratagems of government, so as to prevent the honest-minded from being imposed upon by them. *Shaw.*

[o] Prov. xviii. 2.

as we may observe in the cruel conduct of Lucius Brutus to his own sons, which by the generality was extolled to the skies; yet another said,

"Infelix, utcunque ferent ea facta minores."[p]

So in the discourse betwixt Brutus, Cassius, and others, as to the conspiracy against Cæsar, the question was artfully introduced whether it were lawful to kill a tyrant;[q] the company divided in their opinions about it, some saying it was lawful, and that slavery was the greatest of evils; others denying it, and asserting tyranny to be less destructive than civil war; whilst a third kind, as if followers of Epicurus, made it an unworthy thing that wise men should endanger themselves for fools. But the cases of comparative duties are numerous, among which this question frequently occurs, whether justice may be strained for the safety of one's country, or the like considerable good in future? as to which Jason the Thessalian used to say, Some things must be done unjustly, that many more may be done justly. But the answer is ready,—Present justice is in our power, but of future justice we have no security: let men pursue those things which are good and just at present, and leave futurity to Divine providence.[r] And thus much for the doctrine of the image of good.[s]

CHAPTER III.

The Culture of the Mind divided into the Knowledge of Characteristic Differences of Affections, of Remedies and Cures. Appendix relating to the Harmony between the Pleasures of the Mind and the Body.

WE next proceed to the cultivation of the mind, without which the preceding part of morality is no more than an

---

[p] Virg. Æn. vi. 823.   [q] Plut. Life Brut.
[r] Plutarch, Moral. Præc. Gerend. Reip. i. 24.
[s] Such was the pretext of Titus Quintius Flaminius, who, perceiving that the Achæan league, by which all the Grecian states were associated in one grand confederation, imposed the principal obstacle to the arms of Rome, deceitfully alleged that his sole design was to free each individual state from the thraldom of one dominant power, and leave it to the action of its own laws. The sequel showed, however, that his policy was only an exemplification of the old fable, for the untying the bundle was immediately followed by the subjugation of each community. *Ed.*

image or beautiful statue, without life or motion. Aristotle expressly acknowledges as much,—" It is, therefore, necessary," says he, " to speak of virtue, what it is, and whence it proceeds; for it were in a manner useless to know virtue, and yet be ignorant of the ways to acquire her."[a] Concerning virtue, therefore, we must ascertain both what kind it is and by what means it may be acquired; for we desire a knowledge of the thing itself and the manner of procuring its pleasures.[b] And though he has more than once repeated the same thing, yet himself does not pursue it. And so Cicero gives it as a high commendation to the younger Cato, that he embraced philosophy, not for the sake of disputing, as most do, but of living philosophically.[c] And though at present few have any great regard to the cultivation and discipline of the mind and a regular course of life, as Seneca phrases it,—" De partibus vitæ quisque deliberat, de summa nemo,"[d]—whence this part may appear superfluous, yet we cannot be persuaded to leave it untouched, but rather conclude with the aphorism of Hippocrates, that those who labour under a violent disease, yet seem insensible of their pain, are disordered in their mind. And men in this case want not only a method of cure, but a particular remedy, to bring them to their senses. If any one shall object, that the cure of the mind is the office of divinity, we allow it; yet nothing excludes moral philosophy from the train of theology, whereto it is as a prudent and faithful hand-maid, attending and administering to all its wants. But though, as the Psalmist observes, " the eyes of the maid are perpetually waiting on the hands of the mistress,"[e] yet doubtless many things must be left to the care and judgment of the servant. So ethics ought to be entirely subservient to theology, and obedient to the precepts thereof, though it may still contain many wholesome and useful instructions within its own limits. And therefore, when we consider the excellence of this part of morality, we cannot but greatly wonder it is not hitherto reduced to a body of doctrine, which we are obliged to note as deficient; and shall therefore give some sketch for supplying it.

And first, as in all cases of practice, we must here dis-

[a] Eth. Mag. ad init.   [b] Mag. Moral. i.   [c] Juv. Muræn. xxx. 62.
[d] Epist. lxxi. § 1.   [e] Psal. cxxii. 3.

tinguish the things in our power, and those that are not: for the one may be altered, whilst the other can only be applied. Thus the farmer has no command over the nature of the soil, or the seasons of the year; nor the physician over the constitution of the patient, or the variety of accidents. In the cultivation of the mind, and the cure of its diseases, there are three things to be considered; viz., 1. the different dispositions; 2. the affections; and 3. the remedies: answering in physic to the constitution, the distemper, and the medicines. And of these three, only the last is in our power. Yet we ought as carefully to inquire into the things that are not in our power, as into those that are; because a clear and exact knowledge thereof is to be made the foundation of the doctrine of remedies, in order to their more commodious and successful application. For clothes cannot be made to fit, unless measure of the body be first taken.

The first article, therefore, of the culture of the mind, will regard the different natures or dispositions of men. But here we speak not of the vulgar propensities to virtues and vices, or perturbations and passions, but of such as are more internal and radical. And I cannot sometimes but wonder that this particular should be so generally neglected by the writers both of morality and politics; whereas it might afford great light to both these sciences. In astrological traditions, the natures and dispositions of men are tolerably distinguished according to the influences of the planets; whence some are said to be by nature formed for contemplation, others for politics, others for war, &c. So, likewise, among the poets of all kinds, we everywhere find characters of natures, though commonly drawn with excess, and exceeding the limits of nature. And this subject of the different characters of dispositions is one of those things wherein the common discourse of men is wiser than books—a thing which seldom happens. But much the best matter of all for such a treatise may be derived from the more prudent historians; and not so well from elogies or panegyrics, which are usually written soon after the death of an illustrious person, but much rather from a whole body of history, as often as such a person appears: for such an interwoven account gives a better description than panegyric. And such examples we have in Livy, of Africanus and Cato ; in Tacitus, of Tiberius, Claudius, and Nero ; in Herodian, of Septimius Severus ; in Philip de Comines, of Lewis the Eleventh ; in Guicciardine, of Ferdinand of Spain, the Emperor Maximilian, Pope Leo, and Pope Clement. For these writers having the image of the person to be described constantly before them, scarce ever mention any of their acts, but at the same time introduce something of their natures. So, likewise, some relations which we have seen of the conclaves at Rome give very exact characters of the cardinals : as the letters of ambassadors do of the counsellors of princes. Let, therefore, an accurate and full treatise be wrote upon this fertile and copious subject. But we do not mean, that these characters should be received in ethics as perfect civil images, but rather as outlines, and first draughts of the images themselves, which, being variously compounded and mixed one among another, afford all kinds of portraits. So that an artificial and accurate dissection may be made of men's minds and natures, and the secret disposition of each particular man laid open, that, from a knowledge of the whole, the precepts concerning the cures of the mind may be more rightly formed.[f]

And not only the characters of dispositions impressed by nature should be received into this treatise, but those also which are otherwise imposed upon the mind by the sex, age, country, state of health, make of body, &c. And again, those which proceed from fortune, as in princes, nobles, common people, the rich, the poor, magistrates, the ignorant, the happy, the miserable, &c. Thus we see Plautus makes it a kind of miracle to find an old man beneficent.

"Benignitas quidem hujus oppidò ut adolescentuli est."[g]

And St. Paul, commanding a severity of discipline towards the Cretans, accuses the temper of that nation from the poet:

[f] Compare "Les Caractères des Passions," par M. de la Chambre, ed. Amst. 1658 ; M. Clarmont, "De Conjectandis latentibus Animi Affectibus," reprinted by Conringius ; "Neuheusii Theatrum Ingenii humani, seu de Hominum cognoscenda Indole et Animi Secretis," 1633 ; Mr. Evelyn's digression concerning Physiognomy, in his Discourse of Medals ; "Les Caractères de Théophraste, avec les Mœurs de ce Siècle," par M. de la Bruyère, 1700. See "Stollii Introductio in Historiam Literariam," p. 823. See also more to this purpose above, sect. iv. *Ed.*

[g] Miles Gloriosus, act 3, sc. i. v. 39.

"The Cretans are always liars, evil beasts, and slow bellies."[b] Sallust notes it of the temper of kings, that it is frequent with them to desire contradictories:—"Plerumque regiæ voluntates, ut vehementes sunt; sic mobiles, sæpeque ipsæ sibi adversæ."[i] Tacitus observes, that "honours and dignities commonly change the temper of mankind for the worse." "Solus Vespasianus mutatus in melius.'[k] Pindar remarks that "a sudden flush of good fortune generally enervates and slackens the mind."

"Sunt qui magnam felicitatem concoquere non possunt."[l]

The psalmist intimates, that it is easier to hold a mean in the height, than in the increase of fortune:—"If riches fly to thee, set not thy heart upon them."[m] It is true, Aristotle, in his Rhetorics, cursorily mentions some such observations; and so do others up and down in their writings: but they were never yet incorporated into moral philosophy, whereto they principally belong, as much as treatises of the difference of the soil and glebe belong to agriculture, or discourses of the different complexions or habits of the body to medicine. The thing must, therefore, be now procured, unless we would imitate the rashness of empirics, who employ the same remedies in all diseases and constitutions.

Next to this doctrine of characters follows the doctrine of affections and perturbations, which, we observed above, are the diseases of the mind. For as the ancient politicians said of democracies, that "the people were like the sea, and the orators like the wind;" so it may be truly said, that the nature of the mind would be unruffled and uniform, if the affections, like the winds, did not disturb it. And here, again, we cannot but remember that Aristotle, who wrote so many books of ethics, should never treat of the affections, which are a principal branch thereof; and yet has given them a place in his Rhetorics, where they come to be but secondarily considered:[n] for his discourses of pleasure and pain by no means answer the ends of such a treatise, no more than a discourse of light and splendour would give the doctrine of particular colours: for pleasure and pain are to

---

[b] Epist. Tit. i. 12.   [i] Jugurtha, i. 50.   [k] Hist. i. 53, towards the end.
[l] Or, καταπέψαι μεγὰν ὄλϐον οὐκ ἐδυνάσθη.—Olymp. i. 55.
[m] Psalm lxi. 11.   [n] See b. ii. and cf. Eth. Nic. ii. 4, 1.

particular affections, as light is to colours. The Stoics, so far as may be conjectured from what we have left of them, cultivated this subject better, yet they rather dwelt upon subtile definitions than gave any full and copious treatise upon it. We also find a few short elegant pieces upon some of the affections; as upon anger, false modesty, and two or three more; but to say the truth, the poets and historians are the principal teachers of this science; for they commonly paint to the life in what particular manner the affections are to be raised and inflamed, and how to be soothed and laid; how they are to be checked and restrained from breaking into action; how they discover themselves, though suppressed and smothered; what operations they have; what turns they take; how they mutually intermix; and how they oppose each other, &c. Among which, the latter is of extensive use in moral and civil affairs; I mean, how far one passion may regulate another, and how they employ each other's assistance to conquer some one, after the manner of hunters and fowlers, who take beast with beast, and bird with bird; which man, perhaps, without such assistance, could not so easily do. And upon this foundation rests that excellent and universal use of rewards and punishments in civil life.[o] For these are the supports of states, and suppress all the other noxious affections by those two predominant ones, fear and hope. And, as in civil government, one faction frequently bridles and governs another; the case is the same in the internal government of the mind.[p]

We come now to those things which are within our own power, and work upon the mind, and affect and govern the will and the appetite; whence they have great efficacy in altering the manners. And here philosophers should diligently inquire into the powers and energy of custom, exercise, habit, education, example, imitation, emulation, company, friendship, praise, reproof, exhortation, reputation,

[o] See Butler's "Analogy," chap. on rewards and punishments.
[p] See "Lælius Peregrinus de noscendis et emendandis Animi Affectionibus," ed. Lipsiæ, 1714; "Placcius de Typo Medicinæ moralis;" M. Perault, "De l'Usage des Passions," 1668; "Johan. Francisc. Buddæus de Morbis mentis humanæ, de Sanitate mentis humanæ, et de Remediis morborum, quibus mens laborat," in his "Elementa Philosophiæ Practicæ," lib. de Philosophia morali, sect. iii. cap. 3, 4, 6. See "Stollii Introduct. in Historiam Literariam," pp. 813, 814. *Shaw*.

laws, books, studies, &c.; for these are the things which reign in men's morals. By these agents the mind is formed and subdued; and of these ingredients remedies are prepared, which, so far as human means can reach, conduce to the preservation and recovery of the health of the mind.

To give an instance or two in custom and habit, the opinion of Aristotle seems narrow and careless, which asserts that " custom has no power over those actions which are natural;[q]" using this example, that if a stone be a thousand times thrown up into the air, yet it will acquire no tendency to a spontaneous ascent. And again, that " by often seeing or hearing, we see and hear never the better." For though this may hold in some things, where nature is absolute, yet it is otherwise in things where nature admits intension and remission in a certain latitude. He might have seen, that a strait glove, by being often drawn upon the hand, will become easy; that a stick, by use and continuance, will acquire and retain a bend contrary to its natural one; that the voice, by exercise, becomes stronger and more sonorous; that heat and cold grow more tolerable by custom, &c. And these two last examples come nearer to the point than those he has produced. Be this as it will, the more certain he had found it that virtues and vices depended upon habit, the more he should have endeavoured to prescribe rules how such habits were to be acquired or left off; since numerous precepts may be formed for the prudent directing of exercises, as well those of the mind as the body. We will here mention a few of them.

And the first shall be, that from the beginning we beware of imposing both more difficult, and more superficial tasks than the thing requires. For if too great a burden be laid upon a middling genius, it blunts the cheerful spirit of hope; and if upon a confident one, it raises an opinion, from which he promises himself more than he can perform, which leads to indolence; and in both cases the experiment will not answer expectation. And this always dejects and confounds the mind. But if the tasks are too light, a great loss is sustained in the amount of the progress.

Secondly, to procure a habit in the exercise of any faculty, let two seasons be principally observed: the one when the

[q] Nicom. Eth. ii. last ch.

mind is best, and the other when it is worst disposed for business; that by the former, the greater despatch may be made; and by the latter, the obstructions of the mind may be borne down with a strenuous application; whence the intermediate times slide away the more easily and agreeably.

The third example shall be the precept which Aristotle transiently mentions; viz., to endeavour our utmost against that whereto we are strongly impelled by nature; thus, as it were, rowing against the stream, or bending a crooked stick the contrary way, in order to bring it straight.[r]

A fourth precept may be founded on this sure principle; that the mind is easier, and more agreeably drawn on to those things which are not principally intended by the operator, but conquered or obtained without premeditated design, because our nature is such, as in a manner hates to be commanded. There are many other useful precepts for the regulating of custom; and if custom be prudently and skilfully introduced, it really becomes a second nature; but if unskilfully and casually treated, it will be but the ape of nature, and imitate nothing to the life, or awkwardly, and with deformity.

So, with regard to books, studies, and influence over our manners, there are numerous useful rules and directions. One of the fathers, in great severity, called poetry the devil's wine; as indeed it begets many temptations, desires, and vain opinions. And it is a very prudent saying of Aristotle, deserving to be well considered, that "young men are improper hearers of moral philosophy,"[s] because the heat of their passions is not yet allayed and tempered by time and experience. And to say the truth, the reason why the excellent writings and moral discourses of the ancients have so little effect upon our lives and manners, seems to be, that they are not usually read by men of ripe age and judgment, but wholly left to unexperienced youths and children. And are not young men much less fit for politics than for ethics, before they are well seasoned with religion, and the doctrines of morality and civility? For being, perhaps, depraved and corrupted in their judgment, they are apt to think that moral differences are not real and solid; but that all things are to be measured by utility and success. Thus the poet said,

[r] Nicom. Eth. ii. 95, towards the end.   [s] Nic. Eth. i. 15.

"Successful villany is called virtue"—"Prosperum et felix scelus, virtus vocatur."[t] And again, "Ille crucem pretium sceleris tulit, hic diadema."[u] The poets, indeed, speak in this manner satirically, and through indignation; but some books of politics suppose the same positively, and in earnest. For Machiavel is pleased to say, "if Cæsar had been conquered, he would have become more odious than Catiline:" as if there was no difference, except in point of fortune, betwixt a fury made up of lust and blood, and a noble spirit, of all natural men the most to be admired, but for his ambition. And hence we see how necessary it is for men to be fully instructed in moral doctrines and religious duties, before they proceed to politics. For those bred up from their youth in the courts of princes, and the midst of civil affairs, can scarce ever obtain a sincere and internal probity of manners. Again, caution also is to be used even in moral instructions, or at least in some of them, lest men should thence become stubborn, arrogant, and unsociable. So Cicero says of Cato: "The divine and excellent qualities we see in him are his own; but the things he sometimes fails in are all derived, not from nature, but his instructors."[x] There are many other axioms and directions concerning the things which studies and books beget in the minds of men; for it is true that studies enter our manners, and so do conversation, reputation, the laws, &c.

But there is another cure of the mind, which seems still more accurate and elaborate than the rest; depending upon this foundation, that the minds of all men are, at certain times, in a more perfect, and at others in a more depraved state. The design of this cure is, therefore, to improve the good times, and expunge the bad. There are two practical methods of fixing the good times; viz., 1. determined resolutions; and 2. observances or exercises; which are not of so much significancy in themselves, as because they continually keep the mind in its duty. There are also two ways of expunging the bad times; viz., by some kind of redemption, or expiation of what is past, and a new regulation of life for the future. But this part belongs to religion, whereto

---

[t] Seneca, Herc. Fur. v. 251. [u] Juv. Sat. xiii. 105.
[x] Pro L. Murænа, 39.

moral philosophy is, as we said before, the genuine handmaid.

We will therefore conclude these georgics of the mind with that remedy which of all others is the shortest, noblest, and most effectual for forming the mind to virtue, and placing it near a state of perfection; viz., that we choose and propose to ourselves just and virtuous ends of our lives and actions, yet such as we have in some degree the faculty of obtaining. For if the ends of our actions are good and virtuous, and the resolutions of our mind for obtaining them fixed and constant, the mind will directly mould and form itself at once to all kinds of virtue. And this is certainly an operation resembling the works of nature, whilst the others above mentioned seem only manual. Thus the statuary finishes only that part of the figure upon which his hand is employed, without meddling with the others at that time, which are still but unfashioned marble; whereas nature, on the contrary, when she works upon a flower or an animal, forms the rudiments of all the parts at once.[y] So when virtues are acquired by habit, whilst we endeavour at temperance, we make but little advances towards fortitude or the other virtues; but when we are once entirely devoted to just and honourable ends, whatever the virtue be which those ends recommend and direct, we shall find ourselves ready disposed, and possessed of some propensity to obtain and express it. And this may be that state of mind which Aristotle excellently describes, not as virtuous, but divine.[z] His words are these:—" We may contrast humanity with that virtue which is above it, as being heroic and divine." And a little farther on:—" For as savage creatures are incapable of vice or virtue, so is the Deity." For the divine state is above virtue, which is only the absence of vice. So Pliny proposes the virtue of Trajan, not as an imitation, but

[y] Harvey, who was Bacon's physician, and the most celebrated anatomist of his day, contradicts this doctrine, affirming that nature operates like man by production and elaboration of parts. *Ed.*

[z] " Humanitati autem consentaneum est opponere eam quæ supra humanitatem est heroicam sive divinam virtutem ;" and a little after, "Nam ut feræ neque vitium neque virtus est, hic neque Dei: sed hic quidem status altius quiddam virtute est, ille aliud quiddam a vitio."— Nic. Ethics, vii. 1. *Ed.*

as an example of the divine virtue, when he says, "Men need make no other prayers to the gods than that they would be but as good and propitious to morals as Trajan was."[a] But this savours of the profane arrogance of the heathens, who grasped at shadows larger than the life. The Christian religion comes to the point, by impressing charity upon the minds of men; which is most appositely called the bond of perfection,[b] because it ties up and fastens all the virtues together. And it was elegantly said by Menander of sensual love, which is a bad imitation of the divine, that it was a better tutor for human life than a left-handed sophist; intimating that the grace of carriage is better formed by love than by an awkward preceptor, whom he calls left-handed, as he cannot by all his operose rules and precepts, form a man so dexterously and expeditiously, to value himself justly, and behave gracefully, as love can do. So, without doubt, if the mind be possessed with the fervour of true charity, he will rise to a higher degree of perfection than by all the doctrine of ethics, which is but a sophist compared to charity. And as Xenophon well observed,[c] whilst the other passions, though they raise the mind, yet distort and discompose it by their ecstasies and excesses; whilst love alone, at the same time composes and dilates it; so all other human endowments which we admire, whilst they exalt and enlarge our nature, are yet liable to extravagance: but of charity alone there is no excess. The angels aspiring to be like God in power, transgressed and fell: "I will ascend, and be like the Most High:"[d] and man aspiring to be like God in knowledge, transgressed and fell: "Ye shall be as gods, knowing good and evil:" but in aspiring to be like God in goodness or charity, neither man nor angel can or shall transgress. Nay, we are invited to an imitation of it: "Love your enemies; do good to those that hate you; pray for those that despitefully use and persecute you; that ye may be the children of your Father, which is in heaven: for he maketh his sun to rise upon the good and upon the evil, and sends his rain upon the just and upon the unjust."[e] And thus we conclude this part of moral doctrine, relating to the georgics of the mind.

So in the archetype of the Divine nature—the heathen

[a] Paneg. lxxiv. § 4 and 5.   [b] Colos. iii.   [c] Cyropædia.
[d] Isa. xiv. 14.   [e] Matt. v. 44.

religion,—the words "Optimus maximus," and the Scripture pronounces the mercy of God to be above all his works.[f]

. We have now concluded that portion of morals which appertains to the georgics of the mind; and should any one imagine, in reading the different parts of this science which we have already handled, that all our labour consists in uniting into one digest of the sciences all that has been neglected by other writers, and that such a work is at best only supplying what is clear and evident, and easily arrived at by reflection, let him freely enjoy his judgment; but at the same time we beg him to keep in mind our first assertion, that we sought in these researches, not the flourish and ornament of things, but their use and verity. He may also recall the ancient parable of the Two Gates of Sleep:—

"Sunt geminæ Somni Portæ, quarum altera fertur
Cornea, qua veris facilis datur exitus umbris:
Altera, candenti perfecta nitens elephanto;
Sed falsa ad cœlum mittunt insomnia manes."[g]

A gate of ivory is indeed very stately, but true dreams pass through the gate of horn.

There might, however, be added, by way of appendix, this observation, that there is a certain relation and congruity found between the good of the mind and the good of the body. For as the good of the body consists in,—1. Health; 2. Comeliness; 3. Strength; and, 4. Pleasure;—so the good of the mind, considered in a moral light, tends to render it, —1. sound and calm; 2. graceful; 3. strong and agile for all the offices of life; and, 4. possessed of a constant quick sense of pleasure and noble satisfaction. But as the four former excellencies are seldom found together in the body, so are the four latter seldom found together in the mind.[h] For it is evident that many are full of wit and courage, without being either calm or elegant in their deportment, or beautiful in their person; others again possess an elegant

---

[f] Eccles. xviii. 12.   [g] Virg. Æn. vi. 893.

[h] This doctrine of the georgics of the mind is expressly endeavoured to be supplied by Professor Wesenfeld, in the books he entitles "Arnoldi Wesenfeld Georgica Animi et Vitæ, seu Pathologia practica, moralis nempe et civilis, ex physicis ubique fontibus repetita." Francof. 1695, and 1712. Some account of this work is given in the "Acta Eruditorum." Mens. August, 1696. See also "Joan. Franc. Brudens de Cultura Ingeniorum," ed. Halæ, 1699. *Shaw.*

and fine deportment, and yet eschew honesty and justice; others again have pure minds, but without any qualifications for the business of life;[1] others who perchance unite all these three qualities, possess a sullen humour of stoical sadness and stupidity,—they practise virtue, but refuse to enjoy its pleasures; and if perchance of these qualities two or three are sometimes found together, it seldom if ever happens that all four can be met with in the same person. And thus we have finished that principal branch of human philosophy, which considers man out of society, and as consisting of a body and a soul.

EIGHTH BOOK.

CHAPTER I.

Civil Knowledge divided into the Art of Conversation, the Art of Negotiation, and the Art of State Policy.

THERE goes an old tradition, excellent King, that many Grecian philosophers had a solemn meeting before the ambassador of a foreign prince, where each endeavoured to show his parts, that the ambassador might have somewhat to relate of the Grecian wisdom; but one among the number kept silence, so that the ambassador, turning to him, asked, "But what have you to say, that I may report it?" He answered, "Tell your king that you have found one among the Greeks who knew how to be silent."[a] Indeed, I had forgot in this compendium of arts to insert the art of silence. For as we are now soon to be led, by the course of the work, to treat the subject of government; and knowing that I write to a king who is so perfect a master of this science since his infancy, and being also mindful of the high office I hold under your Majesty, we thought we could not have a better occasion for putting the art of silence in practice.[b] Cicero

---

[1] Mirabeau expressed the same sentiment with his usual felicity. Energy of character is scarcely ever found except in union with violent temperaments. The wicked only are active. *Ed.*   [a] Plut. Moral.
[b] The author here makes a compliment of his silence to King James.

makes mention not only of an art, but even of an eloquence to be found in silence ; and relates in an epistle to Atticus, how once in conversation he made use of this art : "On this occasion," says he, " I assumed a part of your eloquence ; for I said nothing." And Pindar, who peculiarly strikes the mind unexpectedly with some short surprising sentence, has this among the rest : "Things unsaid have sometimes a greater effect than said." And, therefore, I have determined either to be silent upon this subject, or, what is next to it, very concise.

Civil knowledge turns upon a subject of all others the most immersed in matter, and therefore very difficult to reduce to axioms. And yet there are some things that ease the difficulty. For, 1. as Cato said, " that the Romans were like sheep, easier to drive in the flock than single ;" so in this respect the office of ethics is in some degree more difficult than that of politics.[c] 2. Again, ethics endeavours to tinge and furnish the mind with internal goodness, whilst civil doctrine requires no more than external goodness, which is sufficient for society.[d] Whence it often happens, that a reign may be good and the times bad. Thus we sometimes find in sacred history, when mention is made of good and pious kings, that the people had not yet turned their hearts to the Lord God of their fathers. And therefore, in this respect also, ethics has the harder task. 3. States are moved slowly, like machines, and with difficulty ; and consequently not soon put out of order. For, as in Egypt, the seven years of plenty supplied the seven years of famine ; so in governments, the good regulation of former times will not presently suffer the errors of the succeeding to prove destructive. But the resolutions and manners of particular persons are more suddenly subverted ; and this, in the last place, bears hard upon ethics, but favours politics.

deeming it impertinent to speak of the arts of empire, to one who knew them so well ; but the true reason appears to be, that he thought it improper to reveal the mysteries of state. See below, sect. xxv. *Ed.*

[c] Plut. Cato.

[d] Hence there ought to be a due difference preserved betwixt ethics and politics, though many writers seem to mix them together; and form a promiscuous doctrine of the law of nature, morality, policy, and religion together ; as particularly certain scriptural casuists, and political divines. *Shaw.*

Civil knowledge has three parts, suitable to the three principal acts of society; viz., 1. Conversation; 2. Business; and 3. Government. For there are three kinds of good that men desire to procure by civil society; viz., 1. Refuge from solitude; 2. Assistance in the affairs of life; and 3. Protection against injuries. And thus there are three kinds of prudence, very different, and frequently separated from each other; viz., 1. Prudence in conversation; 2. Prudence in business; 3. Prudence in government.[e]

Conversation, as it ought not to be over affected, much less should it be slighted; since a prudent conduct therein not only expresses a certain gracefulness in men's manners, but is also of great assistance in the commodious despatch both of public and private business. For as action, though an external thing, is so essential to an orator as to be preferred before the other weighty and more internal parts of that art, so conversation, though it consist but of externals, is, if not the principal, at least a capital thing in the man of business, and the prudent management of affairs. What effect the countenance may have, appears from the precept of the poet,—"Contradict not your words by your look,"—

"Nec vultu destrue verba tuo."[f]

For a man may absolutely cancel and betray the force of speech by his countenance. And so may actions themselves,

[e] From a mixture of these three parts of civil doctrine, there has of late been formed a new kind of doctrine, which they call by the name of civil prudence. This doctrine has been principally cultivated among the Germans; though hitherto carried to no great length. Hermannus Conringius has dwelt upon it at considerable length, in his book "De Civili Prudentia," published in the year 1662; and Christian Thomasius has treated it excellently in the little piece entitled, "Primæ Lineæ de Jure-consultorum Prudentia Consultatoria," &c., first published in the year 1705, but the third edition, with notes, in 1712. The heads it considers, are, 1. "de Prudentia in genere;" 2. "de Prudentia consultatoria;" 3. "de Prudentia Juris-consultorum;" 4. "de Prudentia consulendi intuitu actionum propriarum;" 5. "de Prudentia dirigendi actiones proprias in conversatione quotidiana;" 6. "de Prudentia in conversatione selecta;" 7. "de Prudentia intuitu societatum domesticarum;" 8. "de Prudentia in societate civili;" and 9. "de Prudentia alios et aliis consulendi." The little piece also of Andr. Bossius, "De Prudentia Civili comparanda," deserves the perusal. See Morhof, "De Prudentiæ Civilis Scriptoribus;" "Struvii Bibliotheca Philosophica," cap. 7; and "Stollii Introductio in Historiam Literariam, de Prudentia Politica." *Shaw.*   [f] Ovid, Ars Amandi, i. 312.

as well as words, be destroyed by the look; according to Cicero, who, recommending affability to his brother towards the provincials, tells him, it did not wholly consist in giving easy access to them, unless he also received them with an obliging carriage. "It is doing nothing," says he, "to admit them with an open door and a locked-up countenance."

"Nil interest habere ostium apertum, vultum clausum."[g]

We learn also that Atticus, previous to the first interview between Cicero and Cæsar, in which the issue of the war was involved, seriously advised his friend, in his letters, to compose his countenance and assume a calm tranquillity. But if the management of the face alone has so great an effect, how much greater is that of familiar conversation, with all its attendants. Indeed the whole of decorum and elegance of manners seems to rest in weighing and maintaining, with an even balance, the dignity betwixt ourselves and others; which is well expressed by Livy, though upon a different occasion, in that character of a person, where he says, that I may neither seem arrogant nor obnoxious; that is, neither forget my own nor others' liberty.[h]

On the other side; a devotion to urbanity and external elegance terminates in an awkward and disagreeable affectation. For what is more preposterous than to copy the theatres in real life? And though we did not fall into this vicious extreme, yet we should waste time and depress the mind too much by attending to such lighter matters. Therefore, as in universities, the students, too fond of company, are usually told by their tutors, that friends are the thieves of time; so the assiduous application to the decorum of conversation steals from the weightier considerations. Again, they who stand in the first rank for urbanity, and seem born, as it were, for this alone, seldom take pleasure in anything else, and scarce ever rise to the higher and more solid virtues. On the contrary, the consciousness of a defect in this particular makes us seek a grace from good opinion, which renders all things else becoming; but where this is wanting, men endea-

[g] De Petit. Consulatus, xi. 44.
[h] Speech of Hanno. "Nunc interroganti senatori, pœniteatne me adhuc suscepti adversus Romanos belli? si reticeam, aut superbus aut obnoxius videar; quorum alterum est hominis alienæ libertatis obliti, alterum suæ." Livy, b. xxiii. c. 12.

vour to supply it by good breeding. And further, there is scarce any greater or more frequent obstruction to business, than an over-curious observance of external decorum, with its attendant too solicitous and scrupulous a choice of times and opportunities. Solomon admirably says, "He that regards the winds shall not sow, and he that regards the clouds shall not reap."[i] For we must make opportunities oftener than we find them. In a word, urbanity is like a garment to the mind, and therefore ought to have the conditions of a garment; that is, 1. it should be fashionable; 2. not too delicate or costly; 3. it should be so made, as principally to show the reigning virtue of the mind, and to supply or conceal deformity; 4. and lastly, above all things, it must not be too strait, so as to cramp the mind and confine its motions in business. But this part of civil doctrine relating to conversation is elegantly treated by some writers, and can by no means be reported as deficient.[k]

CHAPTER II.

The Art of Negotiation divided into the Knowledge of Dispersed Occasions (Conduct in Particular Emergencies), and into the Science of Rising in Life. Examples of the former drawn from Solomon. Precepts relating to Self-advancement.

WE divide the doctrine of business into the doctrine of various occasions, and the doctrine of rising in life. The first includes all the possible variety of affairs, and is as the amanuensis to common life; but the other collects and suggests such things only as regard the improvement of a

[i] Eccles. xi. 4.

[k] It seems of late more cultivated among the French and Germans, than among the English. The "Morale du Monde;" the "Modèles de Conversation;" the "Réflexious sur la Ridicule, and sur les moyens de l'éviter;" "La Politesse des Mœurs;" "L'Art de Plaire dans la Conversation;" and Frid. Geutzkenius's "Doctrina de Decoro," in his Systema Philosophiæ, deserve perusal. This last work, published in Germany, treats 1. of the nature of decorum, and its foundation; 2. of national decorum; 3. of human decorum; 4. the decorum of youth and age; 5. the decorum of men and women; 6. the decorum of husband and wife; 7. the decorum of the clergy; 8. the decorum of princes; and 9. the decorum of the nobility, and men of letters. See "Stollii Introductio in Historiam Literariam, de Doctrina ejus quod est Decorum," p. 795-6. *Shaw.*

man's private fortune, and may therefore serve each person as a private register of his affairs.

No one hath hitherto treated the doctrine of business suitably to its merit, to the great prejudice of the character both of learning and learned men ; for from hence proceeds the mischief, which has fixed it as a reproach upon men of letters, that learning and civil prudence are seldom found together. And if we rightly observe those three kinds of prudence, which we lately said belong to civil life, that of conversation is generally despised by men of learning as a servile thing and an enemy to contemplation ; and for the government of states, though learned men acquit themselves well when advanced to the helm, yet this promotion happens to few of them ; but for the present subject, the prudence of business, upon which our lives principally turn, there are no books extant about it, except a few civil admonitions, collected into a little volume or two, by no means adequate to the copiousness of the subject. But if books were written upon this subject as upon others, we doubt not that learned men, furnished with tolerable experience, would far excel the unlearned, furnished with much greater experience, and outshoot them in their own bow.

Nor need we apprehend that the matter of this science is too various to fall under precept, for it is much less extensive than the doctrine of government, which yet we find very well cultivated. There seem to have been some professors of this kind of prudence among the Romans in their best days ; for Cicero declares it was the custom, a little before his time, among the senators most famous for knowledge and experience, as Coruncanius, Curius, Lælius, &c., to walk the forum at certain hours, where they offered themselves to be consulted by the people, not so much upon law, but upon business of all kinds ; as the marriage of a daughter, the education of a son, the purchasing of an estate, and other occasions of common life.[a] Whence it appears, that there is a certain prudence of advising even in private affairs, and derivable from an universal knowledge of civil business, experience, and general observation of similar cases. So we find the book which Q. Cicero wrote to his brother, De Petitione Consulatus (the only treatise, so far as we know,

[a] Orat. § iii. 33.

extant upon any particular business), though it regarded chiefly the giving advice upon that present occasion, yet contains many particular axioms of politics, which were not only of temporary use, but prescribe a certain permanent rule for popular elections. But in this kind, there is nothing any way comparable to the aphorisms of Solomon, of whom the Scripture bears testimony, that "his heart was as the sand of the sea."[b] For the sand of the sea encompasses the extremities of the whole earth; so his wisdom comprehended all things, both human and divine. And in those aphorisms are found many excellent civil precepts and admonitions, besides things of a more theological nature, flowing from the depth and innermost bosom of wisdom, and running out into a most spacious field of variety. And as we place the doctrine of various occasions among the desiderata of the sciences, we will here dwell upon it a little, and lay down an example thereof, in the way of explaining some of these aphorisms or proverbs of Solomon.

A SPECIMEN OF THE DOCTRINE OF VARIOUS OCCASIONS IN THE COMMON BUSINESS OF LIFE, BY WAY OF APHORISM AND EXPLANATION.

APHORISM I.—*A soft answer appeases anger.*[c]

If the anger of a prince or superior be kindled against you, and it be now your turn to speak, Solomon directs, 1. that an answer be made; and 2. that it be soft. The first rule contains three precepts; viz., 1. to guard against a melancholy and stubborn silence, for this either turns the fault wholly upon you, as if you could make no answer, or secretly impeaches your superior, as if his ears were not open to a just defence. 2. To beware of delaying the thing, and requiring a longer day for your defence; which either accuses your superior of passion, or signifies that you are preparing some artificial turn or colour. So that it is always best directly to say something for the present, in your own excuse, as the occasion requires. And 3. To make a real answer, an answer, not a mere confession or bare submission, but a mixture of apology and excuse. For it is unsafe to do otherwise, unless with very generous and noble spirits, which are extremely rare. Then follows the second rule, that the answer be mild and soft, not stiff and irritating.

[b] 3 Kings iv. 27.   [c] Prov. xv. 1.

II.—*A prudent servant shall rule over a foolish son, and divide the inheritance among the brethren.*[d]

In every jarring family there constantly rises up some servant or humble friend of sway, who takes upon him to compose their differences at his own discretion; to whom, for that reason, the whole family, even the master himself, is subject. If this man has a view to his own ends, he foments and aggravates the differences of the family; but if he prove just and upright, he is certainly very deserving. So that he may be reckoned even as one of the brethren, or at least have the direction of the inheritance in trust.

III.—*If a wise man contends with a fool, whether he be in anger or in jest, there is no quiet.*[e]

We are frequently admonished to avoid unequal conflicts; that is, not to strive with the stronger: but the admonition of Solomon is no less useful, that we should not strive with the worthless; for here the match is very unequal, where it is no victory to conquer, and a great disgrace to be conquered. Nor does it signify if, in such a conquest, we should sometimes deal as in jest, and sometimes in the way of disdain and contempt; for what course soever we take, we are losers, and can never come handsomely off. But the worst case of all is, if our antagonist have something of the fool in him, that is, if he be confident and headstrong.

IV.—*Listen not to all that is spoken, lest thou shouldst hear thy servant curse thee.*[f]

It is scarce credible what uneasiness is created in life by an useless curiosity about the things that concern us; as when we pry into such secrets, as being discovered, give us distaste, but afford no assistance or relief. For, 1. there follows vexation and disquiet of mind, as all human things are full of perfidiousness and ingratitude. So that though we could procure some magic glass, wherein to view the animosities, and all that malice which is any way at work against us, it were better for us to break it directly than to use it. For these things are but as the rustling of leaves, soon over. 2. This curiosity always loads the mind with suspicion, which is a violent enemy to counsels, and renders them unsteady and perplexed. 3. It also frequently fixes the

[d] Prov. xvii. 2. [e] Prov. xxix. 9. [f] Eccles. vii. 22.

evils themselves, which would otherwise have blown over: for it is a dangerous thing to provoke the consciences of men, who, so long as they think themselves concealed, are easily changed for the better; but if they once find themselves discovered, drive out one evil with another. It was therefore justly esteemed the utmost prudence in Pompey that he directly burnt all the papers of Sertorius, unperused by himself or others.

V.—*Poverty comes as a traveller, but want as an armed man.*[g]

This aphorism elegantly describes how prodigals, and such as take no care of their affairs, make shipwreck of their fortunes. For debt, and diminution of the capital, at first steals on gradually and almost imperceptibly like a traveller, but soon after want invades as an armed man; that is, with a hand so strong and powerful as can no longer be resisted; for it was justly said by the ancients, that necessity is of all things the strongest. We must, therefore, prevent the traveller, and guard against the armed man.

VI.—*He who instructs a scoffer, procures to himself reproach; and he who reproves a wicked man, procures to himself a stain.*[h]

This agrees with the precept of our Saviour, not to throw pearls before swine.[i] This aphorism distinguishes betwixt the actions of precept and reproof, and again betwixt the persons of the scorner and the wicked, and lastly, the reward is distinguished. In the former case, precept is repaid by a loss of labour, and in the latter, of reproof, it is repaid with a stain also. For when any one instructs and teaches a scorner, he first loses his time; in the next place, others laugh at his labour, as fruitless and misapplied; and lastly, the scorner himself disdains the knowledge delivered. But there is more danger in reproving a wicked man, who not only lends no ear, but turns again, and either directly rails at his admonisher, who has now made himself odious to him; or, at least, afterwards traduces him to others.

VII.—*A wise son rejoices his father, but a foolish son is a sorrow to his mother.*[k]

The domestic joys and griefs of father and mother from their children are here distinguished; for a prudent and

[g] Prov. vi. 11, and xxiv. 34.   [h] Prov. ix. 7.   [i] Matt. vii. 6.
[k] Prov. x. 1.

hopeful son is a capital pleasure to the father, who knows the value of virtue better than the mother, and therefore rejoices more at his son's disposition to virtue. This joy may also be heightened, perhaps, from seeing the good effect of his own management, in the education of his son, so as to form good morals in him by precept and example. On the other hand, the mother suffers and partakes the most in the calamity of her son, because the maternal affection is the more soft and tender: and again, perhaps, because she is conscious that her indulgence has spoiled and depraved him.

VIII.—*The memory of the just is blessed, but the name of the wicked shall rot.*[l]

We have here that distinction between the character of good and evil men, which usually takes place after death. For in the case of good men, when envy, that pursues them whilst alive, is extinguished, their name presently flourishes, and their fame increases every day. But the fame of bad men, though it may remain for a while, through the favour of friends and faction, yet soon becomes odious, and at length degenerates into infamy, and ends, as it were, in a loathsome odour.

IX.—*He who troubles his own house, shall inherit the wind.*[m]

This is a very useful admonition, as to domestic jars and differences. For many promise themselves great matters from the separation of their wives, the disinheriting of their children, the frequent changing of servants, &c., as if they should thence procure greater peace of mind, or a more successful administration of their affairs; but such hopes commonly turn to wind; these changes being seldom for the better. And such disturbers of their families often meet with various crosses and ingratitude, from those they afterwards adopt and choose. They, by this means, also bring ill reports, and ambiguous rumours upon themselves. For as Cicero well observes, "All men's characters proceed from their domestics."[n] And both these mischiefs Solomon elegantly expresses by the " possession of the wind:" for the frustration of expectation, and the raising of rumours, are justly compared to the winds.

[l] Prov. x. 7.   [m] Prov. xi. 29.   [n] Petit. Consulatus, § 5.

X.—*The end of a discourse is better than the beginning.*[c]

This aphorism corrects a common error, prevailing not only among such as principally study words, but also the more prudent; viz., that men are more solicitous about the beginnings and entrances of their discourses than about the conclusions, and more exactly labour their prefaces and introductions than their closes. Whereas they ought not to neglect the former, but should have the latter, as being things of far the greater consequence, ready prepared beforehand; casting about with themselves, as much as possible, what may be the last issue of the discourse, and how business may be thence forwarded and ripened. They ought further, not only to consider the windings up of discourses relating to business, but to regard also such turns as may be advantageously and gracefully given upon departure, even though they should be quite foreign to the matter in hand. It was the constant practice of two great and prudent privy-counsellors, on whom the weight of the kingdom chiefly rested, as often as they discoursed with their princes upon matters of state, never to end the conversation with what regarded the principal subject; but always to go off with a jest, or some pleasant device; and as the proverb runs, "Washing off their salt-water discourses with fresh at the conclusion." And this was one of the principal arts they had.

XI.—*As dead flies cause the best ointment to yield an ill odour, so does a little folly to a man in reputation for wisdom and honour.*[d]

The condition of men eminent for virtue is, as this aphorism excellently observes, exceeding hard and miserable; because their errors, though ever so small, are not overlooked. But as in a clear diamond, every little grain, or speck, strikes the eye disagreeably, though it would not be observed in a duller stone; so in men of eminent virtue, their smallest vices are readily spied, talked of, and severely censured; whilst in an ordinary man, they would either have lain concealed, or been easily excused. Whence a little folly in a very wise man, a small slip in a very good man, and a little indecency in a polite and elegant man, greatly diminish their characters and reputations. It might, therefore, be no bad policy, for men of uncommon excellencies to intermix with their actions

[c] Eccles vii. 9. [d] Eccles. x. 1.

a few absurdities, that may be committed without vice, in order to reserve a liberty, and confound the observation of little defects.

XII.—*Scornful men ensnare a city, but wise men prevent calamity.*[q]

It may seem strange, that in the description of men, formed, as it were, by nature, for the destruction of states, Solomon should choose the character, not of a proud and haughty, not of a tyrannical and cruel, not of a rash and violent, not of a seditious and turbulent, not of a foolish or incapable man, but the character of a scorner. Yet this choice is becoming the wisdom of that king, who well knew how governments were subverted, and how preserved. For there is scarce such another destructive thing to kingdoms, and commonwealths, as that the counsellors, or senators, who sit at the helm, should be naturally scorners; who, to show themselves courageous advisers, are always extenuating the greatness of dangers, insulting, as fearful wretches, those who weigh them as they ought, and ridiculing the ripening delays of counsel and debate, as tedious matters of oratory, unserviceable to the general issue of business. They despise rumours as the breath of the rabble, and things that will soon pass over, though the counsels of princes are to be chiefly directed from hence. They account the power and authority of laws but nets unfit to hold great matters. They reject, as dreams and melancholy notions, those counsels and precautions that regard futurity at a distance. They satirize and banter such men as are really prudent and knowing in affairs, or such as bear noble minds, and are capable of advising. In short, they sap all the foundations of political government at once—a thing which deserves the greater attention, as it is not effected by open attack, but by secret undermining; nor is it, by any means, so much suspected among mankind as it deserves.

XIII.—*The prince who willingly hearkens to lies, has all his servants wicked.*[r]

When a prince is injudiciously disposed to lend a credulous ear to whisperers and flatterers, pestilent breath seems to proceed from him, corrupting and infecting all his servants; and now some search into his fears, and increase

[q] Prov. xxix. 8. [r] Prov. xxix. 12

them with fictitious rumours; some raise up in him the fury of envy, especially against the most deserving; some, by accusing of others, wash their own stains away; some make room for the preferment and gratification of their friends, by calumniating and traducing their competitors, &c. And these agents are naturally the most vicious servants of the prince. Those again, of better principles and dispositions, after finding little security in their innocence, their master not knowing how to distinguish truth from falsehood, drop their moral honesty, go into the eddy winds of the court, and servilely submit to be carried about with them. For as Tacitus says of Claudius, "There is no safety with that prince, into whose mind all things are infused and directed."[s] And Comines well observes, that "it is better being servant to a prince whose suspicions are endless, than whose credulity is great."[t]

XIV.—*A just man is merciful to the life of his beast, but the mercies of the wicked are cruel.*[u]

Nature has endowed man with a noble and excellent principle of compassion, which extends itself even to the brutes, that by divine appointment are made subject to him. Whence this compassion has some resemblance with that of a prince towards his subjects. And it is certain, that the noblest souls are most extensively merciful; for narrow and degenerate spirits think compassion belongs not to them, but a great soul, the noblest part of the creation, is ever compassionate. Thus under the old law there were numerous precepts not merely ceremonial, as the ordaining of mercy, for example, the not eating of flesh with the blood thereof, &c. So, likewise, the sects of the Essenes and Pythagoreans totally abstained from flesh, as they do also to this day, with an inviolated superstition, in some parts of the empire of Mogul. Nay, the Turks, though a cruel and bloody nation, both in their descent and discipline, give alms to brutes, and suffer them not to be tortured. But lest this principle might seem to countenance all kinds of compassion, Solomon wholesomely subjoins, "That the mercies of the wicked are cruel;" that is, when such great offenders are spared, as ought to be cut off with the sword of justice. For this kind

[s] Annals, xii. 3.   [t] Mémoires et Chroniques du Quinzième Siècle.
[u] Prov. xii. 1

of mercy is the greatest of all cruelties, as cruelty affects but particular persons; whilst impunity lets loose the whole army of evil doers, and drives them upon the innocent.

XV.—*A fool speaks all his mind, but a wise man reserves something for hereafter.*[x]

This aphorism seems principally levelled, not against the futility of light persons, who speak what they should conceal, nor against the pertness with which they indiscriminately and injudiciously fly out upon men and things, nor against the talkative humour with which some men disgust their hearers, but against a more latent failing, viz., a very imprudent and impolitic management of speech; when a man in private conversation so directs his discourse as, in a continued string of words, to deliver all he can say, that any way relates to the subject, which is a great prejudice to business. For, 1. discourse interrupted and infused by parcels, enters deeper than if it were continued and unbroken; in which case the weight of things is not distinctly and particularly felt, as having not time to fix themselves; but one reason drives out another before it had taken root. 2. Again, no one is so powerful or happy in eloquence, as at first setting out to leave the hearer perfectly mute and silent; but he will always have something to answer, and perhaps to object in his turn. And here it happens, that those things which were to be reserved for confutation, or reply, being now anticipated, lose their strength and beauty. 3. Lastly, if a person does not utter all his mind at once, but speaks by starts, first one thing, then another, he will perceive from the countenance and answer of the person spoken to, how each particular affects him, and in what sense he takes it; and thus be directed more cautiously to suppress or employ the matter still in reserve.

XVI.—*If the displeasure of great men rise up against thee, forsake not thy place; for pliant behaviour extenuates great offences.*[y]

This aphorism shows how a person ought to behave, when he has incurred the displeasure of his prince. The precept hath two parts,—1. that the person quit not his post; and 2. that he, with diligence and caution, apply to the cure, as

---

[x] Prov xxix. 11.   [y] Eccles. x. 4.

of a dangerous disease. For when men see their prince incensed against them, what through impatience of disgrace, fear of renewing their wounds by sight, and partly to let their prince behold their contrition and humiliation, it is usual with them to retire from their office or employ, and sometimes to resign their places and dignities into their prince's hands. But Solomon disapproves this method as pernicious. For, 1. it publishes the disgrace too much; whence both our enemies and enviers are more emboldened to hurt us, and our friends the more intimidated from lending their assistance. 2. By this means the anger of the prince, which perhaps would have blown over of itself, had it not been made public, becomes more fixed; and having now begun to displace the person, ends not but in his downfall. 3. This resigning carries something of ill-will with it, and shows a dislike of the times, which adds the evil of indignation to that of suspicion. The following remedies regard the cure: 1. Let him above all things beware how by any insensibility, or elation of mind, he seems regardless of his prince's displeasure, or not affected as he ought. He should not compose his countenance to a stubborn melancholy, but to a grave and decent dejection; and show himself, in all his actions, less brisk and cheerful than usual. It may also be for his advantage to use the assistance and mediation of a friend with the prince, seasonably to insinuate, with how great a sense of grief the person in disgrace is inwardly affected. 2. Let him carefully avoid even the least occasions of reviving the thing which caused the displeasure; or of giving any handle to fresh distaste, and open rebuke. 3. Let him diligently seek all occasions wherein his service may be acceptable to his prince, that he may both show a ready desire of retrieving his past offence, and his prince perceive what a servant he must lose if he quit him. 4. Either let him prudently transfer the blame upon others, or insinuate that the offence was committed with no ill design, or show that their malice, who accused him to the prince, aggravated the thing above measure. 5. Lastly, let him in every respect be watchful and intent upon the cure.

XVII.—*The first in his own cause is just; then comes the other party, and inquires into him.*[z]

The first information in any cause, if it dwell a little with the judge, takes root, tinges, and possesses him so, as hardly to be removed again, unless some manifest falsity be found in the matter itself, or some artifice be discovered in delivering it. For a naked and simple defence, though just and prevalent, can scarce balance the prejudice of a prior information, or of itself reduce to an equilibrium the scale of justice that has once inclined. It is, therefore, safest for the judge to hear nothing as to the merits of a cause, before both parties are convened; and best for the defendant, if he perceive the judge prepossessed, to endeavour, as far as ever the case will allow, principally to detect some artifice, or trick, made use of by the plaintiff to abuse the judge.

XVIII.—*He who brings up his servant delicately, shall find him stubborn in the end.*[a]

Princes and masters are, by the advice of Solomon, to observe moderation in conferring grace and favour upon their servants. This moderation consists in three things. 1. In promoting them gradually, not by sudden starts. 2. In accustoming them sometimes to denial. And 3. as is well observed by Machiavel, in letting them always have something further to hope for. And unless these particulars be observed, princes, in the end, will doubtless find from their servants disrespect and obstinacy, instead of gratitude and duty. For from sudden promotion arises insolence; from a perpetual obtaining one's desires, impatience of denial; and if there be nothing further to wish, there's an end of alacrity and industry.

XIX.—*A man diligent in his business shall stand before kings, and not be ranked among the vulgar.*[b]

Of all the virtues which kings chiefly regard and require in the choice of servants, that of expedition and resolution in the despatch of business is the most acceptable. Men of

[z] Prov. xvii. 17; but the sense is different. [a] Prov. xxix. 21.
[b] Prov. xxii. 29. Franklin cited this aphorism as exemplified in his person. He was caressed by Louis XVI., feared by George III., and lived on terms of easy friendship with the heads of other powers who had combined against England His pre-eminence he attributed entirely to his industry. *Ed.*

depth are held suspected by princes, as inspecting them too close, and being able by their strength of capacity, as by a machine, to turn and wind them against their will and without their knowledge. Popular men are hated, as standing in the light of kings, and drawing the eyes of the multitude upon themselves. Men of courage are generally esteemed turbulent and too enterprising. Honest and just men are accounted morose, and not compliable enough to the will of their masters. Lastly, there is no virtue but has its shade, wherewith the minds of kings are offended; but despatch alone in executing their commands has nothing displeasing to them. Besides, the motions of the minds of kings are swift and impatient of delay; for they think themselves able to effect anything, and imagine that nothing more is wanting but to have it done instantly. Whence despatch is to them the most grateful of all things.

XX.—*I saw all the living which walk under the sun, with the succeeding young prince that shall rise up in his stead.*[c]

This aphorism points out the vanity of those who flock about the next successors of princes. The root of this is the folly naturally implanted in the minds of men; viz. their being too fond of their own hopes: for scarce any one but is more delighted with hope than with enjoyment. Again, novelty is pleasing and greedily coveted by human nature; and these two things, hope and novelty, meet in the successor of a prince. The aphorism hints the same that was formerly said by Pompey to Sylla, and again by Tiberius of Macro, that the sun has more adorers rising than setting.[d] Yet rulers in possession are not much affected with this, or esteem it any great matter, as neither Sylla nor Tiberius did; but rather laugh at the levity of men, and encounter not with dreams; for hope, as was well said, is but a waking dream.[e]

XXI.—*There was a little city manned but by a few, and a mighty king drew his army to it, erecting bulwarks against it, and intrenched it round: now there was found within the walls a poor wise man, and he by his wisdom delivered the city; but none remembered the same poor man.*[f]

This parable describes the corrupt and malevolent nature of men, who, in extremities and difficulties, generally fly to

[c] Eccles. iv. 15. Solomon, in his old age, seeing all his courtiers desert him to pay court to his son Rehoboam, uttered this sentiment. *Ed.*
[d] Tacit. Annals, vi.   [e] Eccles. xiii. 18.   [f] Eccles. ix. 14.

the prudent and the courageous, though they before despised them; and as soon as the storm is over, they show ingratitude to their preservers. Machiavel had reason to put the question, "Which is the more ungrateful towards the well-deserving, the prince or the people?" though he accuses both of ingratitude.[g] The thing does not proceed wholly from the ingratitude either of princes or people, but it is generally attended with the envy of the nobility, who secretly repine at the event, though happy and prosperous, because it was not procured by themselves. Whence they lessen the merit of the author and bear him down.

XXII.—*The way of the slothful is a hedge of thorns.*[h]

This aphorism elegantly shows that sloth is laborious in the end: for diligent and cautious preparation guards the foot from stumbling, and smooths the way before it is trod; but he who is sluggish, and defers all things to the last moment, must of necessity be at every step treading as upon brambles and thorns, which frequently detain and hinder him; and the same may be observed in the government of a family, where, if due care and forethought be used, all things go on calmly, and, as it were, spontaneously, without noise and bustle; but if this caution be neglected, when any great occasion arises, numerous matters crowd in to be done at once, the servants are in confusion, and the house rings.

XXIII.—*He who respects persons in judgment does ill, and will forsake the truth for a piece of bread.*[i]

This aphorism wisely observes, that facility of temper is more pernicious in a judge than bribery; for bribes are not offered by all, but there is no cause wherein something may not be found to sway the mind of the judge, if he be a respecter of persons. Thus, one shall be respected for his country, another for his riches, another for being recommended by a friend, &c. So that iniquity must abound where respect of persons prevails, and judgment be corrupted for a very trifling thing, as it were for a morsel of bread.

XXIV.—*A poor man, that by extortion oppresses the poor, is like a land-flood that causes famine.*[k]

This parable was anciently painted by the fable of the leech, full and empty; for the oppression of a poor and

[g] Discorso sopra Liv. lib. i.   [h] Prov. xv. 19.
[i] Prov. xxviii. 31.   [k] Prov. xxviii. 3.

hungry wretch is much more grievous than the oppression of one who is rich and full ; as he searches into all the corners and arts of exactions and ways of raising contributions. The thing has been also usually resembled to a sponge, which sucks strongly when dry, but less when moist. And it contains an useful admonition to princes, that they commit not the government of provinces or places of power to indigent men, or such as are in debt ; and again to the people, that they permit not their kings to struggle with want.

XXV.—*A just man falling before the wicked, is a troubled fountain and a corrupted spring.*[1]

This is a caution to states, that they should have a capital regard to the passing an unjust or infamous sentence in any great and weighty cause, where not only the guilty is acquitted, but the innocent condemned. To countenance private injuries, indeed, disturbs and pollutes the clear streams of justice, as it were, in the brook ; but unjust and great public sentences, which are afterwards drawn into precedents, infect and defile the very fountain of justice. For when once the court goes on the side of injustice, the law becomes a public robber, and one man really a wolf to another.

XXVI.—*Contract no friendship with an angry man, nor walk with a furious one.*[m]

The more religiously the laws of friendship are to be observed amongst good men, the more caution should be used in making a prudent choice of friends. The nature and humour of friends, so far as concerns ourselves alone, should be absolutely tolerated ; but when they lay us under a necessity, as to the character we should put on towards others, this becomes an exceeding hard and unreasonable condition of friendship. It is therefore of great moment to the peace and security of life, according to the direction of Solomon, to have no friendship with passionate men, and such as easily stir up or enter into debates and quarrels. For such friends will be perpetually entangling us in strifes and contentions, so that we must either break off with them or have no regard to our own safety.

[1] Prov. xxv. 29   [m] Prov. xxii. 24.

XXVII.—*He who conceals a fault seeks friendship, but he who repeats a matter separates friends.*[a]

There are two ways of composing differences and reconciling the minds of men; the one beginning with oblivion and forgiveness, the other with a recollection of the injuries, interweaving it with apologies and excuses. I remember it is the opinion of a very wise politician, "That he who treats of peace without repeating the conditions of the difference, rather deceives the mind with the sweetness of reconciliation than equitably makes up the matter." But Solomon, a still wiser man, is of a contrary opinion, and approves of forgetting, but forbids a repetition of the difference, as being attended with these inconveniences: 1. That it rakes into the old sore; 2. that it may cause a new difference; 3. and lastly, that it brings the matter to end in excuses; whereas both sides had rather seem to forgive the injury than allow of an excuse.

XXVIII.—*In every good work is plenty; but where words abound, there is commonly a want.*[o]

Solomon here distinguishes the fruit of the labour of the tongue, and that of the labour of the hand, as if from the one came want, and from the other abundance. For it almost constantly happens that they who speak much, boast much, and promise largely, are but barren, and receive no fruit from the things they talk of; being seldom industrious or diligent in works, but feed and satisfy themselves with discourse alone as with wind; whilst, as the poet intimates, "he who is conscious to himself that he can really effect," feels the satisfaction inwardly, and keeps silent:

" Qui silet est firmus:"[p]

whereas, he who knows he grasps nothing but empty air, is full of talk and strange stories.

XXIX.—*Open reproof is better than secret affection.*[q]

This aphorism reprehends the indulgence of those who use not the privilege of friendship freely and boldly to admonish their friends as well of their errors as their dangers. "What shall I do?" says an easy, good-natured friend, "or what

---

[a] Prov. xvii. 9.
[p] Ovid, Remedia Amoris, 697.
[o] Prov. xiv. 23.
[q] Prov. xxvii. 5

course shall I take? I love him as well as man can do, and would willingly suffer any misfortune in his stead: but I know his nature; if I deal freely with him, I shall offend him; at least chagrin him, and yet do him no service. Nay, I shall sooner alienate his friendship from me, than win him over from those things he has fixed his mind upon." Such an effeminate and useless friend as this Solomon reprehends, and pronounces that greater advantage may be received from an open enemy; as a man may chance to hear those things from an enemy by way of reproach, which a friend, through too much indulgence, will not speak out.

XXX.—*A prudent man looks well to his steps, but a fool turns aside to deceit.*[r]

There are two kinds of prudence; the one true and sound, the other degenerate and false: the latter Solomon calls by the name of folly. The candidate for the former has an eye to his footings, looking out for dangers, contriving remedies, and by the assistance of good men defending himself against the bad: he is wary in entering upon business, and not unprovided of a retreat; watching for opportunities, powerful against opposition, &c. But the follower of the other is wholly patched up of fallacy and cunning, placing all his hope in the circumventing of others, and forming them to his fancy. And this the aphorism justly rejects as a vicious and even a weak kind of prudence. For, 1. it is by no means a thing in our own power, nor depending upon any constant rule; but is daily inventing of new stratagems as the old ones fail and grow useless. 2. He who has once the character of a crafty, tricking man, is entirely deprived of a principal instrument of business,—trust; whence he will find nothing succeed to his wish. 3. Lastly, however specious and pleasing these arts may seem, yet they are often frustrated; as well observed by Tacitus, when he said, that crafty and bold counsels, though pleasant in the expectation, are hard to execute, and unhappy in the event.

XXXI.—*Be not over-righteous, nor make thyself over-wise: for why shouldst thou suddenly be taken off!*[s]

There are times, says Tacitus, wherein great virtues meet with certain ruin.[t] And this happens to men eminent for

[r] Prov. xv. 21. [s] Eccles. vii. 17. [t] Hist. i. 2.

virtue and justice, sometimes suddenly, and sometimes after it was long foreseen. But if prudence be also joined, so as to make such men cautious and watchful of their own safety, then they gain thus much, that their ruin shall come suddenly, and entirely from secret and dark counsels—whence they may escape envy, and meet destruction unexpected. But for that over-righteousness expressed in the aphorism, it is not understood of virtue itself, in which there is no excess, but of a vain and invidious affectation and show thereof, like what Tacitus intimates of Lepidus—making it a kind of miracle that he never gave any servile opinion, and yet stood safe in severe times.[u]

XXXII.—*Give occasion to a wise man, and his wisdom will be increased.*[x]

This aphorism distinguishes between that wisdom which has grown up and ripened into a true habit, and that which only floats in the brain, or is tossed upon the tongue without having taken root. The former, when occasion offers, is presently roused, got ready, and distended, so as to appear greater than itself; whereas the latter, which was pert before, stands amazed and confounded when occasion calls for it: so that the person who thought himself endowed with this wisdom, begins to question whether his preconceptions about it were not mere dreams and empty speculations.

XXXIII.—*To praise one's friend aloud, rising early, has the same effect as cursing him.*[y]

Moderate and sensible praises, dropped occasionally, are of great service to the reputation and fortunes of men; whilst immoderate, noisy, and fulsome praises do no good, but rather hurt, as the aphorism expresses it. For, 1. they plainly betray themselves to proceed from an excess of good will, or to be purposely designed rather to gain favour with the person by false encomiums, than to paint him justly. 2. Sparing and modest praises generally invite the company somewhat to improve them, but profuse and immoderate ones to detract and take off from them. 3. The principal thing is, that immoderate praises procure envy to the person praised, as all extravagant commendations seem to reproach others that may be no less deserving.

[u] Annals, iv. 20.   [x] Prov. ix. 9.   [y] Prov. xxiv. 14.

XXXIV.—*As the face shines in water, so are men's hearts manifest to the wise.*[z]

This aphorism distinguishes between the minds of prudent men and those of others, by comparing the former to water, or a mirror, which receives the forms and images of things; whilst the latter are like earth, or unpolished stone, which reflects nothing. And the mind of a prudent man is the more aptly compared to a glass, because therein one's own image may, at the same time, be viewed along with those of others, which could not be done by the eye without assistance: but if the mind of a prudent man be so capacious as to observe and distinguish an infinite diversity of natures and manners in men, it remains that we endeavour to render it as various in the application as it is in the representation.

"Qui sapit, innumeris moribus aptus erit."[a]

If we have dwelt too long upon those parables, and used them for higher purposes than mere illustrations, the dignity of both author and subject must be our excuse. For thus, it was not only usual among the Jews, but very common also among the wise men of other ancient nations, when they had, by observation, hit upon anything useful in common life, to reduce and contract it into some short sentence, parable, or fable. Fables anciently supplied the defect of examples; but now that times abound with variety of histories, it is better and more enlivening to draw from real life. But the method of writing best suited to so various and intricate a subject as the different occasions of civil business, is that which Machiavel chose for treating politics; viz., by observation or discourse upon histories and examples.[b] For the knowledge which is newly drawn, and, as it were, under our own eye, from particulars, best finds the way to particulars again. And doubtless it is much more conducive to practice that the discourse follow the example, than that the example follow the discourse: and this regards not only the order, but the thing itself; for when an example is proposed as the basis of a discourse, it is usually proposed with its whole apparatus of circumstances, which may sometimes correct and supply it; whence it becomes as a model for imitation and practice; whilst examples, produced for the sake of the

[z] Prov. xxvii. 19. [a] Ars Amandi, i. 760.
[b] Discorso sopra Liv.

treatise, are but succinctly and nakedly quoted, and, as slaves, wholly attend the call of the discourse.

It is worth while to observe this difference, that as the histories of times afford the best matter for discourses upon politics, such as those of Machiavel,[c] so the histories of lives are most advantageously used for instructions of business, because they contain all the possible variety of occasions and affairs, as well great as small. Yet a more commodious foundation may be had for the precepts of business than either of these histories, and that is, the discoursing upon prudent and serious epistles, such as those of Cicero to Atticus; for epistles represent business nearer and more to the life than either annals or lives. And thus we have treated of the matter and form of the first part of the doctrine of business, which regards variety of occasions, and place it among the desiderata.

There is another part of the doctrine of business differing as much from the former as the being wise in general, and the being wise for one's self;—the one seems to move as from the centre to the circumference, and the other as from the circumference to the centre. For there is a certain prudence of giving counsel to others, and another of looking to one's own affairs. Both these, indeed, are sometimes found united, but oftenest separate; as many are prudent in the management of their own private concerns, and weak in public administration, or the giving advice, like the ant, which is a wise creature for itself, but pernicious in a garden. This virtue of self-wisdom was not unknown even to the Romans, those great lovers of their country; whence, says the comedian, "the wise man forms his own fortune,"—

"Nam pol sapiens fingit fortunam sibi;"[d]

and they had it proverbial amongst them,—" Every man's fortune lies in his own hand,"—" Faber quisque fortunæ propriæ." So Livy gives this character of the elder Cato: "Such was his force of mind and genius, that wherever he had been born he seemed formed for making his own fortune."[e]

But if any one publicly professed or made open show of

[c] Especially his Il Principe, with the notes of Conringius, which was found in the carriage of Napoleon after the battle of Mont St. Jean, with the annotations of the emperor. *Ed.*
[d] Plautus, Trinum. Act ii. sc. 2. v. 84.   [e] Livy, xxxix. 40.

this kind of prudence, it was always accounted not only impolitic, but ominous and unfortunate, as was observed of Timotheus the Athenian, who, after having performed many great exploits for the honour and advantage of his country, and giving an account of his conduct to the people, as the manner then was, he concluded the several particulars thus: "And here fortune had no share;"[f] after which time nothing ever succeeded in his hands. This was, indeed, too arrogant and haughty, like that of Pharaoh in Ezekiel, "Thou sayest, The river is mine, and I made myself;"[g] or that of Habakkuk, "They rejoice, and sacrifice to their net;"[h] or, again, that of Mezentius, who called his hand and javelin his god;

"Dextra mihi deus, et telum, quod missile libro,
Nunc adsint;"[i]

or, lastly, that of Julius Cæsar, the only time that we find him betraying his inward sentiments; for when the Aruspex related to him that the entrails were not prosperous, he muttered softly, "They shall be better when I please," which was said not long before his unfortunate death.[k] And, indeed, this excessive confidence, as it is a profane thing, so it is always unhappy; whence great and truly wise men think proper to attribute all their successes to their felicity, and not to their virtue and industry. So Sylla styled himself happy, not great; and Cæsar, at another time, more advisedly said to the pilot, "Thou carriest Cæsar and his fortune."[l]

But these expressions,—"Every one's fortune is in his own hand," "A wise man shall control the stars," "Every way is passable to virtue," &c.,—if understood, and used rather as spurs to industry than as stirrups to insolence, and rather to beget in men a constancy and firmness of resolution than arrogance and ostentation, they are deservedly esteemed sound and wholesome; and hence, doubtless, it is that they find reception in the breasts of great men, and make

[f] Plut. Sylla.   [g] Ezek. xxix. 3.   [h] Habak. i. 15.
[i] Æneid, x. 773.   [k] Suetonius.
[l] Plutarch. Compare with this a curious letter from Cato to Cicero (ap. Cic. ad Fam. xv. 5), wherein he says, "Supplicationem decretam, si tu, quâ in re nihil fortuito, sed summa tua ratione et continentia reipublicæ, provisum est diis immortalibus gratulari nos quam tibi referre acceptum mavis gau leo."

it sometimes difficult for them to dissemble their thoughts; so we find Augustus Cæsar, who was rather different from than inferior to his uncle, though doubtless a more moderate man, required his friends, as they stood about his death-bed, to give him their applause at his exit,[m] as if conscious to himself that he had acted his part well upon the stage of life. And this part of doctrine also is to be reckoned as deficient, not but that it has been much used and beaten in practice, though not taken notice of in books. Wherefore, according to our custom, we shall here set down some heads upon the subject, under the title of the Self-politician, or the Art of rising in Life.

It may seem a new and odd kind of thing to teach men how to make their fortunes,—a doctrine which every one would gladly learn before he finds the difficulties of it; for the things required to procure fortune are not fewer or less difficult than those to procure virtue. It is as rigid and hard a thing to become a true politician as a true moralist, yet the treating of this subject nearly concerns the merit and credit of learning. It is of great importance to the honour of learning, that men of business should know erudition is not like a lark, which flies high and delights in nothing but singing, but that it is rather like a hawk, which soars aloft indeed, but can stoop when she finds it convenient to pounce upon her prey. Again, this also regards the perfection of learning; for the true rule of a perfect inquiry is, that nothing can be found in the material globe which has not its correspondent in the crystalline globe—the understanding, or that there is nothing found in practice which has not its particular doctrine and theory. But learning esteems the building of a private fortune as a work of an inferior kind; for no man's private fortune can be an end any way worthy of his existence; nay, it frequently happens that men of eminent virtues renounce their fortune to pursue the things of a sublimer nature. Yet even private fortune, as it is the instrument of virtue and doing good, is a particular doctrine, worthy of consideration.

This doctrine has its precepts, some whereof are summary or collective, and others scattered and various. The collective precepts are founded in a just knowledge,—1. of ourselves;

[m] Suetonius.

and, 2. of others. Let this, therefore, be the first whereon the knowledge of the rest principally turns, that we procure to ourselves, as far as possible, the window once required by Momus, who, seeing so many corners and recesses in the structure of the human heart, found fault that it should want a window, through which those dark and crooked turnings might be viewed.ⁿ This window may be procured by diligently informing ourselves of the particular persons we have to deal with,—their tempers, desires, views, customs, habits; the assistances, helps, and assurances whereon they principally rely, and whence they receive their power; their defects and weaknesses, whereat they chiefly lie open and are accessible; their friends, factions, patrons, dependants, enemies, enviers, rivals; their times and manner of access,—

" Sola viri molles aditus et tempora noras;"º

their principles, and the rules they prescribe themselves, &c. But our information should not wholly rest in the persons, but also extend to the particular actions, which from time to time come upon the anvil; how they are conducted, with what success, by whose assistance promoted, by whom opposed, of what weight and moment they are, and what their consequences. For a knowledge of present actions is not only very advantageous in itself, but without it the knowledge of persons will be very fallacious and uncertain; for men change along with their actions, and are one thing whilst entangled and surrounded with business, and another when they return to themselves. And these particular informations, with regard to persons as well as actions, are like the minor propositions in every active syllogism; for no truth, nor excellence of observations or axioms, whence the major political propositions are formed, can give a firm conclusion, if there be an error in the minor proposition. And that such a kind of knowledge is procurable, Solomon assures us, who says, that "counsel in the heart of man is like a deep water, but a wise man will draw it out;"ᵖ for although the knowledge itself does not fall under precept, because it regards individuals, yet instructions may be given of use for fetching it out.

[n] Plato, Reip.; Lucan, Hermot. xx.; and Eras. Chil. i. 74.
[o] Æneid, iv. 423.   [p] Prov. xx. 5.

Men may be known six different ways; viz.,—1. by their countenances; 2. their words; 3. their actions; 4. their tempers; 5. their ends; and, 6. by the relation of others. 1. As to the countenance, there is no great matter in that old proverb, "Fronti nulla fides;"[q] for although this may be said with some truth of the external and general composure of the countenance and gesture, yet there lie concealed certain more subtle motions and actions of the eyes, face, looks, and behaviour, by which the gate, as it were, of the mind is unlocked and thrown open.[r] Who was more close than Tiberius? yet Tacitus observes a difference between his inward thoughts and his language in eulogizing the exploits of Drusus and Germanicus,—thus characterizing his panegyric of the latter: "Magis in speciem verbis adornatis quam ut penitus sentire crederetur;" and then that of Drusus,—"Paucioribus sed intentior, et fidâ oratione."[s] Again, Tacitus sketches the manner of the emperor on other occasions when he was less crafty, and sums up his remarks thus: "Quin ipse compositus alias atque velut eluctantium verborum; solutius promptiusque loquebatur quoties subveniret."[t] And indeed, it is hard to find so great and masterly a dissembler, or a countenance so well broke and commanded, as to carry on an artful and counterfeit discourse without some way or other betraying it.

2. The words of men are full of deceit; but this is well detected in two ways; viz., either when words are spoken on the sudden, or in passion. So Tiberius, being suddenly surprised and hurried beyond himself, with a stinging speech from Agrippina, went a step out of his natural dissimulation; for, says Tacitus, she thus drew an uncommon expression from his secret breast, and he rebuked her as being offended because she did not rule.[u] Whence the poet not unjustly calls these perturbations tortures, mankind being compelled by them to betray their own secrets.

—— "Vino tortus et ira."[x]

---

[q] Martial, i. Ep. 25, v. 4.   [r] Cicero, Petit. Consulatus, § 2.
[s] Annals, i. 52.   [t] Annals, iv. 31.   [u] Annals, iv. 52.
[x] Hor. Ep. ii. 18, v. 38. It must be remembered that Augustus had some intention of conferring the empire upon her husband Germanicus.—*Ed.*

And experience shows that there are very few so true to their own secrets, and of so close a temper, as not sometimes, through anger, ostentation, love to a friend, impotence of mind, or some other affection, to reveal their own thoughts. But nothing searches all the corners of the mind so much as dissimulation practised against dissimulation, according to the Spanish proverb, "Tell a lie and find a truth."

3. Even facts themselves, though the surest pledges of the human mind, are not altogether to be trusted, unless first attentively viewed and considered as to their magnitude and propriety; for it is certain that deceit gets itself a credit in small things, that it may practise to more advantage in larger. And the Italian thinks himself upon the cross with the crier, or put up to sale, when, without manifest cause, he is treated better than usual; for small favours lull mankind, and disarm them both of caution and industry; whence they are properly called by Demosthenes the baits of sloth. Again, we may clearly see the crafty and ambiguous nature of some actions which pass for benefits, from that trick practised by Mucianus upon Antony; for after a pretended reconciliation he most treacherously advanced many of Antony's friends to lieutenancies, tribuneships, &c., and by this cunning entirely disarmed and defeated him; thus winning over Antony's friends to himself.[y]

But the surest key for unlocking the minds of others turns upon searching and sifting either their tempers and natures, or their ends and designs; and the more weak and simple are best judged by their temper, but the more prudent and close by their designs. It was prudently and wittily, though in my judgment not substantially, advised by the pope's nuncio as to the choice of another to succeed him in his residence at a foreign court, that they should by no means send one remarkably but rather tolerably wise; because a man wiser than ordinary could never imagine what the people of that nation were likely to do. It is doubtless a common error, particularly in prudent men, to measure others by the model of their own capacity; whence they frequently overshoot the mark, by supposing that men project and form greater things to themselves, and practise more subtile arts

---

[y] Tacit. Hist. iv

CHAP. II.] HOW TO DISCERN CHARACTER. 323

than ever entered their minds. This is elegantly intimated by the Italian proverb,—

"Di denari, di senno, e di fede,
C' ne manco che non crede;"[z]

and therefore, in men of small capacities, who commit many absurdities, a conjecture must rather be formed from the propensity of their nature than from their ends in view. Whence princes also, though for a quite different reason, are best judged by their tempers as private persons are by their ends; for princes, who are at the top of human desires, have seldom any ends to aspire after with ardour and perseverance, by the situation and distance whereof a direction and measure might be taken of their other actions. And this among others is a principal reason why their hearts, as the Scripture declares, are unsearchable.[a] But every private man is like a traveller, who proceeds intently to the end of his journey, where he sets up: hence one may tolerably conjecture what a private man will or will not do; for if a thing be conducive to his ends, it is probable he will do it; and vice versâ. And this information, from the diversity of the ends and natures of men, may be taken comparatively as well as simply, so as to discover what humour or disposition overrules the rest. Thus Tigellinus, when he found himself outdone by Turpilianus, in administering and suggesting to Nero's pleasures, searched, as Tacitus says, into the fears of Nero, and by this means got rid of his rival.[b]

As for that second-hand knowledge of men's minds which is had from the relation of others, it will be sufficient to observe of it, that defects and vices are best learned from enemies, virtues and abilities from friends, manners and times from servants, and opinions and thoughts from intimate acquaintance; for popular fame is light, and the judgment of superiors uncertain, before whom men walk more masked and secret. The truest character comes from domestics,—"Verior fama e domesticis emanat."[c]

---

[z] "There is always less money, less wisdom, and less honesty, than people imagine."   [a] Prov. xxv. 3.
[b] This expression occurs Tacit. Annal. xiv. 57. It is spoken, however, of the intrigues of Tigellinus against Plautus and Sulla, by which he induced Nero to have both of them murdered. Petronius Turpilianus was put to death by Galba, because he had enjoyed Nero's confidence. Annal. xvi. 18, 19.   [c] Cicero, Petit. Consul.

But the shortest way to this whole inquiry rests upon three particulars; viz.,—1. In procuring numerous friendships with such as have an extensive and general knowledge both of men and things, or at least in securing a set of particular friends, who, according to the diversity of occasions, may be always ready to give a solid information upon any point that shall turn up. 2. In observing a prudent mean and moderation between the freedom of discourse and silence, using frankness of speech most frequently; but when the thing requires it, taciturnity; for openness of speech invites and excites others to use the same towards ourselves, which brings many things to our knowledge; whilst taciturnity procures trust, and makes men willing to deposit their secrets with us as in their own bosom. 3. In gradually acquiring such a habit of watchfulness and intentness in all discourse and action, as at once to promote the business in hand, yet take notice of incidental matters; for, as Epictetus would have a philosopher say to himself in every action, "I will do this, yet keep to my rule,"[d] so a politician should resolve with himself in every business, "I will drive this point, and yet learn somewhat of future use." And, therefore, such tempers as are wholly intent upon a present business without at all regarding what may intervene, which Montaigne acknowledges was his own defect, make excellent ministers of state, but fail in advancing their private fortunes. A principal caution must also be had to restrain the impetuosity and too great alacrity of the mind, lest much knowledge should drive us on to meddle in many matters; for nothing is more unfortunate and rash than such a procedure. Therefore the variety of knowledge to be here procured of men and things comes but to this, that we make a judicious choice both of the matters we undertake and of the persons whose assistance we use, that we may thence know how to manage and dispose all things with the greater dexterity and safety.

Next to the knowledge of others comes the knowledge of ourselves; and it requires no less diligence, but rather more, to get a true and exact information of ourselves than others. For that oracle, "Know thyself," is not only a rule of general prudence, but has also a principal place in politics.

[d] Enchiridion, iv.

And St. James excellently observes of mankind, that "he who views his face in a glass, instantly forgets his features."[e] Whence we had need be often looking. And this also holds in politics. But there is a difference in glasses,—the divine one, wherein we are to behold ourselves, is the Word of God; but the political glass is no other than the state of things and times wherein we live. A man, therefore, must make a thorough examination, not partially like a self-lover, into his own faculties, powers, and abilities, and again into his defects, inabilities, and obstacles, summing up the account, so as to make the latter constantly appear greater, and the former rather less than they are. And upon such an examination the following particulars may come to be considered.

Let the first particular be, how far a man's manners and temper suit with the times; for if they agree in all respects, he may act more freely and at large, and follow the bent of his genius; but if there be any contrariety, then he must walk more cautiously and covertly in the whole scene of his life, and appear less in public, as Tiberius did, who, being conscious that his temper suited not with the age, never frequented the public shows, and for the last twelve years of his life came not to the senate; whereas Augustus lived continually in open sight.[f]

Let the second consideration be, how a man can relish the professions or kinds of life in use and repute, out of which he is to make a choice, so that if his profession be not already entered upon, he may take that which is most suitable to his genius; but if he be already got into a kind of life for which he is unfit, that he may, upon the first opportunity, quit it and take to another,—as Valentine Borgia did, who, being educated by his father for the priesthood, afterwards renounced, followed his own inclination, and appeared in a military character.

Let a third consideration be, how a man stands compared with his equals and rivals, who may also probably be his competitors in his fortune, and let him hold that course of life in which there is the greatest want of eminent men, and wherein it is most likely that himself may rise the highest,

[e] Ep. i. 23, 24.
[f] The expression of Tacitus is, "alia Tiberio morum via." Annals, i. 54.

as Cæsar did, who was first an orator, a pleader, and scarce anything more than a gownman; but when he found that Cicero, Hortensius, and Catullus bore away the prize of eloquence, and that none had greatly signalized themselves in war, except Pompey, he quitted the gown, and taking a long farewell of civil power, went over to the arts of the general and the emperor, whereby he rose to the top pinnacle of sovereignty.

Let the fourth consideration be, to regard one's own nature and temper in the choice of friends and dependants; for different men require different kinds of friends,—some those that are grave and secret, others such as are bold and ostentatious, &c. It is worth observing of what kind the friends of Julius Cæsar were; viz., Antony, Hirtius, Balbus, Dolobella, Pollio, &c., who usually swore to die that he might live ;[g] thereby expressing an infinite affection for Cæsar, but an arrogance and contempt towards everybody else. And they were all men diligent in business, but of no great fame and reputation.

Let a fifth consideration be, to beware of examples, and not fondly square one's self to the imitation of others, as if what was achieved by them must needs be achieved by us, without considering the difference. there may be between our own disposition and manners compared with theirs we propose to imitate. Pompey manifestly fell into this error, who, as Cicero writes of him, had these words often in his mouth,—" Sylla could do this, why shall not I ?"[h] In which particular he greatly imposed upon himself; for Sylla's temper and method of acting differed infinitely from his,—the one's being fierce, violent, and pressing to the end, the other's composed, mindful of the laws, and directing all to majesty and reputation; whence he was greatly curbed and restrained in executing his designs. And these considerations may serve as a specimen of the rest.

But it is not enough for a man to know himself; he must also consider how he may most commodiously and prudently —1. show, 2. express, 3. wind and fashion himself. 1. As for show, we see nothing more frequent in life than for the less capable man to make the greater figure. It is, therefore, no small excellence of prudence, by means of a certain act

[g] Ita vivente Cæsare moriar. [h] Epist. Atticus, ix. Ep. 10.

and grace, to represent one's best side to others, by setting out our own virtues, merits, and fortunes to advantage, which may be done without arrogance or rendering one's self disagreeable; and on the other side artificially concealing our vices, defects, misfortunes, and disgraces, dwelling upon the former, and turning them as it were to the light, but palliating the latter, or effacing them by a well-adapted construction or interpretation, &c. Hence Tacitus says of Mucianus, the most prudent man of his time and the most indefatigable in business, that "he had an art of showing the fair side of whatever he spoke or acted."[i] And certainly it requires some art to prevent this conduct from becoming fulsome and despicable; yet ostentation, though to the first degree of vanity, is a fault in ethics rather than in politics. For as it is usually said of calumny, that if laid on boldly some of it will stick, so it may be said of ostentation, unless perfectly monstrous and ridiculous, " Paint yourself strongly, and some of it will last." Doubtless it will dwell with the crowd, though the wiser sort smile at it; so that the reputation procured with the number will abundantly reward the contempt of a few. But if this ostentation be managed with decency and discretion, it may greatly contribute to raise a man's reputation, as particularly if it carry the appearance of native candour and ingenuity, or be used at times surrounded with dangers, as among the military men in time of war. Or again, if our own praises are let fall as it were by accident, and be not too seriously or largely insisted on, or if any one, in praising himself, at the same time mixes it with censure and ridicule, or lastly, if he does it not spontaneously, but is provoked to it by the insolence and reproach of others. And there are many who, being by nature solid, and consequently wanting in this art of spreading canvas to their own honour, find themselves punished for their modesty, with some diminution of their dignity.

But however persons of weak judgment or too rigid morals may disallow this ostentation of virtue, no one will deny that we should endeavour to keep virtue from being undervalued through our neglect, and less esteemed than it deserves. This diminution in the esteem of virtue happens three ways; viz., 1. When a person presents and thrusts himself and his ser-

[i] Hist. ii. 80.

vice into a business unmasked; for such services are thought sufficiently rewarded by accepting them. 2. When a man at the beginning of a business over-exerts himself, and performs that all at once, which should have been done gradually; though this, indeed, gains early commendation where affairs succeed; but in the end it produces satiety. 3. When a man is too quick and light in receiving the fruit of his virtue—in praise, applause, and favour,—and pleases himself therewith; against which there is this prudent admonition, "Beware lest thou seem unaccustomed to great things, if such small ones delight thee."

A diligent concealment of defects is no less important than a prudent and artful manifestation of virtues. Defects are principally concealed and covered under three cloaks; viz. 1. Caution, 2. Pretext, and 3. Assurance. 1. We call that caution, when a man prudently keeps from meddling in matters to which he is unequal; whilst, on the other hand, daring and restless spirits are injudiciously busying themselves in things they are not acquainted with, and thereby publish and proclaim their own defects. 2. We call that pretext, when a man with sagacity and prudence paves and prepares himself a way for securing a favourable and commodious interpretation of his vices and defects; as proceeding from different principles, or having a different tendency than is generally thought. For as to the concealment of vices, the poet said well, that vice often skulks in the verge of virtue.

"Sæpe latet vitium proximate boni."[1]

Therefore, when we find any defect in ourselves, we must endeavour to borrow the figure and pretext of the neighbouring virtue for a shelter; thus the pretext of dulness is gravity; that of indolence, considerateness, &c. And it is of service to give out some probable reason for not exerting our utmost strength, and so make a necessity appear a virtue. 3. Assurance, indeed, is a daring, but a very certain and effectual remedy, whereby a man professes himself absolutely to slight and despise those things he could not obtain, like crafty merchants, who usually raise the price of their own commodities and sink the price of other men's. Though there is another kind of assurance, more impudent than this, by

[1] Ovid, Ars Amand. i. 661.

which a man brazens out his own defects, and forces them upon others for excellencies; and the better to secure this end, he will feign a distrust of himself in those things wherein he really excels: like poets, who, if you except to any particular verse in their composition, will presently tell you that single line cost them more pains than all the rest; and then produce you another, as suspected by themselves, for your opinion; whilst, of all the number, they know it to be the best and least liable to exception. But above all, nothing conduces more to the well-representing a man's self, and securing his own right, than not to disarm one's self by too much sweetness and good-nature, which exposes a man to injuries and reproaches; but rather, in all cases, at times, to dart out some sparks of a free and generous mind, that have no less of the sting than the honey. This guarded behaviour, attended with a ready disposition to vindicate themselves, some men have from accident and necessity, by means of somewhat inherent in their person or fortune, as we find in the deformed, illegitimate, and disgraced; who, if they do not want virtue, generally prove fortunate.

The expressing or declaring of a man's self is a very different thing from the showing himself, as not relating to virtue, but to the particular actions of life. And here nothing is more politic than to preserve a prudent or sound moderation or medium in disclosing or concealing one's mind as to particular actions. For though profound silence, the hiding of counsels, and managing all things by blind and deaf artifice, is an useful and extraordinary thing; yet it often happens that dissimulation produces errors which prove snares. And we see that the men of greatest repute for politics, scruple not openly and generously to declare their ends without dissimulation: thus Sylla openly declared, "He wished all mortals happy or unhappy, as they were his friends or enemies."[k] So Cæsar, upon his first expedition into Gaul, professed "he had rather be the first man in an obscure village, than the second at Rome."[l] And when the war was begun, he proved no dissembler, if Cicero says truly of him, "That he did not refuse, but in a manner required to be called tyrant, as he was."[m] So we find, in an epistle of Cicero to Atticus, how little of a dissembler Augustus was,

[k] Plut.   [l] Plut.   [m] Epist. ad Att. x. Ep. iv.

who, at his first entrance upon affairs, whilst he remained the delight of the senate, used to swear in this form when he harangued the people: "Ita Parentis honores consequi liceat:"[n] which was no less than tyranny itself. It is true, to salve the matter a little, he would at those times stretch his hand towards the statue of Julius Cæsar erected in the place, whilst the audience smiled, applauded, admired, and cried out among themselves, "What does the youth mean?" but never suspected him of any ill design, who thus candidly and ingenuously spoke his mind.[o] And yet all these we have named were prosperous men. Pompey, on the other hand, who endeavoured at the same ends by more dark and concealed methods,[p] wholly bent himself, by numberless stratagems, to cover his desires and ambition, whilst he brought the state to confusion, that it might then of necessity submit to him, and he thus procure the sovereignty to appearance against his will. And when he thought he had gained his point, as being made sole consul, which no one ever was before him, he found himself never the nearer, because those who would doubtless have assisted him, understood not his intentions; so that at length he was obliged to go in the beaten path, and under pretence of opposing Cæsar, procured himself arms and an army: so slow, casual, and generally unsuccessful, are the counsels covered with dissimulation! And Tacitus seems to have had the same sentiment, when he makes the artifice of dissimulation an inferior prudence, compared with policy, attributing the former to Tiberius, and the latter to Augustus; for speaking of Livia, he says, "She was well tempered with the arts of her husband, and the dissimulation of her son."[q]

As for the bending and forming of the mind, we should doubtless do our utmost to render it pliable, and by no means stiff and refractory to occasions and opportunities; for to continue the same men, when we ought not, is the greatest obstacle business can meet with; that is, if men remain as they did, and follow their own nature after the opportunities are changed.[r] Whence Livy, introducing the elder Cato as a skilful architect of his own fortune, adds

[n] P. xvi. Ep. 15.   [o] Ore probo, animo inverecundo. Sallust.
[p] Occultior, non melior. Tacit. Hist. ii. c. 38.
[q] Annals, v. 1.   [r] Cic. in Brut. speaking of Hortensius, c. 95.

that "he was of a pliant temper:"[s] and hence it is, that grave, solemn, and unchangeable natures generally meet with more respect than felicity. This defect some men have implanted in them by nature, as being in themselves stiff, knotty, and unfit for bending; but in others it is acquired by custom, which is a second nature, or from an opinion, which easily steals into men's minds, that they should never change the method of acting they had once found good and prosperous. Thus Machiavel prudently observes of Fabius Maximus, "That he would obstinately retain his old inveterate custom of delaying and protracting the war, when now the nature was changed and required brisker measures."[t] In others again, the same defect proceeds from want of judgment, when men do not seasonably distinguish the periods of things and actions, but alter too late, after the opportunity is slipped. And something of this kind Demosthenes reprehended in the Athenians, when he said, "They were like rustics in a fencing-school, who always, after a blow, guard the part that was hit, and not before."[u] And lastly, this defect in others, because they are unwilling that the labour they have taken in the way once entered should be lost, and know not how to sound a retreat, but rather trust they shall conquer occasions by perseverance. But this obstinacy and restiveness of the mind, from whatever root it proceeds, is highly prejudicial to business and men's private fortunes: on the contrary, nothing is more politic than to make the wheels of the mind concentric with the wheels of fortune, and capable of turning together with them. And thus much of the two summary or collective precepts for advancing one's fortune.

The scattered precepts for rising in life are numerous: we shall single out a few by way of example. The first is, that the builder of his fortune properly use and apply his rule, that is, accustom his mind to measure and estimate the price and value of things, as they conduce more or less to his particular fortune and ends, and this with diligence, not by halves. It is surprising, yet very true, that many have the logical part of their mind set right and the mathematical wrong, and judge truly of the consequences of things, but very unskilfully of their value. Hence some men are fond

[s] B. xxxix. 40.   [t] Discorso sopra L'v.   [u] Philippic i.

of access to and familiarity with princes ; others of popular
fame, and fancy these to be great enjoyments whereas both
of them are frequently full of envy and dangers. Others,
again, measure things according to their difficulty and the
labour bestowed in procuring them, imagining themselves
must needs have advanced as far as they have moved. So
Cæsar, to describe how diligent and indefatigable the younger
Cato was to little purpose, said in the way of irony, "That
he did all things with great labour." And hence it happens,
that men frequently deceive themselves, when, having the
assistance of some great or honourable personage, they
promise themselves all manner of success ; whilst the truth
is, they are not the greatest, but the fittest instruments that
perform business best and quickest. For improving the true
mathematics of the mind, it should be principally noted what
ought to come first, what second, &c. in the raising and promoting a man's fortune. And, in the first place, we set down
the emendation of the mind ; for by removing the obstacles,
and levelling the inequalities of the mind, a way may be
sooner opened to fortune, than the impediments of the mind
be removed with the assistance of fortune. And, in the
second place, we set down riches, whereto most, perhaps,
would have assigned the first, as their use is so extensive.
But we condemn this opinion for a reason like that of
Machiavel in a similar case; for though it was an established
notion, that "Money is the sinews of war," he said, more
justly, that "War had no sinews but those of good soldiers."
In the same manner, it may be truly affirmed that the sinews
of fortune are not money, but rather the powers of the mind,
address, courage, resolution, intrepidity, perseverance, moderation, industry, &c. In the third place come fame and reputation ; and this the rather, because they have certain tides
and seasons, wherein, if they be not opportunely used, it will
be difficult to recover them again ; for it is a hopeless attempt
to recover a lost reputation. In the last place, we set down
honours, which are easier acquired by any of the former
three, much more by a conjunction of them all, than any one
of them can be procured by honours. But as much depends
upon observing the order of things, so likewise in observing
the order of time, in disturbing of which men frequently err
and hasten to the end, when they should only have consulted

the beginning, and suddenly flying at the greatest things of all, rashly skip over those in the middle—thus neglecting the useful precept, "Attend to what is immediately before you,"—
"Quod nunc instat agamus."*

Our second precept is, to beware of being carried by greatness and presumption of mind to things too difficult, and thus of striving against the stream. It is a prudent advice, in the raising of one's fortune, to yield to necessity.
"Fatis accede, deisque."⁷

Let us look all round us, and observe where things lie open, where they are inclosed and blocked up, where they stoop, and where they mount, and not misemploy our strength where the way is impassable : in doing this we shall prevent repulse, not stick too long in particulars, win a reputation of being moderate, give little offence, and lastly, gain an opinion of felicity ; whilst the things that would probably have happened of themselves, will be attributed to our own industry.

A third precept, which seems somewhat to cross the former, though not when well understood, is, that we do not always wait for opportunities, but sometimes excite and lead them. This Demosthenes intimates in a high strain, when he says, "That as it is a maxim for the general to lead his army, so a wise man should lead things, make them execute his will, and not himself be obliged to follow events."² And if we attend, we shall find two different kinds of men held equal to the management of affairs ; for some know how to make an advantageous use of opportunities, yet contrive or project nothing of themselves ; whilst others are wholly intent upon forming schemes, and neglect the laying hold of opportunities as they offer : but either of these faculties is quite lame without the other.

It is a fourth precept to undertake nothing that necessarily requires much time, but constantly to remember time is ever on the wing,—
"Sed fugit interea, fugit irreparabile tempus."⁸

And the only reason why those who addict themselves to toilsome professions and employs, as lawyers, authors, &c., are

* Virg. Eclog. ix. 66.
⁷ Lucan, viii. 486. Quoted also by Jeremy Taylor in his "Life of Christ," Preface. ² Philippic i. 51. ⁸ Georg. iii. 284.

less versed in making their fortune, is the want of time from their other studies to gain a knowledge of particulars, wait for opportunities, and project their own rising. We see in the courts of princes the most effectual men in making their own fortunes, and invading the fortunes of others, are such as have no public employ, but are continually plotting their own rise and advantage.

A fifth precept is, that we in some measure imitate nature, which does nothing in vain ; and this is not very difficult, if we skilfully mix and interlace our affairs of all kinds : for in every action the mind is to be so instructed and prepared, and our intentions to be so dependent upon and subordinate to each other, that if we cannot gain the highest step, we may contentedly take up with the second, or even the third. But if we can fix on no part of our prospect, then we should direct the pains we have been at to some other end ; so, as if we receive no benefit for the present, yet at least to gain somewhat of future advantage. But if we can obtain no solid good from our endeavours neither in present nor in future, let us endeavour at least to gain a reputation by it, or some one thing or other ; always computing with ourselves, that from every action we receive some advantage more or less, and by no means suffering the mind to despond or be astonished when we fail of our principal end. For there is nothing more contrary to political prudence than to be wholly intent upon any single thing, as he who is so must lose numberless opportunities which come sideways in business, and which perhaps would be more favourable and conducive to the things that shall turn up hereafter, than to those that were before pursued. Let men therefore well understand the rule—" These things should be done, but those should not be omitted."[b]

The sixth precept is, that we do not too peremptorily oblige ourselves to anything, though it seem at first sight not liable to contingency ; but always reserve a window open to fly out, or some secret back-door for retreat.

A seventh precept is, that old one of Bias, provided it be not used treacherously, but only by way of caution and moderation —" Love your friend as if he were to become an enemy, and

---

[b] Which is inculcated by ancient as well as modern wisdom. Epic. Enchir. and Matt. xx. 23, and Luke xi. 42. *Ed.*

hate your enemy as if he were to become your friend:"[c] for it surprisingly betrays and corrupts all sorts of utility, to plunge one's self too far in unhappy friendships, vexations, and turbulent quarrels, or childish and empty emulations. And so much, by way of example, upon the doctrine or art of rising in life.

We are well aware that good fortune may be had upon easier conditions than are here laid down; for it falls almost spontaneously upon some men, whilst others procure it only by diligence and assiduity, without much art, though still with some caution. But as Cicero, when he draws the perfect orator, does not mean that every pleader either could or should be like him; and as in describing the prince or the politician, which some have undertaken, the model is formed to the perfect rules of art, and not according to common life—the same method is observed by us in this sketch of the self-politician.

It must be observed that the precepts we have laid down upon this subject are all of them lawful, and not such immoral artifices as Machiavel speaks of, who directs men to have little regard for virtue itself, but only for the show and public reputation of it: "Because," says he, "the credit and opinion of virtue are a help to a man, but virtue itself a hinderance."[d] He also directs his politician to ground all his prudence on this supposition, that men cannot be truly and safely worked to his purpose but by fear, and therefore advises him to endeavour, by all possible means, to subject them to dangers and difficulties. Whence his politician may seem to be what the Italians call a sower of thorns.[e] So Cicero cites this principle, "Let our friends fall, provided our enemies perish;"[f] upon which the triumvirs acted, in purchasing the death of their enemies by the destruction of their nearest friends. So Catiline became a disturber and incendiary of the state, that he might the better fish his fortune in troubled waters, declaring, that if his fortune was set on

---

[c] Arist. Rhet. ii. 13, 4; and cf. Cic. Læl. xvi. Canning, in one of his speeches, condemns this principle as unworthy of an honourable mind. But it undoubtedly contains much wisdom, when it is restricted to the moderation of the affections. *Ed.*
[d] Libro del Principe.   [e] Il seminatore delle spine.
[f] Cadant amici, dummodo inimici intercidant. Orat. pro reg. Deiot

fire, he would quench it, not with water, but destruction.[g] And so Lysander would say, that children were to be decoyed with sweetmeats and men by false oaths; and there are numerous other corrupt and pernicious maxims of the same kind, more indeed, as in all other cases, than of such as are just and sound. Now if any man delight in this corrupt or tainted prudence, we deny not but he may take a short cut to fortune, as being thus disentangled and set at large from all restraint of laws, good-nature, and virtue, and having no regard but to his own promotion—though it is in life as in a journey, where the shortest road is the dirtiest, and yet the better not much about.

But if men were themselves, and not carried away with the tempest of ambition, they would be so far from studying these wicked arts, as rather to view them, not only in that general map of the world, which shows all to be vanity and vexation of spirit,[h] but also in that more particular one, which represents a life separate from good actions as a curse; that the more eminent this life, the greater the curse; that the noblest reward of virtue is virtue itself; that the extremest punishment of vice is vice itself; and that as Virgil excellently observes, good actions are rewarded, as bad ones also are punished—by the consciousness that attends them.

> "Quæ vobis, quæ digna, viri, pro laudibus istis
> Præmia posse rear solvi? Pulcherrima primum
> Dii moresque dabunt vestri."[i]

And indeed, whilst men are projecting and every way racking their thoughts to provide and take care for their fortunes, they ought, in the midst of all, to have an eye to the Divine Providence, which frequently overturns and brings to naught the machinations and deep devices of the wicked, according to that of the Scripture, "He has conceived iniquity, and shall bring forth vanity."[k] And although men were not in this pursuit to practise injustice and unlawful arts, yet a continual and restless search and striving after fortune, takes up too much of their time, who have nobler things to observe, and prevents them from paying their tribute to God, who exacts from all men the tenth part of their substance and the seventh of their time. Even the heathens observed, that

---

[g] Cicero pro L. Muræna, and Cat. Conspir. 31.   [h] Eccles. i. 2—14.
[i] Æneid, ix. 252.   [k] Psal. vii. 15, but in another sense

man was not made to keep his mind always on the ground; and, like the serpent, eating the dust,—
  "Atque affigit humo divinæ particulam auræ."[1]
And again—
  "Os homini sublime dedit, cœlumque tueri
  Jussit; et erectos ad sidera tollere vultus."[m]

Some, however, may flatter themselves, that, by what sinister means soever their fortune be procured, they are determined to use it well when obtained; when it was said of Augustus Cæsar and Septimus Severus, that "they ought never to have been born, or never to have died:" so much evil they committed in aspiring, and so much good they did when seated. But let such men know that this recompensing of evil with good, though it may be approved after the action, yet is justly condemned in the design. Lastly, it may not be amiss, in this eager pursuit of fortune, for men to cool themselves a little with the saying of Charles the Fifth to his son; viz. "Fortune is like the ladies, who generally scorn and discard their over-earnest admirers." But this last remedy belongs to such as have their taste vitiated by a disease of the mind. Let mankind rather rest upon the corner-stone of divinity and philosophy, both which nearly agree in the thing that ought first to be sought. For Divinity says, "Seek ye first the kingdom of God, and all other things shall be added unto you:"[n] so philosophy directs us first to seek the goods of the mind, and the rest will either be supplied, or are not much wanted. For although this foundation, laid by human hands, is sometimes placed upon the sand, as in the case of Brutus, who, at his death, cried out, "O virtue, I have reverenced thee as a being, but alas, thou art an empty name!"[o] yet the same foundation is ever, by the Divine hand, fixed upon a rock. And here we conclude the doctrine of rising in life, and the general doctrine of business, together.

[1] Hor. Sat. ii. 79.   [m] Ovid. Metam. i. 85.   [n] Matt. vi. 33.
[o] Ὦ τλῆμον ἀρετή, λόγος ἄρ' ἦσθ'· ἐγὼ δέ σε
Ὡς ἔργον ἤσκουν· σὺ δ' ἄρ' ἐδούλευες τύχῃ.—Dio. Cass. xlvii. 49.

CHAPTER III.

The Arts of Empire or State Policy omitted. Two Deficiencies alone noticed. The Art of Enlarging the Bounds of Empire, and the Knowledge of Universal Justice drawn from the Fountains of Law.

WE come now to the art of empire, or the doctrine of governing a state, which includes economics, as a city includes a family. But here, according to my former resolution, I impose silence upon myself; how well qualified soever I might seem to treat the subject, from the constant course of life, studies, employs, and the public posts I have, for a long series of years, sustained, even to the highest in the kingdom, which, through his majesty's favour, and no merit of my own, I held for four years. And this I speak to posterity, not out of ostentation; but because I judge it may somewhat import the dignity of learning, to have a man born for letters rather than anything else, who should, by a certain fatality, and against the bent of his genius, be compelled into active life, and yet be raised, by a prudent king, to the greatest posts of honour, trust, and civil employ. And if I should hereafter have leisure to write upon government, the work will probably either be posthumous or abortive. But in the mean time, having now seated all the sciences, each in its proper place, lest such a high chair as that of government should remain absolutely vacant, we here observe, that two parts of civil doctrine, though belonging not to the secrets of state, but of a more open and vulgar nature, are deficient, and shall, therefore, in our manner, give specimens for supplying them.

The art of government includes the political offices; viz. 1. the preservation; 2. the happiness; and 3. the enlargement of a state. The two former have, in good measure, been excellently treated by some;[a] but there is nothing extant upon the last; which we, therefore, note as deficient, and propose the following sketch, by way of example, for supplying it, under the title of the Military Statesman, or the Doctrine of extending the Bounds of Empire.

---

[a] For an account of these authors, see Morhof's "Polyhist." tom. iii. De Prudentiæ Civilis Scriptoribus; and "Stollii Introduct. in Hist. Literar." cap. v. De Prudentia Politica.

THE MILITARY STATESMAN;

OR, A SPECIMEN OF THE DOCTRINE OF ENLARGING THE BOUNDS OF EMPIRE.

The saying of Themistocles, if applied to himself, was indecent and haughty; but if meant in general, contains a very prudent observation, and as grave a censure. Being asked, at a feast, to touch a lute, he answered, " He could not fiddle; but he could raise a small village to a great city."[b] Which words, if taken in a political sense, excellently describe and distinguish two very different faculties in those who are at the helm of states. For upon an exact survey, we shall find some, though but very few, that, being raised to the council-board, the senate, or other public office, can enlarge a small state, or city, and yet have little skill in music; but many more, who, having a good hand upon the harp, or the lute, that is, at the trifles of a court, are so far from enlarging a state, that they rather seem designed by nature to overturn and ruin it, though ever so happy and flourishing. And, indeed, those base arts and tricks by which many counsellors and men of great place procure the favour of their sovereign, and a popular character, deserve no other name than a certain knack of fiddling; as being things more pleasing for the present, and more ornamental to the practitioner, than useful, and suited to enlarge the bounds, or increase the riches of the state, whereof they are ministers. Again, there are, doubtless, counsellors and governors, who, though equal to business, and of no contemptible abilities, may commodiously manage things so as to preserve them from manifest precipices and inconveniences, though they by no means have the creative power of building and extending an empire. But whatever the workmen be, let us regard the work itself; viz., what is to be deemed the true extent of kingdoms and republics, and by what means this may be procured—a subject well deserving to lie continually before princes, for their diligent meditation; lest, by over-rating their own strength, they should rashly engage in too difficult and vain enterprises, or, thinking too meanly of their power, submit to timorous and effeminate counsels.

The greatness of an empire, in point of bulk and territory, is subject to mensuration, and for its revenue, to calculation.

[b] Plutarch, Tus. Quæst. b. i. 2.

The number of inhabitants may be known by valuation or tax, and the number and extent of cities and towns, by survey and maps; yet in all civil affairs there is not a thing more liable to error than the making a true and intrinsic estimate of the strength and riches of a state. The kingdom of heaven is compared, not to an acorn, or any large nut, but to a grain of mustard-seed; which, though one of the least grains, has in it a certain quick property, and native spirit, whereby it rises soon, and spreads itself wide: so some states of very large compass are little suited to extend their limits, or procure a wider command, whilst others of small dimension prove the foundations of the greatest monarchies.

Fortified towns, well-stored arsenals, noble breeds of war-horses, armed chariots, elephants, engines, all kinds of artillery, arms, and the like, are nothing more than a sheep in a lion's skin, unless the nation itself be, from its origin and temper, stout and warlike. Nor is number of troops itself of any great service, where the soldiers are weak and enervate: for, as Virgil well observes, " The wolf cares not how large the flock is."[c] The Persian army in the plains of Arbela, appeared to the eyes of the Macedonians as an immense ocean of people; insomuch that Alexander's leaders, being struck at the sight, counselled their general to fall upon them by night; but he replied, " I will not steal the victory:"[d] and it was found an easier conquest than he expected. Tigranes, encamped upon a hill, with an army of four hundred thousand men, seeing the Roman army, consisting but of fourteen thousand, making up to him, he jested at it, and said, " Those men are too many for an embassy, but much too few for a battle:"[e] yet before sunset he found them enough to give him chase, with infinite slaughter. And we have abundant examples of the great inequality betwixt number and strength. This, therefore, may be first set down as a sure and certain maxim, and the capital of all the rest, with regard to the greatness of a state, that the people be of a military race,[f] or both by origin and disposition warlike. The sinews of war are not money, if the sinews of men's arms be wanting, as they are in a soft and effeminate nation. It was a just answer of Solon to Crœsus, who showed him all his treasure:

[c] Eclog. vii. 52.
[e] Plut. Lucul.
[d] Quintus Curtius, iv. 15, and Plutarch.
[f] Machi. Discorso sopra Livio, lib. ii.

"Yes, sir, but if another should come with better iron than you, he would be master of all this gold."[g] And, therefore, all princes whose native subjects are not hardy and military, should make a very modest estimate of their power; as, on the other hand, those who rule a stout and martial people, may well enough know their own strength, if they be not otherwise wanting to themselves. As to hired forces, which is the usual remedy when native forces are wanting, there are numerous examples, which clearly show, that whatever state depends upon them, though it may perhaps for a time extend its feathers beyond its nest, yet they will mew soon after.

The blessing of Judah and Issachar can never meet; so that the same tribe, or nation, should be both the lion's whelp, and the ass under the burden:[h] nor can a people, overburdened with taxes, ever be strong and warlike. It is true, that taxes levied by public consent less dispirit and sink the minds of the subject than those imposed in absolute governments; as clearly appears by what is called excise in the Netherlands, and in some measure by the contributions called the subsidies in England. We are now speaking of the minds, and not of the wealth of the people: for tributes by consent, though the same thing with tributes imposed, as to exhausting the riches of a kingdom, yet very differently affect the minds of the subject. So that this also must be a maxim of state, "That a people oppressed with taxes is unfit to rule."

States and kingdoms that aspire to greatness, must be very careful that their nobles and gentry increase not too much; otherwise, the common people will be dispirited, reduced to an abject state, and become little better than slaves to the nobility: as we see in coppices, if the staddles are left too numerous, there will never be clean underwood; but the greatest part degenerates into shrubs and bushes. So in nations, where the nobility is too numerous, the commonalty will be base and cowardly; and, at length, not one head in a hundred among them prove fit for a helmet, especially with regard to the infantry, which is generally the prime strength of an army. Whence, though a nation be full-peopled, its force may be small. We need no clearer proof of this than by comparing England and France. For though England

[g] Plut.   [h] Genesis xlix. 9, 14.

be far inferior in extent and number of inhabitants, yet it has almost constantly got the better of France in war: for this reason, that the rustics, and lower sort of people in England, make better soldiers than the peasants of France. And in this respect it was a very political and deep foresight of Henry the Seventh of England, to constitute lesser settled farms, and houses of husbandry, with a certain fixed and inseparable proportion of land annexed, sufficient for a life of plenty: so that the proprietors themselves, or at least the renters, and not hirelings, might occupy them. For thus a nation may acquire that character which Virgil gives of ancient Italy: "A country strong in arms, and rich of soil,"—

"Terra potens armis, atque ubere glebæ."[1]

We must not here pass over a sort of people, almost peculiar to England, viz., the servants of our nobles and gentry; as the lowest of this kind are no way inferior to the yeomanry for foot-service. And it is certain that the hospitable magnificence and splendour, the attendance and large train, in use among the nobility and gentry of England, add much to our military strength; as, on the other hand, a close retired life among the nobility causes a want of forces.

It must be earnestly endeavoured, that the tree of monarchy, like the tree of Nebuchadnezzar, have its trunk sufficiently large and strong, to support its branches and leaves; or that the natives be sufficient to keep the foreign subjects under: whence those states best consult their greatness, which are liberal of naturalization. For it were vain to think a handful of men, how excellent soever in spirit and counsel, should hold large and spacious countries under the yoke of empire. This, indeed, might perhaps be done for a season, but it cannot be lasting. The Spartans were reserved and difficult in receiving foreigners among them; and, therefore, so long as they ruled within their own narrow bounds, their affairs stood firm and strong; but soon after they began to widen their borders, and extend their dominion farther than the Spartan race could well command the foreign crowd, their power sunk of a sudden. Never did commonwealth receive new citizens so profusely as the Roman; whence its fortune was equal to so prudent a conduct: and thus the

[1] Æneid, i. 531.

Romans acquired the most extensive empire on the globe. It was their custom to give a speedy denization, and in the highest degree; that is, not only a right of commerce of marriage and inheritance, but also the right of suffrage, and of candidature for places and honours.[k] And this not only to particular persons; but they conferred it upon entire families, cities, and sometimes whole nations at once. Add to this their custom of settling colonies, whereby Roman roots were transplanted in foreign soil. And to consider these two practices together, it might be said, that the Romans did not spread themselves over the globe, but that the globe spread itself over the Romans: which is the securest method of extending an empire. I have often wondered how the Spanish government could with so few natives inclose and curb so many kingdoms and provinces. But Spain may be esteemed a sufficiently large trunk, as it contains a much greater tract of country than either Rome or Sparta did at first. And although the Spaniards are very sparing of naturalization, yet they do what comes next to it: promiscuously receive the subjects of all nations into their army; and even their highest military office is often conferred upon foreign leaders. Nay, it appears that Spain at length begins to feel their want of natives, and are now endeavouring to supply it.

It is certain, that the sedentary mechanic arts, practised within doors, and the more curious manufactures, which require the finger rather than the arm, are in their own nature opposite to a military spirit. Men of the sword universally delight in exemption from work, and dread dangers less than labour. And in this temper they must be somewhat indulged, if we desire to keep their minds in vigour. It was, therefore, a great advantage to Sparta, Athens, Rome, and other ancient republics, that they had the use, not of freemen, but generally of slaves for this kind of domestic arts. But after the Christian religion gained ground, the use of slaves was in great measure abolished. What comes nearest this custom is to leave such arts chiefly to strangers, who for that purpose should be invited to come in, or at least be easily admitted. The native vulgar should consist of three kinds; viz., husbandmen, free servants, and

[k] Cic. pro L. C. Bal.

handicraftsmen, used to the strong masculine arts; such as smithery, masonry, carpentry, &c., without including the soldiery.

But above all, it is most conducive to the greatness of empire, for a nation to profess the skill of arms as its principal glory and most honourable employ; for the things hitherto spoken of are but preparatory to the use of arms; and to what end this preparation, if the thing itself be not reduced to action? Romulus, as the story goes, left it in charge to his people at his death, that of all things they should cultivate the art of war, as that which would make their city the head of the world.[1] The whole frame and structure of the Spartan government tended, with more diligence, indeed, than prudence, only to make its inhabitants warriors. Such was also the practice of the Persians and Macedonians, though not so constant and lasting. The Britons, Gauls, Germans, Goths, Saxons, and Normans, for some time also principally cultivated military arts. The Turks did the same, being not a little excited thereto by their law, and still continue the discipline, notwithstanding their soldiery be now on its decline. Of all Christian Europe, the only nation that still retains and professes this discipline is the Spanish. But it is so plain, that every one advances farthest in what he studies most, as to require no enforcing. It is sufficient to intimate, that unless a nation professedly studies and practises arms and military discipline, so as to make them a principal business, it must not expect that any remarkable greatness of empire will come of its own accord. On the contrary, it is the most certain oracle of time, that those nations which have longest continued in the study and profession of arms, as the Romans and the Turks have principally done, make the most surprising progress in enlarging the bounds of empire. And again, those nations which have flourished, though but for a single age, in military glory, yet during that time have obtained such a greatness of empire as has remained with them long after, when their martial discipline was slackened.

It bears some relation to the foregoing precept, that "a state should have such laws and customs as may readily administer just causes, or at least pretexts, of taking arms

[1] Livy, v. 37.

For there is such a natural notion of justice imprinted in men's minds, that they will not make war, which is attended with so many calamities, unless for some weighty or at least some specious reason. The Turks are never unprovided of a cause of war, viz., the propagation of their law and religion. The Romans, though it was a high degree of honour for their emperors to extend the borders of their empire, yet never undertook a war for that sole end. Let it, therefore, be a rule to all nations that aim at empire, to have a quick and lively sensibility of any injury done to their frontier subjects, merchants, or public ministers. And let them not sit too long quiet after the first provocation. Let them also be ready and cheerful in sending auxiliaries to their friends and allies, which the Romans constantly observed, insomuch that if an invasion were made upon any of their allies, who also had a defensive league with others, and the former begged assistance severally, the Romans would ever be the first to give it, and not suffer the honour of the benefit to be snatched from them by others. As for the wars anciently waged from a certain conformity or tacit correspondence of states, I cannot see on what law they stood. Such were the wars undertaken by the Romans for restoring liberty to Greece; such were those of the Lacedæmonians and Athenians, for establishing or overturning democracies or oligarchies; and such sometimes are those entered into by republics or kingdoms, under pretext of protecting the subjects of other nations, or delivering them from tyranny. It may suffice for the present purpose, that no state expect any greatness of empire, unless it be immediately ready to seize any just occasion of a war.

No one body, whether natural or political, can preserve its health without exercise; and honourable war is the wholesome exercise of a kingdom or commonwealth. Civil wars, indeed, are like the heat of a fever, but a war abroad is like the heat of motion—wholesome; for men's minds are enervated and their manners corrupted by sluggish and inactive peace. And, however it may be as to the happiness of a state, it is doubtless best for its greatness to be as it were always in arms. A veteran army, indeed, kept constantly ready for marching, is expensive, yet it gives a state the disposal of things among its neighbours, or at least procures it a great reputation in other respects, as may be clearly seen in the Spaniard, who has now, for a long succession of years, kept a standing army, though not always in the same part of the country.

The dominion of the sea is an epitome of monarchy. Cicero, in a letter to Atticus, writing of Pompey's preparation against Cæsar, says, the designs of Pompey are like those of Themistocles; for he thinks they who command the sea command the empire.[m] And doubtless Pompey would have wearied Cæsar out, and brought him under, had he not, through a vain confidence, abandoned his design. It is plain, from many examples, of how great consequence sea-fights are. The fight at Actium decided the empire of the world; the fight of Lepanto struck a hook in the nose of the Turk; and it has frequently happened that victories or defeats at sea have put a final end to the war, that is, when the whole fortune of it has been committed to them. Doubtless the being master of the sea leaves a nation at great liberty to act, and to take as much or as little of the war as it pleases, whilst those who are superior in land forces have yet numerous difficulties to struggle with. And at present, amongst the European nations, a naval strength, which is the portion of Great Britain, is more than ever of the greatest importance to sovereignty, as well because most of the kingdoms of Europe are not continents, but in good measure surrounded by the sea, as because the treasures of both Indies seem but an accessory to the dominion of the seas.

The wars of later times seem to have been waged in the dark, compared with the variety of glory and honour usually reflected upon the military men of former ages. It is true, we have at this day certain military honours designed perhaps as incentives to courage, though common to men of the gown as well as the sword; we have also some coats of arms and public hospitals, for soldiers worn out and disabled in the service; but among the ancients, when a victory was obtained, there were trophies, funeral orations, and magnificent monuments for such as died in the wars. Civic crowns and military garlands were bestowed upon all the soldiers. The very name of emperor was afterwards borrowed by the greatest kings from leaders in the wars; they had solemn

[m] B. 10, ep. 8.

triumphs for their successful generals; they had donatives and great largesses for the soldiers, when the army was disbanded; these are such great and dazzling things in the eyes of mortals, as to be capable of firing the most frozen spirits and inflaming them for war. In particular, the manner of triumph among the Romans was not a thing of pageantry or empty show, but deserving to be reckoned among the wisest and most noble of their customs, as being attended with these three particulars; viz., 1. The glory and honour of their leaders; 2. The enriching of the treasury with the spoils; and, 3. Donatives to the army. But their triumphal honours were, perhaps, unfit for monarchies, unless in the person of the king or his son, which also obtained at Rome in the times of its emperors, who reserved the honour of the triumph as peculiar to themselves and their sons upon returning from the wars whereat they were present, and had brought to a conclusion, only conferring their vestments and triumphal ensigns upon the other leaders.

But to conclude, though no man, as the Scripture testifies, can by taking care add one cubit to his stature,[n] that is, in the little model of the human body; yet in the vast fabric of kingdoms and commonwealths, it is in the power of kings and rulers to extend and enlarge the bounds of empire; for by prudently introducing such laws, orders, and customs as those above mentioned, and the like, they might sow the seeds of greatness for posterity and future ages. But these counsels seldom reach the ears of princes, who generally commit the whole to the direction and disposal of fortune.

The other desideratum we note in the art of government, is the doctrine of universal justice, or the fountains of law. They who have hitherto written upon laws were either as philosophers or lawyers: the philosophers advance many things that appear beautiful in discourse, but lie out of the road of use; whilst the lawyers, being bound and subject to the decrees of the laws prevailing in their several countries, whether Roman or pontifical, have not their judgment free, but write as in fetters. This doctrine, doubtless, properly belongs to statesmen, who best understand civil society, the good of the people, natural equity, the customs of nations, and the different forms of states; whence they are able to

[n] Matt. vi. 27, and Luke xii. 25.

judge of laws by the principles and precepts, as well of natural justice as of politics. The present view, therefore, is to discover the fountains of justice and public good, and in all the parts of equity to give a certain character and idea of what is just, according whereto those who desire it may examine the laws of particular kingdoms and states, and thence endeavour to amend them. And of this doctrine we shall, in our usual way, give an example, aphoristically, in a single title.

A SPECIMEN OF THE METHOD OF TREATING UNIVERSAL JUSTICE; OR, THE FOUNTAINS OF EQUITY.[o]

Introduction.

APHORISM I. Either law or force prevails in civil society. But there is some force that resembles law, and some law that resembles force more than justice; whence there are three fountains of injustice; viz., 1. Mere force; 2. Malicious ensnaring under colour of law; and, 3. The severity of the law itself.

II. The ground of private right is this: He who does an injury receives profit or pleasure in the action, and incurs danger by the example; whilst others partake not with him in that profit or pleasure, but think the example concerns them; whence they easily agree to defend themselves by laws, lest each particular should be injured in his turn. But if it should happen, from the nature of the times, and a communion of guilt, that the greater or more powerful part should be subject to danger, rather than defended from it by law, faction here disannuls the law; and this case frequently happens.

III. But private right lies under the protection of public laws; for law guards the people, and magistrates guard the laws. But the authority of the magistrate is derived from the majesty of the government, the form of the constitution, and its fundamental laws; whence, if the political constitution be just and right, the laws will be of excellent use; but if otherwise, of little security.

---

[o] Compare Morhof's "Polyhistor," tom. iii. lib. vi. De Jurisprudentia universalis Scriptoribus; "Struvii Bibliothec. Philosoph." cap. 6, 7, De Scriptoribus Politicis; and "Stollii Introduct. in Hist. Liter." p. 753, &c., De Jure Naturali. *Ed.*

IV. Public law is not only the preserver of private right, so as to keep it unviolated and prevent injuries, but extends also to religion, arms, discipline, ornaments, wealth, and all things that regard the good of a state.

V. For the end and scope of laws, whereto all their decrees and sanctions ought to tend, is the happiness of the people; which is procurable,—1. by rightly instructing them in piety, religion, and the duties of morality; 2. securing them by arms against foreign enemies; 3. guarding them by laws against faction and private injuries; 4. rendering them obedient to the government and magistracy; and, 5. thus causing them to flourish in strength and plenty. But laws are the instruments and sinews for procuring all this.

VI. The best laws, indeed, secure this good end, but many other laws fail of it; for laws differ surprisingly from one another, insomuch that some are,—1. excellent; others, 2. of a middle nature; and, 3. others again absolutely corrupt. We shall, therefore, here offer, according to the best of our judgment, certain laws, as it were, of laws;[p] from whence an information may be derived as to what is well or what is ill laid down, or established by particular laws.

VII. But before we proceed to the body of particular laws, we will briefly touch upon the excellencies and dignities of laws in general. Now, that may be esteemed a good law which is,—1. clear and certain in its sense; 2. just in its command; 3. commodious in the execution; 4. agreeable to the form of government; and, 5. productive of virtue in the subject.[q]

TITLE I.
Of that primary dignity of the law, certainty.

VIII. Certainty is so essential to a law, that a law without it cannot be just; for if the trumpet gives an uncertain

[p] As laying down the just foundations and rules of the law; for the law itself is governed by reason, justice, and good sense. But perhaps these aphorisms of the author follow the particular law of England too close to be allowed by other nations for the foundations of universal justice, which is a very extensive subject. See "Struvii Bibliothec. Philosoph." cap. 8, De Scriptoribus Juris Naturæ et Gentium. *Ed.*

[q] These are so many several titles, or general heads, laid down by the author, as if he intended a full treatise upon the subject; but he here only considers the first of them. *Shaw.*

sound, who shall prepare himself to the battle?" So if the law has an uncertain sense, who shall obey it? A law, therefore, ought to give warning before it strikes: and it is a true maxim, that the best law leaves least to the breast of the judge; which is effected by certainty.

IX. Laws have two uncertainties—the one where no law is prescribed, the other when a law is ambiguous and obscure; wherefore we must first speak of cases omitted by the law, that in these also may be found some rules of certainty.

Cases omitted in law.

X. The narrowness of human prudence cannot foresee all the cases that time may produce. Whence new cases, and cases omitted, frequently turn up. And for these there are three remedies or supplies; viz., 1. by proceeding upon analogy; 2. by the use of precedents, though not yet brought into a law; and 3. by juries, which decree according to conscience and discretion, whether in the courts of equity or of common law.

Application and extension of laws.

XI. 1. In cases omitted, the rule of law is to be deduced from similar cases, but with caution and judgment. And here the following rules are to be observed: Let reason be esteemed a fruitful, and custom a barren thing, so as to breed no cases. And therefore what is received against the reason of a law, or where its reason is obscure, should not be drawn into precedents.

XII. A great public good must draw to itself all cases omitted; and therefore, when a law remarkably, and in an extraordinary manner, regards and procures the good of the public, let its interpretation be full and extensive.

XIII. It is a cruel thing to torture the laws, that they may torture men; whence penal laws, much less capital laws, should not be extended to new offences. But if the offence be old, and known to the law, and its prosecution fall upon a new case not provided for by law, the law must rather be forsaken than offences go unpunished.

XIV. Statutes that repeal the common law, especially in common and settled cases, should not be drawn by analogy to cases omitted; for when the republic has long been with-

---

" 1 Cor. xiv. 8.

out an entire law, and that in express cases, there is little danger if cases omitted should wait their remedy from a new statute.

XV. It is enough for such statutes as were plainly temporary laws, enacted upon particular urgent occasions of state, to contain themselves within their proper cases after those occasions cease; for it were preposterous to extend them in any measure to cases omitted.

XVI. There is no precedent of a precedent; but extension should rest in immediate cases, otherwise it would gradually slide on to dissimilar cases, and so the wit of men prevail over the authority of laws.

XVII. In such laws and statutes as are concise, extension may be more freely allowed; but in those which express particular cases, it should be used more cautiously. For as exception strengthens the force of a law in unaccepted cases, so enumeration weakens it in cases not enumerated.

XVIII. An explanatory statute stops the current of a precedent statute; nor does either of them admit extension afterwards. Neither should the judge make a super-extension where the law has once begun one.

XIX. The solemnity of forms and acts admits not of extension to similar cases: for it is losing the nature of solemnity to go from custom to opinion, and the introduction of new things takes from the majesty of the old.

XX. The extension of law is easy to after-cases, which had no existence at the time when the law was made: for where a case could not be described because not then in being, a case omitted is deemed a case expressed, if there be the same reason for it.

Precedents and the use of forms.

XXI. 2. We come next to precedents; from which justice may be derived where the law is deficient, but reserving custom, which is a kind of law, and the precedents which, through frequent use, are passed into custom, as into a tacit law; we shall at present only speak of such precedents as happen but rarely, and have not acquired the force of a law, with a view to show how and with what caution a rule of justice may be derived from them when the law is defective.

XXII. Precedents are to be derived from good and moderate times, and not from such as are tyrannical, factious, or dissolute ; for this latter kind are a spurious birth of time, and prove more prejudicial than instructive.

XXIII. Modern examples are to be held the safest. For why may not what was lately done, without any inconvenience be safely done again ? Yet recent examples have the less authority ; and, where things require a restoration, participate more of their own times than of right reason.

XXIV. Ancient precedents are to be received with caution and choice ; for the course of time alters many things; so that what seems ancient, in time may, for disturbance and unsuitableness, be new at the present ; and therefore the precedents of intermediate times are the best, or those of such times as have most agreement with the present, which ancient times may happen to have more than later.

XXV. Let the limits of a precedent be observed, and rather kept within than exceeded ; for where there is no rule of law, everything should be suspected : and therefore, as this is a dark road, we should not be hasty to follow.

XXVI. Beware of fragments and epitomes of examples, and rather consider the whole of the precedent with all its process ; for if it be absurd to judge upon part of a law without understanding the whole, this should be much rather observed of precedents, the use whereof is precarious, without an evident correspondence.

XXVII. It is of great consequence through what hands the precedents pass, and by whom they have been allowed. For if they have obtained only among clerks and secretaries, by the course of the court, without any manifest knowledge of their superiors ; or have prevailed among that source of errors, the populace, they are to be rejected or lightly esteemed. But if they come before senators, judges, or principal courts, so that of necessity they must have been strengthened, at least by the tacit approval of proper persons, their dignity is the greater.

XXVIII. More authority is to be allowed to those examples which, though less used, have been published and thoroughly canvassed; but less to those that have lain buried and forgotten in the closet or archives : for examples, like waters, are wholesomest in the running stream.

XXIX. Precedents in law should not be derived from history, but from public acts and accurate traditions ; for it is a certain infelicity, even among the best historians, that they dwell not sufficiently upon laws and judicial proceedings; or if they happen to have some regard thereto, yet their accounts are far from being authentic.

XXX. An example rejected in the same, or next succeeding age, should not easily be received again when the same case recurs; for it makes not so much in its favour that men sometimes used it, as in its disfavour that they dropped it upon experience.

XXXI. Examples are things of direction and advice, not rules or orders, and therefore should be so managed as to bend the authority of former times to the service of the present.

Prætorian and censorian courts.

XXXII. 3. There should be both courts and juries, to judge according to conscience and discretion, where the rule of the law is defective; for laws, as we before observed, cannot provide against all cases, but are suited only to such as frequently happen: time, the wisest of all things, daily introducing new cases.

XXXIII. But new cases happen both in criminal matters, which require punishment; and in civil causes, which require relief. The courts that regard the former, we call censorial, or courts of justice; and those that regard the latter, prætorial, or courts of equity.

XXXIV. The courts of justice should have jurisdiction and power, not only to punish new offences, but also to increase the penalties appointed by the laws for old ones, where the cases are flagrant and notorious, yet not capital; for every enormous crime may be esteemed a new one.

XXXV. In like manner, the courts of equity should have power as well to abate the rigour of the law as to supply its defects; for if a remedy be afforded to a person neglected by the law, much more to him who is hurt by the law.

XXXVI. Both the censorial and prætorial courts should absolutely confine themselves to enormous and extraordinary cases, without invading the ordinary jurisdictions; lest otherwise the law should rather be supplanted than supplied.

XXXVII. These jurisdictions should reside only in supreme courts, and not be communicated to the lower;

for the power of supplying, extending, or moderating the laws, differs but little from a power of making them.

XXXVIII. These courts of jurisdiction should not be committed to a single person, but consist of several; and let not their verdict be given in silence, but let the judges produce the reasons of their sentence openly and in full audience of the court; so that what is free in power may yet be limited by regard to fame and reputation.

XXXIX. Let there be no records of blood, nor sentence of capital crimes, passed in any court, but upon known and certain laws: God himself first pronounced, and afterwards inflicted death. Nor should a man lose his life without first knowing that he had forfeited it.

XL. In the courts of justice, let there be three returns of the jury, that the judges may not only lie under no necessity of absolving or condemning, but also have a liberty of pronouncing the case not clear. And let there be, besides penalty, a note of infamy or punishment by way of admonishing others, and chastising delinquents, as it were, by putting them to the blush with shame and scandal.

XLI. In courts of justice, let the first overtures and intermediate parts of all great offences be punished, though the end were not accomplished. And this should be the principal use of such courts; for it is the part of discipline to punish the first buddings of offences; and the part of clemency, to punish the intermediate actions, and prevent their taking effect.

XLII. Great regard must be had in courts of equity, not to afford relief in those cases which the law has not so much omitted as despised for their levity, or, for their odiousness, judged unworthy of a remedy.

XLIII. But above all, it is of the greatest moment to the certainty of the laws we now speak of, that courts of equity keep from swelling and overflowing, lest, under pretence of mitigating the rigour of the law, they should cut its sinews and weaken its strength by wresting all things to their own disposal.

XLIV. No court of equity should have a right of decreeing against a statute, under any pretext of equity whatever; otherwise the judge would become the legislator, and have all things dependent upon his will.

XLV. Some conceive the jurisdiction which decrees according to equity and conscience, and that which proceeds according to strict justice, should be deputed to the same courts, whilst others would have them kept distinct; which seems much the better way. There will be no distinction of cases where there is a mixture of jurisdictions; but arbitration will at length supersede the law.

XLVI. The use of the prætor's table stood upon a good foundation among the Romans, as that wherein he set down and published in what manner he would administer justice. According to which example, the judges in courts of equity should propose to themselves some certain rules to go by, and fix them up to public view: for as that law is ever the best, which leaves least to the breast of the judge; so is that judge the best, who leaves least to himself.[a]

Retrospect and relation of laws.

XLVII. There is also another way of supplying cases omitted; viz., when one law is made upon another, and brings the cases omitted along with it. This happens in those laws or statutes, which, according to the common phrase, look backwards. But laws of this kind are to be seldom used, and with great caution; for a Janus-face is not to be admired in the law.

XLVIII. He who captiously and fraudulently eludes and circumscribes the words or intention of a law, deserves to be hampered by a subsequent law. Whence, in fraudulent and evasive cases, it is just for laws to carry a retrospection, and prove of mutual assistance to each other; so that he who invents loopholes and plots the subversion of present laws, may at least be awed by future.

XLIX. Such laws as strengthen and confirm the true intentions of acts and instruments against the defects of forms and solemnities, very justly include past actions; for the principal fault of a retrospective law is, its causing disturbance; but these confirming laws regard the peace and settlement of transactions. Care, however, must be had not to disturb things once adjudged.

L. It should be carefully observed, that not only such laws as look back to what is past invalidate former transac-

[a] The author made a speech to this effect, upon receiving the seal and taking his place in Chancery.

tions, but such also as prohibit and restrain things future, which are necessarily connected with things past : so, if any law should prohibit certain artificers the sale of their wares in future, this law, though it speaks for hereafter, yet operates upon times past, though such artificers had then no other lawful means of subsisting.

LI. All declaratory laws, though they make no mention of time past, yet are, by the very declaration itself, entirely to regard past matters; for the interpretation does not begin with the declaration, but, as it were, is made contemporary with the law itself. And therefore declaratory laws should not be enacted, except in cases where the law may be retrospected with justice. And so much for the uncertainty of laws, where the law is extant. We proceed to the other part, where the laws, though extant, are perplexed and obscure.

Obscurity of laws.

LII. The obscurity of laws has four sources; viz., 1. An accumulation of laws, especially if mixed with such as are obsolete. 2. An ambiguous description, or want of clear and distinct delivery. 3. A neglect or failure in instituting the method of interpreting justice. 4. And lastly, a clashing and uncertainty of judgments.

Excessive accumulation of laws.

LIII. The prophet says, "It shall rain snares upon them:"[*] but there are no worse snares than the snares of laws, especially the penal, which, growing excessive in number, and useless through time, prove not a lantern, but nets to the feet.

LIV. There are two ways in use of making new statutes; the one confirms and strengthens the former statutes in the like cases, at the same time adding or altering some particulars; the other abrogates and cancels all that was enacted before, and instead thereof, substitutes a new uniform law. And the latter method is the best : for in the former the decrees become complicate and perplexed, and though the business be performed, yet the body of laws in the mean time becomes corrupt; but in the latter, greater diligence must be used when the law itself comes to be weighed anew, and what was before enacted to be reconsidered antecedent

[*] Psal. x. 7.

to its passing; by which means the future agreement and harmony of the laws is well consulted.

LV. It was in use among the Athenians for six persons annually to examine the contradictory titles of their laws, and propose to the people such of them as could not be reconciled, that some certain resolution might be taken about them. According to which example, the legislators of every state should once in three or five years, as it shall seem proper, take a review of these contrarieties in law; but let them first be inspected and prepared by committees appointed for the purpose, and then brought in for the general assembly to fix and establish what shall be approved by vote.

LVI. But let not an over-diligent and scrupulous care be used in reconciling the contradictory titles of laws, by subtile and far-fetched distinctions; for this is the weaving of the wit; and whatever appearance it may have of modesty and reverence, it is to be deemed prejudicial, as rendering the whole body of the laws dissimilar and incoherent. It were, therefore, much better to suppress the worst, and suffer the best to stand alone.

LVII. Obsolete laws, that are grown into disuse, should in the same manner be cancelled. For as an express statute is not regularly abrogated by disuse, it happens that, from a contempt of such as are obsolete, the others also lose part of their authority; whence follows that torture of Mezentius, whereby the living laws are killed in the embraces of the dead ones. But above all things a gangrene in the laws is to be prevented.

LVIII. And let courts of equity have a right of decreeing contrary to obsolete laws and statutes not newly enacted; for although, as is well observed, nobody should be wiser than the laws, yet this should be understood of the laws when they are awake, and not when they sleep. But let it be the privilege, not of judges in the courts of equity, but of kings, solemn councils, and the higher powers, to overrule later statutes found prejudicial to public justice, and to suspend the execution thereof by edicts or public acts, till those meetings are held which have the true power of repealing them, lest otherwise the safety of the people should be endangered.

New digests of laws.

LIX. But if laws heaped upon laws shall swell to such a vast bulk, and labour under such confusion as renders it expedient to treat them anew, and reduce them into one sound and serviceable corps, it becomes a work of the utmost importance, deserving to be deemed heroical, and let the authors of it be ranked among legislators, and the restorers of states and empires.

LX. Such an expurgation and new digest of laws is to be effected by five particulars; viz., 1. By omitting all the obsolete laws, which Justinian calls ancient fables; 2. By receiving the most approved contradictories, and abolishing the rest; 3. By expunging laws of the same purport, and retaining only one, or the most perfect; 4. By throwing out such laws as determine nothing—only propose questions, and leave them undecided; 5. And lastly, by contracting and abridging those that are too verbose and prolix.

LXI. And it would be very useful in such a new digest, separately to range and bring together all those laws received for common law which have a kind of immemorial origin, and on the other side the statutes superadded from time to time; because in numerous particulars in the practice of the law, the interpretation and administration of the common law differs from the statute law. And this method was observed by Trebonianus in his digest and code.

LXII. But in such a second birth of the law, and such a recompilement of the ancient books and laws, the very words and text of the law itself should be retained; and though it were necessary to collect them by fragments and small portions, they may afterwards be regularly wove together. For allowing it might perhaps be more commodious, and with regard to the true reason of the thing, better, to do it by a new text than by such kind of patchwork, yet in the law, style and description are not so much to be regarded as authority, and its patron antiquity; otherwise this might rather seem a work of mere scholarship and method than a corps of majestic laws.

LXIII. 'Twere advisable, in making this new digest, not utterly to abolish the ancient volumes, and give them up to oblivion, but suffer them at least to remain in some library, though with a prohibition of their common use; because in weighty cases it might be proper to consult and inspect the revolutions and series of ancient laws. 'Tis also a solemn thing to intermix antiquity with things present. And such a new body of laws ought to receive the sanction of all those who have any legislative power in the state, lest under a pretence of digesting the old laws new ones should be secretly obtruded.

LXIV. 'Twere to be wished that such a recompilement of the laws might be undertaken in such times as excel the ancient (whose acts and works they model anew) in point of learning and universal knowledge; the contrary whereof happened in the work of Justinian. For 'tis an unfortunate thing to have the works of the ancients mangled, and set together again at the discretion and choice of a less prudent and less learned age. But it often happens that what is necessary is not best.

Obscure and involved exposition of laws.

LXV. Laws are obscurely described either,—1. through their loquacity and superfluity of words; 2. through overconciseness; or, 3. through their preambles contradicting the body of the law.

LXVI. We at present treat of the obscurity which arises from their ill description, and approve not the loquacity and prolixity now used in drawing up the laws, which in no degree obtains what is intended by it, but rather the contrary; for whilst it endeavours to comprehend and express all particular cases in apposite and proper diction (as expecting greater certainty from thence), it raises numerous questions about terms, which renders the true and real design of the law more difficult to come at through a huddle of words.

LXVII. Nor yet can we approve of a too concise and affected brevity, used for the sake of majesty and authority, especially in this age; lest the laws should become like the Lesbian rule.[u] A mediocrity, therefore, is to be observed,

[u] The Lesbians are said to have made their rules from their buildings; so that if the buildings were erroneous, the rules they worked by became so too, and thus propagated the error: so if the laws were written concise, as if drawn up in perfect times, or with an affectation of a sententious or majestic brevity, they might propagate errors, instead of correcting them.

and a well-defined generality of words to be found, which though it does not accurately explain the cases it comprehends, yet clearly excludes those it does not comprehend.

LXVIII. Yet in the ordinary politic laws and edicts, where lawyers are seldom consulted, but the politicians trust to their own judgment, things ought to be largely explained and pointed out to the capacity of the vulgar.

LXIX. Nor do we approve of tedious preambles at the head of laws: they were anciently held impertinent, as introducing laws in the way of dispute, not in the way of command. But as we do not suit ourselves to the manners of the ancients, these prefaces are now generally used of necessity, not only as explanations, but as persuasives to the passing of the law in the assemblies of states, and likewise to satisfy the people; yet as much as possible let preambles be avoided, and the law begin with commanding.

LXX. Though the intent and mind of the law may be sometimes drawn from these preambles, yet its latitude and extent should by no means be derived from them; for the preamble frequently fixes upon a few of the more plausible and specious particulars, by way of example, whilst the law itself contains many more; or on the contrary, the law restrains and limits many things, the reason whereof it were not necessary to insert in the preamble; wherefore the extent of the law is to be derived from the body of the law, the preamble often exceeding or falling short of this extent.

LXXI. There is one very faulty method of drawing up the laws, viz., when the case is largely set forth in the preamble, and then by the force of the word *which*, or some such relative, the body of the law is reflected back upon the preamble, and the preamble inserted and incorporated in the body of the law; whence proceed both obscurity and danger, because the same care is not usually employed in weighing and examining the words of the preamble, as the words of the law itself.

Different methods of expounding laws and solving doubts.

LXXII. There are five ways of interpreting the law, and making it clear; viz., 1. by recording of judgments; 2. by instituting authentic writers; 3. by auxiliary books; 4. by readings; and, 5. by the answers or counsel of qualified persons. A due use of all these affords a great and ready assistance in clearing the laws of their obscurity.

Reports of judgments.

LXXIII. And above all, let the judgments of the supreme and principal courts be diligently and faithfully recorded, especially in weighty causes, and particularly such as are doubtful, or attended with difficulty or novelty. For judgments are the anchors of the laws, as laws are the anchors of states.

LXXIV. And let this be the method of taking them down:—1. Write the case precisely, and the judgments exactly, at length; 2. Add the reasons alleged by the judges for their judgment; 3. Mix not the authority of cases, brought by way of example, with the principal case; 4. And for the pleadings, unless they contain anything very extraordinary, omit them.

LXXV. Let those who take down these judgments be of the most learned counsel in the law, and have a liberal stipend allowed them by the public. But let not the judges meddle in these reports, lest, favouring their own opinions too much, or relying upon their own authority, they exceed the bounds of a recorder.

LXXVI. Let these judgments be digested in the order of time, and not in method and titles; for such writings are a kind of histories or narratives of the laws; and not only the acts themselves, but also their times, afford light to a prudent judge.

Authentic writers.

LXXVII. Let a body of law be wholly compiled, 1. of the laws that constitute the common law; 2. of the statutes; and, 3. of the judgments on record: and besides these, let nothing be deemed authentic, or else be sparingly received.

LXXVIII. Nothing conduces more to the certainty of laws, whereof we now speak, than that the authentic writings should be kept within moderate bounds; and that vast multitude of authors and learned men in the law excluded, which otherwise rend the mind of the laws, distract the judge, make lawsuits endless: and the lawyer himself, finding it impossible to peruse and digest so many books, hence takes up with compendiums. Perhaps some good glossary, a few of the exactest writers, or rather a very few portions of a few authors, might be usefully received for authentic. But let the books be still reserved in libraries, for the judges and counsel to inspect occasionally, without permitting them to be cited in pleading at the bar, or suffering them to pass into authority.

Auxiliary writings.

LXXIX. But let not the knowledge and practice of the law want its auxiliary books, which are of six kinds; viz., 1. Institutes; 2. Explanations of words; 3. The rules of law; 4. The antiquities of law; 5. Summaries or abridgments; and 6. Forms of pleading.

LXXX. Students are to be trained up to the knowledge and higher parts of the law by institutes, which should be written in a clear method. Let the whole of private right, of the laws of Meum and Tuum, be gone over in these elements, not omitting some things and dwelling too much upon others, but giving a little taste of all, that when the student comes to peruse the corps of law, he may meet with nothing entirely new, or without having received some previous notion thereof. But the public law is not to be touched in these institutes, this being to be drawn from the fountains themselves.

LXXXI. Let a commentary be made of the terms of the law, without endeavouring too curiously and laboriously to give their full sense and explanation; the purport hereof being not to search the exact definitions of terms, but to afford such explanations only as may open an easy way to reading the books of the law. And let not this treatise be digested alphabetically,—rather leave that to the index; but place all those words together which relate to the same thing, so that one may help to the understanding of another.

LXXXII. It principally conduces to the certainty of laws, to have a just and exact treatise of the different rules of law; a work deserving the diligence of the most ingenious and prudent lawyers; for we are not satisfied with what is already extant of this kind. Not only the known and common rules are to be here collected, but others also, more subtile and latent, which may be drawn from the harmony of laws and adjudged cases; such as are sometimes found in the best records. And these rules or maxims are general dictates of reason running through the different matters of law, and make, as it were, its ballast.

LXXXIII. But let not the positions or placets of law be taken for rules, as they usually are, very injudiciously; for if this were received, there would be as many rules as there are laws: a law being no other than a commanding rule. But let those be held for rules which cleave to the very form of justice; whence in general the same rules are found through the civil law of different states, unless they sometimes vary with regard to the form of government.

LXXXIV. After the rule is laid down in a short and solid expression, let examples and clear decisions of cases be subjoined by way of explanation; distinctions and exceptions by way of limitation; and things of the same kind by way of amplification to the rule.

LXXXV. It is justly directed not to take laws from rules, but to make the rules from the laws in being: neither must the proof be derived from the words of the rule, as if that were the text of the law; for the rule, like the magnetic needle, does not make, but indicate the law.

LXXXVI. Besides the body of the law, it is proper to take a view of the antiquities of laws, which, though they have lost their authority, still retain their reverence. Those writings upon laws and judgments, whether published or unpublished, are to be held for antiquities of law, which preceded the body of the laws in point of time; for these antiquities should not be lost, but the most useful of them being collected, and such as are frivolous and impertinent rejected, they should be brought into one volume without mixing ancient fables, as Treboninaus calls them, with the laws themselves.

LXXXVII. But for practice, 'tis highly proper to have the whole law orderly digested under heads and titles, whereto any one may occasionally turn on a sudden, as to a storehouse furnished for present use. These summaries bring into order what lay dispersed, and abridge what was diffusive and prolix in the law. But care must be had lest these abridgments should make men ready for practice, and indolent in the science itself; for their office is to serve but as remembrancers, and not as perfect teachers of the law. And they are to be made with great diligence, fidelity, and judgment, that they may fairly represent, and not steal from the laws.

LXXXVIII. Let different forms of pleading be collected in every kind, for this tends to practice; and doubtless they lay open the oracles and mysteries of the law, which conceals many such. And these are better and more fully displayed in forms of pleading than otherwise, as the hand is better seen when opened.

Answers and consultations.

LXXXIX. Some method ought to be taken for solving and putting an end to particular doubts which arise from time to time; for it is a hard thing, if they who desire to keep clear of error, should find no one to set them right, but that their actions must be still, endangered, without any means of knowing the law, before the case is determined.

XC. But we approve not that the answers of prudent men, whether counsellors or professors of law, given to such as ask their advice, should have so great authority, as that the judge might not lawfully depart from their opinion. Let points of law be taken from sworn judges.

XCI. We approve not that judgments should be tried by feigned causes and persons, with a view to predetermine what will be the rule of law; for this dishonours the majesty of laws, and should be judged as a prevarication. Besides, 'tis monstrous for judgments to copy the stage.

XCII. Therefore let as well judgments as answers and advice proceed from none but the judges, the former in suits depending, and the latter in the way of opinion upon difficult points of law. But these notices, whether in private or public affairs, are not to be expected from the judges themselves, for that were to make the judge a pleader; but from the prince or state: and let them recommend it to the judges, who, invested with such authority, are to hear the arguments on both sides, and the pleadings of the counsel employed either by those whom it concerns, or appointed by the judges themselves if necessary; and after the matter is weighed, let the judges declare the law, and give their opinion; and such kind of opinions should be recorded and published among judged cases, and be reckoned of equal authority with them.

Prelections.

XCIII. Let the readings upon the law, and the exercises of such as study it, be so instituted and ordered, that all things may tend to the resolving and putting an end, and not to the raising and maintaining of questions and controversies in the law. But at present a school seems everywhere opened for multiplying disputes, wranglings, and altercations about the laws, in the way of showing the wit of the disputants; though this is also an ancient evil, for it was esteemed a piece of glory of old to support numerous questions of law, as it were by sects and fashions, rather than to end them. But this ought to be prevented.

Instability of judgments.

XCIV. Judgments prove uncertain, either 1. through an untimely and hasty passing of sentence; 2. the emulation of courts; 3. a wrong and unskilful recording of judgments; or, 4. through a too easy and ready way opened for their reversion. Therefore let care be taken, 1. that judgments proceed upon mature deliberation; 2. that courts preserve a due reverence for each other; 3. that judgments be faithfully and prudently recorded; and 4. that the way for reversing of judgments be made narrow, craggy, and thorny.

XCV. If judgment be given upon a case in any principal court, and a like case come into another court, proceed not to judgment before a consultation be held in some considerable assembly of the judges. For if decrees are of necessity to be cut off, at least let them be honourably interred.

XCVI. For courts to quarrel and contend about jurisdiction is a piece of human frailty, and the more, because of a childish opinion, that it is the duty of a good and able judge to enlarge the jurisdiction of his court; whence this disorder is increased, and the spur made use of instead of the bridle. But that courts, through this heat of contention should on all sides uncontrollably reverse each other's decrees which belong not to jurisdiction, is an intolerable evil, and by all means to be suppressed by kings, the senate, or the government. For it is a most pernicious example that courts, which make peace among the subjects, should quarrel among themselves.

XCVII. Let not too easy a passage be opened for the repealing of sentence by appeal, writ of error, rehearing, &c. Some are of opinion, that a cause should be removed to a higher court as a new cause, and the judgment given upon it in the lower be entirely laid aside and suspended; whilst others again would have the judgment remain in its force, and only the execution to be stopped. We approve of neither, unless the court where the sentence passed were of a very inferior nature; but would rather have both the judgment stand and its execution proceed, provided a caveat be put in by the defendant for costs and damages if the sentence should be reversed.

Let this title, of the certainty of laws, serve for a specimen of that digest we propose, and have in hand.[x] And thus we conclude the head of civil doctrine, and with it human philosophy; as with human philosophy, philosophy in general.

And now standing still to breathe, and look back upon the way we have passed, we seem all along to have been but tuning and trying the instruments of the muses, for a concert to be played upon them by other hands; or to have been grating men's ears, that they may have the better music hereafter. And indeed, when I set before me the present state of the times, wherein learning makes her third visit to mankind;[y] and carefully reflect how well she finds us prepared and furnished with all kinds of helps, the sublimity and penetration of many geniuses of the age, those excellent monuments of the ancient writings which shine as so many great lights before us; the art of printing, which largely supplies men of all fortunes with books; the open traffic of the globe,[z] both by sea and land, whence we receive numerous experiments, unknown to former ages, and a large accession to the mass of natural history; the leisure which the greatest minds in the kingdoms and provinces of Europe everywhere enjoy, as being less immersed in business than the ancient Greeks, by reason of their populous states; or the Romans, through the extensiveness of their empire; the peace at present

---

[x] Though the design itself was not executed by the author, some progress was made in the history of the nature, use, and proceedings of the laws of England. *Shaw.*

[y] Alluding only to the two famous ones, among the Greeks and Romans.

[z] He might have added the discovery of a new world. *Ed.*

spread over Britain, Spain, Italy, France, and many other countries; the exhaustion of all that can be invented or said in religious controversies,[a] which have so long diverted many of the best geniuses from the study of other arts; the uncommon learning of his present Britannic majesty, about whom, as about a phœnix, the fine geniuses flock from all quarters; and lastly, the inseparable property of time, which is daily to disclose truth: when all these things, I say, are considered by us, we cannot but be raised into a persuasion that this third period of learning may far exceed the two former of the Greeks and Romans, provided only that men would well and prudently understand their own powers and the defects thereof; receive from each other the lamps of invention, and not the firebrands of contradiction; and esteem the search after truth as a certain noble enterprise, not a thing of delight or ornament, and bestow their wealth and magnificence upon matters of real worth and excellence, not upon such as are vulgar and obvious. As to my own labours, if any one shall please himself or others in reprehending them, let him do it to the full, provided he observe the ancient request, and weigh and consider what he says— "Verbera, sed audi."[b] And certainly the appeal is just, though the thing perhaps may not require it, from men's first thoughts to their second, and from the present age to posterity.

We come, lastly, to that science which the two former periods of time were not blessed with; viz., sacred and inspired theology: the sabbath of all our labours and peregrinations.

[a] This is spoken like one who was versed in ecclesiastical history, and polemical divinity; for scarce any religious dispute is now raised, that has not been previously contested: but many have found the art, by heat and warmth, to revive old doctrines, opinions, and heresies, and pass them upon the crowd for new; rekindling the firebrands of their ancestors, as if religious controversies were to be entailed upon mankind, and descend from one generation to another. *Ed.*

[b] Themistocles to Eurybiades. Plut. Reg. et Imper. Apop

NINTH BOOK.

The Compartments of Theology omitted. Three Deficiencies pointed out. The Right Use of Reason in Matters of Faith. The Knowledge of the Degrees of Unity in the City of God. The Emanations of the Holy Scriptures.

HAVING now, excellent king, with our small bark of knowledge, sailed over, and surrounded the globe of the sciences, as well the old world as the new (let posterity judge with what success), we should pay our vows and conclude; did there not still remain another part to be viewed; viz., sacred or inspired theology. But if we were disposed to survey it, we must quit the small vessel of human reason, and put ourselves on board the ship of the Church, which alone possesses the divine needle for justly shaping the course. Nor will the stars of philosophy, that have hitherto principally lent their light, be of farther service to us; and, therefore, it were not improper to be silent, also, upon this subject, as well as upon that of government. For which reason, we will omit the just distribution of it, and only contribute, according to our slender ability, a few particulars in the way of good wishes. And this we do the rather, because we find no tract in the whole region of divinity, that is absolutely deserted or uncultivated: so great has the diligence of men been, in sowing either wheat or tares. We shall, therefore, only propose three appendages of theology; treating not of the matter already formed, or to be formed by divinity, but only of the manner of forming it. Neither will we here, as we have hitherto practised, give any sketches, annex any specimens, or lay down any precepts for these treatises; but leave all this to divines.

The prerogative of God extends over the whole man, and reaches both to his will and his reason; so that man must absolutely renounce himself, and submit to God: and therefore, as we are obliged to obey the divine law, though our will murmur against it, so are we obliged to believe the word of God, though our reason be shocked at it. For if we should believe only such things as are agreeable to our reason, we assent to the matter, and not to the author:

which is no more than we do to a suspected witness. But the faith imputed to Abraham for righteousness consisted in a particular, laughed at by Sarah,[a] who, in that respect, was an image of the natural reason. And, therefore, the more absurd and incredible any divine mystery is, the greater honour we do to God in believing it; and so much the more noble the victory of faith: as sinners, the more they are oppressed in conscience, yet relying upon the mercy of God for salvation, honour him the more; for all despair is a kind of reproaching the deity. And if well considered, belief is more worthy than knowledge; such knowledge, I mean, as we have at present: for in knowledge, the human mind is acted upon by sense, which results from material things; but in faith, the spirit is affected by spirit, which is the more worthy agent. It is otherwise in the state of glory: for, then, faith shall cease, and we shall know as we are known.[b]

Let us, therefore, conclude, that sacred theology must be drawn from the word and oracles of God;[c] not from the light of nature, or the dictates of reason. It is written, that " the heavens declare the glory of God:" but we nowhere find it, that the heavens declare the will of God, which is pronounced a law, and a testimony, that men should do according to it, &c. Nor does this hold only in the great mysteries of the Godhead, of the creation, and of the redemption, but belongs, also, to the true interpretation of the moral law. " Love your enemies, do good to them that hate you," &c., " that ye may be the children of your heavenly father, who sends his rain upon the just and the unjust."[d] Which words are more than human,—

" Nec vox hominem sonat."[e]

and go beyond the light of nature. So the heathen poets, especially when they speak pathetically, frequently expostulate with laws and moral doctrines, (though these are far more easy and indulgent than divine laws), as if they had a kind of malignant opposition to the freedom of nature,—

—— " Et quod natura remittit
Invida jura negant."[f]

according to the expression of Dendamis, the Indian, to the messengers of Alexander; viz., " That he had heard, indeed,

[a] Gen. xviii. [b] 1 Cor. xiii. 12. [c] Psal. xviii. 2.
[d] Matt. v. 44, 45. [e] Æneid, i. 332. [f] Ovid, Metam. x 330.

somewhat of Pythagoras, and the other wise men of Greece, and believed them to have been great men; but that they held a certain fantastical thing, which they called law and morality, in too great veneration and esteem."g We cannot doubt, therefore, that a large part of the moral law is too sublime to be attained by the light of nature: though it is still certain, that men, even from the light and law of nature, have some notions of virtue, vice, justice, wrong, good, and evil.

We must observe, that the light of nature has two significations; 1. as it arises from sense, induction, reason, and argument, according to the laws of heaven and earth; and 2. as it shines in the human mind, by internal instinct, according to the law of conscience, which is a certain spark, and, as it were, a relique of our primitive purity. And in this latter sense, chiefly, the soul receives some light, for beholding and discerning the perfection of the moral law; though this light be not perfectly clear, but of such a nature as rather to reprehend vice than give a full information of duty; whence religion, both with regard to mysteries and morality, depends upon divine revelation.

Yet the use of human reason in spiritual things is various, and very extensive: for religion is justly called a reasonable service.h The types and ceremonies of the old law were rational and significative, differing widely from the ceremonies of idolatry and magic: which are a kind of deaf and dumb show, and generally uninstructive even by inuendo. But the Christian faith, as in all things else, excels in this, that it preserves the golden mean in the use of reason, and dispute the child of reason, between the laws of the heathens and of Mahomet, which go into extremes: for the heathen religion had no constant belief or confession, and the Mahometan forbids all disputes in religion:i whence one appears with the face of manifold error, the other as a crafty

---

g Strabo, xv. h St. Paul, Rom. xii. 1.
i This is erroneous. The Mohammedan religion, though not divided into so many churches as the Christian, is, notwithstanding, disturbed by the cry of conflicting parties under the generic titles of Soonees and Sheeahs; the former comprise the orthodox, the latter the heretics. It is needless to add that the hatred of the rival sects is most cordial and intense. *Ed.*

and subtile imposture; whilst the sacred Christian faith both receives and rejects the use of reason and dispute under due limitation.[k]

The use of human reason in matters of religion is of two kinds; the one consisting in the explanation of mysteries, the other in the deductions from them. As to the explanation of mysteries, we find that God himself condescends to the weakness of our capacity, and opens his mysteries, so as they may be best understood by us; inoculating, as it were, his revelations into the notions and comprehensions of our reason, and accommodating his inspirations to the opening of our understanding, as a key is fitted to open the lock. Though, in this respect, we should not be wanting to ourselves: for as God makes use of our reason in his illuminations, so ought we likewise to exercise it every way, in order to become more capable of receiving and imbibing mysteries; provided the mind be enlarged, according to its capacity, to the greatness of the mysteries, and not the mysteries contracted to the narrowness of the mind.

With regard to inferences, we must know that we have a certain secondary and respective, not a primitive and absolute, use of reason and arguing left us about mysteries. For after the articles and principles of religion are so seated, as to be entirely removed from the examination of reason, we are then permitted to draw inferences from them, agreeable to their analogy. But this holds not in natural things, where principles themselves are subject to examination by induction, though not by syllogism, and have, besides, no repugnancy to reason: so that both the first and middle propositions are derivable from the same fountain. It is otherwise in religion, where the first propositions are self-existent, and subsist of themselves, uncontrolled by that reason which deduces the subsequent propositions. Nor is this the case in religion alone, but likewise in other sciences, as well the serious as the light, where the primary propositions are postulated: as things wherein the use of reason cannot be absolute. Thus in chess, or other games of the like nature, the first rules and laws of the play are merely positive postulates, which ought to be entirely received, not

[k] Hooker, Eccles. Polit.

disputed : but the skilful playing of the game is a matter of art and reason. So, in human laws, there are numerous maxims, or mere placits of law received, which depend more upon authority than reason, and come not into dispute. But, then, for the inquiry, what is not absolutely, but relatively most just herein : viz., in conformity with those maxims; this, indeed, is a point of reason, and affords a large field for dispute. Such, therefore, is that secondary reason which has place in sacred theology, and is founded upon the good pleasure of God.

And as the use of human reason, in things divine, is of two kinds, so it is attended with two excesses : 1. the one, when it too curiously inquires into the manner of a mystery; 2. the other, when it attributes an equal authority to the inference as to the principles. For he may seem a disciple of Nicodemus, who shall obstinately enquire, " How can a man be born when he is old ?"[l] But he can be esteemed no disciple of St. Paul, who does not sometimes insert in his doctrine, " I, not the Lord," or, according to my judgment,[m] which is the style that generally suits with inferences. Whence it seems a thing of capital use and benefit, to have a sober and diligent treatise wrote concerning the proper use of human reason in divinity, by way of a divine logic. For this would be like an opiate in medicine; and not only lay asleep those empty speculations which sometimes disturb the schools, but also allay that fury of controversy which raises such tumults in the church. This treatise, therefore, we place among the things that are wanted, under the name of the Moderator, or the true Use of human Reason in Theology.

It is of the utmost importance to the peace of the church, to have the covenant of Christians prescribed by our Saviour in two particulars that seem somewhat contradictory, well and clearly explained; the one whereof runs thus : " He who is not with us is against us;"[n] and the other thus : " He who is not against us is for us;"[o] whence it plainly appears, that there are some points wherein he who differs is to be excluded the covenant ; and others again, wherein Christians may differ, and yet keep terms. The bonds of the Christian

[l] John iii. 4. [m] 1 Cor. vii. 12. [n] Matt. xii. 30, and Luke xi. 23.
[o] Luke ix. 50.

communion are, one faith, one baptism,[p] &c., not one ceremony, one opinion, &c. Our Saviour's coat was seamless;[q] but the garment of the church of many colours. The chaff must be separated from the wheat, but the tares in the field are not to be hastily plucked up from the corn. Moses, when he saw the Egyptian contending with the Israelite, did not say, "Why strive ye?" but drew his sword, and killed the Egyptian; but when he saw two Israelites fighting together, though the cause of one of them might have been unjust, yet he says to them, "Ye are brethren, why strive ye?"[r] All which being well considered, it seems a thing of great use and moment to define what, and of how great latitude those matters are, which totally cut off men from the body of the church, and exclude them the communion of the faithful. And if any one shall imagine this done already, we advise him seriously to reflect, with what justice and moderation. But it is highly probable, that whoever speaks of peace will meet with that answer of Jehu to the messenger: "What has peace to do with Jehu?—What hast thou to do with peace?—Turn, and follow me."[s] For the hearts of most men are not set upon peace, but party. And yet we think proper to place among the things wanting, a discourse upon the degrees of unity in the city of God, as a wholesome and useful undertaking.

The holy Scriptures having so great a share in the constitution of theology, a principal regard must be had to their interpretation. We speak not of the authority of interpreting, established by the consent of the church, but of the manner of interpreting, which is either methodical or loose. For the pure waters of divinity are drawn and employed, nearly in the same manner as the natural waters of springs; viz., 1. either received in cisterns, and thence derived through different pipes, for the more commodious use of men; or 2. immediately poured into vessels for present occasions. The former methodical way has produced the scholastic divinity, whereby the doctrine of theology is collected into an art, as in a cistern; and thence distributed around, by the conveyance of axioms and positions.

But the loose way of interpreting has two excesses: the

[p] St. Paul, Eph. ix. 51.   [q] St. John xix. 23.   [r] Exodus ii. 13.
[s] 4 Kings ix. 19.

one supposes such a perfection in the Scriptures, that all philosophy should be derived from their fountains, as if every other philosophy were a profane and heathenish thing. And this distemper principally reigned in the school of Paracelsus, and some others, though originally derived from the rabbies and cabbalists. But these men fail of their end; for they do not, by this means, honour the Scriptures as they imagine, but rather debase and pollute them. For they who seek a material heaven, and a material earth, in the word of God, absurdly seek for transitory things among eternal. To look for theology in philosophy is looking for the living among the dead, and to look for philosophy in theology is to look for the dead among the living.

The other excess, in the manner of interpretation, appears, at first sight, just and sober; yet greatly dishonours the Scriptures, and greatly injures the church, by explaining the inspired writings in the same manner as human writings are explained. For we must remember, that to God, the author of the Scriptures, those two things lie open which are concealed from men; the secrets of the heart, and the successions of time. Therefore, as the dictates of Scripture are directed to the heart, and include the vicissitudes of all ages, along with an eternal and certain foreknowledge of all heresies, contradictions, and the mutable states of the church, as well in general as in particulars, these Scriptures are not to be interpreted barely according to the obvious sense of the place, or with regard to the occasion upon which the words were spoken, or precisely by the context, or the principal scope of the passage, but upon a knowledge of their containing, not only in gross or collectively, but also distributively, in particular words and clauses, numberless rivulets and veins of doctrine, for watering all the parts of the church and all the minds of the faithful. For it is excellently observed, that the answers of our Saviour are not suited to many of the questions proposed to him, but appear, in a manner, impertinent: and this for two reasons, 1. because, as he knew the thoughts of those who put the question, not from their words as men know them, but immediately, and of himself, he answered to their thoughts, and not to their words; and 2. because he spoke not to those alone who were present, but to us, also, now living, and to the men of every age and place, where the gospel shall be preached. And this observation holds in other parts of Scripture.

We find, among theological writings, too many books of controversy; a vast mass of that we call positive theology, common-places, particular treatises, cases of conscience, sermons, homilies, and numerous prolix comments upon the several books of the Scriptures: but the thing we want and propose, as our third appendix to theology, is, a short, sound, and judicious collection of notes and observations upon particular texts of Scripture; without running into commonplace, pursuing controversies, or reducing these notes to artificial method; but leaving them quite loose and native— a thing we find something done in the more learned kind of sermons, which are seldom of long duration, though it has not hitherto prevailed in books designed for posterity. But certainly, as those wines which flow from the first treading of the grape are sweeter and better than those forced out by the press, which gives them the roughness of the husk and the stone; so are those doctrines best and wholesomest, which flow from a gentle crush of the Scripture, and are not wrung into controversies and common-place. And this treatise we set down as wanting, under the title of the first flowings of the Scriptures.

And now we have finished our small globe of the intellectual world with all the exactness we could, marking out and describing those parts of it which we find either not constantly inhabited or not sufficiently cultivated. And if through the course of the work we should anywhere seem to depart from the opinion of the ancients, we would have it remembered that this is not done for the sake of novelty, or striking into different paths from them, but with a desire of improving; for we could neither act consistently with ourselves nor the design, without resolving to add all we could to the inventions of others, at the same time wishing that our own discoveries may be exceeded by those of posterity. And how fairly we have dealt in this matter may appear from hence, that our opinions are everywhere proposed naked and undefended, without endeavouring to bribe the liberty of others by confutations; for where the things advanced prove just, we hope that if any scruple or objection arise in the first reading, an answer will of itself be made in the second. And wherever we have erred, we are certain to have done no violence to the truth by litigious arguments, the effect whereof is the procuring authority to error, and detracting from what is well invented; for error receives honour and truth a repulse from contention.

And here I cannot but reflect how appositely that answer of Themistocles may be applied to myself which he made to the deputy of a small village haranguing upon great things, "Friend, thy words require a city." For so it may be said of my views, that they require an age, perhaps a whole age, to prove, and numerous ages to execute. But as the greatest things are owing to their beginnings, it will be enough for me to have sown for posterity, and the honour of the Immortal Being, whom I humbly entreat, through his Son, our Saviour, favourably to accept these, and the like sacrifices of the human understanding, seasoned with religion, and offered up to his glory!

THE COAST OF THE NEW INTELLECTUAL WORLD;

OR, A RECAPITULATION OF THE DEFICIENCIES OF KNOWLEDGE, POINTED OUT IN THE PRECEDING WORK, TO BE SUPPLIED BY POSTERITY.

The History of Monsters; or irregular productions of nature, in all the three kingdoms,—vegetable, animal, and mineral.

The History of Arts; or nature formed and wrought by human industry.

A well-purged History of Nature in her extent; or the phenomena of the universe.

Inductive History; or historical matters consequentially deduced from phenomena, facts, observations, experiments, arts, and the active sciences.

An Universal Literary History; or the affairs relating to learning and knowledge, in all ages and countries of the world.

Biography; or the lives of all eminent persons.

The History of Prophecy; or the accomplishment of Di-

BOOK IX.] DEFICIENCIES OF KNOWLEDGE. 377

vine predictions, to serve as a guide in the interpretation of prophecies.

The Philosophy of the Ancient Fables; or a just interpretation of the mythology of the ancients.

Primary Philosophy; or a collection of general axioms, subservient to all the sciences.

Physical Astronomy; or a philosophical history of the heavens.

A Just Astrology; or the real effects of the celestial bodies upon the terrestrial.

A Calendar of Doubts; or natural problems, to be continued through all ages, along with a calendar of vulgar errors.

A Collection of the Opinions of the Ancient Philosophers.

An Inquiry into the Simple Forms of Things; or that which constitutes their essences and differences.

Natural Magic; relative to the doctrine of forms.

An Inventory of Knowledge; or an account of the stock of learning among mankind.

A Calendar of leading Experiments; for the better interpretation of nature.

Short and commodious Methods of Calculation, in business, astronomy, &c.

The Doctrine of Gesture; or the motions of the body, with a view to their interpretation.

Comparative Anatomy betwixt different Human Bodies.

A work upon Incurable Diseases, to lessen their number, and fix a true notion of incurable in medicine.

The Laudable Means of procuring easy Deaths.

A Set of approved and effectual Remedies for Diseases.

The Ways of Imitating Natural Springs and Bath Waters.

The Filum Medicinale; or Physician's Clue in Prescription.

A Natural Philosophy fundamental to Physic.

The Ways of Prolonging Life.

An Inquiry into the Nature and Substance of the sensitive Soul.

The Doctrine of Muscular Motion; or the efficacy of the spirits in moving the body.

The Doctrine of Sense and Sensibility; or the difference betwixt perception and sense.

An Inquiry into the Origin and Form of Light; or the foundation of optics.

The Art of Inventing Arts.

The True Use of Induction in Philosophy.

The Art of Indication or Direction in Philosophy.

A Learned or Sagacious Kind of Experience, different from the vulgar, and leading to the direct improvement of arts.

A Particular Topical Invention, directed by the light of leading questions, or proper heads of inquiry.

The Doctrine of Idols; or a detection and confutation of the prejudices, false conceptions, and errors of the mind.

A New Engine; or helps for the mind corresponding to those of the hand.

An Appendix to the Art of Judgment; assigning the kinds of demonstration proper to every subject.

An Interpretation of the Marks, Signatures, or Impressions of things.

A Philosophical Grammar; or an account of the various properties of different languages, in order to form one perfect pattern of speech.

The Traditive Lamp; or the proper method of delivering down the sciences to posterity.

The Doctrine of Prudence in private discourse; or colours of good and ill.

A Collection of Sophisms, with their confutations.

A Collection of studied Antithets; or short and strong sentences, on both sides of the question, in a variety of subjects.

A Collection of lesser Forms of Speech, for all the occasions of writing and speaking.

Sober Satire; or the insides of things.

The Georgics of the Mind; or the means of procuring the true moral habit of virtue.

An Account of the Characters or Natures of Persons.

The Doctrine of the Affections, Passions, or Perturbations of the Mind.

The Secretary to the Uses of Life; or the doctrine of various occasions.

The Doctrine of Business; or books upon all kinds of civil employments, arts, trades, &c.

Self-Policy, the doctrine of rising in life; or the means of advancing a man's private fortune.

The Military Statesman; or the political doctrine of enlarging the bounds of empire.

The Doctrine of Universal Justice; or the fountains of equity.

The Moderator in Divinity; or the true use of human reason in the business of revelation.

The Degrees of Unity in Religion adjusted, with a view to preserve the peace of the Church.

The First Flowings of the Scripture; or a set of short, sound, and judicious notes upon particular texts, tending to use and practice.

NOVUM ORGANUM; see p. 188

OR,

TRUE SUGGESTIONS FOR THE INTERPRETATION OF NATURE

PREFACE.

THEY who have presumed to dogmatize on nature, as on some well investigated subject, either from self-conceit or arrogance, and in the professorial style, have inflicted the greatest injury on philosophy and learning. For they have tended to stifle and interrupt inquiry exactly in proportion as they have prevailed in bringing others to their opinion: and their own activity has not counterbalanced the mischief they have occasioned by corrupting and destroying that of others. They again who have entered upon a contrary course, and asserted that nothing whatever can be known, whether they have fallen into this opinion from their hatred of the ancient sophists, or from the hesitation of their minds, or from an exuberance of learning, have certainly adduced reasons for it which are by no means contemptible. They have not, however, derived their opinion from true sources, and, hurried on by their zeal and some affectation, have certainly exceeded due moderation. But the more ancient Greeks (whose writings have perished), held a more prudent mean, between the arrogance of dogmatism, and the despair of scepticism; and though too frequently intermingling complaints and indignation at the difficulty of inquiry, and the obscurity of things, and champing, as it were, the bit, have still persisted in pressing their point, and pursuing their intercourse with nature; thinking, as it seems, that the better method was not to dispute upon the very point of the possibility of anything being known, but to put it to the test of experience. Yet they themselves, by only employing the power of the understanding, have not adopted a fixed rule, but have laid their whole stress upon intense meditation, and a continual exercise and perpetual agitation of the mind.

Our method, though difficult in its operation, is easily explained. It consists in determining the degrees of certainty, whilst we, as it were, restore the senses to their former rank, but generally reject that operation of the mind which follows close upon the senses, and open and establish a new and certain course for the mind from the first actual perceptions of the senses themselves. This, no doubt, was the view taken by those who have assigned so much to logic; showing clearly thereby that they sought some support for the mind, and suspected its natural and spontaneous mode of action. But this is now employed too late as a remedy, when all is clearly lost, and after the mind, by the daily habit and intercourse of life, has come prepossessed with corrupted doctrines, and filled with the vainest idols. The art of logic therefore being (as we have mentioned), too late a precaution,[a] and in no way remedying the matter, has tended more to confirm errors, than to disclose truth. Our only remaining hope and salvation is to begin the whole labour of the mind again ; not leaving it to itself, but directing it perpetually from the very first, and attaining our end as it were by mechanical aid. If men, for instance, had attempted mechanical labours with their hands alone, and without the power and aid of instruments, as they have not hesitated to carry on the labours of their understanding with the unaided efforts of their mind, they would have been able to move and overcome but little, though they had exerted their utmost and united powers. And just to pause awhile on this comparison, and look into it as a mirror ; let us ask, if any obelisk of a remarkable size were perchance required to be moved, for the purpose of gracing a triumph or any similar pageant, and men were to attempt it with their bare hands, would not any sober spectator avow it to be an act of the greatest madness ? And if they should increase the number of workmen, and imagine that they could thus succeed, would he not think so still more ? But if they chose to make a selection, and to remove the weak, and only employ the strong and vigorous, thinking by this means, at any rate, to achieve their object, would he not say that they were more fondly deranged ? Nay, if not content with this, they were to determine on consulting the athletic art, and were to give orders for all to appear with their hands, arms, and muscles regularly oiled and prepared, would he not exclaim that they were taking pains to rave by method and design ? Yet men are hurried on with the same senseless energy and useless combination in intellectual matters, as long as they expect great results either from the number and agreement, or the excellence and acuteness of their wits ; or even strengthen their minds with logic, which may be considered as an athletic preparation, but yet do not desist (if we rightly consider the matter) from applying their own understandings merely with all this zeal and effort. Whilst nothing is more clear, than that in every great work executed by the hand of man without machines or implements, it is impossible for the strength of individuals to be increased, or for that of the multitude to combine.

Having premised so much, we lay down two points on which we would admonish mankind, lest they should fail to see or to observe them. The first of these is, that it is our good fortune (as we consider it), for the sake of extinguishing and removing contradiction and irritation of mind, to leave the honour and reverence due to the ancients untouched and undiminished, so that we can perform our intended work, and yet enjoy the benefit of our respectful moderation. For if we should profess to offer something better than the ancients, and yet should pursue

---

[a] Because it was idle to draw a logical conclusion from false principles, error being propagated as much by false premises, which logic does not pretend to examine, as by illegitimate inference. Hence, as Bacon says farther on, men being easily led to confound legitimate inference with truth, were confirmed in their errors by the very subtilty of their genius. *Ed.*

the same course as they have done, we could never, by any artifice, contrive to avoid the imputation of having engaged in a contest or rivalry as to our respective wits, excellencies, or talents; which, though neither inadmissible or new (for why should we not blame and point out anything that is imperfectly discovered or laid down by them, of our own right, a right common to all), yet however just and allowable, would perhaps be scarcely an equal match, on account of the disproportion of our strength. But since our present plan leads up to open an entirely different course to the understanding, and one unattempted and unknown to them, the case is altered. There is an end to party zeal, and we only take upon ourselves the character of a guide, which requires a moderate share of authority and good fortune, rather than talents and excellence. The first admonition relates to persons, the next to things.

We make no attempt to disturb the system of philosophy that now prevails, or any other which may or will exist, either more correct or more complete. For we deny not that the received system of philosophy, and others of a similar nature, encourage discussion, embellish harangues, are employed, and are of service in the duties of the professor, and the affairs of civil life. Nay, we openly express and declare that the philosophy we offer will not be very useful in such respects. It is not obvious, nor to be understood in a cursory view, nor does it flatter the mind in its preconceived notions, nor will it descend to the level of the generality of mankind unless by its advantages and effects.

Let there exist then (and may it be of advantage to both), two sources, and two distributions of learning, and in like manner two tribes, and as it were kindred families of contemplators or philosophers, without any hostility or alienation between them; but rather allied and united by mutual assistance. Let there be in short one method of cultivating the sciences, and another of discovering them. And as for those who prefer and more readily receive the former, on account of their haste or from motives arising from their ordinary life, or because they are unable from weakness of mind to comprehend and embrace the other (which must necessarily be the case with by far the greater number), let us wish that they may prosper as they desire in their undertaking, and attain what they pursue. But if any individual desire, and is anxious not merely to adhere to, and make use of present discoveries, but to penetrate still further, and not to overcome his adversaries in disputes, but nature by labour, not in short to give elegant and specious opinions, but to know to a certainty and demonstration, let him, as a true son of science (if such be his wish), join with us; that when he has left the antichambers of nature trodden by the multitude, an entrance may at last be discovered to her inner apartments. And in order to be better understood, and to render our meaning more familiar by assigning determinate names, we have accustomed ourselves to call the one method the anticipation of the mind, and the other the interpretation of nature.

We have still one request left. We have at least reflected and taken pains in order to render our propositions not only true, but of easy and familiar access to men's minds, however wonderfully prepossessed and limited. Yet it is but just that we should obtain this favour from mankind (especially in so great a restoration of learning and the sciences), that whosoever may be desirous of forming any determination upon an opinion of this our work either from his own perceptions, or the crowd of authorities, or the forms of demonstrations, he will not expect to be able to do so in a cursory manner, and whilst attending to other matters; but in order to have a thorough knowledge of the subject, will himself by degrees attempt the course which we describe and maintain; will be accustomed to the subtilty of things which is manifested by experience; and will correct the depraved and deeply rooted habits of his mind by a seasonable, and, as it were, just hesitation: and then, finally (if he will), use his judgment when he has begun to be master of himself.

APHORISMS.—BOOK I.

On the Interpretation of Nature and the Empire of Man.

I. MAN, as the minister and interpreter of nature, does and understands as much as his observations on the order of nature, either with regard to things or the mind, permit him, and neither knows nor is capable of more.

II. The unassisted hand and the understanding left to itself possess but little power. Effects are produced by the means of instruments and helps, which the understanding requires no less than the hand; and as instruments either promote or regulate the motion of the hand, so those that are applied to the mind prompt or protect the understanding.

III. Knowledge and human power are synonymous, since the ignorance of the cause frustrates the effect; for nature is only subdued by submission, and that which in contemplative philosophy corresponds with the cause in practical science becomes the rule.

IV. Man whilst operating can only apply or withdraw natural bodies, nature internally performs the rest.

V. Those who become practically versed in nature are, the mechanic, the mathematician, the physician, the alchemist, and the *magician*,[*] but all (as matters now stand) with faint efforts and meagre success.

[*] Bacon uses the term in its ancient sense, and means one who, knowing the occult properties of bodies, is able to startle the ignorant by drawing out of them wonderful and unforeseen changes. See the 85th aphorism of this book, and the 5th cap. book iii. of the De Augmentis Scientiarum, where he speaks more clearly.

VI. It would be madness and inconsistency to suppose that things which have never yet been performed can be performed without employing some hitherto untried means.

VII. The creations of the mind and hand appear very numerous, if we judge by books and manufactures; but all that variety consists of an excessive refinement, and of deductions from a few well known matters,—*not of a number of axioms*.[b]

VIII. Even the effects already discovered are due to chance and experiment rather than to the sciences; for our present sciences are nothing more than peculiar arrangements of matters already discovered, and not methods for discovery or plans for new operations.

IX. The sole cause and root of almost every defect in the sciences is this, that while we falsely admire and extol the powers of the human mind, we do not search for its real helps.

X. The subtilty of nature is far beyond that of sense or of the understanding; so that the specious meditations, speculations, and theories of mankind are but a kind of insanity, only there is no one to stand by and observe it.

XI. As the present sciences are useless for the discovery of effects, so the present system of logic[c] is useless for the discovery of the sciences.

---

[b] By this term axiomata, Bacon here speaks of general principles, or universal laws. In the 19th aphorism he employs the term to express any proposition collected from facts by induction, and thus fitted to become the starting-point of deductive reasoning. In the last and more rigorous sense of the term, Bacon held they arose from experience. See Whewell's " Philosophy of the Inductive Sciences," vol. i. p. 74; and Mill's "Logic," vol. i. p. 311; and the June "Quarterly," 1841, for the modern phase of the discussion. *Ed.*

[c] Bacon here attributes to the Aristotelian logic the erroneous consequences which sprung out of its abuse. The demonstrative forms it exhibits, whether verbally or mathematically expressed, are necessary to the support, verification, and extension of induction, and when the propositions they embrace are founded on an accurate and close observation of facts, the conclusions to which they lead, even in moral science, may be regarded as certain as the facts wrested out of nature by direct experiment. In physics such forms are absolutely required to generalize the results of experience, and to connect intermediate axioms with laws still more general, as is sufficiently attested by the fact, that no science since Bacon's day has ceased to be experimental by the mere method of induction, and that all become exact only so far as they rise above experience, and connect their isolated phenomena with general laws by the principles of deductive reasoning. So far, then, are these forms from being useless, that they are absolutely essential to the advancement of the sciences, and in no case can be looked on as detrimental, except when obtruded in the place of direct experiment, or employed as a means of deducing conclusions about nature from imaginary hypo-

XII. The present system of logic rather assists in confirming and rendering inveterate the errors founded on vulgar notions than in searching after truth, and is therefore more hurtful than useful.

XIII. The syllogism is not applied to the principles of the sciences, and is of no avail in intermediate axioms,[c] as being very

theses and abstract conceptions. This had been unfortunately the practice of the Greeks. From the rapid development geometry received in their hands, they imagined the same method would lead to results equally brilliant in natural science, and snatching up some abstract principle, which they carefully removed from the test of experiment, imagined they could reason out from it all the laws and external appearances of the universe. The scholastics were impelled along the same path, not only by precedent, but by profession. Theology was the only science which received from them a consistent development, and the *à priori* grounds on which it rested prevented them from employing any other method in the pursuit of natural phenomena. Thus, forms of demonstration, in themselves accurate, and of momentous value in their proper sphere, became confounded with fable, and led men into the idea they were exploring truth when they were only accurately deducing error from error. One principle ever so slightly deflected, like a false quantity in an equation, could be sufficient to infect the whole series of conclusions of which it was the base; and though the philosopher might subsequently deduce a thousand consecutive inferences with the utmost accuracy or precision, he would only succeed in drawing out very methodically nine hundred and ninety-nine errors. *Ed.*

[c] It would appear from this and the two preceding aphorisms, that Bacon fell into the error of denying the utility of the syllogism in the very part of inductive science where it is essentially required; Logic, like mathematics, is purely a formal process, and must, as the scaffolding to the building, be employed to arrange facts in the structure of a science, and not to form any portion of its ground-work, or to supply the materials of which the system is to be composed. The word syllogism, like most other pyschological terms, has no fixed or original signification, but is sometimes employed, as it was by the Greeks, to denote general reasoning, and at others to point out the formal method of deducing a particular inference from two or more general propositions. Bacon does not confine the term within the boundaries of express definition, but leaves us to infer that he took it in the latter sense, from his custom of associating the term with the wranglings of the schools. The scholastics, it is true, abused the deductive syllogism, by employing it in its naked, skeleton-like form, and confounding it with the whole breadth of logical theory; but their errors are not to be visited on Aristotle, who never dreamt of playing with formal syllogisms, and, least of all, mistook the descending for the ascending series of inference. In our mind we are of accord with the Stagyrite, who propounds, as far as we can interpret him, two modes of investigating truth,—the one by which we ascend from particular and singular facts to general laws and axioms, and the other by which we descend

unequal to the subtilty of nature. It forces assent, therefore, and not things.

XIV. The syllogism consists of propositions, propositions of words, words are the signs of notions. If, therefore, the notions (which form the basis of the whole) be confused and carelessly abstracted from things, there is no solidity in the superstructure. Our only hope, then, is in genuine induction.

XV. We have no sound notions either in logic or physics; substance, quality, action, passion, and existence are not clear notions; much less weight, levity, density, tenuity, moisture, dryness, generation, corruption, attraction, repulsion, element, matter, form, and the like. They are all fantastical and ill-defined.

XVI. The notions of less abstract natures, as man, dog, dove, and the immediate perceptions of sense, as heat, cold, white, black, do not deceive us materially, yet even these are sometimes confused by the mutability of matter and the intermixture of things. All the rest which men have hitherto employed are errors, and improperly abstracted and deduced from things.

XVII. There is the same degree of licentiousness and error in forming axioms as in abstracting notions, and that in the first principles, which depend on common induction; still more is this the case in axioms and inferior propositions derived from syllogisms.

XVIII. The present discoveries in science are such as lie immediately beneath the surface of common notions. It is necessary, however, to penetrate the more secret and remote parts of nature, in order to abstract both notions and axioms from things by a more certain and guarded method.

XIX. There are and can exist but two ways of investigating and discovering truth. The one hurries on rapidly from the senses and particulars to the most general axioms, and from them, as principles and their supposed indisputable truth, derives and discovers the intermediate axioms. This is the way now in use. The other constructs its axioms from the senses and particulars, by ascending continually and gradually, till it finally arrives at the most general axioms, which is the true but unattempted way.

XX. The understanding when left to itself proceeds by the from universal propositions to the individual cases which they virtually include. Logic, therefore, must equally vindicate the formal purity of the synthetic illation by which it ascends to the whole, as the analytic process by which it descends to the arts. The deductive and inductive syllogism are of equal significance in building up any body of truth, and whoever restricts logic to either process, mistakes one half of its province for the whole ; and if he acts upon his error, will paralyse his methods, and strike the noblest part of science with sterility. *Ed.*

same way as that which it would have adopted under the guidance of logic, namely, the first; for the mind is fond of starting off to generalities, that it may avoid labour, and after dwelling a little on a subject is fatigued by experiment. But those evils are augmented by logic, for the sake of the ostentation of dispute.

XXI. The understanding, when left to itself in a man of a steady, patient, and reflecting disposition (especially when unimpeded by received doctrines), makes some attempt in the right way, but with little effect, since the understanding, undirected and unassisted, is unequal to and unfit for the task of vanquishing the obscurity of things.

XXII. Each of these two ways begins from the senses and particulars, and ends in the greatest generalities. But they are immeasurably different; for the one merely touches cursorily the limits of experiment and particulars, whilst the other runs duly and regularly through them,—the one from the very outset lays down some abstract and useless generalities, the other gradually rises to those principles which are really the most common in nature.[d]

XXIII. There is no small difference between the idols of the human mind and the ideas of the Divine mind,—that is to say, between certain idle dogmas and the real stamp and impression of created objects, as they are found in nature.

XXIV. Axioms determined upon in argument can never assist in the discovery of new effects; for the subtilty of nature is vastly superior to that of argument. But axioms properly and regularly abstracted from particulars easily point out and define new particulars, and therefore impart activity to the sciences.

XXV. The axioms now in use are derived from a scanty handful, as it were, of experience, and a few particulars of frequent occurrence, whence they are of much the same dimensions or extent as their origin. And if any neglected or unknown instance occurs, the axiom is saved by some frivolous distinction, when it would be more consistent with truth to amend it.

XXVI. We are wont, for the sake of distinction, to call that human reasoning which we apply to nature the anticipation of nature (as being rash and premature), and that which is properly deduced from things the interpretation of nature.

XXVII. Anticipations are sufficiently powerful in producing

[d] The Latin is, *ad ea quæ revera sunt naturæ notiora*. This expression, *naturæ notiora, naturæ notior*, is so frequently employed by Bacon, that we may conclude it to point to some distinguishing feature in the Baconian physics. It properly refers to the most evident principles and laws of nature, and springs from that system which regards the material universe as endowed with intelligence, and acting according to rules either fashioned or clearly understood by itself. *Ed.*

unanimity, for if men were all to become even uniformly mad, they might agree tolerably well with each other.

XXVIII. Anticipations, again, will be assented to much more readily than interpretations, because being deduced from a few instances, and these principally of familiar occurrence, they immediately hit the understanding and satisfy the imagination; whilst on the contrary interpretations, being deduced from various subjects, and these widely dispersed, cannot suddenly strike the understanding, so that in common estimation they must appear difficult and discordant, and almost like the mysteries of faith.

XXIX. In sciences founded on opinions and dogmas, it is right to make use of anticipations and logic if you wish to force assent rather than things.

XXX. If all the capacities of all ages should unite and combine and transmit their labours, no great progress will be made in learning by anticipations, because the radical errors, and those which occur in the first process of the mind, are not cured by the excellence of subsequent means and remedies.

XXXI. It is in vain to expect any great progress in the sciences by the superinducing or engrafting new matters upon old. An instauration must be made from the very foundations, if we do not wish to revolve for ever in a circle, making only some slight and contemptible progress.

XXXII. The ancient authors and all others are left in undisputed possession of their honours; for we enter into no comparison of capacity or talent, but of method, and assume the part of a guide rather than of a critic.

XXXIII. To speak plainly, no correct judgment can be formed either of our method or its discoveries by those anticipations which are now in common use; for it is not to be required of us to submit ourselves to the judgment of the very method we ourselves arraign.

XXXIV. Nor is it an easy matter to deliver and explain our sentiments; for those things which are in themselves new can yet be only understood from some analogy to what is old.

XXXV. Alexander Borgia* said of the expedition of the French into Italy that they came with chalk in their hands to mark up their lodgings, and not with weapons to force their passage. Even so do we wish our philosophy to make its way quietly into those minds that are fit for it, and of good capacity; for we have no need of contention where we differ in first prin-

* This Borgia was Alexander VI., and the expedition alluded to that in which Charles VIII. overran the Italian peninsula in five months. Bacon uses the same illustration in concluding his survey of natural philosophy, in the second book of the "De Augmentis." *Ed.*

ciples, and in our very notions, and even in our forms of demonstration.

XXXVI. We have but one simple method of delivering our sentiments, namely, we must bring men to particulars and their regular series and order, and they must for a while renounce their notions, and begin to form an acquaintance with things.

XXXVII. Our method and that of the sceptics[f] agree in some respects at first setting out, but differ most widely, and are completely opposed to each other in their conclusion; for they roundly assert that nothing can be known; we, that but a small part of nature can be known, by the present method; their next step, however, is to destroy the authority of the senses and understanding, whilst we invent and supply them with assistance.

XXXVIII. The idols and false notions which have already preoccupied the human understanding, and are deeply rooted in it, not only so beset men's minds that they become difficult of access, but even when access is obtained will again meet and trouble us in the instauration of the sciences, unless mankind when forewarned guard themselves with all possible care against them.

XXXIX. Four species of idols beset the human mind,[g] to which (for distinction's sake) we have assigned names, calling the first Idols of the Tribe, the second Idols of the Den, the third Idols of the Market, the fourth Idols of the Theatre.

XL. The formation of notions and axioms on the foundation of true induction is the only fitting remedy by which we can ward off and expel these idols. It is, however, of great service to point them out; for the doctrine of idols bears the same relation to the interpretation of nature as that of the confutation of sophisms does to common logic.[h]

[f] *Ratio eorum qui acatalepsiam tenuerunt.* Bacon alludes to the members of the later academy, who held the ἀκατάληψια, or the impossibility of comprehending anything. His translator, however, makes him refer to the Sceptics, who neither dogmatised about the known or the unknown, but simply held, that as all knowledge was relative, πρὸς πάντα τι, man could never arrive at absolute truth, and therefore could not with certainty affirm or deny anything. *Ed.*

[g] It is argued by Hallam, with some appearance of truth, that idols is not the correct translation of εἴδωλα, from which the original idola is manifestly derived; but that Bacon used it in the literal sense attached to it by the Greeks, as a species of illusion, or false appearance, and not as a species of divinity before which the mind bows down. If Hallam be right, Bacon is saved from the odium of an analogy which his foreign commentators are not far wrong in denouncing as barbarous; but this service is rendered at the expense of the men who have attached an opposite meaning to the word, among whom are Brown, Playfair, and Dugald Stewart. *Ed.*

[h] We cannot see how these idols have less to do with sophistical

XLI. The idols of the tribe are inherent in human nature and the very tribe or race of man; for man's sense is falsely asserted to be the standard of things; on the contrary, all the perceptions both of the senses and the mind bear reference to man and not to the universe, and the human mind resembles those uneven mirrors which impart their own properties to different objects, from which rays are emitted and distort and disfigure them.[1]

XLII. The idols of the den are those of each individual; for everybody (in addition to the errors common to the race of man) has his own individual den or cavern, which intercepts and corrupts the light of nature, either from his own peculiar and singular disposition, or from his education and intercourse with others, or from his reading, and the authority acquired by those whom he reverences and admires, or from the different impressions produced on the mind, as it happens to be preoccupied and predisposed, or equable and tranquil, and the like; so that the spirit of man (according to its several dispositions), is variable, confused, and as it were actuated by chance; and Heraclitus said well that men search for knowledge in lesser worlds, and not in the greater or common world.

XLIII. There are also idols formed by the reciprocal intercourse and society of man with man, which we call idols of the market, from the commerce and association of men with each other; for men converse by means of language, but words are formed at the will of the generality, and there arises from a bad and unapt formation of words a wonderful obstruction to the mind. Nor can the definitions and explanations with which learned men are wont to guard and protect themselves in some instances afford a complete remedy,—words still manifestly force

paralogisms than with natural philosophy. The process of scientific induction involves only the first elements of reasoning, and presents such a clear and tangible surface, as to allow no lurking-place for prejudice; while questions of politics and morals, to which the deductive method, or common logic, as Bacon calls it, is peculiarly applicable, are ever liable to be swayed or perverted by the prejudices he enumerates. After mathematics, physical science is the least amenable to the illusions of feeling; each portion having been already tested by experiment and observation, is fitted into its place in the system, with all the rigour of the geometrical method; affection or prejudice cannot, as in matters of taste, history, or religion, select fragmentary pieces, and form a system of their own. The whole must be admitted, or the structure of authoritative reason razed to the ground. It is needless to say that the idols enumerated present only another interpretation of the substance of logical fallacies. *Ed.*

[1] The propensity to this illusion may be viewed in the spirit of system, or hasty generalization, which is still one of the chief obstacles in the path of modern science. *Ed.*

the understanding, throw everything into confusion, and lead mankind into vain and innumerable controversies and fallacies.

XLIV. Lastly, there are idols which have crept into men's minds from the various dogmas of peculiar systems of philosophy, and also from the perverted rules of demonstration, and these we denominate idols of the theatre: for we regard all the systems of philosophy hitherto received or imagined, as so many plays brought out and performed, creating fictitious and theatrical worlds. Nor do we speak only of the present systems, or of the philosophy and sects of the ancients, since numerous other plays of a similar nature can be still composed and made to agree with each other, the causes of the most opposite errors being generally the same. Nor, again, do we allude merely to general systems, but also to many elements and axioms of sciences which have become inveterate by tradition, implicit credence, and neglect. We must, however, discuss each species of idols more fully and distinctly in order to guard the human understanding against them.

XLV. The human understanding, from its peculiar nature, easily supposes a greater degree of order and equality in things than it really finds; and although many things in nature be *sui generis* and most irregular, will yet invent parallels and conjugates and relatives, where no such thing is. Hence the fiction, that all celestial bodies move in perfect circles, thus rejecting entirely spiral and serpentine lines (except as explanatory terms).[k] Hence also the element of fire is introduced with its peculiar orbit,[l] to keep square with those other three which are

[k] Though Kepler had, when Bacon wrote this, already demonstrated his three great laws concerning the elliptical path of the planets, neither Bacon nor Descartes seem to have known or assented to his discoveries. Our author deemed the startling astronomical announcements of his time to be mere theoretic solutions of the phenomena of the heavens, not so perfect as those advanced by antiquity, but still deserving a praise for the ingenuity displayed in their contrivance. Bacon believed a hundred such systems might exist, and though true in their explanation of phenomena, yet might all more or less differ, according to the preconceived notions which their framers brought to the survey of the heavens. He even thought he might put in his claim to the notice of posterity for his astronomical ingenuity, and, as Ptolemy had laboured by means of epicycles and eccentrics, and Kepler with ellipses, to explain the laws of planetary motion, Bacon thought the mystery would unfold itself quite as philosophically through spiral labyrinths and serpentine lines. What the details of his system were, we are left to conjecture, and that from a very meagre but naïve account of one of his inventions which he has left in his Miscellany MSS. *Ed.*

[l] *Hinc elementum ignis cum orbe suo introductum est.* Bacon saw in fire the mere result of a certain combination of action, and was consequently led to deny its elementary character. The ancient physi-

objects of our senses. The relative rarity of the elements (as they are called) is arbitrarily made to vary in tenfold progression, with many other dreams of the like nature.[m] Nor is this folly confined to theories, but it is to be met with even in simple notions.

XLVI. The human understanding, when any proposition has been once laid down (either from general admission and belief, or from the pleasure it affords), forces everything else to add fresh support and confirmation; and although most cogent and abundant instances may exist to the contrary, yet either does not observe or despises them, or gets rid of and rejects them by some distinction, with violent and injurious prejudice, rather than sacrifice the authority of its first conclusions. It was well answered by him[n] who was shown in a temple the votive tablets suspended by such as had escaped the peril of shipwreck, and was pressed as to whether he would then recognise the power of the gods, by an inquiry, But where are the portraits of those who have perished in spite of their vows? All superstition is much the same, whether it be that of astrology, dreams, omens, retributive judgment, or the like, in all of which the deluded believers observe events which are fulfilled, but neglect and pass over their failure, though it be much more common. But this evil insinuates itself still more craftily in philosophy and the sciences, in which a settled maxim vitiates and governs every other circumstance, though the latter be much more worthy of confidence. Besides, even in the absence of that eagerness and want of thought (which we have mentioned), it is the peculiar and perpetual error of the human understanding to be more moved and excited by affirmatives than negatives, whereas it ought duly and regularly to be impartial; nay, in establishing any true axiom the negative instance is the most powerful.

XLVII. The human understanding is most excited by that which strikes and enters the mind at once and suddenly, and by which the imagination is immediately filled and inflated. It then begins almost imperceptibly to conceive and suppose that everything is similar to the few objects which have taken posses-

cists attributed an orbit to each of the four elements, into which they resolved the universe, and supposed their spheres to involve each other. The orbit of the earth was in the centre, that of fire at the circumference. For Bacon's inquisition into the nature of heat, and its complete failure, see the commencement of the second book of the Novum Organum. *Ed.*

[m] Robert Fludd is the theorist alluded to, who had supposed the gravity of the earth to be ten times heavier than water, that of water ten times heavier than air, and that of air ten times heavier than fire. *Ed.*

[n] Diagoras. The same allusion occurs in the second part of the Advancement of Learning, where Bacon treats of the idols of the mind.

sion of the mind, whilst it is very slow and unfit for the transition to the remote and heterogeneous instances by which axioms are tried as by fire, unless the office be imposed upon it by severe regulations and a powerful authority.

XLVIII. The human understanding is active and cannot halt or rest, but even, though without effect, still presses forward. Thus we cannot conceive of any end or external boundary of the world, and it seems necessarily to occur to us that there must be something beyond. Nor can we imagine how eternity has flowed on down to the present day, since the usually received distinction of an infinity, a parte ante and a parte post° cannot hold good; for it would thence follow that one infinity is greater than another, and also that infinity is wasting away and tending to an end. There is the same difficulty in considering the infinite divisibility of lines arising from the weakness of our minds, which weakness interferes to still greater disadvantage with the discovery of causes; for although the greatest generalities in nature must be positive, just as they are found, and in fact not causable, yet the human understanding, incapable of resting, seeks for something more intelligible. Thus, however, whilst aiming at further progress, it falls back to what is actually less advanced, namely, final causes; for they are clearly more allied to man's own nature, than the system of the universe, and from this source they have wonderfully corrupted philosophy. But he would be an unskilful and shallow philosopher who should seek for causes in the greatest generalities, and not be anxious to discover them in subordinate objects.

XLIX. The human understanding resembles not a dry light, but admits a tincture of the will[p] and passions, which generate

---

[o] A scholastic term, to signify the two eternities of past and future duration, that stretch out on both sides of the narrow isthmus (time) occupied by man. It must be remembered that Bacon lived before the doctrine of limits gave rise to the higher calculus, and therefore could have no conception of different denominations of infinities: on the other hand he would have thought the man insane who should have talked to him about lines infinitely great, inclosing angles infinitely little; that a right line, which is a right line so long as it is finite, by changing infinitely little its direction, becomes an infinite curve, and that a curve may become infinitely less than another curve; that there are infinite squares, and infinite cubes, and infinites of infinites, all greater than one another, and the last but one of which is nothing in comparison with the last. Yet half a century sufficed from Bacon's time, to make this nomenclature, which would have appeared to him the excess of frenzy, not only reasonable but necessary, to grasp the higher demonstrations of physical science. *Ed.*

[p] Spinoza, in his letter to Oldenburg (Op. Posth. p. 398), considers this aphorism based on a wrong conception of the origin of error, and, believing it to be fundamental, was led to reject Bacon's method altogether.

their own system accordingly; for man always believes more readily that which he prefers. He, therefore, rejects difficulties for want of patience in investigation; sobriety, because it limits his hope; the depths of nature, from superstition; the light of experiment, from arrogance and pride, lest his mind should appear to be occupied with common and varying objects; paradoxes, from a fear of the opinion of the vulgar; in short, his feelings imbue and corrupt his understanding in innumerable and sometimes imperceptible ways.

L. But by far the greatest impediment and aberration of the human understanding proceeds from the dulness, incompetency, and errors of the senses; since whatever strikes the senses preponderates over everything, however superior, which does not immediately strike them. Hence contemplation mostly ceases with sight, and a very scanty, or perhaps no regard is paid to invisible objects. The entire operation, therefore, of spirits enclosed in tangible bodies[q] is concealed, and escapes us. All that more delicate change of formation in the parts of coarser substances (vulgarly called alteration, but in fact a change of position in the smallest particles) is equally unknown; and yet, unless the two matters we have mentioned be explored and brought to light, no great effect can be produced in nature. Again, the very nature of common air, and all bodies of less density (of which there are many) is almost unknown; for the senses are weak and erring, nor can instruments be of great use in extending their sphere or acuteness,—all the better interpretations of nature are worked out by instances, and fit and apt experiments, where the senses only judge of the experiment, the experiment of nature and the thing itself.

LI. The human understanding is, by its own nature, prone to abstraction, and supposes that which is fluctuating to be fixed. But it is better to dissect than abstract nature; such was the method employed by the school of Democritus,[r] which made

Spinoza refused to acknowledge in man any such thing as a will, and resolved all his volitions into particular acts, which he considered to be as fatally determined by a chain of physical causes as any effects in nature. *Ed.*

[q] *Operatio spirituum in corporibus tangibilibus.* Bacon distinguished with the schools the gross and tangible parts of bodies, from such as were volatile and untangible. These, in conformity with the scholastic language, he terms spirits, and frequently returns to their operations in the 2nd book. See vii. 4th para. b. 2. *Ed.*

[r] Democritus, of Abdera, a disciple of Leucippus, born B.C. 470, died 360; all his works are destroyed. He is said to be the author of the doctrine of atoms: he denied the immortality of the soul, and first taught that the milky way was occasioned by a confused light from a multitude of stars. He may be considered as the parent of experi-

greater progress in penetrating nature than the rest. It is best to consider matter, its conformation, and the changes of that conformation, its own action,* and the law of this action or motion; for forms are a mere fiction of the human mind, unless you will call the laws of action by that name.†

LII. Such are the idols of the tribe, which arise either from the uniformity of the constitution of man's spirit, or its prejudices, or its limited faculties or restless agitation, or from the interference of the passions. or the incompetency of the senses, or the mode of their impressions.

LIII. The idols of the den derive their origin from the peculiar nature of each individual's mind and body, and also from education, habit, and accident; and although they be various and manifold, yet we will treat of some that require the greatest caution, and exert the greatest power in polluting the understanding.

LIV. Some men become attached to particular sciences and contemplations, either from supposing themselves the authors and inventors of them, or from having bestowed the greatest pains upon such subjects, and thus become most habituated to them.‡ If men of this description apply themselves to philosophy and contemplations of an universal nature, they wrest and corrupt them by their preconceived fancies, of which Aristotle

mental philosophy, in the prosecution of which he was so ardent as to declare that he would prefer the discovery of one of the causes of natural phenomena, to the possession of the diadem of Persia. Democritus imposed on the blind credulity of his contemporaries, and, like Roger Bacon, astonished them by his inventions. *Ed.*

* The Latin is *actus purus*, another scholastic expression to denote the action of the substance, which composes the essence of the body apart from its accidental qualities. For an exposition of the various kind of motions he contemplates, the reader may refer to the 48th aphorism of the 2nd book. *Ed.*

† The scholastics after Aristotle distinguished in a subject three modes of beings: viz., the power or faculty, the act, and the habitude, or in other words that which is able to exist, what exists actually, and what continues to exist. Bacon means that is necessary to fix our attention not on that which can or ought to be, but on that which actually is; not on the right, but on the fact. *Ed.*

‡ The inference to be drawn from this is to suspect that kind of evidence which is most consonant to our inclinations, and not to admit any notion as real except we can base it firmly upon that kind of demonstration which is peculiar to the subject, not to our impression. Sometimes the mode of proof may be consonant to our inclinations, and to the subject at the same time, as in the case of Pythagoras, when he applied his beloved numbers to the solution of astronomical phenomena; or in that of Descartes, when he reasoned geometrically concerning the nature of the soul. Such examples cannot be censured with justice,

affords us a signal instance, who made his natural philosophy completely subservient to his logic, and thus rendered it little more than useless and disputatious. The chemists, again, have formed a fanciful philosophy with the most confined views, from a few experiments of the furnace. Gilbert,[x] too, having employed himself most assiduously in the consideration of the magnet, immediately established a system of philosophy to coincide with his favourite pursuit.

LV. The greatest and, perhaps, radical distinction between different men's dispositions for philosophy and the sciences is this, that some are more vigorous and active in observing the differences of things, others in observing their resemblances; for a steady and acute disposition can fix its thoughts, and dwell upon and adhere to a point, through all the refinements of differences, but those that are sublime and discursive recognise and compare even the most delicate and general resemblances; each of them readily falls into excess, by catching either at nice distinctions or shadows of resemblance.

LVI. Some dispositions evince an unbounded admiration of antiquity, others eagerly embrace novelty, and but few can preserve the just medium, so as neither to tear up what the ancients have correctly laid down, nor to despise the just innovations of the moderns. But this is very prejudicial to the sciences and philosophy, and instead of a correct judgment we have but the factions of the ancients and moderns. Truth is not to be sought in the good fortune of any particular conjuncture of time, which is uncertain, but in the light of nature and experience, which is eternal. Such factions, therefore, are to be abjured, and the understanding must not allow them to hurry it on to assent.

---

inasmuch as the methods pursued were adapted to the end of the inquiry. The remark in the text can only apply to those philosophers who attempt to build up a moral or theological system by the instruments of induction alone, or who rush, with the geometrical axiom, and the *à priori* syllogism, to the investigation of nature. The means in such cases are totally inadequate to the object in view. *Ed.*

[x] Gilbert lived towards the close of the sixteenth century, and was court physician to both Elizabeth and James. In his work alluded to in the text he continually asserts the advantages of the experimental over the *à priori* method in physical inquiry, and succeeded when his censor failed in giving a practical example of the utility of his precepts. His "De Magnete" contains all the fundamental parts of the science, and these so perfectly treated, that we have nothing to add to them at the present day.

Gilbert adopted the Copernican system, and even spoke of the contrary theory as utterly absurd, grounding his argument on the vast velocities which such a supposition requires us to ascribe to the heavenly bodies. *Ed.*

LVII. The contemplation of nature and of bodies in their individual form distracts and weakens the understanding; but the contemplation of nature and of bodies in their general composition and formation stupifies and relaxes it. We have a good instance of this in the school of Leucippus and Democritus compared with others, for they applied themselves so much to particulars as almost to neglect the general structure of things, whilst the others were so astounded whilst gazing on the structure that they did not penetrate the simplicity of nature. These two species of contemplation must, therefore, be interchanged, and each employed in its turn, in order to render the understanding at once penetrating and capacious, and to avoid the inconveniences we have mentioned, and the idols that result from them.

LVIII. Let such, therefore, be our precautions in contemplation, that we may ward off and expel the idols of the den, which mostly owe their birth either to some predominant pursuit, or, secondly, to an excess in synthesis and analysis, or, thirdly, to a party zeal in favour of certain ages, or, fourthly, to the extent or narrowness of the subject. In general, he who contemplates nature should suspect whatever particularly takes and fixes his understanding, and should use so much the more caution to preserve it equable and unprejudiced.

LIX. The idols of the market are the most troublesome of all, those namely which have entwined themselves round the understanding from the associations of words and names. For men imagine that their reason governs words, whilst, in fact, words re-act upon the understanding; and this has rendered philosophy and the sciences sophistical and inactive. Words are generally formed in a popular sense, and define things by those broad lines which are most obvious to the vulgar mind; but when a more acute understanding, or more diligent observation is anxious to vary those lines, and to adapt them more accurately to nature, words oppose it. Hence the great and solemn disputes of learned men often terminate in controversies about words and names, in regard to which it would be better (imitating the caution of mathematicians) to proceed more advisedly in the first instance, and to bring such disputes to a regular issue by definitions. Such definitions, however, cannot remedy the evil in natural and material objects, because they consist themselves of words, and these words produce others;[y] so that we must neces-

[y] The Latin text adds "without end;" but Bacon is scarcely right in supposing that the descent from complex ideas and propositions to those of simple nature, involve the analyst in a series of continuous and interminable definitions. For in the gradual and analytical scale, there is a bar beyond which we cannot go, as there is a summit bounded by the limited variations of our conceptions. Logical definitions, to fulfil their conditions, or indeed to be of any avail, must be given in

sarily have recourse to particular instances, and their regular series and arrangement, as we shall mention when we come to the mode and scheme of determining notions and axioms.

LX. The idols imposed upon the understanding by words are of two kinds. They are either the names of things which have no existence (for as some objects are from inattention left without a name, so names are formed by fanciful imaginations which are without an object), or they are the names of actual objects, but confused, badly defined, and hastily and irregularly abstracted from things. Fortune, the *primum mobile*, the planetary orbits,* the element of fire, and the like fictions, which owe their birth to futile and false theories, are instances of the first kind. And this species of idols is removed with greater facility, because it can be exterminated by the constant refutation or the desuetude of the theories themselves. The others, which are created by vicious and unskilful abstraction, are intricate and deeply rooted. Take some word for instance, as moist, and let us examine how far the different significations of this word are consistent. It will be found that the word moist is nothing but a confused sign of different actions admitted of no settled and defined uniformity. For it means that which easily diffuses itself over another body; that which is indeterminable and cannot be brought to a consistency; that which yields easily in every direction; that which is easily divided and dispersed; that which is easily united and collected; that which easily flows and is put in motion; that which easily adheres to, and wets another body; that which is easily reduced to a liquid state though previously solid. When, therefore, you come to predicate or impose this name, in one sense flame is moist, in another air is not moist, in another fine powder is moist, in another glass is moist; so that it is quite

simpler terms than the object which is sought to be defined; now this, in the case of primordial notions and objects of sense, is impossible; therefore we are obliged to rest satisfied with the mere names of our perceptions. *Ed.*

* The ancients supposed the planets to describe an exact circle round the south. As observations increased and facts were disclosed, which were irreconcileable with this supposition, the earth was removed from the centre to some other point in the circle, and the planets were supposed to revolve in a smaller circle (epicycle) round an imaginary point, which in its turn described a circle of which the earth was the centre. In proportion as observation elicited fresh facts, contradictory to these representations, other epicycles and eccentrics were added, involving additional confusion. Though Kepler had swept away all these complicated theories in the preceding century, by the demonstration of his three laws, which established the elliptical course of the planets, Bacon regarded him and Copernicus in the same light as Ptolemy and Xenophanes. *Ed.*

clear that this notion is hastily abstracted from water only, and common ordinary liquors, without any due verification of it.

There are, however, different degrees of distortion and mistake in words. One of the least faulty classes is that of the names of substances, particularly of the less abstract and more defined species (those then of chalk and mud are good, of earth bad); words signifying actions are more faulty, as to generate, to corrupt, to change; but the most faulty are those denoting qualities (except the immediate objects of sense), as heavy, light, rare, dense. Yet in all of these there must be some notions a little better than others, in proportion as a greater or less number of things come before the senses.

LXI. The idols of the theatre are not innate, nor do they introduce themselves secretly into the understanding, but they are manifestly instilled and cherished by the fictions of theories and depraved rules of demonstration. To attempt, however, or undertake their confutation would not be consistent with our declarations. For since we neither agree in our principles nor our demonstrations, all argument is out of the question. And it is fortunate that the ancients are left in possession of their honours. We detract nothing from them, seeing our whole doctrine relates only to the path to be pursued. The lame (as they say) in the path outstrip the swift who wander from it, and it is clear that the very skill and swiftness of him who runs not in the right direction must increase his aberration.

Our method of discovering the sciences is such as to leave little to the acuteness and strength of wit, and indeed rather to level wit and intellect. For as in the drawing of a straight line, or accurate circle by the hand, much depends on its steadiness and practice, but if a ruler or compass be employed there is little occasion for either; so it is with our method. Although, however, we enter into no individual confutations, yet a little must be said, first, of the sects and general divisions of these species of theories; secondly, something further to show that there are external signs of their weakness; and, lastly, we must consider the causes of so great a misfortune, and so long and general a unanimity in error, that we may thus render the access to truth less difficult, and that the human understanding may the more readily be purified, and brought to dismiss its idols.

LXII. The idols of the theatre, or of theories, are numerous, and may, and perhaps will, be still more so. For unless men's minds had been now occupied for many ages in religious and theological considerations, and civil governments (especially monarchies), had been averse to novelties of that nature even in theory (so that men must apply to them with some risk and injury to their own fortunes, and not only without reward, but subject to contumely and envy), there is no doubt that many other sects of philosophers and theorists would have been introduced, like those which formerly flourished in such diversified abundance amongst the Greeks. For as many imaginary theories of the heavens can be deduced from the phenomena of the sky, so it is even more easy to found many dogmas upon the phenomena of philosophy—and the plot of this our theatre resembles those of the poetical, where the plots which are invented for the stage are more consistent, elegant, and pleasurable than those taken from real history.

In general, men take for the groundwork of their philosophy either too much from a few topics, or too little from many; in either case their philosophy is founded on too narrow a basis of experiment and natural history, and decides on too scanty grounds. For the theoretic philosopher seizes various common circumstances by experiment, without reducing them to certainty or examining and frequently considering them, and relies for the rest upon meditation and the activity of his wit.

There are other philosophers who have diligently and accurately attended to a few experiments, and have thence presumed to deduce and invent systems of philosophy, forming everything to conformity with them.

A third set, from their faith and religious veneration, introduce theology and traditions; the absurdity of some among them having proceeded so far as to seek and derive the sciences from spirits and genii. There are, therefore, three sources of error and three species of false philosophy; the sophistic, empiric, and superstitious.

LXIII. Aristotle affords the most eminent instance of the first; for he corrupted natural philosophy by logic—thus he formed the world of categories, assigned to the human soul, the noblest of substances, a genus determined by words of secondary operation, treated of density and rarity (by which bodies occupy a greater or lesser space), by the frigid distinctions of action and power, asserted that there was a peculiar and proper motion in all bodies, and that if they shared in any other motion, it was owing to an external moving cause, and imposed innumerable arbitrary distinctions upon the nature of things; being everywhere more anxious as to definitions in teaching and the accuracy of the wording of his propositions, than the internal truth of things. And this is best shown by a comparison of his philosophy with the others of greatest repute among the Greeks. For the similar parts of Anaxagoras, the atoms of Leucippus and Democritus, the heaven and earth of Parmenides, the discord and concord of Empedocles,* the resolution of bodies into the com-

* Empedocles, of Agrigentum, flourished 444 B.C. He was the disciple of Telanges the Pythagorean, and warmly adopted the doctrine

mon nature of fire, and their condensation according to Heraclitus, exhibit some sprinkling of natural philosophy, the nature of things, and experiment; whilst Aristotle's physics are mere logical terms, and he remodelled the same subject in his metaphysics under a more imposing title, and more as a realist than a nominalist. Nor is much stress to be laid on his frequent recourse to experiment in his books on animals, his problems, and other treatises; for he had already decided, without having properly consulted experience as the basis of his decisions and axioms, and after having so decided, he drags experiment along as a captive constrained to accommodate herself to his decisions: so that he is even more to be blamed than his modern followers (of the scholastic school) who have deserted her altogether.

LXIV. The empiric school produces dogmas of a more deformed and monstrous nature than the sophistic or theoretic school; not being founded in the light of common notions (which, however poor and superstitious, is yet in a manner universal, and of a general tendency), but in the confined obscurity of a few experiments. Hence this species of philosophy appears probable, and almost certain to those who are daily practised in such experiments, and have thus corrupted their imagination, but incredible and futile to others. We have a strong instance of this in the alchymists and their dogmas; it would be difficult to find another in this age, unless perhaps in the philosophy of Gilbert.[b] We could not, however, neglect to caution others against this school, because we already foresee and augur, that if men be hereafter induced by our exhortations to apply seriously to experiments (bidding farewell to the sophistic doctrines), there will then be imminent danger from empirics, owing to the premature and forward haste of the understanding, and its jumping or flying to generalities and the principles of things. We ought, therefore, already to meet the evil.

LXV. The corruption of philosophy by the mixing of it up with superstition and theology, is of a much wider extent, and is most injurious to it both as a whole and in parts. For the human understanding is no less exposed to the impressions of

of transmigration. He resolved the universe into the four ordinary elements, the principles of whose composition were life and happiness, or concord and amity, but whose decomposition brought forth death and evil, or discord and hatred. Heraclitus held matter to be indifferent to any peculiar form, but as it became rarer or more dense, it took the appearance of fire, air, earth, and water. Fire, however, he believed to be the elementary principle out of which the others were evolved. This was also the belief of Lucretius. See book i. 783, &c.

[b] It is thus the Vulcanists and Neptunians have framed their opposite theories in geology. Phrenology is a modern instance of hasty generalization. *Ed.*

fancy, than to those of vulgar notions. The disputatious and sophistic school entraps the understanding, whilst the fanciful, bombastic, and, as it were, poetical school, rather flatters it. There is a clear example of this among the Greeks, especially in Pythagoras, where, however, the superstition is coarse and overcharged, but it is more dangerous and refined in Plato and his school. This evil is found also in some branches of other systems of philosophy, where it introduces abstracted forms, final and first causes, omitting frequently the intermediate and the like. Against it we must use the greatest caution; for the apotheosis of error is the greatest evil of all, and when folly is worshipped, it is, as it were, a plague spot upon the understanding. Yet some of the moderns have indulged this folly with such consummate inconsiderateness, that they have endeavoured to build a system of natural philosophy on the first chapter of Genesis, the book of Job, and other parts of Scripture; seeking thus the dead amongst the living.[c] And this folly is the more to be prevented and restrained, because not only fantastical philosophy, but heretical religion spring from the absurd mixture of matters divine and human. It is therefore most wise soberly to render unto faith the things that are faith's.

LXVI. Having spoken of the vicious authority of the systems founded either on vulgar notions, or on a few experiments, or on superstition, we must now consider the faulty subjects for contemplation, especially in natural philosophy. The human understanding is perverted by observing the power of mechanical arts, in which bodies are very materially changed by composition or separation, and is induced to suppose that something similar takes place in the universal nature of things. Hence the fiction of elements, and their co-operation in forming natural bodies.[d]

---

[c] In scripture everything which concerns the passing interests of the body is called dead; the only living knowledge having regard to the eternal interest of the soul. *Ed.*

[d] In mechanics and the general sciences, causes compound their effects, or in other words, it is generally possible to deduce *à priori* the consequence of introducing complex agencies into any experiment, by allowing for the effect of each of the simple causes which enter into their composition. In chemistry and physiology a contrary law holds; the causes which they embody generally uniting to form distinct substances, and to introduce unforeseen laws and combinations. The deductive method here is consequently inapplicable, and we are forced back upon experiment.

Bacon in the text is hardly consistent with himself, as he admits in the second book the doctrine, to which modern discovery points, of the reciprocal transmutation of the elements. What seemed poetic fiction in the theories of Pythagoras and Seneca, assumes the appearance of scientific fact in the hands of Baron Caynard. *Ed.*

Again, when man reflects upon the entire liberty of nature, he meets with particular species of things, as animals, plants, minerals, and is thence easily led to imagine that there exist in nature certain primary forms which she strives to produce, and that all variation from them arises from some impediment or error which she is exposed to in completing her work, or from the collision or metamorphosis of different species. The first hypothesis has produced the doctrine of elementary properties, the second that of occult properties and specific powers; and both lead to trifling courses of reflection, in which the mind acquiesces, and is thus diverted from more important subjects. But physicians exercise a much more useful labour in the consideration of the secondary qualities of things, and the operations of attraction, repulsion, attenuation, inspissation, dilatation, astringency, separation, maturation, and the like; and would do still more if they would not corrupt these proper observations by the two systems I have alluded to, of elementary qualities and specific powers, by which they either reduce the secondary to first qualities, and their subtile and immeasurable composition, or at any rate neglect to advance by greater and more diligent observation to the third and fourth qualities, thus terminating their contemplation prematurely. Nor are these powers (or the like) to be investigated only among the medicines for the human body, but also in all changes of other natural bodies.

A greater evil arises from the contemplation and investigation rather of the stationary principles of things from which, than of the active by which things themselves are created. For the former only serve for discussion, the latter for practice. Nor is any value to be set on those common differences of motion which are observed in the received system of natural philosophy, as generation, corruption, augmentation, diminution, alteration, and translation. For this is their meaning: if a body, unchanged in other respects, is moved from its place, this is translation; if the place and species be given, but the quantity changed, it is alteration; but, if from such a change, the mass and quantity of the body do not continue the same, this is the motion of augmentation and diminution; if the change be continued so as to vary the species and substance, and transfuse them to others, this is generation and corruption. All this is merely popular, and by no means penetrates into nature; and these are but the measures and bounds of motion, and not different species of it; they merely suggest how far, and not how or whence. For they exhibit neither the affections of bodies nor the process of their parts, but merely establish a division of that motion, which coarsely exhibits to the senses matter in its varied form. Even when they wish to point out something relative to the causes of motion, and to establish a division of them, they most absurdly introduce natural and violent motion, which is also a popular notion, since every violent motion is also in fact natural, that is to say, the external efficient puts nature in action in a different manner to that which she had previously employed.

But if, neglecting these, any one were for instance to observe that there is in bodies a tendency of adhesion, so as not to suffer the unity of nature to be completely separated or broken, and a *vacuum*[e] to be formed, or that they have a tendency to return to their natural dimensions or tension, so that, if compressed or extended within or beyond it, they immediately strive to recover themselves, and resume their former volume and extent; or that they have a tendency to congregate into masses with similar bodies,—the dense, for instance, towards the circumference of the earth, the thin and rare towards that of the heavens. These and the like are true physical genera of motions, but the others are clearly logical and scholastic, as appears plainly from a comparison of the two.

Another considerable evil is, that men in their systems and contemplations bestow their labour upon the investigation and discussion of the principles of things and the extreme limits of nature, although all utility and means of action consist in the intermediate objects. Hence men cease not to abstract nature till they arrive at potential and shapeless matter,[f] and still persist in their dissection, till they arrive at atoms; and yet were all this true, it would be of little use to advance man's estate.

LXVII. The understanding must also be cautioned against the intemperance of systems, so far as regards its giving or withholding its assent; for such intemperance appears to fix and perpetuate idols, so as to leave no means of removing them.

These excesses are of two kinds. The first is seen in those who decide hastily, and render the sciences positive and dictatorial. The other in those who have introduced scepticism, and vague unbounded inquiry. The former subdues, the latter enervates the understanding. The Aristotelian philosophy, after

---

[e] Galileo had recently adopted the notion that nature abhorred a vacuum for an axiomatic principle, and it was not till Torricelli, his disciple, had given practical proof of the utility of Bacon's method, by the discovery of the barometer (1643), that this error, as also that expressed below, and believed by Bacon, concerning the homœopathic tendencies of bodies, was destroyed. *Ed.*

[f] *Donec ad materiam potentialem et informem ventum fuerit.* Nearly all the ancient philosophers admitted the existence of a certain primitive and shapeless matter as the substratum of things which the creative power had reduced to fixed proportions, and resolved into specific substances. The expression potential matter refers to that substance forming the basis of the Peripatetic system, which virtually contained all the forms that it was in the power of the efficient cause to draw out of it. *Ed.*

destroying other systems (as the Ottomans do their brethren) by its disputatious confutations, decided upon everything, and Aristotle himself then raises up questions at will, in order to settle them; so that everything should be certain and decided, a method now in use among his successors.

The school of Plato introduced scepticism, first, as it were in joke and irony, from their dislike to Protagoras, Hippias,[h] and others, who were ashamed of appearing not to doubt upon any subject. But the new academy dogmatised in their scepticism, and held it as their tenet. Although this method be more honest than arbitrary decision (for its followers allege that they by no means confound all inquiry, like Pyrrho and his disciples, but hold doctrines which they can follow as probable, though they cannot maintain them to be true), yet when the human mind has once despaired of discovering truth, everything begins to languish. Hence men turn aside into pleasant controversies and discussions, and into a sort of wandering over subjects rather than sustain any rigorous investigation. But as we observed at first, we are not to deny the authority of the human senses and understanding, although weak, but rather to furnish them with assistance.

LXVIII. We have now treated of each kind of idols, and their qualities, all of which must be abjured and renounced with firm and solemn resolution, and the understanding must be completely freed and cleared of them, so that the access to the kingdom of man, which is founded on the sciences, may resemble that to the kingdom of heaven, where no admission is conceded except to children.

LXIX. Vicious demonstrations are the muniments and support of idols, and those which we possess in logic, merely subject

---

[g] An allusion to the humanity of the *Sultans*, who, in their earlier histories are represented as signalizing their accession to the throne by the destruction of their family, to remove the danger of rivalry and the terrors of civil war. *Ed.*

[h] The text is "in odium veterum sophistarum, Protagoræ, Hippiæ, et reliquorum." Those were called sophists, who, *ostentationis aut quæstus causa philosophabantur*. (Acad. Prior. ii. 22.) They had corrupted and degraded philosophy before Socrates. Protagoras of Abdera ("Αβδηρα), the most celebrated, taught that man is the measure of all things, by which he meant not only that all which can be known is known only as it related to our faculties, but also that apart from our faculties nothing can be known. The sceptics equally held that knowledge was probable only as it related to our faculties, but they stopped there, and did not, like the sophist, dogmatize about the unknown. The works of Protagoras were condemned for their impiety, and publicly burnt by the ædiles of Athens, who appear to have discharged the office of common hangmen to the literary blasphemers of their day. *Ed.*

and enslave the world to human thoughts, and thoughts to words. But demonstrations are in some manner themselves systems of philosophy and science; for such as they are, and accordingly as they are regularly or improperly established, such will be the resulting systems of philosophy and contemplation. But those which we employ in the whole process leading from the senses and things to axioms and conclusions, are fallacious and incompetent. This process is fourfold, and the errors are in equal number. In the first place the impressions of the senses are erroneous, for they fail and deceive us. We must supply defects by substitutions, and fallacies by their correction. Secondly, notions are improperly abstracted from the senses, and indeterminate and confused when they ought to be the reverse. Thirdly, the induction that is employed is improper, for it determines the principles of sciences by simple enumeration,[1] without adopting exclusions and resolutions, or just separations of nature. Lastly, The usual method of discovery and proof, by first establishing the most general propositions, then applying and proving the intermediate axioms according to them, is the parent of error and the calamity of every science. But we will treat more fully of that which we now slightly touch upon, when we come to lay down the true way of interpreting nature, after having gone through the above expiatory process and purification of the mind.

LXX. But experience is by far the best demonstration, provided it adhere to the experiment actually made, for if that experiment be transferred to other subjects apparently similar, unless with proper and methodical caution it becomes fallacious. The present method of experiment is blind and stupid; hence

[1] Bacon is hardly correct in implying that the *enumerationem per simplicem* was the only light in which the ancients looked upon induction, as they appear to have regarded it as only one, and that the least important, of its species. Aristotle expressly considers induction in a perfect or dialectic sense, and in an imperfect or rhetorical sense. Thus if a genus (G), contains four species (A, B, C, D), the syllogism would lead us to infer, that what is true of G, is true of any of the one four. But perfect induction would reason, that what we can prove of A, B, C, D, separately, we may properly state as true of G, the whole genus. This is evidently a formal argument as demonstrative as the syllogism. In necessary matters, however, legitimate induction may claim a wider province, and infer of the whole genus what is only apparent in a part of the species. Such are those inductive inferences which concern the laws of nature, the immutability of forms, by which Bacon strove to erect his new system of philosophy. The Stagyrite, however, looked upon *enumerationem per simplicem*, without any regard to the nature of the matter, or to the completeness of the species, with as much reprehensive caution as Bacon, and guarded his readers against it as the source of innumerable errors. *Ed.*

men wandering and roaming without any determined course, and consulting mere chance, are hurried about to various points, and advance but little,—at one time they are happy, at another their attention is distracted, and they always find that they want something further. Men generally make their experiments carelessly, and as it were in sport, making some little variation in a known experiment, and then if they fail they become disgusted and give up the attempt; nay, if they set to work more seriously, steadily, and assiduously, yet they waste all their time on probing some solitary matter, as Gilbert on the magnet, and the alchemists on gold. But such conduct shows their method to be no less unskilful than mean; for nobody can successfully investigate the nature of any object by considering that object alone; the inquiry must be more generally extended.

Even when men build any science and theory upon experiment, yet they almost always turn with premature and hasty zeal to practise, not merely on account of the advantage and benefit to be derived from it, but in order to seize upon some security in a new undertaking of their not employing the remainder of their labour unprofitably, and by making themselves conspicuous, to acquire a greater name for their pursuit. Hence, like Atalanta, they leave the course to pick up the golden apple, interrupting their speed, and giving up the victory. But in the true course of experiment, and in extending it to new effects, we should imitate the Divine foresight and order; for God on the first day only created light, and assigned a whole day to that work without creating any material substance thereon. In like manner we must first, by every kind of experiment, elicit the discovery of causes and true axioms, and seek for experiments which may afford light rather than profit. Axioms, when rightly investigated and established, prepare us not for a limited but abundant practice, and bring in their train whole troops of effects. But we will treat hereafter of the ways of experience, which are not less beset and interrupted than those of judgment; having spoken at present of common experience only as a bad species of demonstration, the order of our subject now requires some mention of those external signs of the weakness in practice of the received systems of philosophy and contemplation[b] which we referred to above, and of the causes of a circumstance at first sight so wonderful and incredible. For the knowledge of these external signs prepares the way for assent, and the explanation of the causes removes the wonder; and these two circumstances are of material use in extirpating more easily and gently the idols from the understanding.

LXXI. The sciences we possess have been principally derived

[b] See Ax. lxi. towards the end. This subject extends to Ax. lxxviii.

from the Greeks; for the addition of the Roman, Arabic, or more modern writers, are but few and of small importance, and such as they are, are founded on the basis of Greek invention. But the wisdom of the Greeks was professional and disputatious, and thus most adverse to the investigation of truth. The name, therefore, of sophists, which the contemptuous spirit of those who deemed themselves philosophers, rejected and transferred to the rhetoricians,—Gorgias,[1] Protagoras, Hippias, Polus,— might well suit the whole tribe, such as Plato, Aristotle, Zeno, Epicurus, Theophrastus, and their successors,—Chrysippus, Carneades, and the rest. There was only this difference between them,—the former were mercenary vagabonds, travelling about to different states, making a show of their wisdom, and requiring pay; the latter more dignified and noble, in possession of fixed habitations, opening schools, and teaching philosophy gratuitously. Both, however (though differing in other respects), were professorial, and reduced every subject to controversy, establishing and defending certain sects and dogmas of philosophy, so that their doctrines were nearly (what Dionysius not unaptly objected to Plato) the talk of idle old men to ignorant youths. But the more ancient Greeks, as Empedocles, Anaxagoras, Leucippus, Democritus, Parmenides, Heraclitus, Xenophanes, Philolaus, and the rest[m] (for I omit Pythagoras as being super-

[1] Gorgias of Leontium went to Athens in 424 B.C. He and Polus were disciples of Empedocles, whom we have already noticed (Aphorism 63), where he sustained the three famous propositions, that nothing exists, that nothing can be known, and that it is out of the power of man to transmit or communicate intelligence. He is reckoned one of the earliest writers on the art of rhetoric, and for that reason, Plato called his elegant dialogue on that subject after his name.

[m] Chrysippus, a stoic philosopher of Soli in Cilicia, Campestris, born in 280, died in the 143rd Olympiad, 208 B. C. He was equally distinguished for natural abilities and industry, seldom suffering a day to elapse without writing 500 lines. He wrote several hundred volumes, of which three hundred were on logical subjects; but in all, borrowed largely from others. He was very fond of the *sorites* in argument, which is hence called by Persius the heap of Chrysippus. He was called the Column of the Portico, a name given to the Stoical School from Zeno its founder, who had given his lessons under the portico. *Ed.*

Carneades, born about 215, died in 130. He attached himself to Chrysippus, and sustained with *éclat* the scepticism of the academy. The Athenians sent him with Critolaus and Diogenes as ambassador to Rome, where he attracted the attention of his new auditory by the subtilty of his reasoning, and the fluency and vehemence of his language. Before Galba and Cato the Censor, he harangued with great variety of thought and copiousness of diction in praise of justice. The next day, to establish his doctrine of the uncertainty of human knowledge, he undertook to refute all his arguments. He maintained with the New

stitious), did not (that we are aware) open schools, but betook themselves to the investigation of truth with greater silence and with more severity and simplicity, that is, with less affectation and ostentation. Hence in our opinion they acted more advisedly, however their works may have been eclipsed in course of time by those lighter productions which better correspond with and please the apprehensions and passions of the vulgar; for time, like a river,ᵃ bears down to us that which is light and inflated, and sinks that which is heavy and solid. Nor were even these more ancient philosophers free from the national defect, but inclined too much to the ambition and vanity of forming a sect, and captivating public opinion, and we must despair of any inquiry after truth when it condescends to such trifles. Nor must we omit the opinion, or rather prophecy, of an Egyptian priest with regard to the Greeks, that they would for ever remain children, without any antiquity of knowledge or knowledge of antiquity; for they certainly have this in common with children, that they are prone to talking, and incapable of generation, their wisdom being loquacious and unproductive of

Academy, that the senses, the imagination, and the understanding frequently deceive us, and therefore cannot be infallible judges of truth, but that from the impressions produced on the mind by means of the senses, we infer appearances of truth or probabilities. Nevertheless, with respect to the conduct of life, Carneades held that probable opinions are a sufficient guide.

Xenophanes, a Greek philosopher, of Colophon, born in 556, the founder of the Eleatic school, which owes its fame principally to Parmenides. Wild in his opinions about astronomy, he supposed that the stars were extinguished every morning, and rekindled at night; that eclipses were occasioned by the temporary extinction of the sun, and that there were several suns for the convenience of the different climates of the earth. Yet this man held the chair of philosophy at Athens for seventy years.

Philolaus, a Pythagorian philosopher of Crotona, B.C. 374. He first supported the diurnal motion of the earth round its axis, and its annual motion round the sun. Cicero (Acad. iv. 39), has ascribed this opinion to the Syracusan philosopher Nicetas, and likewise to Plato. From this passage, it is most probable that Copernicus got the idea of the system he afterwards established. Bacon, in the Advancement of Human Learning, charges Gilbert with restoring the doctrines of Philolaus, because he ventured to support the Copernican theory. *Ed.*

ᵃ Bacon is equally conspicuous for the use and abuse of analogical illustrations. The levity, as Stuart Mill very properly observes, by which substances float on a stream, and the levity which is synonymous with worthlessness, have nothing beside the name in common; and to show how little value there is in the figure, we need only change the word into buoyancy, to turn the semblance of Bacon's argument against himself. *Ed.*

effects. Hence the external signs derived from the origin and birthplace of our present philosophy are not favourable.

LXXII. Nor are those much better which can be deduced from the character of the time and age, than the former from that of the country and nation; for in that age the knowledge both of time and of the world was confined and meagre, which is one of the worst evils for those who rely entirely on experience,—they had not a thousand years of history worthy of that name, but mere fables and ancient traditions; they were acquainted with but a small portion of the regions and countries of the world, for they indiscriminately called all nations situated far towards the north Scythians, all those to the west Celts; they knew nothing of Africa but the nearest part of Ethiopia, or of Asia beyond the Ganges, and had not even heard any sure and clear tradition of the regions of the New World. Besides, a vast number of climates and zones, in which innumerable nations live and breathe, were pronounced by them to be uninhabitable; nay, the travels of Democritus, Plato, and Pythagoras, which were not extensive, but rather mere excursions from home, were considered as something vast. But in our times many parts of the New World, and every extremity of the Old are well known, and the mass of experiments has been infinitely increased; wherefore, if external signs were to be taken from the time of the nativity or procreation (as in astrology), nothing extraordinary could be predicted of these early systems of philosophy.

LXXIII. Of all signs there is none more certain or worthy than that of the fruits produced, for the fruits and effects are the sureties and vouchers, as it were, for the truth of philosophy. Now, from the systems of the Greeks and their subordinate divisions in particular branches of the sciences during so long a period, scarcely one single experiment can be culled that has a tendency to elevate or assist mankind, and can be fairly set down to the speculations and doctrines of their philosophy. Celsus candidly and wisely confesses as much, when he observes that experiments were first discovered in medicine, and that men afterwards built their philosophical systems upon them, and searched for and assigned causes, instead of the inverse method of discovering and deriving experiments from philosophy and the knowledge of causes; it is not, therefore, wonderful that the Egyptians (who bestowed divinity and sacred honours on the authors of new inventions) should have consecrated more images of brutes than of men, for the brutes by their natural instinct made many discoveries, whilst men derived but few from discussion and the conclusions of reason.

The industry of the alchemists has produced some effect, by chance, however, and casualty, or from varying their experiments (as mechanics also do), and not from any regular art or theory, the theory they have imagined rather tending to disturb than to assist experiment. Those, too, who have occupied themselves with natural magic (as they term it) have made but few discoveries, and those of small import, and bordering on imposture; for which reason, in the same manner as we are cautioned by religion to show our faith by our works, we may very properly apply the principle to philosophy, and judge of it by its works, accounting that to be futile which is unproductive, and still more so if, instead of grapes and olives, it yield but the thistle and thorns of dispute and contention.

LXXIV. Other signs may be selected from the increase and progress of particular systems of philosophy and the sciences: for those which are founded on nature grow and increase, whilst those which are founded on opinion change and increase not. If, therefore, the theories we have mentioned were not like plants, torn up by the roots, but grew in the womb of nature, and were nourished by her, that which for the last two thousand years has taken place would never have happened, namely, that the sciences still continue in their beaten track, and nearly stationary, without having received any important increase, nay, having on the contrary rather bloomed under the hands of their first author, and then faded away. But we see that the case is reversed in the mechanical arts, which are founded on nature and the light of experience, for they (as long as they are popular) seem full of life, and uninterruptedly thrive and grow, being at first rude, then convenient, lastly polished, and perpetually improved.

LXXV. There is yet another sign (if such it may be termed, being rather an evidence, and one of the strongest nature), namely, the actual confession of those very authorities whom men now follow; for even they who decide on things so daringly, yet at times, when they reflect, betake themselves to complaints about the subtilty of nature, the obscurity of things, and the weakness of man's wit. If they would merely do this, they might perhaps deter those who are of a timid disposition from further inquiry, but would excite and stimulate those of a more active and confident turn to further advances. They are not, however, satisfied with confessing so much of themselves, but consider everything which has been either unknown or unattempted by themselves or their teachers, as beyond the limits of possibility, and thus, with most consummate pride and envy, convert the defects of their own discoveries into a calumny on nature and a source of despair to every one else. Hence arose the New Academy, which openly professed scepticism,* and con-

* We have before observed, that the New Academy did not profess scepticism, but the ἀκατάληψια, or incomprehensibility of the absolute

signed mankind to eternal darkness; hence the notion that forms, or the true differences of things (which are in fact the laws of simple action), are beyond man's reach, and cannot possibly be discovered; hence those notions in the active and operative branches, that the heat of the sun and of fire are totally different, so as to prevent men from supposing that they can elicit or form, by means of fire, anything similar to the operations of nature; and again, that composition only is the work of man and mixture of nature, so as to prevent men from expecting the generation or transformation of natural bodies by art. Men will, therefore, easily allow themselves to be persuaded by this sign not to engage their fortunes and labour in speculations, which are not only desperate, but actually devoted to desperation.

LXXVI. Nor should we omit the sign afforded by the great dissension formerly prevalent among philosophers, and the variety of schools, which sufficiently show that the way was not well prepared that leads from the senses to the understanding, since the same ground-work of philosophy (namely, the nature of things), was torn and divided into such widely differing and multifarious errors. And although in these days the dissensions and differences of opinions with regard to first principles and entire systems are nearly extinct,[p] yet there remain innumerable questions and controversies with regard to particular branches of philosophy. So that it is manifest that there is nothing sure or sound either in the systems themselves or in the methods of demonstration.[q]

LXXVII. With regard to the supposition that there is a general unanimity as to the philosophy of Aristotle, because the other systems of the ancients ceased and became obsolete on its promulgation, and nothing better has been since discovered; whence it appears that it is so well determined and founded, as to have united the suffrages of both ages; we will observe—1st. That the notion of other ancient systems having ceased after the publication of the works of Aristotle is false, for the works

essences of things. Even modern physicists are not wanting, to assert with this school that the utmost knowledge we can obtain is relative, and necessarily short of absolute certainty. It is not without an appearance of truth that these philosophers maintain that our ideas and perceptions do not express the nature of the things which they represent, but only the effects of the peculiar organs by which they are conveyed to the understanding, so that were these organs changed, we should have different conceptions of their nature. That constitution of air which is dark to man is luminous to bats and owls.

[p] Owing to the universal prevalence of Aristotelism.

[q] It must be remembered, that when Bacon wrote, algebra was in its infancy, and the doctrine of units and infinitesimals undiscovered.

of the ancient philosophers subsisted long after that event, even to the time of Cicero, and the subsequent ages. But at a later period, when human learning had, as it were, been wrecked in the inundation of barbarians into the Roman empire, then the systems of Aristotle and Plato were preserved in the waves of ages, like planks of a lighter and less solid nature. 2nd. The notion of unanimity, on a clear inspection, is found to be fallacious. For true unanimity is that which proceeds from a free judgment, arriving at the same conclusion, after an investigation of the fact. Now, by far the greater number of those who have assented to the philosophy of Aristotle, have bound themselves down to it from prejudice and the authority of others, so that it is rather obsequiousness and concurrence than unanimity. But even if it were real and extensive unanimity, so far from being esteemed a true and solid confirmation, it should even lead to a violent presumption to the contrary. For there is no worse augury in intellectual matters than that derived from unanimity, with the exception of divinity and politics, where suffrages are allowed to decide. For nothing pleases the multitude, unless it strike the imagination or bind down the understanding, as we have observed above, with the shackles of vulgar notions. Hence we may well transfer Phocion's remark from morals to the intellect; "That men should immediately examine what error or fault they have committed, when the multitude concurs with, and applauds them."[r] This then is one of the most unfavourable signs. All the signs, therefore, of the truth and soundness of the received systems of philosophy and the sciences are unpropitious, whether taken from their origin, their fruits, their progress, the confessions of their authors, or from unanimity.

LXXVIII. We now come to the causes of errors,[s] and of such perseverance in them for ages. These are sufficiently numerous and powerful to remove all wonder, that what we now offer should have so long been concealed from, and have escaped the notice of mankind, and to render it more worthy of astonishment, that it should even now have entered any one's mind, or become the subject of his thoughts; and that it should have done so, we consider rather the gift of fortune than of any extraordinary talent, and as the offspring of time rather than wit. But, in the first place, the number of ages is reduced to very narrow limits, on a proper consideration of the matter. For out of twenty-five[t]

[r] Because the vulgar make up the overwhelming majority in such decisions, and generally allow their judgments to be swayed by passion or prejudice.
[s] See end of Axiom lxi. The subject extends to Axiom xc.
[t] If we adopt the statement of Herodotus, who places the Homeric

centuries, with which the memory and learning of man are conversant, scarcely six can be set apart and selected as fertile in science and favourable to its progress. For there are deserts and wastes in times as in countries, and we can only reckon up three revolutions and epochs of philosophy. 1. The Greek. 2. The Roman. 3. Our own, that is the philosophy of the western nations of Europe: and scarcely two centuries can with justice be assigned to each. The intermediate ages of the world were unfortunate both in the quantity and richness of the sciences produced. Nor need we mention the Arabs, or the scholastic philosophy, which, in those ages, ground down the sciences by their numerous treatises, more than they increased their weight. The first cause, then, of such insignificant progress in the sciences, is rightly referred to the small proportion of time which has been favourable thereto.

LXXIX. A second cause offers itself, which is certainly of the greatest importance; namely, that in those very ages in which men's wit and literature flourished considerably, or even moderately, but a small part of their industry was bestowed on natural philosophy, the great mother of the sciences. For every art and science torn from this root may, perhaps, be polished, and put into a serviceable shape, but can admit of little growth. It is well known, that after the Christian religion had been acknowledged, and arrived at maturity, by far the best wits were busied upon theology, where the highest rewards offered themselves, and every species of assistance was abundantly supplied, and the study of which was the principal occupation of the western European nations during the third epoch; the rather because literature flourished about the very time when controversies concerning religion first began to bud forth. 2. In the preceding ages, during the second epoch (that of the Romans), philosophical meditation and labour was chiefly

era 400 years back from his time, Homer lived about 900 years before Christ. On adding this number to the sixteen centuries of the Christian era which had elapsed up to Bacon's time, we get the twenty-five centuries he mentions. The Homeric epoch is the furthest point in antiquity from which Bacon could reckon with any degree of certainty. Hesiod, if he were not contemporary, immediately preceded him.

The epoch of Greek philosophy may be included between Thales and Plato, that is, from the 35th to the 88th Olympiad; that of the Roman, between Terence and Pliny. The modern revolution, in which Bacon is one of the central figures, took its rise from the time of Dante and Petrarch, who lived at the commencement of the fourteenth century; and to which, on account of the invention of printing, and the universal spread of literature, which has rendered a second destruction of learning impossible, it is difficult to foresee any other end than the extinction of the race of man. *Ed.*

occupied and wasted in moral philosophy (the theology of the heathens): besides, the greatest minds in these times applied themselves to civil affairs, on account of the magnitude of the Roman empire, which required the labour of many. 3. The age during which natural philosophy appeared principally to flourish among the Greeks, was but a short period, since in the more ancient times the seven sages (with the exception of Thales), applied themselves to moral philosophy and politics, and at a later period, after Socrates had brought down philosophy from heaven to earth, moral philosophy became more prevalent, and diverted men's attention from natural. Nay, the very period during which physical inquiries flourished, was corrupted and rendered useless by contradictions, and the ambition of new opinions. Since, therefore, during these three epochs, natural philosophy has been materially neglected or impeded, it is not at all surprising that men should have made but little progress in it, seeing they were attending to an entirely different matter.

LXXX. Add to this that natural philosophy, especially of late, has seldom gained exclusive possession of an individual free from all other pursuits, even amongst those who have applied themselves to it, unless there may be an example or two of some monk studying in his cell, or some nobleman in his villa.* She has rather been made a passage and bridge to other pursuits.

Thus has this great mother of the sciences been degraded most unworthily to the situation of an handmaid, and made to wait upon medicine or mathematical operations, and to wash the immature minds of youth, and imbue them with a first dye, that they may afterwards be more ready to receive and retain another. In the mean time, let no one expect any great progress in the sciences (especially their operative part), unless natural philosophy be applied to particular sciences, and particular sciences again referred back to natural philosophy. For want of this, astronomy, optics, music, many mechanical arts, medicine itself, and (what perhaps is more wonderful), moral and political philosophy, and the logical sciences have no depth, but only glide over the surface and variety of things; because these sciences, when they have been once partitioned out and established, are no longer nourished by natural philosophy, which would have imparted fresh vigour and growth to them from the sources and genuine contemplation of motion, rays, sounds, texture, and conformation of bodies, and the affections and capacity of the understanding. But we can little wonder that the sciences grow not when separated from their roots.

LXXXI. There is another powerful and great cause of the little advancement of the sciences, which is this; it is impossible

---

* The allusion is evidently to Roger Bacon and René Descartes. *Ed.*

to advance properly in the course when the goal is not properly fixed. But the real and legitimate goal of the sciences, is the endowment of human life with new inventions and riches. The great crowd of teachers know nothing of this, but consist of dictatorial hirelings; unless it so happen that some artisan of an acute genius, and ambitious of fame, gives up his time to a new discovery, which is generally attended with a loss of property. The majority, so far from proposing to themselves the augmentation of the mass of arts and sciences, make no other use of an inquiry into the mass already before them, than is afforded by the conversion of it to some use in their lectures, or to gain, or to the acquirement of a name, and the like. But if one out of the multitude be found, who courts science from real zeal, and on his own account, even he will be seen rather to follow contemplation, and the variety of theories, than a severe and strict investigation of truth. Again, if there even be an unusually strict investigator of truth, yet will he propose to himself, as the test of truth, the satisfaction of his mind and understanding, as to the causes of things long since known, and not such a test as to lead to some new earnest of effects, and a new light in axioms. If, therefore, no one have laid down the real end of science, we cannot wonder that there should be error in points subordinate to that end.

LXXXII. But, in like manner, as the end and goal of science is ill defined, so, even were the case otherwise, men have chosen an erroneous and impassable direction. For it is sufficient to astonish any reflecting mind, that nobody should have cared or wished to open and complete a way for the understanding, setting off from the senses, and regular, well conducted experiment; but that everything has been abandoned either to the mists of tradition, the whirl and confusion of argument, or the waves and mazes of chance, and desultory, ill combined experiment. Now, let any one but consider soberly and diligently the nature of the path men have been accustomed to pursue in the investigation and discovery of any matter, and he will doubtless first observe the rude and inartificial manner of discovery most familiar to mankind: which is no other than this. When any one prepares himself for discovery, he first inquires and obtains a full account of all that has been said on the subject by others, then adds his own reflections, and stirs up and, as it were, invokes his own spirit, after much mental labour, to disclose its oracles. All which is a method without foundation, and merely turns on opinion.

Another, perhaps, calls in logic to assist him in discovery, which bears only a nominal relation to his purpose. For the discoveries of logic are not discoveries of principles and leading axioms, but only of what appears to accord with them.* And when men become curious and importunate, and give trouble, interrupting her about her proofs, and the discovery of principles or first axioms, she puts them off with her usual answer, referring them to faith, and ordering them to swear allegiance to each art in its own department.

There remains but mere experience, which, when it offers itself, is called chance; when it is sought after, experiment.ʸ But this kind of experience is nothing but a loose faggot; and mere groping in the dark, as men at night try all means of discovering the right road, whilst it would be better and more prudent either to wait for day, or procure a light, and then proceed. On the contrary, the real order of experience begins by setting up a light, and then shows the road by it, commencing with a regulated and digested, not a misplaced and vague course of experiment, and thence deducing axioms, and from those axioms new experiments: for not even the divine word proceeded to operate on the general mass of things without due order.

Let men, therefore, cease to wonder if the whole course of science be not run, when all have wandered from the path; quitting it entirely, and deserting experience, or involving themselves in its mazes, and wandering about, whilst a regularly combined system would lead them in a sure track through its wilds to the open day of axioms.

LXXXIII. The evil, however, has been wonderfully increased by an opinion, or inveterate conceit, which is both vainglorious and prejudicial, namely, that the dignity of the human mind is lowered by long and frequent intercourse with experiments and particulars, which are the objects of sense, and confined to matter; especially since such matters generally require labour in investigation, are mean subjects for meditation, harsh in discourse, unproductive in practice, infinite in number, and delicate in their subtilty. Hence we have seen the true path not only deserted, but intercepted and blocked up, experience being rejected with disgust, and not merely neglected or improperly applied.

LXXXIV. Again, the reverence for antiquity,ᶻ and the authority of men who have been esteemed great in philosophy, and general unanimity, have retarded men from advancing in science, and almost enchanted them. As to unanimity, we have spoken of it above.

The opinion which men cherish of antiquity is altogether idle,

* From the abuse of the scholastics, who mistook the *à priori* method, the deductive syllogism for the entire province of logic. *Ed.*
ʸ See Aphorism xcv.
ᶻ The incongruity to which Bacon alludes appears to spring from

and scarcely accords with the term. For the old age and increasing years of the world should in reality be considered as antiquity, and this is rather the character of our own times than of the less advanced age of the world in those of the ancients; for the latter, with respect to ourselves, are ancient and elder, with respect to the world modern and younger. And as we expect a greater knowledge of human affairs, and more mature judgment from an old man than from a youth, on account of his experience, and the variety and number of things he has seen, heard, and meditated upon, so we have reason to expect much greater things of our own age (if it knew but its strength and would essay and exert it) than from antiquity, since the world has grown older, and its stock has been increased and accumulated with an infinite number of experiments and observations.

We must also take into our consideration that many objects in nature fit to throw light upon philosophy have been exposed to our view, and discovered by means of long voyages and travels, in which our times have abounded. It would, indeed, be dishonourable to mankind, if the regions of the material globe, the earth, the sea, and stars, should be so prodigiously developed and illustrated in our age, and yet the boundaries of the intellectual globe should be confined to the narrow discoveries of the ancients.

With regard to authority, it is the greatest weakness to attribute infinite credit to particular authors, and to refuse his own prerogative to time, the author of all authors, and, therefore, of all authority. For truth is rightly named the daughter of time, not of authority. It is not wonderful, therefore, if the bonds of antiquity, authority, and unanimity, have so enchained the power of man, that he is unable (as if bewitched) to become familiar with things themselves.

LXXXV. Nor is it only the admiration of antiquity, authority, and unanimity, that has forced man's industry to rest satisfied with present discoveries, but, also, the admiration of the effects already placed within his power. For whoever passes in review the variety of subjects, and the beautiful apparatus collected and introduced by the mechanical arts for the service of mankind, will certainly be rather inclined to admire our wealth than to perceive our poverty: not considering that the observations of man and operations of nature (which are the souls and first movers of that variety) are few, and not of deep research; the rest must be attributed merely to man's patience, and the deli-

---

confounding two things, which are not only distinct, but affect human knowledge in inverse proportion, viz., the experience which terminates with life, with that experience which one century transmits to another Ed.

cate and well regulated motion of the hand or of instruments. To take an instance, the manufacture of clocks is delicate and accurate, and appears to imitate the heavenly bodies in its wheels, and the pulse of animals in its regular oscillation, yet it only depends upon one or two axioms of nature.

Again, if one consider the refinement of the liberal arts, or even that exhibited in the preparation of natural bodies in mechanical arts and the like, as the discovery of the heavenly motions in astronomy, of harmony in music, of the letters of the alphabet* (still unadopted by the Chinese) in grammar; or, again, in mechanical operations, the productions of Bacchus and Ceres, that is, the preparation of wine and beer, the making of bread, or even the luxuries of the table, distillation, and the like; if one reflect also, and consider for how long a period of ages (for all the above, except distillation, are ancient) these things have been brought to their present state of perfection, and (as we instanced in clocks) to how few observations and axioms of nature they may be referred, and how easily, and as it were, by obvious chance or contemplation, they might be discovered, one would soon cease to admire and rather pity the human lot on account of its vast want and dearth of things and discoveries for so many ages. Yet even the discoveries we have mentioned were more ancient than philosophy and the intellectual arts; so that, (to say the truth) when contemplation and doctrinal science began, the discovery of useful works ceased.

But if any one turn from the manufactories to libraries, and be inclined to admire the immense variety of books offered to our view, let him but examine and diligently inspect the matter and contents of these books, and his astonishment will certainly change its object: for when he finds no end of repetitions, and how much men do and speak the same thing over again, he will pass from admiration of this variety to astonishment at the poverty and scarcity of matter, which has hitherto possessed and filled men's minds.

But if any one should condescend to consider such sciences as are deemed rather curious than sound, and take a full view of the operations of the alchymists or magi, he will perhaps hesitate whether he ought rather to laugh or to weep. For the alchemist cherishes eternal hope, and when his labours succeed not, accuses his own mistakes, deeming, in his self-accusation, that he has not properly understood the words of art or of his authors; upon which he listens to tradition and vague whispers, or imagines there is some slight unsteadiness in the minute details of his practice, and then has recourse to an endless repe-

---

* The Chinese characters resemble, in many respects, the hieroglyphics of the Egyptians, being adapted to represent ideas, not sounds.

tition of experiments: and in the mean time, when, in his casual experiments, he falls upon something in appearance new, or of some degree of utility, he consoles himself with such an earnest, and ostentatiously publishes them, keeping up his hope of the final result. Nor can it be denied that the alchemists have made several discoveries, and presented mankind with useful inventions. But we may well apply to them the fable of the old man, who bequeathed to his sons some gold buried in his garden, pretending not to know the exact spot, whereupon they worked diligently in digging the vineyard, and though they found no gold, the vintage was rendered more abundant by their labour.

The followers of natural magic, who explain everything by sympathy and antipathy, have assigned false powers and marvellous operations to things by gratuitous and idle conjectures: and if they have ever produced any effects, they are rather wonderful and novel than of any real benefit or utility.

In superstitious magic (if we say anything at all about it) we must chiefly observe, that there are only some peculiar and definite objects with which the curious and superstitious arts have, in every nation and age, and even under every religion, been able to exercise and amuse themselves. Let us, therefore, pass them over. In the mean time we cannot wonder that the false notion of plenty should have occasioned want.

LXXXVI. The admiration of mankind with regard to the arts and sciences, which is of itself sufficiently simple and almost puerile, has been increased by the craft and artifices of those who have treated the sciences, and delivered them down to posterity. For they propose and produce them to our view so fashioned, and as it were masked, as to make them pass for perfect and complete. For if you consider their method and divisions, they appear to embrace and comprise everything which can relate to the subject. And although this frame be badly filled up and resemble an empty bladder, yet it presents to the vulgar understanding the form and appearance of a perfect science.

The first and most ancient investigators of truth were wont, on the contrary, with more honesty and success, to throw all the knowledge they wished to gather from contemplation, and to lay up for use, into aphorisms, or short scattered sentences unconnected by any method, and without pretending or professing to comprehend any entire art. But according to the present system, we cannot wonder that men seek nothing beyond that which is handed down to them as perfect, and already extended to its full complement.

LXXXVII. The ancient theories have received additional support and credit from the absurdity and levity of those who have promoted the new, especially in the active and practical part of natural philosophy. For there have been many silly and fantastical fellows who, from credulity or imposture, have loaded mankind with promises, announcing and boasting of the prolongation of life, the retarding of old age, the alleviation of pains, the remedying of natural defects, the deception of the senses, the restraint and excitement of the passions, the illumination and exaltation of the intellectual faculties, the transmutation of substances, the unlimited intensity and multiplication of motion, the impressions and changes of the air, the bringing into our power the management of celestial influences, the divination of future events, the representation of distant objects, the revelation of hidden objects, and the like. One would not be very wrong in observing with regard to such pretenders, that there is as much difference in philosophy, between their absurdity and real science, as there is in history between the exploits of Cæsar or Alexander, and those of Amadis de Gaul and Arthur of Britain. For those illustrious generals are found to have actually performed greater exploits than such fictitious heroes are even pretended to have accomplished, by the means, however, of real action, and not by any fabulous and portentous power. Yet it is not right to suffer our belief in true history to be diminished, because it is sometimes injured and violated by fables. In the mean time we cannot wonder that great prejudice has been excited against any new propositions (especially when coupled with any mention of effects to be produced), by the conduct of impostors who have made a similar attempt; for their extreme absurdity, and the disgust occasioned by it, has even to this day overpowered every spirited attempt of the kind.

LXXXVIII. Want of energy, and the littleness and futility of the tasks that human industry has undertaken, have produced much greater injury to the sciences: and yet (to make it still worse) that very want of energy manifests itself in conjunction with arrogance and disdain.

For, in the first place, one excuse, now from its repetition become familiar, is to be observed in every art, namely, that its promoters convert the weakness of the art itself into a calumny upon nature: and whatever it in their hands fails to effect, they pronounce to be physically impossible. But how can the art ever be condemned whilst it acts as judge in its own cause? Even the present system of philosophy cherishes in its bosom certain positions or dogmas, which (it will be found on diligent inquiry) are calculated to produce a full conviction that no difficult, commanding, and powerful operation upon nature ought to be anticipated through the means of art; we instanced[b] above the alleged different quality of heat in the sun and fire, and composition and mixture. Upon an accurate observation the

[b] See Axiom 75.

whole tendency of such positions is wilfully to circumscribe man's power, and to produce a despair of the means of invention and contrivance, which would not only confound the promises of hope, but cut the very springs and sinews of industry, and throw aside even the chances of experience. The only object of such philosophers is to acquire the reputation of perfection for their own art, and they are anxious to obtain the most silly and abandoned renown, by causing a belief that whatever has not yet been invented and understood can never be so hereafter. But if any one attempt to give himself up to things, and to discover something new, yet he will only propose and destine for his object the investigation and discovery of some one invention, and nothing more; as the nature of the magnet, the tides, the heavenly system, and the like, which appear enveloped in some degree of mystery, and have hitherto been treated with but little success. Now it is the greatest proof of want of skill, to investigate the nature of any object in itself alone; for that same nature, which seems concealed and hidden in some instances, is manifest and almost palpable in others, and excites wonder in the former, whilst it hardly attracts attention in the latter.[c] Thus the nature of consistency is scarcely observed in wood or stone, but passed over by the term solid without any further inquiry about the repulsion of separation or the solution of continuity. But in water-bubbles the same circumstance appears matter of delicate and ingenious research, for they form themselves into thin pellicles, curiously shaped into hemispheres, so as for an instant to avoid the solution of continuity.

In general those very things which are considered as secret are manifest and common in other objects, but will never be clearly seen if the experiments and contemplation of man be directed to themselves only. Yet it commonly happens, that if, in the mechanical arts, any one bring old discoveries to a finer polish, or more elegant height of ornament, or unite and compound them, or apply them more readily to practice, or exhibit them on a less heavy and voluminous scale, and the like, they will pass off as new.

We cannot, therefore, wonder that no magnificent discoveries, worthy of mankind, have been brought to light, whilst men are satisfied and delighted with such scanty and puerile tasks, nay,

[c] The methods by which Newton carried the rule and compass to the boundaries of creation is a sufficient comment on the sagacity of the text. The same cause which globulizes a bubble, has rounded the earth, and the same law which draws a stone to its surface, keeps the moon in her orbit. It was by calculating and ascertaining these principles upon substances entirely at his disposal that this great philosopher was enabled to give us a key to unlock the mysteries of the universe. *Ed.*

even think that they have pursued or attained some great object in their accomplishment.

LXXXIX. Nor should we neglect to observe that natural philosophy has, in every age, met with a troublesome and difficult opponent: I mean superstition, and a blind and immoderate zeal for religion. For we see that, among the Greeks, those who first disclosed the natural causes of thunder and storms to the yet untrained ears of man were condemned as guilty of impiety towards the gods.[d] Nor did some of the old fathers of Christianity treat those much better who showed by the most positive proofs (such as no one now disputes) that the earth is spherical, and thence asserted that there were antipodes.[e]

Even in the present state of things the condition of discussions on natural philosophy is rendered more difficult and dangerous by the summaries and methods of divines, who, after reducing divinity into such order as they could, and brought it into a scientific form, have proceeded to mingle an undue proportion of the contentious and thorny philosophy of Aristotle with the substance of religion.[f]

The fictions of those who have not feared to deduce and confirm the truth of the Christian religion by the principles and authority of philosophers, tend to the same end, though in a different manner.[g] They celebrate the union of faith and the senses as though it were legitimate, with great pomp and solemnity, and gratify men's pleasing minds with a variety, but in the meantime confound most improperly things divine and human. Moreover, in these mixtures of divinity and philosophy the received doctrines of the latter are alone included, and any novelty,

---

[d] See the "Clouds" of Aristophanes, where Socrates is represented as chasing Jupiter out of the sky, by resolving thunder-storms into aërial concussions and whirlwinds. *Ed.*

[e] Robespierre was the latest victim of this bigotry. In his younger days he attempted to introduce Franklin's lightning conductor into France, but was persecuted by those whose lives he sought to protect, as one audaciously striving to avert the designs of Providence. *Ed.*

[f] We can hardly agree with the text. The scholastics, in building up a system of divinity, certainly had recourse to the deductive syllogism, because the inductive was totally inapplicable, except as a verificatory process. With regard to the technical form in which they marshalled their arguments, which is what our author aims at in his censure, they owed nothing at all to Aristotle, the conducting a dispute in naked syllogistic fashion having originated entirely with themselves. *Ed.*

[g] Bacon cannot be supposed to allude to those divines who have attempted to show that the progress of physical science is confirmatory of revelation, but only to such as have built up a system of faith out of their own refinements on nature and revelation, as Patricius and Emanuel Swedenborg. *Ed.*

even though it be an improvement, scarcely escapes banishment and extermination.

In short, you may find all access to any species of philosophy, however pure, intercepted by the ignorance of divines. Some in their simplicity are apprehensive that a too deep inquiry into nature may penetrate beyond the proper bounds of decorum, transferring and absurdly applying what is said of sacred mysteries in Holy Writ against those who pry into divine secrets, to the mysteries of nature, which are not forbidden by any prohibition. Others with more cunning imagine and consider, that if secondary causes be unknown, everything may more easily be referred to the Divine hand and wand, a matter, as they think, of the greatest consequence to religion, but which can only really mean that God wishes to be gratified by means of falsehood. Others fear, from past example, lest motion and change in philosophy should terminate in an attack upon religion. Lastly, there are others who appear anxious lest there should be something discovered in the investigation of nature to overthrow, or at least shake, religion, particularly among the unlearned. The two last apprehensions appear to resemble animal instinct, as if men were diffident, in the bottom of their minds and secret meditations, of the strength of religion and the empire of faith over the senses, and therefore feared that some danger awaited them from an inquiry into nature. But any one who properly considers the subject will find natural philosophy to be, after the Word of God, the surest remedy against superstition, and the most approved support of faith. She is, therefore, rightly bestowed upon religion as a most faithful attendant, for the one exhibits the will and the other the power of God. Nor was he wrong who observed, "Ye err, not knowing the Scriptures and the power of God," thus uniting in one bond the revelation of his will and the contemplation of his power. In the meanwhile, it is not wonderful that the progress of natural philosophy has been restrained, since religion, which has so much influence on men's minds, has been led and hurried to oppose her through the ignorance of some and the imprudent zeal of others.

XC. Again, in the habits and regulations of schools, universities, and the like assemblies, destined for the abode of learned men and the improvement of learning, everything is found to be opposed to the progress of the sciences; for the lectures and exercises are so ordered, that anything out of the common track can scarcely enter the thoughts and contemplations of the mind. If, however, one or two have perhaps dared to use their liberty, they can only impose the labour on themselves, without deriving any advantage from the association of others; and if they put up with this, they will find their industry and spirit of no slight disadvantage to them in making their fortune; for the pursuits of men in such situations are, as it were, chained down to the writings of particular authors, and if any one dare to dissent from them he is immediately attacked as a turbulent and revolutionary spirit. Yet how great is the difference between civil matters and the arts, for there is not the same danger from new activity and new light. In civil matters even a change for the better is suspected on account of the commotion it occasions, for civil government is supported by authority, unanimity, fame, and public opinion, and not by demonstration. In the arts and sciences, on the contrary, every department should resound, as in mines, with new works and advances. And this is the rational, though not the actual view of the case, for that administration and government of science we have spoken of is wont too rigorously to repress its growth.

XCI. And even should the odium I have alluded to be avoided, yet it is sufficient to repress the increase of science that such attempts and industry pass unrewarded; for the cultivation of science and its reward belong not to the same individual. The advancement of science is the work of a powerful genius, the prize and reward belong to the vulgar or to princes, who (with a few exceptions) are scarcely moderately well informed. Nay, such progress is not only deprived of the rewards and beneficence of individuals, but even of popular praise; for it is above the reach of the generality, and easily overwhelmed and extinguished by the winds of common opinions. It is not wonderful, therefore, that little success has attended that which has been little honoured.

XCII. But by far the greatest obstacle to the advancement of the sciences, and the undertaking of any new attempt or department, is to be found in men's despair and the idea of impossibility; for men of a prudent and exact turn of thought are altogether diffident in matters of this nature, considering the obscurity of nature, the shortness of life, the deception of the senses, and weakness of the judgment. They think, therefore, that in the revolutions of ages and of the world there are certain floods and ebbs of the sciences, and that they grow and flourish at one time, and wither and fall off at another, that when they have attained a certain degree and condition they can proceed no further.

If, therefore, any one believe or promise greater things, they impute it to an uncurbed and immature mind, and imagine that such efforts begin pleasantly, then become laborious, and end in confusion. And since such thoughts easily enter the minds of men of dignity and excellent judgment, we must really take heed lest we should be captivated by our affection for an excellent and most beautiful object, and relax or diminish the severity of our judgment; and we must diligently examine what gleam of hope shines upon us, and in what direction it manifests itself, so that, banishing her lighter dreams, we may discuss and weigh whatever appears of more sound importance. We must consult the prudence of ordinary life, too, which is diffident upon principle, and in all human matters augurs the worst. Let us, then, speak of hope, especially as we are not vain promisers, nor are willing to enforce or ensnare men's judgment, but would rather lead them willingly forward. And although we shall employ the most cogent means of enforcing hope when we bring them to particulars, and especially those which are digested and arranged in our Tables of Invention (the subject partly of the second, but principally of the fourth part of the Instauration), which are, indeed, rather the very object of our hopes than hope itself; yet to proceed more leniently we must treat of the preparation of men's minds, of which the manifestation of hope forms no slight part; for without it all that we have said tends rather to produce a gloom than to encourage activity or quicken the industry of experiment, by causing them to have a worse and more contemptuous opinion of things as they are than they now entertain, and to perceive and feel more thoroughly their unfortunate condition. We must, therefore, disclose and prefix our reasons for not thinking the hope of success improbable, as Columbus, before his wonderful voyage over the Atlantic, gave the reasons of his conviction that new lands and continents might be discovered besides those already known; and these reasons, though at first rejected, were yet proved by subsequent experience, and were the causes and beginnings of the greatest events.

XCIII. Let us begin from God, and show that our pursuit from its exceeding goodness clearly proceeds from him, the author of good and father of light. Now, in all divine works the smallest beginnings lead assuredly to some result, and the remark in spiritual matters that "the kingdom of God cometh without observation," is also found to be true in every great work of Divine Providence, so that everything glides quietly on without confusion or noise, and the matter is achieved before men either think or perceive that it is commenced. Nor should we neglect to mention the prophecy of Daniel, of the last days of the world, "Many shall run to and fro, and knowledge shall be increased,"[b] thus plainly hinting and suggesting that fate (which is Providence) would cause the complete circuit of the globe (now accomplished, or at least going forward by means of so many distant voyages), and the increase of learning to happen at the same epoch.

XCIV. We will next give a most potent reason for hope deduced from the errors of the past, and the ways still unattempted; for well was an ill-governed state thus reproved,

[b] Daniel xii. 4.

"That which is worst with regard to the past should appear most consolatory for the future; for if you had done all that your duty commanded, and your affairs proceeded no better, you could not even hope for their improvement; but since their present unhappy situation is not owing to the force of circumstances, but to your own errors, you have reason to hope that by banishing or correcting the latter you can produce a great change for the better in the former." So if men had, during the many years that have elapsed, adhered to the right way of discovering and cultivating the sciences without being able to advance, it would be assuredly bold and presumptuous to imagine it possible to improve; but if they have mistaken the way and wasted their labour on improper objects, it follows that the difficulty does not arise from things themselves, which are not in our power, but from the human understanding, its practice and application, which is susceptible of remedy and correction. Our best plan, therefore, is to expose these errors; for in proportion as they impeded the past, so do they afford reason to hope for the future. And although we have touched upon them above, yet we think it right to give a brief, bare, and simple enumeration of them in this place.

XCV. Those who have treated of the sciences have been either empirics or dogmatical.[i] The former like ants only heap up and use their store, the latter like spiders spin out their own webs. The bee, a mean between both, extracts matter from the flowers of the garden and the field, but works and fashions it by its own efforts. The true labour of philosophy resembles hers, for it neither relies entirely or principally on the powers of the mind, nor yet lays up in the memory the matter afforded by the experiments of natural history and mechanics in its raw state, but changes and works it in the understanding. We have good reason, therefore, to derive hope from a closer and purer alliance of these faculties (the experimental and rational) than has yet been attempted.

XCVI. Natural philosophy is not yet to be found unadulterated, but is impure and corrupted,—by logic in the school of Aristotle, by natural theology in that of Plato,[k] by mathematics

[i] Bacon, in this Aphorism, appears to have entertained a fair idea of the use of the inductive and deductive methods in scientific inquiry, though his want of geometrical knowledge must have hindered him from accurately determining the precise functions of each, as it certainly led him in other parts of the Organon (V. Aph. 82), to undervalue the deductive, and, as he calls it, the dogmatic method, and to rely too much upon empiricism. *Ed.*

[k] The reader may consult the note of the 23rd Aphorism for the fault which Bacon censures, and, if he wish to pursue the subject further, may read Plato's Timæus, where that philosopher explains his

in the second school of Plato (that of Proclus and others)[1] which ought rather to terminate natural philosophy than to generate or create it. We may, therefore, hope for better results from pure and unmixed natural philosophy.

XCVII. No one has yet been found possessed of sufficient firmness and severity to resolve upon and undertake the task of entirely abolishing common theories and notions, and applying the mind afresh, when thus cleared and levelled, to particular researches; hence our human reasoning is a mere farrago and crude mass made up of a great deal of credulity and accident, and the puerile notions it originally contracted.

But if a man of mature age, unprejudiced senses, and clear mind, would betake himself anew to experience and particulars, we might hope much more from such a one; in which respect we promise ourselves the fortune of Alexander the Great, and let none accuse us of vanity till they have heard the tale, which is intended to check vanity.

For Æschines spoke thus of Alexander and his exploits: "We live not the life of mortals, but are born at such a period that posterity will relate and declare our prodigies;" as if he considered the exploits of Alexander to be miraculous.

But in succeeding ages[m] Livy took a better view of the fact, and has made some such observation as this upon Alexander: "That he did no more than dare to despise insignificance." So in our opinion posterity will judge of us, that we have achieved no great matters, but only set less account upon what is considered important; for the meantime (as we have before observed)

---

system in detail. Bacon, however, is hardly consistent in one part of his censure, for he also talks about the spirit and appetites of inanimate substances, and that so frequently, as to preclude the supposition that he is employing metaphor. *Ed.*

[1] Proclus flourished about the beginning of the fifth century, and was the successor of Plotinus, Porphyry, and Iamblicus, who, in the two preceding centuries, had revived the doctrines of Plato, and assailed the Christian religion. The allusion in the text must be assigned to Iamblicus, who, in the fourth century, had republished the Pythagorean theology of numbers, and endeavoured to construct the world out of arithmetic, thinking everything could be solved by the aid of proportions and geometry. Bacon must not be understood in the text to censure the use but the abuse of mathematics and physical investigations, as in the "De Augmentis" (lib. iv. c. 6), he enumerates the multiplicity of demonstration scientific facts admit of, from this source. *Ed.*

[m] See Livy, lib. x. c. 17, where, in a digression on the probable effect of a contest between Rome and Alexander the Great, he says: "Non cum Dario rem esse dixisset: quem mulierum ac spadonum agmen trahentem inter purpuram atque aurum, oneratum fortunæ apparatibus, prædam verius quam hostem, nihil aliud quam ausus vana contemnere, incruentus devicit."

our only hope is in the regeneration of the sciences, by regularly raising them on the foundation of experience and building them anew, which I think none can venture to affirm to have been already done or even thought of.

XCVIII. The foundations of experience (our sole resource) have hitherto failed completely or have been very weak; nor has a store and collection of particular facts, capable of informing the mind or in any way satisfactory, been either sought after or amassed. On the contrary, learned, but idle and indolent, men have received some mere reports of experience, traditions as it were of dreams, as establishing or confirming their philosophy, and have not hesitated to allow them the weight of legitimate evidence. So that a system has been pursued in philosophy with regard to experience resembling that of a kingdom or state which would direct its councils and affairs according to the gossip of city and street politicians, instead of the letters and reports of ambassadors and messengers worthy of credit. Nothing is rightly inquired into, or verified, noted, weighed, or measured, in natural history; indefinite and vague observation produces fallacious and uncertain information. If this appear strange, or our complaint somewhat too unjust (because Aristotle himself, so distinguished a man and supported by the wealth of so great a king, has completed an accurate history of animals, to which others with greater diligence but less noise have made considerable additions, and others again have composed copious histories and notices of plants, metals, and fossils), it will arise from a want of sufficiently attending to and comprehending our present observations; for a natural history compiled on its own account, and one collected for the mind's information as a foundation for philosophy, are two different things. They differ in several respects, but principally in this,—the former contains only the varieties of natural species without the experiments of mechanical arts; for as in ordinary life every person's disposition, and the concealed feelings of the mind and passions are most drawn out when they are disturbed,—so the secrets of nature betray themselves more readily when tormented by art than when left to their own course. We must begin, therefore, to entertain hopes of natural philosophy then only, when we have a better compilation of natural history, its real basis and support.

XCIX. Again, even in the abundance of mechanical experiments, there is a very great scarcity of those which best inform and assist the understanding. For the mechanic, little solicitous about the investigation of truth, neither directs his attention, nor applies his hand to anything that is not of service to his business. But our hope of further progress in the sciences will then only be well founded, when numerous experiments shall be received and collected into natural history, which, though of no use in themselves, assist materially in the discovery of causes and axioms; which experiments we have termed enlightening, to distinguish them from those which are profitable. They possess this wonderful property and nature, that they never deceive or fail you; for being used only to discover the natural cause of some object, whatever be the result, they equally satisfy your aim by deciding the question.

C. We must not only search for, and procure a greater number of experiments, but also introduce a completely different method, order, and progress of continuing and promoting experience. For vague and arbitrary experience is (as we have observed), mere groping in the dark, and rather astonishes than instructs. But when experience shall proceed regularly and uninterruptedly by a determined rule, we may entertain better hopes of the sciences.

CI. But after having collected and prepared an abundance and store of natural history, and of the experience required for the operations of the understanding or philosophy, still the understanding is as incapable of acting on such materials of itself, with the aid of memory alone, as any person would be of retaining and achieving, by memory, the computation of an almanack. Yet meditation has hitherto done more for discovery than writing, and no experiments have been committed to paper. We cannot, however, approve of any mode of discovery without writing, and when that comes into more general use, we may have further hopes.

CII. Besides this, there is such a multitude and host, as it were, of particular objects, and lying so widely dispersed, as to distract and confuse the understanding; and we can, therefore, hope for no advantage from its skirmishing, and quick movements and incursions, unless we put its forces in due order and array, by means of proper and well arranged, and, as it were, living tables of discovery of these matters, which are the subject of investigation, and the mind then apply itself to the ready prepared and digested aid which such tables afford.

CIII. When we have thus properly and regularly placed before the eyes a collection of particulars, we must not immediately proceed to the investigation and discovery of new particulars or effects, or, at least, if we do so, must not rest satisfied therewith. For, though we do not deny that by transferring the experiments from one art to another (when all the experiments of each have been collected and arranged, and have been acquired by the knowledge, and subjected to the judgment of a single individual), many new experiments may be discovered tending to benefit society and mankind, by what we term literate experience; yet comparatively insignificant results are to be expected thence, whilst the more important are to be derived from the new light of axioms, deduced by certain method and rule from the above particulars, and pointing out and defining new particulars in their turn. Our road is not a long plain, but rises and falls, ascending to axioms, and descending to effects.

CIV. Nor can we suffer the understanding to jump and fly from particulars to remote and most general axioms (such as are termed the principles of arts and things), and thus prove and make out their intermediate axioms according to the supposed unshaken truth of the former. This, however, has always been done to the present time from the natural bent of the understanding, educated too, and accustomed to this very method, by the syllogistic mode of demonstration. But we can then only augur well for the sciences, when the ascent shall proceed by a true scale and successive steps, without interruption or breach, from particulars to the lesser axioms, thence to the intermediate (rising one above the other), and lastly, to the most general. For the lowest axioms differ but little from bare experiment;[a] the highest and most general (as they are esteemed at present), are notional, abstract, and of no real weight. The intermediate are true, solid, full of life, and upon them depend the business and fortune of mankind; beyond these are the really general, but not abstract, axioms, which are truly limited by the intermediate.

We must not then add wings, but rather lead and ballast to the understanding, to prevent its jumping or flying, which has not yet been done; but whenever this takes place, we may entertain greater hopes of the sciences.

CV. In forming axioms, we must invent a different form of

---

[a] The lowest axioms are such as spring from simple experience,—such as in chemistry, that animal substances yield no fixed salt by calcination; in music, that concords intermixed with discords make harmony, &c. Intermediate axioms advance a step further, being the result of reflection, which, applied to our experimental knowledge, deduces laws from them, such as in optics of the first degree of generality, that the angle of incidence is equal to the angle of reflection; and in mechanics, Kepler's three laws of motion, while his general law, that all bodies attract each other with forces proportional to their masses, and inversely as the squares of their distances, may be taken as one of the highest axioms. Yet so far is this principle from being only notional or abstract, it has presented us with a key which fits into the intricate wards of the heavens, and has laid bare to our gaze the principal mechanism of the universe. But natural philosophy in Bacon's day had not advanced beyond intermediate axioms, and the term notional or abstract is applied to those general axioms then current, not founded on the solid principles of inductive inquiry, but based up n à *priori* reasoning and airy metaphysics. *Ed.*

induction from that hitherto in use; not only for the proof and discovery of principles (as they are called), but also of minor, intermediate, and, in short, every kind of axioms. The induction which proceeds by simple enumeration is puerile, leads to uncertain conclusions, and is exposed to danger from one contradictory instance, deciding generally from too small a number of facts, and those only the most obvious. But a really useful induction for the discovery and demonstration of the arts and sciences, should separate nature by proper rejections and exclusions, and then conclude for the affirmative, after collecting a sufficient number of negatives. Now this has not been done, nor even attempted, except perhaps by Plato, who certainly uses this form of induction in some measure, to sift definitions and ideas. But much of what has never yet entered the thoughts of man must necessarily be employed, in order to exhibit a good and legitimate mode of induction or demonstration, so as even to render it essential for us to bestow more pains upon it than have hitherto been bestowed on syllogisms. The assistance of induction is to serve us not only in the discovery of axioms, but also in defining our notions. Much indeed is to be hoped from such an induction as has been described.

CVI. In forming our axioms from induction, we must examine and try whether the axiom we derive be only fitted and calculated for the particular instances from which it is deduced, or whether it be more extensive and general. If it be the latter, we must observe, whether it confirm its own extent and generality by giving surety, as it were, in pointing out new particulars, so that we may neither stop at actual discoveries, nor with a careless grasp catch at shadows and abstract forms, instead of substances of a determinate nature: and as soon as we act thus, well authorized hope may with reason, be said to beam upon us.

CVII. Here, too, we may again repeat what we have said above, concerning the extending of natural philosophy and reducing particular sciences to that one, so as to prevent any schism or dismembering of the sciences; without which we cannot hope to advance.

CVIII. Such are the observations we would make in order to remove despair and excite hope, by bidding farewell to the errors of past ages, or by their correction. Let us examine whether there be other grounds for hope. And, first, if many useful discoveries have occurred to mankind by chance or opportunity, without investigation or attention on their part, it must necessarily be acknowledged that much more may be brought to light by investigation and attention, if it be regular and orderly, not hasty and interrupted. For although it may now and then happen that one falls by chance upon something that had before escaped considerable efforts and laborious inquiries, yet undoubtedly the reverse is generally the case. We may, therefore, hope for further, better, and more frequent results from man's reason, industry, method, and application, than from chance and mere animal instinct, and the like, which have hitherto been the sources of invention.

CIX. We may also derive some reason for hope from the circumstance of several actual inventions being of such a nature, that scarcely any one could have formed a conjecture about them previously to their discovery, but would rather have ridiculed them as impossible. For men are wont to guess about new subjects from those they are already acquainted with, and the hasty and vitiated fancies they have thence formed: than which there cannot be a more fallacious mode of reasoning, because much of that which is derived from the sources of things does not flow in their usual channel.

If, for instance, before the discovery of cannon, one had described its effects in the following manner: There is a new invention by which walls and the greatest bulwarks can be shaken and overthrown from a considerable distance; men would have begun to contrive various means of multiplying the force of projectiles and machines by means of weights and wheels, and other modes of battering and projecting. But it is improbable that any imagination or fancy would have hit upon a fiery blast, expanding and developing itself so suddenly and violently, because none would have seen an instance at all resembling it, except perhaps in earthquakes or thunder, which they would have immediately rejected as the great operations of nature, not to be imitated by man.

So, if before the discovery of silk thread, any one had observed, That a species of thread had been discovered, fit for dresses and furniture, far surpassing the thread of worsted or flax in fineness, and at the same time in tenacity, beauty, and softness; men would have begun to imagine something about Chinese plants, or the fine hair of some animals, or the feathers or down of birds, but certainly would never have had an idea of its being spun by a small worm, in so copious a manner, and renewed annually. But if any one had ventured to suggest the silkworm, he would have been laughed at as if dreaming of some new manufacture from spiders.

So again, if before the discovery of the compass, any one had said, That an instrument had been invented, by which the quarters and points of the heavens could be exactly taken and distinguished, men would have entered into disquisitions on the refinement of astronomical instruments, and the like, from the excitement of their imaginations; but the thought of anything being discovered, which, not being a celestial body, but a mere mineral or metallic substance, should yet in its motion agree with that of such bodies, would have appeared absolutely incredible. Yet were these facts, and the like (unknown for so many ages) not discovered at last either by philosophy or reasoning, but by chance and opportunity; and (as we have observed), they are of a nature most heterogeneous, and remote from what was hitherto known, so that no previous knowledge could lead to them.

We may, therefore, well hope° that many excellent and useful matters are yet treasured up in the bosom of nature, bearing no relation or analogy to our actual discoveries, but out of the common track of our imagination, and still undiscovered, and which will doubtless be brought to light in the course and lapse of years, as the others have been before them; but in the way we now point out, they may rapidly and at once be both represented and anticipated.

CX. There are, moreover, some inventions which render it probable that men may pass and hurry over the most noble discoveries which lie immediately before them. For however the discovery of gunpowder, silk, the compass, sugar, paper, or the like, may appear to depend on peculiar properties of things and nature, printing at least involves no contrivance which is not clear and almost obvious. But from want of observing that although the arrangement of the types of letters required more trouble than writing with the hand, yet these types once arranged serve for innumerable impressions, whilst manuscript only affords one copy; and again, from want of observing that ink might be thickened so as to stain without running (which was necessary, seeing the letters face upwards, and the impression is made from above), this most beautiful invention (which assists so materially the propagation of learning) remained unknown for so many ages.

The human mind is often so awkward and ill-regulated in the career of invention that it is at first diffident, and then despises itself. For it appears at first incredible that any such discovery should be made, and when it has been made, it appears incredible that it should so long have escaped men's research. All which affords good reason for the hope that a vast mass of inventions yet remains, which may be deduced not only from the investigation of new modes of operation, but also from transferring, comparing, and applying these already known, by the method of what we have termed literate experience.

° This hope has been abundantly realized in the discovery of gravity and the decomposition of light, mainly by the inductive method. To a better philosophy we may also attribute the discovery of electricity, galvanism, and their mutual connection with each other, and magnetism, the inventions of the air-pump, steam-engine, and the chronometer.

CXI. Nor should we omit another ground of hope. Let men only consider (if they will) their infinite expenditure of talent, time, and fortune, in matters and studies of far inferior importance and value; a small portion of which applied to sound and solid learning would be sufficient to overcome every difficulty. And we have thought right to add this observation, because we candidly own that such a collection of natural and experimental history as we have traced in our own mind, and as is really necessary, is a great and as it were royal work, requiring much labour and expense.

CXII. In the meantime let no one be alarmed at the multitude of particulars, but rather inclined to hope on that very account. For the particular phenomena of the arts and nature are in reality but as a handful, when compared with the fictions of the imagination removed and separated from the evidence of facts. The termination of our method is clear, and I had almost said near at hand; the other admits of no termination, but only of infinite confusion. For men have hitherto dwelt but little, or rather only slightly touched upon experience, whilst they have wasted much time on theories and the fictions of the imagination. If we had but any one who could actually answer our interrogations of nature, the invention of all causes and sciences would be the labour of but a few years.

CXIII. We think some ground of hope is afforded by our own example, which is not mentioned for the sake of boasting, but as a useful remark. Let those who distrust their own powers observe myself, one who have amongst my contemporaries been the most engaged in public business, who am not very strong in health (which causes a great loss of time), and am the first explorer of this course, following the guidance of none, nor even communicating my thoughts to a single individual; yet having once firmly entered in the right way, and submitting the powers of my mind to things, I have somewhat advanced (as I make bold to think) the matter I now treat of. Then let others consider what may be hoped from men who enjoy abundant leisure, from united labours, and the succession of ages, after these suggestions on our part, especially in a course which is not confined, like theories, to individuals, but admits of the best distribution and union of labour and effect, particularly in collecting experiments. For men will then only begin to know their own power, when each performs a separate part, instead of undertaking in crowds the same work.

CXIV. Lastly, though a much more faint and uncertain breeze of hope were to spring up from our new continent, yet we consider it necessary to make the experiment, if we would not show a dastard spirit. For the risk attending want of success is not to be compared with that of neglecting the attempt; the former is attended with the loss of a little human labour, the latter with that of an immense benefit. For these and other reasons it appears to us that there is abundant ground to hope, and to induce not only those who are sanguine to make experiment, but even those who are cautious and sober to give their assent.

CXV. Such are the grounds for banishing despair, hitherto one of the most powerful causes of the delay and restraint to which the sciences have been subjected; in treating of which we have at the same time discussed the signs and causes of the errors, idleness, and ignorance, that have prevailed; seeing especially that the more refined causes, which are not open to popular judgment and observation, may be referred to our remarks on the idols of the human mind.

Here, too, we should close the demolishing branch of our instauration, which is comprised in three confutations : 1, the confutation of natural human reason left to itself; 2, the confutation of demonstration; 3, the confutation of theories, or received systems of philosophy and doctrines. Our confutation has followed such a course as was open to it, namely, the exposing of the signs of error, and the producing evidence of the causes of it: for we could adopt no other, differing as we do both in first principles and demonstrations from others.

It is time for us therefore to come to the art itself, and the rule for the interpretation of nature: there is, however, still something which must not be passed over. For the intent of this first book of aphorisms being to prepare the mind for understanding, as well as admitting, what follows, we must now, after having cleansed, polished, and levelled its surface, place it in a good position, and as it were a benevolent aspect towards our propositions; seeing that prejudice in new matters may be produced not only by the strength of preconceived notions, but also by a false anticipation or expectation of the matter proposed. We shall therefore endeavour to induce good and correct opinions of what we offer, although this be only necessary for the moment, and as it were laid out at interest, until the matter itself be well understood.

CXVI. First, then, we must desire men not to suppose that we are ambitious of founding any philosophical sect, like the ancient Greeks, or some moderns, as Telesius, Patricius, and Severinus.[p] For neither is this our intention, nor do we think

[p] As Bacon very frequently cites these authors, a slight notice of their labours may not be unacceptable to the reader. Bernardinus Telesius, born at Cosenza, in 1508, combated the Aristotelian system in a work entitled " De Rerum Natura juxta propria principia," *i. e.* according to principles of his own. The proem of the work announces his design was to show that " the construction of the world, the magnitude and

that peculiar abstract opinions on nature and the principles of things are of much importance to men's fortunes, since it were easy to revive many ancient theories, and to introduce many new ones; as for instance, many hypotheses with regard to the heavens can be formed, differing in themselves, and yet sufficiently according with the phenomena.

We bestow not our labour on such theoretical, and, at the same time, useless topics. On the contrary, our determination is that of trying, whether we can lay a firmer foundation, and extend to a greater distance the boundaries of human power and dignity. And although here and there, upon some particular points, we hold (in our own opinion) more true and certain, and I might even say, more advantageous tenets than those in general repute (which we have collected in the fifth part of our Instauration), yet we offer no universal or complete theory. The time does not yet appear to us to be arrived, and we entertain no hope of our life being prolonged to the completion of the sixth part of the instauration (which is destined for philosophy discovered by the interpretation of nature), but are content if we proceed quietly and usefully in our intermediate pursuit, scattering, in the mean time, the seeds of less adulterated truth for posterity, and, at least, commence the great work.

nature of the bodies contained in it, are not to be investigated by reasoning, which was done by the ancients, but are to be apprehended by the senses, and collected from the things themselves." He had, however, no sooner laid down this principle than he departed from it in practice, and pursued the deductive method he so much condemned in his predecessors. His first step was an assumption of principles as arbitrary as any of the empirical notions of antiquity; at the outset of his book he very quietly takes it for granted that heat is the principle of motion, cold of immobility, matter being assumed as the corporeal substratum, in which these incorporeal and active agents carry on their operations. Out of these abstract and ill-defined conceptions Telesius builds up a system quite as complete, symmetrical, and imaginative as any of the structures of antiquity.

Francis Patricius, born at Cherso, in Dalmatia, about 1529, was another physicist who rose up against Aristotle, and announced the dawn of a new philosophy. In 1593 appeared his "Nova de Universis Philosophia." He lays down a string of axioms, in which scholastic notions, physical discoveries, and theological dogmas, are strangely commingled, and erects upon them a system which represents all the grotesque features of theological empiricism.

Severinus, born in Jutland, in 1529, published an attack on Aristotle's natural history, but adopted fantasies which the Stagyrite ridiculed in his own day. He was a follower of Paracelsus, a Swiss enthusiast of the fifteenth century, who ignored the ancient doctrine of the four elements for salt, sulphur, and mercury, and allied chemistry and medicine with mysticism. *Ed.*

CXVII. And, as we pretend not to found a sect, so do we neither offer nor promise particular effects; which may occasion some to object to us, that since we so often speak of effects, and consider everything in its relation to that end, we ought also to give some earnest of producing them. Our course and method, however (as we have often said, and again repeat), is such as not to deduce effects from effects, nor experiments from experiments (as the empirics do), but in our capacity of legitimate interpreters of nature, to deduce causes and axioms from effects and experiments; and new effects and experiments from those causes and axioms.

And although any one of moderate intelligence and ability will observe the indications and sketches of many noble effects in our tables of inventions (which form the fourth part of the Instauration), and also in the examples of particular instances cited in the second part, as well as in our observations on history (which is the subject of the third part); yet we candidly confess that our present natural history, whether compiled from books or our own inquiries, is not sufficiently copious and well ascertained to satisfy, or even assist, a proper interpretation.

If, therefore, there be any one who is more disposed and prepared for mechanical art, and ingenious in discovering effects, than in the mere management of experiment, we allow him to employ his industry in gathering many of the fruits of our history and tables in this way, and applying them to effects, receiving them as interest till he can obtain the principal. For our own part, having a greater object in view, we condemn all hasty and premature rest in such pursuits as we would Atalanta's apple (to use a common allusion of ours); for we are not childishly ambitious of golden fruit, but use all our efforts to make the course of art outstrip nature, and we hasten not to reap moss or the green blade, but wait for a ripe harvest.

CXVIII. There will be some, without doubt, who, on a perusal of our history and tables of invention, will meet with some uncertainty, or perhaps fallacy, in the experiments themselves, and will thence perhaps imagine that our discoveries are built on false foundations and principles. There is, however, really nothing in this, since it must needs happen in beginnings.[q] For

---

[q] Bacon's apology is sound, and completely answers those German and French critics, who have refused him a niche in the philosophical pantheon. One German commentator, too modest to reveal his name, accuses Bacon of ignorance of the calculus, though, in his day, Wallis had not yet stumbled upon the laws of continuous fractions; while Count de Maistre, in a coarse attack upon his genius, expresses his astonishment at finding Bacon unacquainted with discoveries which were not heard of till a century after his death. *Ed.*

it is the same as if in writing or printing one or two letters were wrongly turned or misplaced, which is no great inconvenience to the reader, who can easily by his own eye correct the error; let men in the same way conclude, that many experiments in natural history may be erroneously believed and admitted, which are easily expunged and rejected afterwards, by the discovery of causes and axioms. It is, however, true, that if these errors in natural history and experiments become great, frequent, and continued, they cannot be corrected and amended by any dexterity of wit or art. If then, even in our natural history, well examined and compiled with such diligence, strictness, and (I might say) reverential scruples, there be now and then something false and erroneous in the details, what must we say of the common natural history, which is so negligent and careless when compared with ours? or of systems of philosophy and the sciences, based on such loose soil (or rather quicksand)? Let none then be alarmed by such observations.

CXIX. Again, our history and experiments will contain much that is light and common, mean and illiberal, too refined and merely speculative, and, as it were, of no use, and this perhaps may divert and alienate the attention of mankind.

With regard to what is common; let men reflect, that they have hitherto been used to do nothing but refer and adapt the causes of things of rare occurrence to those of things which more frequently happen, without any investigation of the causes of the latter, taking them for granted and admitted.

Hence, they do not inquire into the causes of gravity, the rotation of the heavenly bodies, heat, cold, light, hardness, softness, rarity, density, liquidity, solidity, animation, inanimation, similitude, difference, organic formation, but taking them to be self-evident, manifest, and admitted, they dispute and decide upon other matters of less frequent and familiar occurrence.

But we (who know that no judgment can be formed of that which is rare or remarkable, and much less anything new brought to light, without a previous regular examination and discovery of the causes of that which is common, and the causes again of those causes) are necessarily compelled to admit the most common objects into our history. Besides, we have observed that nothing has been so injurious to philosophy as this circumstance, namely, that familiar and frequent objects do not arrest and detain men's contemplation, but are carelessly admitted, and their causes never inquired after; so that information on unknown subjects is not more often wanted than attention to those which are known.

CXX. With regard to the meanness, or even the filthiness of particulars, for which (as Pliny observes), an apology is requisite, such subjects are no less worthy of admission into natural history than the most magnificent and costly; nor do they at all pollute natural history, for the sun enters alike the palace and the privy, and is not thereby polluted. We neither dedicate nor raise a capitol or pyramid to the pride of man, but rear a holy temple in his mind, on the model of the universe, which model therefore we imitate. For that which is deserving of existence is deserving of knowledge, the image of existence. Now the mean and splendid alike exist. Nay, as the finest odours are sometimes produced from putrid matter (such as musk and civet), so does valuable light and information emanate from mean and sordid instances. But we have already said too much, for such fastidious feelings are childish and effeminate.

CXXI. The next point requires a more accurate consideration, namely, that many parts of our history will appear to the vulgar, or even any mind accustomed to the present state of things, fantastically and uselessly refined. Hence, we have in regard to this matter said from the first, and must again repeat, that we look for experiments that shall afford light rather than profit, imitating the divine creation, which, as we have often observed, only produced light on the first day, and assigned that whole day to its creation, without adding any material work.

If any one, then, imagine such matters to be of no use, he might equally suppose light to be of no use, because it is neither solid nor material. For, in fact, the knowledge of simple natures, when sufficiently investigated and defined, resembles light, which, though of no great use in itself, affords access to the general mysteries of effects, and with a peculiar power comprehends and draws with it whole bands and troops of effects, and the sources of the most valuable axioms. So also the elements of letters have of themselves separately no meaning, and are of no use, yet are they, as it were, the original matter in the composition and preparation of speech. The seeds of substances, whose effect is powerful, are of no use except in their growth, and the scattered rays of light itself avail not unless collected.

But if speculative subtilties give offence, what must we say of the scholastic philosophers who indulged in them to such excess? And those subtilties were wasted on words, or, at least, common notions (which is the same thing), not on things or nature, and alike unproductive of benefit in their origin and their consequences: in no way resembling ours, which are at present useless, but in their consequences of infinite benefit. Let men be assured that all subtle disputes and discursive efforts of the mind are late and preposterous, when they are introduced subsequently to the discovery of axioms, and that their true, or, at any rate, chief opportunity is, when experiment is to be weighed and axioms to be derived from it. They otherwise catch and grasp at nature, but never seize or detain her: and we may well apply to nature that which has been said of opportunity or fortune, that she wears a lock in front, but is bald behind.

In short, we may reply decisively to those who despise any part of natural history as being vulgar, mean, or subtile, and useless in its origin, in the words of a poor woman to a haughty prince,[r] who had rejected her petition as unworthy, and beneath the dignity of his majesty: "Then cease to reign," for it is quite certain that the empire of nature can neither be obtained nor administered by one who refuses to pay attention to such matters as being poor and too minute.

CXXII. Again, it may be objected to us as being singular and harsh, that we should with one stroke and assault, as it were, banish all authorities and sciences, and that too by our own efforts, without requiring the assistance and support of any of the ancients.

Now we are aware, that had we been ready to act otherwise than sincerely, it was not difficult to refer our present method to remote ages, prior to those of the Greeks (since the sciences in all probability flourished more in their natural state, though silently, than when they were paraded with the fifes and trumpets of the Greeks); or even (in parts, at least), to some of the Greeks themselves, and to derive authority and honour from thence; as men of no family labour to raise and form nobility for themselves in some ancient line, by the help of genealogies. Trusting, however, to the evidence of facts, we reject every kind of fiction and imposture; and think it of no more consequence to our subject, whether future discoveries were known to the ancients, and set or rose according to the vicissitudes of events and lapse of ages, than it would be of importance to mankind to know whether the new world be the island of Atlantis,[s] and known to the ancients, or be now discovered for the first time.

With regard to the universal censure we have bestowed, it is quite clear to any one who properly considers the matter, that it is both more probable and more modest than any partial one could have been. For if the errors had not been rooted in the primary notions, some well conducted discoveries must have corrected others that were deficient. But since the errors were fundamental, and of such a nature, that men may be said rather to have neglected or passed over things, than to have formed a wrong or false judgment of them, it is little to be wondered at, that they did not obtain what they never aimed at, nor arrive at

---

[r] Philip of Macedon.   [s] See Plato's Timæus.

a goal which they had not determined, nor perform a course which they had neither entered upon nor adhered to.

With regard to our presumption, we allow that if we were to assume a power of drawing a more perfect straight line or circle than any one else, by superior steadiness of hand or acuteness of eye, it would lead to a comparison of talent; but if one merely assert that he can draw a more perfect line or circle with a ruler or compasses, than another can by his unassisted hand or eye, he surely cannot be said to boast of much. Now this applies not only to our first original attempt, but also to those who shall hereafter apply themselves to the pursuit. For our method of discovering the sciences merely levels men's wits, and leaves but little to their superiority, since it achieves everything by the most certain rules and demonstrations. Whence (as we have often observed), our attempt is to be attributed to fortune rather than talent, and is the offspring of time rather than of wit. For a certain sort of chance has no less effect upon our thoughts than on our acts and deeds.

CXXIII. We may, therefore, apply to ourselves the joke of him who said, that water and wine drinkers could not think alike,[*] especially as it hits the matter so well. For others, both ancients and moderns, have in the sciences drank a crude liquor like water, either flowing of itself from the understanding, or drawn up by logic as the wheel draws up the bucket. But we drink and pledge others with a liquor made of many well ripened grapes, collected and plucked from particular branches, squeezed in the press, and at last clarified and fermented in a vessel. It is not, therefore, wonderful that we should not agree with others.

CXXIV. Another objection will without doubt be made, namely, that we have not ourselves established a correct, or the best goal or aim of the sciences (the very defect we blame in others). For they will say that the contemplation of truth is more dignified and exalted than any utility or extent of effects; but that our dwelling so long and anxiously on experience and matter, and the fluctuating state of particulars, fastens the mind to earth, or rather casts it down into an abyss of confusion and disturbance, and separates and removes it from a much more divine state, the quiet and tranquillity of abstract wisdom. We willingly assent to their reasoning, and are most anxious to effect the very point they hint at and require. For we are founding a real model of the world in the understanding, such as it is found to be, not such as man's reason has distorted. Now this cannot be done without dissecting and anatomizing the world

[*] The saying of Philocrates when he differed from Demosthenes. *Ed.*

most diligently; but we declare it necessary to destroy completely the vain little, and as it were, apish imitations of the world, which have been formed in various systems of philosophy by men's fancies. Let men learn (as we have said above), the difference that exists between the idols of the human mind and the ideas of the divine mind. The former are mere arbitrary abstractions; the latter the true marks of the Creator on his creatures, as they are imprinted on, and defined in matter, by true and exquisite touches. Truth, therefore, and utility, are here perfectly identical, and the effects are of more value as pledges of truth than from the benefit they confer on men.

CXXV. Others may object that we are only doing that which has already been done, and that the ancients followed the same course as ourselves. They may imagine, therefore, that, after all this stir and exertion, we shall at last arrive at some of those systems that prevailed among the ancients: for that they, too, when commencing their meditations, laid up a great store of instances and particulars, and digested them under topics and titles in their common-place books, and so worked out their systems and arts, and then decided upon what they discovered, and related now and then some examples to confirm and throw light upon their doctrine; but thought it superfluous and troublesome to publish their notes, minutes, and common-places, and therefore followed the example of builders who remove the scaffolding and ladders when the building is finished. Nor can we indeed believe the case to have been otherwise. But to any one, not entirely forgetful of our previous observations, it will be easy to answer this objection or rather scruple; for we allow that the ancients had a particular form of investigation and discovery, and their writings show it. But it was of such a nature, that they immediately flew from a few instances and particulars (after adding some common notions, and a few generally received opinions most in vogue) to the most general conclusions or the principles of the sciences, and then by their intermediate propositions deduced their inferior conclusions, and tried them by the test of the immoveable and settled truth of the first, and so constructed their art. Lastly, if some new particulars and instances were brought forward, which contradicted their dogmas, they either with great subtilty reduced them to one system, by distinctions or explanations of their own rules, or got rid of them clumsily as exceptions, labouring most pertinaciously in the mean time to accommodate the causes of such as were not contradictory to their own principles. Their natural history and their experience were both far from being what they ought to have been, and their flying off to generalities ruined everything.

CXXVI. Another objection will be made against us, that we

prohibit decisions, and the laying down of certain principles, till we arrive regularly at generalities by the intermediate steps, and thus keep the judgment in suspense and lead to uncertainty. But our object is not uncertainty but fitting certainty, for we derogate not from the senses but assist them, and despise not the understanding but direct it. It is better to know what is necessary, and not to imagine we are fully in possession of it, than to imagine that we are fully in possession of it, and yet in reality to know nothing which we ought.

CXXVII. Again, some may raise this question rather than objection, whether we talk of perfecting natural philosophy alone according to our method, or the other sciences also, such as logic, ethics, politics. We certainly intend to comprehend them all. And as common logic, which regulates matters by syllogisms, is applied not only to natural, but also to every other science, so our inductive method likewise comprehends them all.[a] For we form a history and tables of invention for anger, fear, shame, and the like, and also for examples in civil life, and the mental operations of memory, composition, division, judgment, and the rest, as well as for heat and cold, light, vegetation, and the like. But since our method of interpretation, after preparing and arranging a history, does not content itself with examining the operations and disquisitions of the mind like common logic, but also inspects the nature of things, we so regulate the mind that it may be enabled to apply itself in every respect correctly to that nature. On that account we deliver numerous and various precepts in our doctrine of interpretation, so that they may apply in

---

[a] The old error of placing the deductive syllogism in antagonism to the inductive, as if they were not both parts of one system or refused to cohere together. So far from there being any radical opposition between them, it would not be difficult to show that Bacon's method was syllogistic in his sense of the term. For the suppressed premiss of every Baconian enthymeme, viz. the acknowledged uniformity of the laws of nature as stated in the axiom, whatever has once occurred will occur again, must be assumed as the basis of every conclusion which he draws before we can admit its legitimacy. The opposition, therefore, of Bacon's method could not be directed against the old logic, for it assumed and exemplified its principles, but rather to the abusive application which the ancients made of this science, in turning its powers to the development of abstract principles which they imagined to be pregnant with the solution of the latent mysteries of the universe. Bacon justly overthrew these ideal notions, and accepted of no principle as a basis which was not guaranteed by actual experiment and observation; and so far he laid the foundations of a sound philosophy by turning the inductive logic to its proper account in the interpretation of nature.

some measure to the method of discovering the quality and condition of the subject matter of investigation.

CXXVIII. Let none even doubt whether we are anxious to destroy and demolish the philosophy, arts, and sciences, which are now in use. On the contrary, we readily cherish their practice, cultivation, and honour; for we by no means interfere to prevent the prevalent system from encouraging discussion, adorning discourses, or being employed serviceably in the chair of the professor or the practice of common life, and being taken, in short, by general consent as current coin. Nay, we plainly declare, that the system we offer will not be very suitable for such purposes, not being easily adapted to vulgar apprehensions, except by effects and works. To show our sincerity in professing our regard and friendly disposition towards the received sciences, we can refer to the evidence of our published writings (especially our books on the Advancement of Learning). We will not, therefore, endeavour to evince it any further by words; but content ourselves with steadily and professedly premising, that no great progress can be made by the present methods in the theory or contemplation of science, and that they cannot be made to produce any very abundant effects.

CXXIX. It remains for us to say a few words on the excellence of our proposed end. If we had done so before, we might have appeared merely to express our wishes, but now that we have excited hope and removed prejudices, it will perhaps have greater weight. Had we performed and completely accomplished the whole, without frequently calling in others to assist in our labours, we should then have refrained from saying any more, lest we should be thought to extol our own deserts. Since, however, the industry of others must be quickened, and their courage roused and inflamed, it is right to recall some points to their memory.

First, then, the introduction of great inventions appears one of the most distinguished of human actions, and the ancients so considered it; for they assigned divine honours to the authors of inventions, but only heroic honours to those who displayed civil merit (such as the founders of cities and empires, legislators, the deliverers of their country from lasting misfortunes, the quellers of tyrants, and the like). And if any one rightly compare them, he will find the judgment of antiquity to be correct; for the benefits derived from inventions may extend to mankind in general, but civil benefits to particular spots alone; the latter, moreover, last but for a time, the former for ever. Civil reformation seldom is carried on without violence and confusion, whilst inventions are a blessing and a benefit without injuring or afflicting any.

Inventions are also, as it were, new creations and imitations of divine works, as was expressed by the poet:[x]—

> "Primum frugiferos fœtus mortalibus ægris
> Dididerant quondam præstanti nomine Athenæ
> Et *recreaverunt* vitam legesque rogarunt."

And it is worthy of remark in Solomon, that whilst he flourished in the possession of his empire, in wealth, in the magnificence of his works, in his court, his household, his fleet, the splendour of his name, and the most unbounded admiration of mankind, he still placed his glory in none of these, but declared[y] that it is the glory of God to conceal a thing, but the glory of a king to search it out.

Again, let any one but consider the immense difference between men's lives in the most polished countries of Europe, and in any wild and barbarous region of the new Indies, he will think it so great, that man may be said to be a god unto man, not only on account of mutual aid and benefits, but from their comparative states—the result of the arts, and not of the soil or climate.

Again, we should notice the force, effect, and consequences of inventions, which are nowhere more conspicuous than in those three which were unknown to the ancients; namely, printing, gunpowder, and the compass. For these three have changed the appearance and state of the whole world: first in literature, then in warfare, and lastly in navigation; and innumerable changes have been thence derived, so that no empire, sect, or star, appears to have exercised a greater power and influence on human affairs than these mechanical discoveries.

It will, perhaps, be as well to distinguish three species and degrees of ambition. First, that of men who are anxious to enlarge their own power in their country, which is a vulgar and degenerate kind; next, that of men who strive to enlarge the power and empire of their country over mankind, which is more dignified but not less covetous; but if one were to endeavour to renew and enlarge the power and empire of mankind in general over the universe, such ambition (if it may be so termed) is both more sound and more noble than the other two. Now the empire

---

[x] This is the opening of the sixth book of Lucretius. Bacon probably quoted from memory; the lines are,—

> "Primæ frugiferos fœtus mortalibus ægris
> Dididerunt quondam præclaro nomine Athenæ
> Et recreaverunt, &c."

> The teeming corn, that feeble mortals crave,
> First, and long since, renowned Athens gave,
> And cheered their life—then taught to frame their laws.

[y] Prov. xxv. 2.

of man over things is founded on the arts and sciences alone, for nature is only to be commanded by obeying her.

Besides this, if the benefit of any particular invention has had such an effect as to induce men to consider him greater than a man, who has thus obliged the whole race, how much more exalted will that discovery be, which leads to the easy discovery of everything else! Yet (to speak the truth) in the same manner as we are very thankful for light which enables us to enter on our way, to practise arts, to read, to distinguish each other, and yet sight is more excellent and beautiful than the various uses of light; so is the contemplation of things as they are, free from superstition or imposture, error or confusion, much more dignified in itself than all the advantage to be derived from discoveries.

Lastly, let none be alarmed at the objection of the arts and sciences becoming depraved to malevolent or luxurious purposes and the like, for the same can be said of every worldly good; talent, courage, strength, beauty, riches, light itself, and the rest. Only let mankind regain their rights over nature, assigned to them by the gift of God, and obtain that power, whose exercise will be governed by right reason and true religion.

CXXX. But it is time for us to lay down the art of interpreting nature, to which we attribute no absolute necessity (as if nothing could be done without it) nor perfection, although we think that our precepts are most useful and correct. For we are of opinion, that if men had at their command a proper history of nature and experience, and would apply themselves steadily to it, and could bind themselves to two things: 1. to lay aside received opinions and notions; 2. to restrain themselves, till the proper season, from generalization, they might, by the proper and genuine exertion of their minds, fall into our way of interpretation without the aid of any art. For interpretation is the true and natural act of the mind, when all obstacles are removed: certainly, however, everything will be more ready and better fixed by our precepts.

Yet do we not affirm that no addition can be made to them; on the contrary, considering the mind in its connection with things, and not merely relatively to its own powers, we ought to be persuaded that the art of invention can be made to grow with the inventions themselves.

APHORISMS.—BOOK II.

On the Interpretation of Nature, or the Reign of Man.

I. To generate and superinduce a new nature or new natures, upon a given body, is the labour and aim of human power: whilst to discover the form or true difference of a giving nature, or the nature[a] to which such nature is owing, or source from which it emanates (for these terms approach nearest to an explanation of our meaning), is the labour and discovery of human knowledge; and subordinate to these primary labours are two others of a secondary nature and inferior stamp. Under the first must be ranked the transformation of concrete bodies from one to another, which is possible within certain limits; under the second, the discovery, in every species of generation and motion, of the latent and uninterrupted process from the manifest efficient and manifest subject matter up to the given form: and a like discovery of the latent conformation of bodies which are at rest instead of being in motion.

II. The unhappy state of man's actual knowledge is manifested even by the common assertions of the vulgar. It is rightly laid down that true knowledge is that which is deduced from causes. The division of four causes also is not amiss: matter, form, the efficient, and end or final cause.[b] Of these, however, the latter is so far from being beneficial, that it even corrupts the sciences, except in the intercourse of man with man. The discovery of form is considered desperate. As for the efficient cause and matter (according to the present system of inquiry and the received opinions concerning them, by which they are placed remote from, and without any latent process towards form), they are but desultory and superficial, and of scarcely any avail to real and active knowledge. Nor are we unmindful of our having pointed out and corrected above the error of the human mind, in assign-

---

[a] Τὸ τί ἦν εἶναι, or ἦν οὐσία of Aristotle.—See lib. iii. Metap.

[b] These divisions are from Aristotle's Metaphysics, where they are termed, 1. ὕλη ἢ τὸ ὑποκείμενον. 2. τὸ τί ἦν εἶναι. 3. ὅθεν ἡ ἀρχὴ τῆς κινήσεως. 4. τὸ οὗ ἕνεκεν—καὶ τὸ ἀγαθόν.

ing the first qualities of essence to forms.[c] For although nothing exists in nature except individual bodies,[d] exhibiting clear individual effects according to particular laws, yet in each branch of learning, that very law, its investigation, discovery, and development, are the foundation both of theory and practice. This law, therefore, and its parallel in each science, is what we understand by the term form,[e] adopting that word because it has grown into common use, and is of familiar occurrence.

[c] See Aphorism li. and second paragraph of Aphorism lxv. in the first book.

[d] Bacon means, that although there exist in nature only individualities, yet a certain number of these may have common properties, and be controlled by the same laws. Now, these homogeneous qualities which distinguish them from other individuals, lead us to class them under one expression, and sometimes under a single term. Yet these classes are only pure conceptions in Bacon's opinion, and cannot be taken for distinct substances. He evidently here aims a blow at the Realists, who concluded that the essence which united individualities in a class was the only real and immutable existence in nature, inasmuch as it entered into their ideas of individual substances as a distinct and essential property, and continued in the mind as the mould, type, or pattern of the class, while its individual forms were undergoing perpetual renovation and decay. *Ed.*

[e] Bacon's definition is obscure. All the idea we have of a law of nature consists in invariable sequence between certain classes of phenomena; but this cannot be the complete sense attached by Bacon to the term form, as he employs it in the fourth aphorism as convertible with the nature of any object; and again in the first aphorism, as the *natura naturans*, or general law or condition in any substance or quality,—*natura naturata*—which is whatever its form is, or that particular combination of forces which impresses a certain nature upon matter subject to its influence. Thus, in the Newtonian sense, the form of whiteness would be that combination of the seven primitive rays of light which give rise to that colour. In combination with this word, and affording a still further insight into its meaning, we have the phrases, *latens processus ad formam, et latens schematismus corporum.* Now, the *latens schematismus* signifies the internal texture, structure, or configuration of bodies, or the result of the respective situation of all the parts of a body; while the *latens processus ad formam* points out the gradation of movements which takes place among the molecula of bodies when they either conserve or change their figure. Hence we may consider the form of any quality in body as something convertible with that quality, *i.e.*, when it exists the quality is present, and *vice versâ*. In this sense, the form of a thing differs only from its efficient cause in being permanent, whereas we apply cause to that which exists in order of time. The *latens processus* and *latens schematismus* are subordinate to form, as concrete exemplifications of its essence. The former is the secret and invisible process by which change is effected, and involves

III. He who has learnt the cause of a particular nature (such as whiteness or heat), in particular subjects only, has acquired but an imperfect knowledge: as he who can induce a certain effect upon particular substances only, among those which are susceptible of it, has acquired but an imperfect power. But he who has only learnt the efficient and material cause (which causes are variable and mere vehicles conveying form to particular substances) may perhaps arrive at some new discoveries in matters of a similar nature, and prepared for the purpose, but does not stir the limits of things which are much more deeply rooted: whilst he who is acquainted with forms, comprehends the unity of nature in substances apparently most distinct from each other. He can disclose and bring forward, therefore, (though it has never yet been done) things which neither the vicissitudes of nature, nor the industry of experiment, nor chance itself, would ever have brought about, and which would for ever have escaped man's thoughts; from the discovery of forms, therefore, results genuine theory and free practice.

IV. Although there is a most intimate connection, and almost an identity between the ways of human power and human knowledge, yet, on account of the pernicious and inveterate habit of dwelling upon abstractions, it is by far the safest method to commence and build up the sciences from those foundations which bear a relation to the practical division, and to let them mark out and limit the theoretical. We must consider, therefore, what precepts, or what direction or guide, a person would most desire, in order to generate and superinduce any nature upon a given body: and this not in abstruse, but in the plainest language.

For instance, if a person should wish to superinduce the yellow colour of gold upon silver, or an additional weight (observing always the laws of matter) or transparency on an opaque stone, or tenacity in glass, or vegetation on a substance which is not

---

the principle since called the law of continuity. Thus, the succession of events between the application of the match to the expulsion of the bullet is an instant of latent progress which we can now trace with some degree of accuracy. It also more directly refers to the operation by which one form or condition of being is induced upon another. For example, when the surface of iron becomes rusty, or when water is converted into steam, some change has taken place, or latent process from one form to another. Mechanics afford many exemplifications of the first latent process we have denoted, and chemistry of the second. The *latens schematismus* is that visible structure of bodies on which so many of their properties depend. When we inquire into the constitution of crystals, and into the internal structure of plants, we are examining into their latent schematism. *Ed.*

vegetable, we must (I say) consider what species of precept or guide this person would prefer. And firstly, he will doubtless be anxious to be shown some method that will neither fail in effect, nor deceive him in the trial of it; secondly, he will be anxious that the prescribed method should not restrict him and tie him down to peculiar means, and certain particular methods of acting; for he will, perhaps, be at loss, and without the power or opportunity of collecting and procuring such means. Now if there be other means and methods (besides those prescribed) of creating such a nature, they will perhaps be of such a kind as are in his power, yet by the confined limits of the precept he will be deprived of reaping any advantage from them; thirdly, he will be anxious to be shown something not so difficult as the required effect itself, but approaching more nearly to practice.

We will lay this down, therefore, as the genuine and perfect rule of practice, that it should be certain, free, and preparatory, or having relation to practice. And this is the same thing as the discovery of a true form; for the form of any nature is such, that when it is assigned the particular nature infallibly follows. It is, therefore, always present when that nature is present, and universally attests such presence, and is inherent in the whole of it. The same form is of such a character, that if it be removed the particular nature infallibly vanishes. It is, therefore, absent, whenever that nature is absent, and perpetually testifies such absence, and exists in no other nature. Lastly, the true form is such, that it deduces the particular nature from some source of essence existing in many subjects, and more known (as they term it) to nature, than the form itself. Such, then, is our determination and rule with regard to a genuine and perfect theoretical axiom, that a nature be found convertible with a given nature, and yet such as to limit the more known nature, in the manner of a real genus. But these two rules, the practical and theoretical, are in fact the same, and that which is most useful in practice is most correct in theory.

V. But the rule or axiom for the transformation of bodies is of two kinds. The first regards the body as an aggregate or combination of simple natures. Thus, in gold are united the following circumstances: it is yellow, heavy, of a certain weight, malleable and ductile to a certain extent; it is not volatile, loses part of its substance by fire, melts in a particular manner, is separated and dissolved by particular methods, and so of the other natures observable in gold. An axiom, therefore, of this kind deduces the subject from the forms of simple natures; for he who has acquired the forms and methods of superinducing yellowness, weight, ductility, stability, deliquescence, solution, and the like, and their degrees and modes, will consider and contrive how to unite them in any body, so as to transform¹ it into gold. And this method of operating belongs to primary action; for it is the same thing to produce one or many simple natures, except that man is more confined and restricted in his operations, if many be required, on account of the difficulty of uniting many natures together. It must, however, be observed, that this method of operating (which considers natures as simple though in a concrete body) sets out from what is constant, eternal, and universal in nature, and opens such broad paths to human power, as the thoughts of man can in the present state of things scarcely comprehend or figure to itself.

The second kind of axiom (which depends on the discovery of the latent process) does not proceed by simple natures, but by concrete bodies, as they are found in nature and in its usual course. For instance, suppose the inquiry to be, from what beginnings, in what manner, and by what process gold or any metal or stone is generated from the original menstruum, or its elements, up to the perfect mineral: or, in like manner, by what process plants are generated, from the first concretion of juices in the earth, or from seeds, up to the perfect plant, with the whole successive motion, and varied and uninterrupted efforts of nature; and the same inquiry be made as to a regularly deduced system of the generation of animals from coition to birth, and so on of other bodies.

Nor is this species of inquiry confined to the mere generation of bodies, but it is applicable to other changes and labours of nature. For instance, where an inquiry is made into the whole series and continued operation of the nutritive process, from the first reception of the food to its complete assimilation to the recipient;² or into the voluntary motion of animals, from the first impression of the imagination, and the continuous effects of the spirits, up to the bending and motion of the joints; or into the free motion of the tongue and lips, and other accessories which give utterance to articulate sounds. For all these investigations relate to concrete or associated natures artificially brought together, and take into consideration certain particular and special habits of nature, and not those fundamental and general laws which constitute forms. It must, however, be plainly owned, that this method appears more prompt and easy, and of greater promise than the primary one.

In like manner the operative branch, which answers to this

---

¹ By the recent discoveries in electric magnetism, copper wires, or, indeed, wires of any metal, may be transformed into magnets; the magnetic law, or form, having been to that extent discovered.

² Haller has pursued this investigation in his "Physiology," and has left his successors little else to do than repeat his discoveries. *Ed.*

contemplative branch, extends and advances its operation from that which is usually observed in nature, to other subjects immediately connected with it, or not very remote from such immediate connexion. But the higher and radical operations upon nature depend entirely on the primary axioms. Besides, even where man has not the means of acting, but only of acquiring knowledge, as in astronomy (for man cannot act upon, change, or transform the heavenly bodies), the investigation of facts or truth, as well as the knowledge of causes and coincidences, must be referred to those primary and universal axioms that regard simple natures; such as the nature of spontaneous rotation, attraction, or the magnetic force, and many others which are more common than the heavenly bodies themselves. For let no one hope to determine the question whether the earth or heaven revolve in the diurnal motion, unless he have first comprehended the nature of spontaneous rotation.

VI. But the latent process of which we speak, is far from being obvious to men's minds, beset as they now are. For we mean not the measures, symptoms, or degrees of any process which can be exhibited in the bodies themselves, but simply a continued process, which, for the most part, escapes the observation of the senses.

For instance, in all generations and transformations of bodies, we must inquire, what is in the act of being lost and escaping, what remains, what is being added, what is being diluted, what is being contracted, what is being united, what is being separated, what is continuous, what is broken off, what is urging forward, what impedes, what predominates, what is subservient, and many other circumstances.

Nor are these inquiries again to be made in the mere generation and transformation of bodies only, but in all other alterations and fluctuations, we must in like manner inquire; what precedes, what succeeds, what is quick, what is slow, what produces and what governs motion, and the like. All which matters are unknown and unattempted by the sciences, in their present heavy and inactive state. For, since every natural act is brought about by the smallest efforts,[b] or, at least, such as are too small to strike our senses, let no one hope that he will be able to direct or change nature unless he have properly comprehended and observed these efforts.

VII. In like manner, the investigation and discovery of the latent conformation in bodies is no less new, than the discovery of the latent process and form. For we as yet are doubtless

---

[b] Bacon here first seems pregnant with the important development of the higher calculus, which, in the hands of Newton and Descartes, was to effect as great a revolution in philosophy as his method. *Ed.*

only admitted to the ante-chamber of nature, and do not prepare an entrance into her presence-room. But nobody can endue a given body with a new nature, or transform it successfully and appropriately into a new body, without possessing a complete knowledge of the body so to be changed or transformed. For he will run into vain, or, at least, into difficult and perverse methods, ill adapted to the nature of the body upon which he operates. A clear path, therefore, towards this object also must be thrown open, and well supported.

Labour is well and usefully bestowed upon the anatomy of organized bodies, such as those of men and animals, which appears to be a subtile matter, and an useful examination of nature. The species of anatomy, however, is that of first sight, open to the senses, and takes place only in organized bodies. It is obvious, and of ready access, when compared with the real anatomy of latent conformation in bodies which are considered similar, particularly in specific objects and their parts; as those of iron, stone, and the similar parts of plants and animals, as the root, the leaf, the flower, the flesh, the blood, and bones, &c. Yet human industry has not completely neglected this species of anatomy; for we have an instance of it in the separation of similar bodies by distillation, and other solutions, which shows the dissimilarity of the compound by the union of the homogeneous parts. These methods are useful, and of importance to our inquiry, although attended generally with fallacy: for many natures are assigned and attributed to the separate bodies, as if they had previously existed in the compound, which, in reality, are recently bestowed and superinduced by fire and heat, and the other modes of separation. Besides, it is, after all, but a small part of the labour of discovering the real conformation in the compound, which is so subtile and nice, that it is rather confused and lost by the operation of the fire, than discovered and brought to light.

A separation and solution of bodies, therefore, is to be effected, not by fire indeed, but rather by reasoning and true induction, with the assistance of experiment, and by a comparison with other bodies, and a reduction to those simple natures and their forms which meet, and are combined in the compound; and we must assuredly pass from Vulcan to Minerva, if we wish to bring to light the real texture and conformation of bodies, upon which every occult and (as it is sometimes called) specific property and virtue of things depends, and whence also every rule of powerful change and transformation is deduced.

For instance, we must examine what spirit is in every body,[1] what tangible assence; whether that spirit is copious and ex-

[1] By spirit, Bacon here plainly implies material fluid too fine to be grasped by the unassisted sense, which rather operates than reasons.

uberant, or meagre and scarce, fine or coarse, aeriform or igniform, active or sluggish, weak or robust, progressive or retrograde, abrupt or continuous, agreeing with external and surrounding objects, or differing from them, &c. In like manner must we treat tangible essence (which admits of as many distinctions as the spirit), and its hairs, fibres, and varied texture. Again, the situation of the spirit in the corporeal mass, its pores, passages, veins, and cells, and the rudiments or first essays of the organic body, are subject to the same examination. In these, however, as in our former inquiries, and therefore in the whole investigation of latent conformation, the only genuine and clear light which completely dispels all darkness and subtile difficulties, is admitted by means of the primary axioms.

VIII. This method will not bring us to atoms,[k] which takes for granted the vacuum, and immutability of matter (neither of which hypotheses is correct), but to the real particles such as we discover them to be. Nor is there any ground for alarm at this refinement as if it were inexplicable, for, on the contrary, the more inquiry is directed to simple natures, the more will everything be placed in a plain and perspicuous light, since we transfer our attention from the complicated to the simple, from the incommensurable to the commensurable, from surds to rational quantities, from the indefinite and vague to the definite and certain; as when we arrive at the elements of letters, and the simple tones of concords. The investigation of nature is best conducted when mathematics are applied to physics. Again, let none be alarmed at vast numbers and fractions, for in calculation it is as easy to set down or to reflect upon a thousand as an unit, or the thousandth part of an integer as an integer itself.

IX.[1] From the two kinds of axioms above specified, arise the

---

We sometimes adopt the same mode of expression, as in the words spirits of nitre, spirits of wine. Some such agency has been assumed by nearly all the modern physicists, a few of whom, along with Bacon, would leave us to gather from their expressions, that they believe such bodies endowed with the sentient powers of perception. As another specimen of his sentiment on this subject, we may refer to a paragraph on the decomposition of compounds, in his essay on death, beginning—"The spirit which exists in all living bodies, keeps all the parts in due subjection; when it escapes, the body decomposes, or the similar parts unite." *Ed.*

[k] The theory of the Epicureans and others. The atoms are supposed to be invisible, inalterable particles, endued with all the properties of the given body, and forming that body by their union. They must be separated, of course, which either takes a vacuum for granted, or introduces a tertium quid into the composition of the body.

[1] Compare the three following aphorisms with the three last chapters of the third book of the "De Augmentis Scientiarum."

two divisions of philosophy and the sciences, and we will use the commonly adopted terms which approach the nearest to our meaning, in our own sense. Let the investigation of forms, which (in reasoning at least, and after their own laws), are eternal and immutable, constitute metaphysics,[m] and let the investigation of the efficient cause of matter, latent process, and latent conformation (which all relate merely to the ordinary course of nature, and not to her fundamental and eternal laws), constitute physics. Parallel to these, let there be two practical divisions; to physics that of mechanics, and to metaphysics that of magic, in the purest sense of the term, as applied to its ample means, and its command over nature.

X. The object of our philosophy being thus laid down, we proceed to precepts, in the most clear and regular order. The signs for the interpretation of nature comprehend two divisions, the first regards the eliciting or creating of axioms from experiment, the second the deducing or deriving of new experiments from axioms. The first admits of three subdivisions into ministrations 1. To the senses. 2. To the memory. 3. To the mind or reason.

For we must first prepare as a foundation for the whole, a complete and accurate natural and experimental history. We must not imagine or invent, but discover the acts and properties of nature.

[m] Bacon gives this unfortunate term its proper signification; μετα, in composition, with the Greeks signifying change or mutation. Most of our readers, no doubt, are aware that the obtrusion of this word into technical philosophy was purely capricious, and is of no older date than the publication of Aristotle's works by Andronicus of Rhodes, one of the learned men into whose hands the manuscripts of that philosopher fell, after they were brought by Sylla from Athens to Rome. To fourteen books in these MSS. with no distinguishing title, Andronicus is said to have prefixed the words τα μετα τα φυσικα, to denote the place which they ought to hold either in the order of Aristotle's arrangement, or in that of study. These books treat first of those subjects which are common to matter and mind; secondly, of things separate from matter, *i. e.* of God, and of the subordinate spirits, which were supposed by the Peripatetics to watch over particular portions of the universe. The followers of Aristotle accepted the whimsical title of Andronicus, and in their usual manner allowed a word to unite things into one science, which were plainly heterogeneous. Their error was adopted by the Peripatetics of the Christian Church. The schoolmen added to the notion of ontology, the science of the mind, or pneumatology, and as that genus of being has since become extinct with the schools, metaphysics thus in modern parlance comes to be synonymous with psychology. It were to be wished that Bacon's definition of the term had been accepted, and mental science delivered from one of the greatest monstrosities in its nomenclature, yet Bacon whimsically enough in his De Augmentis includes mathematics in metaphysics. *Ed.*

But natural and experimental history is so varied and diffuse, that it confounds and distracts the understanding unless it be fixed and exhibited in due order. We must, therefore, form tables and co-ordinations of instances, upon such a plan, and in such order, that the understanding may be enabled to act upon them.

Even when this is done, the understanding, left to itself and to its own operation, is incompetent and unfit to construct its axioms without direction and support. Our third ministration, therefore, must be true and legitimate induction, the very key of interpretation. We must begin, however, at the end, and go back again to the others.

XI. The investigation of forms proceeds thus: a nature being given, we must first present to the understanding all the known instances which agree in the same nature, although the subject matter be considerably diversified. And this collection must be made as a mere history, and without any premature reflection, or too great degree of refinement. For instance; take the investigation of the form of heat.

Instances agreeing in the Form of Heat.

1. The rays of the sun, particularly in summer, and at noon.
2. The same reflected and condensed, as between mountains, or along walls, and particularly in burning mirrors.
3. Ignited meteors.
4. Burning lightning.
5. Eruptions of flames from the cavities of mountains, &c.
6. Flame of every kind.
7. Ignited solids.
8. Natural warm baths.
9. Warm or heated liquids.
10. Warm vapours and smoke; and the air itself, which admits a most powerful and violent heat if confined, as in reverberating furnaces.
11. Damp hot weather, arising from the constitution of the air, without any reference to the time of the year.
12. Confined and subterraneous air in some caverns, particularly in winter.
13. All shaggy substances, as wool, the skins of animals, and the plumage of birds, contain some heat.
14. All bodies, both solid and liquid, dense and rare (as th air itself), placed near fire for any time.
15. Sparks arising from the violent percussion of flint an steel.
16. All bodies rubbed violently, as stone, wood, cloth, &c., so that rudders, and axles of wheels, sometimes catch fire, and the West Indians obtain fire by attrition.
17. Green and moist vegetable matter confined and rubbed

together, as roses, peas in baskets; so hay, if it be damp when stacked, often catches fire.

18. Quick lime sprinkled with water.

19. Iron, when first dissolved by acids in a glass, and without any application to fire; the same of tin, but not so intensely.

20. Animals, particularly internally; although the heat is not perceivable by the touch in insects, on account of their small size.

21. Horse dung, and the like excrement from other animals, when fresh.

22. Strong oil of sulphur and of vitriol exhibit the operation of heat in burning linen.

23. As does the oil of marjoram, and like substances, in burning the bony substance of the teeth.

24. Strong and well rectified spirits of wine exhibit the same effects; so that white of eggs when thrown into it grows hard and white, almost in the same manner as when boiled, and bread becomes burnt and brown as if toasted.

25. Aromatic substances and warm plants, as the dracunculus [arum], old nasturtium, &c., which, though they be not warm to the touch (whether whole or pulverized), yet are discovered by the tongue and palate to be warm and almost burning when slightly masticated.

26. Strong vinegar and all acids, on any part of the body not clothed with the epidermis, as the eye, tongue, or any wounded part, or where the skin is removed, excite a pain differing but little from that produced by heat.

27. Even a severe and intense cold produces a sensation of burning.[a]

"Nec Boreæ penetrabile frigus adurit."

28. Other instances.

We are wont to call this a table of existence and presence.

XII. We must next present to the understanding instances which do not admit of the given nature, for form (as we have observed) ought no less to be absent where the given nature is absent, than to be present where it is present. If, however, we were to examine every instance, our labour would be infinite.

Negatives, therefore, must be classed under the affirmatives, and the want of the given nature must be inquired into more particularly in objects which have a very close connection with those others in which it is present and manifest. And this we are wont to term a table of deviation or of absence in proximity.

[a] "Ne tenues pluviæ, rapidive potentia solis
Acrior, aut Boreæ penetrabile frigus adurat."
Virg. Georg. i. 92, 93.

Proximate Instances wanting the Nature of Heat.

The rays of the moon, stars, and comets, are not found to be warm to the touch, nay, the severest cold has been observed to take place at the full of the moon. Yet the larger fixed stars are supposed to increase and render more intense the heat of the sun, as he approaches them, when the sun is in the sign of the lion for instance, and in the dog-days.º

The rays of the sun in what is called the middle region of the air give no heat, to account for which the commonly assigned reason is satisfactory; namely, that that region is neither sufficiently near to the body of the sun whence the rays emanate, nor to the earth whence they are reflected. And the fact is manifested by snow being perpetual on the tops of mountains, unless extremely lofty. But it is observed on the other hand by some, that at the Peak of Teneriffe, and also among the Andes of Peru, the tops of the mountains are free from snow, which only lies in the lower part as you ascend. Besides, the air on the summit of these mountains is found to be by no means cold, but only thin and sharp; so much so, that in the Andes it pricks and hurts the eyes from its extreme sharpness, and even excites the orifice of the stomach and produces vomiting. The ancients also observed, that the rarity of the air on the summit of Olympus was such, that those who ascended it were obliged to carry sponges moistened with vinegar and water, and to apply them now and then to their nostrils, as the air was not dense enough for their respiration; on the summit of which mountain it is also related, there reigned so great a serenity and calm, free from rain, snow, or wind, that the letters traced upon the ashes of the sacrifices on the altar of Jupiter, by the fingers of those who had offered them, would remain undisturbed till the next year. Those even, who at this day go to the top of the Peak of Teneriffe, walk by night and not in the day-time, and are advised and pressed by their guides, as soon as the sun rises, to make haste in their descent, on account of the danger (apparently arising from the rarity of the atmosphere), lest their breathing should be relaxed and suffocated.ᵖ

º This notion, which he repeats again, and particularizes in the 18th aph. of this book, is borrowed from the ancients, and we need not say is as wise as their other astronomical conjectures. The sun also approaches stars quite as large in other quarters of the zodiac, when it looks down upon the earth through the murky clouds of winter. When that luminary is in Leo, the heat of the earth is certainly greater than at any other period, but this arises from the accumulation of heat after the solstice, for the same reason that the maximum heat of the day is at two o'clock instead of noon. *Ed.*

ᵖ Bouguer, employed by Louis XIV. in philosophical researches,

The reflection of the solar rays in the polar regions is found to be weak and inefficient in producing heat, so that the Dutch, who wintered in Nova Zembla, and expected that their vessel would be freed about the beginning of July from the obstruction of the mass of ice which had blocked it up, were disappointed and obliged to embark in their boat. Hence the direct rays of the sun appear to have but little power even on the plain, and when reflected, unless they are multiplied and condensed, which takes place when the sun tends more to the perpendicular; for, then, the incidence of the rays occurs at more acute angles, so that the reflected rays are nearer to each other, whilst, on the contrary, when the sun is in a very oblique position, the angles of incidence are very obtuse, and the reflected rays at a greater distance. In the mean time it must be observed, that there may be many operations of the solar rays, relating, too, to the nature of heat, which are not proportioned to our touch, so that, with regard to us, they do not tend to produce warmth, but, with regard to some other bodies, have their due effect in producing it.

Let the following experiment be made. Take a lens the reverse of a burning glass, and place it between the hand and the solar rays, and observe whether it diminish the heat of the sun as a burning glass increases it. For it is clear, with regard to the visual rays, that in proportion as the lens is made of unequal thickness in the middle and at its sides, the images appear either more diffused or contracted. It should be seen, therefore, if the same be true with regard to heat.

Let the experiment be well tried, whether the lunar rays can be received and collected by the strongest and best burning glasses, so as to produce even the least degree of heat.[q] But if that degree be, perhaps, so subtile and weak, as not to be perceived or ascertained by the touch, we must have recourse to those glasses which indicate the warm or cold state of the atmosphere, and let the lunar rays fall through the burning glass on

ascended the Andes to discover the globular form of the earth, and published an account of his passage, which verifies the statement of Bacon.

[q] Montanari asserts in his book against the astrologers that he had satisfied himself by numerous and oft-repeated experiments, that the lunar rays gathered to a focus produced a sensible degree of heat. Muschenbröck, however, adopts the opposite opinion, and asserts that himself, De la Hire, Villet, and Tschirnhausen had tried with that view the strongest burning-glasses in vain. (Opera de Igne.) De la Lande makes a similar confession in his Astronomy (vol. ii. vii. § 1413). Bouguer, whom we have just quoted, demonstrated that the light of the moon was 300,000 degrees less than that of the sun : it would consequently be necessary to invent a glass with an absorbing power 300,000 degrees greater than those ordinarily in use, to try the experiment Bacon speaks of. *Ed.*

the top of this thermometer, and then notice if the water be depressed by the heat.[r]

Let the burning glass be tried on warm objects which emit no luminous rays, as heated but not ignited iron or stone, or hot water, or the like; and observe whether the heat become increased and condensed, as happens with the solar rays.

Let it be tried on common flame.

The effect of comets (if we can reckon them amongst meteors[s]) in augmenting the heat of the season is not found to be constant or clear, although droughts have generally been observed to follow them. However, luminous lines, and pillars, and openings, and the like, appear more often in winter than in summer, and especially with the most intense cold but joined with drought. Lightning, and coruscations, and thunder, however, rarely happen in winter, and generally at the time of the greatest heats. The appearances we term falling stars are generally supposed to consist of some shining and inflamed viscous substance, rather than of violently hot matter; but let this be further investigated.

Some coruscations emit light without burning, but are never accompanied by thunder.

Eructations and eruptions of flame are to be found in cold climates as well as in hot, as in Iceland and Greenland; just as the trees of cold countries are sometimes inflammable and more pitchy and resinous than in warm, as the fir, pine, and the like. But the position and nature of the soil, where such eruptions are

---

[r] In this thermometer, mercury was not dilated by heat or contracted by cold, as the one now in use, but a mass of air employed instead, which filled the cavity of the bulb. This being placed in an inverted position to ours, that is to say, with the bulb uppermost, pressed down the liquor when the air became dilated by heat, as ours press it upward; and when the heat diminished, the liquor rose to occupy the place vacated by the air, as the one now in use descends. It consequently was liable to be affected by a change in the temperature, as by the weight of air, and could afford only a rude standard of accuracy in scientific investigations. This thermometer was not Bacon's own contrivance, as is commonly supposed, but that of Drebbel. *Ed.*

[s] Lalande is indignant that the Chaldeans should have more correct notions of the nature of comets than the modern physicists, and charges Bacon with entertaining the idea that they were the mere effects of vapour and heat. This passage, with two others more positive, in the "De Aug." (cap. xl.) and the "Descript. Globi Intellect." (cap. vi.) certainly afford ground for the assertion; but if Bacon erred, he erred with Galileo, and with the foremost spirits of the times. It is true that Pythagoras and Seneca had asserted their belief in the solidity of these bodies, but the wide dominion which Aristotle subsequently exercised, threw their opinions into the shade, and made the opposite doctrine everywhere paramount. *Ed.*

wont to happen, is not yet sufficiently investigated to enable us to subjoin a negative instance to the affirmative.

All flame is constantly more or less warm, and this instance is not altogether negative; yet it is said that the ignis fatuus (as it is called), and which sometimes is driven against walls, has but little heat; perhaps it resembles that of spirits of wine, which is mild and gentle. That flame, however, appears yet milder, which in some well authenticated and serious histories is said to have appeared round the head and hair of boys and virgins, and instead of burning their hair, merely to have played about it. And it is most certain that a sort of flash, without any evident heat, has sometimes been seen about a horse when sweating at night, or in damp weather. It is also a well known fact,[t] and it was almost considered as a miracle, that a few years since a girl's apron sparkled when a little shaken or rubbed, which was, perhaps, occasioned by the alum or salts with which the apron was imbued, and which, after having been stuck together and incrusted rather strongly, were broken by the friction. It is well known that all sugar, whether candied or plain, if it be hard, will sparkle when broken or scraped in the dark. In like manner sea and salt water is sometimes found to shine at night when struck violently by the oar. The foam of the sea when agitated by tempests also sparkles at night, and the Spaniards call this appearance the sea's lungs. It has not been sufficiently ascertained what degree of heat attends the flame which the ancient sailors called Castor and Pollux, and the moderns call St. Ermus' fire.

Every ignited body that is red-hot is always warm, although without flame, nor is any negative instance subjoined to this affirmative. Rotten wood, however, approaches nearly to it, for it shines at night, and yet is not found to be warm; and the putrefying scales of fish which shine in the same manner are not warm to the touch, nor the body of the glowworm, or of the fly called Lucciola.[u]

The situation and nature of the soil of natural warm baths has not been sufficiently investigated, and therefore a negative instance is not subjoined.

To the instances of warm liquids we may subjoin the negative one of the peculiar nature of liquids in general; for no tangible liquid is known that is at once warm in its nature and constantly continues warm; but their heat is only superinduced as an adventitious nature for a limited time, so that those which are extremely warm in their power and effect, as spirits of wine, chemical aromatic oils, the oils of vitriol and sulphur, and the

---

[t] Was it a silk apron which exhibited electric sparks? Silk was then scarce.   [u] The Italian fire-fly.

like, and which speedily burn, are yet cold at first to the touch, and the water of natural baths, poured into any vessel and separated from its source, cools down like water heated by the fire. It is, however, true that oily substances are rather less cold to the touch than those that are aqueous, oil for instance than water, silk than linen; but this belongs to the table of degrees of cold.

In like manner we may subjoin a negative instance to that of warm vapour, derived from the nature of vapour itself, as far as we are acquainted with it. For exhalations from oily substances, though easily inflammable, are yet never warm unless recently exhaled from some warm substance.

The same may be said of the instance of air; for we never perceive that air is warm unless confined or pressed, or manifestly heated by the sun, by fire, or some other warm body.

A negative instance is exhibited in weather by its coldness with an east or north wind, beyond what the season would lead us to expect, just as the contrary takes place with the south or west winds. An inclination to rain (especially in winter) attends warm weather, and to frost cold weather.

A negative instance as to air confined in caverns may be observed in summer. Indeed, we should make a more diligent inquiry into the nature of confined air. For in the first place the qualities of air in its own nature with regard to heat and cold may reasonably be the subject of doubt; for air evidently derives its heat from the effects of celestial bodies, and possibly its cold from the exhalation of the earth, and in the mid region of air (as it is termed) from cold vapours and snow, so that no judgment can be formed of the nature of air by that which is out of doors and exposed, but a more correct one might be derived from confined air. It is necessary, however, that the air should be enclosed in a vessel of such materials as would not imbue it with heat or cold of themselves, nor easily admit the influence of the external atmosphere. The experiment should be made therefore with an earthen jar, covered with folds of leather to protect it from the external air, and the air should be kept three or four days in this vessel well closed. On opening the jar, the degree of heat may be ascertained either by the hand or a graduated glass tube.

There is a similar doubt as to whether the warmth of wool, skins, feathers, and the like, is derived from a slight inherent heat, since they are animal excretions, or from their being of a certain fat and oily nature that accords with heat, or merely from the confinement and separation of air which we spoke of in the preceding paragraph;[*] for all air appears to possess a cer-

---

[*] This last is found to be the real reason, air not being a good con-

tain degree of warmth when separated from the external atmosphere. Let an experiment be made, therefore with fibrous substances of linen, and not of wool, feathers, or silk, which are animal excretions. For it is to be observed that all powders (where air is manifestly enclosed) are less cold than the substances when whole, just as we imagine froth (which contains air) to be less cold than the liquid itself.

We have here no exactly negative instance, for we are not acquainted with any body tangible or spirituous which does not admit of heat when exposed to the fire. There is, however, this difference, that some admit it more rapidly, as air, oil, and water, others more slowly, as stone and metals.[7] This, however, belongs to the table of degrees.

No negative is here subjoined, except the remark that sparks are not kindled by flint and steel, or any other hard substance, unless some small particles of the stone or metal are struck off, and that the air never forms them by friction, as is commonly supposed; besides, the sparks from the weight of the ignited substance, have a tendency to descend rather than to rise, and when extinguished becomes a sort of dark ash.

We are of opinion that here again there is no negative; for we are not acquainted with any tangible body which does not become decidedly warm by friction, so that the ancients feigned that the gods had no other means or power of creating heat than the friction of air, by rapid and violent rotation. On this point, however, further inquiry must be made, whether bodies projected by machines (as balls from cannon) do not derive some degree of heat from meeting the air, which renders them somewhat warm when they fall. The air in motion rather cools than heats, as in the winds, the bellows, or breath when the mouth is contracted. The motion, however, in such instances is not sufficiently rapid to excite heat, and is applied to a body of air, and not to its component parts, so that it is not surprising that heat should not be generated.

We must make a more diligent inquiry into this instance; for herbs and green and moist vegetables appear to possess a latent heat, so small, however, as not to be perceived by the touch in single specimens, but when they are united and confined, so that their spirit cannot exhale into the air, and they rather warm each other, their heat is at once manifested, and even flame occasionally in suitable substances.

ductor, and therefore not allowing the escape of heat. The confined air is disengaged when these substances are placed under an exhausted receiver.

[7] This is erroneous. Air, in fact, is one of the worst, and metals are the best conductors of heat.

Here, too, we must make a more diligent inquiry; for quick lime, when sprinkled with water, appears to conceive heat, either from its being collected into one point (as we observed of herbs when confined), or from the irritation and exasperation of the fiery spirit by water, which occasions a conflict and struggle. The true reason will more readily be shown if oil be used instead of water, for oil will equally tend to collect the confined spirit, but not to irritate. The experiment may be made more general, both by using the ashes and calcined products of different bodies and by pouring different liquids upon them.

A negative instance may be subjoined of other metals which are more soft and soluble; for leaf gold dissolved by aqua regia, or lead by aqua fortis, are not warm to the touch whilst dissolving, no more is quicksilver (as far as I remember), but silver excites a slight heat, and so does copper, and tin yet more plainly, and most of all iron and steel, which excite not only a powerful heat, but a violent bubbling. The heat, therefore, appears to be occasioned by the struggle which takes place when these strong dissolvents penetrate, dig into, and tear asunder the parts of those substances, whilst the substances themselves resist. When, however, the substances yield more easily, scarcely any heat is excited.

There is no negative instance with regard to the heat of animals, except in insects (as has been observed), owing to their small size; for in fishes, as compared with land animals, a lower degree rather than a deprivation of heat is observable. In plants and vegetables, both as to their exudations and pith when freshly exposed, there is no sensible degree of heat. But in animals there is a great difference in the degree, both in particular parts (for the heat varies near the heart, the brain, and the extremities) and in the circumstances in which they are placed, such as violent exercise and fevers.

Here, again, there is scarcely a negative instance. I might add that the excrements of animals, even when they are no longer fresh, possess evidently some effective heat, as is shown by their enriching the soil.

Such liquids (whether oily or watery) as are intensely acrid exhibit the effects of heat, by the separation and burning of bodies after some little action upon them, yet they are not at first warm to the touch, but they act according to their affinity and the pores of the substances to which they are applied; for aqua regia dissolves gold but not silver,—on the contrary, aqua fortis dissolves silver but not gold; neither of them dissolves glass, and so of the rest.

Let spirits of wine be tried on wood, or butter, wax, or pitch, to see if this will melt them at all by their heat; for the twenty-fourth instance shows that they possess properties resembling those of heat in causing incrustation. Let an experiment also be made with a graduated glass or calendar,* concave at the top, by pouring well-rectified spirits of wine into the cavity, and covering it up in order that they may the better retain their heat, then observe whether their heat make the water descend.

Spices and acrid herbs are sensibly warm to the palate, and still more so when taken internally; one should see, therefore, on what other substances they exhibit the effects of heat. Now, sailors tell us that when large quantities of spices are suddenly opened, after having been shut up for some time, there is some danger of fever and inflammation to those who stir them or take them out. An experiment might, therefore, be made whether such spices and herbs, when produced, will, like smoke, dry fish and meat hung up over them.

There is an acrid effect and a degree of penetration in cold liquids, such as vinegar and oil of vitriol, as well as in warm, such as oil of marjoram and the like; they have, therefore, an equal effect in causing animated substances to smart, and separating and consuming inanimate parts. There is not any negative instance as to this, nor does there exist any animal pain unaccompanied by the sensation of heat.

There are many effects common to cold and heat, however different in their process; for snowballs appear to burn boys' hands after a little time, and cold no less than fire preserves bodies from putrefaction,—besides both heat and cold contract bodies. But it is better to refer these instances and the like to the investigation of cold.

XIII. In the third place we must exhibit to the understanding the instances in which that nature, which is the object of our inquiries, is present in a greater or less degree, either by comparing its increase and decrease in the same object, or its degree in different objects; for since the form of a thing is its very essence, and the thing only differs from its form as the apparent from the actual object, or the exterior from the interior, or that which is considered with relation to man from that which is considered with relation to the universe; it necessarily follows that no nature can be considered a real form which does not uniformly diminish and increase with the given nature. We are wont to call this our Table of Degrees, or Comparative Instances.

Table of the Degrees or Comparative Instances of Heat.

We will first speak of those bodies which exhibit no degree of heat sensible to the touch, but appear rather to possess a potential heat, or disposition and preparation for it. We will then go

---

* See No. 38 in the table of the degrees of heat.

on to others, which are actually warm to the touch, and observe the strength and degree of it.

1. There is no known solid or tangible body which is by its own nature originally warm; for neither stone, metal, sulphur, fossils, wood, water, nor dead animal carcasses are found warm. The warm springs in baths appear to be heated accidentally, by flame, subterraneous fire (such as is thrown up by Etna and many other mountains), or by the contact of certain bodies, as heat is exhibited in the dissolution of iron and tin. The degree of heat, therefore, in inanimate objects is not sensible to our touch; but they differ in their degrees of cold, for wood and metal are not equally cold.* This, however, belongs to the Table of Degrees of Cold.

2. But with regard to potential heat and predisposition to flame, we find many inanimate substances wonderfully adapted to it, as sulphur, naphtha, and saltpetre.

3. Bodies which have previously acquired heat, as horse-dung from the animal, or lime, and perhaps ashes and soot from fire, retain some latent portion of it. Hence distillations and separations of substances are effected by burying them in horse-dung, and heat is excited in lime by sprinkling it with water (as has been before observed).

4. In the vegetable world we know of no plant, nor part of any plant (as the exudations or pith) that is warm to man's touch. Yet (as we have before observed) green weeds grow warm when confined, and some vegetables are warm and others cold to our internal touch, *i. e.* the palate and stomach, or even after a while to our external skin (as is shown in plasters and ointments).

5. We know of nothing in the various parts of animals, when dead or detached from the rest, that is warm to the touch; for horse-dung itself does not retain its heat, unless it be confined and buried. All dung, however, appears to possess a potential heat, as in manuring fields; so also dead bodies are endued with this latent and potential heat to such a degree, that in cemeteries where people are interred daily the earth acquires a secret heat, which consumes any recently-deposited body much sooner than pure earth; and they tell you that the people of the East are acquainted with a fine soft cloth, made of the down of birds, which can melt butter wrapped gently up in it by its own warmth.

---

* Bacon here mistakes sensation confined to ourselves for an internal property of distinct substances. Metals are denser than wood, and our bodies consequently coming into contact with more particles of matter when we touch them, lose a greater quantity of heat than in the case of lighter substances. *Ed.*

6. Manures, such as every kind of dung, chalk, sea-sand, salt, and the like, have some disposition towards heat.

7. All putrefaction exhibits some slight degree of heat, though not enough to be perceptible by the touch; for neither the substances which by putrefaction are converted into animalculæ,[b] as flesh and cheese, nor rotten wood which shines in the dark, are warm to the touch. The heat, however, of putrid substances displays itself occasionally in a disgusting and strong scent.

8. The first degree of heat, therefore, in substances which are warm to the human touch appears to be that of animals, and this admits of a great variety of degrees, for the lowest (as in insects) is scarcely perceptible, the highest scarcely equals that of the sun's rays in warm climates and weather, and is not so acute as to be insufferable to the hand. It is said, however, of Constantius, and some others of a very dry constitution and habit of body, that when attacked with violent fevers, they became so warm as to appear almost to burn the hand applied to them.

9. Animals become more warm by motion and exercise, wine and feasting, venery, burning fevers, and grief.

10. In the paroxysm of intermittent fevers the patients are at first seized with cold and shivering, but soon afterwards become more heated than at first,—in burning and pestilential fevers they are hot from the beginning.

11. Let further inquiry be made into the comparative heat of different animals, as fishes, quadrupeds, serpents, birds, and also of the different species, as the lion, the kite, or man; for, according to the vulgar opinion, fishes are the least warm internally, and birds the most, particularly doves, hawks, and ostriches.

12. Let further inquiry be made as to the comparative heat in different parts and limbs of the same animal; for milk, blood, seed, and eggs are moderately warm, and less hot than the outward flesh of the animal when in motion or agitated. The degree of heat of the brain, stomach, heart, and the rest, has not yet been equally well investigated.

13. All animals are externally cold in winter and cold weather, but are thought to be internally warmer.

14. The heat of the heavenly bodies, even in the warmest climates and seasons, never reaches such a pitch as to light or burn the driest wood or straw, or even tinder without the aid of burning-glasses. It can, however, raise vapour from moist substances.

15. Astronomers tell us that some stars are hotter than others.

[b] This was the ancient opinion, but the moderns incline to the belief that these insects are produced by generation or fecundity from seeds deposited by their tribes in bodies on the verge of putrefaction. *Ed.*

Mars is considered the warmest after the Sun, then Jupiter, then Venus. The Moon and, above all, Saturn, are considered to be cold. Among the fixed stars Sirius is thought the warmest, then Cor Leonis or Regulus, then the lesser Dog-star.

16. The sun gives out more heat as it approaches towards the perpendicular or zenith, which may be supposed to be the case with the other planets, according to their degree of heat; for instance, that Jupiter gives out more heat when situated beneath Cancer or Leo than when he is beneath Capricorn and Aquarius.

17. It is to be supposed that the sun and other planets give more heat in perigee, from their approximation to the earth, than when in apogee. But if in any country the sun should be both in its perigee and nearer to the perpendicular at the same time, it must necessarily give out more heat than in a country where it is also in perigee, but situated more obliquely; so that the comparative altitude of the planets should be observed, and their approach to or declination from the perpendicular in different countries.

18. The sun and other planets are thought also to give out more heat in proportion as they are nearer to the larger fixed stars, as when the sun is in Leo he is nearer Cor Leonis, Cauda Leonis, Spica Virginis, Sirius, and the lesser Dog-star, than when he is in Cancer, where, however, he approaches nearer to the perpendicular. It is probable, also, that the quarters of the heavens produce a greater heat (though not perceptibly), in proportion as they are adorned with a greater number of stars, particularly those of the first magnitude.

19. On the whole, the heat of the heavenly bodies is augmented in three ways; 1. The approach to the perpendicular; 2. Proximity or their perigee; 3. The conjunction or union of stars.

20. There is a very considerable difference between the degree of heat in animals, and even in the rays of the heavenly bodies (as they reach us), and the heat of the most gentle flame, and even of all ignited substances, nay liquids, or the air itself when unusually heated by fire. For the flame of spirit of wine, though diffused and uncollected, is yet able to set straw, linen, or paper on fire, which animal heat, or that of the sun, will never accomplish without a burning-glass.

21. There are, however, many degrees of strength and weakness in flame and ignited bodies: but no diligent inquiry has been made in this respect, and we must, therefore, pass it hastily over. Of all flames, that of spirits of wine appears to be the most gentle, except, perhaps, the *Ignis Fatuus*, or the flashes from the perspiration of animals. After this we should be inclined to place the flame of light and porous vegetables, such

as straw, reeds, and dried leaves; from which the flame of hair or feathers differs but little. Then, perhaps, comes the flame of wood, particularly that which contains but little rosin or pitch; that of small wood, however (such as is usually tied up in fagots), is milder than that of the trunks or roots of trees. This can be easily tried in iron furnaces, where a fire of fagots or branches of trees is of little service. Next follows the flame of oil, tallow, wax, and the like oily and fat substances, which are not very violent. But a most powerful heat is found in pitch and rosin, and a still greater in sulphur, camphire, naphtha, saltpetre, and salts (after they have discharged their crude matter), and in their compounds; as in gunpowder, Greek fire (vulgarly called wild fire), and its varieties, which possess such a stubborn heat as scarcely to be extinguished by water.

22. We consider that the flame which results from some imperfect metals is very strong and active; but on all these points further inquiry should be made.

23. The flame of vivid lightning appears to exceed all the above, so as sometimes to have melted even wrought iron into drops, which the other flames cannot accomplish.

24. In ignited bodies there are different degrees of heat, concerning which, also, a diligent inquiry has not been made. We consider the faintest heat to be that of tinder, touchwood, and dry rope match, such as is used for discharging cannon. Next follows that of ignited charcoal or cinders, and even bricks, and the like; but the most violent is that of ignited metals, as iron, copper, and the like. Further inquiry, however, must be made into this also.

25. Some ignited bodies are found to be much warmer than some flames; for instance, red hot iron is much warmer, and burns more than the flame of spirits of wine.

26. Some bodies even not ignited, but only heated by the fire, as boiling water, and the air confined in reverberatories, surpass in heat many flames and ignited substances.

27. Motion increases heat,[c] as is shown in the bellows and the blow-pipe; for the harder metals are not dissolved or melted by steady quiet fire, without the aid of the blow-pipe.

28. Let an experiment be made with burning-glasses; in which respect I have observed, that if a glass be placed at the distance of ten inches, for instance, from the combustible object, it does not kindle or burn it so readily, as if the glass be placed

---

[c] The correct measure of the activity of flame may be obtained by multiplying its natural force into the square of its velocity. On this account the flame of vivid lightning mentioned in No. 23, contains so much vigour, its velocity being greater than that arising from other heat. *Ed.*

at the distance of five inches (for instance), and be then gradually and slowly withdrawn to the distance of ten inches. The cone and focus of the rays, however, are the same, but the mere motion increases the effect of the heat.

29. Conflagrations, which take place with a high wind, are thought to make greater way against than with the wind, because when the wind slackens, the flame recoils more rapidly than it advances when the wind is favourable.

30. Flame does not burst out or arise unless it have some hollow space to move and exert itself in, except in the exploding flame of gunpowder, and the like, where the compression and confinement of the flame increase its fury.

31. The anvil becomes so hot by the hammer, that if it were a thin plate it might probably grow red, like ignited iron by repeated strokes. Let the experiment be tried.

32. But in ignited bodies that are porous, so as to leave room for the fire to move itself, if its motion be prevented by strong compression, the fire is immediately extinguished; thus it is with tinder, or the burning snuff of a candle, or lamp, or even hot charcoal or cinders; for when they are squeezed by snuffers, or the foot, and the like, the effect of the fire instantly ceases.

33. The approach towards a hot body increases heat in proportion to the approximation; a similar effect to that of light, for the nearer any object is placed towards the light, the more visible it becomes.

34. The[d] union of different heats increases heat, unless the substances be mixed; for a large and small fire in the same spot tend mutually to increase each other's heat, but lukewarm water poured into boiling water cools it.

35. The continued neighbourhood of a warm body increases heat. For the heat, which perpetually passes and emanates from it, being mixed with that which preceded it, multiplies the whole. A fire, for instance, does not warm a room in half an hour as much as the same fire would in an hour. This does not apply to light, for a lamp or candle placed in a spot gives no more light by remaining there, than it did at first.

36. The irritation of surrounding cold increases heat, as may be seen in fires during a sharp frost. We think that this is owing not merely to the confinement and compression of the heat (which forms a sort of union), but also by the exasperation of it, as when the air or a stick are violently compressed or bent, they recoil, not only to the point they first occupied, but still

---

[d] The fires supply fresh heat, the water has only a certain quantity of heat, which being diffused over a fresh supply of cooler water, must be on the whole lowered.

further back. Let an accurate experiment, therefore, be made with a stick, or something of the kind, put into the flame, in order to see whether it be not sooner burnt at the sides than in the middle of it.[e]

37. There are many degrees in the susceptibility of heat. And, first, it must be observed how much a low gentle heat changes and partially warms even the bodies least susceptible of it. For even the heat of the hand imparts a little warmth to a ball of lead or other metal held a short time in it; so easily is heat transmitted and excited, without any apparent change in the body.

38. Of all bodies that we are acquainted with, air admits and loses heat the most readily, which is admirably seen in weather-glasses, whose construction is as follows. Take a glass with a hollow belly, and a thin and long neck; turn it upside down, and place it with its mouth downwards into another glass vessel containing water; the end of the tube touching the bottom of the vessel, and the tube itself leaning a little on the edge, so as to be fixed upright. In order to do this more readily, let a little wax be applied to the edge, not however so as to block up the orifice, lest by preventing the air from escaping, the motion, which we shall presently speak of, and which is very gentle and delicate, should be impeded.

Before the first glass be inserted in the other, its upper part (the belly) should be warmed at the fire. Then upon placing it as we have described, the air (which was dilated by the heat), after a sufficient time has been allowed for it to lose the additional temperature, will restore and contract itself to the same dimensions as that of the external or common atmosphere at the moment of immersion, and the water will be attracted upwards in the tube to a proportionate extent. A long narrow slip of paper should be attached to the tube, divided into as many degrees as you please. You will then perceive, as the weather grows warmer or colder, that the air contracts itself into a narrower space in cold weather and dilates in the warm, which will be exhibited by the rising of the water as the air contracts itself, and its depression as the air dilates. The sensibility of the air with regard to heat or cold is so delicate and exquisite, that it far exceeds the human touch, so that a ray of sunshine, the heat of the breath, and much more, that of the hand placed on the top of the tube, immediately causes an evident depression of the water. We think, however, that the spirit of animals

[e] If condensation were the cause of the greater heat, Bacon concludes the centre of the flame would be the hotter part, and vice versâ. The fact is, neither of the causes assigned by Bacon is the true one; for the fire burns more quickly only because the draught of air is more rapid, the cold dense air pressing rapidly into the heated room and towards the chimney.

possesses a much more delicate susceptibility of heat and cold, only that it is impeded and blunted by the grossness of their bodies.

39. After air, we consider those bodies to be most sensible of heat, which have been recently changed and contracted by cold, as snow and ice; for they begin to be dissolved and melt with the first mild weather. Next, perhaps, follows quicksilver; then greasy substances, as oil, butter, and the like; then wood; then water; lastly, stones and metals, which do not easily grow hot, particularly towards their centre.ᶠ When heated, however, they retain their temperature for a very long time; so that a brick or stone, or hot iron, plunged in a basin of cold water, and kept there for a quarter of an hour or thereabouts, retains such a heat as not to admit of being touched.

40. The less massive the body is, the more readily it grows warm at the approach of a heated body, which shows that heat with us is somewhat averse to a tangible mass.ᵍ

41. Heat with regard to the human senses and touch is various and relative, so that lukewarm water appears hot if the hand be cold, and cold if the hand be hot.

XIV. Any one may readily see how poor we are in history, since in the above tables, besides occasionally inserting traditions and report instead of approved history and authentic instances (always, however, adding some note if their credit or authority be doubtful), we are often forced to subjoin, " Let the experiment be tried—Let further inquiry be made."

XV. We are wont to term the office and use of these three tables the presenting a review of instances to the understanding; and when this has been done, induction itself is to be brought into action. For on an individual review of all the instances a nature is to be found, such as always to be present and absent with the given nature, to increase and decrease with it, and, as we have said, to form a more common limit of the nature. If the mind attempt this affirmatively from the first (which it always will when left to itself), there will spring up phantoms,

---

ᶠ Bacon appears to have confounded combustibility and fusibility with susceptibility of heat; for though the metals will certainly neither dissolve as soon as ice or butter, nor be consumed as soon as wood, that only shows that different degrees of heat are required to produce similar effects on different bodies; but metals much more readily acquire and transmit the same degree of heat than any of the above substances. The rapid transmission renders them generally cold to the touch. The convenience of fixing wooden handles to vessels containing hot water illustrates these observations.

ᵍ Another singular error, the truth being, that solid bodies are the best conductors; but of course where heat is diffused over a large mass, it is less in each part, than if that part alone absorbed the whole quantum of heat. *Ed.*

mere theories and ill-defined notions, with axioms requiring daily correction. These will, doubtless, be better or worse, according to the power and strength of the understanding which creates them. But it is only for God (the bestower and creator of forms), and perhaps for angels and intelligences, at once to recognise forms affirmatively at the first glance of contemplation: man, at least, is unable to do so, and is only allowed to proceed first by negatives, and then to conclude with affirmatives, after every species of exclusion.

XVI. We must, therefore, effect a complete solution and separation of nature; not by fire, but by the mind, that divine fire. The first work of legitimate induction, in the discovery of forms, is rejection, or the exclusive instances of individual natures, which are not found in some one instance where the given nature is present, or are found in any one instance where it is absent, or are found to increase in any one instance where the given nature decreases, or the reverse. After an exclusion correctly effected, an affirmative form will remain as the residuum, solid, true, and well defined, whilst all volatile opinions go off in smoke. This is readily said; but we must arrive at it by a circuitous rout. We shall perhaps, however, omit nothing that can facilitate our progress.

XVII. The first and almost perpetual precaution and warning which we consider necessary is this; that none should suppose from the great part assigned by us to forms, that we mean such forms as the meditations and thoughts of men have hitherto been accustomed to. In the first place, we do not at present mean the concrete forms, which (as we have observed) are in the common course of things compounded of simple natures, as those of a lion, an eagle, a rose, gold, or the like. The moment for discussing these will arrive when we come to treat of the latent process and latent conformation, and the discovery of them as they exist in what are called substances, or concrete natures.

Nor again, would we be thought to mean (even when treating of simple natures) any abstract forms or ideas, either undefined or badly defined in matter. For when we speak of forms, we mean nothing else than those laws and regulations of simple action which arrange and constitute any simple nature, such as heat, light, weight, in every species of matter, and in a susceptible subject. The form of heat or form of light, therefore, means no more than the law of heat or the law of light. Nor do we ever abstract or withdraw ourselves from things, and the operative branch of philosophy. When, therefore, we say (for instance) in our investigation of the form of heat, Reject rarity, or, Rarity is not of the form of heat, it is the same as if we were to say, Man can superinduce heat on a dense body, or the reverse, Man can abstract or ward off heat from a rare body.

But if our forms appear to any one to be somewhat abstracted, from their mingling and uniting heterogeneous objects (the heat for instance of the heavenly bodies appears to be very different from that of fire; the fixed red of the rose and the like, from that which is apparent in the rainbow, or the radiation of opal or the diamond;[h] death by drowning, from that by burning, the sword, apoplexy, or consumption; and yet they all agree in the common natures of heat, redness, and death), let him be assured that his understanding is enthralled by habit, by general appearances and hypotheses. For it is most certain that, however heterogeneous and distinct, they agree in the form or law which regulates heat, redness, or death; and that human power cannot be emancipated and freed from the common course of nature, and expanded and exalted to new efficients and new modes of operation, except by the revelation and invention of forms of this nature. But after this[i] union of nature, which is the principal point, we will afterwards, in its proper place, treat of the divisions and ramifications of nature, whether ordinary or internal and more real.

XVIII. We must now offer an example of the exclusion or rejection of natures found by the tables of review, not to be of the form of heat; first premising that not only each table is sufficient for the rejection of any nature, but even each single instance contained in them. For it is clear from what has been said that every contradictory instance destroys an hypothesis as to the form. Still, however, for the sake of clearness, and in order to show more plainly the use of the tables, we redouble or repeat the exclusive.

An Example of the Exclusive Table, or of the Rejection of Natures from the Form of Heat.

1. On account of the sun's rays, reject elementary (or terrestrial) nature.

2. On account of common fire, and particularly subterranean fires (which are the most remote and secluded from the rays of the heavenly bodies), reject celestial nature.

3. On account of the heat acquired by every description of substances (as minerals, vegetables, the external parts of animals,

---

[h] This general law or form has been well illustrated by Newton's discovery of the decomposition of colours.

[i] *I. e.* the common link or form which connects the various kinds of natures, such as the different hot or red natures enumerated above. —See Aphorism iii. part 2

water, oil, air, &c.) by mere approximation to the fire or any warm body, reject all variety and delicate texture of bodies.

4. On account of iron and ignited metals, which warm other bodies, and yet neither lose their weight nor substance, reject the imparting or mixing of the substance of the heating body.

5. On account of boiling water and air, and also those metals and other solid bodies which are heated, but not to ignition, or red heat, reject flame or light.

6. On account of the rays of the moon and other heavenly bodies (except the sun), again reject flame or light.

7. On account of the comparison between red-hot iron and the flame of spirits of wine (for the iron is more hot and less bright, whilst the flame of spirits of wine is more bright and less hot), again reject flame and light.

8. On account of gold and other ignited metals, which are of the greatest specific density, reject rarity.

9. On account of air, which is generally found to be cold and yet continues rare, reject rarity.

10. On account of ignited iron,[k] which does not swell in bulk, but retains the same apparent dimension, reject the absolute expansive motion of the whole.

11. On account of the expansion of the air in thermometers and the like, which is absolutely moved and expanded to the eye, and yet acquires no manifest increase of heat, again reject absolute or expansive motion of the whole.

12. On account of the ready application of heat to all substances without any destruction or remarkable alteration of them, reject destructive nature or the violent communication of any new nature.

13. On account of the agreement and conformity of the effects produced by cold and heat, reject both expansive and contracting motion as regards the whole.

14. On account of the heat excited by friction, reject principal nature, by which we mean that which exists positively, and is not caused by a preceding nature.

There are other natures to be rejected; but we are merely offering examples, and not perfect tables.

None of the above natures are of the form of heat; and man is freed from them all in his operation upon heat.

XIX. In the exclusive table are laid the foundations of true induction, which is not, however, completed until the affirmative be attained. Nor is the exclusive table perfect, nor can it be so at first. For it is clearly a rejection of simple natures; but if we have not as yet good and just notions of simple natures, how can the exclusive table be made correct? Some of the above, as the

---

[k] This is erroneous,—all metals expand considerably when heated.

notion of elementary and celestial nature, and rarity, are vague and ill-defined. We, therefore, who are neither ignorant nor forgetful of the great work which we attempt, in rendering the human understanding adequate to things and nature, by no means rest satisfied with what we have hitherto enforced, but push the matter farther, and contrive and prepare more powerful aid for the use of the understanding, which we will next subjoin. And, indeed, in the interpretation of nature the mind is to be so prepared and formed, as to rest itself on proper degrees of certainty, and yet to remember (especially at first) that what is present depends much upon what remains behind.

XX. Since, however, truth emerges more readily from error than confusion, we consider it useful to leave the understanding at liberty to exert itself and attempt the interpretation of nature in the affirmative, after having constructed and weighed the three tables of preparation, such as we have laid them down, both from the instances there collected, and others occurring elsewhere. Which attempt we are wont to call the liberty of the understanding, or the commencement of interpretation, or the first vintage.

The First Vintage of the Form of Heat.

It must be observed that the form of anything is inherent (as appears clearly from our premises) in each individual instance in which the thing itself is inherent, or it would not be a form. No contradictory instance, therefore, can be alleged. The form, however, is found to be much more conspicuous and evident in some instances than in others; in those (for example) where its nature is less restrained and embarrassed, and reduced to rule by other natures. Such instances we are wont to term coruscations, or conspicuous instances. We must proceed, then, to the first vintage of the form of heat.

From the instances taken collectively, as well as singly, the nature whose limit is heat appears to be motion. This is chiefly exhibited in flame, which is in constant motion, and in warm or boiling liquids, which are likewise in constant motion. It is also shown in the excitement or increase of heat by motion, as by bellows and draughts: for which see Inst. 29, Tab. 3, and by other species of motion, as in Inst. 28 and 31, Tab. 3. It is also shown by the extinction of fire and heat upon any strong pressure, which restrains and puts a stop to motion; for which see Inst. 30 and 32, Tab. 3. It is further shown by this circumstance, namely, that every substance is destroyed, or at least materially changed, by strong and powerful fire and heat: whence it is clear that tumult and confusion are occasioned by heat, together with a violent motion in the internal parts of bodies; and this gradually tends to their dissolution.

What we have said with regard to motion must be thus understood, when taken as the genus of heat: it must not be thought that heat generates motion, or motion heat (though in some respects this be true), but that the very essence of heat, or the substantial self[1] of heat, is motion and nothing else, limited, however, by certain differences which we will presently add, after giving some cautions for avoiding ambiguity.

Sensible heat is relative, and regards man, not universe; and is rightly held to be merely the effect of heat on animal spirit. It is even variable in itself, since the same body (in different states of sensation) excites the feeling of heat and of cold; this is shown by Inst. 41, Tab. 3.

Nor should we confound the communication of heat or its transitive nature, by which a body grows warm at the approach of a heated body, with the form of heat; for heat is one thing and heating another. Heat can be excited by friction without any previous heating body, and, therefore, heating is excluded from the form of heat. Even when heat is excited by the approach of a hot body, this depends not on the form of heat, but on another more profound and common nature; namely, that of assimilation and multiplication, about which a separate inquiry must be made.

The notion of fire is vulgar, and of no assistance; it is merely compounded of the conjunction of heat and light in any body, as in ordinary flame and red-hot substances.

Laying aside all ambiguity, therefore, we must lastly consider the true differences which limit motion and render it the form of heat.

I. The first difference is, that heat is an expansive motion, by which the body strives to dilate itself, and to occupy a greater space than before. This difference is principally seen in flame, where the smoke or thick vapour is clearly dilated and bursts into flame.

It is also shown in all boiling liquids, which swell, rise, and boil up to the sight, and the process of expansion is urged forward till they are converted into a much more extended and dilated body than the liquid itself, such as steam, smoke, or air.

It is also shown in wood and combustibles where exudation sometimes takes place, and evaporation always.

It is also shown in the melting of metals, which, being very compact, do not easily swell and dilate, but yet their spirit, when dilated and desirous of further expansion, forces and urges its thicker parts into dissolution, and if the heat be pushed still farther, reduces a considerable part of them into a volatile state.

It is also shown in iron or stones, which, though not melted or

---

[1] "Quid ipsum," the τὸ τί ἦν εἶναι of Aristotle.

BOOK II.] APHORISMS. 479

dissolved, are however softened. The same circumstance takes place in sticks of wood, which become flexible when a little heated in warm ashes.

It is most readily observed in air, which instantly and manifestly expands with a small degree of heat, as in Inst. 38, Tab. 3.

It is also shown in the contrary nature of cold; for cold contracts and narrows every substance;[m] so that in intense frosts nails fall out of the wall and brass cracks, and heated glass exposed suddenly to the cold cracks and breaks. So the air by a slight degree of cold, contracts itself, as in Inst. 38, Tab. 3. More will be said of this in the inquiry into cold.

Nor is it to be wondered at if cold and heat exhibit many common effects (for which see Inst. 32, Tab 2), since two differences, of which we shall presently speak, belong to each nature: although in the present difference the effects be diametrically opposed to each other. For heat occasions an expansive and dilating motion, but cold a contracting and condensing motion.

II. The second difference is a modification of the preceding, namely, that heat is an expansive motion, tending towards the exterior, but at the same time bearing the body upwards. For there is no doubt that there be many compound motions, as an arrow or dart, for instance, has both a rotatory and progressive motion. In the same way the motion of heat is both expansive and tending upwards.

This difference is shown by putting the tongs or poker into the fire. If placed perpendicularly with the hand above, they soon burn it, but much less speedily if the hand hold them sloping or from below.

It is also conspicuous in distillations *per descensum*, which men are wont to employ with delicate flowers, whose scent easily evaporates. Their industry has devised placing the fire above instead of below, that it may scorch less; for not only flame but all heat has an upward tendency.

Let an experiment be made on the contrary nature of cold, whether its contraction be downwards, as the expansion of heat is upwards. Take, therefore, two iron rods or two glass tubes, alike in other respects, and warm them a little, and place a sponge, dipped in cold water, or some snow, below the one and above the other. We are of opinion that the extremities will grow cold in that rod first where it is placed beneath, as the contrary takes place with regard to heat.

[m] To show the error of the text, we need only mention the case of water, which, when confined in corked vases, and exposed to the action of a freezing atmosphere, is sure to swell out and break those vessels which are not sufficiently large to contain its expanded volume. Megalotti narrates a hundred other instances of a similar character. *Ed.*

III. The third difference is this; that heat is not a uniform expansive motion of the whole, but of the small particles of the body; and this motion being at the same time restrained, repulsed, and reflected, becomes alternating, perpetually hurrying, striving, struggling, and irritated by the repercussion, which is the source of the violence of flame and heat.

But this difference is chiefly shown in flame and boiling liquids, which always hurry, swell, and subside again in detached parts.

It is also shown in bodies of such hard texture as not to swell or dilate in bulk, such as red-hot iron, in which the heat is most violent.

It is also shown by the fires burning most briskly in the coldest weather.

It is also shown by this, that when the air is dilated in the thermometer uniformly and equably, without any impediment or repulsion, the heat is not perceptible. In confined draughts also, although they break out very violently, no remarkable heat is perceived, because the motion affects the whole, without any alternating motion in the particles; for which reason try whether flame do not burn more at the sides than in its centre.

It is also shown in this, that all burning proceeds by the minute pores of bodies,—undermining, penetrating, piercing, and pricking them as if with an infinite number of needle-points. Hence all strong acids (if adapted to the body on which they act) exhibit the effects of fire, from their corroding and pungent nature.

The difference of which we now speak is common also to the nature of cold, in which the contracting motion is restrained by the resistance of expansion, as in heat the expansive motion is restrained by the resistance of contraction.

Whether, therefore, the particles of matter penetrate inwards or outwards, the reasoning is the same, though the power be very different, because we have nothing on earth which is intensely cold.

IV. The fourth difference is a modification of the preceding, namely, that this stimulating or penetrating motion should be rapid and never sluggish, and should take place not in the very minutest particles, but rather in those of some tolerable dimensions.

It is shown by comparing the effects of fire with those of time. Time dries, consumes, undermines, and reduces to ashes as well as fire, and perhaps to a much finer degree; but as its motion is very slow, and attacks very minute particles, no heat is perceived.

It is also shown in a comparison of the dissolution of iron and gold; for gold is dissolved without the excitement of any heat, but iron with a vehement excitement of it, although most in the same time, because in the former the penetration of the separating acid is mild, and gently insinuates itself, and the particles of gold yield easily, but the penetration of iron is violent, and attended with some struggle, and its particles are more obstinate.

It is partially shown, also, in some gangrenes and mortifications of flesh, which do not excite great heat or pain, from the gentle nature of the putrefaction.

Let this suffice for a first vintage, or the commencement of the interpretation of the form of heat by the liberty of the understanding.

From this first vintage the form or true definition of heat (considered relatively to the universe and not to the sense) is briefly thus:—Heat is an expansive motion restrained, and striving to exert itself in the smaller particles." The expansion is modified by its tendency to rise, though expanding towards the exterior; and the effort is modified by its not being sluggish, but active and somewhat violent.

With regard to the operative definition, the matter is the same. If you are able to excite a dilating or expansive motion in any natural body, and so to repress that motion and force it on itself as not to allow the expansion to proceed equally, but only to be partially exerted and partially repressed, you will beyond all doubt produce heat, without any consideration as to whether the body be of earth (or elementary, as they term it), or imbued with celestial influence, luminous or opaque, rare or dense, locally expanded or contained within the bounds of its first dimensions, verging to dissolution or remaining fixed, animal, vegetable, or

" Bacon's inquisition into the nature of heat, as an example of the mode of interpreting nature, cannot be looked upon otherwise than as a complete failure. Though the exact nature of this phenomenon is still an obscure and controverted matter, the science of thermotics now consists of many important truths, and to none of these truths is there so much as an approximation in Bacon's process. The steps by which this science really advanced were the discovery of a measure of a heat or temperature, the establishment of the laws of conduction and radiation, of the laws of specific heat, latent heat, and the like. Such advances have led to Ampère's hypothesis, that heat consists in the vibrations of an imponderable fluid; and to Laplace's theory, that temperature consists in the internal radiation of a similar medium. These hypotheses cannot yet be said to be even probable, but at least they are so modified as to include some of the preceding laws which are firmly established, whereas Bacon's "form," or true definition of heat, as stated in the text, includes no laws of phenomena, explains no process, and is indeed itself an example of illicit generalization.

In all the details of his example of heat he is unfortunate. He includes in his collection of instances, the *hot* tastes of aromatic plants, the caustic effects of acids, and many other facts which cannot be ascribed to heat without a studious laxity in the use of the word. *Ed.*

mineral, water, or oil, or air, or any other substance whatever susceptible of such motion. Sensible heat is the same, but considered relatively to the senses. Let us now proceed to further helps.

XXI. After our tables of first review, our rejection or exclusive table, and the first vintage derived from them, we must advance to the remaining helps of the understanding with regard to the interpretation of nature, and a true and perfect induction, in offering which we will take the examples of cold and heat where tables are necessary, but where fewer instances are required, we will go through a variety of others, so as neither to confound investigation nor to narrow our doctrine.

In the first place, therefore, we will treat of prerogative instances;° 2. Of the supports of induction; 3. Of the correction of induction; 4. Of varying the investigation according to the

> By this term Bacon understands general phenomena, taken in order from the great mass of indiscriminative facts, which, as they lie in nature, are apt to generate confusion by their number, indistinctness, and complication. Such classes of phenomena, as being peculiarly suggestive of causation, he quaintly classes under the title of prerogative inquiries, either seduced by the fanciful analogy, which such instances bore to the *prerogativa centuria* in the Roman Comitia, or justly considering them as Herschell supposes to hold a kind of prerogative dignity from being peculiarly suggestive of causation.
>
> Two high authorities in physical science (v. Herschell, Nat. Phil. art. 192; Whewell's Philosophy of the Inductive Sciences, vol. ii. p. 243) pronounce these instances of little service in the task of induction, being for the most part classed not according to the ideas which they involve, or to any obvious circumstance in the facts of which they consist, but according to the extent and manner of their influence upon the inquiry in which they are employed. Thus we have solitary instances, migrating instances, ostensive instances, clandestine instances, so termed according to the degree in which they exhibit, or seem to exhibit, the property, whose nature we would examine. We have guidepost instances, crucial instances, instances of the parted road, of the doorway, of the lamp, according to the guidance they supply to our advance. Whewell remarks that such a classification is much of the same nature as if, having to teach the art of building, we were to describe tools with reference to the amount and place of the work which they must do, instead of pointing out their construction and use; as if we were to inform the pupil that we must have tools for lifting a stone up, tools for moving it side-ways, tools for laying it square, and tools for cementing it firmly. The means are thus lost in the end, and we reap the fruits of unmethodical arrangement in the confusion of cross division. In addition, all the instances are leavened with the error of confounding the laws with the causes of phenomena, and we are urged to adopt the fundamental error of seeking therein the universal agents, or general causes of phenomena, without ascending the gradual steps of intermediate laws. *Ed.*

nature of the subject; 5. Of the prerogative natures with respect to investigation, or of what should be the first or last objects of our research; 6. Of the limits of investigation, or a synopsis of all natures that exist in the universe; 7. Of the application to practical purposes, or of what relates to man; 8. Of the preparations for investigation; 9. And lastly, of the ascending and descending scale of axioms.[p]

XXII. Amongst the prerogative instances we will first mention solitary instances. Solitary instances are those which exhibit the required nature in subjects that have nothing in common with any other subject than the nature in question, or which do not exhibit the required nature in subjects resembling others in every respect except that of the nature in question; for these instances manifestly remove prolixity, and accelerate and confirm exclusion, so that a few of them are of as much avail as many.

For instance, let the inquiry be the nature of colour. Prisms, crystalline gems, which yield colours not only internally but on the wall, dews, &c., are solitary instances; for they have nothing in common with the fixed colours in flowers and coloured gems, metals, woods, &c., except the colour itself. Hence we easily deduce that colour is nothing but a modification of the image of the incident and absorbed light, occasioned in the former case by the different degrees of incidence, in the latter by the various textures and forms of bodies.[q] These are solitary instances as regards similitude.

Again, in the same inquiry the distinct veins of white and black in marble, and the variegated colours of flowers of the same species, are solitary instances; for the black and white of marble, and the spots of white and purple in the flowers of the stock, agree in every respect but that of colour. Thence we easily deduce that colour has not much to do with the intrinsic natures of any body, but depends only on the coarser and as it were mechanical arrangement of the parts. These are solitary instances as regards difference. We call them both solitary or wild, to borrow a word from the astronomers.

XXIII. In the second rank of prerogative instances we will consider migrating instances. In these the required nature passes towards generation, having no previous existence, or towards corruption, having first existed. In each of these divisions, therefore, the instances are always twofold, or rather it is one instance, first in motion or on its passage, and then brought

[p] Of these nine general heads no more than the first is prosecuted by the author.
[q] This very nearly approaches to Sir I. Newton's discovery of the decomposition of light by the prism.

to the opposite conclusion. These instances not only hasten and confirm exclusion, but also reduce affirmation, or the form itself, to a narrow compass; for the form must be something conferred by this migration, or, on the contrary, removed and destroyed by it; and although all exclusion advances affirmation, yet this takes place more directly in the same than in different subjects; but if the form (as it is quite clear from what has been advanced) exhibit itself in one subject, it leads to all. The more simple the migration is, the more valuable is the instance. These migrating instances are, moreover, very useful in practice, for since they manifest the form, coupled with that which causes or destroys it, they point out the right practice in some subjects, and thence there is an easy transition to those with which they are most allied. There is, however, a degree of danger which demands caution, namely, lest they should refer the form too much to its efficient cause, and imbue, or at least tinge, the understanding with a false notion of the form from the appearance of such cause, which is never more than a vehicle or conveyance of the form. This may easily be remedied by a proper application of exclusion.

Let us then give an example of a migrating instance. Let whiteness be the required nature. An instance which passes towards generation is glass in its entire and in its powdered state, or water in its natural state, and when agitated to froth; for glass when entire, and water in its natural state, are transparent and not white, but powdered glass and the froth of water are white and not transparent. We must inquire, therefore, what has happened to the glass or water in the course of this migration; for it is manifest that the form of whiteness is conveyed and introduced by the bruising of the glass and the agitation of the water; but nothing is found to have been introduced but a diminishing of the parts of the glass and water and the insertion of air. Yet this is no slight progress towards discovering the form of whiteness, namely, that two bodies, in themselves more or less transparent (as air and water, or air and glass), when brought into contact in minute portions, exhibit whiteness from the unequal refraction of the rays of light.

But here we must also give an example of the danger and caution of which we spoke; for instance, it will readily occur to an understanding perverted by efficients, that air is always necessary for producing the form of whiteness, or that whiteness is only generated by transparent bodies, which suppositions are both false, and proved to be so by many exclusions; nay, it will rather appear (without any particular regard to air or the like), that all bodies which are even in such of their parts as affect the sight exhibit transparency, those which are uneven and of simple texture whiteness, those which are uneven and of compound but regular texture all the other colours except black, but those which are uneven and of a compound irregular and confused texture exhibit blackness. An example has been given, therefore, of an instance migrating towards generation in the required nature of whiteness. An instance migrating towards corruption in the same nature is that of dissolving froth or snow, for they lose their whiteness and assume the transparency of water in its pure state without air.

Nor should we by any means omit to state, that under migrating instances we must comprehend not only those which pass towards generation and destruction, but also those which pass towards increase or decrease, for they, too, assist in the discovery of the form, as is clear from our definition of a form and the Table of Degrees. Hence paper, which is white when dry, is less white when moistened (from the exclusion of air and admission of water), and tends more to transparency. The reason is the same as in the above instances.[r]

XXIV. In the third rank of prerogative instances we will class conspicuous instances, of which we spoke in our first vintage of the form of heat, and which we are also wont to call coruscations, or free and predominant instances. They are such as show the required nature in its bare substantial shape, and at its height or greatest degree of power, emancipated and free from all impediments, or at least overcoming, suppressing, and restraining them by the strength of its qualities; for since every body is susceptible of many united forms of natures in the concrete, the consequence is that they mutually deaden, depress, break, and confine each other, and the individual forms are obscured. But there are some subjects in which the required nature exists in its full vigour rather than in others, either from the absence of any impediment, or the predominance of its quality. Such instances are eminently conspicuous. But even in these care must be taken, and the hastiness of the understanding checked, for whatever makes a show of the form, and forces it forward, is to be suspected, and recourse must be had to severe and diligent exclusion.

For example, let heat be the required nature. The thermometer is a conspicuous instance of the expansive motion, which (as has been observed) constitutes the chief part of the form of heat; for although flame clearly exhibits expansion, yet from its being extinguished every moment, it does not exhibit the progress of expansion. Boiling water again, from its rapid conver-

[r] The mineral kingdom, as displaying the same nature in all its gradations, from the shells so perfect in structure in limestone to the finer marbles in which their nature gradually disappears, is the great theatre for instances of migration. *Ed.*

sion into vapour, does not so well exhibit the expansion of water in its own shape, whilst red-hot iron and the like are so far from showing this progress, that, on the contrary, the expansion itself is scarcely evident to the senses, on account of its spirit being repressed and weakened by the compact and coarse particles which subdue and restrain it. But the thermometer strikingly exhibits the expansion of the air as being evident and progressive, durable and not transitory.[a]

Take another example. Let the required nature be weight. Quicksilver is a conspicuous instance of weight; for it is far heavier than any other substance except gold, which is not much heavier, and it is a better instance than gold for the purpose of indicating the form of weight; for gold is solid and consistent, which qualities must be referred to density, but quicksilver is liquid and teeming with spirit, yet much heavier than the diamond and other substances considered to be most solid; whence it is shown that the form of gravity or weight predominates only in the quantity of matter, and not in the close fitting of it.[b]

XXV. In the fourth rank of prerogative instances we will class clandestine instances, which we are also wont to call twilight instances; they are as it were opposed to the conspicuous instances, for they show the required nature in its lowest state of efficacy, and as it were its cradle and first rudiments, making an effort and a sort of first attempt, but concealed and subdued by a contrary nature. Such instances are, however, of great importance in discovering forms, for as the conspicuous tend easily to differences, so do the clandestine best lead to genera, that is, to those common natures of which the required natures are only the limits.

As an example, let consistency, or that which confines itself, be the required nature, the opposite of which is a liquid or flowing state. The clandestine instances are such as exhibit some weak and low degree of consistency in fluids, as a water bubble, which is a sort of consistent and bounded pellicle formed out of the

---

[a] Bacon was not aware of the fact since brought to light by Römer, that down to fourteen fathoms from the earth's mean level the thermometer remains fixed at the tenth degree, but that as the thermometer descends below that depth the heat increases in a ratio proportionate to the descent, which happens with little variation in all climates. Buffon considers this a proof of a central fire in our planet. *Ed.*

[b] All the diversities of bodies depend upon two principles, *i. e.* the quantity and the position of the elements that enter into their composition. The primary difference is not that which depends on the greatest or least quantity of material elements, but that which depends on their position. It was the quick perception of this truth that made Leibnitz say that to complete mathematics it was necessary to join to the analysis of quantity the analysis of position. *Ed.*

substance of the water. So caves' droppings, if there be enough water to follow them, draw themselves out into a thin thread, not to break the continuity of the water, but if there be not enough to follow, the water forms itself into a round drop, which is the best form to prevent a breach of continuity; and at the moment the thread ceases, and the water begins to fall in drops, the thread of water recoils upwards to avoid such a breach. Nay, in metals, which when melted are liquid but more tenacious, the melted drops often recoil and are suspended. There is something similar in the instance of the child's looking-glass, which little boys will sometimes form of spittle between rushes, and where the same pellicle of water is observable; and still more in that other amusement of children, when they take some water rendered a little more tenacious by soap, and inflate it with a pipe, forming the water into a sort of castle of bubbles, which assumes such consistency, by the interposition of the air, as to admit of being thrown some little distance without bursting. The best example is that of froth and snow, which assume such consistency as almost to admit of being cut, although composed of air and water, both liquids. All these circumstances clearly show that the terms liquid and consistent are merely vulgar notions adapted to the sense, and that in reality all bodies have a tendency to avoid a breach of continuity, faint and weak in bodies composed of homogeneous parts (as is the case with liquids), but more vivid and powerful in those composed of heterogeneous parts, because the approach of heterogeneous matter binds bodies together, whilst the insinuation of homogeneous matter loosens and relaxes them.

Again, to take another example, let the required nature be attraction or the cohesion of bodies. The most remarkable conspicuous instance with regard to its form is the magnet. The contrary nature to attraction is non-attraction, though in a similar substance. Thus iron does not attract iron, lead lead, wood wood, nor water water. But the clandestine instance is that of the magnet armed with iron, or rather that of iron in the magnet so armed. For its nature is such that the magnet when armed does not attract iron more powerfully at any given distance than when unarmed; but if the iron be brought in contact with the armed magnet, the latter will sustain a much greater weight than the simple magnet, from the resemblance of substance in the two portions of iron, a quality altogether clandestine and hidden in the iron until the magnet was introduced. It is manifest, therefore, that the form of cohesion is something which is vivid and robust in the magnet, and hidden and weak in the iron. It is to be observed, also, that small wooden arrows without an iron point, when discharged from large mortars, penetrate further into wooden substances (such as the ribs of ships or the like), than the same arrows pointed with iron,ᵘ owing to the similarity of substance, though this quality was previously latent in the wood. Again, although in the mass air does not appear to attract air, nor water water, yet when one bubble is brought near another, they are both more readily dissolved, from the tendency to contact of the water with the water, and the air with the air.ˣ These clandestine instances (which are, as has been observed, of the most important service) are principally to be observed in small portions of bodies, for the larger masses observe more universal and general forms, as will be mentioned in its proper place.ʸ

XXVI. In the fifth rank of prerogative instances we will class constitutive instances, which we are wont also to call collective instances. They constitute a species or lesser form, as it were, of the required nature. For since the real forms (which are

ᵘ Query?

ˣ The real cause of this phenomenon is the attraction of the surface-water in the vessel by the sides of the bubbles. When the bubbles approach, the sides nearest each other both tend to raise the small space of water between them, and consequently less water is raised by each of these nearer sides than by the exterior part of the bubble, and the greater weight of the water raised on the exterior parts pushes the bubbles together. In the same manner a bubble near the side of a vessel is pushed towards it; the vessel and bubble both drawing the water that is between them. The latter phenomenon cannot be explained on Bacon's hypothesis.

ʸ Modern discoveries appear to bear out the sagacity of Bacon's remark, and the experiments of Baron Cagnard may be regarded as a first step towards its full demonstration. After the new facts elicited by that philosopher, there can be little doubt that the solid, liquid, and aëriform state of bodies are merely stages in a progress of gradual transition from one extreme to the other, and that however strongly marked the distinctions between them may appear, they will ultimately turn out to be separated by no sudden or violent line of demarcation, but slide into each other by imperceptible gradations. Bacon's suggestion, however, is as old as Pythagoras, and perhaps simultaneous with the first dawn of philosophic reason. The doctrine of the reciprocal transmutation of the elements underlies all the physical systems of the ancients, and was adopted by the Epicureans as well as the Stoics. Ovid opens his last book of the Metamorphoses with the poetry of the subject, where he expressly points to the hint of Bacon :—

—— " Tenuatus in auras
Aëraque humor abit, &c. &c.
* * * * *
Inde retro redeunt, idemque retexitur ordo."—xv. 246—249.

and Seneca, in the third book of his Natural Philosophy, quest. iv states the opinion in more precise language than either the ancient bard or the modern philosopher. *Ed.*

always convertible with the given nature) lie at some depth, and are not easily discovered, the necessity of the case and the infirmity of the human understanding require that the particular forms, which collect certain groups of instances (but by no means all) into some common notion, should not be neglected, but most diligently observed. For whatever unites nature, even imperfectly, opens the way to the discovery of the form. The instances, therefore, which are serviceable in this respect are of no mean power, but endowed with some degree of prerogative.

Here, nevertheless, great care must be taken that, after the discovery of several of these particular forms, and the establishing of certain partitions or divisions of the required nature derived from them, the human understanding do not at once rest satisfied, without preparing for the investigation of the great or leading form, and taking it for granted that nature is compound and divided from its very root, despise and reject any farther union as a point of superfluous refinement, and tending to mere abstraction.

For instance, let the required nature be memory, or that which excites and assists memory. The constitutive instances are order or distribution, which manifestly assists memory; topics or common-places in artificial memory, which may be either places in their literal sense, as a gate, a corner, a window, and the like, or familiar persons and marks, or anything else (provided it be arranged in a determinate order), as animals, plants, and words, letters, characters, historical persons, and the like, of which, however, some are more convenient than others. All these common-places materially assist memory, and raise it far above its natural strength. Verse, too, is recollected and learnt more easily than prose. From this group of three instances—order, the common-places of artificial memory, and verses—is constituted one species of aid for the memory,[1] which may be well termed a separation from infinity. For when a man strives to recollect or recall anything to memory, without a preconceived notion or perception of the object of his search, he inquires about, and labours, and turns from point to point, as if involved in infinity. But if he have any preconceived notion, this infinity is separated off, and the range of his memory is brought within closer limits. In the three instances given above, the preconceived notion is clear and determined. In the first, it must be something that agrees with order; in the second, an image which

[1] The author's own system of Memoria Technica may be found in the De Augmentis, chap. xv. We may add that, notwithstanding Bacon's assertion that he intended his method to apply to religion, politics, and morals, this is the only lengthy illustration he has adduced of any subject out of the domain of physical science. *Ed.*

has some relation or agreement with the fixed common-places; in the third, words which fall into a verse: and thus infinity is divided off. Other instances will offer another species, namely, that whatever brings the intellect into contact with something that strikes the sense (the principal point of artificial memory), assists the memory. Others again offer another species, namely, whatever excites an impression by any powerful passion, as fear, wonder, shame, delight, assists the memory. Other instances will afford another species: thus those impressions remain most fixed in the memory which are taken from the mind when clear and least occupied by preceding or succeeding notions, such as the things we learn in childhood, or imagine before sleep, and the first time of any circumstance happening. Other instances afford the following species: namely, that a multitude of circumstances or handles assist the memory, such as writing in paragraphs, reading aloud, or recitation. Lastly, other instances afford still another species: thus the things we anticipate, and which rouse our attention, are more easily remembered than transient events; as if you read any work twenty times over, you will not learn it by heart so readily as if you were to read it but ten times, trying each time to repeat it, and when your memory fails you looking into the book. There are, therefore, six lesser forms, as it were, of things which assist the memory: namely—1, the separation of infinity; 2, the connection of the mind with the senses; 3, the impression in strong passion; 4, the impression on the mind when pure; 5, the multitude of handles; 6, anticipation.

Again, for example's sake, let the required nature be taste or the power of tasting. The following instances are constitutive: 1. Those who do not smell, but are deprived by nature of that sense, do not perceive or distinguish rancid or putrid food by their taste, nor garlic from roses, and the like. 2. Again, those whose nostrils are obstructed by accident (such as a cold) do not distinguish any putrid or rancid matter from anything sprinkled with rose-water. 3. If those who suffer from a cold blow their noses violently at the very moment in which they have anything fetid or perfumed in their mouth, or on their palate, they instantly have a clear perception of the fetor or perfume. These instances afford and constitute this species or division of taste, namely, that it is in part nothing else than an internal smelling, passing and descending through the upper passages of the nostrils to the mouth and palate. But, on the other hand, those whose power of smelling is deficient or obstructed, perceive what is salt, sweet, pungent, acid, rough, and bitter, and the like, as well as any one else: so that the taste is clearly something compounded of the internal smelling, and an exquisite species of touch which we will not here discuss.

Again, as another example, let the required nature be the communication of quality, without intermixture of substance. The instance of light will afford or constitute one species of communication, heat and the magnet another. For the communication of light is momentary and immediately arrested upon the removal of the original light. But heat, and the magnetic force, when once transmitted to or excited in another body, remain fixed for a considerable time after the removal of the source.

In fine, the prerogative of constitutive instances is considerable, for they materially assist the definitions (especially in detail) and the divisions or partitions of natures, concerning which Plato has well said, "He who can properly define and divide is to be considered a god."*

* The collective instances here meant are no other than general facts or laws of some degree of generality, and are themselves the result of induction. For example, the system of Jupiter, or Saturn with its satellites, is a collective instance, and materially assisted in securing the admission of the Copernican system. We have here in miniature, and displayed at one view, a system analogous to that of the planets about the sun, of which, from the circumstance of our being involved in it, and unfavourably situated for seeing it otherwise than in detail, we are incapacitated from forming a general idea, but by slow and progressive efforts of reason.

But there is a species of collective instance which Bacon does not seem to have contemplated, in which particular phenomena are presented in such numbers at once, as to make the induction of their law a matter of ocular inspection. For example, the parabolic form assumed by a jet of water spouted out of a hole is a collective instance of the velocities and directions of the motions of all the particles which compose it seen together, and which thus leads us without trouble to recognize the law of the motion of a projectile. Again, the beautiful figures exhibited by sand strewed on regular plates of glass or metal set in vibration, are collective instances of an infinite number of points which remain at rest while the remainder of the plate vibrates, and in consequence afford us an insight into the law which regulates their arrangement and sequence throughout the whole surface. The richly coloured lemniscates seen around the optic axis of crystals exposed to polarized light afford a striking instance of the same kind, pointing at once to the general mathematical expression of the law which regulates their production. Such collective instances as these lead us to a general law by an induction which offers itself spontaneously, and thus furnish advanced posts in philosophical exploration. The laws of Kepler, which Bacon ignored on account of his want of mathematical taste, may be cited as a collective instance. The first is, that the planets move in elliptical orbits, having the sun for their common focus. The second, that about this focus the *radius vector* of each planet describes equal areas in equal times. The third, that the squares of the periodic times of the planets are as the cubes of their mean distance from the sun. This collective instance "opened the way" to the discovery of the Newtonian law of gravitation. *Ed.*

XXVII. In the sixth rank of prerogative instances we will place similar or proportionate instances, which we are also wont to call physical parallels, or resemblances. They are such as exhibit the resemblances and connection of things, not in minor forms (as the constitutive do), but at once in the concrete. They are therefore, as it were, the first and lowest steps towards the union of nature; nor do they immediately establish any axiom, but merely indicate and observe a certain relation of bodies to each other. But although they be not of much assistance in discovering forms, yet they are of great advantage in disclosing the frame of parts of the universe, upon whose members they practise a species of anatomy, and thence occasionally lead us gently on to sublime and noble axioms, especially such as relate to the construction of the world, rather than to simple natures and forms.

As an example, take the following similar instances: a mirror and the eye; the formation of the ear, and places which return an echo. From such similarity, besides observing the resemblance (which is useful for many purposes), it is easy to collect and form this axiom. That the organs of the senses, and bodies which produce reflections to the senses, are of a similar nature. Again, the understanding once informed of this, rises easily to a higher and nobler axiom; namely, that the only distinction between sensitive and inanimate bodies, in those points in which they agree and sympathise, is this; in the former, animal spirit is added to the arrangement of the body, in the latter it is wanting. So that there might be as many senses in animals as there are points of agreement with inanimate bodies, if the animated body were perforated, so as to allow the spirit to have access to the limb properly disposed for action, as a fit organ. And, on the other hand, there are, without doubt, as many motions in an inanimate as there are senses in the animated body, though the animal spirit be absent. There must, however, be many more motions in inanimate bodies than senses in the animated, from the small number of organs of sense. A very plain example of this is afforded by pains. For, as animals are liable to many kinds and various descriptions of pains (such as those of burning, of intense cold, of pricking, squeezing, stretching, and the like), so is it most certain, that the same circumstances, as far as motion is concerned, happen to inanimate bodies, such as wood or stone when burnt, frozen, pricked, cut, bent, bruised, and the like; although there be no sensation, owing to the absence of animal spirit.

Again, wonderful as it may appear, the roots and branches of trees are similar instances. For every vegetable swells and throws out its constituent parts towards the circumference, both upwards and downwards. And there is no difference between the roots and branches, except that the root is buried in the earth, and the branches are exposed to the air and sun. For if one take a young and vigorous shoot, and bend it down to a small portion of loose earth, although it be not fixed to the ground, yet will it immediately produce a root, and not a branch. And, *vice versâ*, if earth be placed above, and so forced down with a stone or any hard substance, as to confine the plant and prevent its branching upwards, it will throw out branches into the air downwards.

The gums of trees, and most rock gems, are similar instances; for both of them are exudations and filtered juices, derived in the former instance from trees, in the latter from stones; the brightness and clearness of both arising from a delicate and accurate filtering. For nearly the same reason, the hair of animals is less beautiful and vivid in its colour than the plumage of most birds, because the juices are less delicately filtered through the skin than through the quills.

The scrotum of males and matrix of females are also similar instances; so that the noble formation which constitutes the difference of the sexes appears to differ only as to the one being internal and the other external; a greater degree of heat causing the genitals to protrude in the male, whilst the heat of the female being too weak to effect this, they are retained internally.

The fins of fishes and the feet of quadrupeds, or the feet and wings of birds, are similar instances; to which Aristotle adds the four folds in the motion of serpents;[b] so that in the formation of the universe, the motion of animals appears to be chiefly effected by four joints or bendings.

The teeth of land animals, and the beaks of birds, are similar instances, whence it is clear, that in all perfect animals there is a determination of some hard substance towards the mouth.

Again, the resemblance and conformity of man to an inverted plant is not absurd. For the head is the root of the nerves and animal faculties, and the seminal parts are the lowest, not including the extremities of the legs and arms. But in the plant, the root (which resembles the head) is regularly placed in the lowest, and the seeds in the highest part.[c]

Lastly, we must particularly recommend and suggest, that

[b] Is not this very hasty generalization? Do serpents move with four folds only? Observe also the motion of centipedes and other insects.

[c] Shaw states another point of difference between the objects cited in the text,—animals having their roots within, while plants have theirs without; for their lacteals nearly correspond with the fibres of the roots in plants; so that animals seem nourished within themselves as plants are without. *Ed.*

man's present industry in the investigation and compilation of natural history be entirely changed, and directed to the reverse of the present system. For it has hitherto been active and curious in noting the variety of things, and explaining the accurate differences of animals, vegetables, and minerals, most of which are the mere sport of nature, rather than of any real utility as concerns the sciences. Pursuits of this nature are certainly agreeable, and sometimes of practical advantage, but contribute little or nothing to the thorough investigation of nature. Our labour must therefore be directed towards inquiring into and observing resemblances and analogies, both in the whole and its parts, for they unite nature, and lay the foundation of the sciences.

Here, however, a severe and rigorous caution must be observed, that we only consider as similar and proportionate instances, those which (as we first observed) point out physical resemblances; that is, real and substantial resemblances, deeply founded in nature, and not casual and superficial, much less superstitious or curious; such as those which are constantly put forward by the writers on natural magic (the most idle of men, and who are scarcely fit to be named in connection with such serious matters as we now treat of), who, with much vanity and folly, describe, and sometimes too, invent, unmeaning resemblances and sympathies.

But leaving such to themselves, similar instances are not to be neglected, in the greater portions of the world's conformation; such as Africa and the Peruvian continent, which reaches to the Straits of Magellan; both of which possess a similar isthmus and similar capes, a circumstance not to be attributed to mere accident.

Again, the new and old world are both of them broad and expanded towards the north, and narrow and pointed towards the south.

Again, we have very remarkable similar instances in the intense cold, towards the middle regions (as it is termed) of the air, and the violent fires which are often found to burst from subterraneous spots, the similarity consisting in both being ends and extremes; the extreme of the nature of cold, for instance, is towards the boundary of heaven, and that of the nature of heat towards the centre of the earth, by a similar species of opposition or rejection of the contrary nature.

Lastly, in the axioms of the sciences, there is a similarity of instances worthy of observation. Thus the rhetorical trope which is called surprise, is similar to that of music termed the declining of a cadence. Again,—the mathematical postulate, that things which are equal to the same are equal to one another, is similar to the form of the syllogism in logic, which unites things agreeing in the middle term.[d] Lastly, a certain degree of sagacity in collecting and searching for physical points of similarity, is very useful in many respects.[e]

XXVIII. In the seventh rank of prerogative instances, we will place singular instances, which we are also wont to call irregular or heteroclite (to borrow a term from the grammarians). They are such as exhibit bodies in the concrete, of an apparently extravagant and separate nature, agreeing but little with other things of the same species. For, whilst the similar instances resemble each other, those we now speak of are only like themselves. Their use is much the same with that of clandestine instances: they bring out and unite nature, and discover genera or common natures, which must afterwards be limited by real differences. Nor should we desist from inquiry, until the properties and qualities of those things, which may be deemed miracles, as it were, of nature, be reduced to, and comprehended in, some form or certain law; so that all irregularity or singularity may be found to depend on some common form; and the miracle only consists in accurate differences, degree, and rare coincidence, not in the species itself. Man's meditation proceeds no farther at present, than just to consider things of this kind as the secrets and vast efforts of nature, without an assignable cause, and, as it were, exceptions to general rules.

As examples of singular instances, we have the sun and moon amongst the heavenly bodies; the magnet amongst minerals; quicksilver amongst metals; the elephant amongst quadrupeds; the venereal sensation amongst the different kinds of touch; the

---

[d] Bacon falls into an error here in regarding the syllogism as something distinct from the reasoning faculty, and only one of its forms. It is not generally true that the syllogism is only a form of reasoning by which we unite ideas which accord with the middle term. This agreement is not even essential to accurate syllogisms; when the relation of the two things compared to the third is one of equality or similitude, it of course follows that the two things compared may be pronounced equal, or like to each other. But if the relation between these terms exist in a different form, then it is not true that the two extremes stand in the same relation to each other as to the middle term. For instance, if A is double of B, and B double of C, then A is quadruple of C. But then the relation of A to C is different from that of A to B and of B to C. *Ed.*

[e] Comparative anatomy is full of analogies of this kind. Those between natural and artificial productions are well worthy of attention, and sometimes lead to important discoveries. By observing an analogy of this kind between the plan used in hydraulic engines for preventing the counter-current of a fluid, and a similar contrivance in the blood-vessels, Harvey was led to the discovery of the circulation of the blood. *Ed.*

scent of sporting dogs amongst those of smell. The letter S, too, is considered by the grammarians as sui generis, from its easily uniting with double or triple consonants, which no other letter will. These instances are of great value, because they excite and keep alive inquiry, and correct an understanding depraved by habit and the common course of things.

XXIX. In the eighth rank of prerogative instances, we will place deviating instances, such as the errors of nature, or strange and monstrous objects, in which nature deviates and turns from her ordinary course. For the errors of nature differ from singular instances, inasmuch as the latter are the miracles of species, the former of individuals. Their use is much the same, for they rectify the understanding in opposition to habit, and reveal common forms. For with regard to these, also, we must not desist from inquiry, till we discern the cause of the deviation. The cause does not, however, in such cases rise to a regular form, but only to the latent process towards such a form. For he who is acquainted with the paths of nature, will more readily observe her deviations; and, *vice versâ*, he who has learnt her deviations, will be able more accurately to describe her paths.

They differ again from singular instances, by being much more apt for practice and the operative branch. For it would be very difficult to generate new species, but less so to vary known species, and thus produce many rare and unusual results.[f] The passage from the miracles of nature to those of art is easy; for if nature be once seized in her variations, and the cause be manifest, it will be easy to lead her by art to such deviation as she was at first led to by chance; and not only to that but others, since deviations on the one side lead and open the way to others in every direction. Of this we do not require any examples, since they are so abundant. For a compilation, or particular natural history, must be made of all monsters and prodigious births of nature; of everything, in short, which is new, rare, and unusual in nature. This should be done with a rigorous selection, so as to be worthy of credit. Those are most to be suspected which depend upon superstition, as the prodigies of Livy, and those perhaps, but little less, which are found in the works of writers on natural magic, or even alchymy, and the like; for such men, as it were, are the very suitors and lovers of fables; but our instances should be derived from some grave and credible history, and faithful narration.

XXX. In the ninth rank of prerogative instances, we will

---

[f] This is well illustrated in plants, for the gardener can produce endless varieties of any known species, but can never produce a new species itself.

place bordering instances, which we are also wont to term participants. They are such as exhibit those species of bodies which appear to be composed of two species, or to be the rudiments between the one and the other. They may well be classed with the singular or heteroclite instances; for in the whole system of things, they are rare and extraordinary. Yet from their dignity, they must be treated of and classed separately, for they point out admirably the order and constitution of things, and suggest the causes of the number and quality of the more common species in the universe, leading the understanding from that which is, to that which is possible.

We have examples of them in moss, which is something between putrescence and a plant;[g] in some comets, which hold a place between stars and ignited meteors; in flying fishes, between fishes and birds; and in bats, between birds and quadrupeds.[h] Again,

Simia quam similis turpissima bestia nobis.

We have also biformed fœtus, mingled species, and the like.

XXXI. In the tenth rank of prerogative instances, we will place the instances of power, or the fasces (to borrow a term from the insignia of empire), which we are also wont to call the wit or hands of man. These are such works as are most noble and perfect, and, as it were, the masterpieces in every art. For since our principal object is to make nature subservient to the state and wants of man, it becomes us well to note and enumerate the works, which have long since been in the power of man, especially those which are most polished and perfect: because the passage from these to new and hitherto undiscovered works, is more easy and feasible. For if any one, after an attentive contemplation of such works as are extant, be willing to push forward in his design with alacrity and vigour, he will undoubtedly either advance them, or turn them to something within their immediate reach, or even apply and transfer them to some more noble purpose.

Nor is this all: for as the understanding is elevated and raised by rare and unusual works of nature, to investigate and discover the forms which include them also, so is the same effect frequently produced by the excellent and wonderful works of art; and even to a greater degree, because the mode of effecting and constructing the miracles of art is generally plain, whilst that of

[g] The discoveries of Tournefort have placed moss in the class of plants. The fish alluded to below are to be found only in the tropics. *Ed.*

[h] There is, however, no real approximation to birds in either the flying-fish or bat, any more than a man approximates to a fish because he can swim. The wings of the flying-fish and bat are mere expansions of skin, bearing no resemblance whatever to those of birds.

effecting the miracles of nature is more obscure. Great care, however, must be taken, that they do not depress the understanding, and fix it, as it were, to earth.

For there is some danger, lest the understanding should be astonished and chained down, and as it were bewitched, by such works of art, as appear to be the very summit and pinnacle of human industry, so as not to become familiar with them, but rather to suppose that nothing of the kind can be accomplished, unless the same means be employed, with perhaps a little more diligence, and more accurate preparation.

Now, on the contrary, it may be stated as a fact, that the ways and means hitherto discovered and observed, of effecting any matter or work, are for the most part of little value, and that all really efficient power depends, and is really to be deduced from the sources of forms, none of which have yet been discovered.

Thus (as we have before observed), had any one meditated on balistic machines, and battering rams, as they were used by the ancients, whatever application he might have exerted, and though he might have consumed a whole life in the pursuit, yet would he never have hit upon the invention of flaming engines, acting by means of gunpowder; nor would any person, who had made woollen manufactories and cotton the subject of his observation and reflection, have ever discovered thereby the nature of the silkworm or of silk.

Hence all the most noble discoveries have (if you observe) come to light, not by any gradual improvement and extension of the arts, but merely by chance; whilst nothing imitates or antipates chance (which is wont to act at intervals of ages) but the invention of forms.

There is no necessity for adducing any particular examples of these instances, since they are abundant. The plan to be pursued is this: all the mechanical, and even the liberal arts (as far as they are practical), should be visited and thoroughly examined, and thence there should be formed a compilation or particular history of the great masterpieces, or most finished works in each, as well as of the mode of carrying them into effect.

Nor do we confine the diligence to be used in such a compilation to the leading works and secrets only of every art, and such as excite wonder; for wonder is engendered by rarity, since that which is rare, although it be compounded of ordinary natures, always begets wonder.

On the contrary, that which is really wonderful, from some specific difference distinguishing it from other species, is carelessly observed, if it be but familiar. Yet the singular instances of art should be observed no less than those of nature, which we have before spoken of: and as in the latter we have classed the sun, the moon, the magnet, and the like, all of them most familiar to us, but yet in their nature singular, so should we proceed with the singular instances of art.

For example: paper, a very common substance, is a singular instance of art; for if you consider the subject attentively, you will find that artificial substances are either woven by straight and transverse lines, as silk, woollen, or linen cloth, and the like; or coagulated from concrete juices, such as brick, earthenware, glass, enamel, porcelain, and the like, which admit of a polish if they be compact, but if not, become hard without being polished; all which latter substances are brittle, and not adherent or tenacious. On the contrary, paper is a tenacious substance, which can be cut and torn, so as to resemble and almost rival the skin of any animal, or the leaf of vegetables, and the like works of nature; being neither brittle like glass, nor woven like cloth, but having fibres and not distinct threads, just as natural substances, so that scarcely anything similar can be found amongst artificial substances, and it is absolutely singular. And in artificial works we should certainly prefer those which approach the nearest to an imitation of nature, or, on the other hand, powerfully govern and change her course.

Again, in these instances which we term the wit and hands of man, charms and conjuring should not be altogether despised, for although mere amusements, and of little use, yet they may afford considerable information.

Lastly, superstition and magic (in its common acceptation) are not to be entirely omitted; for although they be overwhelmed by a mass of lies and fables, yet some investigation should be made, to see if there be really any latent natural operation in them; as in fascination, and the fortifying of the imagination, the sympathy of distant objects, the transmission of impressions from spirit to spirit no less than from body to body, and the like.

XXXII. From the foregoing remarks, it is clear that the five last species of instances (the similar, singular, deviating, and bordering instances, and those of power) should not be reserved for the investigation of any given nature, as the preceding and many of the succeeding instances must, but a collection of them should be made at once, in the style of a particular history, so that they may arrange the matter which enters the understanding, and correct its depraved habit, for it is necessarily imbued, corrupted, perverted, and distorted by daily and habitual impressions.

They are to be used, therefore, as a preparative, for the purpose of rectifying and purifying the understanding; for whatever withdraws it from habit, levels and planes down its surface for the reception of the dry and pure light of true notions.

These instances, moreover, level and prepare the way for the operative branch, as we will mention in its proper place when speaking of the practical deductions.

XXXIII. In the eleventh rank of prerogative instances we will place accompanying and hostile instances. These are such as exhibit any body or concrete, where the required nature is constantly found, as an inseparable companion, or, on the contrary, where the required nature is constantly avoided, and excluded from attendance, as an enemy. From these instances may be formed certain and universal propositions, either affirmative or negative; the subject of which will be the concrete body, and the predicate the required nature. For particular propositions are by no means fixed, when the required nature is found to fluctuate and change in the concrete, either approaching and acquired, or receding and laid aside. Hence particular propositions have no great prerogative, except in the case of migration, of which we have spoken above. Yet such particular propositions are of great use, when compared with the universal, as will be mentioned in its proper place. Nor do we require absolute affirmation or negation, even in universal propositions, for if the exceptions be singular or rare, it is sufficient for our purpose.

The use of accompanying instances is to narrow the affirmative of form; for as it is narrowed by the migrating instances, where the form must necessarily be something communicated or destroyed by the act of migration, so it is narrowed by accompanying instances, where the form must necessarily be something which enters into the concretion of the body, or, on the contrary, is repugnant to it; and one who is well acquainted with the constitution or formation of the body, will not be far from bringing to light the form of the required nature.

For example: let the required nature be heat. Flame is an accompanying instance; for in water, air, stone, metal, and many other substances, heat is variable, and can approach or retire; but all flame is hot, so that heat always accompanies the concretion of flame. We have no hostile instance of heat; for the senses are unacquainted with the interior of the earth, and there is no concretion of any known body which is not susceptible of heat.

Again, let solidity be the required nature. Air is an hostile instance; for metals may be liquid or solid, so may glass; even water may become solid by congelation, but air cannot become solid or lose its fluidity.

With regard to these instances of fixed propositions, there are two points to be observed, which are of importance. First, that if there be no universal affirmative or negative, it be carefully noted as not existing. Thus, in heat, we have observed that there exists no universal negative, in such substances, at least, as have come to our knowledge. Again, if the required nature be eternity or incorruptibility, we have no universal affirmative within our sphere, for these qualities cannot be predicated of any bodies below the heavens, or above the interior of the earth. Secondly, to our general propositions as to any concrete, whether affirmative or negative, we should subjoin the concretes which appear to approach nearest to the non-existing substances; such as the most gentle or least-burning flames in heat, or gold in incorruptibility, since it approaches nearest to it. For they all serve to show the limit of existence and non-existence, and circumscribe forms, so that they cannot wander beyond the conditions of matter.

XXXIV. In the twelfth rank of prerogative instances, we will class those subjunctive instances, of which we spoke in the last aphorism, and which we are also wont to call instances of extremity or limits; for they are not only serviceable when subjoined to fixed propositions, but also of themselves and from their own nature. They indicate with sufficient precision the real divisions of nature, and measures of things, and the "how far" nature effects or allows of anything, and her passage thence to something else. Such are gold in weight, iron in hardness, the whale in the size of animals, the dog in smell, the flame of gunpowder in rapid expansion, and others of a like nature. Nor are we to pass over the extremes in defect, as well as in abundance, as spirits of wine in weight, the touchstone in softness, the worms upon the skin in the size of animals, and the like.

XXXV. In the thirteenth rank of prerogative instances, we will place those of alliance or union. They are such as mingle and unite natures held to be heterogeneous, and observed and marked as such in received classifications.

These instances show that the operation and effect, which is considered peculiar to some one of such heterogeneous natures, may also be attributed to another nature styled heterogeneous, so as to prove that the difference of the natures is not real nor essential, but a mere modification of a common nature. They are very serviceable, therefore, in elevating and carrying on the mind, from differences to genera, and in removing those phantoms and images of things, which meet it in disguise in concrete substances.

For example: let the required nature be heat. The classification of heat into three kinds, that of the celestial bodies, that of animals, and that of fire, appears to be settled and admitted; and these kinds of heat, especially one of them compared with the other two, are supposed to be different, and clearly heterogeneous in their essence and species, or specific nature, since the heat of the heavenly bodies and of animals generates and cherishes, whilst that of fire corrupts and destroys. We have an instance of alliance, then, in a very common experiment, that of a vine branch admitted into a building where there is a constant fire, by which the grapes ripen a whole month sooner than in the air; so that fruit upon the tree can be ripened by fire, although this appear the peculiar effect of the sun. From this beginning, therefore, the understanding rejects all essential difference, and easily ascends to the investigation of the real differences between the heat of the sun and that of fire, by which their operation is rendered dissimilar, although they partake of a common nature.

These differences will be found to be four in number. 1. The heat of the sun is much milder and gentler in degree than that of fire. 2. It is much more moist in quality, especially as it is transmitted to us through the air. 3. Which is the chief point, it is very unequal, advancing and increased at one time, retiring and diminished at another, which mainly contributes to the generation of bodies. For Aristotle rightly asserted, that the principal cause of generation and corruption on the surface of the earth, was the oblique path of the sun in the zodiac, whence its heat becomes very unequal, partly from the alternation of night and day, partly from the succession of summer and winter. Yet must he immediately corrupt and pervert his discovery, by dictating to nature according to his habit, and dogmatically assigning the cause of generation to the approach of the sun, and that of corruption to its retreat; whilst, in fact, each circumstance indifferently and not respectively contributes both to generation and corruption; for unequal heat tends to generate and corrupt, as equable heat does to preserve. 4. The fourth difference between the heat of the sun and fire is of great consequence; namely, that the sun, gradually, and for a length of time, insinuates its effects, whilst those of fire (urged by the impatience of man) are brought to a termination in a shorter space of time. But if any one were to pay attention to the tempering of fire, and reducing it to a more moderate and gentle degree (which may be done in various ways), and then were to sprinkle and mix a degree of humidity with it; and, above all, were to imitate the sun in its inequality; and lastly, were patiently to suffer some delay (not such, however, as is proportioned to the effects of the sun, but more than men usually admit of in those of fire), he would soon banish the notion of any difference, and would attempt, or equal, or perhaps sometimes surpass the effect of the sun, by the heat of fire. A like instance of alliance is that of reviving butterflies, benumbed and nearly dead from cold, by the gentle warmth of fire; so that fire is no less able to revive animals than to ripen vegetables. We may also mention the celebrated invention of Fracastorius, of applying a pan considerably heated to the head in desperate cases of apoplexy, which clearly expands the animal spirits, when compressed and almost extinguished by the humours and obstructions of the brain, and excites them to action, as the fire would operate on water or air, and in the result produces life. Eggs are sometimes hatched by the heat of fire, an exact imitation of animal heat; and there are many instances of the like nature, so that no one can doubt that the heat of fire, in many cases, can be modified till it resemble that of the heavenly bodies and of animals.

Again, let the required natures be motion and rest. There appears to be a settled classification, grounded on the deepest philosophy, that natural bodies either revolve, move in a straight line, or stand still and rest. For there is either motion without limit, or continuance within a certain limit, or a translation towards a certain limit. The eternal motion of revolution appears peculiar to the heavenly bodies, rest to this our globe, and the other bodies (heavy and light, as they are termed, that is to say, placed out of their natural position) are borne in a straight line to masses or aggregates which resemble them, the light towards the heaven, the heavy towards the earth; and all this is very fine language.

But we have an instance of alliance in low comets, which revolve, though far below the heavens; and the fiction of Aristotle, of the comet being fixed to, or necessarily following some star, has been long since exploded; not only because it is improbable in itself, but from the evident fact of the discursive and irregular motion of comets through various parts of the heavens.[1]

Another instance of alliance is that of the motion of air, which appears to revolve from east to west within the tropics, where the circles of revolution are the greatest.

The flow and ebb of the sea would perhaps be another instance, if the water were once found to have a motion of revolution, though slow and hardly perceptible, from east to west, subject, however, to a reaction twice a day. If this be so, it is clear that the motion of revolution is not confined to the celestial bodies, but is shared, also, by air and water.

Again,—the supposed peculiar disposition of light bodies to rise is rather shaken; and here we may find an instance of alliance in a water bubble. For if air be placed under water, it rises rapidly towards the surface by that striking motion (as Democritus terms it) with which the descending water strikes the air and raises it, not by any struggle or effort of the air itself; and when it has reached the surface of the water, it is prevented from ascending

---

[1] Seneca was a sounder astronomer than Bacon. He ridiculed the idea of the motion of any heavenly bodies being irregular, and predicted that the day would come, when the laws which guided the revolution of these bodies would be proved to be identical with those which controlled the motions of the planets. The anticipation was realized by Newton. *Ed*

any further, by the slight resistance it meets with in the water, which does not allow an immediate separation of its parts, so that the tendency of the air to rise must be very slight.

Again, let the required nature be weight. It is certainly a received classification, that dense and solid bodies are borne towards the centre of the earth, and rare and light bodies to the circumference of the heavens, as their appropriate places. As far as relates to places (though these things have much weight in the schools), the notion of there being any determinate place is absurd and puerile. Philosophers trifle, therefore, when they tell you, that if the earth were perforated, heavy bodies would stop on their arrival at the centre. This centre would indeed be an efficacious nothing, or mathematical point, could it affect bodies or be sought by them, for a body is not acted upon except by a body.[k] In fact, this tendency to ascend and descend is either in the conformation of the moving body, or in its harmony and sympathy with another body. But if any dense and solid body be found, which does not, however, tend towards the earth, the classification is at an end. Now, if we allow of Gilbert's opinion, that the magnetic power of the earth, in attracting heavy bodies, is not extended beyond the limit of its peculiar virtue (which operates always at a fixed distance and no further),[1] and this be proved by some instance, such an instance will be one of alliance in our present subject. The nearest approach to it is that of waterspouts, frequently seen by persons navigating the Atlantic towards either of the Indies. For the force and mass of the water suddenly effused by waterspouts, appears to be so considerable, that the water must have been collected previously, and have remained fixed where it was formed, until it was afterwards forced down by some violent cause, rather than made to fall by the natural motion of gravity: so that it may be conjectured that a dense and compact mass, at a great distance from the earth, may be suspended as the earth itself is, and would not fall, unless forced down. We do not, however, affirm this as

[k] But see Bacon's own corollary at the end of the Instances of Divorce, Aphorism xxxvii. If Bacon's remark be accepted, the censure will fall upon Newton and the system so generally received at the present day. It is, however, unjust, as the centre of which Newton so often speaks is not a point with an active inherent force, but only the result of all the particular and reciprocal attractions of the different parts of the planet acting upon one spot. It is evident, that if all these forces were united in this centre, that the sum would be equal to all their partial effects. *Ed.*

[1] Since Newton's discovery of the law of gravitation, we find that the attractive force of the earth must extend to an infinite distance. Bacon himself alludes to the operation of this attractive force at great distances in the Instances of the Rod, Aphorism xlv.

certain. In the mean while, both in this respect and many others, it will readily be seen how deficient we are in natural history, since we are forced to have recourse to suppositions for examples, instead of ascertained instances.

Again, let the required nature be the discursive power of the mind. The classification of human reason and animal instinct appears to be perfectly correct. Yet there are some instances of the actions of brutes which seem to show that they, too, can syllogise. Thus it is related, that a crow, which had nearly perished from thirst in a great drought, saw some water in the hollow trunk of a tree, but as it was too narrow for him to get into it, he continued to throw in pebbles, which made the water rise till he could drink; and it afterwards became a proverb.

Again, let the required nature be vision. The classification appears real and certain, which considers light as that which is originally visible, and confers the power of seeing; and colour, as being secondarily visible, and not capable of being seen without light, so as to appear a mere image or modification of light. Yet there are instances of alliance in each respect; as in snow when in great quantities, and in the flame of sulphur; the one being a colour originally and in itself light, the other a light verging towards colour.[m]

XXXVI. In the fourteenth rank of prerogative instances, we will place the instances of the cross, borrowing our metaphor from the crosses erected where two roads meet, to point out the different directions. We are wont also to call them decisive and judicial instances, and in some cases instances of the oracle and of command. Their nature is as follows. When in investigating any nature the understanding is, at it were, balanced, and uncertain to which of two or more natures the cause of the required nature should be assigned, on account of the frequent and usual concurrence of several natures, the instances of the cross show that the union of one nature with the required nature is firm and indissoluble, whilst that of the other is unsteady and separable; by which means the question is decided, and the first is received as the cause, whilst the other is dismissed and rejected. Such instances, therefore, afford great light, and are of great weight, so that the course of interpretation sometimes terminates, and is completed in them. Sometimes, however, they are found amongst the instances already observed, but they are generally new, being expressly and purposely sought for and applied, and brought to light only by attentive and active diligence.

For example: let the required nature be the flow and ebb of the sea, which is repeated twice a day, at intervals of six hours

[m] Snow reflects light, but is not a source of light.

between each advance and retreat, with some little difference, agreeing with the motion of the moon. We have here the following cross-ways.

This motion must be occasioned either by the advancing and the retiring of the sea, like water shaken in a basin, which leaves one side while it washes the other; or by the rising of the sea from the bottom, and its again subsiding, like boiling water. But a doubt arises, to which of these causes we should assign the flow and ebb. If the first assertion be admitted, it follows, that when there is a flood on one side, there must at the same time be an ebb on another, and the question therefore is reduced to this. Now Acosta, and some others, after a diligent inquiry, have observed that the flood tide takes place on the coast of Florida, and the opposite coasts of Spain and Africa, at the same time, as does also the ebb; and that there is not, on the contrary, a flood tide at Florida when there is an ebb on the coasts of Spain and Africa. Yet if one consider the subject attentively, this does not prove the necessity of a rising motion, nor refute the notion of a progressive motion. For the motion may be progressive, and yet inundate the opposite shores of a channel at the same time; as if the waters be forced and driven together from some other quarter, for instance, which takes place in rivers, for they flow and ebb towards each bank at the same time, yet their motion is clearly progressive, being that of the waters from the sea entering their mouths. So it may happen, that the waters coming in a vast body from the eastern Indian Ocean are driven together, and forced into the channel of the Atlantic, and therefore inundate both coasts at once. We must inquire, therefore, if there be any other channel by which the waters can at the same time sink and ebb: and the Southern Ocean at once suggests itself, which is not less than the Atlantic, but rather broader and more extensive than is requisite for this effect.

We at length arrive, then, at an instance of the cross, which is this. If it be positively discovered, that when the flood sets in towards the opposite coasts of Florida and Spain in the Atlantic, there is at the same time a flood tide on the coasts of Peru and the back part of China, in the Southern Ocean, then assuredly, from this decisive instance, we must reject the assertion, that the flood and ebb of the sea, about which we inquire, takes place by progressive motion; for no other sea or place is left where there can be an ebb. But this may most easily be learnt, by inquiring of the inhabitants of Panama and Lima (where the two oceans are separated by a narrow isthmus), whether the flood and ebb takes place on the opposite sides of the isthmus at the same time, or the reverse. This decision or rejection appears certain, if it be granted that the earth is fixed;

but if the earth revolves, it may perhaps happen, that from the unequal revolution (as regards velocity) of the earth and the waters of the sea, there may be a violent forcing of the waters into a mass, forming the flood, and a subsequent relaxation of them (when they can no longer bear the accumulation), forming the ebb. A separate inquiry must be made into this. Even with this hypothesis, however, it remains equally true, that there must be an ebb somewhere, at the same time that there is a flood in another quarter.

Again, let the required nature be the latter of the two motions we have supposed; namely, that of a rising and subsiding motion, if it should happen that upon diligent examination the progressive motion be rejected. We have, then, three ways before us, with regard to this nature. The motion, by which the waters raise themselves, and again fall back, in the floods and ebbs, without the addition of any other water rolled towards them, must take place in one of the three following ways. Either the supply of water emanates from the interior of the earth, and returns back again; or there is really no greater quantity of water, but the same water (without any augmentation of its quantity) is extended or rarefied, so as to occupy a greater space and dimension, and again contracts itself; or there is neither an additional supply nor any extension, but the same waters (with regard to quantity, density, or rarity) raise themselves and fall from sympathy, by some magnetic power attracting and calling them up, as it were, from above. Let us then (passing over the first two motions) reduce the investigation to the last, and inquire if there be any such elevation of the water by sympathy or a magnetic force; and it is evident, in the first place, that the whole mass of water being placed in the trench or cavity of the sea, cannot be raised at once, because there would not be enough to cover the bottom, so that if there be any tendency of this kind in the water to raise itself, yet it would be interrupted and checked by the cohesion of things, or (as the common expression is) that there may be no vacuum. The water, therefore, must rise on one side, and for that reason be diminished and ebb on another. But it will again necessarily follow that the magnetic power not being able to operate on the whole, operates most intensely on the centre, so as to raise the waters there, which, when thus raised successively, desert and abandon the sides.[a]

We at length arrive, then, at an instance of the cross, which is this: if it be found, that during the ebb the surface of the waters at sea is more curved and round, from the waters rising in the middle, and sinking at the sides or coast, and if, during a

---

[a] Bacon's sagacity here foreshadows Newton's theory of the tides.

flood, it be more even and level, from the waters returning to their former position, then assuredly, by this decisive instance, the raising of them by a magnetic force can be admitted; if otherwise, it must be entirely rejected. It is not difficult to make the experiment (by sounding in straits), whether the sea be deeper towards the middle in ebbs, than in floods. But it must be observed, if this be the case, that (contrary to common opinion) the waters rise in ebbs, and only return to their former position in floods, so as to bathe and inundate the coast.

Again, let the required nature be the spontaneous motion of revolution, and particularly, whether the diurnal motion, by which the sun and stars appear to us to rise and set, be a real motion of revolution in the heavenly bodies, or only apparent in them, and real in the earth. There may be an instance of the cross of the following nature. If there be discovered any motion in the ocean from east to west, though very languid and weak, and if the same motion be discovered rather more swift in the air (particularly within the tropics, where it is more perceptible from the circles being greater). If it be discovered also in the low comets, and be already quick and powerful in them; if it be found also in the planets, but so tempered and regulated as to be slower in those nearest the earth, and quicker in those at the greatest distance, being quickest of all in the heavens, then the diurnal motion should certainly be considered as real in the heavens, and that of the earth must be rejected; for it will be evident that the motion from east to west is part of the system of the world and universal; since it is most rapid in the height of the heavens, and gradually grows weaker, till it stops and is extinguished in rest at the earth.

Again, let the required nature be that other motion of revolution, so celebrated amongst astronomers, which is contrary to the diurnal, namely, from west to east,—and which the ancient astronomers assign to the planets, and even to the starry sphere, but Copernicus and his followers to the earth also,—and let it be examined whether any such motion be found in nature, or it be rather a fiction and hypothesis for abridging and facilitating calculation, and for promoting that fine notion of effecting the heavenly motions by perfect circles; for there is nothing which proves such a motion in heavenly objects to be true and real, either in a planet's not returning in its diurnal motion to the same point of the starry sphere, or in the pole of the zodiac being different from that of the world, which two circumstances have occasioned this notion. For the first phenomenon is well accounted for by the spheres overtaking or falling behind each other, and the second by spiral lines; so that the inaccuracy of the return and declination to the tropics may be rather modifications of the one diurnal motion than contrary motions, or about different poles. And it is most certain, if we consider ourselves for a moment as part of the vulgar (setting aside the fictions of astronomers and the school, who are wont undeservedly to attack the senses in many respects, and to affect obscurity), that the apparent motion is such as we have said, a model of which we have sometimes caused to be represented by wires in a sort of a machine.

We may take the following instances of the cross upon this subject. If it be found in any history worthy of credit, that there has existed any comet, high or low, which has not revolved in manifest harmony (however irregularly) with the diurnal motion, then we may decide so far as to allow such a motion to be possible in nature. But if nothing of the sort be found, it must be suspected, and recourse must be had to other instances of the cross.

Again, let the required nature be weight or gravity. Heavy and ponderous bodies must, either of their own nature, tend towards the centre of the earth by their peculiar formation, or must be attracted and hurried by the corporeal mass of the earth itself, as being an assemblage of similar bodies, and be drawn to it by sympathy. But if the latter be the cause, it follows that the nearer bodies approach to the earth, the more powerfully and rapidly they must be borne towards it, and the further they are distant, the more faintly and slowly (as is the case in magnetic attractions), and that this must happen within a given distance; so that if they be separated at such a distance from the earth that the power of the earth cannot act upon them, they will remain suspended like the earth, and not fall at all.º

The following instance of the cross may be adopted. Take a clock moved by leaden weights,ᵖ and another by a spring, and

* The error in the text arose from Bacon's impression that the earth was immoveable. It is evident, since gravitation acts at an infinite distance, that no such point could be found; and even supposing the impossible point of equilibrium discovered, the body could not maintain its position an instant, but would be hurried, at the first movement of the heavenly bodies, in the direction of the dominant gravitating power. *Ed.*

ᵖ Fly clocks are referred to in the text, not pendulum clocks, which were not known in England till 1662. The former, though clumsy and rude in their construction, still embodied sound mechanical principles. The comparison of the effect of a spring with that of a weight in producing certain motions in certain times on altitudes and in mines, has recently been tried by Professors Airy and Whewell in Dalcoath mine, by means of a pendulum, which is only a weight moved by gravity, and a chronometer balance moved and regulated by a spring. In his thirty-seventh Aphorism, Bacon also speaks of gravity as an incorporeal power, acting at a distance, and requiring time for its transmission;

let them be set well together, so that one be neither quicker nor slower than the other; then let the clock moved by weights be placed on the top of a very high church, and the other be kept below, and let it be well observed, if the former move slower than it did, from the diminished power of the weights. Let the same experiment be made at the bottom of mines worked to a considerable depth, in order to see whether the clock move more quickly from the increased power of the weights. But if this power be found to diminish at a height, and to increase in subterraneous places, the attraction of the corporeal mass of the earth may be taken as the cause of weight.

Again, let the required nature be the polarity of the steel needle when touched with the magnet. We have these two ways with regard to this nature:—Either the touch of the magnet must communicate polarity to the steel towards the north and south, or else it may only excite and prepare it, whilst the actual motion is occasioned by the presence of the earth, which Gilbert considers to be the case, and endeavours to prove with so much labour. The particulars he has inquired into with such ingenious zeal amount to this:—1. An iron bolt placed for a long time towards the north and south acquires polarity from this habit, without the touch of the magnet, as if the earth itself operating but weakly from its distance (for the surface or outer

---

a consideration which occurred at a later period to Laplace in one of his most delicate investigations.

Crucial instances, as Herschel remarks, afford the readiest and securest means of eliminating extraneous causes, and deciding between the claims of rival hypotheses; especially when these, running parallel to each other, in the explanation of great classes of phenomena, at length come to be placed at issue upon a single fact. A curious example is given by M. Fresnel, as decisive in his mind of the question between the two great theories on the nature of light, which, since the time of Newton and Huyghens have, divided philosophers. When two very clean glasses are laid one on the other, if they be not perfectly flat, but one or both, in an almost imperceptible degree, convex or prominent, beautiful and vivid colours will be seen between them; and if these be viewed through a red glass, their appearance will be that of alternate dark and bright stripes. These stripes are formed between the two surfaces in apparent contact, and being applicable on both theories, are appealed to by their respective supporters as strong confirmatory facts; but there is a difference in one circumstance, according as one or other theory is employed to explain them. In the case of the Huyghenian theory, the intervals between the bright stripes ought to appear absolutely black, when a prism is used for the upper glass, in the other half bright. This curious case of difference was tried, as soon as the opposing consequences of the two theories were noted by M. Fresnel, and the result is stated by him to be decisive in favour of that theory which makes light to consist in the vibrations of an elastic medium. *Ed.*

crust of the earth does not, in his opinion, possess the magnetic power), yet, by long continued motion, could supply the place of the magnet, excite the iron, and convert and change it when excited. 2. Iron, at a red or white heat, when quenched in a direction parallel to the north and south, also acquires polarity without the touch of the magnet, as if the parts of iron being put in motion by ignition, and afterwards recovering themselves, were, at the moment of being quenched, more susceptible and sensitive of the power emanating from the earth, than at other times, and therefore as it were excited. But these points, though well observed, do not completely prove his assertion.

An instance of the cross on this point might be as follows: Let a small magnetic globe be taken, and its poles marked, and placed towards the east and west, not towards the north and south, and let it continue thus. Then let an untouched needle be placed over it, and suffered to remain so for six or seven days. Now, the needle (for this is not disputed), whilst it remains over the magnet, will leave the poles of the world and turn to those of the magnet, and therefore, as long as it remains in the above position, will turn to the east and west. But if the needle, when removed from the magnet and placed upon a pivot, be found immediately to turn to the north and south, or even by degrees to return thither, then the presence of the earth must be considered as the cause, but if it remains turned as at first, towards the east and west, or lose its polarity, then that cause must be suspected, and farther inquiry made.

Again, let the required nature be the corporeal substance of the moon, whether it be rare, fiery, and aërial (as most of the ancient philosophers have thought), or solid and dense (as Gilbert and many of the moderns, with some of the ancients, hold).[q] The reasons for this latter opinion are grounded chiefly upon this, that the moon reflects the sun's rays, and that light does not appear capable of being reflected except by solids. The instances of the cross will therefore (if any) be such as to exhibit reflection by a rare body, such as flame, if it be but sufficiently dense. Now, certainly, one of the reasons of twilight is the reflection[r] of the rays of the sun by the upper part of the atmosphere. We see the sun's rays also reflected on fine evenings by streaks of moist clouds, with a splendour not less, but

[q] Bacon plainly, from this passage, was inclined to believe that the moon, like the comets, was nothing more than illuminated vapour. The Newtonian law, however, has not only established its solidity, but its density and weight. A sufficient proof of the former is afforded by the attraction of the sea, and the moon's motion round the earth. *Ed.*

[r] Rather the refraction, the sky or air, however, *reflects* the blue rays of light.

perhaps more bright and glorious than that reflected from the body of the moon, and yet it is not clear that those clouds have formed into a dense body of water. We see, also, that the dark air behind the windows at night reflects the light of a candle in the same manner as a dense body would do.* The experiment should also be made of causing the sun's rays to fall through a hole upon some dark and bluish flame. The unconfined rays of the sun when falling on faint flames, do certainly appear to deaden them, and render them more like white smoke than flames. These are the only instances which occur at present of the nature of those of the cross, and better perhaps can be found. But it must always be observed that reflection is not to be expected from flame, unless it be of some depth, for otherwise it becomes nearly transparent. This at least may be considered certain, that light is always either received and transmitted or reflected by an even surface.

Again, let the required nature be the motion of projectiles (such as darts, arrows, and balls) through the air. The school, in its usual manner, treats this very carelessly, considering it enough to distinguish it by the name of violent motion, from that which they term natural, and as far as regards the first percussion or impulse, satisfies itself by its axiom, that two bodies cannot exist in one place, or there would be a penetration of dimensions. With regard to this nature we have these two cross-ways :—The motion must arise either from the air carrying the projected body, and collecting behind it, like a stream behind boats, or the wind behind straws; or from the parts of the body itself not supporting the impression, but pushing themselves forward in succession to ease it. Fracastorius, and nearly all those who have entered into any refined inquiry upon the subject, adopt the first. Nor can it be doubted that the air has some effect, yet the other motion is without doubt real, as is clear from a vast number of experiments. Amongst others we may take this instance of the cross, namely, that a thin plate or wire of iron rather stiff, or even a reed or pen split in two, when drawn up and bent between the finger and thumb, will leap forward; for it is clear that this cannot be attributed to the air's being collected behind the body, because the source of motion is in the centre of the plate or pen, and not in its extremities.

Again, let the required nature be the rapid and powerful motion of the explosion of gunpowder, by which such vast

---

* The polished surface of the glass causes the reflection in this case, and not the air; and a hat or other black surface, put behind the window in the day-time, will enable the glass to reflect distinctly for the same reason, namely, that the reflected rays are not mixed and confused with those transmitted from the other side of the window.

masses are upheaved, and such weights discharged as we observe in large mines and mortars, there are two cross-ways before us with regard to this nature. This motion is excited either by the mere effort of the body expanding itself when inflamed, or by the assisting effort of the crude spirit, which escapes rapidly from fire, and bursts violently from the surrounding flame as from a prison. The school, however, and common opinion only consider the first effort; for men think that they are great philosophers when they assert that flame, from the form of the element, is endowed with a kind of necessity of occupying a greater space than the same body had occupied when in the form of powder, and that thence proceeds the motion in question. In the mean time they do not observe, that although this may be true, on the supposition of flame being generated, yet the generation may be impeded by a weight of sufficient force to compress and suffocate it, so that no such necessity exists as they assert. They are right, indeed, in imagining that the expansion and the consequent emission or removal of the opposing body, is necessary if flame be once generated, but such a necessity is avoided if the solid opposing mass suppress the flame before it be generated; and we in fact see that flame, especially at the moment of its generation, is mild and gentle, and requires a hollow space where it can play and try its force. The great violence of the effect, therefore, cannot be attributed to this cause; but the truth is, that the generation of these exploding flames and fiery blasts arises from the conflict of two bodies of a decidedly opposite nature,—the one very inflammable, as is the sulphur, the other having an antipathy to flame, namely, the crude spirit of the nitre; so that an extraordinary conflict takes place whilst the sulphur is becoming inflamed as far as it can (for the third body, the willow charcoal, merely incorporates and conveniently unites the two others), and the spirit of nitre is escaping, as far also as it can, and at the same time expanding itself (for air, and all crude substances, and water are expanded by heat), fanning thus, in every direction, the flame of the sulphur by its escape and violence, just as if by invisible bellows.

Two kinds of instances of the cross might here be used,—the one of very inflammable substances, such as sulphur and camphire, naphtha and the like, and their compounds, which take fire more readily and easily than gunpowder if left to themselves (and this shows that the effort to catch fire does not of itself produce such a prodigious effect); the other of substances which avoid and repel flame, such as all salts; for we see that when they are cast into the fire, the aqueous spirit escapes with a crackling noise before flame is produced, which also happens in a less degree in stiff leaves, from the escape of the aqueous part before the oily part has caught fire. This is more particularly observed in quicksilver, which is not improperly called mineral water, and which, without any inflammation, nearly equals the force of gunpowder by simple explosion and expansion, and is said, when mixed with gunpowder, to increase its force.

Again, let the required nature be the transitory nature of flame and its momentaneous extinction; for to us the nature of flame does not appear to be fixed or settled, but to be generated from moment to moment, and to be every instant extinguished; it being clear that those flames which continue and last, do not owe their continuance to the same mass of flame, but to a continued succession of new flame regularly generated, and that the same identical flame does not continue. This is easily shown by removing the food or source of the flame, when it at once goes out. We have the two following cross-ways with regard to this nature: —This momentary nature either arises from the cessation of the cause which first produced it, as in light, sounds, and violent motions, as they are termed, or flame may be capable, by its own nature, of duration, but is subjected to some violence from the contrary natures which surround it, and is destroyed.

We may therefore adopt the following instance of the cross. We see to what a height the flames rise in great conflagrations; for as the base of the flame becomes more extensive, its vertex is more lofty. It appears, then, that the commencement of the extinction takes place at the sides, where the flame is compressed by the air, and is ill at ease; but the centre of the flame, which is untouched by the air and surrounded by flame, continues the same, and is not extinguished until compressed by degrees by the air attacking it from the sides. All flame, therefore, is pyramidal, having its base near the source, and its vertex pointed from its being resisted by the air, and not supplied from the source. On the contrary, the smoke, which is narrow at the base, expands in its ascent, and resembles an inverted pyramid, because the air admits the smoke, but compresses the flame; for let no one dream that the lighted flame is air, since they are clearly heterogeneous.

The instance of the cross will be more accurate, if the experiment can be made by flames of different colours. Take, therefore, a small metal sconce, and place a lighted taper in it, then put it in a basin, and pour a small quantity of spirits of wine round the sconce, so as not to reach its edge, and light the spirit. Now the flame of the spirit will be blue, and that of the taper yellow; observe, therefore, whether the latter (which can easily be distinguished from the former by its colour, for flames do not mix immediately, as liquids do) continue pyramidal, or tend more to a globular figure, since there is nothing to destroy or compress it. If the latter result be observed, it must be considered as settled, that flame continues positively the same, whilst inclosed within another flame, and not exposed to the resisting force of the air.

Let this suffice for the instances of the cross. We have dwelt the longer upon them in order gradually to teach and accustom mankind to judge of nature by these instances, and enlightening experiments, and not by probable reasons.[1]

XXXVII. We will treat of the instances of divorce as the fifteenth of our prerogative instances. They indicate the separation of natures of the most common occurrence. They differ, however, from those subjoined to the accompanying instances; for the instances of divorce point out the separation of a particular nature from some concrete substance with which it is usually found in conjunction, whilst the hostile instances point out the total separation of one nature from another. They differ, also, from the instances of the cross, because they decide nothing, but only inform us that the one nature is capable of being separated from the other. They are of use in exposing false forms, and dissipating hasty theories derived from obvious facts; so that they add ballast and weight, as it were, to the understanding.

For instance, let the required natures be those four which

---

[1] These instances, which Bacon seems to consider as a great discovery, are nothing more than disjunctive propositions combined with dilemmas. In proposing to explain an effect, we commence with the enumeration of the different causes which seem connected with its production; then with the aid of one or more dilemmas, we eliminate each of the phenomena accidental to its composition, and conclude with attributing the effect to the residue. For instance, a certain phenomenon (a) is produced either by phenomenon (B) or phenomenon (C); but C cannot be the cause of a, for it is found in D, E, F, neither of which are connected with a. Then the true cause of phenomenon (a) must be phenomenon (B).

This species of reasoning is liable to several paralogisms, against which Bacon has not guarded his readers, from the very fact that he stumbled into them unwittingly himself. The two principal ones are false exclusions and defective enumerations. Bacon, in his survey of the causes which are able to concur in producing the phenomena of the tides, takes no account of the periodic melting of the Polar ice, or the expansion of water by the solar heat: nor does he fare better in his exclusions. For the attraction of the planets and the progression and retrograde motion communicated by the earth's diurnal revolution, can plainly affect the sea together, and have a simultaneous influence on its surface.

Bacon is hardly just or consistent in his censure of Ramus; the end of whose dichotomy was only to render reasoning by dilemma, and crucial instances, more certain in their results, by reducing the divisions which composed their parts to two sets of contradictory propositions. The affirmative or negative of one would then necessarily have led to the acceptance or rejection of the other. *Ed.*

Telesius terms associates, and of the same family, namely, heat, light, rarity, and mobility, or promptitude to motion; yet many instances of divorce can be discovered between them. Air is rare and easily moved, but neither hot nor light; the moon is light but not hot; boiling water is warm but not light; the motion of the needle in the compass is swift and active, and yet its substance is cold, dense, and opaque; and there are many similar examples.

Again, let the required natures be corporeal nature and natural action. The latter appears incapable of subsisting without some body, yet may we, perhaps, even here find an instance of divorce, as in the magnetic motion, which draws the iron to the magnet, and heavy bodies to the globe of the earth; to which we may add other actions which operate at a distance. For such action takes place in time, by distinct moments, not in an instant; and in space, by regular degrees and distances. There is, therefore some one moment of time and some interval of space, in which the power or action is suspended betwixt the two bodies creating the motion. Our consideration, then, is reduced to this, whether the bodies which are the extremes of motion prepare or alter the intermediate bodies, so that the power advances from one extreme to the other by succession and actual contact, and in the mean time exists in some intermediate body; or whether there exists in reality nothing but the bodies, the power, and the space? In the case of the rays of light, sounds, and heat, and some other objects which operate at a distance, it is indeed probable that the intermediate bodies are prepared and altered, the more so because a qualified medium is required for their operation. But the magnetic or attractive power admits of an indifferent medium, and it is not impeded in any. But if that power or action is independent of the intermediate body, it follows that it is a natural power or action existing in a certain time and space without any body, since it exists neither in the extreme nor in the intermediate bodies. Hence the magnetic action may be taken as an instance of divorce of corporeal nature and natural action; to which we may add, as a corollary and an advantage not to be neglected, that it may be taken as a proof of essence and substance being separate and incorporeal, even by those who philosophize according to the senses. For if natural power and action emanating from a body can exist at any time and place entirely without any body, it is nearly a proof that it can also emanate originally from an incorporeal substance; for a corporeal nature appears to be no less necessary for supporting and conveying, than for exciting or generating natural action.

XXXVIII. Next follow five classes of instances which we are wont to call by the general term of instances of the lamp, or of immediate information. They are such as assist the senses; for since every interpretation of nature sets out from the senses, and

BOOK II.] INSTANCES OF THE DOOR. 517

leads, by a regular fixed and well-established road, from the perceptions of the senses to those of the understanding (which are true notions and axioms), it necessarily follows, that in proportion as the representatives or ministerings of the senses are more abundant and accurate, everything else must be more easy and successful.

The first of these five sets of instances of the lamp, strengthen, enlarge, and correct the immediate operations of the senses; the second reduce to the sphere of the senses such matters as are beyond it; the third indicate the continued process or series of such things and motions, as for the most part are only observed in their termination, or in periods; the fourth supply the absolute wants of the senses; the fifth excite their attention and observation, and at the same time limit the subtilty of things. We will now proceed to speak of them singly.

XXXIX. In the sixteenth rank, then, of prerogative instances, we will place the instances of the door or gate, by which name we designate such as assist the immediate action of the senses. It is obvious, that sight holds the first rank among the senses, with regard to information, for which reason we must seek principally helps for that sense. These helps appear to be threefold, either to enable it to perceive objects not naturally seen, or to see them from a greater distance, or to see them more accurately and distinctly.

We have an example of the first (not to speak of spectacles and the like, which only correct and remove the infirmity of a deficient sight, and therefore give no further information) in the lately invented microscopes, which exhibit the latent and invisible minutiæ of substances, and their hidden formation and motion, by wonderfully increasing their apparent magnitude. By their assistance we behold with astonishment the accurate form and outline of a flea, moss, and animalculæ, as well as their previously invisible colour and motion. It is said, also, that an apparently straight line, drawn with a pen or pencil, is discovered by such a microscope to be very uneven and curved, because neither the motion of the hand, when assisted by a ruler, nor the impression of ink or colour, are really regular, although the irregularities are so minute as not to be perceptible without the assistance of the microscope. Men have (as is usual in new and wonderful discoveries) added a superstitious remark, that the microscope sheds a lustre on the works of nature, and dishonour on those of art, which only means that the tissue of nature is much more delicate than that of art. For the microscope is only of use for minute objects, and Democritus, perhaps, if he had seen it, would have exulted in the thought of a means being discovered for seeing his atom, which he affirmed to be entirely invisible. But the inadequacy of these microscopes, for the observation of any but the most minute bodies, and even of those if parts of a larger body, destroys their utility; for if the invention could be extended to greater bodies, or the minute parts of greater bodies, so that a piece of cloth would appear like a net, and the latent minutiæ and irregularities of gems, liquids, urine, blood, wounds, and many other things could be rendered visible, the greatest advantage would, without doubt, be derived.

We have an instance of the second kind in the telescope, discovered by the wonderful exertions of Galileo; by the assistance of which a nearer intercourse may be opened (as by boats or vessels) between ourselves and the heavenly objects. For by its aid we are assured that the Milky Way is but a knot or constellation of small stars, clearly defined and separate, which the ancients only conjectured to be the case; whence it appears to be capable of demonstration, that the spaces of the planetary orbits (as they are termed) are not quite destitute of other stars, but that the heaven begins to glitter with stars before we arrive at the starry sphere, although they may be too small to be visible without the telescope. By the telescope, also, we can behold the revolutions of smaller stars round Jupiter, whence it may be conjectured that there are several centres of motion among the stars. By its assistance, also, the irregularity of light and shade on the moon's surface is more clearly observed and determined, so as to allow of a sort of selenography.[u] By the telescope we see the spots in the sun, and other similar phenomena; all of which are most noble discoveries, as far as credit can be safely given to demonstrations of this nature, which are on this account very suspicious, namely, that experiment stops at these few, and nothing further has yet been discovered by the same method, among objects equally worthy of consideration.

We have instances of the third kind in measuring-rods, astrolabes, and the like, which do not enlarge, but correct and guide the sight. If there be other instances which assist the other senses in their immediate and individual action, yet if they add nothing further to their information they are not apposite to our present purpose, and we have therefore said nothing of them.

XL. In the seventeenth rank of prerogative instances we will place citing instances (to borrow a term from the tribunals), because they cite those things to appear, which have not yet appeared. We are wont also to call them invoking instances, and their property is that of reducing to the sphere of the senses objects which do not immediately fall within it.

Objects escape the senses either from their distance, or the intervention of other bodies, or because they are not calculated to make an impression upon the senses, or because they are not

---

* Père Snenier first pointed out the spots on the sun's disk, and by the marks which they afforded him, computed its revolution to be performed in twenty-five days and some hours. *Ed.*

in sufficient quantity to strike the senses, or because there is not sufficient time for their acting upon the senses, or because the impression is too violent, or because the senses are previously filled and possessed by the object, so as to leave no room for any new motion. These remarks apply principally to sight, and next to touch, which two senses act extensively in giving information, and that too upon general objects, whilst the remaining three inform us only, as it were, by their immediate action, and as to specific objects.

There can be no reduction to the sphere of the senses in the first case, unless in the place of the object, which cannot be perceived on account of the distance, there be added or substituted some other object, which can excite and strike the sense from a greater distance, as in the communication of intelligence by fires, bells, and the like.

In the second case we effect this reduction by rendering those things which are concealed by the interposition of other bodies, and which cannot easily be laid open, evident to the senses by means of that which lies at the surface, or proceeds from the interior; thus the state of the body is judged of by the pulse, urine, &c.

The third and fourth cases apply to many subjects, and the reduction to the sphere of the senses must be obtained from every quarter in the investigation of things. There are many examples. It is obvious that air, and spirit, and the like, whose whole substance is extremely rare and delicate, can neither be seen nor touched—a reduction, therefore, to the senses becomes necessary in every investigation relating to such bodies.

Let the required nature, therefore, be the action and motion of the spirit enclosed in tangible bodies; for every tangible body with which we are acquainted, contains an invisible and intangible spirit, over which it is drawn, and which it seems to clothe. This spirit being emitted from a tangible substance, leaves the body contracted and dry; when retained, it softens and melts it; when neither wholly emitted nor retained, it models it, endows it with limbs, assimilates, manifests, organizes it, and the like. All these points are reduced to the sphere of the senses by manifest effects.

For in every tangible and inanimate body the enclosed spirit at first increases, and as it were feeds on the tangible parts which are most open and prepared for it; and when it has digested and modified them, and turned them into spirit, it escapes with them. This formation and increase of spirit is rendered sensible by the diminution of weight; for in every desiccation something is lost in quantity, not only of the spirit previously existing in the body, but of the body itself, which was previously tangible, and has been recently changed, for the spirit itself has no weight. The departure or emission of spirit is rendered sensible in the rust of metals, and other putrefactions of a like nature, which stop before they arrive at the rudiments of life, which belong to the third species of process.[x] In compact bodies the spirit does not find pores and passages for its escape, and is therefore obliged to force out, and drive before it, the tangible parts also, which consequently protrude, whence arises rust and the like. The contraction of the tangible parts, occasioned by the emission of part of the spirit (whence arises desiccation), is rendered sensible by the increased hardness of the substance, and still more by the fissures, contractions, shrivelling, and folds of the bodies thus produced. For the parts of wood split and contract, skins become shrivelled, and not only that, but, if the spirit be emitted suddenly by the heat of the fire, become so hastily contracted as to twist and roll themselves up.

On the contrary, when the spirit is retained, and yet expanded and excited by heat or the like (which happens in solid and tenacious bodies), then the bodies are softened, as in hot iron; or flow, as in metals; or melt, as in gums, wax, and the like. The contrary effects of heat, therefore (hardening some substances and melting others), are easily reconciled,[y] because the spirit is emitted in the former, and agitated and retained in the latter; the latter action is that of heat and the spirit, the former that of the tangible parts themselves, after the spirit's emission.

But when the spirit is neither entirely retained nor emitted, but only strives and exercises itself, within its limits, and meets with tangible parts, which obey and readily follow it wherever it leads them, then follows the formation of an organic body, and of limbs, and the other vital actions of vegetables and animals. These are rendered sensible chiefly by diligent observation of the first beginnings, and rudiments or effects of life in animalculæ sprung from putrefaction, as in the eggs of ants, worms, mosses, frogs after rain, &c. Both a mild heat and a pliant substance, however, are necessary for the production of life, in order that the spirit may neither hastily escape, nor be restrained by the obstinacy of the parts, so as not to be able to bend and model them like wax.

Again, the difference of spirit which is important and of effect in many points (as unconnected spirit, branching spirit, branching and cellular spirit, the first of which is that of all inanimate

---

[x] Rust is now well known to be a chemical combination of oxygen with the metal, and the metal when rusty acquires additional weight. His theory as to the generation of animals, is deduced from the erroneous notion of the possibility of spontaneous generation (as 't was termed). See the next paragraph but one.

[y] "Limus ut hic durescit, et hæc ut cera liquescit
Uno eodemque igni."—Virg. Ecl. viii.

substances, the second of vegetables, and the third of animals), is placed, as it were, before the eyes by many reducing instances.

Again, it is clear that the more refined tissue and conformation of things (though forming the whole body of visible or tangible objects) are neither visible nor tangible. Our information, therefore, must here also be derived from reduction to the sphere of the senses. But the most radical and primary difference of formation depends on the abundance or scarcity of matter within the same space or dimensions. For the other formations which regard the dissimilarity of the parts contained in the same body, and their collocation and position, are secondary in comparison with the former.

Let the required nature then be the expansion or coherence of matter in different bodies, or the quantity of matter relative to the dimensions of each. For there is nothing in nature more true than the twofold proposition,—that nothing proceeds from nothing and that nothing is reduced to nothing, but that the quantum, or sum total of matter, is constant, and is neither increased nor diminished. Nor is it less true, that out of this given quantity of matter, there is a greater or less quantity, contained within the same space or dimensions according to the difference of bodies; as, for instance, water contains more than air. So that if any one were to assert that a given content of water can be changed into an equal content of air, it is the same as if he were to assert that something can be reduced into nothing. On the contrary, if any one were to assert that a given content of air can be changed into an equal content of water, it is the same as if he were to assert that something can proceed from nothing. From this abundance or scarcity of matter are properly derived the notions of density and rarity, which are taken in various and promiscuous senses.

This third assertion may be considered as being also sufficiently certain; namely, that the greater or less quantity of matter in this or that body, may, by comparison, be reduced to calculation, and exact, or nearly exact, proportion. Thus, if one should say that there is such an accumulation of matter in a given quantity of gold, that it would require twenty-one times the quantity in dimension of spirits of wine, to make up the same quantity of matter, it would not be far from the truth.

The accumulation of matter, however, and its relative quantity, are rendered sensible by weight; for weight is proportionate to the quantity of matter, as regards the parts of a tangible substance, but spirit and its quantity of matter are not to be computed by weight, which spirit rather diminishes than augments.

We have made a tolerably accurate table of weight, in which we have selected the weights and size of all the metals, the principal minerals, stones, liquids, oils, and many other natural and artificial bodies: a very useful proceeding both as regards theory and practice, and which is capable of revealing many unexpected results. Nor is this of little consequence, that it serves to demonstrate that the whole range of the variety of tangible bodies with which we are acquainted (we mean tolerably close, and not spongy, hollow bodies, which are for a considerable part filled with air), does not exceed the ratio of one to twenty-one. So limited is nature, or at least that part of it to which we are most habituated.

We have also thought it deserving our industry, to try if we could arrive at the ratio of intangible or pneumatic bodies to tangible bodies, which we attempted by the following contrivance. We took a vial capable of containing about an ounce, using a small vessel in order to effect the subsequent evaporation with less heat. We filled this vial, almost to the neck, with spirits of wine, selecting it as the tangible body which, by our table, was the rarest, and contained a less quantity of matter in a given space than all other tangible bodies which are compact and not hollow. Then we noted exactly the weight of the liquid and vial. We next took a bladder, containing about two pints, and squeezed all the air out of it, as completely as possible, and until the sides of the bladder met. We first, however, rubbed the bladder gently with oil, so as to make it air-tight, by closing its pores with the oil. We tied the bladder tightly round the mouth of the vial, which we had inserted in it, and with a piece of waxed thread to make it fit better and more tightly, and then placed the vial on some hot coals in a brazier. The vapour or steam of the spirit, dilated and become aeriform by the heat, gradually swelled out the bladder, and stretched it in every direction like a sail. As soon as that was accomplished, we removed the vial from the fire and placed it on a carpet, that it might not be cracked by the cold; we also pricked the bladder immediately, that the steam might not return to a liquid state by the cessation of heat, and confound the proportions. We then removed the bladder, and again took the weight of the spirit which remained; and so calculated the quantity which had been converted into vapour, or an aeriform shape, and then examined how much space had been occupied by the body in its form of spirits of wine in the vial, and how much, on the other hand, had been occupied by it in its aeriform shape in the bladder, and subtracted the results; from which it was clear, that the body, thus converted and changed, acquired an expansion of one hundred times beyond its former bulk.

Again, let the required nature be heat or cold, of such a degree as not to be sensible from its weakness. They are rendered sensible by the thermometer, as we described it above;[*] for the cold and heat are not actually perceived by the touch, but heat expands and cold contracts the air. Nor, again, is that expansion or contraction of the air in itself visible, but the air when expanded depresses the water, and when contracted raises it, which is the first reduction to sight.

Again, let the required nature be the mixture of bodies; namely, how much aqueous, oleaginous or spirituous, ashy or salt parts they contain; or, as a particular example, how much butter, cheese, and whey there is in milk, and the like? These things are rendered sensible by artificial and skilful separations in tangible substances; and the nature of the spirit in them, though not immediately perceptible, is nevertheless discovered by the various motions and efforts of bodies. And, indeed, in this branch men have laboured hard in distillations and artificial separations, but with little more success than in their other experiments now in use; their methods being mere guesses and blind attempts, and more industrious than intelligent; and what is worst of all, without any imitation or rivalry of nature, but rather by violent heats and too energetic agents, to the destruction of any delicate conformation, in which principally consist the hidden virtues and sympathies. Nor do men in these separations ever attend to or observe what we have before pointed out; namely, that in attacking bodies by fire, or other methods, many qualities are superinduced by the fire itself, and the other bodies used to effect the separation, which were not originally in the compound. Hence arise most extraordinary fallacies; for the mass of vapour which is emitted from water by fire, for instance, did not exist as vapour or air in the water, but is chiefly created by the expansion of the water by the heat of the fire.

So, in general, all delicate experiments on natural or artificial bodies, by which the genuine are distinguished from the adulterated, and the better from the more common, should be referred to this division; for they bring that which is not the object of the senses within their sphere. They are therefore to be everywhere diligently sought after.

With regard to the fifth cause of objects escaping our senses, it is clear that the action of the sense takes place by motion, and this motion is time. If, therefore, the motion of any body be either so slow or so swift as not to be proportioned to the necessary momentum which operates on the senses, the object is not perceived at all; as in the motion of the hour hand, and that, again, of a musket-ball. The motion which is imperceptible by the senses from its slowness, is readily and usually rendered

[*] See Table of Degrees, No. 38.

sensible by the accumulation of motion; that which is imperceptible from its velocity, has not as yet been well measured; it is necessary, however, that this should be done in some cases, with a view to a proper investigation of nature.

The sixth case, where the sense is impeded by the power of the object, admits of a reduction to the sensible sphere, either by removing the object to a greater distance, or by deadening its effects by the interposition of a medium, which may weaken and not destroy the object; or by the admission of its reflection where the direct impression is too strong, as that of the sun in a basin of water.

The seventh case, where the senses are so overcharged with the object as to leave no further room, scarcely occurs except in the smell or taste, and is not of much consequence as regards our present subject. Let what we have said, therefore, suffice with regard to the reduction to the sensible sphere of objects not naturally within its compass.

Sometimes, however, this reduction is not extended to the senses of man, but to those of some other animal, whose senses, in some points, exceed those of man; as (with regard to some scents) to that of the dog, and with regard to light existing imperceptibly in the air, when not illuminated from any extraneous source, to the sense of the cat, the owl, and other animals which see by night. For Telesius has well observed, that there appears to be an original portion of light even in the air itself,[a] although but slight and meagre, and of no use for the most part to the eyes of men, and those of the generality of animals; because those animals to whose senses this light is proportioned can see by night, which does not, in all probability, proceed from their seeing either without light or by any internal light.

Here, too, we would observe, that we at present discuss only the wants of the senses, and their remedies; for their deceptions must be referred to the inquiries appropriated to the senses, and sensible objects; except that important deception, which makes them define objects in their relation to man, and not in their relation to the universe, and which is only corrected by universal reasoning and philosophy.[b]

[a] Riccati, and all modern physicists, discover some portion of light in every body, which seems to confirm the passage in Genesis that assigns to this substance priority in creation. *Ed.*

[b] As instances of this kind, which the progress of science since the time of Bacon afford, we may cite the air-pump and the barometer, for manifesting the weight and elasticity of air: the measurement of the velocity of light, by means of the occultation of Jupiter's satellites and the aberration of the fixed stars: the experiments in electricity and galvanism, and in the greater part of pneumatic chemistry. In

XLI In the eighteenth rank of prerogative instances we will class the instances of the road, which we are also wont to call itinerant and jointed instances. They are such as indicate the gradually continued motions of nature. This species of instances escapes rather our observation than our senses; for men are wonderfully indolent upon this subject, consulting nature in a desultory manner, and at periodic intervals, when bodies have been regularly finished and completed, and not during her work. But if any one were desirous of examining and contemplating the talents and industry of an artificer, he would not merely wish to see the rude materials of his art, and then his work when finished, but rather to be present whilst he is at labour, and proceeding with his work. Something of the same kind should be done with regard to nature. For instance, if any one investigate the vegetation of plants, he should observe from the first sowing of any seed (which can easily be done, by pulling up every day seeds which have been two, three, or four days in the ground, and examining them diligently), how and when the seed begins to swell and break, and be filled, as it were, with spirit; then how it begins to burst the bark and push out fibres, raising itself a little at the same time, unless the ground be very stiff; then how it pushes out these fibres, some downwards for roots, others upwards for the stem, sometimes also creeping laterally, if it find the earth open and more yielding on one side, and the like. The same should be done in observing the hatching of eggs, where we may easily see the process of animation and organization, and what parts are formed of the yolk, and what of the white of the egg, and the like. The same may be said of the inquiry into the formation of animals from putrefaction; for it would not be so humane to inquire into perfect and terrestrial animals, by cutting the fœtus from the womb; but opportunities may perhaps be offered of abortions, animals killed in hunting, and the like. Nature, therefore, must, as it were, be watched, as being more easily observed by night than by day: for contemplations of this kind may be considered as carried on by night, from the minuteness and perpetual burning of our watch-light.

The same, must be attempted with inanimate objects, which we have ourselves done by inquiring into the opening of liquids by fire. For the mode in which water expands is different from that observed in wine, vinegar, or verjuice, and very different, again, from that observed in milk and oil, and the like; and this was easily seen by boiling them with slow heat, in a glass vessel, through which the whole may be clearly perceived. But we all these cases scientific facts are elicited, which sense could never have revealed to us. *Ed.*

merely mention this, intending to treat of it more at large and more closely when we come to the discovery of the latent process; for it should always be remembered that we do not here treat of things themselves, but merely propose examples.^c

XLII. In the nineteenth rank of prerogative instances we will class supplementary or substitutive instances, which we are also wont to call instances of refuge. They are such as supply information, where the senses are entirely deficient, and we therefore have recourse to them when appropriate instances cannot be obtained. This substitution is twofold, either by approximation or by analogy. For instance, there is no known medium which entirely prevents the effect of the magnet in attracting iron,—neither gold, nor silver, nor stone, nor glass, wood, water, oil, cloth, or fibrous bodies, air, flame, or the like. Yet by accurate experiment, a medium may perhaps be found which would deaden its effect, more than another comparatively and in degree; as, for instance, the magnet would not perhaps attract iron through the same thickness of gold as of air, or the same quantity of ignited as of cold silver, and so on; for we have not ourselves made the experiment, but it will suffice as an example. Again, there is no known body which is not susceptible of heat, when brought near the fire; yet air becomes warm much sooner than stone. These are examples of substitution by approximation.

Substitution by analogy is useful, but less sure, and therefore to be adopted with some judgment. It serves to reduce that which is not the object of the senses to their sphere, not by the perceptible operations of the imperceptible body, but by the consideration of some similar perceptible body. For instance, let the subject for inquiry be the mixture of spirits, which are invisible bodies. There appears to be some relation between bodies and their sources or support. Now, the source of flame seems to be oil and fat; that of air, water, and watery sub-

^c The itinerant instances, as well as frontier instances, are cases in which we are enabled to trace the general law of continuity which seems to pervade all nature, and which has been aptly embodied in the sentence, "natura non agit per saltum." The pursuit of this law into phenomena where its application is not at first sight obvious, has opened a mine of physical discovery, and led us to perceive an intimate connection between facts which at first seemed hostile to each other. For example, the transparency of gold-leaf, which permits a bluish-green light to pass through it, is a frontier instance between transparent and opaque bodies, by exhibiting a body of the glass generally regarded the most opaque in nature, as still possessed of some slight degree of transparency. It thus proves that the quality of opacity is not a contrary or antagonistic quality to that of transparency, but only its extreme lowest degree.

stances; for flame increases over the exhalation of oil, and air over that of water. One must therefore consider the mixture of oil and water, which is manifest to the senses, since that of air and flame in general escapes the senses. But oil and water mix very imperfectly by composition or stirring, whilst they are exactly and nicely mixed in herbs, blood, and the parts of animals. Something similar, therefore, may take place in the mixture of flame and air in spirituous substances, not bearing mixture very well by simple collision, whilst they appear, however, to be well mixed in the spirits of plants and animals.

Again, if the inquiry do not relate to perfect mixtures of spirits, but merely to their composition, as whether they easily incorporate with each other, or there be rather (as an example) certain winds and exhalations, or other spiritual bodies, which do not mix with common air, but only adhere to and float in it in globules and drops, and are rather broken and pounded by the air, than received into, and incorporated with it; this cannot be perceived in common air, and other aeriform substances, on account of the rarity of the bodies, but an image, as it were, of this process may be conceived in such liquids as quicksilver, oil, water, and even air, when broken and dissipated it ascends in small portions through water, and also in the thicker kinds of smoke; lastly, in dust, raised and remaining in the air, in all of which there is no incorporation: and the above representation in this respect is not a bad one, if it be first diligently investigated, whether there can be such a difference of nature between spirituous substances, as between liquids, for then these images might conveniently be substituted by analogy.

And although we have observed of these supplementary instances, that information is to be derived from them, when appropriate instances are wanting, by way of refuge, yet we would have it understood, that they are also of great use, when the appropriate instances are at hand, in order to confirm the information afforded by them; of which we will speak more at length, when our subject leads us, in due course, to the support of induction.

XLIII. In the twentieth rank of prerogative instances we will place lancing instances, which we are also wont (but for a different reason) to call twitching instances. We adopt the latter name, because they twitch the understanding, and the former because they pierce nature, whence we style them occasionally the instances of Democritus.[d] They are such as warn the understanding of the admirable and exquisite subtilty of nature, so that it becomes roused and awakened to attention, observation, and proper inquiry; as, for instance, that a little drop of ink should

---

[d] Alluding to his theory of atoms.

be drawn out into so many letters; that silver merely gilt on its surface should be stretched to such a length of gilt wire; that a little worm, such as you may find on the skin, should possess both a spirit and a varied conformation of its parts; that a little saffron should imbue a whole tub of water with its colour; that a little musk or aroma should imbue a much greater extent of air with its perfume; that a cloud of smoke should be raised by a little incense; that such accurate differences of sounds as articulate words should be conveyed in all directions through the air, and even penetrate the pores of wood and water (though they become much weakened), that they should be, moreover, reflected, and that with such distinctness and velocity; that light and colour should for such an extent and so rapidly pass through solid bodies, such as glass and water, with so great and so exquisite a variety of images, and should be refracted and reflected; that the magnet should attract through every description of body, even the most compact; but (what is still more wonderful) that in all these cases the action of one should not impede that of another in a common medium, such as air; and that there should be borne through the air, at the same time, so many images of visible objects, so many impulses of articulation, so many different perfumes, as of the violet, rose, &c., besides cold and heat, and magnetic attractions; all of them, I say, at once, without any impediment from each other, as if each had its paths and peculiar passage set apart for it, without infringing against or meeting each other.

To these lancing instances, however, we are wont, not without some advantage, to add those which we call the limits of such instances. Thus, in the cases we have pointed out, one action does not disturb or impede another of a different nature, yet those of a similar nature subdue and extinguish each other; as the light of the sun does that of the candle, the sound of a cannon that of the voice, a strong perfume a more delicate one, a powerful heat a more gentle one, a plate of iron between the magnet and other iron the effect of the magnet. But the proper place for mentioning these will be also amongst the supports of induction.

XLIV. We have now spoken of the instances which assist the senses, and which are principally of service as regards information; for information begins from the senses. But our whole labour terminates in practice, and as the former is the beginning, so is the latter the end of our subject. The following instances, therefore, will be those which are chiefly useful in practice. They are comprehended in two classes, and are seven in number. We call them all by the general name of practical instances. Now there are two defects in practice, and as many divisions of important instances. Practice is either deceptive or too laborious. It is generally deceptive (especially after a diligent examination of natures), on account of the power and actions of bodies being ill defined and determined. Now the powers and actions of bodies are defined and determined either by space or by time, or by the quantity at a given period, or by the predominance of energy; and if these four circumstances be not well and diligently considered, the sciences may indeed be beautiful in theory, but are of no effect in practice. We call the four instances referred to this class, mathematical instances and instances of measure.

Practice is laborious either from the multitude of instruments, or the bulk of matter and substances requisite for any given work. Those instances, therefore, are valuable, which either direct practice to that which is of most consequence to mankind, or lessen the number of instruments or of matter to be worked upon. We assign to the three instances relating to this class, the common name of propitious or benevolent instances. We will now separately discuss these seven instances, and conclude with them that part of our work which relates to the prerogative or illustrious instances.

XLV. In the twenty-first rank of prerogative instances we will place the instances of the rod or rule, which we are also wont to call the instances of completion or *non ultrà*. For the powers and motions of bodies do not act and take effect through indefinite and accidental, but through limited and certain spaces; and it is of great importance to practice that these should be understood and noted in every nature which is investigated, not only to prevent deception, but to render practice more extensive and efficient. For it is sometimes possible to extend these powers, and bring the distance, as it were, nearer, as in the example of telescopes.

Many powers act and take effect only by actual touch, as in the percussion of bodies, where the one does not remove the other, unless the impelling touch the impelled body. External applications in medicine, as ointment and plasters, do not exercise their efficacy except when in contact with the body. Lastly, the objects of touch and taste only strike those senses when in contact with their organs.

Other powers act at a distance, though it be very small, of which but few have as yet been noted, although there be more than men suspect; this happens (to take everyday instances) when amber or jet attracts straws, bubbles dissolve bubbles, some purgative medicines draw humours from above, and the like. The magnetic power by which iron and the magnet, or two magnets, are attracted together, acts within a definite and narrow sphere, but if there be any magnetic power emanating from the earth a little below its surface, and affecting the needle in its polarity, it must act at a great distance.

Again, if there be any magnetic force which acts by sympathy between the globe of the earth and heavy bodies, or between that of the moon and the waters of the sea (as seems most probable from the particular floods and ebbs which occur twice in the month), or between the starry sphere and the planets, by which they are summoned and raised to their apogees, these must all operate at very great distances.* Again, some conflagrations and the kindling of flames take place at very considerable distances with particular substances, as they report of the naphtha of Babylon. Heat, too, insinuates itself at wide distances, as does also cold, so that the masses of ice which are broken off and float upon the Northern Ocean, and are borne through the Atlantic to the coast of Canada, become perceptible by the inhabitants, and strike them with cold from a distance. Perfumes also (though here there appears to be always some corporeal emission) act at remarkable distances, as is experienced by persons sailing by the coast of Florida, or parts of Spain, where there are whole woods of lemons, oranges, and other odoriferous plants, or rosemary and marjoram bushes, and the like. Lastly, the rays of light and the impressions of sound act at extensive distances.

* Observe the approximation to Newton's theory. The same notion repeated still more clearly in the ninth motion. Newton believed that the planets might so conspire as to derange the earth's annual revolution, and to elongate the line of the apsides and ellipsis that the earth describes in its annual revolution round the sun. In the supposition that all the planets meet on the same straight line, Venus and Mercury on one side of the sun, and the earth, moon, Mars, Jupiter, and Saturn on the side diametrically opposite; then Saturn would attract Jupiter, Jupiter Mars, Mars the moon, which must in its turn attract the earth in proportion to the force with which it was drawn out of its orbit. The result of this combined action on our planet would elongate its ecliptic orbit, and so far draw it from the source of heat, as to produce an intensity of cold destructive to animal life. But this movement would immediately cease with the planetary concurrence which produced it, and the earth, like a compressed spring, bound almost as near to the sun as she had been drawn from it, the reaction of the heat on its surface being about as intense as the cold caused by the first removal was severe. The earth, until it gained its regular track, would thus alternately vibrate between each side of its orbit, with successive changes in its atmosphere, proportional to the square of the variation of its distance from the sun. In no place is Bacon's genius more conspicuous than in these repeated guesses at truth. He would have been a strong Copernican, had not Gilbert defended the system. *Ed*

Yet all these powers, whether acting at a small or great distance, certainly act within definite distances, which are well ascertained by nature; so that there is a limit depending either on the mass or quantity of the bodies, the vigour or faintness of the powers, or the favourable or impeding nature of the medium, all of which should be taken into account and observed. We must also note the boundaries of violent motions, such as missiles, projectiles, wheels, and the like, since they are also manifestly confined to certain limits.

Some motions and virtues are to be found of a directly contrary nature to these, which act in contact but not at a distance; namely, such as operate at a distance and not in contact, and again act with less force at a less distance, and the reverse. Sight, for instance, is not easily effective in contact, but requires a medium and distance; although I remember having heard from a person deserving of credit, that in being cured of a cataract (which was done by putting a small silver needle within the first coat of the eye, to remove the thin pellicle of the cataract, and force it into a corner of the eye), he had distinctly seen the needle moving across the pupil. Still, though this may be true, it is clear that large bodies cannot be seen well or distinctly, unless at the vertex of a cone, where the rays from the object meet at some distance from the eye. In old persons the eye sees better if the object be moved a little farther, and not nearer. Again, it is certain that in projectiles the impact is not so violent at too short a distance as a little afterwards.¹ Such are the observations to be made on the measure of motions as regards distance.

There is another measure of motion in space which must not be passed over, not relating to progressive but spherical motion, —that is, the expansion of bodies into a greater, or their contraction into a lesser sphere. For in our measure of this motion we must inquire what degree of compression or extension bodies easily and readily admit of, according to their nature, and at what point they begin to resist it, so as at last to bear it no further,—as when an inflated bladder is compressed, it allows a certain compression of the air, but if this be increased, the air does not suffer it, and the bladder is burst.

---

¹ This is not true except when the projectile acquires greater velocity at every successive instant of its course, which is never the case except with falling bodies. Bacon appears to have been led into the opinion from observing that gun-shots pierce many objects at a distance from which they rebound when brought within a certain proximity of contact. This apparent inconsistency, however, arises from the resistance of the parts of the object, which velocity combined with force is necessary to overcome. *Ed.*

We have proved this by a more delicate experiment. We took a metal bell, of a light and thin sort, such as is used for salt-cellars, and immerged it in a basin of water, so as to carry the air contained in its interior down with it to the bottom of the basin. We had first, however, placed a small globe at the bottom of the basin, over which we placed the bell. The result was, that if the globe were small compared with the interior of the bell, the air would contract itself, and be compressed without being forced out, but if it were too large for the air readily to yield to it, the latter became impatient of the pressure, raised the bell partly up, and ascended in bubbles.

To prove, also, the extension (as well as the compression) which air admits of, we adopted the following method:—We took a glass egg, with a small hole at one end; we drew out the air by violent suction at this hole, and then closed the hole with the finger, immersed the egg in water, and then removed the finger. The air being constrained by the effort made in suction, and dilated beyond its natural state, and therefore striving to recover and contract itself (so that if the egg had not been immersed in water, it would have drawn in the air with a hissing sound), now drew in a sufficient quantity of water to allow the air to recover its former dimensions.[g]

It is well ascertained that rare bodies (such as air) admit of considerable contraction, as has been before observed; but tangible bodies (such as water) admit of it much less readily, and to a less extent. We investigated the latter point by the following experiment:—

We had a leaden globe made, capable of containing about two pints, wine measure, and of tolerable thickness, so as to support considerable pressure. We poured water into it through an aperture, which we afterwards closed with melted lead, as soon as the globe was filled with water, so that the whole became perfectly solid. We next flattened the two opposite sides with a heavy hammer, which necessarily caused the water to occupy a less space, since the sphere is the solid of greatest content; and when hammering failed from the resistance of the water, we made use of a mill or press, till at last the water, refusing to submit to a greater pressure, exuded like a fine dew through the solid lead. We then computed the extent to which the original space had been reduced, and concluded that water admitted such a degree of compression when constrained by great violence.

The more solid, dry, or compact bodies, such as stones, wood, and metals, admit of much less, and indeed scarcely any perceptible compression or expansion, but escape by breaking, slipping

[g] This passage shows that the pressure of the external atmosphere, which forces the water into the egg, was not in Bacon's time understood

forward, or other efforts; as appears in bending wood, or steel for watch-springs, in projectiles, hammering, and many other motions, all of which, together with their degrees, are to be observed and examined in the investigation of nature, either to a certainty, or by estimation, or comparison, as opportunity permits.

XLVI. In the twenty-second rank of prerogative instances we will place the instances of the course, which we are also wont to call water instances, borrowing our expression from the water hour-glasses employed by the ancients instead of those with sand. They are such as measure nature by the moments of time, as the last instances do by the degrees of space. For all motion or natural action takes place in time, more or less rapidly, but still in determined moments well ascertained by nature. Even those actions which appear to take effect suddenly, and in the twinkling of an eye (as we express it), are found to admit of greater or less rapidity.

In the first place, then, we see that the return of the heavenly bodies to the same place takes place in regular times, as does the flood and ebb of the sea. The descent of heavy bodies towards the earth, and the ascent of light bodies towards the heavenly sphere, take place in definite times,[h] according to the nature of the body, and of the medium through which it moves. The sailing of ships, the motions of animals, the transmission of projectiles, all take place in times the sums of which can be computed. With regard to heat, we see that boys in winter bathe their hands in the flame without being burnt; and conjurers, by quick and regular movements, overturn vessels filled with wine or water, and replace them without spilling the liquid, with several similar instances. The compression, expansion, and eruption of several bodies, take place more or less rapidly, according to the nature of the body and its motion, but still in definite moments.

In the explosion of several cannon at once (which are some

[h] We have already alluded, in a note prefixed to the same aphorism of the first book, to Newton's error of the absolute lightness of bodies. In speaking again of the volatile or spiritual substances (Aph. xl. b. ii.), which he supposed with the Platonists and some of the schoolmen to enter into the composition of every body, he ascribes to them a power of lessening the weight of the material coating in which he supposes them inclosed. It would appear from these passages and the text that Bacon had no idea of the relative density of bodies, and the capability which some have to diminish the specific gravity of the heavier substances by the dilation of their parts; or if he had, the reveries in which Aristotle indulged in treating of the soul, about the appetency of bodies to fly to kindred substances,—flame and spirit to the sky, and solid opaque substances to the earth, must have vitiated his mind. *Ed.*

times heard at the distance of thirty miles), the sound of those nearest to the spot is heard before that of the most distant. Even in sight (whose action is most rapid), it is clear that a definite time is necessary for its exertion, which is proved by certain objects being invisible from the velocity of their motion, such as a musket-ball; for the flight of the ball is too swift to allow an impression of its figure to be conveyed to the sight.

This last instance, and others of a like nature, have sometimes excited in us a most marvellous doubt, no less than whether the image of the sky and stars is perceived as at the actual moment of its existence, or rather a little after, and whether there is not (with regard to the visible appearance of the heavenly bodies) a true and apparent time, as well as a true and apparent place, which is observed by astronomers in parallaxes. It appeared so incredible to us, that the images or radiations of heavenly bodies could suddenly be conveyed through such immense spaces to the sight, and it seemed that they ought rather to be transmitted in a definite time.[i] That doubt, however (as far as regards any great difference between the true and apparent time), was subsequently completely set at rest, when we considered the infinite loss and diminution of size as regards the real and apparent magnitude of a star, occasioned by its distance, and at the same time observed at how great a distance (at least sixty miles) bodies which are merely white can be suddenly seen by us. For there is no doubt, that the light of the heavenly bodies not only far surpasses the vivid appearance of white, but even the light of any flame (with which we are acquainted) in the vigour of its radiation. The immense velocity of the bodies themselves, which is perceived in their diurnal motion, and has so astonished thinking men, that they have been more ready to believe in the motion of the earth, renders the motion of radiation from them (marvellous as it is in its rapidity) more worthy of belief. That which has weighed most with us, however, is, that if there were any considerable interval of time between the reality and the appearance, the images would often be interrupted and confused by clouds formed in the mean time, and similar disturbances of the medium. Let this suffice with regard to the simple measures of time.

It is not merely the absolute, but still more the relative measure of motions and actions which must be inquired into, for this latter is of great use and application. We perceive that

---

Römer, a Danish astronomer, was the first to demonstrate, by connecting the irregularities of the eclipses of Jupiter's satellites with their distances from the earth, the necessity of time for the propagation of light. The idea occurred to Dominic Cassini as well as Bacon, but both allowed the discovery to slip out of their hands. *Ed.*

the flame of fire-arms is seen sooner than the sound is heard, although the ball must have struck the air before the flame, which was behind it, could escape: the reason of which is, that light moves with greater velocity than sound. We perceive, also, that visible images are received by the sight with greater rapidity than they are dismissed, and for this reason, a violin string touched with the finger appears double or triple, because the new image is received before the former one is dismissed. Hence, also, rings when spinning appear globular, and a lighted torch, borne rapidly along at night, appears to have a tail. Upon the principle of the inequality of motion, also, Galileo attempted an explanation of the flood and ebb of the sea, supposing the earth to move rapidly, and the water slowly, by which means the water, after accumulating, would at intervals fall back, as is shown in a vessel of water made to move rapidly. He has, however, imagined this on data which cannot be granted (namely, the earth's motion), and besides, does not satisfactorily account for the tide taking place every six hours.

An example of our present point (the relative measure of motion), and, at the same time, of its remarkable use of which we have spoken, is conspicuous in mines filled with gunpowder, where immense weights of earth, buildings, and the like, are overthrown and prostrated by a small quantity of powder; the reason of which is decidedly this, that the motion of the expansion of the gunpowder is much more rapid than that of gravity,[k] which would resist it, so that the former has terminated before the latter has commenced. Hence, also, in missiles, a strong blow will not carry them so far as a sharp and rapid one. Nor could a small portion of animal spirit in animals, especially in such vast bodies as those of the whale and elephant, have ever bent or directed such a mass of body, were it not owing to the velocity of the former, and the slowness of the latter in resisting its motion.

In short, this point is one of the principal foundations of the magic experiments (of which we shall presently speak), where a small mass of matter overcomes and regulates a much larger, if there but be an anticipation of motion, by the velocity of one before the other is prepared to act.

Finally, the point of the first and last should be observed in all natural actions. Thus, in an infusion of rhubarb the purgative property is first extracted, and then the astringent; we have experienced something of the same kind in steeping violets in vinegar, which first extracts the sweet and delicate odour of

---

[k] The author in the text confounds inertness, which is a simple indifference of bodies to action, with gravity, which is a force acting always in proportion to their density. He falls into the same error further on. *Ed.*

the flower, and then the more earthy part, which disturbs the perfume; so that if the violets be steeped a whole day, a much fainter perfume is extracted than if they were steeped for a quarter of an hour only, and then taken out; and since the odoriferous spirit in the violet is not abundant, let other and fresh violets be steeped in the vinegar every quarter of an hour, as many as six times, when the infusion becomes so strengthened, that although the violets have not altogether remained there for more than one hour and a half, there remains a most pleasing perfume, not inferior to the flower itself, for a whole year. It must be observed, however, that the perfume does not acquire its full strength, till about a month after the infusion. In the distillation of aromatic plants macerated in spirits of wine, it is well known that an aqueous and useless phlegm rises first, then water containing more of the spirit, and lastly, water containing more of the aroma; and many observations of the like kind, well worthy of notice, are to be made in distillations. But let these suffice as examples.[1]

[1] The experiments of the two last classes of instances are considered only in relation to practice, and Bacon does not so much as mention their infinitely greater importance in the theoretical part of induction. The important law of gravitation in physical astronomy could never have been demonstrated but by such observations and experiments as assigned accurate geometrical measures to the quantities compared. It was necessary to determine with precision the demi-diameter of the earth, the velocity of falling bodies at its surface, the distance of the moon, and the speed with which she describes her orbit, before the relation could be discovered between the force which draws a stone to the ground and that which retains the moon in her sphere.

In many cases the result of a number of particular facts, or the collective instances rising out of them, can only be discovered by geometry, which so far becomes necessary to complete the work of induction. For instance, in the case of optics, when light passes from one transparent medium to another, it is refracted, and the angle which the ray of incidence makes with the superficies which bounds the two media determines that which the refracted ray makes with the same superficies. Now, all experiment can do for us in this case is, to determine for any particular angle of incidence the corresponding angle of refraction. But with respect to the general rule which in every possible case deduces one of these angles from the other, or expresses the constant and invariable relation which subsists between them, experiment gives no direct information. Geometry must, consequently, be called in, which, when a constant though unknown relation subsists between two angles, or two variable qualities of any kind, and when an indefinite number of values of those quantities are assigned, furnishes infallible means of discovering that unknown relation either accurately or by approximation. In this way it has been found, when the two media remain the same, the cosines of the above-mentioned angles have a constant ratio to each other. Hence, when the relations of the simple elements of pheno-

INSTANCES OF QUANTITY.

XLVII. In the twenty-third rank of prerogative instances we will place instances of quantity, which we are also wont to call the doses of nature (borrowing a word from medicine). They are such as measure the powers by the quantity of bodies, and point out the effect of the quantity in the degree of power. And in the first place, some powers only subsist in the universal quantity, or such as bears a relation to the confirmation and fabric of the universe. Thus the earth is fixed, its parts fall. The waters in the sea flow and ebb, but not in the rivers, except by the admission of the sea. Then, again, almost all particular powers act according to the greater or less quantity of the body. Large masses of water are not easily rendered foul, small are. New wine and beer become ripe and drinkable in small skins much more readily than in large casks. If an herb be placed in a considerable quantity of liquid, infusion takes place rather than impregnation; if in less, the reverse. A bath, therefore, and a light sprinkling, produce different effects on the human body. Light dew, again, never falls, but is dissipated and incorporated with the air; thus we see that in breathing on gems, the slight quantity of moisture, like a small cloud in the air, is immediately dissolved. Again, a piece of the same magnet does not attract so much iron as the whole magnet did. There are some powers where the smallness of the quantity is of more avail; as in boring, a sharp point pierces more readily than a blunt one; the diamond, when pointed, makes an impression on glass, and the like.

Here, too, we must not rest contented with a vague result, but inquire into the exact proportion of quantity requisite for a particular exertion of power; for one would be apt to suppose that the power bears an exact proportion to the quantity; that if a leaden bullet of one ounce, for instance, would fall in a given time, one of two ounces ought to fall twice as rapidly, which is most erroneous. Nor does the same ratio prevail in every kind of power, their difference being considerable. The measure,

mena are discovered to afford a general rule which will apply to any concrete case, the deductive method must be applied, and the elementary principles made through its agency to account for the laws of their more complex combinations. The reflection and refraction of light by the rain falling from a cloud opposite to the sun was thought, even before Newton's day, to contain the *form* of the rainbow. This philosopher transformed a probable conjecture into a certain fact when he deduced from the known laws of reflection and refraction the breadth of the coloured arch, the diameter of the circle of which it is a part, and the relation of the latter to the place of the spectator and the sun. Doubt was at once silenced when there came out of his calculus a combination of the same laws of the simple elements of optics answering to the phenomena in nature. *Ed.*

therefore, must be determined by experiment, and not by probability or conjecture.

Lastly, we must in all our investigations of nature observe what quantity, or dose, of the body is requisite for a given effect, and must at the same time be guarded against estimating it at too much or too little.

XLVIII. In the twenty-fourth rank of prerogative instances we will place wrestling instances, which we are also wont to call instances of predominance. They are such as point out the predominance and submission of powers compared with each other, and which of them is the more energetic and superior, or more weak and inferior. For the motions and effects of bodies are compounded, decomposed, and combined, no less than the bodies themselves. We will exhibit, therefore, the principal kinds of motions or active powers, in order that their comparative strength, and thence a demonstration and definition of the instances in question, may be rendered more clear.

Let the first motion be that of the resistance of matter, which exists in every particle, and completely prevents its annihilation; so that no conflagration, weight, pressure, violence, or length of time can reduce even the smallest portion of matter to nothing, or prevent it from being something, and occupying some space, and delivering itself (whatever straits it be put to), by changing its form or place, or, if that be impossible, remaining as it is; nor can it ever happen that it should either be nothing or nowhere. This motion is designated by the schools (which generally name and define everything by its effects and inconveniences rather than by its inherent cause) by the axiom, that two bodies cannot exist in the same place, or they call it a motion to prevent the penetration of dimensions. It is useless to give examples of this motion, since it exists in every body.

Let the second motion be that which we term the motion of connection, by which bodies do not allow themselves to be separated at any point from the contact of another body, delighting, as it were, in the mutual connection and contact. This is called by the schools a motion to prevent a vacuum. It takes place when water is drawn up by suction or a syringe, the flesh by cupping, or when the water remains without escaping from perforated jars, unless the mouth be opened to admit the air, and innumerable instances of a like nature.

Let the third be that which we term the motion of liberty, by which bodies strive to deliver themselves from any unnatural pressure or tension, and to restore themselves to the dimensions suited to their mass; and of which, also, there are innumerable examples. Thus, we have examples of their escaping from pressure, in the water in swimming, in the air in flying, in the water again in rowing, and in the air in the undulation of the winds, and in springs of watches. An exact instance of the motion of compressed air is seen in children's popguns, which they make by scooping out elder-branches or some such matter, and forcing in a piece of some pulpy root or the like, at each end; then they force the root or other pellet with a ramrod to the opposite end, from which the lower pellet is emitted and projected with a report, and that before it is touched by the other piece of root or pellet, or by the ramrod. We have examples of their escape from tension, in the motion of the air that remains in glass eggs after suction, in strings, leather, and cloth, which recoil after tension, unless it be long continued. The schools define this by the term of motion from the form of the element; injudiciously enough, since this motion is to be found not only in air, water, or fire, but in every species of solid, as wood, iron, lead, cloth, parchment, &c., each of which has its own proper size, and is with difficulty stretched to any other. Since, however, this motion of liberty is the most obvious of all, and to be seen in an infinite number of cases, it will be as well to distinguish it correctly and clearly; for some most carelessly confound this with the two others of resistance and connection; namely, the freedom from pressure with the former, and that from tension with the latter, as if bodies when compressed yielded or expanded to prevent a penetration of dimensions, and when stretched rebounded and contracted themselves to prevent a vacuum. But if the air, when compressed, could be brought to the density of water, or wood to that of stone, there would be no need of any penetration of dimensions, and yet the compression would be much greater than they actually admit of. So if water could be expanded till it became as rare as air, or stone as rare as wood, there would be no need of a vacuum, and yet the expansion would be much greater than they actually admit of. We do not, therefore, arrive at a penetration of dimensions or a vacuum before the extremes of condensation and rarefaction, whilst the motion we speak of stops and exerts itself much within them, and is nothing more than a desire of bodies to preserve their specific density (or, if it be preferred, their form), and not to desert them suddenly, but only to change by degrees, and of their own accord. It is, however, much more necessary to intimate to mankind (because many other points depend upon this), that the violent motion which we call mechanical, and Democritus (who, in explaining his primary motions, is to be ranked even below the middling class of philosophers) termed the motion of a blow, is nothing else than this motion of liberty, namely, a tendency to relaxation from compression. For in all simple impulsion or flight through the air, the body is not displaced or moved in space, until its parts are placed in an unnatural state, and compressed by the impelling force. When that takes place, the different parts urging the other in succession, the whole is moved, and that with a rotatory as well as progressive motion, in order that the parts may, by this means also, set themselves at liberty, or more readily submit. Let this suffice for the motion in question.

Let the fourth be that which we term the motion of matter, and which is opposed to the last; for in the motion of liberty, bodies abhor, reject, and avoid a new size or volume, or any new expansion or contraction (for these different terms have the same meaning), and strive, with all their power, to rebound and resume their former density; on the contrary, in the motion of matter, they are anxious to acquire a new volume or dimension, and attempt it willingly and rapidly, and occasionally by a most vigorous effort, as in the example of gunpowder. The most powerful, or at least most frequent, though not the only instruments of this motion, are heat and cold. For instance, the air, if expanded by tension (as by suction in the glass egg), struggles anxiously to restore itself; but if heat be applied, it strives, on the contrary, to dilate itself, and longs for a larger volume, regularly passing and migrating into it, as into a new form (as it is termed); nor after a certain degree of expansion is it anxious to return, unless it be invited to do so by the application of cold, which is not indeed a return, but a fresh change. So also water, when confined by compression, resists, and wishes to become as it was before, namely, more expanded; but if there happen an intense and continued cold, it changes itself readily, and of its own accord, into the condensed state of ice; and if the cold be long-continued, without any intervening warmth (as in grottos and deep caves), it is changed into crystal or similar matter, and never resumes its form.

Let the fifth be that which we term the motion of continuity We do not understand by this simple and primary continuity with any other body (for that is the motion of connection), but the continuity of a particular body in itself; for it is most certain that all bodies abhor a solution of continuity, some more and some less, but all partially. In hard bodies (such as steel and glass) the resistance to an interruption of continuity is most powerful and efficacious, whilst although in liquids it appears to be faint and languid, yet it is not altogether null, but exists in the lowest degree, and shows itself in many experiments, such as bubbles, the round form of drops, the thin threads which drip from roofs, the cohesion of glutinous substances, and the like. It is most conspicuous, however, if an attempt be made to push this separation to still smaller particles. Thus, in mortars, the pestle produces no effect after a certain degree of contusion, water does not penetrate small fissures, and the air itself, notwithstanding its subtilty, does not penetrate the pores of solid vessels at once, but only by long-continued insinuation.

Let the sixth be that which we term the motion of acquisition, or the motion of need.[m] It is that by which bodies placed amongst others of a heterogeneous and, as it were, hostile nature, if they meet with the means or opportunity of avoiding them, and uniting themselves with others of a more analogous nature, even when these latter are not closely allied to them, immediately seize and, as it were, select them, and appear to consider it as something acquired (whence we derive the name), and to have need of these latter bodies. For instance, gold, or any other metal in leaf, does not like the neighbourhood of air; if, therefore, they meet with any tangible and thick substance (such as the finger, paper, or the like), they immediately adhere to it, and are not easily torn from it. Paper, too, and cloth, and the like, do not agree with the air, which is inherent and mixed in their pores. They readily, therefore, imbibe water or other liquids, and get rid of the air. Sugar, or a sponge, dipped in water or wine, and though part of it be out of the water or wine, and at some height above it, will yet gradually absorb them.[n]

Hence an excellent rule is derived for the opening and dissolution of bodies; for (not to mention corrosive and strong waters, which force their way) if a body can be found which is more adapted, suited, and friendly to a given solid, than that with which it is by some necessity united, the given solid immediately opens and dissolves itself to receive the former, and excludes or removes the latter.[o] Nor is the effect or power of this motion confined to contact, for the electric energy (of which Gilbert and others after him have told so many fables) is only the energy excited in a body by gentle friction, and which does not endure the air, but prefers some tangible substance if there be any at hand.

Let the seventh be that which we term the motion of greater congregation, by which bodies are borne towards masses of a similar nature, for instance, heavy bodies towards the earth, light to the sphere of heaven. The schools termed this natural motion, by a superficial consideration of it, because produced by no external visible agent, which made them consider it innate in the substances; or perhaps because it does not cease, which is

---

[m] As far as this motion results from attraction and repulsion, it is only a simple consequence of the two last. *Ed.*

[n] These two cases are now resolved into the property of the capillary tubes, and present only another feature of the law of attraction. *Ed.*

[o] This is one of the most useful practical methods in chemistry at the present day.

little to be wondered at, since heaven and earth are always present, whilst the causes and sources of many other motions are sometimes absent and sometimes present. They therefore called this perpetual and proper, because it is never interrupted, but instantly takes place when the others are interrupted, and they called the others adscititious. The former, however, is in reality weak and slow, since it yields, and is inferior to the others as long as they act, unless the mass of the body be great; and although this motion have so filled men's minds, as almost to have obscured all others, yet they know but little about it, and commit many errors in its estimate.

Let the eighth be that which we term the motion of lesser congregation, by which the homogeneous parts in any body separate themselves from the heterogeneous and unite together, and whole bodies of a similar substance coalesce and tend towards each other, and are sometimes congregated, attracted, and meet, from some distance; thus in milk the cream rises after a certain time, and in wine the dregs and tartar sink; which effects are not to be attributed to gravity and levity only, so as to account for the rising of some parts and the sinking of others, but much more to the desire of the homogeneous bodies to meet and unite. This motion differs from that of need in two points: 1st, because the latter is the stimulus of a malignant and contrary nature, whilst in this of which we treat (if there be no impediment or restraint), the parts are united by their affinity, although there be no foreign nature to create a struggle; 2ndly, because the union is closer and more select. For in the other motion, bodies which have no great affinity unite, if they can but avoid the hostile body, whilst in this, substances which are connected by a decided kindred resemblance come together and are moulded into one. It is a motion existing in all compound bodies, and would be readily seen in each, if it were not confined and checked by the other affections and necessities of bodies which disturb the union.

This motion is usually confined in the three following manners: by the torpor of the bodies; by the power of the predominating body; by external motion. With regard to the first, it is certain that there is more or less sluggishness in tangible bodies, and an abhorrence of locomotion; so that unless excited they prefer remaining contented with their actual state, to placing themselves in a better position. There are three means of breaking through this sluggishness,—heat; the active power of a similar body; vivid and powerful motion. With regard to the first, heat is, on this account, defined as that which separates heterogeneous, and draws together homogeneous substances; a definition of the Peripatetics which is justly ridiculed by Gilbert, who says it is as if one were to define man to be that which sows wheat and plants vineyards; being only a definition deduced from effects, and those but partial. But it is still more to be blamed, because those effects, such as they are, are not a peculiar property of heat, but a mere accident (for cold, as we shall afterwards show, does the same), arising from the desire of the homogeneous parts to unite; the heat then assists them in breaking through that sluggishness which before restrained their desire. With regard to the assistance derived from the power of a similar body, it is most conspicuous in the magnet when armed with steel, for it excites in the steel a power of adhering to steel, as a homogeneous substance, the power of the magnet breaking through the sluggishness of the steel. With regard to the assistance of motion, it is seen in wooden arrows or points, which penetrate more deeply into wood than if they were tipped with iron, from the similarity of the substance, the swiftness of the motion breaking through the sluggishness of the wood; of which two last experiments we have spoken above in the aphorism on clandestine instances.[p]

The confinement of the motion of lesser congregation, which arises from the power of the predominant body, is shown in the decomposition of blood and urine by cold. For as long as these substances are filled with the active spirit, which regulates and restrains each of their component parts, as the predominant ruler of the whole, the several different parts do not collect themselves separately on account of the check; but as soon as that spirit has evaporated, or has been choked by the cold, then the decomposed parts unite, according to their natural desire. Hence it happens, that all bodies which contain a sharp spirit (as salts and the like), last without decomposition, owing to the permanent and durable power of the predominating and imperious spirit.

The confinement of the motion of lesser congregation, which arises from external motion, is very evident in that agitation of bodies which preserves them from putrefaction. For all putrefaction depends on the congregation of the homogeneous parts, whence, by degrees, there ensues a corruption of the first form (as it is called), and the generation of another. For the decomposition of the original form, which is itself the union of the homogeneous parts, precedes the putrefaction, which prepares the way for the generation of another. This decomposition, if not interrupted, is simple; but if there be various obstacles, putrefactions ensue, which are the rudiments of a new generation. But if (to come to our present point) a frequent agitation be excited by external motion, the motion towards union (which is delicate and gentle, and requires to be free from all external

[p] See Aphorism xxv.

influence) is disturbed, and ceases; which we perceive to be the case in innumerable instances. Thus, the daily agitation or flowing of water prevents putrefaction; winds prevent the air from being pestilent; corn turned about and shaken in granaries continues clean: in short, everything which is externally agitated will with difficulty rot internally.

We must not omit that union of the parts of bodies which is the principal cause of induration and desiccation. When the spirit or moisture, which has evaporated into spirit, has escaped from a porous body (such as wood, bone, parchment, and the like), the thicker parts are drawn together, and united with a greater effort, and induration or desiccation is the consequence; and this we attribute not so much to the motion of connection (in order to prevent a vacuum), as to this motion of friendship and union.

Union from a distance is rare, and yet is to be met with in more instances than are generally observed. We perceive it when one bubble dissolves another, when medicines attract humours from a similarity of substance, when one string moves another in unison with it on different instruments, and the like. We are of opinion that this motion is very prevalent also in animal spirits, but are quite ignorant of the fact. It is, however, conspicuous in the magnet, and magnetized iron. Whilst speaking of the motions of the magnet, we must plainly distinguish them, for there are four distinct powers or effects of the magnet which should not be confounded, although the wonder and astonishment of mankind has classed them together. 1. The attraction of the magnet to the magnet, or of iron to the magnet, or of magnetized iron to iron. 2. Its polarity towards the north and south, and its variation. 3. Its penetration through gold, glass, stone, and all other substances. 4. The communication of power from the mineral to iron, and from iron to iron, without any communication of the substances. Here, however, we only speak of the first. There is also a singular motion of attraction between quicksilver and gold, so that the gold attracts quicksilver even when made use of in ointment; and those who work surrounded by the vapours of quicksilver, are wont to hold a piece of gold in their mouths, to collect the exhalations, which would otherwise attack their heads and bones, and this piece soon grows white.[q] Let this suffice for the motion of lesser congregation.

Let the ninth be the magnetic motion, which, although of the nature of that last mentioned, yet, when operating at great distances, and on great masses, deserves a separate inquiry, especially if it neither begin in contact, as most motions of con-

[q] Query.

gregation do, nor end by bringing the substances into contact, as all do, but only raise them, and make them swell without any further effect. For if the moon raise the waters, or cause moist substances to swell, or if the starry sphere attract the planets towards their apogees, or the sun confine the planets Mercury and Venus to within a certain distance of his mass;[r] these motions do not appear capable of being classed under either of those of congregation, but to be, as it were, intermediately and imperfectly congregative, and thus to form a distinct species.

Let the tenth motion be that of avoidance, or that which is opposed to the motion of lesser congregation, by which bodies, with a kind of antipathy, avoid and disperse, and separate themselves from, or refuse to unite themselves with others of a hostile nature. For although this may sometimes appear to be an accidental motion, necessarily attendant upon that of the lesser congregation, because the homogeneous parts cannot unite, unless the heterogeneous be first removed and excluded, yet it is still to be classed separately,[s] and considered as a distinct species, because, in many cases, the desire of avoidance appears to be more marked than that of union.

It is very conspicuous in the excrements of animals, nor less, perhaps, in objects odious to particular senses, especially the smell and taste; for a fetid smell is rejected by the nose, so as to produce a sympathetic motion of expulsion at the mouth of the stomach; a bitter and rough taste is rejected by the palate or throat, so as to produce a sympathetic concussion and shivering of the head. This motion is visible also in other cases. Thus it is observed in some kinds of antiperistasis, as in the middle region of the air, the cold of which appears to be occasioned by the rejection of cold from the regions of the heavenly bodies; and also in the heat and combustion observed in subterranean spots, which appear to be owing to the rejection of heat from the centre of the earth. For heat and cold, when in small quantities, mutually destroy each other, whilst in larger quantities, like armies equally matched, they remove and eject each other in open conflict. It is said, also, that cinnamon and other perfumes retain their odour longer when placed near privies and foul places, because they will not unite and mix with stinks. It is well known that quicksilver, which would otherwise reunite into a complete mass, is prevented from so doing by man's spittle, pork lard, turpentine, and the like, from the little affinity of its

[r] Observe this approximation to Newton's theory.
[s] Those differences which are generated by the masses and respective distances of bodies are only differences of quantity, and not specific; consequently those three classes are only one. *Ed.*

parts with those substances, so that when surrounded by them it draws itself back, and its avoidance of these intervening obstacles is greater than its desire of reuniting itself to its homogeneous parts; which is what they term the mortification of quicksilver. Again, the difference in weight of oil and water is not the only reason for their refusing to mix, but it is also owing to the little affinity of the two; for spirits of wine, which are lighter than oil, mix very well with water. A very remarkable instance of the motion in question is seen in nitre, and crude bodies of a like nature, which abhor flame, as may be observed in gunpowder, quicksilver, and gold. The avoidance of one pole of the magnet by iron is not (as Gilbert has well observed), strictly speaking, an avoidance, but a conformity, or attraction to a more convenient situation.

Let the eleventh motion be that of assimilation, or self-multiplication, or simple generation, by which latter term we do not mean the simple generation of integral bodies, such as plants or animals, but of homogeneous bodies. By this motion homogeneous bodies convert those which are allied to them, or at least well disposed and prepared, into their own substance and nature. Thus flame multiplies itself over vapours and oily substances, and generates fresh flame; the air over water and watery substances multiplies itself and generates fresh air; the vegetable and animal spirit, over the thin particles of a watery or oleaginous spirit contained in its food, multiplies itself and generates fresh spirit; the solid parts of plants and animals, as the leaf, flower, the flesh, bone, and the like, each of them assimilate some part of the juices contained in their food, and generate a successive and daily substance. For let none rave with Paracelsus, who (blinded by his distillations) would have it, that nutrition takes place by mere separation, and that the eye, nose, brain, and liver, lie concealed in bread and meat, the root, leaf, and flower, in the juice of the earth; asserting that just as the artist brings out a leaf, flower, eye, nose, hand, foot, and the like, from a rude mass of stone or wood by the separation and rejection of what is superfluous; so the great artist within us brings out our several limbs and parts by separation and rejection. But to leave such trifling, it is most certain that all the parts of vegetables and animals, as well the homogeneous as organic, first of all attract those juices contained in their food, which are nearly common, or at least not very different, and then assimilate and convert them into their own nature. Nor does this assimilation, or simple generation, take place in animated bodies only, but the inanimate also participate in the same property (as we have observed of flame and air), and that languid spirit, which is contained in every tangible animated substance, is perpetually working upon the coarser parts, and converting them into spirit, which afterwards is exhaled, whence ensues a diminution of weight, and a desiccation of which we have spoken elsewhere.[1] Nor should we, in speaking of assimilation, neglect to mention the accretion which is usually distinguished from aliment, and which is observed when mud grows into a mass between stones, and is converted into a stony substance, and the scaly substance round the teeth is converted into one no less hard than the teeth themselves; for we are of opinion that there exists in all bodies a desire of assimilation, as well as of uniting with homogeneous masses. Each of these powers, however, is confined, although in different manners, and should be diligently investigated, because they are connected with the revival of old age. Lastly, it is worthy of observation, that in the nine preceding motions, bodies appear to aim at the mere preservation of their nature, whilst in this they attempt its propagation.

Let the twelfth motion be that of excitement, which appears to be a species of the last, and is sometimes mentioned by us under that name. It is, like that, a diffusive, communicative, transitive, and multiplying motion; and they agree remarkably in their effect, although they differ in their mode of action, and in their subject matter. The former proceeds imperiously, and with authority; it orders and compels the assimilated to be converted and changed into the assimilating body. The latter proceeds by art, insinuation, and stealth, inviting and disposing the excited towards the nature of the exciting body. The former both multiplies and transforms bodies and substances; thus a greater quantity of flame, air, spirit, and flesh is formed; but in the latter, the powers only are multiplied and changed, and heat, the magnetic power, and putrefaction, in the above instances, are increased. Heat does not diffuse itself when heating other bodies by any communication of the original heat, but only by exciting the parts of the heated body to that motion which is the form of heat, and of which we spoke in the first vintage of the nature of heat. Heat, therefore, is excited much less rapidly and readily in stone or metal than in air, on account of the inaptitude and sluggishness of those bodies in acquiring that motion, so that it is probable, that there may be some substances, towards the centre of the earth, quite incapable of being heated, on account of their density, which may deprive them of the spirit by which the motion of excitement is usually commenced. Thus also the magnet creates in the iron a new disposition of its parts, and a conformable motion, without losing any of its virtue. So the leaven of bread, yeast, rennet, and some poisons, excite and invite successive and continued motion in dough, beer, cheese, or

[1] See the citing instances, Aphorism xl.

the human body; not so much from the power of the exciting, as the predisposition and yielding of the excited body.

Let the thirteenth motion be that of impression, which is also a species of motion of assimilation, and the most subtle of diffusive motions. We have thought it right, however, to consider it as a distinct species, on account of its remarkable difference from the two last; for the simple motion of assimilation transforms the bodies themselves, so that if you remove the first agent, you diminish not the effect of those which succeed; thus, neither the first lighting of flame, nor the first conversion into air, are of any importance to the flame or air next generated. So, also, the motion of excitement still continues for a considerable time after the removal of the first agent, as in a heated body on the removal of the original heat, in the excited iron on the removal of the magnet, and in the dough on the removal of the leaven. But the motion of impression, although diffusive and transitive, appears, nevertheless, to depend on the first agent, so that upon the removal of the latter the former immediately fails and perishes; for which reason also it takes effect in a moment, or at least a very short space of time. We are wont to call the two former motions the motions of the generation of Jupiter, because when born they continue to exist; and the latter, the motion of the generation of Saturn, because it is immediately devoured and absorbed. It may be seen in three instances: 1. In the rays of light; 2. in the percussions of sounds; 3. in magnetic attractions as regards communication. For, on the removal of light, colours and all its other images disappear, as on the cessation of the first percussion and the vibration of the body, sound soon fails, and although sounds are agitated by the wind, like waves, yet it is to be observed, that the same sound does not last during the whole time of the reverberation. Thus, when a bell is struck, the sound appears to be continued for a considerable time, and one might easily be led into the mistake of supposing it to float and remain in the air during the whole time, which is most erroneous.[u] For the reverberation is not one identical sound, but the repetition of sounds, which is made manifest by stopping and confining the

---

[u] Aristotle's doctrine, that sound takes place when bodies strike the air, which the modern science of acoustics has completely established, was rejected by Bacon in a treatise upon the same subject: "The collision or thrusting of air," he says, "which they will have to be the cause of sound, neither denotes the form nor the latent process of sound, but is a term of ignorance and of superficial contemplation." To get out of the difficulty, he betook himself to his theory of spirits, a species of phenomena which he constantly introduces to give himself the air of explaining things he could not understand, or would not admit upon the hypothesis of his opponents. *Ed.*

sonorous body; thus, if a bell be stopped and held tightly, so as to be immovable, the sound fails, and there is no further reverberation, and if a musical string be touched after the first vibration, either with the finger (as in the harp), or a quill (as in the harpsichord), the sound immediately ceases. If the magnet be removed the iron falls. The moon, however, cannot be removed from the sea, nor the earth from a heavy falling body, and we can, therefore, make no experiment upon them; but the case is the same.

Let the fourteenth motion be that configuration or position, by which bodies appear to desire a peculiar situation, collocation, and configuration with others, rather than union or separation. This is a very abstruse notion, and has not been well investigated; and, in some instances, appears to occur almost without any cause, although we be mistaken in supposing this to be really the case. For if it be asked, why the heavens revolve from east to west, rather than from west to east, or why they turn on poles situate near the Bears, rather than round Orion or any other part of the heaven, such a question appears to be unreasonable, since these phenomena should be received as determinate and the objects of our experience. There are, indeed, some ultimate and self-existing phenomena in nature, but those which we have just mentioned are not to be referred to that class: for we attribute them to a certain harmony and consent of the universe, which has not yet been properly observed. But if the motion of the earth from west to east be allowed, the same question may be put, for it must also revolve round certain poles, and why should they be placed where they are, rather than elsewhere? The polarity and variation of the needle come under our present head. There is also observed in both natural and artificial bodies, especially solids rather than fluids, a particular collocation and position of parts, resembling hairs or fibres, which should be diligently investigated, since, without a discovery of them, bodies cannot be conveniently controlled or wrought upon. The eddies observable in liquids by which, when compressed, they successively raise different parts of their mass before they can escape, so as to equalize the pressure, is more correctly assigned to the motion of liberty.

Let the fifteenth motion be that of transmission or of passage, by which the powers of bodies are more or less impeded or advanced by the medium, according to the nature of the bodies and their effective powers, and also according to that of the medium. For one medium is adapted to light, another to sound, another to heat and cold, another to magnetic action, and so on with regard to the other actions.

Let the sixteenth be that which we term the royal or political motion, by which the predominant and governing parts of any body check, subdue, reduce, and regulate the others, and force them to unite, separate, stand still, move, or assume a certain position, not from any inclination of their own, but according to a certain order, and as best suits the convenience of the governing part, so that there is a sort of dominion and civil government exercised by the ruling part over its subjects. The motion is very conspicuous in the spirits of animals, where, as long as it is in force, it tempers all the motions of the other parts. It is found in a less degree in other bodies, as we have observed in blood and urine, which are not decomposed until the spirit, which mixed and retained their parts, has been emitted or extinguished. Nor is this motion peculiar to spirits only, although in most bodies the spirit predominates, owing to its rapid motion and penetration; for the grosser parts predominate in denser bodies, which are not filled with a quick and active spirit (such as exists in quicksilver or vitriol), so that unless this check or yoke be thrown off by some contrivance, there is no hope of any transformation of such bodies. And let not any one suppose that we have forgotten our subject, because we speak of predominance in this classification of motions, which is made entirely with the view of assisting the investigation of wrestling instances, or instances of predominance. For we do not now treat of the general predominance of motions or powers, but of that of parts in whole bodies, which constitutes the particular species here considered.

Let the seventeenth motion be the spontaneous motion of revolution, by which bodies having a tendency to move, and placed in a favourable situation, enjoy their peculiar nature, pursuing themselves and nothing else, and seeking, as it were, to embrace themselves. For bodies seem either to move without any limit, or to tend towards a limit, arrived at which they either revolve according to their peculiar nature, or rest. Those which are favourably situated, and have a tendency to motion, move in a circle with an eternal and unlimited motion; those which are favourably situated and abhor motion, rest. Those which are not favourably situated move in a straight line (as their shortest path), in order to unite with others of a congenial nature. This motion of revolution admits of nine differences: 1. with regard to the centre about which the bodies move; 2. the poles round which they move; 3. the circumference or orbit relatively to its distance from the centre; 4. the volocity, or greater or less speed with which they revolve; 5. the direction of the motion as from east to west, or the reverse; 6. the deviation from a perfect circle, by spiral lines at a greater or less distance from the centre; 7. the deviation from the circle, by spiral lines at a greater or less distance from the poles; 8. the greater or less distance of these spirals from each other; 9. and lastly, the variation of the poles if they be moveable; which, however, only affects revolution when circular. The motion in question is, according to common and long-received opinion, considered to be that of the heavenly bodies. There exists, however, with regard to this, a considerable dispute between some of the ancients as well as moderns, who have attributed a motion of revolution to the earth. A much more reasonable controversy, perhaps, exists (if it be not a matter beyond dispute), whether the motion in question (on the hypothesis of the earth's being fixed) is confined to the heavens, or rather descends and is communicated to the air and water. The rotation of missiles, as in darts, musket-balls, and the like, we refer entirely to the motion of liberty.

Let the eighteenth motion be that of trepidation,[a] to which (in the sense assigned to it by astronomers) we do not give much credit; but in our serious and general search after the tendencies of natural bodies, this motion occurs, and appears worthy of forming a distinct species. It is the motion of an (as it were) eternal captivity; when bodies, for instance, being placed not altogether according to their nature, and yet not exactly ill, constantly tremble, and are restless, not contented with their position, and yet not daring to advance. Such is the motion of the heart and pulse of animals, and it must necessarilly occur in all bodies which are situated in a mean state, between conveniences and inconveniences; so that being removed from their proper position, they strive to escape, are repulsed, and again continue to make the attempt.

Let the nineteenth and last motion be one which can scarcely be termed a motion, and yet is one; and which we may call the motion of repose, or of abhorrence of motion. It is by this motion that the earth stands by its own weight, whilst its extremes move towards the middle, not to an imaginary centre, but in order to unite. It is owing to the same tendency, that all bodies of considerable density abhor motion, and their only tendency is not to move, which nature they preserve, although excited and urged in a variety of ways to motion. But if they be compelled to move, yet do they always appear anxious to recover their former state, and to cease from motion, in which respect they certainly appear active, and attempt it with sufficient swiftness and rapidity, as if fatigued, and impatient of delay. We can only have a partial representation of this tendency, because with us every tangible substance is not only not con-

---

[a] The motion of trepidation, as Bacon calls it, was attributed by the ancient astronomers to the eight spheres, relative to the precession of the equinoxes. Galileo was the first to observe this kind of lunar motion. *Ed.*

densed to the utmost, but even some spirit is added, owing to the action and concocting influence of the heavenly bodies.

We have now, therefore, exhibited the species, or simple elements of the motions, tendencies, and active powers, which are most universal in nature; and no small portion of natural science has been thus sketched out. We do not, however, deny that other instances can perhaps be added, and our divisions changed according to some more natural order of things, and also reduced to a less number; in which respect we do not allude to any abstract classification, as if one were to say, that bodies desire the preservation, exaltation, propagation, or fruition of their nature; or, that motion tends to the preservation and benefit either of the universe (as in the case of those of resistance and connection), or of extensive wholes, as in the case of those of the greater congregation, revolution, and abhorrence of motion, or of particular forms, as in the case of the others. For although such remarks be just, yet, unless they terminate in matter and construction, according to true definitions, they are speculative, and of little use. In the mean time, our classification will suffice, and be of much use in the consideration of the predominance of powers, and examining the wrestling instances which constitute our present subject.

For of the motions here laid down, some are quite invincible, some more powerful than others, which they confine, check, and modify; others extend to a greater distance, others are more immediate and swift, others strengthen, increase, and accelerate the rest.

The motion of resistance is most adamantine and invincible. We are yet in doubt whether such be the nature of that of connection; for we cannot with certainty determine whether there be a vacuum, either extensive or intermixed with matter. Of one thing, however, we are satisfied, that the reason assigned by Leucippus and Democritus for the introduction of a vacuum (namely, that the same bodies could not otherwise comprehend, and fill greater and less spaces) is false. For there is clearly a folding of matter, by which it wraps and unwraps itself in space within certain limits, without the intervention of a vacuum. Nor is there two thousand times more of vacuum in air than in gold, as there should be on this hypothesis; a fact demonstrated by the very powerful energies of fluids (which would otherwise float like fine dust *in vacuo*), and many other proofs. The other motions direct, and are directed by each other, according to their strength, quantity, excitement, emission, or the assistance or impediments they meet with.

For instance; some armed magnets hold and support iron of sixty times their own weight; so far does the motion of lesser congregation predominate over that of the greater; but if the weight be increased, it yields. A lever of a certain strength will raise a given weight, and so far the motion of liberty predominates over that of the greater congregation, but if the weight be greater, the former motion yields. A piece of leather stretched to a certain point does not break, and so far the motion of continuity predominates over that of tension, but if the tension be greater, the leather breaks, and the motion of continuity yields. A certain quantity of water flows through a chink, and so far the motion of greater congregation predominates over that of continuity, but if the chink be smaller it yields. If a musket be charged with ball and powdered sulphur alone, and fire be applied, the ball is not discharged, in which case the motion of greater congregation overcomes that of matter; but when gunpowder is used, the motion of matter in the sulphur predominates, being assisted by that motion, and the motion of avoidance in the nitre; and so of the rest. For wrestling instances (which show the predominance of powers, and in what manner and proportion they predominate and yield) must be searched for with active and industrious diligence.

The methods and nature of this yielding must also be diligently examined, as for instance, whether the motions completely cease, or exert themselves, but are constrained. For in the bodies with which we are acquainted, there is no real but an apparent rest, either in the whole or in parts. This apparent rest is occasioned either by equilibrium, or the absolute predominance of motions. By equilibrium, as in the scales of the balance, which rest if the weights be equal. By predominance, as in perforated jars, in which the water rests, and is prevented from falling by the predominance of the motion of connection. It is, however, to be observed (as we have said before), how far the yielding motions exert themselves. For if a man be held stretched out on the ground against his will, with arms and legs bound down, or otherwise confined, and yet strive with all his power to get up, the struggle is not the less, although ineffectual. The real state of the case (namely, whether the yielding motion be, as it were, annihilated by the predominance, or there be rather a continued, although an invisible effort) will, perhaps, appear in the concurrence of motions, although it escape our notice in their conflict. For instance; let an experiment be made with muskets; whether a musket-ball, at its utmost range in a straight line, or (as it is commonly called) point blank, strike with less force when projected upwards, where the motion of the blow is simple, than when projected downwards, where the motion of gravity concurs with the blow.

The rules of such instances of predominance as occur should be collected: such as the following; the more general the desired advantage is, the stronger will be the motion; the motion of connection, for instance, which relates to the intercourse of the parts of the universe, is more powerful than that of gravity, which relates to the intercourse of dense bodies only. Again, the desire of a private good does not in general prevail against that of a public one, except where the quantities are small. Would that such were the case in civil matters!

XLIX. In the twenty-fifth rank of prerogative instances we will place suggesting instances; such as suggest, or point out, that which is advantageous to mankind; for bare power and knowledge in themselves exalt rather than enrich human nature. We must, therefore, select from the general store, such things as are most useful to mankind. We shall have a better opportunity of discussing these when we treat of the application to practice, besides, in the work of interpretation, we leave room, on every subject, for the human or optative chart; for it is a part of science to make judicious inquiries and wishes.

L. In the twenty-sixth rank of prerogative instances we will place the generally useful instances. They are such as relate to various points, and frequently occur, sparing by that means considerable labour and new trials. The proper place for treating of instruments and contrivances, will be that in which we speak of the application to practice, and the methods of experiment. All that has hitherto been ascertained, and made use of, will be described in the particular history of each art. At present, we will subjoin a few general examples of the instances in question.

Man acts, then, upon natural bodies (besides merely bringing them together or removing them) by seven principal methods: 1. By the exclusion of all that impedes and disturbs; 2. by compression, extension, agitation, and the like; 3. by heat and cold; 4. by detention in a suitable place; 5. by checking or directing motion; 6. by peculiar harmonies; 7. by a seasonable and proper alternation, series, and succession of all these, or, at least, of some of them.

1. With regard to the first,—common air, which is always at hand, and forces its admission, as also the rays of the heavenly bodies, create much distu. oance. Whatever, therefore, tends to exclude them may well be considered as generally useful. The substance and thickness of vessels in which bodies are placed when prepared for operations may be referred to this head. So also may the accurate methods of closing vessels by consolidation, or the *lutum sapientiæ*, as the chemists call it. The exclusion of air by means of liquids at the extremity is also very useful, as when they pour oil on wine, or the juices of herbs, which by spreading itself upon the top like a cover, preserves them uninjured from the air. Powders, also, are serviceable, for although they contain air mixed up in them, yet they ward off the power of the mass of circumambient air, which is seen in the preservation of grapes and other fruits in sand or flour. Wax, honey, pitch, and other resinous bodies, are well used in order

to make the exclusion more perfect, and to remove the air and celestial influence. We have sometimes made an experiment by placing a vessel or other bodies in quicksilver, the most dense of all substances capable of being poured round others. Grottos and subterraneous caves are of great use in keeping off the effects of the sun, and the predatory action of air, and in the north of Germany are used for granaries. The depositing of bodies at the bottom of water may be also mentioned here; and I remember having heard of some bottles of wine being let down into a deep well in order to cool them, but left there by chance, carelessness, and forgetfulness for several years, and then taken out; by which means the wine not only escaped becoming flat or dead, but was much more excellent in flavour, arising (as it appears) from a more complete mixture of its parts. But if the case require that bodies should be sunk to the bottom of water, as in rivers or the sea, and yet should not touch the water, nor be inclosed in sealed vessels, but surrounded only by air, it would be right to use that vessel which has been sometimes employed under water above ships that have sunk, in order to enable the divers to remain below and breathe occasionally by turns. It was of the following nature:—A hollow tub of metal was formed, and sunk so as to have its bottom parallel with the surface of the water; it thus carried down with it to the bottom of the sea all the air contained in the tub. It stood upon three feet (like a tripod), being of rather less height than a man, so that, when the diver was in want of breath, he could put his head into the hollow of the tub, breathe, and then continue his work. We hear that some sort of boat or vessel has now been invented, capable of carrying men some distance under water. Any bodies, however, can easily be suspended under some such vessel as we have mentioned, which has occasioned our remarks upon the experiment.

Another advantage of the careful and hermetical closing of bodies is this,—not only the admission of external air is prevented (of which we have treated), but the spirit of bodies also is prevented from making its escape, which is an internal operation. For any one operating on natural bodies must be certain as to their quantity, and that nothing has evaporated or escaped, since profound alterations take place in bodies, when art prevents the loss or escape of any portion, whilst nature prevents their annihilation. With regard to this circumstance, a false idea has prevailed (which if true would make us despair of preserving quantity without diminution), namely, that the spirit of bodies, and air when rarefied by a great degree of heat, cannot be so kept in by being inclosed in any vessel as not to escape by the small pores. Men are led into this idea by the common experiments of a cup inverted over water, with a candle or piece of lighted paper in it, by which the water is drawn up, and of those cups which, when heated, draw up the flesh. For they think that in each experiment the rarefied air escapes, and that its quantity is therefore diminished, by which means the water or flesh rises by the motion of connection. This is, however, most incorrect. For the air is not diminished in quantity, but contracted in dimensions,[y] nor does this motion of the rising of the water begin till the flame is extinguished, or the air cooled, so that physicians place cold sponges, moistened with water, on the cups, in order to increase their attraction. There is, therefore, no reason why men should fear much from the ready escape of air: for although it be true that the most solid bodies have their pores, yet neither air, nor spirit, readily suffers itself to be rarefied to such an extreme degree; just as water will not escape by a small chink.

2. With regard to the second of the seven above-mentioned methods, we must especially observe, that compression and similar violence have a most powerful effect either in producing locomotion, and other motions of the same nature, as may be observed in engines and projectiles, or in destroying the organic body, and those qualities, which consist entirely in motion (for all life, and every description of flame and ignition are destroyed by compression, which also injures and deranges every machine); or in destroying those qualities which consist in position and a coarse difference of parts, as in colours; for the colour of a flower when whole, differs from that it presents when bruised, and the same may be observed of whole and powdered amber; or in tastes, for the taste of a pear before it is ripe, and of the same pear when bruised and softened, is different, since it becomes perceptibly more sweet. But such violence is of little avail in the more noble transformations and changes of homogeneous bodies, for they do not, by such means, acquire any constantly and permanently new state, but one that is transitory, and always struggling to return to its former habit and freedom. It would not, however, be useless to make some more diligent experiments with regard to this; whether, for instance, the condensation of a perfectly homogeneous body (such as air, water, oil, and the like) or their rarefaction, when effected by violence, can become permanent, fixed, and, as it were, so changed, as to become a nature. This might at first be tried by simple perseverance, and then by means of helps and harmonies. It might readily have been attempted (if we had but thought of

---

[y] Part of the air is expanded and escapes, and part is consumed by the flame. When condensed, therefore, by the cold application, it cannot offer sufficient resistance to the external atmosphere to prevent the liquid or flesh from being forced into the glass

it), when we condensed water (as was mentioned above), by hammering and compression, until it burst out. For we ought to have left the flattened globe untouched for some days, and then to have drawn off the water, in order to try whether it would have immediately occupied the same dimensions as it did before the condensation. If it had not done so, either immediately, or soon afterwards, the condensation would have appeared to have been rendered constant; if not, it would have appeared that a restitution took place, and that the condensation had been transitory. Something of the same kind might have been tried with the glass eggs; the egg should have been sealed up suddenly and firmly, after a complete exhaustion of the air, and should have been allowed to remain so for some days, and it might then have been tried whether, on opening the aperture, the air would be drawn in with a hissing noise, or whether as much water would be drawn into it when immersed, as would have been drawn into it at first, if it had not continued sealed. For it is probable (or, at least, worth making the experiment) that this might have happened, or might happen, because perseverance has a similar effect upon bodies which are a little less homogeneous. A stick bent together for some time does not rebound, which is not owing to any loss of quantity in the wood during the time, for the same would occur (after a larger time) in a plate of steel, which does not evaporate. If the experiment of simple perseverance should fail, the matter should not be given up, but other means should be employed. For it would be no small advantage, if bodies could be endued with fixed and constant natures by violence. Air could then be converted into water by condensation, with other similar effects; for man is more the master of violent motions than of any other means.

3. The third of our seven methods is referred to that great practical engine of nature, as well as of art, cold and heat. Here, man's power limps, as it were, with one leg. For we possess the heat of fire, which is infinitely more powerful and intense than that of the sun (as it reaches us), and that of animals. But we want cold,[1] except such as we can obtain in winter, in caverns, or by surrounding objects with snow and ice, which, perhaps, may be compared in degree with the noontide heat of the sun in tropical countries, increased by the reflection of mountains and walls. For this degree of heat and cold can be borne for a short period only by animals, yet it is nothing compared with the heat of a burning furnace, or the corresponding degree of cold.[2] Everything with us has a tendency to

[1] Heat can now be abstracted by a very simple process, till the degree of cold be of almost any required intensity.
[2] It is impossible to compare a degree of heat with a degree of cold,

become rarefied, dry, and wasted, and nothing to become condensed or soft, except by mixtures, and, as it were, spurious methods. Instances of cold, therefore, should be searched for most diligently, such as may be found by exposing bodies upon buildings in a hard frost, in subterraneous caverns, by surrounding bodies with snow and ice in deep places excavated for that purpose, by letting bodies down into wells, by burying bodies in quicksilver and metals, by immersing them in streams which petrify wood, by burying them in the earth (which the Chinese are reported to do with their china, masses of which, made for that purpose, are said to remain in the ground for forty or fifty years, and to be transmitted to their heirs as a sort of artificial mine), and the like. The condensations which take place in nature, by means of cold, should also be investigated, that by learning their causes, they may be introduced into the arts; such as are observed in the exudation of marble and stones, in the dew upon the panes of glass in a room towards morning after a frosty night, in the formation and the gathering of vapours under the earth into water, whence spring fountains, and the like.

Besides the substances which are cold to the touch, there are others which have also the effect of cold, and condense; they appear, however, to act only upon the bodies of animals, and scarcely any further. Of these we have many instances, in medicines and plasters. Some condense the flesh and tangible parts, such as astringent and inspissating medicines, others the spirits, such as soporifics. There are two modes of condensing the spirits, by soporifics or provocatives to sleep; the one by calming the motion, the other by expelling the spirit. The violet, dried roses, lettuces, and other benign or mild remedies, by their friendly and gently cooling vapours, invite the spirits to unite, and restrain their violent and perturbed motion. Rosewater, for instance, applied to the nostrils in fainting fits, causes the resolved and relaxed spirits to recover themselves, and, as it were, cherishes them. But opiates, and the like, banish the spirits by their malignant and hostile quality. If they be applied, therefore, externally, the spirits immediately quit the part and no longer readily flow into it; but if they be taken internally, their vapour, mounting to the head, expels, in all directions, the spirits contained in the ventricles of the brain, and

without the assumption of some arbitrary test, to which the degrees are to be referred. In the next sentence Bacon appears to have taken the power of animal life to support heat or cold as the test, and then the comparison can only be between the degree of heat or of cold that will produce death.

The zero must be arbitrary which divides equally a certain degree heat from a certain degree of cold.

since these spirits retreat, but cannot escape, they consequently meet and are condensed, and are sometimes completely extinguished and suffocated; although the same opiates, when taken in moderation, by a secondary accident (the condensation which succeeds their union), strengthen the spirits, render them more robust, and check their useless and inflammatory motion, by which means they contribute not a little to the cure of diseases, and the prolongation of life.

The preparations of bodies, also, for the reception of cold should not be omitted, such as that water a little warmed is more easily frozen than that which is quite cold, and the like.

Moreover, since nature supplies cold so sparingly, we must act like the apothecaries, who, when they cannot obtain any simple ingredient, take a succedaneum, or *quid pro quo*, as they term it, such as aloes for xylobalsamum, cassia for cinnamon. In the same manner we should look diligently about us, to ascertain whether there may be any substitutes for cold, that is to say, in what other manner condensation can be effected, which is the peculiar operation of cold. Such condensations appear hitherto to be of four kinds only. 1. By simple compression, which is of little avail towards permanent condensation, on account of the elasticity of substances, but may still however be of some assistance. 2. By the contraction of the coarser, after the escape or departure of the finer parts of a given body; as is exemplified in induration by fire, and the repeated heating and extinguishing of metals, and the like. 3. By the cohesion of the most solid homogeneous parts of a given body, which were previously separated, and mixed with others less solid, as in the return of sublimated mercury to its simple state, in which it occupies much less space than it did in powder, and the same may be observed of the cleansing of all metals from their dross. 4. By harmony or the application of substances which condense by some latent power. These harmonies are as yet but rarely observed, at which we cannot be surprised, since there is little to hope for from their investigation, unless the discovery of forms and confirmation be attained. With regard to animal bodies, it is not to be questioned that there are many internal and external medicines which condense by harmony, as we have before observed, but this action is rare in inanimate bodies. Written accounts, as well as report, have certainly spoken of a tree in one of the Tercera or Canary Islands (for I do not exactly recollect which) that drips perpetually, so as to supply the inhabitants, in some degree, with water; and Paracelsus says that the herb called *ros solis* is filled with dew at noon, whilst the sun gives out its greatest heat, and all other herbs around it are dry. We treat both these accounts as fables; they would, however, if true, be of the most important service, and most worthy of examination. As to the honey-dew, resembling manna, which is found in May on the leaves of the oak, we are of opinion that it is not condensed by any harmony or peculiarity of the oak leaf, but that whilst it falls equally upon other leaves it is retained and continues on those of the oak, because their texture is closer, and not so porous as that of most of the other leaves.[b]

With regard to heat, man possesses abundant means and power; but his observation and inquiry are defective in some respects, and those of the greatest importance, notwithstanding the boasting of quacks. For the effects of intense heat are examined and observed, whilst those of a more gentle degree of heat, being of the most frequent occurrence in the paths of nature, are, on that very account, least known. We see, therefore, the furnaces, which are most esteemed, employed in increasing the spirits of bodies to a great extent, as in the strong acids, and some chymical oils; whilst the tangible parts are hardened, and, when the volatile part has escaped, become sometimes fixed; the homogeneous parts are separated, and the heterogeneous incorporated and agglomerated in a coarse lump; and (what is chiefly worthy of remark) the junction of compound bodies, and the more delicate conformations are destroyed and confounded. But the operation of a less violent heat should be tried and investigated, by which more delicate mixtures, and regular conformations may be produced and elicited, according to the example of nature, and in imitation of the effect of the sun, which we have alluded to in the aphorism on the instances of alliance. For the works of nature are carried on in much smaller portions, and in more delicate and varied positions than those of fire, as we now employ it. But man will then appear to have really augmented his power, when the works of nature can be imitated in species, perfected in power, and varied in quantity; to which should be added the acceleration in point of time. Rust, for instance, is the result of a long process, but *crocus martis* is obtained immediately; and the same may be observed of natural verdigris and ceruse. Crystal is formed slowly, whilst glass is blown immediately: stones increase slowly, whilst bricks are baked immediately, &c. In the mean time (with regard to our present subject) every different species of heat should, with its peculiar effects, be diligently collected and inquired into; that of the heavenly bodies, whether their rays be direct, reflected, or refracted, or condensed by a burning-glass; that of lightning, flame, and ignited charcoal; that of fire of different materials, either open or confined, straitened or overflowing, qualified by the different forms of the furnaces, excited by the bellows, or quiescent, removed to a greater or less

[b] It may often be observed on the leaves of the lime and other trees.

distance, or passing through different media; moist heats, such as the *balneum Mariæ*, and the dunghill; the external and internal heat of animals; dry heats, such as the heat of ashes, lime, warm sand; in short, the nature of every kind of heat, and its degrees.

We should, however, particularly attend to the investigation and discovery of the effects and operations of heat, when made to approach and retire by degrees, regularly, periodically, and by proper intervals of space and time. For this systematical inequality is in truth the daughter of heaven and mother of generation, nor can any great result be expected from a vehement, precipitate, or desultory heat. For this is not only most evident in vegetables, but in the wombs of animals also there arises a great inequality of heat, from the motion, sleep, food, and passions of the female. The same inequality prevails in those subterraneous beds where metals and fossils are perpetually forming, which renders yet more remarkable the ignorance of some of the reformed alchymists, who imagined they could attain their object by the equable heat of lamps, or the like, burning uniformly. Let this suffice concerning the operation and effects of heat; nor is it time for us to investigate them thoroughly before the forms and conformations of bodies have been further examined and brought to light. When we have determined upon our models, we may seek, apply, and arrange our instruments.

4. The fourth mode of action is by continuance, the very steward and almoner, as it were, of nature. We apply the term continuance to the abandonment of a body to itself for an observable time, guarded and protected in the meanwhile from all external force. For the internal motion then commences to betray and exert itself when the external and adventitious is removed. The effects of time, however, are far more delicate than those of fire. Wine, for instance, cannot be clarified by fire as it is by continuance. Nor are the ashes produced by combustion so fine as the particles dissolved or wasted by the lapse of ages. The incorporations and mixtures, which are hurried by fire, are very inferior to those obtained by continuance; and the various conformations assumed by bodies left to themselves, such as mouldiness, &c., are put a stop to by fire or a strong heat. It is not, in the mean time, unimportant to remark that there is a certain degree of violence in the motion of bodies entirely confined; for the confinement impedes the proper motion of the body. Continuance in an open vessel, therefore, is useful for separations, and in one hermetically sealed for mixtures, that in a vessel partly closed, but admitting the air, for putrefaction. But instances of the operation and effect of continuance must be collected diligently from every quarter

5. The direction of motion (which is the fifth method of action) is of no small use. We adopt this term, when speaking of a body which, meeting with another, either arrests, repels, allows, or directs its original motion. This is the case principally in the figure and position of vessels. An upright cone, for instance, promotes the condensation of vapour in alembics, but when reversed, as in inverted vessels, it assists the refining of sugar. Sometimes a curved form, or one alternately contracted and dilated, is required. Strainers may be ranged under this head, where the opposed body opens a way for one portion of another substance and impedes the rest. Nor is this process or any other direction of motion carried on externally only, but sometimes by one body within another. Thus, pebbles are thrown into water to collect the muddy particles, and syrups are refined by the white of an egg, which glues the grosser particles together so as to facilitate their removal. Telesius, indeed, rashly and ignorantly enough attributes the formation of animals to this cause, by means of the channels and folds of the womb. He ought to have observed a similar formation of the young in eggs which have no wrinkles or inequalities. One may observe a real result of this direction of motion in casting and modelling.

6. The effects produced by harmony and aversion (which is the sixth method) are frequently buried in obscurity; for these occult and specific properties (as they are termed), the sympathies and antipathies, are for the most part but a corruption of philosophy. Nor can we form any great expectation of the discovery of the harmony which exists between natural objects, before that of their forms and simple conformations, for it is nothing more than the symmetry between these forms and conformations.

The greater and more universal species of harmony are not, however, so wholly obscure, and with them, therefore, we must commence. The first and principal distinction between them is this; that some bodies differ considerably in the abundance and rarity of their substance, but correspond in their conformation; others, on the contrary, correspond in the former and differ in the latter. Thus the chymists have well observed, that in their trial of first principles sulphur and mercury, as it were, pervade the universe; their reasoning about salt, however, is absurd, and merely introduced to comprise earthy dry fixed bodies. In the other two, indeed, one of the most universal species of natural harmony manifests itself. Thus there is a correspondence between sulphur, oil, greasy exhalations, flame, and, perhaps, the substance of the stars. On the other hand, there is a like correspondence between mercury, water, aqueous vapour, air, and perhaps, pure inter-sideral æther. Yet do these two quaternions, or great natural tribes (each within its own limits), differ immensely in quantity and density of substance, whilst they generally agree in conformation, as is manifest in many instances. On the other hand, the metals agree in such quantity and density (especially when compared with vegetables, &c.), but differ in many respects in conformation. Animals and vegetables, in like manner, vary in their almost infinite modes of conformation, but range within very limited degrees of quantity and density of substance.

The next most general correspondence is that between individual bodies and those which supply them by way of menstruum or support. Inquiry, therefore, must be made as to the climate, soil, and depth at which each metal is generated, and the same of gems, whether produced in rocks or mines, also as to the soil in which particular trees, shrubs, and herbs, mostly grow and, as it were, delight; and as to the best species of manure, whether dung, chalk, sea sand, or ashes, &c., and their different propriety and advantage according to the variety of soils. So also the grafting and setting of trees and plants (as regards the readiness of grafting one particular species on another) depends very much upon harmony, and it would be amusing to try an experiment I have lately heard of, in grafting forest trees (garden trees alone having hitherto been adopted), by which means the leaves and fruit are enlarged, and the trees produce more shade. The specific food of animals again should be observed, as well as that which cannot be used. Thus the carnivorous cannot be fed on herbs, for which reason the order of feuilletans, the experiment having been made, has nearly vanished; human nature being incapable of supporting their regimen, although the human will has more power over the bodily frame than that of other animals. The different kinds of putrefaction from which animals are generated should be noted.

The harmony of principal bodies with those subordinate to them (such indeed may be deemed those we have alluded to above) are sufficiently manifest, to which may be added those that exist between different bodies and their objects, and, since these latter are more apparent, they may throw great light when well observed and diligently examined upon those which are more latent.

The more internal harmony and aversion, or friendship and enmity (for superstition and folly have rendered the terms of sympathy and antipathy almost disgusting), have been either falsely assigned, or mixed with fable, or most rarely discovered from neglect. For if one were to allege that there is an enmity between the vine and the cabbage, because they will not come up well when sown together, there is a sufficient reason for it in the succulent and absorbent nature of each plant, so that the one defrauds the other. Again, if one were to say that there is a harmony and friendship between the corn and the corn-flower, or the wild poppy, because the latter seldom grow anywhere but in cultivated soils, he ought rather to say, there is an enmity between them, for the poppy and the cornflower are produced and created by those juices which the corn has left and rejected, so that the sowing of the corn prepares the ground for their production. And there are a vast number of similar false assertions. As for fables, they must be totally exterminated. There remains, then, but a scanty supply of such species of harmony as has borne the test of experiment, such as that between the magnet and iron, gold and quicksilver, and the like. In chemical experiments on metals, however, there are some others worthy of notice, but the greatest abundance (where the whole are so few in numbers) is discovered in certain medicines, which, from their occult and specific qualities (as they are termed), affect particular limbs, humours, diseases, or constitutions. Nor should we omit the harmony between the motion and phenomena of the moon, and their effects on lower bodies, which may be brought together by an accurate and honest selection from the experiments of agriculture, navigation, and medicine, or of other sciences. By as much as these general instances, however, of more latent harmony, are rare, with so much the more diligence are they to be inquired after, through tradition, and faithful and honest reports, but without rashness and credulity, with an anxious and, as it were, hesitating degree of reliance. There remains one species of harmony which, though simple in its mode of action, is yet most valuable in its use, and must by no means be omitted, but rather diligently investigated. It is the ready or difficult coition or union of bodies in composition, or simple juxta-position. For some bodies readily and willingly mix, and are incorporated, others tardily and perversely; thus powders mix best with water, chalk and ashes with oils, and the like. Nor are these instances of readiness and aversion to mixture to be alone collected, but others, also, of the collocation, distribution, and digestion of the parts when mingled, and the predominance after the mixture is complete

7. Lastly, there remains the seventh, and last of the seven, modes of action; namely, that by the alternation and interchange of the other six; but of this, it will not be the right time to offer any examples, until some deeper investigation shall have taken place of each of the others. The series, or chain of this alternation, in its mode of application to separate effects, is no less powerful in its operation, than difficult to be traced. But men are possessed with the most extreme impatience, both of such inquiries, and their practical application, although it be the clue of the labyrinth in all greater works. Thus far of the generally useful instances.

LI. The twenty-seventh and last place we will assign to the magical instances, a term which we apply to those where the matter or efficient agent is scanty or small, in comparison with the grandeur of the work or effect produced; so that even when common they appear miraculous, some at first sight, others even upon more attentive observation. Nature, however, of herself, supplies these but sparingly. What she will do when her whole store is thrown open, and after the discovery of forms, processes, and conformation, will appear hereafter. As far as we can yet conjecture, these magic effects are produced in three ways, either by self-multiplication, as in fire, and the poisons termed specific, and the motions transferred and multiplied from wheel to wheel; or by the excitement, or, as it were, invitation of another substance, as in the magnet, which excites innumerable needles without losing or diminishing its power; and again in leaven, and the like; or by the excess of rapidity of one species of motion over another, as has been observed in the case of gunpowder, cannon, and mines. The two former require an investigation of harmonies, the latter of a measure of motion. Whether there be any mode of changing bodies *per minima* (as it is termed), and transferring the delicate conformations of matter, which is of importance in all transformations of bodies, so as to enable art to effect, in a short time, that which nature works out by divers expedients, is a point of which we have as yet no indication. But, as we aspire to the extremest and highest results in that which is solid and true, so do we ever detest, and, as far as in us lies, expel all that is empty and vain.

LII. Let this suffice as to the respective dignity of prerogatives of instances. But it must be noted, that in this our organ, we treat of logic, and not of philosophy. Seeing, however, that our logic instructs and informs the understanding, in order that it may not, with the small hooks, as it were, of the mind, catch at, and grasp mere abstractions, but rather actually penetrate nature, and discover the properties and effects of bodies, and the determinate laws of their substance (so that this science of ours springs from the nature of things, as well as from that of the mind); it is not to be wondered at, if it have been continually interspersed and illustrated with natural observations and experiments, as instances of our method. The prerogative instances are, as appears from what has preceded, twenty-seven in number, and are termed, solitary instances, migrating instances, conspicuous instances, clandestine instances, constitutive instances, similar instances, singular instances, deviating instances, bordering instances, instances of power, accompanying and hostile instances, subjunctive instances, instances of alliance, instances of the cross, instances of divorce, instances of the gate, citing instances, instances of the road, supplementary instances, lancing instances, instances of the rod, instances of the course, doses of nature, wrestling instances, suggesting instances, generally useful instances, and magical instances. The advantage, by which these instances excel the more ordinary, regards specifically either theory or practice, or both. With regard to theory, they assist either the senses or the understanding; the senses, as in the five instances of the lamp; the understanding, either by expediting the exclusive mode of arriving at the form, as in solitary instances, or by confining, and more immediately indicating the affirmative, as in the migrating, conspicuous, accompanying, and subjunctive instances; or by elevating the understanding, and leading it to general and common natures, and that either immediately, as in the clandestine and singular instances, and those of alliance; or very nearly so, as in the constitutive; or still less so, as in the similar instances; or by correcting the understanding of its habits, as in the deviating instances; or by leading to the grand form or fabric of the universe, as in the bordering instances; or by guarding it from false forms and causes, as in those of the cross and of divorce. With regard to practice, they either point it out, or measure, or elevate it. They point it out, either by showing where we must commence in order not to repeat the labours of others, as in the instances of power; or by inducing us to aspire to that which may be possible, as in the suggesting instances; the four mathematical instances measure it. The generally useful and the magical elevate it.

Again, out of these twenty-seven instances, some must be collected immediately, without waiting for a particular investigation of properties. Such are the similar, singular, deviating, and bordering instances, those of power, and of the gate, and suggesting, generally useful, and magical instances; for these either assist and cure the understanding and senses, or furnish our general practice. The remainder are to be collected when we finish our synoptical tables for the work of the interpreter, upon any particular nature; for these instances, honoured and gifted with such prerogatives, are like the soul amid the vulgar crowd of instances, and (as we from the first observed) a few of them are worth a multitude of the others. When, therefore, we are forming our tables they must be searched out with the greatest zeal, and placed in the table. And, since mention must be made of them in what follows, a treatise upon their nature has necessarily been prefixed. We must next, however, proceed to the supports and corrections of induction, and thence to concretes, the latent process, and latent conformations, and the other matters, which we have enumerated in their order in the twenty-first aphorism, in order that, like good and faithful guardians, we may yield up their fortune to mankind, upon the emancipation and majority of their understanding; from which must necessarily follow an improvement of their estate, and an increase of their power over nature. For man, by the fall, lost at once his state of innocence, and his empire over creation, both of which can be partially recovered even in this life, the first by religion and faith, the second by the arts and sciences. For creation did not become entirely and utterly rebellious by the curse, but in consequence of the Divine decree, "in the sweat of thy brow shalt thou eat bread," she is compelled by our labours (not assuredly by our disputes or magical ceremonies), at length, to afford mankind in some degree his bread, that is to say, to supply man's daily wants.

THE END.

CATALOGUE OF
BOHN'S LIBRARIES.

N.B.—It is requested that all orders be accompanied by payment. Books are sent carriage free on the receipt of the published price in stamps or otherwise.

The Works to which the letters 'N. S.' (denoting New Style) are appended are kept in neat cloth bindings of various colours, as well as in the regular Library style. All Orders are executed in the New binding, unless the contrary is expressly stated.

Complete Sets or Separate Volumes can be had at short notice, half-bound in calf or morocco.

New Volumes of Standard Works in the various branches of Literature are constantly being added to this Series, which is already unsurpassed in respect to the number, variety, and cheapness of the Works contained in it. The Publishers have to announce the following Volumes as recently issued or now in preparation:—

Seneca's Minor Works. Translated by Aubrey Stewart, M.A. *[In the press.*

Elze's Life of Shakespeare. Translated by L. Dora Schmitz. *[In the press.*

Julian the Apostate. By the Rev. C. W. King. *[In the press.*

Adam Smith's Wealth of Nations. Printed from the Fourth Edition, with Introduction by E. Belfort Bax. *[Ready, see p.* 8.

Dunlop's History of Fiction. With Introduction and Supplement bringing the Work down to recent times. By Henry Wilson. 3 vols. *[In the press.*

Letters and Works of Lady Mary Wortley Montagu. *[Ready, see p.* 7.

Heaton's Concise History of Painting. *[In the press.*

Lucian's Dialogues of the Gods, the Sea Gods, and the Dead. *[In the press.*

Strickland's Lives of the Tudor and Stuart Princesses. In one vol. *[In the press.*

February, 1888.

BOHN'S LIBRARIES.

STANDARD LIBRARY.

317 *Vols. at* 3*s.* 6*d. each, excepting those marked otherwise.* (56*l.* 1*s. per set.*)

ADDISON'S Works. Notes of Bishop Hurd. Short Memoir, Portrait, and 8 Plates of Medals. 6 vols. *N. S.* This is the most complete edition of Addison's Works issued.

ALFIERI'S Tragedies. In English Verse. With Notes, Arguments, and Introduction, by E. A. Bowring, C.B. 2 vols. *N. S.*

AMERICAN POETRY. — *See* Poetry *of America.*

BACON'S Moral and Historical Works, including Essays, Apophthegms, Wisdom of the Ancients, New Atlantis, Henry VII., Henry VIII., Elizabeth, Henry Prince of Wales, History of Great Britain, Julius Cæsar, and Augustus Cæsar. With Critical and Biographical Introduction and Notes by J. Devey, M.A. Portrait. *N. S.*
— *See also Philosophical Library.*

BALLADS AND SONGS of the Peasantry of England, from Oral Recitation, private MSS., Broadsides, &c. Edit. by R. Bell. *N. S.*

BEAUMONT AND FLETCHER. Selections. With Notes and Introduction by Leigh Hunt.

BECKMANN (J.) History of Inventions, Discoveries, and Origins. With Portraits of Beckmann and James Watt. 2 vols. *N. S.*

BELL (Robert).—*See Ballads, Chaucer, Green.*

BOSWELL'S Life of Johnson, with the TOUR in the HEBRIDES and JOHNSONIANA. New Edition, with Notes and Appendices, by the Rev. A. Napier, M.A., Trinity College, Cambridge, Vicar of Holkham, Editor of the Cambridge Edition of the 'Theological Works of Barrow.' With Frontispiece to each vol. 6 vols. *N.S.*

BREMER'S (Frederika) Works. Trans. by M. Howitt. Portrait. 4 vols. *N.S.*

BRINK (B. T.) Early English Literature (to Wiclif). By Bernhard Ten Brink. Trans. by Prof. H. M. Kennedy. *N. S.*

BRITISH POETS, from Milton to Kirke White. Cabinet Edition. With Frontispiece. 4 vols. *N. S.*

BROWNE'S (Sir Thomas) Works. Edit. by S. Wilkin, with Dr. Johnson's Life of Browne. Portrait. 3 vols.

BURKE'S Works. 6 vols. *N. S.*
—— **Speeches on the Impeachment** of Warren Hastings; and Letters. 2 vols. *N. S.*
—— **Life.** By J. Prior. Portrait. *N. S.*

BURNS (Robert). Life of. By J. G. Lockhart, D.C.L. A new and enlarged edition. With Notes and Appendices by W. S. Douglas. Portrait. *N. S.*

BUTLER'S (Bp.) Analogy of Religion; Natural and Revealed, to the Constitution and Course of Nature; with Two Dissertations on Identity and Virtue, and Fifteen Sermons. With Introductions, Notes, and Memoir. Portrait. *N. S.*

CAMOEN'S Lusiad, or the Discovery of India. An Epic Poem. Trans. from the Portuguese, with Dissertation, Historical Sketch, and Life, by W. J. Mickle. 5th edition. *N. S.*

CARAFAS (The) of Maddaloni. Naples under Spanish Dominion. Trans. by Alfred de Reumont. Portrait of Massaniello.

CARREL. The Counter-Revolution in England for the Re-establishment of Popery under Charles II. and James II., by Armand Carrel; with Fox's History of James II. and Lord Lonsdale's Memoir of James II. Portrait of Carrel.

CARRUTHERS. — *See Pope, in Illustrated Library.*

CARY'S Dante. The Vision of Hell, Purgatory, and Paradise. Trans. by Rev. H. F. Cary, M.A. With Life, Chronological View of his Age, Notes, and Index of Proper Names. Portrait. *N. S.*
This is the authentic edition, containing Mr. Cary's last corrections, with additional notes.

CELLINI (Benvenuto). Memoirs of, by himself. With Notes of G. P. Carpani. Trans. by T. Roscoe. Portrait. *N. S.*

CERVANTES' Galatea. A Pastoral Romance. Trans. by G. W. J. Gyll. *N. S.*

—— **Exemplary Novels.** Trans. by W. K. Kelly. *N. S.*

—— **Don Quixote de la Mancha.** Motteux's Translation revised. With Lockhart's Life and Notes. 2 vols. *N. S.*

CHAUCER'S Poetical Works. With Poems formerly attributed to him. With a Memoir, Introduction, Notes, and a Glossary, by R. Bell. Improved edition, with Preliminary Essay by Rev. W. W. Skeat, M.A. Portrait. 4 vols. *N. S.*

CLASSIC TALES, containing Rasselas, Vicar of Wakefield, Gulliver's Travels, and The Sentimental Journey. *N. S.*

COLERIDGE'S (S. T.) Friend. A Series of Essays on Morals, Politics, and Religion. Portrait. *N. S.*

—— **Aids to Reflection. Confessions of an Inquiring Spirit;** and Essays on Faith and the Common Prayer-book. New Edition, revised. *N. S.*

—— **Table-Talk and Omniana.** By T. Ashe, B.A. *N. S.*

—— **Lectures on Shakspere and** other Poets. Edit. by T. Ashe, B.A. *N. S.* Containing the lectures taken down in 1811-12 by J. P. Collier, and those delivered at Bristol in 1813.

—— **Biographia Literaria;** or, Biographical Sketches of my Literary Life and Opinions; with Two Lay Sermons. *N. S.*

—— **Miscellanies, Æsthetic and** Literary; to which is added, THE THEORY OF LIFE. Corrected and arranged by T. Ashe, B.A. *N. S.*

COMMINES.—*See Philip.*

CONDÉ'S History of the Dominion of the Arabs in Spain. Trans. by Mrs. Foster. Portrait of Abderahmen ben Moavia. 3 vols.

COWPER'S Complete Works, Poems, Correspondence, and Translations. Edit. with Memoir by R. Southey. 45 Engravings. 8 vols.

COXE'S Memoirs of the Duke of Marlborough. With his original Correspondence, from family records at Blenheim. Revised edition. Portraits. 3 vols.
*** An Atlas of the plans of Marlborough's campaigns, 4to. 10s. 6d.

—— **History of the House of Austri**a From the Foundation of the Monarchy by Rhodolph of Hapsburgh to the Death of Leopold II., 1218-1792. By Archdn. Coxe With Continuation from the Accession of Francis I. to the Revolution of 1848 4 Portraits. 4 vols.

CUNNINGHAM'S Lives of the most Eminent British Painters. With Notes and 16 fresh Lives by Mrs. Heaton. 3 vols. *N. S.*

DEFOE'S Novels and Miscellaneous Works. With Prefaces and Notes, including those attributed to Sir W. Scott. Portrait. 7 vols. *N. S.*

DE LOLME'S Constitution of England, in which it is compared both with the Republican form of Government and the other Monarchies of Europe. Edit., with Life and Notes, by J. Macgregor, M.P.

DUNLOP'S History of Fiction. With Introduction and Supplement adapting the work to present requirements. By Henry Wilson. 3 vols. [*In the press*

ELZE'S Life of Shakespeare. Translated by L. Dora Schmitz. [*In the press*

EMERSON'S Works. 3 vols. Most complete edition published. *N. S.*
Vol. I.—Essays, Lectures, and Poems.
Vol. II.—English Traits, Nature, and Conduct of Life.
Vol. III.—Society and Solitude—Letters and Social Aims—Miscellaneous Papers (hitherto uncollected)—May-Day, &c.

FOSTER'S (John) Life and Correspondence. Edit. by J. E. Ryland. Portrait. 2 vols. *N. S.*

—— **Lectures at Broadmead Chapel.** Edit. by J. E. Ryland. 2 vols. *N. S.*

—— **Critical Essays contributed to** the 'Eclectic Review.' Edit. by J. E. Ryland. 2 vols. *N. S.*

—— **Essays: On Decision of Charac**ter; on a Man's writing Memoirs of Himself; on the epithet Romantic; on the aversion of Men of Taste to Evangelical Religion. *N. S.*

—— **Essays on the Evils of Popular** Ignorance, and a Discourse on the Propagation of Christianity in India. *N. S.*

—— **Essay on the Improvement of** Time, with Notes of Sermons and other Pieces. *N. S.*

—— **Fosteriana:** selected from periodical papers, edit. by H. G. Bohn. *N. S.*

FOX (Rt. Hon. C. J.)—*See Carrel.*

GIBBON'S Decline and Fall of the Roman Empire. Complete and unabridged, with variorum Notes; including those of Guizot, Wenck, Niebuhr, Hugo, Neander, and others. 7 vols. 2 Maps and Portrait. *N. S.*

GOETHE'S Works. Trans. into English by E. A. Bowring, C.B., Anna Swanwick, Sir Walter Scott, &c. &c. 13 vols. *N. S.*
  Vols. I. and II.—Autobiography and Annals. Portrait.
  Vol. III.—Faust. Complete.
  Vol. IV.—Novels and Tales; containing Elective Affinities, Sorrows of Werther, The German Emigrants, The Good Women, and a Nouvelette.
  Vol. V.—Wilhelm Meister's Apprenticeship.
  Vol. VI.—Conversations with Eckerman and Soret.
  Vol. VII.—Poems and Ballads in the original Metres, including Hermann and Dorothea.
  Vol. VIII.—Götz von Berlichingen, Torquato Tasso, Egmont, Iphigenia, Clavigo, Wayward Lover, and Fellow Culprits.
  Vol. IX.—Wilhelm Meister's Travels. Complete Edition.
  Vol. X.—Tour in Italy. Two Parts. And Second Residence in Rome.
  Vol. XI.—Miscellaneous Travels, Letters from Switzerland, Campaign in France, Siege of Mainz, and Rhine Tour.
  Vol. XII.—Early and Miscellaneous Letters, including Letters to his Mother, with Biography and Notes.
  Vol. XIII.—Correspondence with Zelter.

—— **Correspondence with Schiller.** 2 vols.—*See Schiller.*

GOLDSMITH'S Works. 5 vols. *N.S.*
  Vol. I.—Life, Vicar of Wakefield, Essays, and Letters.
  Vol. II.—Poems, Plays, Bee, Cock Lane Ghost.
  Vol. III.—The Citizen of the World, Polite Learning in Europe.
  Vol. IV.—Biographies, Criticisms, Later Essays.
  Vol. V.—Prefaces, Natural History, Letters, Goody Two-Shoes, Index.

GREENE, MARLOW, and BEN JONSON (Poems of). With Notes and Memoirs by R. Bell. *N. S.*

GREGORY'S (Dr.) The Evidences, Doctrines, and Duties of the Christian Religion.

GRIMM'S Household Tales. With the Original Notes. Trans. by Mrs. A. Hunt. Introduction by Andrew Lang, M.A. 2 vols. *N. S.*

GUIZOT'S History of Representative Government in Europe. Trans. by A. R. Scoble.

—— **English Revolution of 1640.** From the Accession of Charles I. to his Death. Trans. by W. Hazlitt. Portrait.

—— **History of Civilisation.** From the Roman Empire to the French Revolution. Trans. by W. Hazlitt. Portraits. 3 vols.

HALL'S (Rev. Robert) Works and Remains. Memoir by Dr. Gregory and Essay by J. Foster. Portrait.

HAUFF'S Tales. The Caravan—The Sheikh of Alexandria—The Inn in the Spessart. Translated by Prof. S. Mendel. *N. S.*

HAWTHORNE'S Tales. 3 vols. *N. S.*
  Vol. I.—Twice-told Tales, and the Snow Image.
  Vol. II.—Scarlet Letter, and the House with Seven Gables.
  Vol. III.—Transformation, and Blithedale Romance.

HAZLITT'S (W.) Works. 7 vols. *N.S.*

—— **Table-Talk.**

—— **The Literature of the Age of Elizabeth** and Characters of Shakespeare's Plays. *N. S.*

—— **English Poets and English Comic Writers.** *N. S.*

—— **The Plain Speaker.** Opinions on Books, Men, and Things. *N. S.*

—— **Round Table.** Conversations of James Northcote, R.A.; Characteristics. *N. S.*

—— **Sketches and Essays,** and Winterslow. *N. S.*

—— **Spirit of the Age;** or, Contemporary Portraits. To which are added Free Thoughts on Public Affairs, and a Letter to William Gifford. New Edition, by W. Carew Hazlitt. *N. S.*

HEINE'S Poems. Translated in the original Metres, with Life by E. A. Bowring, C.B. *N. S.*

—— **Travel-Pictures.** The Tour in the Harz, Norderney, and Book of Ideas, together with the Romantic School. Trans. by F. Storr. With Maps and Appendices. *N. S.*

HOFFMANN'S Works. The Serapion Brethren. Vol. I. Trans. by Lt.-Col. Ewing. *N. S.* [*Vol. II. in the press.*

HUGO'S (Victor) Dramatic Works. Hernani—Ruy Blas—The King's Diversion. Translated by Mrs. Newton Crosland and F. L. Slous. *N. S.*

—— **Poems,** chiefly Lyrical. Collected by H. L. Williams. *N. S.*
This volume contains contributions from F. S. Mahoney, G. W. M. Reynolds, Andrew Lang, Edwin Arnold, Mrs. Newton Crosland, Miss Fanny Kemble, Bishop Alexander, Prof. Dowden, &c.

HUNGARY: its History and Revolution, with Memoir of Kossuth. Portrait.

HUTCHINSON (Colonel). Memoirs of. By his Widow, with her Autobiography, and the Siege of Lathom House. Portrait. *N. S.*

IRVING'S (Washington) Complete Works. 15 vols. *N. S.*

—— **Life and Letters.** By his Nephew, Pierre E. Irving. With Index and a Portrait. 2 vols. *N. S.*

JAMES'S (G. P. R.) Life of Richard Cœur de Lion. Portraits of Richard and Philip Augustus. 2 vols.

—— **Louis XIV.** Portraits. 2 vols.

JAMESON (Mrs.) Shakespeare's Heroines. Characteristics of Women. By Mrs. Jameson. *N. S.*

JEAN PAUL.—*See Richter.*

JONSON (Ben). Poems of.—*See Greene.*

JUNIUS'S Letters. With Woodfall's Notes. An Essay on the Authorship. Facsimiles of Handwriting. 2 vols. *N. S.*

LA FONTAINE'S Fables. In English Verse, with Essay on the Fabulists. By Elizur Wright. *N. S.*

LAMARTINE'S The Girondists, or Personal Memoirs of the Patriots of the French Revolution. Trans. by H. T. Ryde. Portraits of Robespierre, Madame Roland, and Charlotte Corday. 3 vols.

—— **The Restoration of Monarchy in France** (a Sequel to The Girondists). 5 Portraits. 4 vols.

—— **The French Revolution of 1848.** 6 Portraits.

LAMB'S (Charles) Elia and Eliana. Complete Edition. Portrait. *N. S.*

—— **Specimens of English Dramatic Poets of the time of Elizabeth.** Notes, with the Extracts from the Garrick Plays. *N. S.*

—— **Talfourd's Letters of Charles Lamb.** New Edition, by W. Carew Hazlitt. 2 vols. *N. S.*

LANZI'S History of Painting in Italy, from the Period of the Revival of the Fine Arts to the End of the 18th Century. With Memoir of the Author. Portraits of Raffaelle, Titian, and Correggio, after the Artists themselves. Trans. by T. Roscoe. 3 vols.

LAPPENBERG'S England under the Anglo-Saxon Kings. Trans. by B. Thorpe, F.S.A. 2 vols. *N. S.*

LESSING'S Dramatic Works. Complete. By E. Bell, M.A. With Memoir by H. Zimmern. Portrait. 2 vols. *N. S.*

—— **Laokoon, Dramatic Notes,** and Representation of Death by the Ancients. Frontispiece. *N. S.*

LOCKE'S Philosophical Works, containing Human Understanding, with Bishop of Worcester, Malebranche's Opinions, Natural Philosophy, Reading and Study. With Preliminary Discourse, Analysis, and Notes, by J. A. St. John. Portrait. 2 vols. *N. S.*

—— **Life and Letters,** with Extracts from his Common-place Books. By Lord King.

LOCKHART (J. G.)—*See Burns.*

LONSDALE (Lord).—*See Carrel.*

LUTHER'S Table-Talk. Trans. by W. Hazlitt. With Life by A. Chalmers, and LUTHER'S CATECHISM. Portrait after Cranach. *N. S.*

—— **Autobiography.**—*See Michelet.*

MACHIAVELLI'S History of Florence, THE PRINCE, Savonarola, Historical Tracts, and Memoir. Portrait. *N. S.*

MARLOWE. Poems of.—*See Greene.*

MARTINEAU'S (Harriet) History of England (including History of the Peace from 1800-1846. 5 vols. *N. S.*

MENZEL'S History of Germany, from the Earliest Period to the Crimean War. 3 Portraits. 3 vols.

MICHELET'S Autobiography of Luther. Trans. by W. Hazlitt. With Notes. *N. S.*

—— **The French Revolution** to the Flight of the King in 1791. *N. S.*

MIGNET'S The French Revolution from 1789 to 1814. Portrait of Napoleon. *N. S.*

MILTON'S Prose Works. With Preface, Preliminary Remarks by J. A. St. John, and Index. 5 vols.

MITFORD'S (Miss) Our Village. Sketches of Rural Character and Scenery. 2 Engravings. 2 vols. *N. S.*

MOLIÈRE'S Dramatic Works. In English Prose, by C. H. Wall. With a Life and a Portrait. 3 vols. *N. S.*

'It is not too much to say that we have here probably as good a translation of Molière as can be given.'—*Academy.*

MONTAGU. Letters and Works of Lady Mary Wortley Montagu. Lord Wharncliffe's Third Edition. Edited by W. Moy Thomas. With steel plates. 2 vols. 5s. each. *N. S.*

MONTESQUIEU'S Spirit of Laws. Revised Edition, with D'Alembert's Analysis, Notes, and Memoir. 2 vols. *N. S.*

NEANDER (Dr. A.) History of the Christian Religion and Church. Trans. by J. Torrey. With Short Memoir. 10 vols.

—— **Life of Jesus Christ, in its Historical** Connexion and Development. *N. S.*

—— **The Planting and Training of** the Christian Church by the Apostles. With the Antignosticus, or Spirit of Tertullian. Trans. by J. E. Ryland. 2 vols.

—— **Lectures on the History of** Christian Dogmas. Trans. by J. E. Ryland. 2 vols.

—— **Memorials of Christian Life in** the Early and Middle Ages; including Light in Dark Places. Trans. by J. E. Ryland.

OCKLEY (S.) History of the Saracens and their Conquests in Syria, Persia, and Egypt. Comprising the Lives of Mohammed and his Successors to the Death of Abdalmelik, the Eleventh Caliph. By Simon Ockley, B.D., Prof. of Arabic in Univ. of Cambridge. Portrait of Mohammed.

PERCY'S Reliques of Ancient English Poetry, consisting of Ballads, Songs, and other Pieces of our earlier Poets, with some few of later date. With Essay on Ancient Minstrels, and Glossary. 2 vols. *N. S.*

PHILIP DE COMMINES. Memoirs of. Containing the Histories of Louis XI. and Charles VIII., and Charles the Bold, Duke of Burgundy. With the History of Louis XI., by J. de Troyes. With a Life and Notes by A. R. Scoble. Portraits. 2 vols.

PLUTARCH'S LIVES. Newly Translated, with Notes and Life, by A Stewart, M.A., late Fellow of Trinity College, Cambridge, and G. Long, M.A. 4 vols. *N. S.*

POETRY OF AMERICA. Selections from One Hundred Poets, from 1776 to 1876. With Introductory Review, and Specimens of Negro Melody, by W. J. Linton. Portrait of W. Whitman. *N. S.*

RANKE (L.) History of the Popes, their Church and State, and their Conflicts with Protestantism in the 16th and 17th Centuries. Trans. by E. Foster. Portraits of Julius II. (after Raphael), Innocent X. (after Velasquez), and Clement VII. (after Titian). 3 vols. *N. S.*

—— **History of Servia.** Trans. by Mrs. Kerr. To which is added, The Slave Provinces of Turkey, by Cyprien Robert. *N. S.*

—— **History of the Latin and Teutonic** Nations. 1494-1514. Trans. by P. A. Ashworth, translator of Dr. Gneist's 'History of the English Constitution.' *N.S.*

REUMONT (Alfred de).—*See Carafas.*

REYNOLDS' (Sir J.) Literary Works. With Memoir and Remarks by H. W. Beechy. 2 vols. *N. S.*

RICHTER (Jean Paul). Levana, a Treatise on Education; together with the Autobiography, and a short Memoir. *N. S.*

—— **Flower, Fruit, and Thorn Pieces,** or the Wedded Life, Death, and Marriage of Siebenkaes. Translated by Alex. Ewing. *N. S.*

The only complete English translation.

ROSCOE'S (W.) Life of Leo X., with Notes, Historical Documents, and Dissertation on Lucretia Borgia. 3 Portraits. 2 vols.

—— **Lorenzo de' Medici,** called 'The Magnificent,' with Copyright Notes, Poems, Letters, &c. With Memoir of Roscoe and Portrait of Lorenzo.

RUSSIA, History of, from the earliest Period to the Crimean War. By W. K. Kelly. 3 Portraits. 2 vols.

SCHILLER'S Works. 6 vols. *N. S.*

Vol. I.—Thirty Years' War—Revolt in the Netherlands. Rev A. J. W. Morrison, M.A. Portrait.

Vol. II.—Revolt in the Netherlands, *completed*—Wallenstein. By J. Churchill and S. T. Coleridge.—William Tell. Sir Theodore Martin. Engraving (after Vandyck).

Vol. III.—Don Carlos. R. D. Boylan —Mary Stuart. Mellish — Maid of Orleans. Anna Swanwick—Bride of Messina. A. Lodge, M.A. Together with the Use of the Chorus in Tragedy (a short Essay). Engravings.

These Dramas are all translated in metre.

Vol. IV.—Robbers—Fiesco—Love and Intrigue—Demetrius—Ghost Seer—Sport of Divinity.

The Dramas in this volume are in prose.

Vol. V.—Poems. E. A. Bowring, C.B.

Vol. VI.—Essays, Æsthetical and Philosophical, including the Dissertation on the Connexion between the Animal and Spiritual in Man.

SCHILLER and GOETHE. Correspondence between, from A.D. 1794-1805. With Short Notes by L. Dora Schmitz. 2 vols. *N. S.*

SCHLEGEL'S (F.) Lectures on the Philosophy of Life and the Philosophy of Language. By A. J. W. Morrison.

—— **The History of Literature,** Ancient and Modern.

—— **The Philosophy of History.** With Memoir and Portrait.

—— **Modern History,** with the Lectures entitled Cæsar and Alexander, and The Beginning of our History. By L. Purcel and R. H. Whitelock.

—— **Æsthetic and Miscellaneous Works,** containing Letters on Christian Art, Essay on Gothic Architecture, Remarks on the Romance Poetry of the Middle Ages, on Shakspeare, the Limits of the Beautiful, and on the Language and Wisdom of the Indians. By E. J. Millington.

SCHLEGEL (A. W.) Dramatic Art and Literature. By J. Black. With Memoir by A. J. W. Morrison. Portrait.

SCHUMANN (Robert), His Life and Works. By A. Reissmann. Trans. by A. L. Alger. *N. S.*

SHAKESPEARE'S Dramatic Art. The History and Character of Shakspeare's Plays. By Dr. H. Ulrici. Trans. by L. Dora Schmitz. 2 vols. *N. S.*

SHERIDAN'S Dramatic Works. With Memoir. Portrait (after Reynolds). *N. S.*

SKEAT (Rev. W. W.)—*See Chaucer.*

SISMONDI'S History of the Literature of the South of Europe. With Notes and Memoir by T. Roscoe. Portraits of Sismondi and Dante. 2 vols.
The specimens of early French, Italian, Spanish, and Portugese Poetry, in English Verse, by Cary and others.

SMITH'S (Adam) The Wealth of Nations. An Inquiry into the Nature and Causes of. Reprinted from the Sixth Edition. With an Introduction by Ernest Belfort Bax. 2 vols. *N. S.*

SMITH'S (Adam) Theory of Moral Sentiments; with Essay on the First Formation of Languages, and Critical Memoir by Dugald Stewart.

SMYTH'S (Professor) Lectures on Modern History; from the Irruption of the Northern Nations to the close of the American Revolution. 2 vols.

—— **Lectures on the French Revolution.** With Index. 2 vols.

SOUTHEY.—*See Cowper, Wesley, and (Illustrated Library) Nelson.*

STURM'S Morning Communings with God, or Devotional Meditations for Every Day. Trans. by W. Johnstone, M.A.

SULLY. Memoirs of the Duke of, Prime Minister to Henry the Great. With Notes and Historical Introduction. 4 Portraits. 4 vols.

TAYLOR'S (Bishop Jeremy) Holy Living and Dying, with Prayers, containing the Whole Duty of a Christian and the parts of Devotion fitted to all Occasions. Portrait. *N. S.*

THIERRY'S Conquest of England by the Normans; its Causes, and its Consequences in England and the Continent. By W. Hazlitt. With short Memoir. 2 Portraits. 2 vols. *N. S.*

TROYE'S (Jean de).—*See Philip de Commines.*

ULRICI (Dr.)—*See Shakespeare.*

VASARI. Lives of the most Eminent Painters, Sculptors, and Architects. By Mrs. J. Foster, with selected Notes. Portrait. 6 vols., Vol. VI. being an additional Volume of Notes by J. P. Richter. *N. S.*

WERNER'S Templars in Cyprus. Trans. by E. A. M. Lewis. *N. S.*

WESLEY, the Life of, and the Rise and Progress of Methodism. By Robert Southey. Portrait. 5s. *N. S.*

WHEATLEY. A Rational Illustration of the Book of Common Prayer, being the Substance of everything Liturgical in all former Ritualist Commentators upon the subject. Frontispiece. *N. S.*

HISTORICAL LIBRARY.

21 Volumes at 5s. each. (5l. 5s. per set.)

EVELYN'S Diary and Correspondence, with the Private Correspondence of Charles I and Sir Edward Nicholas, and between Sir Edward Hyde (Earl of Clarendon) and Sir Richard Browne. Edited from the Original MSS. by W. Bray, F.A.S. 4 vols. *N. S.* 45 Engravings (after Vandyke, Lely, Kneller, and Jamieson, &c.).

N.B.—This edition contains 130 letters from Evelyn and his wife, contained in no other edition.

PEPYS' Diary and Correspondence. With Life and Notes, by Lord Braybrooke. 4 vols. *N. S.* With Appendix containing additional Letters, an Index, and 31 Engravings (after Vandyke, Sir P. Lely, Holbein, Kneller, &c.).

JESSE'S Memoirs of the Court of England under the Stuarts, including the Protectorate. 3 vols. With Index and 42 Portraits (after Vandyke, Lely, &c.).

—— Memoirs of the Pretenders and their Adherents. 7 Portraits.

NUGENT'S (Lord) Memorials of Hampden, his Party and Times. With Memoir. 12 Portraits (after Vandyke and others). *N. S.*

STRICKLAND'S (Agnes) Lives of the Queens of England from the Norman Conquest. From authentic Documents, public and private. 6 Portraits. 6 vols. *N. S.*

—— Life of Mary Queen of Scots. 2 Portraits. 2 vols. *N. S.*

—— Lives of the Tudor and Stuart Princesses. [*In the press.*

PHILOSOPHICAL LIBRARY.

16 Vols. at 5s. each, excepting those marked otherwise. (3l. 14s. per set.)

BACON'S Novum Organum and Advancement of Learning. With Notes by J. Devey, M.A.

BAX. A Handbook of the History of Philosophy, for the use of Students. By E. Belfort Bax, Editor of Kant's 'Prolegomena.' 5s. *N. S.*

COMTE'S Philosophy of the Sciences. An Exposition of the Principles of the *Cours de Philosophie Positive.* By G. H. Lewes, Author of 'The Life of Goethe.'

DRAPER (Dr. J. W.) A History of the Intellectual Development of Europe. 2 vols. *N. S.*

HEGEL'S Philosophy of History. By J. Sibree, M.A.

KANT'S Critique of Pure Reason. By J. M. D. Meiklejohn. *N. S.*

—— Prolegomena and Metaphysical Foundations of Natural Science, with Biography and Memoir by E. Belfort Bax. Portrait. *N. S.*

LOGIC, or the Science of Inference. A Popular Manual. By J. Devey.

MILLER (Professor). History Philosophically Illustrated, from the Fall of the Roman Empire to the French Revolution. With Memoir. 4 vols. 3s. 6d. each.

SPINOZA'S Chief Works. Trans. with Introduction by R. H. M. Elwes. 2 vols. *N.S.*

Vol. I.—Tractatus Theologico-Politicus —Political Treatise.

Vol. II.—Improvement of the Understanding—Ethics—Letters.

TENNEMANN'S Manual of the History of Philosophy. Trans. by Rev. A. Johnson, M.A.

THEOLOGICAL LIBRARY.

15 Vols. at 5s. each, excepting those marked otherwise. (3*l.* 13*s.* 6*d.* per set.)

BLEEK. Introduction to the Old Testament. By Friedrich Bleek. Trans. under the supervision of Rev. E. Venables, Residentiary Canon of Lincoln. 2 vols. *N. S.*

CHILLINGWORTH'S Religion of Protestants. 3*s.* 6*d.*

EUSEBIUS. Ecclesiastical History of Eusebius Pamphilius, Bishop of Cæsarea. Trans. by Rev. C. F. Cruse, M.A. With Notes, Life, and Chronological Tables.

EVAGRIUS. History of the Church. —*See Theodoret.*

HARDWICK. History of the Articles of Religion; to which is added a Series of Documents from A.D. 1536 to A.D. 1615. Ed. by Rev. F. Proctor. *N. S.*

HENRY'S (Matthew) Exposition of the Book of Psalms. Numerous Woodcuts.

PEARSON (John, D.D.) Exposition of the Creed. Edit. by E. Walford, M.A. With Notes, Analysis, and Indexes. *N. S.*

PHILO-JUDÆUS, Works of. The Contemporary of Josephus. Trans. by C. D. Yonge. 4 vols.

PHILOSTORGIUS. Ecclesiastical History of.—*See Sozomen.*

SOCRATES' Ecclesiastical History Comprising a History of the Church from Constantine, A.D. 305, to the 38th year of Theodosius II. With Short Account of the Author, and selected Notes.

SOZOMEN'S Ecclesiastical History A.D. 324-440. With Notes, Prefatory Remarks by Valesius, and Short Memoir. Together with the ECCLESIASTICAL HISTORY OF PHILOSTORGIUS, as epitomised by Photius. Trans. by Rev. E. Walford, M.A. With Notes and brief Life.

THEODORET and EVAGRIUS. Histories of the Church from A.D. 332 to the Death of Theodore of Mopsuestia, A.D. 427; and from A.D. 431 to A.D. 544. With Memoirs.

WIESELER'S (Karl) Chronological Synopsis of the Four Gospels. Trans. by Rev. Canon Venables. *N. S.*

ANTIQUARIAN LIBRARY.

35 Vols. at 5s. each. (8*l.* 15*s.* per set.)

ANGLO-SAXON CHRONICLE.—*See Bede.*

ASSER'S Life of Alfred.—*See Six O. E. Chronicles.*

BEDE'S (Venerable) Ecclesiastical History of England. Together with the ANGLO-SAXON CHRONICLE. With Notes, Short Life, Analysis, and Map. Edit. by J. A. Giles, D.C.L.

BOETHIUS'S Consolation of Philosophy. King Alfred's Anglo-Saxon Version of. With an English Translation on opposite pages, Notes, Introduction, and Glossary, by Rev. S. Fox, M.A. To which is added the Anglo-Saxon Version of the METRES OF BOETHIUS, with a free Translation by Martin F. Tupper, D.C.L.

BRAND'S Popular Antiquities of England, Scotland, and Ireland. Illustrating the Origin of our Vulgar and Provincial Customs, Ceremonies, and Superstitions. By Sir Henry Ellis, K.H., F.R.S. Frontispiece. 3 vols.

CHRONICLES of the CRUSADES Contemporary Narratives of Richard Cœur de Lion, by Richard of Devizes and Geoffrey de Vinsauf; and of the Crusade at Saint Louis, by Lord John de Joinville. With Short Notes. Illuminated Frontispiece from an old MS.

DYER'S (T. F. T.) British Popular Customs, Present and Past. An Account of the various Games and Customs associated with different Days of the Year in the British Isles, arranged according to the Calendar. By the Rev. T. F. Thiselton Dyer, M.A.

EARLY TRAVELS IN PALESTINE Comprising the Narratives of Arculf, Willibald, Bernard, Sæwulf, Sigurd, Benjamin of Tudela, Sir John Maundeville De la Brocquière, and Maundrell; all unabridged. With Introduction and Notes by Thomas Wright. Map of Jerusalem.

ELLIS (G.) Specimens of Early English Metrical Romances, relating to Arthur, Merlin, Guy of Warwick, Richard Cœur de Lion, Charlemagne, Roland, &c. &c. With Historical Introduction by J. O. Halliwell, F.R.S. Illuminated Frontispiece from an old MS.

ETHELWERD. Chronicle of.—*See Six O. E. Chronicles.*

FLORENCE OF WORCESTER'S Chronicle, with the Two Continuations: comprising Annals of English History from the Departure of the Romans to the Reign of Edward I. Trans., with Notes, by Thomas Forester, M.A.

GEOFFREY OF MONMOUTH. Chronicle of.—*See Six O. E. Chronicles.*

GESTA ROMANORUM, or Entertaining Moral Stories invented by the Monks. Trans. with Notes by the Rev. Charles Swan. Edit. by W. Hooper, M.A.

GILDAS. Chronicle of.—*See Six O. E. Chronicles.*

GIRALDUS CAMBRENSIS' Historical Works. Containing Topography of Ireland, and History of the Conquest of Ireland, by Th. Forester, M.A. Itinerary through Wales, and Description of Wales, by Sir R. Colt Hoare.

HENRY OF HUNTINGDON'S History of the English, from the Roman Invasion to the Accession of Henry II.; with the Acts of King Stephen, and the Letter to Walter. By T. Forester, M.A. Frontispiece from an old MS.

INGULPH'S Chronicles of the Abbey of Croyland, with the CONTINUATION by Peter of Blois and others. Trans. with Notes by H. T. Riley, B.A.

KEIGHTLEY'S (Thomas) Fairy Mythology, illustrative of the Romance and Superstition of Various Countries. Frontispiece by Cruikshank. *N. S.*

LEPSIUS'S Letters from Egypt, Ethiopia, and the Peninsula of Sinai; to which are added, Extracts from his Chronology of the Egyptians, with reference to the Exodus of the Israelites. By L. and J. B. Horner. Maps and Coloured View of Mount Barkal.

MALLET'S Northern Antiquities, or an Historical Account of the Manners, Customs, Religions, and Literature of the Ancient Scandinavians. Trans. by Bishop Percy. With Translation of the PROSE EDDA, and Notes by J. A. Blackwell. Also an Abstract of the 'Eyrbyggia Saga' by Sir Walter Scott. With Glossary and Coloured Frontispiece.

MARCO POLO'S Travels; with Notes and Introduction. Edit. by T. Wright.

MATTHEW PARIS'S English History, from 1235 to 1273. By Rev. J. A. Giles, D.C.L. With Frontispiece. 3 vols.— *See also Roger of Wendover.*

MATTHEW OF WESTMINSTER'S Flowers of History, especially such as relate to the affairs of Britain, from the beginning of the World to A.D. 1307. By C. D. Yonge. 2 vols.

NENNIUS. Chronicle of.—*See Six O. E. Chronicles.*

ORDERICUS VITALIS' Ecclesiastical History of England and Normandy. With Notes, Introduction of Guizot, and the Critical Notice of M. Delille, by T. Forester, M.A. To which is added the CHRONICLE OF ST. EVROULT. With General and Chronological Indexes. 4 vols.

PAULI'S (Dr. R.) Life of Alfred the Great. To which is appended Alfred's ANGLO-SAXON VERSION OF OROSIUS. With literal Translation interpaged, Notes, and an ANGLO-SAXON GRAMMAR and Glossary, by B. Thorpe, Esq. Frontispiece.

RICHARD OF CIRENCESTER. Chronicle of.—*See Six O. E. Chronicles.*

ROGER DE HOVEDEN'S Annals of English History, comprising the History of England and of other Countries of Europe from A.D. 732 to A.D. 1201. With Notes by H. T. Riley, B.A. 2 vols.

ROGER OF WENDOVER'S Flowers of History, comprising the History of England from the Descent of the Saxons to A.D. 1235, formerly ascribed to Matthew Paris. With Notes and Index by J. A. Giles, D.C.L. 2 vols.

SIX OLD ENGLISH CHRONICLES: viz., Asser's Life of Alfred and the Chronicles of Ethelwerd, Gildas, Nennius, Geoffrey of Monmouth, and Richard of Cirencester. Edit., with Notes, by J. A. Giles, D.C.L. Portrait of Alfred.

WILLIAM OF MALMESBURY'S Chronicle of the Kings of England, from the Earliest Period to King Stephen. By Rev. J. Sharpe. With Notes by J. A. Giles, D.C.L. Frontispiece.

YULE-TIDE STORIES. A Collection of Scandinavian and North-German Popular Tales and Traditions, from the Swedish, Danish, and German. Edit. by B. Thorpe.

ILLUSTRATED LIBRARY.

86 Vols. at 5s. each, excepting those marked otherwise. (23*l.* 4*s. per set.*)

ALLEN'S (Joseph, R.N.) Battles of the British Navy. Revised edition, with Indexes of Names and Events, and 57 Portraits and Plans. 2 vols.

ANDERSEN'S Danish Fairy Tales. By Caroline Peachey. With Short Life and 120 Wood Engravings.

ARIOSTO'S Orlando Furioso. In English Verse by W. S. Rose. With Notes and Short Memoir. Portrait after Titian, and 24 Steel Engravings. 2 vols.

BECHSTEIN'S Cage and Chamber Birds: their Natural History, Habits, &c. Together with SWEET'S BRITISH WARBLERS. 43 Plates and Woodcuts. *N. S.*

—— or with the Plates Coloured, 7*s.* 6*d.*

BONOMI'S Nineveh and its Palaces. The Discoveries of Botta and Layard applied to the Elucidation of Holy Writ. 7 Plates and 294 Woodcuts. *N. S.*

BUTLER'S Hudibras, with Variorum Notes and Biography. Portrait and 28 Illustrations.

CATTERMOLE'S Evenings at Haddon Hall. Romantic Tales of the Olden Times. With 24 Steel Engravings after Cattermole.

CHINA, Pictorial, Descriptive, and Historical, with some account of Ava and the Burmese, Siam, and Anam. Map, and nearly 100 Illustrations.

CRAIK'S (G. L.) Pursuit of Knowledge under Difficulties. Illustrated by Anecdotes and Memoirs. Numerous Woodcut Portraits. *N. S.*

CRUIKSHANK'S Three Courses and a Dessert; comprising three Sets of Tales, West Country, Irish, and Legal; and a Mélange. With 50 Illustrations by Cruikshank. *N. S.*

—— **Punch and Judy.** The Dialogue of the Puppet Show; an Account of its Origin, &c. 24 Illustrations by Cruikshank. *N. S.*

—— With Coloured Plates. 7*s.* 6*d.*

DIDRON'S Christian Iconography; a History of Christian Art in the Middle Ages. By the late A. N. Didron. Trans. by E. J. Millington, and completed, with Additions and Appendices, by Margaret Stokes. 2 vols. With numerous Illustrations.
Vol. I. The History of the Nimbus, the Aureole, and the Glory; Representations of the Persons of the Trinity.
Vol. II. The Trinity; Angels; Devils; The Soul; The Christian Scheme. Appendices.

DANTE, in English Verse, by I. C. Wright, M.A. With Introduction and Memoir. Portrait and 34 Steel Engravings after Flaxman. *N. S.*

DYER (Dr. T. H.) Pompeii: its Buildings and Antiquities. An Account of the City, with full Description of the Remains and Recent Excavations, and an Itinerary for Visitors. By T. H. Dyer, LL.D. Nearly 300 Wood Engravings, Map, and Plan. 7*s.* 6*d.* *N. S.*

—— **Rome**: History of the City, with Introduction on recent Excavations. 8 Engravings, Frontispiece, and 2 Maps.

GIL BLAS. The Adventures of From the French of Lesage by Smollett. 24 Engravings after Smirke, and 10 Etchings by Cruikshank. 612 pages. 6*s.*

GRIMM'S Gammer Grethel; or, German Fairy Tales and Popular Stories containing 42 Fairy Tales. By Edgar Taylor. Numerous Woodcuts after Cruikshank and Ludwig Grimm. 3*s.* 6*d.*

HOLBEIN'S Dance of Death and Bible Cuts. Upwards of 150 Subjects, engraved in facsimile, with Introduction and Descriptions by the late Francis Douce and Dr. Dibdin. 7*s.* 6*d.*

HOWITT'S (Mary) Pictorial Calendar of the Seasons; embodying AIKIN'S CALENDAR OF NATURE. Upwards of 100 Woodcuts.

INDIA, Pictorial, Descriptive, and Historical, from the Earliest Times. 100 Engravings on Wood and Map.

JESSE'S Anecdotes of Dogs. With 40 Woodcuts after Harvey, Bewick, and others. *N. S.*

—— With 34 additional Steel Engravings after Cooper, Landseer, &c. 7*s.* 6*d.* *N. S.*

KING'S (C. W.) Natural History of Gems or Decorative Stones. Illustrations. 6*s.*

—— **Natural History of Precious Stones and Metals.** Illustrations. 6*s.*

KITTO'S Scripture Lands. Described in a series of Historical, Geographical, and Topographical Sketches. 42 Maps.

—— With the Maps coloured, 7*s.* 6*d.*

KRUMMACHER'S Parables. 40 Illustrations.

LINDSAY'S (Lord) Letters on Egypt, Edom, and the Holy Land. 36 Wood Engravings and 2 Maps.

LODGE'S Portraits of Illustrious Personages of Great Britain, with Biographical and Historical Memoirs. 240 Portraits engraved on Steel, with the respective Biographies unabridged. Complete in 8 vols.

LONGFELLOW'S Poetical Works, including his Translations and Notes. 24 full-page Woodcuts by Birket Foster and others, and a Portrait. *N. S.*

—— Without the Illustrations, 3*s*. 6*d*. *N. S.*

—— **Prose Works.** With 16 full-page Woodcuts by Birket Foster and others.

LOUDON'S (Mrs.) Entertaining Naturalist. Popular Descriptions, Tales, and Anecdotes, of more than 500 Animals. Numerous Woodcuts. *N. S.*

MARRYAT'S (Capt., R.N.) Masterman Ready; or, the Wreck of the *Pacific*. (Written for Young People.) With 93 Woodcuts. 3*s*. 6*d*. *N. S.*

—— **Mission; or, Scenes in Africa.** (Written for Young People.) Illustrated by Gilbert and Dalziel. 3*s*. 6*d*. *N. S.*

—— **Pirate and Three Cutters.** (Written for Young People.) With a Memoir. 8 Steel Engravings after Clarkson Stanfield, R.A. 3*s*. 6*d*. *N. S.*

—— **Privateersman.** Adventures by Sea and Land One Hundred Years Ago. (Written for Young People.) 8 Steel Engravings. 3*s*. 6*d*. *N. S.*

—— **Settlers in Canada.** (Written for Young People.) 10 Engravings by Gilbert and Dalziel. 3*s*. 6*d*. *N. S.*

—— **Poor Jack.** (Written for Young People.) With 16 Illustrations after Clarkson Stanfield, R.A. 3*s*. 6*d*. *N. S.*

MAXWELL'S Victories of Wellington and the British Armies. Frontispiece and 4 Portraits.

MICHAEL ANGELO and RAPHAEL, Their Lives and Works. By Duppa and Quatremère de Quincy. Portraits and Engravings, including the Last Judgment, and Cartoons. *N. S.*

MILLER'S History of the Anglo-Saxons, from the Earliest Period to the Norman Conquest. Portrait of Alfred, Map of Saxon Britain, and 12 Steel Engravings.

MILTON'S Poetical Works, with a Memoir and Notes by J. Montgomery, an Index to Paradise Lost, Todd's Verbal Index to all the Poems, and Notes. 120 Wood Engravings. 2 vols. *N. S.*

MUDIE'S History of British Birds. Revised by W. C. L. Martin. 52 Figures of Birds and 7 Plates of Eggs. 2 vols. *N.S.*

—— With the Plates coloured, 7*s*. 6*d*. per vol.

NAVAL and MILITARY HEROES of Great Britain; a Record of British Valour on every Day in the year, from William the Conqueror to the Battle of Inkermann. By Major Johns, R.M., and Lieut. P. H. Nicolas, R.M. Indexes. 24 Portraits after Holbein, Reynolds, &c. 6*s*.

NICOLINI'S History of the Jesuits: their Origin, Progress, Doctrines, and Designs. 8 Portraits.

PETRARCH'S Sonnets, Triumphs, and other Poems, in English Verse. With Life by Thomas Campbell. Portrait and 15 Steel Engravings.

PICKERING'S History of the Races of Man, and their Geographical Distribution; with AN ANALYTICAL SYNOPSIS OF THE NATURAL HISTORY OF MAN. By Dr. Hall. Map of the World and 12 Plates.

—— With the Plates coloured, 7*s*. 6*d*.

PICTORIAL HANDBOOK OF Modern Geography on a Popular Plan. Compiled from the best Authorities, English and Foreign, by H. G. Bohn. 150 Woodcuts and 51 Maps. 6*s*.

—— With the Maps coloured, 7*s*. 6*d*.

—— Without the Maps, 3*s*. 6*d*.

POPE'S Poetical Works, including Translations. Edit., with Notes, by R. Carruthers. 2 vols.

—— **Homer's Iliad,** with Introduction and Notes by Rev. J. S. Watson, M.A. With Flaxman's Designs. *N. S.*

—— **Homer's Odyssey,** with the BATTLE OF FROGS AND MICE, Hymns, &c., by other translators, including Chapman. Introduction and Notes by J. S. Watson, M.A. With Flaxman's Designs. *N. S.*

—— **Life,** including many of his Letters. By R. Carruthers. Numerous Illustrations.

POTTERY AND PORCELAIN, and other objects of Vertu. Comprising an Illustrated Catalogue of the Bernal Collection, with the prices and names of the Possessors. Also an Introductory Lecture on Pottery and Porcelain, and an Engraved List of all Marks and Monograms. By H. G. Bohn. Numerous Woodcuts.

—— With coloured Illustrations, 10*s*. 6*d*.

PROUT'S (Father) Reliques. Edited by Rev. F. Mahony. Copyright edition, with the Author's last corrections and additions. 21 Etchings by D. Maclise, R.A. Nearly 600 pages. 5*s*. *N. S.*

RECREATIONS IN SHOOTING. With some Account of the Game found in the British Isles, and Directions for the Management of Dog and Gun. By 'Craven.' 62 Woodcuts and 9 Steel Engravings after A. Cooper, R.A.

REDDING'S History and Descriptions of Wines, Ancient and Modern. 20 Woodcuts.

RENNIE. Insect Architecture. Revised by Rev. J. G. Wood, M.A. 186 Woodcuts. *N. S.*

ROBINSON CRUSOE. With Memoir of Defoe, 12 Steel Engravings and 74 Woodcuts after Stothard and Harvey.

—— Without the Engravings, 3s. 6d.

ROME IN THE NINETEENTH CENtury. An Account in 1817 of the Ruins of the Ancient City, and Monuments of Modern Times. By C. A. Eaton. 34 Steel Engravings. 2 vols.

SHARPE (S.) The History of Egypt, from the Earliest Times till the Conquest by the Arabs, A.D. 640. 2 Maps and upwards of 400 Woodcuts. 2 vols. *N. S.*

SOUTHEY'S Life of Nelson. With Additional Notes, Facsimiles of Nelson's Writing, Portraits, Plans, and 50 Engravings, after Birket Foster, &c. *N. S.*

STARLING'S (Miss) Noble Deeds of Women; or, Examples of Female Courage, Fortitude, and Virtue. With 14 Steel Portraits. *N. S.*

STUART and REVETT'S Antiquities of Athens, and other Monuments of Greece; with Glossary of Terms used in Grecian Architecture. 71 Steel Plates and numerous Woodcuts.

SWEET'S British Warblers. 5s.—*See Bechstein.*

TALES OF THE GENII; or, the Delightful Lessons of Horam, the Son of Asmar. Trans. by Sir C. Morrell. Numerous Woodcuts.

TASSO'S Jerusalem Delivered. In English Spenserian Verse, with Life, by J. H. Wiffen. With 8 Engravings and 24 Woodcuts. *N. S.*

WALKER'S Manly Exercises; containing Skating, Riding, Driving, Hunting, Shooting, Sailing, Rowing, Swimming, &c. 44 Engravings and numerous Woodcuts.

WALTON'S Complete Angler, or the Contemplative Man's Recreation, by Izaak Walton and Charles Cotton. With Memoirs and Notes by E. Jesse. Also an Account of Fishing Stations, Tackle, &c., by H. G. Bohn. Portrait and 203 Woodcuts. *N. S.*

—— With 26 additional Engravings on Steel, 7s. 6d.

—— **Lives of Donne, Wotton, Hooker,** &c., with Notes. A New Edition, revised by A. H. Bullen, with a Memoir of Izaak Walton by William Dowling. 6 Portraits, 6 Autograph Signatures, &c. *N. S.*

WELLINGTON, Life of. From the Materials of Maxwell. 18 Steel Engravings.

—— **Victories of.**—*See Maxwell.*

WESTROPP (H. M.) A Handbook of Archæology, Egyptian, Greek, Etruscan, Roman. By H. M. Westropp. Numerous Illustrations. 7s. 6d. *N. S.*

WHITE'S Natural History of Selborne, with Observations on various Parts of Nature, and the Naturalists' Calendar. Sir W. Jardine. Edit., with Notes and Memoir, by E. Jesse. 40 Portraits. *N. S.*

—— With the Plates coloured, 7s. 6d. *N. S.*

YOUNG LADY'S BOOK, The. A Manual of Recreations, Arts, Sciences, and Accomplishments. 1200 Woodcut Illustrations. 7s. 6d.

—— cloth gilt, gilt edges, 9s.

CLASSICAL LIBRARY.

TRANSLATIONS FROM THE GREEK AND LATIN.

98 *Vols. at 5s. each, excepting those marked otherwise.* (24*l*. 0s. 6d. per set.)

ÆSCHYLUS, The Dramas of. In English Verse by Anna Swanwick. 4th edition. *N. S.*

—— **The Tragedies of.** In Prose, with Notes and Introduction, by T. A. Buckley, B.A. Portrait. 3s. 6d.

AMMIANUS MARCELLINUS. History of Rome during the Reigns of Constantius, Julian, Jovianus, Valentinian, and Valens, by C. D. Yonge, B.A. Double volume. 7s. 6d.

ANTONINUS (M. Aurelius), The Thoughts of. Translated literally, with Notes, Biographical Sketch, and Essay on the Philosophy, by George Long, M.A. 3s. 6d. *N. S.*

APULEIUS, The Works of. Comprising the Golden Ass, God of Socrates, Florida, and Discourse of Magic. With a Metrical Version of Cupid and Psyche, and Mrs. Tighe's Psyche. Frontispiece.

CLASSICAL LIBRARY.

ARISTOPHANES' Comedies. Trans., with Notes and Extracts from Frere's and other Metrical Versions, by W. J. Hickie. Portrait. 2 vols.

ARISTOTLE'S Nicomachean Ethics. Trans., with Notes, Analytical Introduction, and Questions for Students, by Ven. Archdn. Browne.

—— **Politics and Economics.** Trans., with Notes, Analyses, and Index, by E. Walford, M.A., and an Essay and Life by Dr. Gillies.

—— **Metaphysics.** Trans., with Notes, Analysis, and Examination Questions, by Rev. John H. M'Mahon, M.A.

—— **History of Animals.** In Ten Books. Trans., with Notes and Index, by R. Cresswell, M.A.

—— **Organon;** or, Logical Treatises, and the Introduction of Porphyry. With Notes, Analysis, and Introduction, by Rev. O. F. Owen, M.A. 2 vols. 3s. 6d. each.

—— **Rhetoric and Poetics.** Trans., with Hobbes' Analysis, Exam. Questions, and Notes, by T. Buckley, B.A. Portrait.

ATHENÆUS. The Deipnosophists; or, the Banquet of the Learned. By C. D. Yonge, B.A. With an Appendix of Poetical Fragments. 3 vols.

ATLAS of Classical Geography. 22 large Coloured Maps. With a complete Index. Imp. 8vo. 7s. 6d.

BION.—*See Theocritus.*

CÆSAR. Commentaries on the Gallic and Civil Wars, with the Supplementary Books attributed to Hirtius, including the complete Alexandrian, African, and Spanish Wars. Trans. with Notes. Portrait.

CATULLUS, Tibullus, and the Vigil of Venus. Trans. with Notes and Biographical Introduction. To which are added, Metrical Versions by Lamb, Grainger, and others. Frontispiece.

CICERO'S Orations. Trans. by C. D. Yonge, B.A. 4 vols.

—— **On Oratory and Orators.** With Letters to Quintus and Brutus. Trans., with Notes, by Rev. J. S. Watson, M.A.

—— **On the Nature of the Gods,** Divination, Fate, Laws, a Republic, Consulship. Trans., with Notes, by C. D. Vonge, B.A.

—— **Academics,** De Finibus, and Tusculan Questions. By C. D. Yonge, B.A. With Sketch of the Greek Philosophers mentioned by Cicero.

CICERO'S Orations.—*Continued.*

—— **Offices;** or, Moral Duties. Cato Major, an Essay on Old Age; Lælius, an Essay on Friendship; Scipio's Dream; Paradoxes; Letter to Quintus on Magistrates. Trans., with Notes, by C. R. Edmonds. Portrait. 3s. 6d.

DEMOSTHENES' Orations. Trans., with Notes, Arguments, a Chronological Abstract, and Appendices, by C. Rann Kennedy. 5 vols.

DICTIONARY of LATIN and GREEK Quotations; including Proverbs, Maxims, Mottoes, Law Terms and Phrases. With the Quantities marked, and English Translations.

—— With Index Verborum (622 pages). 6s.

—— Index Verborum to the above, with the *Quantities* and Accents marked (56 pages), limp cloth. 1s.

DIOGENES LAERTIUS. Lives and Opinions of the Ancient Philosophers. Trans., with Notes, by C. D. Vonge, B.A.

EPICTETUS. The Discourses of. With the Encheiridion and Fragments. With Notes, Life, and View of his Philosophy, by George Long, M.A. N. S.

EURIPIDES. Trans., with Notes and Introduction, by T. A. Buckley, B.A. Portrait. 2 vols.

GREEK ANTHOLOGY. In English Prose by G. Burges, M.A. With Metrical Versions by Bland, Merivale, Lord Denman, &c.

GREEK ROMANCES of Heliodorus, Longus, and Achilles Tatius; viz., The Adventures of Theagenes and Chariclea; Amours of Daphnis and Chloe; and Loves of Clitopho and Leucippe. Trans., with Notes, by Rev. R. Smith, M.A.

HERODOTUS. Literally trans. by Rev. Henry Cary, M.A. Portrait.

HESIOD, CALLIMACHUS, and Theognis. In Prose, with Notes and Biographical Notices by Rev. J. Banks, M.A. Together with the Metrical Versions of Hesiod, by Elton; Callimachus, by Tytler; and Theognis, by Frere.

HOMER'S Iliad. In English Prose, with Notes by T. A. Buckley, B.A. Portrait.

—— **Odyssey,** Hymns, Epigrams, and Battle of the Frogs and Mice. In English Prose, with Notes and Memoir by T. A. Buckley, B.A.

HORACE. In Prose by Smart, with Notes selected by T. A. Buckley, B.A. Portrait. 3s. 6d.

JULIAN THE APOSTATE. By the Rev. C. W. King, M.A. [*In the press.*

JUSTIN, CORNELIUS NEPOS, and Eutropius. Trans., with Notes, by Rev. J. S. Watson, M.A.

JUVENAL, PERSIUS, SULPICIA, and Lucilius. In Prose, with Notes, Chronological Tables, Arguments, by L. Evans, M.A. To which is added the Metrical Version of Juvenal and Persius by Gifford. Frontispiece.

LIVY. The History of Rome. Trans. by Dr. Spillan and others. 4 vols. Portrait.

LUCAN'S Pharsalia. In Prose, with Notes by H. T. Riley.

LUCIAN'S Dialogues of the Gods, of the Sea Gods, and of the Dead. Trans. by Howard Williams, M.A. [*In the press.*

LUCRETIUS. In Prose, with Notes and Biographical Introduction by Rev. J. S. Watson, M.A. To which is added the Metrical Version by J. M. Good.

MARTIAL'S Epigrams, complete. In Prose, with Verse Translations selected from English Poets, and other sources. Dble. vol. (670 pages). 7s. 6d.

MOSCHUS.—*See Theocritus.*

OVID'S Works, complete. In Prose, with Notes and Introduction. 3 vols.

PAUSANIAS' Description of Greece. Translated into English, with Notes and Index. By Arthur Richard Shilleto, M.A., sometime Scholar of Trinity College, Cambridge. 2 vols.

PHALARIS. Bentley's Dissertations upon the Epistles of Phalaris, Themistocles, Socrates, Euripides, and the Fables of Æsop. With Introduction and Notes by Prof. W. Wagner, Ph.D.

PINDAR. In Prose, with Introduction and Notes by Dawson W. Turner. Together with the Metrical Version by Abraham Moore. Portrait.

PLATO'S Works. Trans., with Introduction and Notes. 6 vols.

—— **Dialogues.** A Summary and Analysis of. With Analytical Index to the Greek text of modern editions and to the above translations, by A. Day, LL.D.

PLAUTUS'S Comedies. In Prose, with Notes and Index by H. T. Riley, B.A. 2 vols.

PLINY'S Natural History. Trans., with Notes, by J. Bostock, M.D., F.R.S., and H. T. Riley, B.A. 6 vols.

PLINY. The Letters of Pliny the Younger. Melmoth's Translation, revised with Notes and short Life, by Rev. F. C. T. Bosanquet, M.A.

PLUTARCH'S Morals. Theosophical Essays. Trans. by C. W. King, M.A. *N.S.*

—— **Lives.** *See page* 7.

PROPERTIUS, The Elegies of. With Notes, Literally translated by the Rev. P. J. F. Gantillon, M.A., with metrical versions of Select Elegies by Nott and Elton. 3s. 6d.

QUINTILIAN'S Institutes of Oratory. Trans., with Notes and Biographical Notice, by Rev. J. S. Watson, M.A. 2 vols.

SALLUST, FLORUS, and **VELLEIUS** Paterculus. Trans., with Notes and Biographical Notices, by J. S. Watson, M.A.

SENECA DE BENEFICIIS. Newly translated by Aubrey Stewart, M.A. 3s. 6d. *N.S.*

SENECA'S Minor Works. Translated by A. Stewart, M.A. [*In the press.*

SOPHOCLES. The Tragedies of. In Prose, with Notes, Arguments, and Introduction. Portrait.

STRABO'S Geography. Trans., with Notes, by W. Falconer, M.A., and H. C. Hamilton. Copious Index, giving Ancient and Modern Names. 3 vols.

SUETONIUS' Lives of the Twelve Cæsars and Lives of the Grammarians. The Translation of Thomson, revised, with Notes, by T. Forester.

TACITUS. The Works of. Trans. with Notes. 2 vols.

TERENCE and PHÆDRUS. In English Prose, with Notes and Arguments, by H. T. Riley, B.A. To which is added Smart's Metrical Version of Phædrus. With Frontispiece.

THEOCRITUS, BION, MOSCHUS and Tyrtæus. In Prose, with Notes and Arguments, by Rev. J. Banks, M.A. To which are appended the METRICAL VERSIONS of Chapman. Portrait of Theocritus.

THUCYDIDES. The Peloponnesian War. Trans., with Notes, by Rev. H. Dale. Portrait. 2 vols. 3s. 6d. each.

TYRTÆUS.—*See Theocritus.*

VIRGIL. The Works of. In Prose, with Notes by Davidson. Revised, with additional Notes and Biographical Notice by T. A. Buckley, B.A. Portrait. 3s. 6d.

XENOPHON'S Works. Trans., with Notes, by J. S. Watson, M.A., and others. Portrait. In 3 vols.

COLLEGIATE SERIES.

10 *Vols. at* 5s. *each.* (2l. 10s. *per set.*)

DANTE. The Inferno. Prose Trans., with the Text of the Original on the same page, and Explanatory Notes, by John A. Carlyle, M.D. Portrait. *N. S.*

—— **The Purgatorio.** Prose Trans., with the Original on the same page, and Explanatory Notes, by W. S. Dugdale. *N. S.*

NEW TESTAMENT (The) in Greek. Griesbach's Text, with the Readings of Mill and Scholz at the foot of the page, and Parallel References in the margin. Also a Critical Introduction and Chronological Tables. Two Fac-similes of Greek Manuscripts. 650 pages. 3s. 6d.

—— or bound up with a Greek and English Lexicon to the New Testament (250 pages additional, making in all 900). 5s. The Lexicon may be had separately, price 2s.

DOBREE'S Adversaria. (Notes on the Greek and Latin Classics.) Edited by the late Prof. Wagner. 2 vols.

DONALDSON (Dr.) The Theatre of the Greeks. With Supplementary Treatise on the Language, Metres, and Prosody of the Greek Dramatists. Numerous Illustrations and 3 Plans. By J. W. Donaldson, D.D. *N. S.*

KEIGHTLEY'S (Thomas) Mythology of Ancient Greece and Italy. Revised by Leonhard Schmitz, Ph.D., LL.D. 12 Plates. *N. S.*

HERODOTUS, Notes on. Original and Selected from the best Commentators. By D. W. Turner, M.A. Coloured Map.

—— **Analysis and Summary of,** with a Synchronistical Table of Events—Tables of Weights, Measures, Money, and Distances—an Outline of the History and Geography—and the Dates completed from Gaisford, Baehr, &c. By J. T. Wheeler.

THUCYDIDES. An Analysis and Summary of. With Chronological Table of Events, &c., by J. T. Wheeler.

SCIENTIFIC LIBRARY.

59 *Vols. at* 5s. *each, excepting those marked otherwise.* (15l. 6s. 6d. *per set.*)

AGASSIZ and GOULD. Outline of Comparative Physiology touching the Structure and Development of the Races of Animals living and extinct. For Schools and Colleges. Enlarged by Dr. Wright. With Index and 300 Illustrative Woodcuts.

BOLLEY'S Manual of Technical Analysis; a Guide for the Testing and Valuation of the various Natural and Artificial Substances employed in the Arts and Domestic Economy, founded on the work of Dr. Bolley. Edit. by Dr. Paul. 100 Woodcuts.

BRIDGEWATER TREATISES.

—— **Bell (Sir Charles) on the Hand;** its Mechanism and Vital Endowments, as evincing Design. Preceded by an Account of the Author's Discoveries in the Nervous System by A. Shaw. Numerous Woodcuts.

—— **Kirby on the History, Habits, and Instincts of Animals.** With Notes by T. Rymer Jones. 100 Woodcuts. 2 vols.

—— **Whewell's Astronomy and General Physics,** considered with reference to Natural Theology. Portrait of the Earl of Bridgewater. 3s. 6d.

BRIDGEWATER TREATISES.—
Continued.

—— **Chalmers on the Adaptation of External Nature to the Moral and Intellectual Constitution of Man.** With Memoir by Rev. Dr. Cumming. Portrait.

—— **Prout's Treatise on Chemistry, Meteorology, and the Function of Digestion,** with reference to Natural Theology. Edit. by Dr. J. W. Griffith. 2 Maps.

—— **Buckland's Geology and Mineralogy.** With Additions by Prof. Owen, Prof. Phillips, and R. Brown. Memoir of Buckland. Portrait. 2 vols. 15s. Vol. I. Text. Vol. II. 90 large plates with letterpress.

—— **Roget's Animal and Vegetable Physiology.** 463 Woodcuts. 2 vols. 6s. each.

—— **Kidd on the Adaptation of External Nature to the Physical Condition of Man.** 3s. 6d.

CARPENTER'S (Dr. W. B.) Zoology. A Systematic View of the Structure, Habits, Instincts, and Uses of the principal Families of the Animal Kingdom, and of the chief Forms of Fossil Remains. Revised by W. S. Dallas, F.L.S. Numerous Woodcuts. 2 vols. 6s. each.

CARPENTER'S Works.—*Continued.*
— **Mechanical Philosophy, Astronomy, and Horology.** A Popular Exposition. 181 Woodcuts.
— **Vegetable Physiology and Systematic Botany.** A complete Introduction to the Knowledge of Plants. Revised by E. Lankester, M.D., &c. Numerous Woodcuts. 6s.
— **Animal Physiology.** Revised Edition. 300 Woodcuts. 6s.

CHEVREUL on Colour. Containing the Principles of Harmony and Contrast of Colours, and their Application to the Arts; including Painting, Decoration, Tapestries, Carpets, Mosaics, Glazing, Staining, Calico Printing, Letterpress Printing, Map Colouring, Dress, Landscape and Flower Gardening, &c. Trans. by C. Martel. Several Plates.
— With an additional series of 16 Plates in Colours, 7s. 6d.

ENNEMOSER'S History of Magic. Trans. by W. Howitt. With an Appendix of the most remarkable and best authenticated Stories of Apparitions, Dreams, Second Sight, Table-Turning, and Spirit-Rapping, &c. 2 vols.

HIND'S Introduction to Astronomy. With Vocabulary of the Terms in present use. Numerous Woodcuts. 3s. 6d. *N.S.*

HOGG'S (Jabez) Elements of Experimental and Natural Philosophy. Being an Easy Introduction to the Study of Mechanics, Pneumatics, Hydrostatics, Hydraulics, Acoustics, Optics, Caloric, Electricity, Voltaism, and Magnetism. 400 Woodcuts.

HUMBOLDT'S Cosmos; or, Sketch of a Physical Description of the Universe. Trans. by E. C. Otté, B. H. Paul, and W. S. Dallas, F.L.S. Portrait. 5 vols. 3s. 6d. each, excepting vol. v., 5s.
— **Personal Narrative of his Travels in America during the years 1799-1804.** Trans., with Notes, by T. Ross. 3 vols.
— **Views of Nature; or, Contemplations of the Sublime Phenomena of Creation, with Scientific Illustrations.** Trans. by E. C. Otté.

HUNT'S (Robert) Poetry of Science; or, Studies of the Physical Phenomena of Nature. By Robert Hunt, Professor at the School of Mines.

JOYCE'S Scientific Dialogues. A Familiar Introduction to the Arts and Sciences. For Schools and Young People. Numerous Woodcuts.
— **Introduction to the Arts and Sciences, for Schools and Young People.** Divided into Lessons with Examination Questions. Woodcuts. 3s. 6d.

JUKES-BROWNE'S Student's Handbook of Physical Geology. By A. J. Jukes-Browne, of the Geological Survey of England. With numerous Diagrams and Illustrations, 6s. *N.S.*
— **The Student's Handbook of Historical Geology.** By A. J. Jukes-Brown, B.A., F.G.S., of the Geological Survey of England and Wales. With numerous Diagrams and Illustrations. 6s. *N.S.*

KNIGHT'S (Charles) Knowledge is Power. A Popular Manual of Political Economy.

LECTURES ON PAINTING by the Royal Academicians, Barry, Opie, Fuseli. With Introductory Essay and Notes by R. Wornum. Portrait of Fuseli.

LILLY. Introduction to Astrology. With a Grammar of Astrology and Tables for calculating Nativities, by Zadkiel.

MANTELL'S (Dr.) Geological Excursions through the Isle of Wight and along the Dorset Coast. Numerous Woodcuts and Geological Map.
— **Medals of Creation; or, First Lessons in Geology:** including Geological Excursions. Coloured Plates and several hundred Woodcuts. 2 vols. 7s. 6d. each.
— **Petrifactions and their Teachings.** Handbook to the Organic Remains in the British Museum. Numerous Woodcuts. 6s.
— **Wonders of Geology; or, a Familiar Exposition of Geological Phenomena.** A coloured Geological Map of England, Plates, and 200 Woodcuts. 2 vols. 7s. 6d. each.

MORPHY'S Games of Chess, being the Matches and best Games played by the American Champion, with explanatory and analytical Notes by J. Löwenthal. With short Memoir and Portrait of Morphy.

SCHOUW'S Earth, Plants, and Man. Popular Pictures of Nature. And Kobell's Sketches from the Mineral Kingdom. Trans. by A. Henfrey, F.R.S. Coloured Map of the Geography of Plants.

SMITH'S (Pye) Geology and Scripture; or, the Relation between the Scripture and Geological Science. With Memoir.

STANLEY'S Classified Synopsis of the Principal Painters of the Dutch and Flemish Schools, including an Account of some of the early German Masters. By George Stanley.

STAUNTON'S Chess-Player's Handbook. A Popular and Scientific Introduction to the Game, with numerous Diagrams and Coloured Frontispiece. *N.S.*

STAUNTON.—*Continued.*

—— **Chess Praxis.** A Supplement to the Chess-player's Handbook. Containing the most important modern Improvements in the Openings; Code of Chess Laws; and a Selection of Morphy's Games. Annotated. 636 pages. Diagrams. 6s.

—— **Chess-Player's Companion.** Comprising a Treatise on Odds, Collection of Match Games, including the French Match with M. St. Amant, and a Selection of Original Problems. Diagrams and Coloured Frontispiece.

—— **Chess Tournament of 1851.** A Collection of Games played at this celebrated assemblage. With Introduction and Notes. Numerous Diagrams.

STOCKHARDT'S Experimental Chemistry. A Handbook for the Study of the Science by simple Experiments. Edit. by C. W. Heaton, F.C.S. Numerous Woodcuts. *N. S.*

URE'S (Dr. A.) Cotton Manufacture of Great Britain, systematically investigated; with an Introductory View of its Comparative State in Foreign Countries. Revised by P. L. Simmonds. 150 Illustrations. 2 vols.

—— **Philosophy of Manufactures,** or an Exposition of the Scientific, Moral, and Commercial Economy of the Factory System of Great Britain. Revised by P. L. Simmonds. Numerous Figures. 800 pages. 7s. 6d.

ECONOMICS AND FINANCE.

GILBART'S History, Principles, and Practice of Banking. Revised to 1881 by A. S. Michie, of the Royal Bank of Scotland. Portrait of Gilbart. 2 vols. 10s. *N. S.*

REFERENCE LIBRARY.

28 Volumes at Various Prices. (8l. 10s. *per set.*)

BLAIR'S Chronological Tables. Comprehending the Chronology and History of the World, from the Earliest Times to the Russian Treaty of Peace, April 1856. By J. W. Rosse. 800 pages. 10s.

—— **Index of Dates.** Comprehending the principal Facts in the Chronology and History of the World, from the Earliest to the Present, alphabetically arranged; being a complete Index to the foregoing. By J. W. Rosse. 2 vols. 5s. each.

BOHN'S Dictionary of Quotations from the English Poets. 4th and cheaper Edition. 6s.

BUCHANAN'S Dictionary of Science and Technical Terms used in Philosophy, Literature, Professions, Commerce, Arts, and Trades. By W. H. Buchanan, with Supplement. Edited by Jas. A. Smith. 6s.

CHRONICLES OF THE TOMBS. A Select Collection of Epitaphs, with Essay on Epitaphs and Observations on Sepulchral Antiquities. By T. J. Pettigrew, F.R.S., F.S.A. 5s.

CLARK'S (Hugh) Introduction to Heraldry. Revised by J. R. Planché. 5s. 950 Illustrations.

—— *With the Illustrations coloured,* 15s. *N. S.*

COINS, Manual of.—*See Humphreys.*

DATES, Index of.—*See Blair.*

DICTIONARY of Obsolete and Provincial English. Containing Words from English Writers previous to the 19th Century. By Thomas Wright, M.A., F.S.A., &c. 2 vols. 5s. each.

EPIGRAMMATISTS (The). A Selection from the Epigrammatic Literature of Ancient, Mediæval, and Modern Times. With Introduction, Notes, Observations, Illustrations, an Appendix on Works connected with Epigrammatic Literature, by Rev. H. Dodd, M.A. 6s. *N. S.*

GAMES, Handbook of. Comprising Treatises on above 40 Games of Chance, Skill, and Manual Dexterity, including Whist, Billiards, &c. Edit. by Henry G. Bohn. Numerous Diagrams. 5s. *N. S.*

HENFREY'S Guide to English Coins. Revised Edition, by C. F. Keary, M.A., F.S.A. With an Historical Introduction. 6s. *N. S.*

HUMPHREYS' Coin Collectors' Manual. An Historical Account of the Progress of Coinage from the Earliest Time, by H. N. Humphreys. 140 Illustrations. 2 vols. 5s. each. *N. S.*

LOWNDES' Bibliographer's Manual of English Literature. Containing an Account of Rare and Curious Books published in or relating to Great Britain and Ireland, from the Invention of Printing, with Biographical Notices and Prices, by W. T. Lowndes. Parts I.-X. (A to Z), 3s. 6d. each. Part XI. (Appendix Vol.), 5s. Or the 11 parts in 4 vols., half morocco, 2l. 2s.

MEDICINE, Handbook of Domestic, Popularly Arranged. By Dr. H. Davies. 700 pages. 5s.

NOTED NAMES OF FICTION. Dictionary of. Including also Familiar Pseudonyms, Surnames bestowed on Eminent Men, &c. By W. A. Wheeler, M.A. 5s. *N. S.*

POLITICAL CYCLOPÆDIA. A Dictionary of Political, Constitutional, Statistical, and Forensic Knowledge; forming a Work of Reference on subjects of Civil Administration, Political Economy, Finance, Commerce, Laws, and Social Relations. 4 vols. 3s. 6d. each.

PROVERBS, Handbook of. Containing an entire Republication of Ray's Collection, with Additions from Foreign Languages and Sayings, Sentences, Maxims, and Phrases. 5s.

—— **A Polyglot of Foreign.** Comprising French, Italian, German, Dutch, Spanish, Portuguese, and Danish. With English Translations. 5s.

SYNONYMS and ANTONYMS; or, Kindred Words and their Opposites, Collected and Contrasted by Ven. C. J. Smith, M.A. 5s. *N. S.*

WRIGHT (Th.)—*See Dictionary.*

NOVELISTS' LIBRARY.

11 Volumes at 3s. 6d. each, excepting those marked otherwise. (2l. 1s. 6d. per set.)

BURNEY'S Evelina; or, a Young Lady's Entrance into the World. By F. Burney (Mme. D'Arblay). With Introduction and Notes by A. R. Ellis, Author of 'Sylvestra,' &c. *N. S.*

—— **Cecilia.** With Introduction and Notes by A. R. Ellis. 2 vols. *N. S.*

EBERS' Egyptian Princess. Trans. by Emma Buchheim. *N. S.*

FIELDING'S Joseph Andrews and his Friend Mr. Abraham Adams. With Roscoe's Biography. *Cruikshank's Illustrations. N. S.*

—— **Amelia.** Roscoe's Edition, revised. *Cruikshank's Illustrations.* 5s. *N. S.*

FIELDING.—*Continued.*

—— **History of Tom Jones, a Foundling.** Roscoe's Edition. *Cruikshank's Illustrations.* 2 vols. *N. S.*

GROSSI'S Marco Visconti. Trans. by A. F. D. *N. S.*

MANZONI. The Betrothed: being a Translation of 'I Promessi Sposi.' Numerous Woodcuts. 1 vol. (732 pages 5s. *N. S.*

STOWE (Mrs. H. B.) Uncle Tom's Cabin; or, Life among the Lowly. 8 full-page Illustrations. *N. S.*

ARTISTS' LIBRARY.

7 Volumes at Various Prices. (1l. 18s. 6d. per set.)

BELL (Sir Charles). The Anatomy and Philosophy of Expression, as Connected with the Fine Arts. 5s. *N. S.*

DEMMIN. History of Arms and Armour from the Earliest Period. By Auguste Demmin. Trans. by C. C. Black, M.A., Assistant Keeper, S. K. Museum. 1900 Illustrations. 7s. 6d. *N. S.*

FAIRHOLT'S Costume in England. Third Edition. Enlarged and Revised by the Hon. H. A. Dillon, F.S.A. With more than 700 Engravings. 2 vols. 5s. each. *N. S.*
Vol. I. History. Vol. II. Glossary.

FLAXMAN. Lectures on Sculpture. With Three Addresses to the R.A. by Sir R. Westmacott, R.A., and Memoir of Flaxman. Portrait and 53 Plates. 6s. *N.S.*

HEATON'S Concise History of Painting. [*In the press.*]

LEONARDO DA VINCI'S Treatise on Painting. Trans. by J. F. Rigaud, R.A. With a Life and an Account of his Works by J. W. Brown. Numerous Plates. 5s. *N. S.*

PLANCHÉ'S History of British Costume, from the Earliest Time to the 19th Century. By J. R. Planché. 400 Illustrations. 5s. *N. S.*

BOHN'S CHEAP SERIES.

PRICE ONE SHILLING EACH.

A Series of Complete Stories or Essays, mostly reprinted from Vols. in Bohn's Libraries, and neatly bound in stiff paper cover, with cut edges, suitable for Railway Reading.

ASCHAM (ROGER).—
   SCHOLEMASTER. By Professor Mayor.

CARPENTER (DR. W. B.).—
   PHYSIOLOGY OF TEMPERANCE AND TOTAL ABSTINENCE.

EMERSON.—
   ENGLAND AND ENGLISH CHARACTERISTICS. Lectures on the Race, Ability, Manners, Truth, Character, Wealth, Religion, &c. &c.
   NATURE: An Essay. To which are added Orations, Lectures, and Addresses.
   REPRESENTATIVE MEN: Seven Lectures on Plato, Swedenborg, Montaigne, Shakespeare, Napoleon, and Goethe.
   TWENTY ESSAYS on Various Subjects.
   THE CONDUCT OF LIFE.

FRANKLIN (BENJAMIN).—
   AUTOBIOGRAPHY. Edited by J. Sparks.

HAWTHORNE (NATHANIEL).—
   TWICE-TOLD TALES. Two Vols. in One.
   SNOW IMAGE, and other Tales.
   SCARLET LETTER.
   HOUSE WITH THE SEVEN GABLES.
   TRANSFORMATION; or the Marble Fawn. Two Parts.

HAZLITT (W.).—
   TABLE-TALK: Essays on Men and Manners. Three Parts.
   PLAIN SPEAKER: Opinions on Books, Men, and Things. Three Parts.
   LECTURES ON THE ENGLISH COMIC WRITERS.
   LECTURES ON THE ENGLISH POETS.

HAZLITT (W.).—*Continued.*
    LECTURES ON THE CHARACTERS OF SHAKE-
        SPEARE'S PLAYS.
    LECTURES ON THE LITERATURE OF THE AGE OF
        ELIZABETH, chiefly Dramatic.

IRVING (*WASHINGTON*).—
    LIFE OF MOHAMMED. With Portrait.
    LIVES OF SUCCESSORS OF MOHAMMED.
    LIFE OF GOLDSMITH.
    SKETCH-BOOK.
    TALES OF A TRAVELLER.
    TOUR ON THE PRAIRIES.
    CONQUESTS OF GRANADA AND SPAIN. Two Parts.
    LIFE AND VOYAGES OF COLUMBUS. Two Parts.
    COMPANIONS OF COLUMBUS: Their Voyages and Dis-
        coveries.
    ADVENTURES OF CAPTAIN BONNEVILLE in the Rocky
        Mountains and the Far West.
    KNICKERBOCKER'S HISTORY OF NEW YORK, from the
        Beginning of the World to the End of the Dutch Dynasty.
    TALES OF THE ALHAMBRA.
    CONQUEST OF FLORIDA UNDER HERNANDO DE
        SOTO.
    ABBOTSFORD AND NEWSTEAD ABBEY.
    SALMAGUNDI; or, The Whim-Whams and Opinions of
        LAUNCELOT LANGSTAFF, Esq.
    BRACEBRIDGE HALL; or, The Humourists.
    ASTORIA; or, Anecdotes of an Enterprise beyond the Rocky
        Mountains.
    WOLFERT'S ROOST, and Other Tales.

LAMB (*CHARLES*).—
    ESSAYS OF ELIA. With a Portrait.
    LAST ESSAYS OF ELIA.
    ELIANA. With Biographical Sketch.

MARRYAT (*CAPTAIN*).
    PIRATE AND THE THREE CUTTERS. With a Memoir of
        the Author.

The only authorised Edition; no others published in England contain the Derivations and Etymological Notes of Dr. Mahn, who devoted several years to this portion of the Work.

WEBSTER'S DICTIONARY
OF THE ENGLISH LANGUAGE.

Thoroughly revised and improved by CHAUNCEY A. GOODRICH, D.D., LL.D., and NOAH PORTER, D.D., of Yale College.

THE GUINEA DICTIONARY.

New Edition [1880], with a Supplement of upwards of 4600 New Words and Meanings.
1628 Pages. 3000 Illustrations.

The features of this volume, which render it perhaps the most useful Dictionary for general reference extant, as it is undoubtedly one of the cheapest books ever published, are as follows :—

1. COMPLETENESS.—It contains 114,000 words.
2. ACCURACY OF DEFINITION.
3. SCIENTIFIC AND TECHNICAL TERMS.
4. ETYMOLOGY.
5. THE ORTHOGRAPHY is based, as far as possible, on Fixed Principles.
6. PRONUNCIATION.
7. THE ILLUSTRATIVE CITATIONS.
8. THE SYNONYMS.
9. THE ILLUSTRATIONS, which exceed 3000.

Cloth, 21s.; half-bound in calf, 30s.; calf or half russia, 31s. 6d.; russia, 2l.

With New Biographical Appendix, containing over 9700 Names.

THE COMPLETE DICTIONARY

Contains, in addition to the above matter, several valuable Literary Appendics, and 70 extra pages of Illustrations, grouped and classified.
1 vol. 1919 pages, cloth, 31s. 6d.

'Certainly the best practical English Dictionary extant.'—*Quarterly Review*, 1873.

Prospectuses, with Specimen Pages, sent post free on application.

To be obtained through all Booksellers.

(24)

BOHN'S SELECT LIBRARY

OF STANDARD WORKS.

THE texts in all cases will be printed without abridgment, where Introductions, Biographical Notices and Notes appear to be of use to the Student, they will be given. The volumes, well printed and on good paper, will be issued at 1s. in paper covers, and 1s. 6d. in cloth.

NOW READY.

BACON'S ESSAYS. With Introduction and Notes.

LESSING'S LAOKOON. Beasley's Translation, revised with Introduction, Notes, &c., by Edward Bell, M.A.

DANTE'S INFERNO. Translated, with Notes, by Rev. H. F. Cary.

GOETHE'S FAUST. Part I. Translated, with Introduction, by Anna Swanwick.

GOETHE'S BOYHOOD. Being Part I. of the Autobiography. Translated by J. Oxenford.

SCHILLER'S MARY STUART and THE MAID OF ORLEANS. Translated by J. Mellish and Anna Swanwick.

To be followed at intervals of a fortnight by

THE QUEEN'S ENGLISH. By the late Dean Alford.

HELPS' LIFE OF THE LATE THOMAS BRASSEY.

THE VICAR OF WAKEFIELD.

GOLDSMITH'S PLAYS.

PLATO'S APOLOGY, CRITO, PHAEDO, and PROTAGORAS.

HAUFF'S CARAVAN.

MOLIÈRE'S PLAYS.

STEWART'S LIFE OF THE DUKE OF WELLINGTON, &c. &c.

LONDON:

www.ingramcontent.com/pod-product-compliance
Lightning Source LLC
Chambersburg PA
CBHW021229300426
44111CB00007B/478